I0896768

Content Generation Through Narrative Communication and Simulation

Takashi Ogata
Iwate Prefectural University, Japan

Shin Asakawa
Tokyo Woman's Christian University, Japan

A volume in the Advances in Linguistics and Communication Studies (ALCS) Book Series

IGI Global
DISSEMINATOR OF KNOWLEDGE

Published in the United States of America by
IGI Global
Information Science Reference (an imprint of IGI Global)
701 E. Chocolate Avenue
Hershey PA, USA 17033
Tel: 717-533-8845
Fax: 717-533-8661
E-mail: cust@igi-global.com
Web site: http://www.igi-global.com

Copyright © 2018 by IGI Global. All rights reserved. No part of this publication may be reproduced, stored or distributed in any form or by any means, electronic or mechanical, including photocopying, without written permission from the publisher. Product or company names used in this set are for identification purposes only. Inclusion of the names of the products or companies does not indicate a claim of ownership by IGI Global of the trademark or registered trademark.

Library of Congress Cataloging-in-Publication Data

Names: Ogata, Takashi, 1958- editor. | Asakawa, Shin, 1962- editor.
Title: Content generation through narrative communication and simulation / Takashi Ogata and Shin Asakawa, editors.
Description: Hershey : Information Science Reference, [2018]
Identifiers: LCCN 2017032862| ISBN 9781522547754 (hardcover) | ISBN 9781522547761 (ebook)
Subjects: LCSH: Communication models.
Classification: LCC P93.55 .C66 2018 | DDC 302.201/1--dc23 LC record available at https://lccn.loc.gov/2017032862

This book is published in the IGI Global book series Advances in Linguistics and Communication Studies (ALCS) (ISSN: 2372-109X; eISSN: 2372-1111)

British Cataloguing in Publication Data
A Cataloguing in Publication record for this book is available from the British Library.

All work contributed to this book is new, previously-unpublished material. The views expressed in this book are those of the authors, but not necessarily of the publisher.

For electronic access to this publication, please contact: eresources@igi-global.com.

Advances in Linguistics and Communication Studies (ALCS) Book Series

Abigail G. Scheg
Western Governors University, USA

ISSN:2372-109X
EISSN:2372-1111

Mission

The scope of language and communication is constantly changing as society evolves, new modes of communication are developed through technological advancement, and novel words enter our lexicon as the result of cultural change. Understanding how we communicate and use language is crucial in all industries and updated research is necessary in order to promote further knowledge in this field.

The **Advances in Linguistics and Communication Studies (ALCS)** book series presents the latest research in diverse topics relating to language and communication. Interdisciplinary in its coverage, ALCS presents comprehensive research on the use of language and communication in various industries including business, education, government, and healthcare.

Coverage

- Computer-Mediated Communication
- Forensic Linguistics
- Dialectology
- Computational linguistics
- Sociolinguistics
- Cross-Cultural Communication
- Language Acquisition
- Media and Public Communications
- Non-Verbal Communication
- Discourse Analysis

IGI Global is currently accepting manuscripts for publication within this series. To submit a proposal for a volume in this series, please contact our Acquisition Editors at Acquisitions@igi-global.com or visit: http://www.igi-global.com/publish/.

The Advances in Linguistics and Communication Studies (ALCS) Book Series (ISSN 2372-109X) is published by IGI Global, 701 E. Chocolate Avenue, Hershey, PA 17033-1240, USA, www.igi-global.com. This series is composed of titles available for purchase individually; each title is edited to be contextually exclusive from any other title within the series. For pricing and ordering information please visit http://www.igi-global.com/book-series/advances-linguistics-communication-studies/78950. Postmaster: Send all address changes to above address. Copyright © 2018 IGI Global. All rights, including translation in other languages reserved by the publisher. No part of this series may be reproduced or used in any form or by any means – graphics, electronic, or mechanical, including photocopying, recording, taping, or information and retrieval systems – without written permission from the publisher, except for non commercial, educational use, including classroom teaching purposes. The views expressed in this series are those of the authors, but not necessarily of IGI Global.

Titles in this Series

For a list of additional titles in this series, please visit: www.igi-global.com/book-series

Establishing and Evaluating Digital Ethos and Online Credibility
Moe Folk (Kutztown University of Pennsylvania, USA) and Shawn Apostel (Bellarmine University, USA)
Information Science Reference • copyright 2017 • 400pp • H/C (ISBN: 9781522510727) • US $200.00 (our price)

Computational and Cognitive Approaches to Narratology
Takashi Ogata (Iwate Prefectural University, Japan) and Taisuke Akimoto (The University of Electoro-Communications, Japan)
Information Science Reference • copyright 2016 • 467pp • H/C (ISBN: 9781522504320) • US $215.00 (our price)

Analyzing Language and Humor in Online Communication
Rotimi Taiwo (Obafemi Awolowo University, Nigeria) Akinola Odebunmi (University of Ibadan, Nigeria) and Akin Adetunji (Emmanuel Alayande College of Education, Nigeria)
Information Science Reference • copyright 2016 • 324pp • H/C (ISBN: 9781522503385) • US $185.00 (our price)

Discourse Analysis as a Tool for Understanding Gender Identity, Representation, and Equality
Nazmunnessa Mahtab (University of Dhaka, Bangladesh) Sara Parker (John Moores University, UK) Farah Kabir (Action Aid, Bangladesh) Tania Haque (University of Dhaka, Bangladesh) Aditi Sabur (University of Dhaka, Bangladesh) and Abu Saleh Mohammad Sowad (University of Dhaka, Bangladesh)
Information Science Reference • copyright 2016 • 323pp • H/C (ISBN: 9781522502258) • US $185.00 (our price)

Revealing Gender Inequalities and Perceptions in South Asian Countries through Discourse Analysis
Nazmunnessa Mahtab (University of Dhaka, Bangladesh) Sara Parker (John Moores University, UK) Farah Kabir (Action Aid, Bangladesh) Tania Haque (University of Dhaka, Bangladesh) Aditi Sabur (University of Dhaka, Bangladesh) and Abu Saleh Mohammad Sowad (University of Dhaka, Bangladesh)
Information Science Reference • copyright 2016 • 286pp • H/C (ISBN: 9781522502791) • US $185.00 (our price)

Interdisciplinary Perspectives on Contemporary Conflict Resolution
Paulo Novais (University of Minho, Portugal) and Davide Carneiro (University of Minho, Portugal)
Information Science Reference • copyright 2016 • 363pp • H/C (ISBN: 9781522502456) • US $185.00 (our price)

Handbook of Research on Effective Communication, Leadership, and Conflict Resolution
Anthony H. Normore (California State University Dominguez Hills, USA & International Academy of Public safety, USA) Larry W. Long (Illinois State University, USA & International Academy of Public Safety, USA) and Mitch Javidi (North Carolina State University, USA & International Academy of Public Safety, USA)
Information Science Reference • copyright 2016 • 733pp • H/C (ISBN: 9781466699700) • US $315.00 (our price)

IGI Global
DISSEMINATOR OF KNOWLEDGE

701 East Chocolate Avenue, Hershey, PA 17033, USA
Tel: 717-533-8845 x100 • Fax: 717-533-8661
E-Mail: cust@igi-global.com • www.igi-global.com

Editorial Advisory Board

Akinori Abe, *Chiba University, Japan*
Ryutaro Ichise, *National Institute of Informatics, Japan*
Akihito Kanai, *Hosei University, Japan*
Yoji Kawamura, *Kindai University, Japan*
Tetsuya Nasukawa, *IBM Research – Tokyo, Japan*
Yoshihiko Nitta, *Nihon University, Japan*
Tadashi Nomoto, *The Graduate University for Advanced Studies, Japan*
Kai Seino, *National Institute of Vocational Rehabilitation, Japan*
Koichi Takeuchi, *Okayama University, Japan*

List of Reviewers

Taisuke Akimoto, *Kyushu Institute of Technology, Japan*
Hiroki Fukushima, *Kyushu Women's University, Japan*
Eugene Schneider Kitamura, *Kobe University, Japan*
Mitsunori Matsushita, *Kansai University, Japan*
Jumpei Ono, *Iwate Prefectural University, Japan*
Tatsuji Takahashi, *Tokyo Denki University, Japan*
Akira Utsumi, *The University of Electro-Communications, Japan*

Table of Contents

Detailed Table of Contents

Today more than ever, narrative content generation has become important. This is due to the advances and accessibility of computational devices. As these devices become more familiar to people and easier to handle, there will be greater expectations for autonomous functioning and desires for a natural communication with the users. To achieve such demands, computational devices need to process and generate higher levels of meanings such as context and abstraction of topics. This chapter gives a background on topics that have been developed so far in content analysis and content generation, but focuses mainly on the figure-ground impression model, for both analysis and generating narrative context. By focusing on the characters and their attributes in the text, not only is this model able to represent the figure-ground impressions qualitatively, but also quantitatively. Such a feature may be useful to execute in computational devices such as artificial intelligence.

In this chapter, the author develops a computational model of the narrative ability for artificial agents. To illustrate an overview of this study, the author addresses an architectural and conceptual systematization of the narrative ability. The proposed model consists of two essential elements: the "mental world" as the internal representation of the world that is formed from many stories, and the mechanism of "narrating" as the act of expressing part of the mental world. In this chapter, the basic concepts and system frameworks of the narrative ability, mental world, and narrating are presented.

In this chapter, the author proposes a multifaceted representation model for the sensory domain of taste, especially the taste of sake. The author aims to bridge the domain of taste and the domain of words and, on the basis of the findings of the first-person-singular study, proposes that the pictorial description, together with the verbal description, can achieve the aim. As the results of the study, the author finds the difference between the manner of description of the PTG (primary taste group for sake: sweetness, umami, and acidity) and the STG (stimulus taste group: astringency and dryness). The PTG tends to be described in curvy shapes; in contrast, the STG tends to be represented in linear patterns.

Aesthetic sentences often behave freely from ordinary grammatical constraints; nevertheless, they maintain rich message transmitting power. This is apparently a mysterious language phenomenon, which dexterously gives full play to its strong narrative power on the reader's soul. In this chapter, the author takes haiku, classical Japanese short poetic sentence, as a model of aesthetic sentence. By using

research was to obtain suggestions regarding business solutions that could be used to provide employment support for students with developmental disabilities by conducting text mining and narrative theory analysis. Furthermore, the "narrative generation system" is advocated as a comprehensive framework which organically unifies the whole "narrative phenomenon" from various sides. Furthermore, these researches apply the knowledge of other fields, such as pedagogy on developmental disability, personal support, text mining, and a narratology; psychology; engineering; and literature. Therefore, the authors believe that this research corresponds to "narrative generation system" theory research. Thus, it may be possible for suggestions regarding narrative generation to be produced as a secondary result of this chapter's process of analysis.

Toward the building of a social/consumption simulation model, the objectives of this chapter are to understand in detail the practice of advertising communication through a framework aiming at quantification, to elucidate the goals and techniques of advertising communication, and to create a model for advertising communication strategies. First, the advertising communications goals, the advertising communications techniques, the motivations to become involved, and the consumer-generated contents are categorized. Next, the relationships between these categorized items are identified. Finally, the typical advertising communications strategies are identified and organized into three types models (two types of sender-driven strategies and one type of receiver-driven strategy). These models can be utilized to establish strategic rules for social simulations that include both senders and receivers of advertising.

Problem-solving behavior in a situation where the problem is not defined creates problems. However, concrete examples of the phenomenon are not shown. In order to capture this phenomenon, the authors investigated the process of pedal development for automobiles. The name of the pedal is called "Naruse pedal." Naruse pedal reduces accidents caused by mistakes in pressing foot on accelerator pedal and brake pedal. Naruse pedal has been reported by many media including the New York Times. The authors surveyed the development process of Naruse pedal. They show this development case and confirm the existence of simultaneity of needs and solution.

The goal of this chapter is to explore a system to assist elderly travelers who are not familiar with computers in externalizing information about their travel experiences and in accumulating this information in the

Preface

This book, *Content Generation through Narrative Communication and Simulation*, deals with models, systems, theories, and analyses for the generation of contents, especially narrative contents, in various genres. "Narrative" in this book is used in a broad sense that includes folktales, various types of narration (descriptions of travel experiences or the taste of Japanese sake, free answers of people with developmental disabilities), novels, poems, metaphors, *haiku*s, dramas and scenarios, *kabuki* and performing arts, pictures, games, advertisements, social networks, management problem solving, and narratives in the narrow sense. "Narrative content" refers to the informational content to be conveyed to such receivers as readers and audiences; the concept is associated with reception and consumption through the communication process between the sender and the receiver. Further, this book also includes various narrative levels, namely, the personal and social or collective levels and the automatic, semi-automatic, and interactive levels. In particular, this book examines the challenges of automated narrative content generation based on narrative communication and simulation technologies. This research plan will be conducted through interdisciplinary methods in such areas as informatics, literary studies, and the social sciences. Results of this study will contribute to the scientific and technological expansion of information science and engineering and literary studies in the future. Additionally, it will also be usefully applied to novel digital content ideas as well as creations in more practical fields.

OBJECTIVE AND TARGETS

This book presents theories, models, systems, and analyses of the generation of narrative contents in various genres based on interdisciplinary methods from informatics, literary studies, and social sciences. The chapters in this book treat the wide variety of narrative forms mentioned above to show the diversity of narrative genres. At the same time, the book shows that various narrative phenomena can be analyzed, modeled, and systematized based on a methodological framework, the method of narrative content generation. This methodological framework integrates previous academic genres into a group. Chapters in this book concern a diverse range of academic areas, such as the informatics (artificial intelligence, cognitive science, game and entertainment informatics, natural language processing, media technologies, human creative aid, collaborative problem solving, and neuroscience and deep learning), literary (narratology, literary theories, *kabuki* studies, film studies, logics, philosophy, linguistics, discourse theory, and creativity), and social science areas (management science, marketing and advertising studies, communication studies). However, these can all be grouped under the perspective of narrative content generation study.

The following people will find this text useful in furthering their research exposure to pertinent interdisciplinary topics in content generation through narrative communication and simulation and in supporting their own research efforts in this field: Researchers and advanced students of information science and engineering (including AI and cognitive science); researchers and advanced students of literary studies (including narratology, modern literary theories, semiotics, discourse linguistics, and sociological approaches); and designers, creators, developers, and researchers of advanced digital content creation (including for computer games, digital novels, and automated text generation).

BOOK ORGANIZATION

Although it is difficult to clearly categorize these studies, the editors organized them into the following four sections: (1) "Introduction" includes a chapter by the editors of this book. (2) "Systems and Models for Narrative Generation and Simulation": The three chapters in this section discuss systems and models for generating or simulating narratives. (3) "Computational and Cognitive Modeling to Narrative Communication and Simulation": The seven chapters in this section propose narrative models using various narrative genres and methods. (4) "Analyses, Models, and Systems for Social Narratives": These three chapters focus on social aspects of narratives, such as those frequently encountered in marketing, advertising, and management.

Section 1: Introduction

"Aspects of Content Generation Through Narrative Communication and Simulation" by Takashi Ogata (Iwate Prefectural University) and Shin Asakawa (Tokyo Woman's Christian University), the introductory chapter in this book, describes the problems this book treats, such as content generation, narrative communication, and narrative simulation, based on the Integrated Narrative Generation System (INGS) and *Geino* Information System (GIS) that Ogata has presented as its central core. In this sense, this chapter shows the authors' synthesized approach to and paradigm of narrative generation study. This study also holds developmental possibilities for the micro and macro directions of narrative generation. In the micro direction, the authors will further the implementation of and experimentation on INGS positively in the future, and these results will be linked to the distributive and social development of the narrative generation system, especially GIS, in the macro direction. In addition, this chapter refers to neural network models as a possible technique for future narrative generation systems.

Section 2: Systems and Models for Narrative Generation and Simulation

In "An Integrated Approach to Narrative Generation: From Mishima and *Kabuki* to Narrative Generation Systems," Takashi Ogata undertakes a comprehensive description of the structure of his narrative generation research. In particular, this chapter has the indirect purpose of compactly showing the whole of the author's narrative generation studies by presenting several concrete examples, and the direct purpose of considering and discussing these contents. This chapter shows an entire framework of narrative analyses in relation to narrative generation systems, mainly the Integrated Narrative Generation System and *Geino* Information System, and conducts analyses of a novel by Yukio Mishima and several aspects of *kabuki* as two examples of the narrative multiplicity or multiple narrative structures model of Ogata.

Furthermore, the chapter concludes with directions for partially incorporating the results of these narrative analyses as a kind of narrative simulation into the above narrative generation systems. This chapter mainly treats the two narrative genres of novel and *kabuki* in relation to various research areas, including AI, cognitive science, narratology, literary theories, narrative analysis, and *kabuki* studies.

"Narrative Simulation for Film Rhetoric Composition With or Without Story and Nostalgia Effects" by Akihito Kanai (Hosei University) shows that the indeterminacy created by the non-story and nostalgia aspects of rhetoric is an essential issue of narrative simulation in the composition of non-story film rhetoric with reference to Eisenstein, Chatman, and Deleuze in addition to Kanai's theories of film rhetoric and story or narrative simulation. Per Kanai, the narrative simulation of film can test cognitive effects created through the interaction between cognitive process, story, discourse, and the rhetoric of a film. Non-story film editing can be classified according to the categories of rhythm and nostalgia and can be used for narrative film rhetoric simulation. Nostalgia may emerge from the determinacy of the place and time and the indeterminacy of non-story aspects of rhetoric. Non-nostalgia narrative may emerge from the indeterminacy of the place and time and can be simulated by the use of non-story editing in accordance with the rhythm categories. Based on the above theoretical framework, this chapter presents a film narrative simulation mechanism and discusses the results and future directions of this approach.

Next, Jumpei Ono (Graduate School of Iwate Prefectural University) and Takashi Ogata, in "Surprise-Based Narrative Generation in an Automatic Narrative Generation Game," present an approach to automated game systems aiming at narrative generation through the interaction between the system and the user(s). In particular, they have been developing an automatic narrative generation game using the method of the Table-Talk Role Playing Game (TRPG), which is an analog game based on the interactive processes of real humans. The proposed system progresses by repeating the interaction between a Game Master (GM) and Players (PLs). The PLs can detail and change the story whose basis the GM had prepared. On the theoretical side, a basic idea is that a "gap" between the original story of the GM and the changed story creates a variety of impressive effects for an interesting story or narrative, especially a kind of "surprise." This proposed system and its mechanisms are implemented using the Integrated Narrative Generation System of Ogata.

Section 3: Computational and Cognitive Modeling to Narrative Communication and Simulation

The first chapter in this section, "Narratology and Creativity" by Akinori Abe (Chiba University), discusses the creativity in the "Innovation Marketplace on Data Jacket" (IMDJ). IMDF is an Innovation Game in which a new production will be obtained during the combination of various techniques, materials, and previous products. The chapter discusses this problem from the perspective of abduction. Further, the author discusses the role of comfortable communication in the creative situation as well as the usual situation. This chapter presents a new approach for expanding previous narratological and literary theories for creative narrative or literary production.

Next, with "Literary Psychology-Modeling Figure-Ground Structures in Narrative Stories: Towards a Narrative Content Generation," Eugene Schneider Kitamura (Kobe University) tries to describe stories in mathematical terms—rough set theory—to both analyze and generate narrative content. The source of the basic idea lies in gestalt psychology. In particular, readers should remember the famous drawing consisting of two faces alternating with a vase named after Danish gestalt psychologist Edgar Rubin. Rubin's face/vase drawing is an example of switching figure and ground. The face would be never noticed when the perception of the vase has been established, just as the perception of two faces would not occur when we see the vase in the figure. This situation is analogous to our understanding of novels. The figure-ground properties of the most famous of Shakespeare's plays, *Romeo and Juliet*, is described in terms of graph theory. Each character was assigned to value in terms of the figure-ground relations which was also derived from lattice structure, then was interpreted as its story. The method that Kitamura's paper proposed might open for us remarkable ways to generate content.

The purpose of "Narratives of an Artificial Agents: Mental Worlds and Narrating" by Taisuke Akimoto (Kyushu Institute of Technology) is to develop a computational model of narrative ability for artificial agents based on multidimensional narrative structures and hierarchical narrative graphs. The proposed model consists of two elements: the "mental world" as the internal representation of the world that is formed from many stories, and the mechanism of "narrating" as the act of expressing part of the mental world. In this chapter, the basic concepts and system frameworks of narrative ability, the mental world, and narrating are presented based on computational narrative studies, including those of Schank and his colleagues, cognitive approaches, and narrative discourse generation.

"A Phenomenological Model for Generating the Tasting Description of Japanese Sake" by Hiroki Fukushima (Kyushu Women's University) proposes a comprehensive "multifaceted" representation or model for describing the taste of Japanese sake as a core material. The author bridges the domains of taste and words on the basis of the findings of a first-person-singular study in cognitive science. In particular, this chapter achieves its goal by using pictorial descriptions together with verbal descriptions. As a result of this approach, the author discovered the difference between the manner of description of the PTG (Primary Taste Group for sake: sweetness, *umami*, and acidity) and the STG (Stimulus Taste Group: astringency and dryness); the PTG tends to be described in curvy Shapes, whereas in contrast the STG tends to be represented in linear Patterns. This challenging research shows a new approach for describing or narrating the vague object of the taste of sake to extend the range of cognitive science and narratology.

In "Haiku-Like Aesthetic Sentence Composition Through the Narrative Process" by Yoshihiko Nitta (Nihon University), the Haiku, a very short poem genre originated by Japanese poets in the Edo era, is treated and formally modeled for future automated Haiku generation or simulation. Per the author, aesthetic sentences often behave free from ordinary grammatical constraints but still preserve the power to transmit rich messages. Various events and situations that tacitly suggest the deep emotion and feelings of writer are embedded in a very short sentence composed of words or phrases in a 5-7-5-syllable pattern. Using numerous examples of Haiku, a season-word ontology or knowledge base for Haiku, and functional grammar, the model systematically describes Haiku interpretations and the composition process.

Akira Utsumi's (The University of Electro-Communications) "Literary Metaphor Comprehension and Production: A Unified View" focuses on "literary metaphors" that are used in literary works to enrich meanings and evoke aesthetic effects. Metaphors clearly are important elements in narratives and literary works, and Utsumi's unified approach to metaphors seeks to develop basic methods for metaphor comprehension and generation or simulation. Based on the author's theories of metaphor, such as the "interpretive diversity theory of nominal metaphors" and the "indirect categorization theory of predicative metaphors," the chapter introduces a unified view of literary metaphor comprehension and metaphor production, and finally discusses how people generate literary metaphors.

As the last chapter in this section, "Logic as a Narrative" by Koji Sawa (International Christian University High School) sheds light on logic as narrative generations. Complex network theories such as those proposed by Erdos and Renyi, Watts and Strogatz, and Barabasi and Albert were adopted in this chapter. Deductive logic exemplified by "All men are mortal. Socrates is a man. Therefore, Socrates is mortal" together with complex networks might be interpreted as a tool to describe stories. Since the collection of networks would exhibit the power law in spite of the fact that local deductive logic was not assumed throughout the whole of the network, this power law might suggest that when a complex network is considered, the transformation and integration of logic might be useful as a narrative.

Section 4: Analyses, Models, and Systems for Social Narratives

In the final section, first, three authors, Kai Seino, Yoko Enomoto, and Shiho Miyazawa (National Institute of Vocational Rehabilitation), in "Narrative Analysis of Employment Support for Students with Developmental Disabilities: Using an Objective Analysis of Free-Expression Answers," aim to obtain suggestions for employment support for students with developmental disabilities by conducting text mining and narrative analysis. In this chapter, the text data of the free-expression answers regarding the employment support of students with developmental disabilities are regarded as a kind of narrative. In addition to obtaining a variety of suggestions for actual employment support processing, the authors show the relationships of their text analysis research with narrative or story generation research. In particular, although the subjects' perspectives are limited to the existing situation, the acquired knowledge in this chapter enables us to bridge to narrative or story generation in order to expand their limited perspectives to encompass wider or alternative possibilities.

Next, Yoji Kawamura (Kindai University), through "Practice and Modeling of Advertising Communication Strategy: Sender-Driven and Receiver-Driven," presents an approach to building a social and consumption simulation model in an advertising and marketing narrative communication area. Therefore, this chapter moves to the social level of narrative communication and simulation. The author especially concentrates on the reception or consumption side of narrative communication, and this chapter also presents an approach to narrative communication and simulation models by analyzing consumer behavior. However, a difference from many marketing and advertising studies is that the author proposes narrative simulation strategies, including two types of sender-driven strategies and one type of receiver-driven strategy, as well as further concrete techniques or rhetoric, for an automated advertising model or system.

In " 'The Dialogue Triangle' Effect and Structure for Prototyping on 'Need-Solution Pairs': The Development of the "'Naruse Pedal.' Which Prevents Mistakes When Stepping on a Vehicle Pedal," Akimitsu Hirota (Kindai University) also deals with a social study related to the problem of narrative communication, in particular the topic of problem-solving behavior in product development (the process of pedal development for automobiles) in a situation where the problem is not defined. The background of this chapter's author is primarily management science. This study considers the process of simultaneously discovering and resolving problems through the case study of a user developing a product and the role of prototyping in this process based on several theoretical concepts, such as "need-solution pairs," "two behaviors in trial and error," and "dialogue triangle."

The final chapter in this section, as well as the book as a whole, "Collaboration for Supporting the Externalization of the Travel Narratives of the Elderly: A Case Study" by Nanae Shirozu and Mitsunori Matsushita (Kansai University), explores a system to assist elderly travelers who are not familiar with computers in externalizing information about their travel experiences and in accumulating this information in the form of travel narratives. In this chapter, a travel experience and the description of the experience and feelings evoked by it are understood as a narrative. This is similar to Fukushima's chapter on the experience of drinking sake and describing the taste. In a co-creation dialogue environment involving a speaker and a listener, the authors conduct participatory observation and externalization interviews about travel experiences. As a result of this experiment, the authors found that subjects became more involved and responsive and related more cohesive stories when paired with a listener equipped with relevant information. This observation indicates an aspect of cooperative story generation.

As these chapters show, this book covers diverse narrative genres and academic methods relating to content generation, narrative communication, and simulation. Such an integrated study has crucial and fundamental academic value, and will be useful in practical fields for the personal and social creation and distribution of novel narrative contents in the future.

Takashi Ogata
Iwate Prefectural University, Japan

Shin Asakawa
Tokyo Woman's Christian University, Japan

Acknowledgment

The editors would like to acknowledge the help of all the people involved in this project. Without their great contributions, this book would not have been completed. First, the editors wish to thank all the authors for their high-quality contributions and the reviewers for their valuable advices in improving the quality of the book. Second, the editors acknowledge the comprehensive support of the editorial advisory board members. Finally, the editors thank IGI Global for their assistance in the entire process.

Takashi Ogata
Iwate Prefectural University, Japan

Shin Asakawa
Tokyo Woman's Christian University, Japan

Section 1
Introduction

Chapter 1
Aspects of Content Generation Through Narrative Communication and Simulation

Takashi Ogata
Iwate Prefectural University, Japan

Shin Asakawa
Tokyo Woman's Christian University, Japan

ABSTRACT

In this chapter, the authors focus on narrative contents by considering and analyzing narrative communication and simulation. In particular, the authors present the multiple narrative structures model and informational narratology as original theoretical frameworks in seeking to undertake narrative hierarchical and multiple structures and micro and macro structures. The authors also introduce, as designing and developing systems, the integrated narrative generation system (INGS) for implementing the narrative micro mechanism, and the geinō information system (GIS) for designing the macro mechanism. Furthermore, neural network technologies including deep learning are also introduced to show the technological possibility of implementing narrative generation systems. These show a synthesized approach or establish a paradigm for narrative generation studies.

INTRODUCTION

In this chapter, the author understands narrative contents from the viewpoint of communication and simulation. In particular, the central issue is to consider narrative simulation systems based on the characteristics of narrative communication, namely the problem of narrative generation systems. Previously, there has been little research dealing with narrative contents from the viewpoints of narrative communication and simulation, and aimed at systematic realization and modeling as narrative generation systems. Based on the above key terms or concepts, this chapter presents both concrete models of narrative generation and narrative generation systems as narrative simulation. This chapter also describes

DOI: 10.4018/978-1-5225-4775-4.ch001

Copyright © 2018, IGI Global. Copying or distributing in print or electronic forms without written permission of IGI Global is prohibited.

an approach to combining narrative communication and simulation with new technologies, particularly neural networks and deep learning.

The author begins by presenting the key terms or concepts in this chapter and throughout the whole of this book. "Content" means the semantic aspect of information, in contrast to the formal aspect of information, which also exists. For example, the composition of a novel, such as chapter 1 and chapter 2, corresponds to a formal aspect and event sequence that can be summarized as a story, while the plot is a semantic aspect of that content. Further, by the term "narrative content," the author means a type of content that represents narrative or includes the element of narrative in various forms. "Narrative communication" means various types of communication structure that appear in various aspects of a narrative, while "narrative simulation" is equal to simulated narrative creation or collection by a human and narrative generation system, and artificial intelligence systems to perform and collect the narrative simulation. "Narrative content" refers to informational content to be sent to such receivers as readers and audiences; the concept is associated with reception and consumption through the communication process between the sender and receiver.

Originally, "narrative" in the title of this book was used in the broad sense, from novels, poems, and films to games, advertisements, and psychological narratives. The chapter appendix shows a comprehensive list of narrative genres as compiled by Ogata (1999a), based in particular on Japanese narrative phenomena.

The authors have divided the background research areas into the following two fields: application fields and the fields of methods, theories, and technologies. The authors' main application fields include narrative or story generation, natural language generation, dialogue generation, media (image, music, and so on) generation, interactive generation, and other related content generation fields. The next main methods, theories, and technologies include various fields in artificial intelligence and cognitive science, in particular knowledge representation, natural language processing and generation, conceptual dictionaries and ontology, media technologies, knowledge acquisition and text mining, neural network and deep learning, and other related fields. In this study, although the applicable technological objective is to develop narrative generation systems, the development approach is supported by theoretical studies.

The first two parts in the "BACKGROUND" section, i.e., content generation and narrative generation, comprise the applicable and technological systems. After the "BACKGROUND", Ogata discusses problems of "narrative communication" and "narrative simulation." Regarding the former, in its association with multiple narrative structures as one of Ogata's (2016a) theoretical foundations, the author presents an entire framework of narrative generation in which micro and macro narratives exist and are related to each other. As an architecture that simulates both of the above mechanisms under an organic mechanism, the author continuously introduces an integrated narrative generation system called the INGS (Ogata, 2016a) and a *geinō* information system called the GIS (Ogata, 2016b). Although there are various narrative levels, including personal and social or collective levels, automatic, semi-automatic, and interactive levels, and so on, the authors have been tackling automated narrative content generation based on narrative simulation technologies, mainly using artificial intelligence. On the other hand, Asakawa, who is an author of this chapter, provides a simple explanation of content generation studies using neural networks and deep learning (Asakawa, 2015a, 2015b, 2016). In the future, it will be possible to integrate the approaches of Ogata and Asakawa in their narrative generation systems.

This research plan will be conducted using interdisciplinary methods, including informatics (artificial intelligence, cognitive science, natural language processing, media technologies, neuroscience, deep learning), literary studies (narratology, literary theories), and social science areas (management science, marketing, and advertising studies). In the future, the results of this study in relation to narrative content communication and simulation through narrative generation systems such as those introduced in this book, will contribute to the scientific and technological expansion of information science and engineering, and literary studies. At the same time, it will also be useful for application to novel digital content ideas as well as the creations in more practical fields. This book presents theories, models, systems, and analyses of the generation of narrative contents in various genres based on interdisciplinary methods from informatics, literary studies, and social sciences. In particular, the authors seek to undertake diverse themes, including the following difficult topics: content generation (creation/production and reception/consumption) models and systems for narratives including novels, stories, poems, texts, films, games, advertisements, news, psychological narratives, rhetorical representations such as metaphors, marketing brands, and new products. Such integrated study of narrative content generation has a crucial and fundamental academic value, and in practical fields, will be useful for the future personal and social creation and distribution of novel narrative contents. In "FUTURE RESEARCH DIRECTIONS," the authors will list research topics from the above interdisciplinary perspective.

BACKGROUND

In content generation, for example, automatic document production has partially reached the stage of actual business. For example, the "Wordsmith" system by Automated Insights, Inc. (https://automatedinsights.com/) transforms structured data in industrial genres, such as ecommerce, financial services, real estate, media, entertainment, personal fitness, business intelligence, etc., into story forms. The "Qull" system by Narrative Science, Inc. (https://www.narrativescience.com/) is a data-driven storytelling system for business fields. However, in this chapter, the authors mainly describe narrative generation and story generation. Narrative generation and story generation relevant to human creativity have also been important and major themes for automatic document production.

The core background of this chapter is narrative generation. The authors will provide a comprehensive description of the situation relating to narrative generation (or narrative simulation in this chapter). Further, the author will summarize, principally based on Ogata (2016a), the expanded literary theory, which is a concept of the research and development by Ogata and the multiple narrative structures model that comprises the above concept.

Narrative Generation Systems for Narrative Simulation

This section overviews the research into narrative generation systems for narrative simulation. First, the author summarizes the description in Ogata (2016a) in the authors' previous book (Ogata & Akimoto, 2016) regarding comparatively classical narrative generation studies and then introduces new related studies.

An Overview of Narrative Generation System Studies

The human imagination has created devices or systems to automatically produce documents and narratives. To give an old example, Oda (2007) explained a conceptual mechanism called the *Lullian circle* in "Ars Magna Generalis et Ultima" (1305-1308) presented by Ramon Llull or Raimundus Lullus (1232-1315).

Jonathan Swift (1667-1745) described a kind of automatic document production machine in Part III of *Gulliver's Travels* (Swift, 2005). In relatively new examples, "An Imaginary Number" by Stanislaw Lem (1921-2006) (1984) collected novels written by a narrative generation machine in a fictional situation and Richard Powers (1957-), in his *Galatea 2.2* (Powers, 1995), drew the developmental process of a story generation program using a neural network. Additionally, experimental novels (Kihara, 2017).

Ogata (2016a) divided the majority of computer-based narrative generation systems into two approaches, namely a problem-solving approach (Newell & Simon, 1972) and a structural approach, depending on the AI techniques used to support their design and development.

A chief strategy of the problem-solving approach was the planning method based on a goal or goals by Schank and Abelson (1977). Schank's group presented various ideas and systems for story or narrative generation. For example, the TALE-SPIN program (Meehan, 1980) automatically generates different stories, an event sequence, from a story world based on characters planning actions to achieve specific goals. Each event in a generated story is described or defined using the conceptual dependency theory by Schank and Abelson (1977), is a formal method for describing the semantics of each event. This first method for story generation by the planning or problem-solving method was inherited by the following systems. For instance, Turner (1994) presented the MINSTREL system, which automatically generates stories according to material in *King Arthur and the Knights of the Round Table*. As an idea relating to narrative or story generation is case-based reasoning by Schank and Riesbeck (1981), as a method utilizing an example to apply to different problems than the original one. It is similar to the literary or narratological theory of intertextuality (Kristeva, 1980; Genette, 1982), which states the mutual using relationships of several or many literary contents. Various narrative generation systems and models, such as MEXICA (Pérez y Pérez & Sharples, 2001) and Sharples' (1996) engagement-reflection theory have used case-based reasoning.

On the other hand, the structural approach involves a narrative generation process based on narrative or story structural formalizations, such as story grammar and story schemas (Rumelhart, 1975). GESTER (Pemberton, 1989) and JOSEPH (Lang, 1999) consist of an interpreter with both a story grammar and a world model to simulate story developments according to their knowledge. The story grammar defines the abstract structure of the stories, while the world model contains elements embodied within the story structure: actors or characters, objects, and causal relations between events. This is a kind of hierarchical system to show a story's dynamic structure. In addition, Propp's (1968) folk tale theory, which Ogata uses as part of the story generation mechanism in the INGS and for other previous story generation systems (Ogata & Terano, 1991; Ogata, Hori, & Ohsuga, 1996), is a type of story grammar proposed from the side of narratology or literary theory.

Furthermore, as a system of different classifications, Ogata (2016a) also focused on the following systems that synthesize various narrative generation methods. Lebowitz (1985) proposed the conceptual design of a synthetic narrative generation framework involving character planning as well as the author's goals and planning. DAYDREAMER by Mueller (1990) is a computer program that simulates the consciousness of daydreaming, with a consistent character and a narrator, using various planning methods. A story generation system based on Aesop's world by Okada and Endo (1992) generates stories based on problem-solving or goal-oriented planning methods according to the goals of specific characters. Further, this system uses a mind model comprising both intelligent processing and sensitive processing, and conceptual dictionaries to describe the story's world and define the rules of goal planning. MINSTREL (Turner, 1994), mentioned above, is also classified in this group. The BRUTUS system by Bringsjord and Ferrucci (1999) has a synthetic narrative generation system architecture and uses the goal-based problem-solving simulation of characters and natural language generation by story grammar and literary rhetoric. Many previous narrative generation systems were basically story generation systems. By contrast, Ogata and Morita (2001) discussed the relation and difference between story and discourse in a narrative and designing and implementing for the narrative generation systems. A synthetic interactive fiction system, or IF, by Montfort (2007) also realized narrative variations, using the narrative discourse theory proposed by Genette (1972) to introduce structural techniques of "how a story is narrated," namely the problem of narrative discourse or plot, into the system.

Recent Narrative Generation System Studies

This section surveys recent narrative generation system studies and the related genres in books, doctoral dissertations, and papers, although they are not necessarily comprehensive or systematic.

First, Calvo, Daza-Arévalo, and Figueroa-Nazuno (2016) discuss the problem of creativity through computer programs using storytelling as the material and present a heuristic storytelling method based on simple syntactic and semantic properties found in a text corpus, in order to generate novel and coherent fictional texts according to what has already been written. Yılmaz (2017) treats new forms of advertisement creativity through digital media to provide the implementation of narration and storytelling in contemporary advertising and related areas, including digital games, viral advertising, and interactive media. In this book, Erdem (2017) deals with narrative advertisement. Lu and Zhang (2002) explore the possibility of a full life cycle automation of computer animation generation, in particular the generation process of computer animation from a children's story in natural language text form to the final animated movie. Gerhard (2010) provides a history and a detailed overview of prominent procedures of algorithmic music composition, in particular a specific class of algorithm in a compositional context using markov models, generative grammars, transition networks, chaos and self-similarity, genetic algorithms, cellular automata, artificial neural networks, and artificial intelligence.

There are also related doctoral dissertations. For example, Lee (2012) presents a Sports Commentary Recommendation System (SCoReS) to automatically suggest stories for commentators to tell during games using automated narration and human-computer interaction to keep the viewer informed and entertained. Finlayson (2012) presents a new machine learning algorithm called the Analogical Story Merging (ASM) that can extract and learn "culturally-relevant plot patterns" from sets of folktales, in particular a substantive portion, "functions" and "moves," of Vladimir Propp's (1968) in a theory of the structure of folktale plots, based on a developed text annotation mechanism. Sarlej (2014) explores the automatic generation of stories with morals by focusing on six common morals identified in Aesopâs fables: retribution, greed, pride, realistic expectations, recklessness, and reward. And this thesis defines the relationship between the moral of a story and the patterns of character emotions that arise in that story to generate stories. As a study related to computer games, Hollister (2016) presents and evaluates a narrative generation method called the CAMPFIRE Story Telling System with input from the listener based on the Cooperating Context Method (CCM) to generate and tell dynamic stories in real time. Cutumisu (2009) provides non-repetitive and more entertaining behaviors for the non-player characters (NPCs) in role-playing games without investing programming effort in describe describing custom non-trivial scripts for each NPC. Likewise, Dubbelman (2013) discusses the practice of narrative design from the perspective of embodied presence so that narrative designer challenges express fictional worlds without disrupting this feeling of "being-there" from insights and practices in game, film, performance, architecture, and literature studies. The study subsequently proposes alternative narrative devices, more compatible with the interactive and spatial nature of computer games. Langxuan (2015) introduces the drama-guided narrative health game framework to develop games for health according to two key constructs: engagement and adherence.

In addition, recently, Swartjes (2010), for instance, provided a multi-agent narrative generation system, while Si (2010) developed a narrative generation system using interaction between characters and the user. Riedl and colleagues have conducted the Scheherazade project (Li & Riedl, 2015). Kybartas and Bidarra (2016) present a comprehensive survey for story generation techniques. In particular, divides narrative components into "narrative," "story," "plot," "space," and "discourse" to survey the degree of automation in computational narrative based on many examples of story and narrative generation systems. Furthermore, Martin, Ammanabrolu, Hancock, Singh, Harrison, and Riedl (2017) deals with both the event generation from an event and the sentence generation from an event in the pipeline architecture of story generation. In particular, based on recurrent encoder-decoder neural networks, both two neural techniques called *event2event* and *event2sentence* for event and sentence generation.

Expanded Literary Theory and Multiple Narrative Structures Model for Dealing With Narrative Multiplicity

In this section, the author introduces, mainly based on the description by Ogata (2016a) and other of his previous studies (Ogata, 1997, 2000, 2002a, 2002b, 2014, 2016b, etc.), the concept of "expanded literary theory (ELT)," as one of his ideas for the research into and development of treating narrative multiplicity at various levels, and the multiple narrative structures model as part of ELT.

ELT was originally presented as a concept for research fields in which narratology and literary theories are organically introduced into computational and cognitive approaches, such as AI and cognitive science, or into narrative generation systems. Ogata also aimed at an extended narratology or literary theory for designing and developing digital narratives or information contents in ELT. ELT has the following two features: (1) in the wide sense, it develops and analyzes narratives as information contents and (2) in the narrow sense, it develops narrative generation systems. The second narrow aspect is related to the point that a narrative work as an information content has an automatic narrative generation mechanism as a narrative engine. This point will be associated with his research plan as represented by, so to speak, an information content including or using a narrative generation system (Ogata, in press-a). ELT is related to the creation of literary or entertaining narrative works over existing styles that either use a narrative generation function or are supported by such. In these viewpoints, ELT is the most significant concept for pursuing Ogata's (2016a) INGS project. In fact, by proposing the concept of ELT, Ogata is presenting several attempts at mixing informatics and literature to design and develop narrative generation systems and their applicable mechanisms.

The following description shows the characteristics of ELT as compared to previous approaches to narratology using three criteria: object, direction or concern, and method. In the previous narratology, non-digital texts were studied and the analysis and interpretation thereof were the main directions or concerns. Moreover, a variety of methods were proposed based on very rich literary knowledge. In contrast, Ogata's ELT deals with narratives and literary works using information media, including automatic narrative generation systems. The major objects are narrative generation systems and narratives or literary works that use or include them. The narrative generation systems need to be opened toward a variety of applications and work to achieve various purposes. Next, the primary direction or concern is the generation or creation of texts, as well as the invention or development of new genres and styles in narratives or literary works. One of the reasons for the invention or development of narrative innovation is as follows. Previous narratology dealt with narratives and literary works that had a very long history; therefore, the analysis and interpretation thereof were the most important issues. By contrast, the history of narratives or literary works using information technologies is currently very short and this new narratology has not fully accumulated a wealth of knowledge on works and theories. ELT is necessary to create a theoretical framework for generation and production through narrative innovation. Finally, as stated previously, ELT, with its short history has not acquired a wealth of theoretical and experiential knowledge and methods. The current important topic is to introduce the experiential knowledge of previous narratology and literary theories into ELT to effectively adapt to the new field for the future expansion of target texts and for the constitution of an expanded original narrative theory.

One of the current goals of ELT is the synthesis of literary theories in INGS. ELT is required to function as a background design idea to concretize the INGS. The current experimental version of the INGS also mixes, organically and partially, three literary theories: the story structure theory by Propp (1968) story structure theory, Genette's (1972) narrative discourse theory (these have already been mentioned above), and Jauss's (1970) reception theory. Although the objective in ELT, from a larger perspective, is to develop and propose a new narratology by mixing both information science and literary theories, a purely descriptive method is adopted to achieve this objective. Rather, ELT is implemented through, so to speak, a practical theory in which a variety of narratologies and literary theories are introduced or fused into the narrative generation systems to be developed.

An important issue in the future of ELT is to newly treat Japanese literary theories for, so to speak, "cultural-dependent narrative generation systems." In the old or traditional literature, for instance *Kagerō Nikki* (Fujiwara no Michitsuna no Haha, 1989), *Genji Monogatari* by Murasaki Shikibu (1993-1997). On the other hand, in modern Japanese literature, many works have proposed original theoretical literary studies by blending Japanese and European literary traditions: Sōseki Natsume (1867-1916) (1907) analyzed literary works from the perspective of relations of emotional and logial elements. Takaaki Yoshimoto (1924-2012) (1965) analyzed the historical process of Japanese literature by a theoretical framework based on instructional and poetic language expression. As other theoretical or narratological authors, there are Shigehiko Hasumi (1936-) (1985), Kōjin Karatani (1941-) (1993), Naomi Watanabe (1952-) (2012), and so on. Moreover, Riichi Yokomitsu published novels such as *Kikai* [*Machine*] (1931) to show an experimental description of narrative discourse, while Kenzaburō Ōe (1935-) published experimental novels, including *Dōjidai game* [*The game of contemporaneity*] (1979) to introduce narratology and literary theories into the narrative structures.

ELT has been extended towards constructing a comprehensive concept that includes several concepts for directing generation acts in a narrative generation system or the aspects of narratives to be generated thereby. Further, the objectives also include creating narrative generation systems and new narrative works. The following three are also concepts to be composed of ELT in this extended sense.

- **Circular Narrative Control:** This is a design plan of narrative generation by Ogata, in particular the INGS. The first meaning is iterative narrative generation. An example is an experimentally implemented mechanism for the narrative discourse phase (Akimoto & Ogata, 2012, 2013a). It will be connected to a method through which a narrative generation cycle continues to acquire many generated results, and is synthesized to an edited and individual narrative work. In contrast, the second meaning is the free and flexible control of the applicable order of narrative generation phases. This concept is gradually being implemented in the INGS. A perfectly free processing order among the modules will also be related to the following concept of "fluidity and fixation."

- **Fluidity and Fixation:** This concept was adopted for the design and use of various information contents, including narrative contents generated by the INGS, related to narrative generation. Information contents have the following characteristics: the capacities of free compilation, self-organization, and automatic generation. The concepts of fluidity and fixation are also related to these characteristics. In the cases of previous and traditional contents, these kinds of floating characteristics of contents may be able to be treated as the phenomena in a human brain that write texts for a narrative work. The texts are then fixed as outside content through the social process of a human group or organization. In contrast, information contents enable the fluidity itself to be brought out. A novel that a writer has written is equivalent to a work in the world of traditional contents, whereas the writing or creating process involved in writing a novel can be considered a work in the world of information contents and narrative generation. The creation by a narrative generation system will enable the representation and visualization of the narrative content generation at any stage of the narrative generation process. It may be regarded as a literary or artistic work. The following two forms or styles are considered from the author's viewpoint on work as an information content: (1) the style in which the fluidity itself is equivalent to a work (the fixation), and (2) the form in which various means of processing are used to fix one or more works based on many or a huge number of works and the fragments generated through a fluid narrative generation process. Some previous studies can be re-considered from the viewpoint of fluidity and fixation. For instance, the Jauss-based mechanism by Akimoto and Ogata (2012, 2013a) indicates that the circulative process corresponding to the fluidity and user-viewing of one or more generated results is equivalent to fixation.
- **Norm and Deviation:** This is a narrative control method based on the norm, which is the standard framework by which a narrative generation process should be performed, and on the deviation from the norm. This is related to the literary concept of "defamiliarization" by Shklovsky (1990). The defamiliarization techniques presented by Ogata were originally acquired by analyzing television commercials (Abe, Ogata, & Hanada, 2008; Zhang, Ono, & Ogata, 2011, 2012)

In television commercials, various techniques for defamiliarizing or deviating from realistic events are employed to differentiate and make appealing a commercial product. Ogata, who generalized this methodology into one of the universal narrative generation techniques, considered that, in the relative sense, each cycle of narrative generation corresponds to a system of deviation from the current state (norm). For instance, he seeks to undertake the application of this concept into the INGS by considering that preliminarily constructed scripts and dictionaries correspond to the norm, whereas various rhetorical techniques perform the deviation.

Moreover, the multiple narrative structure model is not only a concept composed of ELT in the extended sense as stated above but is a concept positioned in the higher level to be related to narrative generation systems, narrative works created using the systems, and further, the entire structure of Ogata's research.

The multiple narrative structures model is a comprehensive research plan, including its methods. The basic idea is as follows: A basis of narrative generation is set on the concept of "multiplicity" and the narrative generation studies are required to be designed and developed on it. The basic concept of multiplicity is based on the complexity of narrative structures and representations of a folkloric typical communication structure. Changing from a typical folkloric narrative structure, narratives that transform to diverse genres are multiply extended, for example, at the level of elements or components such as story and character. The section "MULTIPLE NARRATIVE STRUCTURES OF *KABUKI*: STORIES AND PEOPLE" in the chapter titled, "An Integrated Approach to Narrative Generation: From Mishima and *Kabuki* to Narrative Generation Systems," in this book, describes in detail how an actor who appears in a *kabuki* play demonstrates multiplicity: He plays one or more characters in the drama; he is a person with a real body; and he has his own personal life history with a real name, in addition to playing a character with a name that has been inherited historically.

This type of phenomenon indicates that a narrative, a *kabuki* play in the aforementioned example, has multiple structures. Although it is partially similar to the multiplicity of voices by Bakhtin (1984), Ogata clearly divides the phenomenon of narrative generation into the following two levels for designing and developing narrative generation systems that cover multiple structures with a wider range: (1) the level of the generation (and reception) process of a single narrative work and the work itself, and (2) the level of the production (and consumption) process of two or more narrative works and the sequential narrative including each of the narrative works. Multiple voices and structures are derived in each of the narratives. Of course, each of the narratives has various relationships with the narrative works by other authors. However, a narrative also has diverse associations with a sequence of narratives as the historical and social process in the production and consumption level or organizational level. The production and consumption level or organizational level contain the generation and reception level of a single narrative work.

Based on the recognition of multiplicity or plurality of narratives, the narrative generation research described in this chapter was conducted according to a broad framework, including a wide range of narratives, from narrative generation systems in a narrow sense, i.e., systems as computer programs, to narrative generation systems in a wide sense, i.e., systems as a method of dealing with collective societies of humans as a symbolic narrative generation system. Ogata (2011, 2016a), based on the fundamental consideration in Ogata (1995) and Ogata and Kanai (2010), divided this comprehensive framework for research in narrative generation into five fields. The core portion covers narrative generation systems such as computer programs. Beyond this are two interdisciplinary areas: literary studies (primarily narratology and literary theories) and information studies (chiefly AI and cognitive science). A new narratological area, created by blending these two areas, has been called ELT as stated above. The next level contains a variety of narratological approaches to a number of fields, such as folklore, cultural anthropology, history, sociology, philosophy, psychology, marketing and advertising, business administration, architecture, and biology. The outermost level consists of spaces occupied by various fields relevant to the narrative. The authors' approaches to narrative generation and content generation such as computer programs are founded on this overall and comprehensive narrative perspective.

Finally, as stated above, the expanded literary theory as an extended concept, aims, in the most direct manner, to construct a new narratology and a new literary theory by blending both human studies, such as narratology and literary theories, and informational studies, such as AI and cognitive science. At the same time, it is an overall concept to include the multiple narrative structures model that tries to seize narratives and narrative generation from the viewpoint of multiplicity, and several further concepts, such as circular narrative control, norm-deviation and fluidity-fixation, to direct both narrative generation mechanisms and narratives to be generated using the narrative generation mechanisms.

NARRATIVE COMMUNICATION AND SIMULATION: A FRAMEWORK OF INFORMATIONAL NARRATOLOGY

In this section, the authors consider the problem of narrative communication and narrative simulation through the following three frameworks: the informational narratology by Ogata, Kawamura, and Kanai (in press) and chapter 1 (Kawamura, Ogata, & Kanai, in press), the integrated narrative generation system (INGS) by Ogata (2016a), and the *geinō* information system (GIS) by Ogata (2016b). Although this informational narratology proposes a synthesized narrative model that is related to the multiple narrative structures model in the expanded literary theory described above, it particularly positions the narrative generation by the sender in addition to the narrative generation by the receiver clearly on the model. This model also deals with narratives or narrative phenomena as the existences of both micro narratives and macro narratives, and their respective mutual relationships. In particular, the informational narratology, similar to the multiple narrative structures model that composes a part of the narrative generation studies by Ogata, but from a slightly different perspective, sees an important characteristic of narrative communication in the aspect of multiple structure of both micro and macro narratives. Related to this framework, the computer architecture for simulating this micro narrative generation is the INGS and similarly, the architecture for simulating this macro narrative production corresponds to the GIS.

A Narrative Communication Framework by Informational Narratology

This section simply introduces the informational narratology by Kawamura, Ogata, and Kanai (in press). Although this partially overlaps with Ogata's multiple narrative structures model, the main difference is that the multiple narrative structures model focuses on the concrete structuring of narrative generation techniques and the knowledge on the sender side, while informational narratology emphasizes the aspect of image generation on the narrative receiver side and the reception-oriented generation methods.

Contents and Narratives

In the informational narratology, a content generated by the sender is called a narrative or narrative content. It divides the generation and reception of a narrative content into the following two forms: "created content = narrative" and "content' (through the interaction between the sender and receiver) = narrative."

- **Created Content = Narrative (Figure 1):** This is a model in which a content is provided to a sender as a package (such as a book). In this model, the sender who generates the content decides a medium through which the content is distributed, and creates the content to utilize the characteristics of the medium and to represent any intentions and world views (including no intentions and no world views). The receiver then receives this created content. This is the process of "created content = narrative."

Figure 1. A simple model of the generation and reception of a content
Source: Kawamura, Ogata, and Kanai (in press).

- **A Content' Through the Interaction Between the Sender and Receiver (Figure 2):** In the case that a content is provided to a receiver through a stage instead of a package, the content is called "content'." In this case, the sender (including the performers) basically plays the content conscious of the response of the receiver of the content (including applause, cheers, and laughter). Thus, there are two types of content, both the content provided by the sender and the content' to which the receiver's response is added. The latter means the content' created in entertainments, dramas, live music, and so on. In these cases, although the subject who generates the content' is the sender, the receiver's response contributes to changing the content'. Thus, this type of content' is generated through the interaction between the sender and receiver.

Reception and Narrative, Visible Narrative, and Invisible Narrative

First, "story," which is one of the most important terms in a narrative, means a temporal line or sequence of events. The "event" is a unit of occurrences that change any states in the story. The receiver of a narrative receives a content to interpret the story from the sequence of events. Thus, although a story is an element at the abstract level, it can be structured and symbolized as a temporal line and sequence of events. An abstract or synopsis of a narrative is often equivalent to the simple description of the story. On the other hand, the receiver does not necessarily interpret only the structuralized story. Rather, the receiver feels the style and atmosphere in the overall content, associates the representation elements of a content with various things, and moves the mind by connecting the content with his/her experiences. These are largely related to each receiver's unique knowledge and experiences and the reception methods also differ from each other. Therefore, it is difficult to symbolize their elements as structured phenomena. In this chapter, all elements except for story are called "images."

The following two contrasting concepts are introduced here: "visible narrative" or "narrative as external representation" and "invisible narrative" or "narrative as internal representation." Firstly, regarding the visible narrative and narrative as external representation, the contents shown in Figures 1 and 2 are the representation itself generated by the sender and are composed of elements that the receiver can directly perceive. On the other hand, regarding the visible narrative or narrative as internal representation, the receiver, who is in a place to receive a content, interprets any stories and holds any images in the mind (Figure 3). These are called "reception stories" or "reception images." Further, by triggering the content in the receiver, the mutual interaction of both the afterimage of the memory of the content

Figure 2. A model for which the response of the content is considered
Source: Kawamura, Ogata, and Kanai (in press).

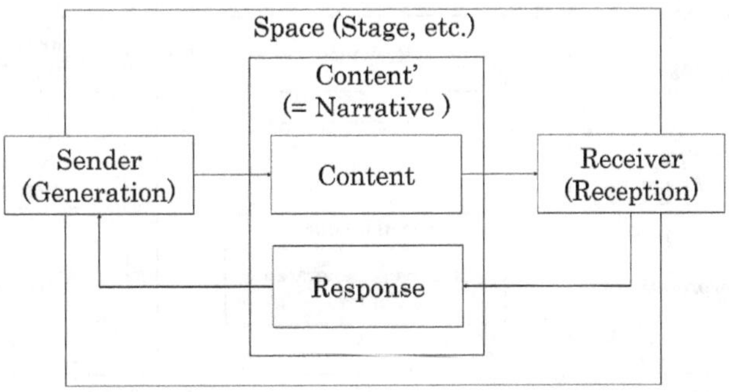

Figure 3. A model considering the receiver's internal representation
Source: Kawamura, Ogata, and Kanai (in press).

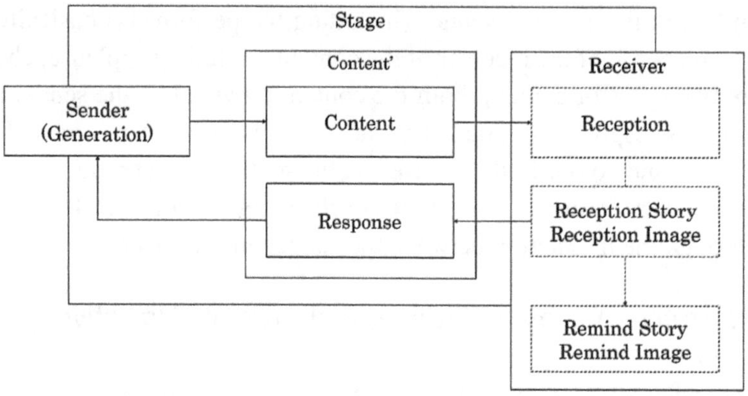

and the knowledge and experiences enables the receiver to re-structure the stories and images, which are called "reminding story" and "reminding image," for the content and to construct the life images of the receiver. Because such stories and images exist within the receiver, they are basically elements that cannot be perceived, or invisible elements. The frame by the dotted line in Figure 3 shows invisible elements.

Who is the subject that generates these stories and images? The sender who generates the content itself is the first subject. As shown in Figure 4, the sender generates content based on the unique stories and images. However, there generally exist gaps between the sender's stories/images contained in the content and the stories/images received by the receivers. To speak in extremes, the sender's stories and images themselves, which were expressed once as contents, do not already have any meanings, at least in the social process. Different receivers may have different stories and images from each other based on the same content. Concurrently, various interactions between a content and the receivers generate diverse stories and images. This is the idea of the "stories and images through the interactions between a content and the receivers = narrative."

Figure 4. A model considering the generation by the receiver
Source: Kawamura, Ogata, and Kanai (in press).

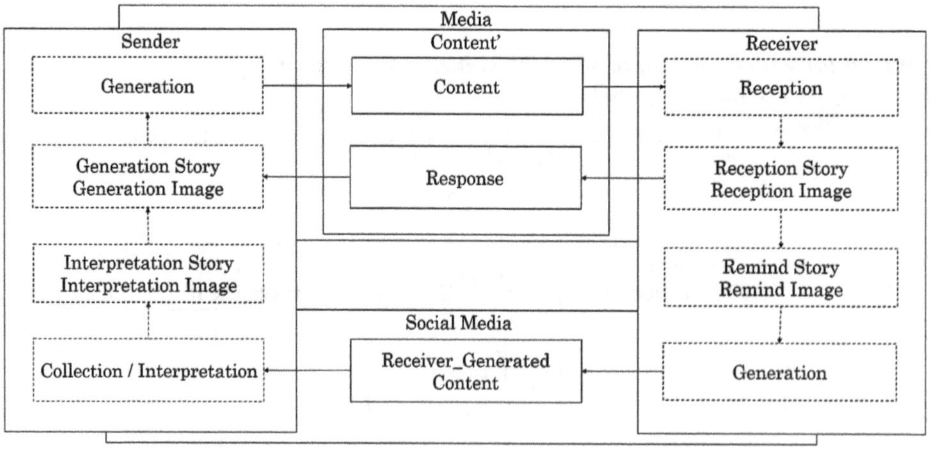

Media and Narrative

Informational narratology differentiates the "representation form" that the media uses to represent the content itself, such as letters and moving images, from simple "media" that are the means of social content distribution. A previous important role of narrative-relating media was to distribute the content generated by the sender. On the other hand, social media through which the receivers can send their information, have been increasing in recent times. They enable the stories and images generated by the receivers to be socially distributed as narratives that are externally represented. When a sender generates a content, he or she collects and interprets the receivers' responses and receiver-generated contents to utilize them for the next content generation (Figure 4). The utilization includes the following methods: the first is the method whereby the sender interprets stories and images from the receivers' responses and receiver-generated contents to plan the next story generation and image generation dependent on them. The next method is that the sender introduces some of the receivers' responses and the receiver-generated contents into the content to be generated.

A point to focus on here is that social narratives are generated through the mutual interactions of the contents generated by the sender and receivers, the reception and reminding, interpreted stories and images, and so on. The basis or starting point of a narrative to be generated is the content generated by the sender, and the stories and images received by the receivers. However, the narrative is transformed into diverse stories, images, and contents by the knowledge and experiences of each receiver, social situations, and events influencing each receiver, receiver-generated contents, and the situation and intention of the sender. If a collection of these stories, images, and contents can be regarded as a narrative in the wide sense, a narrative author means an entire society, including the senders and receivers.

Another issue to be focused on here is that the interaction between the sender and receiver based on a content draws a cycle in any form. Narratives to be generated dynamically perform through the interaction between the sender and receiver. Sometimes, the cycle is fixed into one narrative and a narrative content transforms into extraordinary new narratives by amplified change. It is too difficult to predict the futures of narrative phenomena their complexity. What controls the turning point of narrative fixation and transformation is frequently unclear in the sender and receiver.

Narrative Generation and Strategy: The Narrative Generation–Reception Process

Although it is difficult to decide where the starting point in the circulative process shown in Figure 4 lies, the authors regard a narrative generation process as one that begins with the imagination and planning of the stories and images to be generated by the sender. The sender, based on his or her knowledge, experiences, and various data, generates content as visible elements according to stories and images as invisible elements. Diverse processings are performed in the process whereby invisible elements are transformed into visible elements, including the process for forming and planning invisible elements. More diverse and variable processings can be conducted when the content is a complex representation object.

Next, in a situation where the interaction between the sender and receiver is repeated, the sender, for the narrative generation, sets any intentions and strategies for generating the generating stories and generating images, depending on the receivers' responses and the interpretation stories and interpretation images by the sender (Figure 5).

Although there are frequently differences between the story or image generated by the sender and those imagined by the receiver, the sender basically generates a content so that his/her generating story

Figure 5. A model considering a sender's strategy
Source: Kawamura, Ogata, and Kanai (in press).

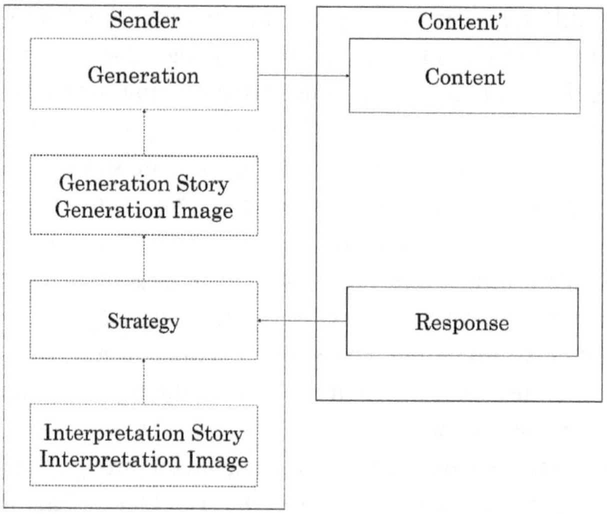

and image are correctly transmitted to the receivers. Additionally, the sender, based on the receivers' responses, confirms whether his/her generating story and image have been correctly understood by the receiver to generate the content. This method corresponds to a "sender-driven" strategy, where the initiative for the story and image are positioned on the sender. In this case, the sender tries to transmit the stories and images as faithfully as possible to the receiver.

By contrast, in some cases, the sender intentionally generates a content using the representation form, with which it is too difficult to relate the story and image to the receiver. Alternatively, the sender generates a content so that the receiver can easily create the sender's story and image instead of forcing the receiver to receive them. This means a "receiver-driven" strategy in which the initiative for the story and image is set on the receiver's side. In this case, the sender transmits any incompatibility or feeling of difference or omission to the receiver to extract the reminding stories and reminding images from the receiver. Additionally, the sender also receives these responses and receiver-generated contents to utilize them for the generation of the sender's content generation.

Moreover, in an extreme situation, the receiver arbitrarily amplifies the stories and images differently from the story generated by the sender. This is, so to speak, the state of "divergence" where the initiative for story generation and image generation is moved to the receiver beyond the sender's strategy. An extreme example is, so to speak, "burst into flames," which means a state triggered by an event or content where the receivers' responses and contents are spread violently through social media, etc., to occupy the media. The intentional realization of such a situation will be possible through strategic control (Figure 5).

Viewpoints of Informational Narratology: Two Types of Direction

The final goal of the informational narratology approach is to create information systems for generating narratives using such narrative informational modeling. The research perspectives in the informational narratology can be divided into the following two types: the micro perspective and macro perspective.

- **Informational Modeling of Micro Narratives:** Informational narratology aims at modeling the elements and structures of micro narratives. It analyzes narratives in diverse genres and media to extract the visible elements and invisible elements and systematizes the commonality and structures of the relationships among their elements. The systematized narrative structures can be used as informational models for narrative generation. Further, cognitive experiments relating to narrative reception processes enable the effects on the receivers of narrative techniques and rhetoric to be explored and for the reception process from the visible to invisible elements to be made clear. Furthermore, it develops information systems that implement the techniques and rhetoric for narrative generation to simulate the generation process from the visible to invisible elements through narrative generation experiments.
- **Informational Modeling of Macro Narratives:** Informational narratology aims at modeling elements and structures in macro narratives. It visualizes the relationships between narrative societies that are composed of diverse types of subjects, and narratives as visible and invisible elements as an informational modeling, by analyzing social phenomena related to the performing arts, advertisement, and so on. Further, informational narratology considers the directions for embodying social narrative generation systems towards developing information systems that simulate the aspects of narrative societies.

A Simulation Framework of Micro Narratives: An Integrated Narrative Generation System

The multiple narrative structures model by Ogata, in addition to the above informational narratology, is linked to the design and development of the integrated narrative generation system (INGS), namely a micro direction, and the *geinō* information system (GIS), namely a macro direction.

The INGS is a mechanism that systematizes the narrative generation-reception process. In this narrative generation study, narrative generation in the wide sense stems from two types of process: the narrative generation and reception process and the narrative production and consumption process. To give an overview, the former corresponds to personal level narrative generation, while the latter corresponds to social distribution level narrative generation. The INGS is a personal level narrative generation system, while the GIS's narrative generation system framework treats of narrative generation as social narrative distribution.

Ogata (2016a), relying on his framework of expanded literary theory, divided the components in the largest level of a narrative generation mechanism into the following four parts to demonstrate the important narratological concepts and a set of cognitive and computational techniques used to realize those concepts: (1) the generation of a story or narrative world, mainly including characters, places, and objects to appear in the story or to be narrated, (2) the manner of narrative discourse for narrating or re-structuring the story made in the above (the deep structure generation aspect of the narrative discourse processing), (3) the manner of narrative discourse for expressing language and other surface representations based on the above deep level narrative discourse (the surface level generation in the narrative discourse processing), and (4) the narrator or sender and narratee or receiver that correspond to the two necessary types of main object for narrating or generating a narrative, including a story and narrative discourse. These basically comprise an exemplary set of narrative possibilities and the narrative generation mechanism of the INGS does not necessarily use all of the modules in the current development stage. However, they show a division based on a large framework of narrative generation.

Moreover, as the computational techniques for implementing those elements as possibilities, the following elements, which correspond to the above (1) to (4), can be listed: (1) Story Generation: the technological methods or theories including the frame, semantic network, rule base, story grammar, knowledge base, agent, conceptual system, ontology, problem solving, planning, inference, case-based reasoning, case grammar, discourse theory, etc.; (2) Narrative Discourse: namely, structure transformation, grammatical and rhetorical knowledge structures, etc., are included; (3) Narrative Expression: natural language generation, image processing technologies, automatic musical composition and variation, etc., correspond to the technologies; (4) Narrator and Narratee: agent, knowledge representation, generation control technique, etc., are considered.

Figure 6 shows the overall structure of the INGS. At the macro level, it is composed of the following three generation mechanisms: story, discourse, and representation or expression. Parts corresponding to the mechanisms in this figure concern the "story-generation mechanism," "narrative-discourse mechanism," several "narrative-expression mechanisms," and several "control mechanisms." On the other hand, elements corresponding to the content or knowledge in this figure are part of a "state-event transformation knowledge base," several "conceptual dictionaries," "several language notation dictionaries," and "narrative-content knowledge bases." In his study, Ogata (2016a) presented a detailed list of all the modules in the newest version of the INGS.

The story generation mechanism is a mechanism corresponding to the above (1) and the INGS is implemented using the techniques including frame, semantic network, rule base, story grammar, knowledge base, problem solving, planning, discourse theory, etc. At the same time, the story generation mechanism uses the revised and extended version of Propp's folktale morphology (1968) to show an aspect of Ogata's expanded literary theory. The mechanism is related to the above state-event transformation knowledge base and the conceptual dictionaries. These are classified as the components to be included in the framework of the story generation mechanism in the above grouping. These knowledge-base

Figure 6. INGS architecture

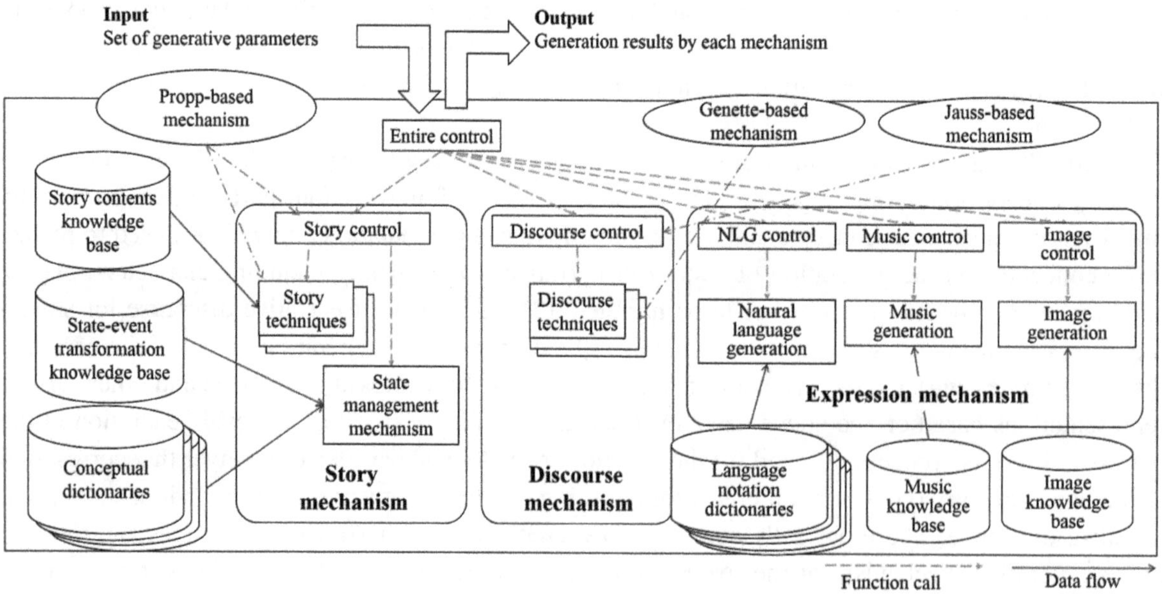

and conceptual dictionaries are implemented by using techniques including frame, semantic network, knowledge base, conceptual system, ontology, case grammar, and so on. The second narrative discourse mechanism corresponds to the above (2) to use techniques such as structure transformation and grammatical and rhetorical knowledge structure. This part is strongly related to narratology and literary theories and is the most narratological and literary part of the INGS's narrative generation processes. In fact, narratology, in the narrow sense, deals with narrative discourse. As expanded literary theory, the INGS has utilized a revised and extended version of Genette's (1972) narratology or narrative discourse theory. Next, the narrative representation or expression mechanism is a part corresponding to (3) above to treat the techniques, including natural language generation, image processing technology, automatic musical composition, and variation. Finally, the control mechanism, mainly in the current INGS, deals with the ordering control of modules and mutual control by the virtual narrator-narratee. The latter in particular is a mechanism overlapping with (4) above to be implemented by introducing the idea of Jauss's reception theory (1970) into a portion.

In addition, the purpose of the INGS is to simulate narrative generation at a single or personal level different from the GIS. Therefore, there are corresponding relationships between the INGS and humans. For example, the conceptual dictionaries in the INGS are equivalent to the conceptual memory of a personal human and the narrative content knowledge bases are similar to human episodic memory. Further, narrative generation techniques, such as the story generation techniques in the INGS, are equivalent to the knowledge required to create and operate event sequences in the human brain.

However, the levels of narrator and narratee in a narrative are not necessarily clearly modeled in the current design and implementation through the INGS. These are difficult problems that raise various questions concerning narrative subjects, such as who is the narrator in a narrative?; who is the narratee in a narrative?; who is the author in a narrative? These considerations will be described in the next part of this chapter.

A problem or issue to be considered or solved is that subjects of narrative generation, including characters, narrators, sender(s), and receiver(s), are not described explicitly in the current version of the INGS. Although, for instance, the knowledge of each character is now formed using conceptual dictionaries in this system, they are not formed as, so to speak, thick knowledge structures. However, each character is explicitly defined in the system as a substance. By contrast, narrator(s), sender(s), and receiver(s) do not exist in the system in the form of substantial descriptions of each. Although it is necessary to substantiate these at a time appropriate to each in the narrative generation process, the problem of timing will be discussed in the next section.

All the program components of the implementation in the current version were listed in Table 2 in Ogata (2016a). Although the main development program language is Common Lisp, several types of development tool are also partially used for particular purposes. The following description provides an overview of each of the mechanisms according to Table 2 in Ogata (2016a).

- **Conceptual Structure Generation Mechanism:** This is a collection of various types of narrative technique, including story generation techniques (to generate story structures), narrative discourse techniques (to generate narrative discourse structures based on the story structures).
    - **Story Generation Mechanism:** Although the current INGS contains various types of story generation technique that generate the hierarchical story structures based on fragmental scriptural and "temporal event sequences" (Ogata, Hori, & Ohsuga, 1996), "Propp-based story content grammar," and "pair relationships between events" (Ogata, 2007; Imabuchi

& Ogata, 2012, 2013), "defamiliarization rhetoric" (Zhang, Ono, & Ogata, 2011, 2012), and so on, the group of story generation techniques is a central portion of the story generation mechanism and, further, the whole of the INGS. This formal mechanism is required to systematically reflect previous studies and future expansion concerning semantic studies of narrative temporal knowledge and to learn such huge volumes of fragmental data from various current corpora. The sub-mechanisms in the story generation mechanism have an "event concepts generation mechanism," including event generation functions based on verb concepts and instances, and "state generation rules based on events and states" (Onodera, Akimoto, & Ogata, 2012).

  - **Narrative Discourse Generation Mechanism:** The central parts include narrative discourse techniques and narrative discourse techniques selection functions, narrative discourse techniques application functions. Other mechanisms help the actual usage. Regarding this phase, Ogata (1999b, 2004) has analyzed and formalized "Genette-based narrative discourse techniques" for a systematic collection of narrative discourse techniques, including other discourse techniques in addition to the Genette-based ones, for implementation in the INGS. Further, discourse generation functions based on variation music are also included in the INGS as a music mechanism.
  - **Surface Expression Generation Mechanisms:** These techniques for surface narrative representation include mechanisms for language ("sentence generation mechanism" (Kumagai, Funakoshi, Akimoto, & Ogata, 2012)), music ("music generation mechanism" (Kobayashi & Ogata, 2004; Ogata & Akimoto, 2007; Akimoto & Ogata, 2013b)), and image ("image generation mechanism" (Ogata, 2008)). The language generation mechanism has functions for diverse linguistic elements including single sentence, word order, language notation, and complex sentence. The music generation mechanism contains various kinds of transformation function, including "from story to original music, from original music to original music, from variation music to original music," and "from narrative discourse to variation music" (Akimoto & Ogata, 2014). These musical functions are a symbolic design of the circulative narrative control, stated in the section titled "Expanded Literary Theory and Multiple Narrative Structures Model for Dealing with Narrative Multiplicity" in this chapter in the INGS.

- **Dictionaries:** These mainly comprise "conceptual dictionaries" (Ogata, 2015) ("noun conceptual dictionary," "verb conceptual dictionary," "adjective conceptual dictionary," and "adjective verb conceptual dictionary") and "language notation dictionaries" (Ono & Ogata, 2015) ("noun notation dictionary," "verb notation dictionary," "adjective notation dictionary," "adjective verb notation dictionary," and "particle notation dictionary"). The verb and noun conceptual dictionaries are especially important in the INGS because the former provide such fundamental information about an event, which is a basic unit in a story and narrative discourse, as the semantic element or case structure, while the latter provide concrete information and the ontological position of each event.
- **Knowledge Bases:** This group is used for the above several types of narrative technique. The "story content knowledge bases" are, in particular, the most important set for use in story generation. In particular, each story technique is a formal operational definition, while the corresponding element in a story knowledge base is the content knowledge required to concretely achieve a story structure construction. The "Propp-based story content grammar" is also divided into two parts:

formal grammatical rules and the concrete knowledge to be used by those rules. Further, differentiating from the Propp-based knowledge base itself, various knowledge bases that subdivide the Propp-based knowledge base into fragment knowledge units are stored, for "cause-effect," "villainy-liquidation," "interdiction-violation," "lack-liquidation," "order-obey, pursuit-rescue," "reconnaissance-delivery," "struggle-victory," "transfer-return," and "trickery-complicity." The knowledge bases for narrative expression include "knowledge bases for music," "animation," and "pictures."

- **Main Functions and Common Libraries:** The main functions, which are positioned amongst the highest functions of an entire INGS, should correspond to the control portion. Although this module currently plays several basic control works related to deciding the order of processing, they remain partial primitive control in comparison with the conceptual design of the INGS. Thus, this part is an important topic for the future.

A Simulation Framework of Macro Narratives: The *Geinō* Information System

This section comprehensively introduces the concept and plan of the "*Geinō* Information System (GIS)," which corresponds to macro narrative generation in Ogata's narrative generation framework. The GIS is, in the multiple narrative structures model, equivalent to the narrative production-consumption mechanism that contains the INGS as a narrative generation-reception mechanism.

Towards the GIS: Geinō *and Multiple Narrative Structures*

In Japanese, the words *monogatari* (narrative) and *geinō* (performing arts) have unique meanings. *Monogatari* does not simply indicate a genre, such as folktales and novels, while, similarly, *geinō* does not simply mean the performing arts. Simply speaking, those words or concepts have folkloric, religious, social, and cultural meanings based on the history and culture of Japan. Originally, although Japanese culture is often seen as a simple culture on the surface, it has, in fact, reached contemporary society replete with the aftereffects of the historical phenomena of conquering/being conquered and dominating/being dominated in ancient society. In this historical process, other lines of narration and narrative that differ from the power narrative, namely an orthodox history, such as narrations and narratives by the conquerors, the ruled, the losers, and inconspicuous people, were spun out before and behind the power relationship. Murasaki Shikibu (1993-1997), in the chapter of *Hotaru* ("Firefly") in *Genji Monogatari*," used a figure to illustrate the contrasting relationship between orthodox histories and fictional narratives to claim the superiority of the latter.

In many cases, narratives that have such an origin have been sent to the receivers as narrations, dances, and through their *gei* (*geinō* techniques) rather than in the form of books like contemporary novels. In particular, narratives have frequently developed that are associated with *geinō*. If we do not privilege the narrative reception phenomena in the modern age, narratives and *geinō* must be seized as having a strong association. Although this claim is extreme, if literary traditions such as *geinō* in Japan continue as hidden figures in the age of modern and contemporary literature, narratives that substantially inherit the mind and concrete techniques may be created through different routes from this direct inheritance, or it will be required. For Ogata, narrative generation research is such an approach. In this sense, the direction that Ogata's narrative generation research aims at, or the ultimate goal at which Ogata aims, is related to the "commonplace" and "thing without property" and lies far from objects represented by words such as advanced, avant garde, and innovative. Although *Kabuki* and other Japanese dramas and *geinō*s have been evaluated as an advanced artistic genre by advanced film and drama theories such as Eisenstein (1898-1948) (1981) and Meyerhold (1874-1940) (2001), this was, in fact, only an ironic fact.

On the other hand, *geinō* frequently shows the style or form in which various genres and works mix together because it does not aim at purity as an artistic genre or at independence as a work. Ogata understands this characteristic of "various genres and works mixing" as the viewpoint of multiplicity. For instance, in the multiple narrative structures in *kabuki*, each narrative, like a *geinō* work, always exists in combination with the narrative of the actor who plays it. For many audiences, an important purpose of *kabuki* stages may be to view a specific actor rather than the *kabuki* play itself, or the scenario, author(s), and direction. In different performances of the same *kabuki* work, their popularity is strongly influenced by who is actually acting in the play the play. Although a similar situation may also be seen in, for instance, the case of cinema, a special characteristic of *geinō* like *kabuki* is that actors, various music performers, and others, have, in many cases, held and inherited their narrative over many generations. For many audience members who view Ichikawa Ebizō XI (1977-) before their eyes, as he performs *kabuki* on stage, they are reminded of the figure(s) and face(s) of past Ebizo(s) whom they have viewed and think of his father, Ichikawa Danjūrō VII (1946 -2013), as well as Ichikawa Ebizōs and Ichikawa Danjūrōs in their history. Many *kabuki* plays have been acted by many actors throughout the history of *kabuki*. By contrast, an actor may perform in many different works to create his performing history. Thus, *geinō* narratives like *kabuki* conspicuously show various types of a narrative's multiple structures, including the narrative as a work to be performed, the narrative of the life that each actor has, and the narrative of each character. The characters also appear in many *kabuki* plays transversely, and frequently cross different genres).

As stated above, the multiplicity of *geinō* is not necessarily the most important in a single work. This characteristic is, rather, more important in the repetitive production-consumption among many works. As a *geinōjin*, an actor has his/her life story and, in the progression process, repeats their narrative generation, while the receiver or audience also continues to pursue the circulative process. Narrative powers and their connections are continuously strengthened at various levels, in this narrative production-consumption process as repetition.

The *Geinō* Information System (GIS), which Ogata created together with Kawamura (Kawamura & Ogata, 2000a, 2000b), is a model that comprises a concretization of the multiple narrative structures model and the model as a synthesis from the perspective of Ogata. In addition, Kawamura has studied his GIS based chiefly on *geinō* production organizations and enterprises, such as Yoshimoto Kogyou, which is a representative *geinō* production company that has mainly treated of comical *geinō* performances in modern and contemporary Japan (Kawamura & Ogata, 2000a, 2000b). In contrast, Ogata has conducted original research on the GIS based on Japan's folkloric and *geinō* studies, its history from ancient to modern and contemporary, and especially such concrete *geinō* genres as *kabuki* and *ningyō jōruri* (Ogata & Kawamura, 1997a, 1997b, 1999). The GIS, which is to be continued and developed, will aim at an implementation as a kind of *geinō* production mechanism such as an engineering model, dependent on the diverse results of *geinō works* and research in Japan, from ancient society to the modern and contemporary one.

The GIS is related to the narrative production-consumption model as a multiple narrative structures model. The narrative production-consumption model is a model that contains several narrative generation-reception mechanisms and enables, for example, transformation from a single model, such as a news scenario generation system, to a social model as a collection of single systems, such as a television studio. The multiple narrative structures model, which is a basic concept in this research, regards narrative generation as a multiple and multi-layered process. This multiplicity is, in the generation-reception mechanism, associated with the division between story, narrative discourse, and narrative representation. On the other hand, viewing the axis of a narrative production-consumption mechanism, the generation-reception mechanisms included in the above can be comprehended as the state based on fluidity, which is one of the central concepts in Ogata's theoretical framework for narrative generation. In particular, an element required for each narrative generation mechanism becomes an element in a narrative production-consumption mechanism, which is a mechanism in which the fluid, continuous, repetitive, and circulative generation in the narrative generation mechanism is fixed in any timing to form an element in the larger narrative generation. Viewed on a more macro level, this means that, in the narrative situation in which various narratives continue to be generated through the circulative mechanism, a narrative is fixed in any timing and a large narrative is generated through collection or continuation. For instance, in a television studio, a single-level narrative generation by each reporter is always performed with various types of reception act within the television studio. However, the particular parts are externalized and fixed to form a sequence of narrative production-consumption. The GIS is intended to be a concrete implementation of the narrative production-consumption model based on the multiple narrative structures model.

In addition, this model is partially related to Bakhtin's (1984) theory of polyphony and to Kristeva's (1980) theory of intertextuality. Bakhtin calls novels that are not integrated by the author's single voice "polyphony novels." Kristeva's idea was that a document exists in a network that contains many documents or fragments, including novels and other genres, whether or not the author is aware of that fact. In the contemporary situation, this idea of literature is strongly originally related to the documents and narratives produced on the Web. These ideas are mainly based on literary studies. At the same time, one of the origins of Bakhtin's polyphonic theory is also the special Western literary tradition that mixes with performing arts. Concurrently, although Bakhtin's theory must, of course, have different characteristics from *geinō* in Japan, it may be partially related to GIS and the multiple narrative structures.

A Design Overview of the GIS

A conceptual composition of the GIS is shown in Figure 7. This is an original design by Kawamura and Ogata (2000a) and it will be revised and changed in future progressions. Regarding previous attempts, refer to papers such as Kawamura and Ogata (2000b) and Amino, Kawamura, and Ogata (2002). The GIS corresponds to a narrative production-consumption mechanism that includes the multiple use of the INGS as a narrative generation-reception mechanism. The system is, at the highest level, composed of a sender mechanism, a receiver mechanism, and a *geinō* history.

Simply speaking, the GIS can be summarized as a system that continuously generates *geinō* contents through the interaction between the sender mechanism and receiver mechanism. In the sender mechanism, a variety of methods coexist and, at the highest level, it divides into two types of sender mechanism: *geinō* works and *geinōjins*. Thus, the GIS is also a system that creates contents relating to the subjects of *geinō* works called *geinōjins* in addition to simply creating contents as *geinō* works. Further, as mentioned in the above overview of informational narratology, receivers of a narrative frequently realize the level at which they themselves are the senders, beyond their positioning as simply pure reception subjects. In this sense, the receivers can also be regarded as the subjects that generate narratives. The GIS produces various types of content through the above mutuality between sender and receivers. However, the production-consumption process results in a sequence of contents in addition to a content

Figure 7. Overall architecture of the GIS

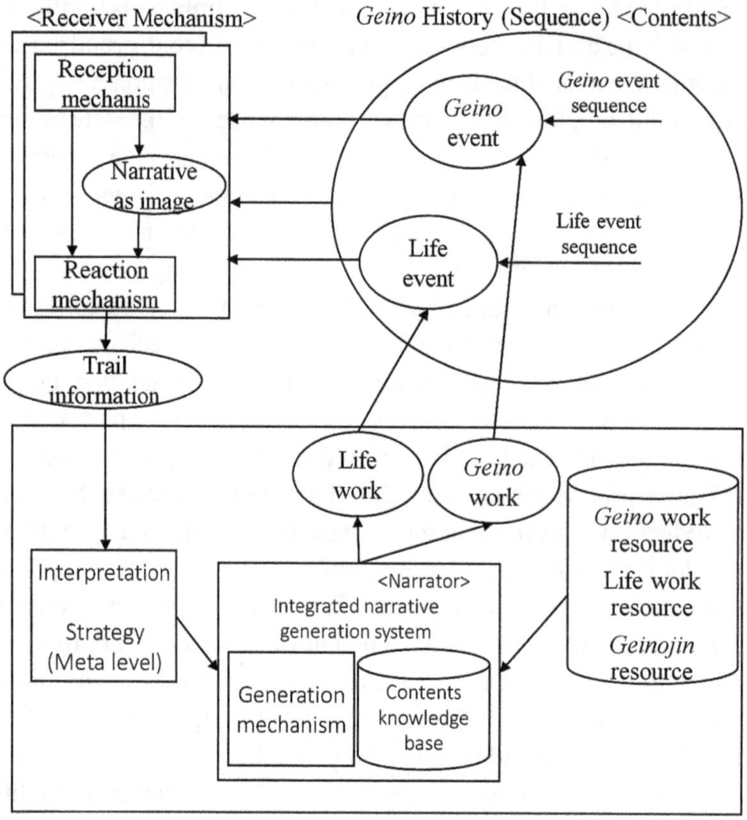

as a simple object. A sequence of contents is here called "*geinō* history." Namely, from a more macro viewpoint, the GIS can be defined as a system that produces *geinō* histories according to the mutuality between the sender and receivers.

GIS Including INGS and Geinō *History*

The concrete mechanism of the GIS is designed as a complex mechanism in which, ordinarily, several INGSs are contained. As stated above, although a *geinō* history is gradually extended through the mutual association between the sender and receiver mechanisms, the author will consider this problem based on the viewpoints of the following several narrative generation concepts covered by Ogata's narrative generation research (2016a): (1) circular narrative control, (2) narrative fluidity and fixation, (3) narrative norm-deviation, and (4) narrative generation-reception and production-consumption. Further, the relationships between the INGS and GIS are also included within this perspective.

Figure 8 shows the execution principle of the GIS (including the INGS) that has the above elements. This figure indicates that, in a narrative generation process as a generation-reception or single form, a narrative generation is performed iteratively and cyclically. This narrative state, seen as a synthetic whole, corresponds to a fluid state in narrative generation. In this iterative and cyclical narrative genera-

Figure 8. The execution principle of the GIS in the relationship with the INGS

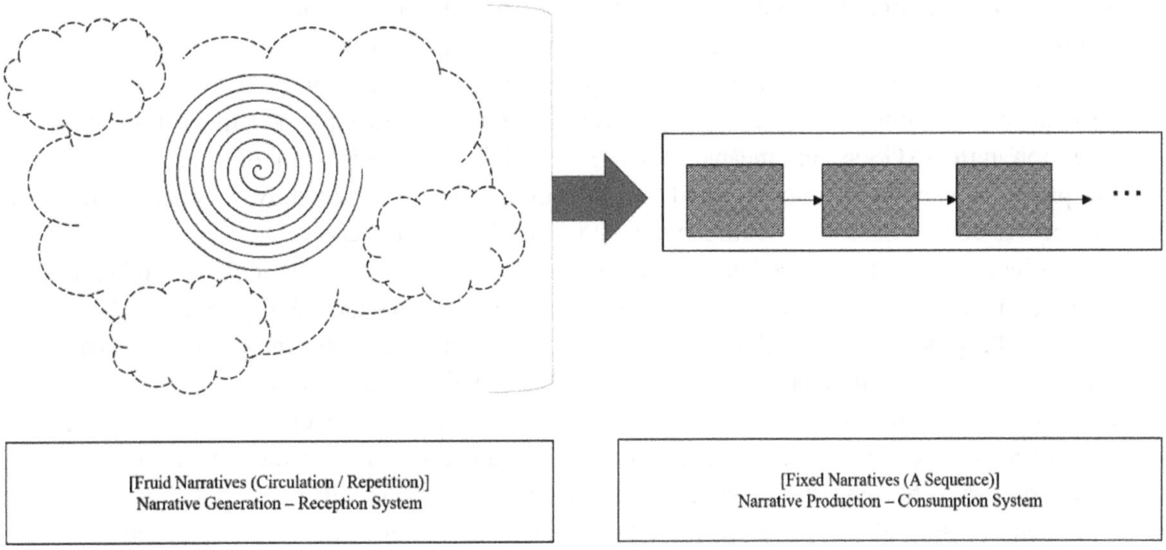

tion process as a fluid state, the receiver side, comprising one or more humans or one or more artificial subjects created virtually within a system, functions as a kind of control mechanism for the narrative generation. A content as a thing that is relatively fixed is frequently pushed to the outside of the cyclical process through the interaction between the narrator side and receiver side. In particular, in the fluid, iterative, and cyclical generation process, a fixed narrative content frequently jumps to the outside from the ring of the circulation. This external or outside world is, for instance, the world of narrative distribution. This theoretical framework calls the level of generating externalized and fixed narrative contents themselves the narrative production-consumption process or system. Concurrently, the level of narrative generation in the above fluid situation is called the narrative generation-reception process or system. A kind of communication as generation control is also performed among the receivers who form a part of this narrative production-consumption process. Additionally, the receiver, in the production-consumption process in addition to the narrative generation-reception process, can be seen as the receiver as a single or collective object. Furthermore, in the narrative production-consumption process, the interaction, which is similar to the association between the sender and receiver in the narrative generation-reception process, is performed to form an iterative and cyclical process.

As described above, by *geinō* history in the framework of the GIS, the author means a sequence of contents at various levels that the sender and receiver mechanisms gradually create through their mutual relationships. This repeated and circulative narrative generation is a core part of the GIS.

However, this iterative and cyclical characteristic is also formed, in several respects, in the generation-reception process of the INGS as a single system. One is the circulative and iterative generation between music and a conceptual narrative, and the INGS enables the generation order from music to a conceptual structure in addition to music from a conceptual structure (Kobayashi & Ogata, 2004; Ogata & Akimoto, 2007; Akimoto & Ogata, 2013b, Akimoto & Ogata, 2014). The circulative and repeated characteristic here also means the non-specification of the processing order. The INGS mechanism aims to realize the circulation and repetition in such a sense in all sides of generation. Similarly, the circular narrative control is also used in the narrative discourse control mechanism that introduces the theory by Jause mentioned above to perform the circular and iterative processing of narrative discourse that theoretically goes on ad infinitum, through the interaction between the narrator and narratee who are virtually set in the system. This is a mechanism that models a narrative generation process as the response and intentional deviation by the narrator (sender) of the requirement and expectation by the narratee (receiver) to repeat narrative discourse generation based on their relationship. As explained above, the circulation and repetition in the INGS system means, at first, free and flexible control that does not determine the order of processing among the modules and representation forms, and, secondly, is concretized as narrative discourse control based on the informational feedback from the receiver.

The GIS including the INGS need, in addition to the above, to have unique circulation and repetition. First, the idea of narrative discourse control using reception theory (Akimoto & Ogata, 2012, 2013a) can be extended to the production-reception process. Next, in the framework of the informational narratology (Ogata, Kawamura & Kanai, in press), Kawamura (2016) and Kanai (2016) rather understand narrative generation processing from the perspective of reception. The large framework is that the receiver side subjectively proposes the parameters for generation and production, while, on the other hand, the sender side purely performs the generation and production according to the receiver's proposition. This reversal is, in itself, not special technologically. At the level of GIS strategy, this type of mechanism means multiplization whereby sender- and receiver-oriented strategies are treated equally. The flexibility of the processing order is also related to the narrative's plural characteristic. An important point is how narrative production-reception can be multiplexed and an entire narrative diversified, including the generation-reception. In the future, discussing narrative multiplicity and diversity using *kabuki* as material will be concretely linked to the design and development of such system architecture.

Next, the author would like to think from the perspective of the fluidity and fixation of narrative generation. The INGS is divided into the following large level generation phases of story, narrative discourse, and narrative representation, and this division shows that each side of a narrative is generated by respective generation phases. "Finally, a whole narrative is formed" can be considered to indicate that diverse narrative possibilities are hidden in each step of the generation, namely the fluid state, and they are finally fixed into a narrative. In the GIS, as stated above, the INGS is placed in the mechanism to exercise a relatively more fluid narrative generation and the specific parts in the GIS in the narrow sense, except for the part of the INGS, are positioned in the same way in the mechanism to ensure more fixed narrative generation or production.

However, to create a more essential mechanism, the processing of fluidity and fixation needs to be performed recursively. The above description comprised a model in which the narrative generation process as a single substance is considered an undifferentiated and fluid processing, and each content that was fixed in the fluid situation forms a narrative sequence in the production-consumption. Moreover, there can be a situation where this sequence itself becomes fluid. Next, the iterative process, in which the fluid state in this next step again results in a fixed state, recursively occurs and the movement of the re-fixation regarding a sequence of fixed narrative contents as a fluid situation occurs once more. Ultimately, such circulation and repetition continues ad infinitum. A possibility of a method for implementing such a model in the GIS is the processing through which fixed narrative contents by the GIS or the sequence are returned to the INGS once more as some knowledge elements. In addition, because the fact that such processing and process are themselves fixed is clearly a problem, it is also necessary to make such situations fluid at the meta-level or from different perspectives. When an entire society is seized as a large narrative production-consumption apparatus, each narrative generation and reception within the society also becomes a fluid process that aims at fixation on a higher level. Although its scale is relatively small, the GIS is a mechanism that can be considered more technologically and explicitly and is a system, viewed as a whole, that multiply stores the fluid narrative generation-consumption processes. When the author considers the concepts of fluidity and fixation through the recursive feature, the framework itself will be able to be regarded as fluid.

Sender Mechanism

The following three parts explain the design of the main mechanisms of which the GIS is composed. The first sender mechanism receives the external information, which mainly includes traces of information that are outputted by the reception mechanism in the GIS through the GIS mechanism of "interpretation strategy" to select an interpretation according to an interpretation framework. Lastly, the sender mechanism generates the information based on this interpretation. However, this process does not necessarily mean that the GIS simply generates narratives according to the desire and expectation of the receivers. The INGS is placed in the central position of narrative generation by the sender mechanism.

The sequence and repetition of generation by the sender mechanism forms "*geinō* histories." In order to continuously generate *geinō* histories, the GIS uses special knowledge bases called "work resource," "life resource," and "*geinōjin* resource," which are not included in the INGS. Although these are similar to the narrative content knowledge bases in the INGS, the unique content knowledge is contained in the GIS.

The *geinōjin* resource is equivalent to a place where *geinōjin* information is stored. The *geinōjin* information includes the information on *geinō* performers and actors/actresses as well as their personal information. In particular, the life resource is the part from which only the life histories are extracted in the *geinōjin* resource. The work resource means the knowledge used to process *geinō* works using various methods. In particular, it comprises information based on more specific narratives in comparison with the content knowledge to be stored in the narrative content knowledge bases in the INGS. Further, in this mechanism, the author aims to store the narrative content knowledge with a focus on *kabuki* and *ningyō jōruri*. The *life* resource comprises the information that analyzes and processes the information relating to *geinō* works using various methods.

The work resource in the GIS is prepared to store more specific and concrete narrative information compared to the knowledge representation of the narrative content in the narrative content knowledge bases in the INGS. For example, analyzing and studying *kabuki* aims at the storage of the specific narrative content knowledge, including various information and knowledge relating to a *kabuki* work. In particular, knowledge in the INGS is more general and several of the dictionaries in the INGS are placed into the most general knowledge group. The knowledge of the GIS is also categorized into two major groups on the axis of generality/specialty. Although the most special knowledge is private and personal knowledge of the author in Ogata's research plan (Ogata, hakuto, chapter 17), various knowledge resources are prepared in the GIS as general knowledge more than the above knowledge type.

Receiver Mechanism

A receiver mechanism outputs, through various methods, the reactive information based on the reception experiences of contents including a work, a sequence of works, and the life history of a *geinojin*. The receiver for the GIS includes humans and, further, virtual existences that are programmed, such as artificial readers and artificial audiences. The subject of a narrator also includes both virtual existence or an artificial author and a real existence or human, from the viewpoints of functions or agents. From the level of the GIS, one of the narrative generation-reception functions, such as the INGS, can also be human. Designing the GIS for an entire narrative generation system by a human-machine system is one of the real and actual methods used. This does not necessarily mean that humans compromise the processing for which complete automation is impossible by a machine. The GIS sequentially forms a *geinō* history through the iterative and circulative interaction between the sender and receiver mechanisms. Of course, the receiver mechanism can be comprised entirely of reception subjects where each of the subjects is a machinery mechanism.

The receiver mechanism evaluates, by some method, generated narratives, including single works, and further their sequence, to represent them as responses in some form. In particular, the receiver mechanism outputs the response information based on the reception experiences for a *geinō* work, a sequence of *geinō* works, the life histories of *geinōjins*, and so on. In the original architecture of the GIS in Figure 7, the term "trace information" means fragmental information in various forms of the evaluations and responses from receivers. The trace information, in the content phenomena of real societies, includes providing direct information to the sender using language, such as discourse, e-mail, blogs, critiques, and *geinō*-related news as more indirect methods, as well as rumors, reputations, word-of-mouth communication, scandals, and so on. The trace information in the GIS is equivalent to various expressions of the reception information by both real and virtual receivers and is regarded as a parameter referred to in various senses by the sender mechanism.

Although literary theories, including reception theory and reader-centric criticism, are certainly newly focused on the side of receivers in literary works, there are no clearly systematized studies that efficiently enable the application and usage in narrative generation systems in these areas. Evaluating a narrative is always very subjective and vague. Although literary histories are considered to be described and constructed based on objective evaluation of literary works as far as possible, it is also clear that each literary history is a very ideological institution or social system. Further, the reception theories of Jauss (1970) and Izer (1976) clearly demonstrated the historical variability of literary evaluations. The GIS will utilize the basic idea of Akimoto and Ogata (2013a) that attempted a very simple experimentation of the evaluation and generation cycle using virtual or artificial receivers, in the narrative discourse mechanism in the INGS.

Narrative and literary evaluation is also very difficult with respect to psychological meaning. For example, people often use language representations such as "interesting (面白い)" in reading a literary or narrative work. This word, "interesting" or "interestingness," is frequently used for research and is a complex and subtle concept that synthesizes a variety of senses and nuances in this case. The "interestingness" of a narrative is a more general word, although the synthetic and complex characteristics of narratives are not different from those of research. However, the evaluation criteria for "interestingness" are not so simple, even though or perhaps because people frequently and ordinarily use them. There are also historical differences in terms of what people find interesting. For instance, in the local situation in contemporary Japan, in the personal opinion of Ogata, from approximately the 1970s to 1980s, very readable and understandable texts were lionized, excessively distributed, and flourished. The trend of this age was linked to the dislike for unreadable and incomprehensible texts. The trend of hating such discourse as "difficult works are interesting" has recently risen to an extreme and, for instance, some people, who name "authors of novels," have published a book criticizing "difficult literary works that they have not read" as if boasting of this fact. This may, however, be a symptom of returning to an age in which people find "difficult literary works" interesting. On the other hand, from personal experience, the feeling of reading Joyce's *Ulysses* (1922) and finding it extremely interesting can also be regarded as a fact. Although it is, perhaps, influenced by the tide of liberal principles in the current age, what is interesting or what people ought to find interesting is a kind of institutional norm and there are also people who efficiently feel the interestingness of such works that are generally recognized to be difficult. Additionally, as a related topic, the narrative generation game system by Ono and Ogata (in press) is conducting a study analyzing the functions and techniques of "surprise" in stories and narratives.

Another problem is related to the point that the evaluation by the receiver in the GIS is directed to various objects. It may be directed to a single work, the life contents and events of *geinōjins*, and the sequences of the respective contents. The evaluation and response from, so to speak, a fixed point for a single work form the complicated information that makes up the traces of narrative reception, in the relationships with the evaluation and response through a temporal flow for the history and sequence of works that include the first work. To process this kind of trace information within a system, it will be necessary to classify and analyze the objects to be evaluated. Further, because a closed evaluation within a system is not actually useful, experiments will also be necessary in the form opened to business-like narrative distribution processes. In this case, if only evaluations by receivers and consumers are privileged, more specific public works will be evaluated as good. However, this kind of majority rule is only one of the possibilities of narrative and literary evaluations. Moreover, evaluating one's own works from the sender side will be able to be an element to be considered. In particular, a work that has not even one reader has been read by the author through the writing process. Therefore, the author can also be a receiver of the work at a minimum. For example, the self-satisfaction by an author herself or himself may also be a possible evaluation criterion. This standpoint emphasizes self-satisfaction rather than selling or being read by many readers. In such cases, a perverted logic will also exist, such as that not selling proves the high evaluation.

In addition, this problem of multiple or plural evaluations is related to a merit in the multiple narrative structures model. In particular, if, in this model, the narrative evaluations can be diverse and plural, the narrative generation and distribution can be operated in a direction where diverse and plural evaluations are retrieved from the receivers. This may be a merit in considering narrative social distribution.

Contents Generated by GIS

Although the contents generated by the sender mechanism of the GIS include contents of life works, in the wide sense, such as scandals (documents) of *geinōjins* relating to *geinō* works, in addition to the narrative contents in the narrow sense, this discussion focuses on *geinō* works in the narrow sense, such as dramas. To give an overview for the production, first, GIS mainly decides the following elements: "authors" (single or several), "performers" or "actors/actresses" (ordinarily several), and "chronicle (the part or parts)." One or more authors decided here first create the "story" of a narrative and, for this story, the "characters" and "places, stages" (of which there are usually several) are selected and decided upon. Based on the above, the INGS in the GIS exercises the entire narrative generation process from the overview stage to the detailed stage. Both the INGS and GIS enact the entire process by performing their unique respective tasks and through their mutual interaction. In addition, of course, in case of such narratives as dramas, the stage performance occurs after the scenario is produced. If the INGS can enact this process, the possibilities to be considered may include the CG and robot representation, mainly through the narrative representation mechanism. However, here, with the limitation to the generation at the level of scenario, the author would like to describe the various concepts that appear in the sender mechanisms.

First, the GIS has several authors similar to authors working in the theatre in *kabuki*. In this sense, the author her/himself is also a kind of *geinōjin* and has her/his life story. In the case of a dramatic or theatrical narrative, the author, for specific performers, chooses and sets particular places = stages and the historical context to produce a narrative content where specific characters are actively performing. A GIS system is akin to a theatrical group and also holds a collection of limited numbers of performers (actors, actresses, or *geinōjins*). Each performer also holds the stories of their respective life histories. The performers are related to the *geinōjin* resources and life resources in Figure 7. Technologically, the main body of an author is equivalent to the INGS, which generates each work utilizing the knowledge resources involved in the GIS in addition to unique knowledge.

The knowledge resources also include the "characters" extracted from existing *kabuki*, *ningyō jōruri*, modern and contemporary novels, et cetera. The characters in *kabuki* and *ningyō jōruri* are already fluidized as they commonly appear among many works in ordinary cases. By contrast, in modern and contemporary novels, although there are examples of a specific character appearing in many works by the same author, they do not reach such sufficient fluidity as do *kabuki* and *ningyō jōruri* narratives in which a specific character freely plays an active part in the different works written by different authors, although this phenomenon may, from a larger perspective, be considered to be the fixation of a character. An experimental direction will also be possible to intentionally create such a narrative situation. This is related to the work resource in Figure 7, in addition to the next topics of places = stages and chronicle. The GIS also stocks or organizes the typical places and stages that have appeared in previous narrative works. Furthermore, they can be designed as a knowledge base based on the reference of the works (work resource) from *ningyō jōruri* and *kabuki* to modern and contemporary novels.

Kabuki and *ningyō jōruri* have prepared typical epochs, such as the eras of Sugawara no Michizane (845-903) and *Heike Monogatari* (1991-1993), particularly in their association with places = stages. These correspond to main components along with characters and places = stages. "Worlds" similar to them in *kabuki* are not explicitly defined in modern and contemporary narratives. However, in fact, many narratives are produced according to the framework of each age divided by the Meiji restoration (1868), the Pacific War (1941-1945), the age of high economic growth (1954-1973), and so on, although, as in the following description, they still do not seem to reach the stage that is established as a kind of historical or chronic common illusion. One research (very distant) possibility is to inductively construct a chronicle in each epoch from existing narrative works to be utilized by the GIS and INGS.

Here, the author would like to mention the problem with respect to chronicle and narrator. In the following description, the narrative representation mechanism is placed in the narrative discourse mechanism in the INGS. The content, as the thing narrated, which means a narrative discourse structure in the wide sense, is divided into the structural and deep level and the representative and surface level. The latter level also includes the generation of music and image in addition to language generation. A basic method is to process all surface representation mechanisms in the semiotic level similar to language. The generation subject in the narrative representation mechanism is also called a narrator. Thus, the narrator in the INGS is a mechanism covering both the narrative discourse mechanism and narrative representation mechanism. Additionally, the former is called the narrative discourse mechanism in the wide sense and a whole mixing both the former and latter is called the narrative discourse mechanism in the wide sense.

On the other hand, the story generation mechanism is a qualitatively different mechanism. In the current INGS, the author clearly calls the generation subject in the narrative discourse mechanism "narrator" (in addition, Hasumi (2014), perhaps dependent on his idea that "novel" is different from "narrative," uses the word "speaker" instead of "narrator"). However, the generation subject in the story generation mechanism is not named clearly, although clearly a different mechanism from that of a narrator needs to be used for the story generation mechanism.

Compared to the "historical narratology" by Noe (1996), Kan (2010), etc., the above narrator means a subject who concretely narrates a historical material. The thing that corresponds to this "historical material" is a story or narrative content in the present components of the INGS. Who produces, composes, and prepares this content? This problem is not necessarily clear in the case of a real history. However, in the historical case, it will be possible to differentiate the thing called a "chronicle" from the layer corresponding to a story. In this case, the layer of chronicle + story is set on the stage before the narrative discourse by the narrator. Further, a chronicle or story must be constructed by subjects who differ from the narrator in the case of narrative discourse. The author regards a chronicle or story as one subject here. Who created them? A chronicle means a discourse as itself in which events that occurred are described within a specific temporal range. Although a history uses past events as its materials, it needs to be edited and organized in chronicle form because people cannot witness the real occurrence themselves from the materials. The subject of such a chronicle must differ from the narrator who, in a sense, freely narrates the materials. It is straightforward to say, the name of the "chronicle author" or simply "author" may be given to the existence. Namely, it also includes the meaning of an author of real events or materials. However, the materials of a chronicle are themselves frequently a fiction, in the case of a fictional narrative. At the same time, from the viewpoint of the narrator of a narrative discourse, a group of events for the materials will be relatively able to be interpreted as real events. Thus, the following shows the possible division: the generation subject of the story generation mechanism (including a chronicle author) is simply called an "author"; the generation subject in the narrative discourse mechanism is called a "narrator."

The author would like to consider the above problem using the example of the story composition of, so to speak, *jidai-mono* in *ningyō jōroru* and *kabuki*. Imao (2010) discussed the classification between *jidai-mono* and *sewa-mono*, which is in contrast to the *jidai-mono*. Generally, a *jidai-mono* story is produced dependent on a history that preliminarily exists as a so-called "common illusion" (Yoshimoto, 1968). Such a history corresponds to the chronicle prior to the story and the narrative discourse (in the narrow and wide senses). The story of *jidai-mono* arranges and rearranges, as if it slips through in the chronicle, many historical facts, including characters, places = stages, and times in an attempt to create the reverse story, which is hidden in the lower layers of the story, according to the framework of necessary chronological and historical facts. Concurrently, in this case, a better or appropriate direction is to define the composition of "chronicle/story/narrative discourse" rather than the above composition of "chronicle+story/narrative discourse." In the method of narrative production based on such composition, the chronicle layer in the three stages of chronicle/story/narrative discourse is simply an existing fact that is too difficult to shift. In this case, the author may be able instead to regard both story and narrative discourse as the level corresponding to the narrative discourse in the INGS, such as "chronicle/story+narrative discourse." When this *kabuki* method is applied, it will be able to treat the level of a chronicle as that which corresponds to a part of the narrative content knowledge stored in the knowledge bases. Thus, the present story generation mechanism and narrative discourse mechanism are equivalent to the narrator who alters and edits those structures and contents. This is a possible method to be considered.

On the other hand, however, Japanese history from modern to contemporary, which will be dealt with in Ogata's narrative study (particularly in the phase of future actual narrative production), has not still been holding, so to speak, provisions and determinism as seen in histories that authors of *kabuki* and *ningyō jōruri* had previously treated as their objectives or materials. In current society, people are in a whirlpool, a fluid situation, where histories, which are not limited, are being generated. This means that we are existing in the way that chronicles themselves are produced, defined, and determined. Although a minimum "chronicle as a historical chronology" exists, it has not been established in the case of modern and contemporary ages as a common illusion of people as it was in previous ages. Alternatively, although there may be various possibilities of fixation, a fluid situation that does not result in the ending is continuing. This is because, through the temporal flow from modern to contemporary, many events for which the evaluation and positioning have not been established are proliferating and the world of historical events has not been boiled down to a common illusion. At the same time, there have many attempts to bring out a chronicle or chronicles from prewar days to after the war via media, literature, and cinema in present-day Japan. The present situation must be a step wherein the hot composition process of a history or histories, a chronicle or chronicles as a common illusion is just progressing. Concurrently, in this situation, the evaluation of what has really occurred is also shaking in a complex manner. The basis itself of story or narrative generation, which is dependent on a determined chronicle or chronicles that believe in a common illusion, as past *kabuki* writers did, has not been established in the above fluid situation.

Therefore, even in the case of treating history, a chronicle itself does not exist as the proposition and background of the story. At the practical level, a possible method to be considered is to spin stories to fill the gap between existing historical facts (which exist in a huge number). In this case, a chronicle is a kind of framework for the mere background situation or information for establishing a story. A chronicle is also defined as a type of macro framework at a similar level to characters and places = stages. Concurrently, because story generation continues according to a chronicle as a framework that has neither efficient meaning nor basis, and based on recognizing its fact, the chronicle itself frequently changes. Alternatively, an essential issue regarding the present narrative is in the work of creating a chronicle, and further in the acts of not creating some chronicle.

An essential problem regards what narrative information is to be given preliminarily. This means the starting point of the narration by the narrator in the narrative discourse. In particular, should a chronicle be given or not? In the first case, the author (as a tentative term) of a story creates a story on the basis of this chronicle and the narrator transforms it into a narrative discourse. On the other hand, the second case requires the author for the chronicle. Further, based on the chronicle, both the author of the story and the narrator are required for a narrative discourse. Another idea of the conceptual division is to instead integrate the author of the story and the narrator of the narrative discourse into the same category described as "narrator A/narrator B" to indicate the difference of levels. Alternatively, the chronicle and story could be given the name of the author to describe them as "author A/author B." The latter, author B, is a naming method or concept definition for a relatively non-deterministic chronicle. In contrast, the former, author A, is set for a relatively deterministic chronicle. These refer to a method or model for defining the different features of authors according to the characteristics of the chronicles. Another method or model is, dependent on a preliminarily given chronicle, to define both the author who is the subject that composes and edits the chronicle and the narrator who is the subject of the narrative discourse.

According to the above discussion, from the perspective of the relationships between the INGS and GIS, what relationships exist among chronicle, story, and narrative discourse? If chronicles are previously stored in the knowledge base, the level of an author corresponds to that of a subject who generates various stories using those chronicles. On the other hand, a narrator corresponds to a subject who narrates the generated story using various methods, namely narrative discourse techniques. However, there are several levels in chronicles. If a chronicle description itself is preliminarily given to the GIS as an already completed object, it is not necessary to especially set the level of the authors of chronicles. By contrast, if anyone must describe a chronicle by a considerable effort, the descriptive subject must be added to a part of the subject of narration as an independent author of the chronicle. Thus, as a possibility, the GIS includes three types of subject: the author of the chronicle, the author (or author of the story), and the narrator. Most fundamentally, although the chronicle's author is a unique subject for the GIS, the author of the story and the narrator are the subjects of narration in the INGS. On the other hand, as a more special form, there is the author of the story at the level of *geinō* history. A *geinō* history is, of course, a story composed as a result and the author cannot create it completely intentionally. However, if story generation at the level of planning also exists, the story generation of a *geinō* history can also exist, at the level of planning at least. Furthermore, the narrative discourse corresponding to a story at this level will also be able to exist efficiently. The subjects of narration for these narratives, including the story as a *geinō* history and the narrative discourse, are considered to be contained in the GIS.

Finally, in this study, the definition of the INGS and GIS may not be narrative generation systems at a personal level. They are, rather, narrative generation systems that strongly consider the narratological, structural, and communal levels. If structural and narratological ideas are inserted into the idea of communal illusion by Yoshimoto (1968), the characteristic as communal illusion is the degree issue and the narrative discourse techniques can also be interpreted at the communal level. Of course, the layer of chronicle is the communal level. In terms of the degree issue, the narrator of a story (and chronicle) is a narrator at the more communal and structural levels, while the narrator of a narrative discourse is a narrator at the more personal level. Concurrently, it is necessary to prepare mechanisms to properly utilize the level of "narrator" as a large framework in accordance with the stages of narrative generation or to change the degree of usage.

NEURAL NETWORKS, DEEP LEARNING, AND CONTENT GENERATION

Thus far, the authors have reviewed narrative content generation based on the INGS. In this section, we review neural network models for content generation. The recent success of neural networks, especially image recognition and translation, has brought many researchers into the field of narratology. For those who are interested in narratives or content generation, this section will provide a brief summary of the models related to content generation. In this section, we selected the following five models:

1. Introduction of recurrent neural network models
2. Word embedding models
3. Encoder/Decoder models
4. Variational autoencoders
5. Memory augmented recurrent neural networks

Although all the models above were proposed in different but related areas against content generation, we selected them in order to prompt progression in terms of content generation. In advance of our introducing these models, we have provided a brief description of recurrent neural networks (RNN, henceforth) to prompt understanding in readers of this section of common basic knowledge about the most successful models for processing sequential information.

Introduction of Recurrent Neural Networks

RNNs are amongst the most successful recent models in deep learning. The key features of RNNs as well as other deep learning models can be summarized as:

1. End-to-End
2. Differentiable

Although quite a lot of data is required, RNNs can be used to generate content because of these key features. End-to-End claims that no special prior knowledge is required to generate content. Differentiable refers to the claim that all the parameters to be tuned are learnable with adequate neural network models such as RNNs.

RNNs consist of a bunch of groups of neurons with feedback connections. These feedback connections play essential roles in processing and generating sequential information. The ability to process sequential information might be a key function of content generation. RNNs were originally proposed because of the need to deal with such sequential information. This feature might be prominent compared with other deep learning models such as convolutional neural networks (CNN) and reinforcement learning (RL). Although it might be possible for both CNN and RL to deal with sequential information, these models have not in general been proposed for the purpose of processing sequential information. These models process sequential information as unfolding static data in turn.

Neural networks are universal function approximators, meaning that they can express any function that we may wish to model, including a function that accurately predicts our predictive probability for the ensuing data. These simple frameworks are well-known, particularly in areas like natural language processing (NLP). Context generation usually depends on NLP, and it is worth mentioning the basic findings recently developed in NLP.

The authors briefly formalize the basic RNN (Elman, 1990), which has three layers: the input, hidden, and output layers respectively. The state of hidden layer ($\boldsymbol{h}$) can be written as:

$$\boldsymbol{h}_t = f\left(\boldsymbol{W}\boldsymbol{x}_t + \boldsymbol{U}\boldsymbol{h}_{t-1} + \boldsymbol{b}\right), \tag{1}$$

where $\boldsymbol{W}$ is a weight matrix from input to hidden, $\boldsymbol{x}t$ is an input vector, $\boldsymbol{U}$ is a recurrent matrix to reflect the influence from the previous hidden state, and $\boldsymbol{b}$ is a bias. The only difference from the multilayered perceptron (MLP) is that the previous hidden state just one time previously is added as an input. Despite the fact that only one previous state is considered, the RNN has the ability to remember a much more distant history. The previous hidden state might be influenced by previous states from the entire past. This is called long term dependency (LTD). The solution to controlling previous states is, in essence, one of the tendencies of recent RNN research.

In the final layer, we must calculate the target vector $\boldsymbol{y}$. The probability of the target y is calculated by the softmax function:

$$p_j = \frac{\exp\left(x_j\right)}{\sum_i \exp\left(x_i\right)}. \tag{2}$$

By taking the exponent and dividing by the sum of the values over the entire candidates, these scores can be turned into probabilities that are between and and add up to . This is called the softmax function.

Now, the only remaining missing link is how to acquire the parameters $), consisting of the weight matrix and bias . Basically, the way we do so is by attempting to find parameters that fit the training corpus well. To do so, we use standard machine learning methods for optimizing parameters. First, we define a loss function, which is a function expressing how poorly we are doing in respect of the training data. In most cases, we assume that this loss is equal to the negative log likelihood:

$$\ell\left(\theta \middle| y\right) = -\sum \log P\left(y \middle| \theta\right). \tag{3}$$

Then, we must optimize all the parameters to reduce this loss. While there are many methods for so doing, in recent years one of the go-to methods is stochastic gradient descent (SGD) (Bottou & Bousquet, 2007). SGD is an iterative process whereby we randomly pick a single word and take a step to improve the likelihood with respect to it. In order to do so, we first calculate the derivative of the loss with respect to each of the features in the full feature set θ:

$$\frac{d\ell}{d\left(y,\theta\right)}. \tag{4}$$

We can then use this information to take a step in the direction that will reduce the loss according to the objective function:

$$\theta \leftarrow \theta - \eta \frac{d\ell}{d\left(y,\theta\right)} \tag{5}$$

where η is one of the hyperparameters, the learning rate, specifying the amount by which we update the parameters every time we perform an update. By so doing, we can find parameters for our model that reduce the loss, or increase the likelihood, in the training data. This is quite simple, but it is well-known to work well for almost all problems.

Word Embedding Models

Natural language processing systems traditionally treat words as discrete atomic symbols. These encodings are arbitrary, and provide no useful information to the system regarding the relationships that may exist between the individual symbols. This means that the model can leverage very little of what it has learned about word meanings. Representing words as unique, discrete ids also leads to data sparsity, and usually means that we may require more data in order to successfully train statistical models. Using word embedding models (vector representations) can overcome some of these obstacles.

Word embedding models (Word2vec and its relatives) are computationally-efficient predictive models for learning word meanings from raw text. They come in two flavors: the Continuous Bag-of-Words model (CBOW) and the Skip-Gram model (Mikolov et al., 2013). Algorithmically, these models are similar, except that CBOW predicts target words from source context words, while the skip-gram does the inverse and predicts source context-words from the target words. This inversion might seem like an arbitrary choice, but statistically it has the effect that CBOW smooths over much of the distributional information.

Encoder/Decoder Models

The basic idea of the Encoder/Decoder model is relatively simple. We have two RNNs, Enc and Dec. The name Encoder/Decoder originally comes from the idea that the first RNN running to encode its information as a vector. Then, the second RNN is used to predict that Enc decodes this information into the target (Sutskever et al., 2014; Bahdanau et al., 2015).

Theoretically, a sufficiently large and well-trained Encoder/Decoder model should be able to perform machine translations well. However, in some ways, this view is over-simplified. An attention mechanism is introduced to overcome dealing with more complex information, and the attention might play an important role against generating content generation schema.

Variational Autoencoders

The variational auto-encoder (VAE) model is rooted in Bayesian inference, i.e., it wants to model the underlying probability distribution of data so that it can sample new data from that distribution. VAEs allow us to formalize this problem in the framework of probabilistic graphical models where we are maximizing a lower bound on the log likelihood of the data. Kingma and Wellings (2014) introduced a flexible and computationally scalable method for improving the accuracy of variational inference. In particular, most VAEs have so far been trained using crude approximate posteriors, where every latent variable is independent. Recent extensions have addressed this problem by conditioning each latent variable on the others before it in a chain, but this is computationally inefficient due to the sequential dependencies that are introduced. The core contribution of their work, termed inverse autoregressive flow (IAF), is a new approach that, unlike previous work, allows us to parallelize the computation of rich approximate posteriors, and make them almost arbitrarily flexible.

Bowman et al., (2015) introduced an RNN-based variational autoencoder generative model that incorporates distributed latent representations of entire sentences. This factorization allows it to explicitly model the holistic properties of sentences, such as style, topic, and high-level syntactic features. Samples from the prior distribution over these sentence representations produced diverse but well-formed sentences. By examining paths through this latent space, they could generate coherent novel sentences that interpolate between known sentences.

Memory Augmented RNN

The basic RNN design struggles with longer sequences. Such models have been found to be very powerful, achieving remarkable results in many tasks including machine translation, voice recognition, and image captioning. As a result, RNNs have become widespread in the last few years. We have seen a growing number of attempts to augment RNNs with new properties. Among them, the Neural Turing Machines (NTM) (Graves et al., 2015) combined RNN with external memories, and showed a powerful competence to deal with content generation. By controlling external memories, NTM could be one of the candidates for modeling content generation. The NTMs consist of controllers and memory ticks. The controllers in the NTM can process both external command and internal memory at the same time, and therefore, they could deal with complex sequences such as sorting algorithms and so on. The RNN outputs an attention distribution that describes how we spread out the amount we care about different memory positions. As such, the result of the read operation is a weighted sum.

The authors would like to give a brief explanation of the working mechanisms of NTMs. They actually use a combination of two different methods: content-based attention and location-based attention. Content-based attention allows NTMs to search through their memory and focus on places that match what they are looking for, while location-based attention allows relative movement in memory, enabling the NTM to loop. These kinds of mechanism might be a promising way to generate some volume of content. The NTM's controller provides a query vector and each memory entry is scored for similarity with the query. The scores are then converted into a distribution using softmax. It might be interpolated that the attention might be control sequences from the previous time step.

We convolve the attention with a shift filter, which allows the controller to move its focus. Then, NTM sharpens the attention distribution. This final attention distribution is fed to the read or write operation.

This capability to read and write allows NTMs to perform many simple algorithms, previously beyond the capability of neural networks. For example, they can learn to store a long sequence in memory, and then loop over it, repeating it back repeatedly.

Summary and Discussion of RNN-Based Content Generation Models

This section has covered RNN-based content generation models. These models now represent the state-of-the-art in many modeling tasks. It should be noted that this is an active research field, and there are a number of advanced research topics that are beyond the scope of this section. Readers might have questions about the discrepancy between abilities that RNN models demonstrate and the problems with which content generation models must grapple. However, recent RNN-based models, like Encoder/Decoder and memory augmented models, possess mechanisms to deal with LTD as well as attention. These mechanisms could be considered as essentially the same as the models described in other sections of this chapter. While the gap remains between RNNs (deep learning models) and content generation, it seems to be worth paying attention to RNN-based models.

FUTURE RESEARCH DIRECTIONS

This section will present future research work on the following four topics.

- **Multiple Narrative Structures Model and Informational Narratology for Narrative Communication:** The multiple narrative structures model aims to contribute to the narrative generation system studies by Ogata. On the other hand, the informational narratology is a synthesized model for considering and analyzing from diverse aspects if selecting one. Although this is the difference between the models, they have substantially in common the point that both models grasp a narrative or narratives as the multiplicity of the micro and macro levels. One purpose, from an awareness of this issue, is to develop these models in the direction of a process model of multiple narrative generation from the perspective of hierarchical evolution linking the micro to the macro levels. This will be a basic model for implementing interaction between the INGS and GIS. Another topic is to contrive a process model that goes toward the sender's generation from the receiver's reception instead of vice-versa. In particular, this reverse model will be able to function as an initiative model for expanding narrative generation in the direction of social distribution through the GIS.

- **Integrated Narrative Generation System for Micro-Level Narrative Simulation:** Since Ogata (2016), Ogata has been continuing the research on various partial components of the INGS as follows: (1) Ogata, for the story content knowledge base, conducted several studies regarding the storing of fragmental event sequences or scripts by manual and automatic acquisition (Ogata, Arai, & Ono, 2016). (2) Concerning the conceptual dictionaries, Ogata (2015), rather than changing the structures, automatically acquired as the properties the elements of each general noun concept and proper noun concept to utilize the knowledge for an explanation generation mechanism as a kind of sentence generation mechanism in the narrative representation or expression mechanism. Further, Ogata and Ono (2016) acquired the appearance frequency information and co-occurrence information of the concepts from a text corpus of Japanese modern and contemporary literature called "Aozora Bunko" (Aozorabunko, 2017) to control the concrete use of elements in the conceptual dictionaries. Ogata is currently introducing into the INGS systems the respective developed and experimented elements as each single level to further expand the INGS. The above (1) is particularly effective for the development of the INGS in terms of its acquiring the ability to continuously and always generate narratives if it is operated on random narrative generation. In particular, Ogata (2016a) plans to realize a mechanism that gradually revises the results by random generation through a learning process.
- ***Geinō* Information System for Macro-Level Narrative Simulation:** Although this GIS first aims to advise the phase of concrete design and implementation, several central works must be prepared in the implementation phase. In particular, Ogata plans to extend concrete works of the implementation based on the specified works. One is, by organically introducing an INGS that is already implemented as a whole, or several INGSs into the GIS, to realize a mechanism through which the INGS sequentially and continuously performs the narrative generation processing derived by the control mechanism of the GIS and to experiment to open the GIS including the INGS into the social distribution process. This is certainly a kind of open direction or fluidity. At the same time, it is also a fixation and convergence in contrast to the fluidity, and therefore means placing various constraints on the narrative generation that were to be performed originally in an unconstrained way. The second issue is to make thinner and more substantial such elements as "world" in *kabuki*, including characters, places and stages, objects, ages, and the forms of a story or plot, beyond the level of basic definitions of concepts in the conceptual dictionaries in the current version of the INGS. This means that we grasp the GIS as a kind of troupe. The word troupe is considered adequate rather than saying a *geinō* production (entertainment production), as the characteristic of a troupe is to hold diverse settings for stage composition and decoration in addition to the human resources. In this sense, the GIS must be defined as the metaphor of a troupe despite the *geino* production organization that the authors originally envisaged. Through these works, both the INGS that performs the micro narrative generation or narrative simulation and the GIS that performs the macro level thereof are organically integrated into an overall system to embody the multiple narrative structures model and the informational narratology.

- **Neural Network Based Story Generation**: Although much progressions of neural networks in machine translations, image captioning, and short conversations have been done so far, a lot of studies still must be done for computational story generation studies. Although recent recurrent neural network models such as encoder/decoder, VAE, and memory augmented RNNs would not be able to generate long stories sufficiently, these models would still be one of the possible candidates for computational story generations. Another way to deal with rather longer sentences like paragraphs, or a bunch of documents would be natural extensions of vector space models in which meanings of words could be represented (word2vec and its relatives). When we will extend the vector space models not only to word meanings, but also to sentences, paragraphs, and documents meaning, all the other methods employed in this book might use them in order to generate narratives. Therefore, vector space representations might be one of the fundamental tools for content generations. Recurrent network based story generation modeling with vector space representation of contents might indicate one possible direction to bring this area to the more excitements.

CONCLUSION

An important feature of the authors' research is to seek to undertake the problems of narrative communication and simulation from the perspective of narrative generation and narrative generation systems. Further, the authors focus in particular on narrative contents in existing diverse contents from the perspective of the humanistic significance and interesting diversity. Based on the above points, this chapter has provided several discussions on the aspects of narrative communication and their relationships based on the multiple narrative structures model and the relating model in which narrative characteristics are seen in the multiplicity and multi-layered features of various information points that Ogata and other researchers have been presenting. In this research, the micro level, which is the level corresponding to a personal narrative generation mechanism, has been designed and implemented as an integrated narrative generation system (INGS). On the other hand, the macro level, which is particularly the level equivalent to a narrative production system that contains several or diverse personal-level narrative generation mechanisms, has been considered and designed through a *geinō* information system (GIS). These systems mean the models and systems that perform narrative simulation through narrative communications at various levels. This chapter has modeled and systematized respectively the macro and micro levels in the framework of the multiple narrative structures model as in the INGS and GIS. At the same time, although the authors have chiefly used so-called symbolic processing methods, such as knowledge representation, conceptual or ontological mechanisms and rule-based mechanisms, as technologies or techniques for designing and developing narrative generation systems including the INGS and GIS, so-called pattern processing technologies such as neural networks and deep learning will be available for use and introduced in the future. This chapter has also referred to these methods as new technological possibilities for narrative generation.

As stated above, in this chapter, the authors have described such problems as content generation, narrative communication, and narrative simulation using the INGS and GIS as the core. In this sense, this chapter shows the authors' synthesized approach or paradigm to narrative generation study. This study holds the possibility of expansion in both the micro and macro directions. In the macro direction, the authors will positively advance the implementation and experiments of the INGS to introduce the results into the GIS for linking to the distributive and social development of the narrative generation system. At the same time, in the macro direction, popularizing the authors' ideas and plans for narrative generation will also be an important issue by further propelling the systematization as narrative generation research.

ACKNOWLEDGMENT

This chapter's research was supported by JSPS KAKENHI Grant Numbers 26330258, Support Center for Advanced Telecommunications Technologies Research Grant (2015-2017), and Kayamori Foundation of Information Science Advancement Research Grant (2017).

REFERENCES

Abe, H., Ogata, T., & Hanada, K. (2008). Televi kōkoku no shot ni okeru brand dōnyū rhetoric no bunseki - Kōkoku no monogatari seisei system no ichi kikō no tameni [An analysis of brand introduction rhetoric in a shot in television commercial films: For a mechanism of an advertising narrative generation system]. In *Proceedings of the 16th Meeting of Literature, Cognition, and Computer Rereserch Group II in the Japanese Cognitive Science Society* (16G-05). Retrieved from http://www.ogata.soft.iwate-pu.ac.jp/LCC2_Web/LCC(II)Proceedings/Proceedings(16)/2008.11.15AbeOgataHanata.pdf

Akimoto, T., & Ogata, T. (2012). A narratological approach for narrative discourse: Implementation and evaluation of the system based on Genette and Jauss. In *Proceedings of the 34th Annual Conference of the Cognitive Science Society* (pp. 1272-1277). Tokyo: Japanese Cognitive Science Society.

Akimoto, T., & Ogata, T. (2013a). Discourse mechanism in narrative generation system: Proposal of a system introducing narrative discourse theory and reception theory. *Cognitive Studies*, *20*(4), 396–420.

Akimoto, T., & Ogata, T. (2013b). The expansion of paths in the mutual transformation mechanism of music and narrative. *International Journal of Cognitive Informatics and Natural Intelligence*, *7*(4), 44–63. doi:10.4018/ijcini.2013100103

Akimoto, T., & Ogata, T. (2014). Circulative narrative generation based on the mutual transformation between narrative conceptual structures and music in the integrated narrative generation system. *Journal of Robotics. Networking and Artificial Life*, *1*(3), 198–202. doi:10.2991/jrnal.2014.1.3.6

Amino, T., Kawamura, Y., & Ogata, T. (2002). Hierarchical generation of *geino*-idol stories: Toward *geino* information system and narrative marketing. In *Proceedings of* the *17th Congress of the International Association of Empirical Aesthetics* (pp. 549-552). Rome, Italy: University of Rome Tre.

Aozorabunko. (2017). *Aozora bunko*. Retrieved October 5, 2017, from http://www.aozora.gr.jp/

Asakawa, S. (2015a). *Deep learning, big data, kikai gakushū mataha sono shinrigaku* [Deep learning, big data, machine learning or the psychology]. Tokyo: Shin'yōsha.

Asakawa, S. (2015b). Neural network monogatari seisei model [A neural network narrative generation model]. In *Proceedings of the 49th Special Interest Group on Language Sense Processing Engineering in Japaniese Society for Artificial Intelligence* (pp. 15-21). Tokyo: Japaniese Society for Artificial Intelligence.

Asakawa, S. (2016). *Python de taikensuru shinsō gakushū* [Deep learning to experience by Python]. Tokyo: Koronasha.

Bahdanau, D., Cho, K., & Bengio, Y. (2015). *Neural machine translation by jointly learning to align and translate*. Paper presented at The International Conference on Learning Representations (ICLR), San Diego, CA.

Bakhtin, M. (1984). *Problems of Dostoevsky's poetics* (C. Emerson, Trans.). University of Minnesota Press. (Original work published 1963)

Bottou, L., & Bousquet, O. (2007). The tradeoffs of large scale learning. In Advances in Neural Information Processing Systems (vol. 20). Cambridge, MA: MIT Press.

Bowman, S. R., Vilnis, L., Vinyals, O., Dai, A. M., Jozefowicz, R., & Bengio, S. (2015). *Generating sentences from a continuous space*. arXiv, 1511.06349.

Bringsjord, S., & Ferrucci, D. A. (1999). *Artificial intelligence and literary creativity: Inside the mind of BRUTUS, a storytelling machine*. Lawrence Erlbaum.

Calvo, H., Daza-Arévalo, J. A., & Figueroa-Nazuno, J. (2016). Automatic story generation by learning from literary structures. Marietta, GA: Scholars' Press.

Cutumisu, M. (2009). *Using behaviour patterns to generate scripts for computer role-playing games* (Doctoral dissertation). Department of Computing Science, University of Alberta, Edmonton, Canada.

Dubbelman, T. (2013). *Narratives of being there: Computer games, presence and fictional worlds* (Doctoral dissertation). Universiteit Utrecht, Utrecht, The Netherlands.

Eisenstein, S. M. (1981). Montage [Montage]. In Eisenstein Zenshū Kankō Iinkai [Selected Writings of Eisenstein Publishing Committee], Tokyo: Kinema-Junpo. (Original works written 1936-1940)

Elman, J. L. (1990). Finding structure in time. *Cognitive Science*, *14*(2), 179–211. doi:10.1207/s15516709cog1402_1

Erdem, M. N. (2017). Narrative 3.0: Generating of user integrated narrative. In R. Yılmaz (Ed.), Narrative advertising models and conceptualization in the digital age (pp. 97-116). Hershey, PA: Information Science Reference (IGI Global).

Finlayson, M. A. (2012) *Learning narrative structure from annotated folktales* (Doctoral dissertation). Electrical Engineering and Computer Science, Massachusetts Institute of Technology, Cambridge, MA.

Fujiwara no Michitsuna no Haha. (1989). Kagerō nikki [Dragonfly diary]. In *Shin nihon koten bungaku taikei 24* [New Japanese classic literature collection 24]. Tokyo: Iwanamishoten. (Original work published around 975)

Genette, G. (1972). *Discours du récit, Essai de méthode, Figures III*. Paris: Seuil.

Genette, G. (1982). *Palimpsestes: La littérature au second degré*. Paris: Seuil.

Gerhard, N. (2010). *Algorithmic composition: Paradigms of automated music generation*. Berlin: Springer.

Graves, A., Wayne, G., & Danihelka, I. (2014). *Neural Turing machines*. arXiv:1410.5401

Hasumi, S. (1985). *Monogatari hihan josetsu* [An introduction to narrative criticism]. Tokyo: Chūōkōronsha.

Hasumi, S. (2014). *Bovary fujin ron* [A Theory of "Madam Bovary"]. Tokyo: Chikumashobō.

Hollister, J. (2016). *A contextual approach to real time, interactive narrative generation* (Doctoral dissertation). University of Central Florida, Orlando, FL.

Imabuchi, S., & Ogata, T. (2012). A story generation system based on Propp theory: As a mechanism in an integrated narrative generation system. In *Lecture Notes in Artificial Intelligence* (Vol. 7614, pp. 312–321). Berlin: Springer. doi:10.1007/978-3-642-33983-7_31

Imabuchi, S., & Ogata, T. (2013). Methods for generalizing the Propp-based story generation mechanism. In Lecture Notes in Computer Science (Vol. 8210, pp. 333–344). Berlin: Springer. doi:10.1007/978-3-319-02750-0_36

Imao, T. (1970). *Henshin no shisō* [The theory of metamorphosis]. Tokyo: Hōsei University Press.

Iser, W. (1976). *Der akt des lesens*. Munchen, Germany: Wilhelm Fink Verlag.

Jauss, H. R. (1970). Literaturgeschichte als provokation. Frankfurt am Main: Suhrkamp Verlag.

Joyce, J. (1922). *Ulysses*. Paris: Sylvia Beach.

Kan, S. (2010). *Rekishi no tetsugaku - Monogatari wo koete* [The philosophy of history: Beyond narratives]. Tokyo: Keisōshobō.

Kanai, A. (2016). Non-story, nostalgia, and film cognition: Nostalgia-based narrative rhetoric composition. In T. Ogata & T. Akimoto (Eds.), Computational and cognitive approaches to narratology (pp. 385-399). Hershey, PA: Information Science Reference (IGI Global).

Karatani, K. (1993). *Origins of modern Japanese literature*. Durham, UK: Duke University Press. (Original work published 1980)

Kawamura, Y. (2016). An attempt of the commercial film production support system based on the image rhetoric of commercial film. In T. Ogata & T. Akimoto (Eds.), Computational and cognitive approaches to narratology (pp. 117-139). Hershey, PA: Information Science Reference (IGI Global). doi:10.4018/978-1-5225-0432-0.ch004

Kawamura, Y., & Ogata, T. (2000a). *Geinō* soshiki model to image senryaku [A *geinō* organization model and the image strategies]. *Journal of Ōsaka University of Economics and Law*, *23*(2), 130–164.

Kawamura, Y., & Ogata, T. (2000b). A conceptual framework on *geinō* organization model for artificial *geinō* performers with lives. In *Proceedings of the 5th International Symposium on Artificial Life and Robotics* (pp. 793-796). Ōita, Japan: International Society of Artificial Life and Robotics.

Kawamura, Y., Ogata, T., & Kanai, A. (in press). Monogatari no wakugumi. [The framework of narrative] In T. Ogata, Y. Kawamura, & A. Kanai (Eds.), *Jōhō monogatariron - Jinkō chinō, ninchi, shakai katei to monogatari seisei* [Informational narratology: Artificial intelligence/cognition/social process and narrative generation]. Tokyo: Hakutōshobō.

Kihara, Y. (2017). *Jikkensuru shousetsu tachi - Monogataru toha betssu no shikata de* [Experimental fiction: Otherwise than narrating]. Tokyo: Sairyūsha.

Kingma, D. P., & Welling, M. (2014). *Auto-encoding variational Bayes.* arXiv:1312.6114

Kobayashi, F., & Ogata, T. (2004). Narrative and music as variation: Transformation of musical structure based on narrative discourse theory. In *Proceedings of the 9th International Symposium on Artificial Life and Robotics* (Vol. 1, pp. 170-173). Ōita, Japan: International Society of Artificial Life and Robotics.

Kristeva, J. (1980). *Desire in language: A semiotic approach to literature and art.* Columbia University Press. (Original work published 1969)

Kumagai, S., Funakoshi, S., Akimoto, T., & Ogata, T. (2012). Development of a language dictionary and a simple narrative sentence generation mechanism. In *Proceedings of the 26th Annual Conference of the Japanese Society for Artificial Intelligence* (1N1-OS-1a-3). Tokyo: Japanese Society for Artificial Intelligence.

Kybartas, B., & Bidarra, R. (2016). A survey on story generation techniques for authoring computational narratives. *IEEE Transactions on Computational Intelligence and AI in Games*, *9*(3), 39–253. doi:10.1109/TCIAIG.2016.2546063

Lang, R. R. (1999). A declarative model for simple narratives. In *Narrative intelligence: Papers from the 1999 AAAI fall symposium, Technical Report* (FS-99-01; pp. 134-141). Palo Alto, CA: Association for the Advancement of Artificial Intelligence.

Langxuan, Y. (2015). *The construction and evaluation of a design framework for narrative games for health* (Doctoral dissertation). Computer Science Program, Northeastern University, Boston, MA.

Lebowitz, M. (1985). Story-telling as planning and learning. *Poetics*, *14*(6), 483–502. doi:10.1016/0304-422X(85)90015-4

Lee, G. M. K. (2012). *Automated story-based commentary for sports* (Doctoral dissertation). Department of Computing Science, University of Alberta, Edmonton, Canada.

Lem, S. (1984). *Imaginary Magnitude.* Orland, FL: Harcourt Brace Jevanovich. (Original work published 1973)

Li, B., & Riedl, M. O. (2015). Scheherazade: Crowd-powered interactive narrative generation. In *Proceedings of the 29th AAAI Conference on Artificial Intelligence* (pp. 4305-4306). Palo Alto, CA: Association for the Advancement of Artificial Intelligence.

Lu, R., & Zhang, S. (2002). *Automatic generation of computer animation: Using AI for movie animation.* Berlin: Springer. doi:10.1007/3-540-45590-6

Martin, L. J., Ammanabrolu, P., Hancock, W., Singh, S., Harrison, B., & Riedl, M. O. (2017). Event representations for automated story generation with deep neural nets. In *Proceedings of KDD 2017 Workshop on Machine Learning for Creativity*. Retrieved from http://ml4creativity.mybluemix.net/papers/MartinEtAl-Event_Representations_for_Automated_Story-camera_ready.pdf

Meehan, J. R. (1980). *The metanovel: Writing stories by computer*. Garland Publishing.

Meyerhold, V., Isahaya, Y., Iwate, T., & Ura, M. et al.. (2001). *Meyehold best selection* [Vsevolod Meyerhold Selected Writings]. Tokyo: Sakuhinsha.

Mikolov, T., Sutskever, I., Chen, K., Corrado, G. S., & Dean, J. (2013). Distributed representations of words and phrases and their compositionality. In C. J. C. Burges, L. Bottou, M. Welling, Z. Ghahramani, & K. Weinberger (Eds.), Advances in neural information processing systems (Vol. 26, pp. 3111–3119). Curran Associates, Inc.

Mikolov, T., & Yih, W., & Zweig, G. (2013). *Linguistic regularities in continuous space-word representations*. Paper presented at the 2013 Conference of the North American Chapter of the Association for Computational Linguistics: Human Language Technologies.

Montfort, N. (2007). *Generating narrative variation in interactive fiction* (Doctoral dissertation). University of Pennsylvania, Philadelphia, PA.

Mueller, E. T. (1990). *Daydreaming in humans and machines*. Ablex.

Murasaki Shikibu. (1993-1997). Genji monogatari (1-5). Tokyo: Iwanamishoten.

Natsume, S. (1907). *Bungaku ron* [A theory of literature]. Tokyo: Ōkurashoten, Hattorishoten.

Newell, A., & Simon, H. A. (1972). *Human problem solving*. Prentice Hall.

Noe, K. (1996). *Monogatari no tetsugaku - Yanagita Kunio to rekishi no hakken* [The philosophy of narrative: Yanagita Kunio and the invention of a history]. Tokyo: Iwanamishoten.

Oda, J. (2007). Re-reinvestigation of Raimundus Lullus on creativity. In *Proceedings of the 26th Special Interest Group on Language Sense Engineering Research Group in Japanese Artificial Intelligence Society* (pp. 47-51). Tokyo: Japanese Artificial Intelligence Society.

Ōe, K. (1979). *Dōjidai game* [The game of contemporaneity]. Tokyo: Shinchōsha.

Ogata, T. (1995). *Monogatari seisei - Monogatari no tameno gihō to senryaku ni motozuku approach* [Narrative generation: An approach based on techniques and strategies for narrative] (Doctoral dissertation). The University of Tokyo, Tokyo, Japan.

Ogata, T. (1997). Tajū monogatari kōzō no model [A model of multiple narrative structures]. In *Proceedings of the 9th Annual Conference of Japan Simulation & Gaming Association* (pp. 107-110). Tokyo: Japan Simulation & Gaming Association.

Ogata, T. (1999a). Monogatari genre taikei no mōrateki kentō [A comprehensive consideration of a narrative genre system]. In N. Yoshimine, H. Akama & A. Tokosumi (Eds.), Literature and Cognition/Computer 2: The Expansion of Literature. Japanese Cognitive Science Society Technical Report (00-No. 40).

Ogata, T. (1999b). An attempt for systematization of narrative discourse theory from the viewpoint of narrative generation system. *Proceedings of IPSJ SIG Computers and the Humanities*, *99*(85), 31–38.

Ogata, T. (2000). Tajū monogatari kōzō no macro model - Simulation toshite no monogatari josetsu [The macro model of multiple narrative structures: an introduction to a narrative as a simulation]. *Simulation & Gaming*, *10*(1), 35–46.

Ogata, T. (2002a). Expanded literary theory: Cognitive/computational expansion of literary theories and narratology. In *Proceedings of the 17th Congress of the International Association of Empirical Aesthetics* (pp. 163-166). Rome, Italy: University of Rome Tre.

Ogata, T. (2002b). The concept of system narratology: From the viewpoint of expanded literary theory. In *Proceedings of the 3rd International Workshop of Literature in Cognition and Computer in held in PRICAI2002* (W7-1, pp. 1-10). Tokyo: Japanese Society of Cognitive Studies.

Ogata, T. (2004): Toward the consistent simulation of narrative discourse based on narratology. In *Proceedings of the 9th International Symposium on Artificial Life and Robotics* (Vol. 2, pp. 579-584). Oita, Japan: International Society of Artificial Life and Robotics.

Ogata, T. (2007). To the rhetoric of story from Propp: Centering around the rhetoric of de-composition and re-composition. *Cognitive Studies*, *14*(4), 532–558.

Ogata, T. (2008). Monogatari seisei system ni okeru eizō kosei he mukete [Towards image editing in a narrative generation system]. In A. Kanai & Y. Niwa (Eds.), *Eizō henshū no riron to jissen* [Theories and practices of image editing] (pp. 165–235). Tokyo: Hōsei University Press.

Ogata, T. (2011). Narrative generation system as the practice of "informatics of narratology.". *Journal of Japan Society for Fazzy Theory and Intelligent Informatics*, *23*(5), 14–24.

Ogata, T. (2014). Expanded literary theory for automatic narrative generation. In *Proceedings of Joint 7th International Conference on Soft Computing and Intelligent Systems and 15th International Symposium on Advanced Intelligent Systems* (pp. 1558-1563). Tokyo: Japan Society of Fuzzy Theory and Intelligent Informatics.

Ogata, T. (2015). Building conceptual dictionaries for an integrated narrative generation system. *Journal of Robotics. Networking and Artificial Life*, *1*(4), 270–284. doi:10.2991/jrnal.2015.1.4.6

Ogata, T. (2016a). Computational and cognitive approaches to narratology from the perspective of narrative generation. In T. Ogata & T. Akimoto (Eds.), Computational and cognitive approaches to narratology (pp. 1-73). Hershey, PA: Information Science Reference (IGI Global). doi:10.4018/978-1-5225-0432-0.ch001

Ogata, T. (2016b). Kabuki as multiple narrative structures. In T. Ogata & T. Akimoto (Eds.), Computational and cognitive approaches to narratology (pp. 400-431). Hershey, PA: Information Science Reference (IGI Global).

Ogata, T. (n.d.a). Gaibu heno monogatari seisei mataha geinō jōhō system ni mukete [Narrative generation to outside or toward a geino information system]. In T. Ogata, Y. Kawamura & A. Kanai (Eds.), Jōhō monogatariron - Jinkō chinō, ninchi, shakai katei to monogatari seisei [Informational narratology: Artificial intelligence/cognition/social process and narrative generation]. Tokyo: Hakutōshobō. (in press)

Ogata, T. (n.d.b). Naibu heno monogatari seisei mataha watakushi monogatari ni mukete [Narrative generation to inside or toward I narratives]. In Jōhō monogatariron - Jinkō chinō, ninchi, shakai katei to monogatari seisei [Informational narratology: artificial intelligence/cognition/social process and narrative generation]. Tokyo: Hakutōshobō. (in press)

Ogata, T., & Akimoto, T. (2007). Towards the circular narrative generation based on the correspondences between language-based narrative and music: Systems development based on narrative rhetoric and fundamental considerations about the systems and the circular narrative generation. *Cognitive Studies, 14*(3), 355–379.

Ogata, T., & Akimoto, T. (Eds.). (2016). Computational and cognitive approaches to narratology. Hershey, PA: Information Science Reference (IGI Global). doi:10.4018/978-1-5225-0432-0

Ogata, T., Arai, T., & Ono, J. (2016). Using synthetically collected scripts for story generation. In *Proceedings of the 26th International Conference on Computational Linguistics: System Demonstrations* (pp. 253-257). Tokyo: The COLING 2016 Organizing Committee.

Ogata, T., Hori, K., & Ohsuga, S. (1996). A basic framework for narrative conceptual structure generation based on narrative techniques and strategies. *Jinkō Chinō Gakkaishi, 11*(1), 148–159.

Ogata, T., & Kanai, A. (2010). *Monogatariron no jōhōgaku josetsu - Monogatari seisei no shisō to gijutsu wo megutte* [An introduction to informatics of narratology: Towards the thoughts and technologies of narrative generation]. Tokyo: Gakubunsha.

Ogata, T., & Kawamura, Y. (1997a). Historical process of contents creation and current strategy. In *Proceedings of the 7th International Forum on Tehcnology Management* (pp. 400-405). Kyōto, Japan: International Forum on Tehcnology Management.

Ogata, T., & Kawamura, Y. (1997b). Gendai minzoku kōgaku kōsō - Kenkyū keika to kongo no vision [A plan of contemporary folk engineering: The research process and future vision]. In *Proceedins of the 1997 Spring Conference of the Japanese Society of Management and Information* (pp. 161–164). Tokyo: Japanese Society of Management and Information.

Ogata, T., & Kawamura, Y. (1999). Monogatari sanshutsu soshikiron to *geinō* soshiki model [Narrative production organization and a geino organization model]. In *Proceedings of the 1999 Meeting of the Academic Association of Organizational Science* (pp. 219-222). Tokyo: Academic Association of Organizational Science.

Ogata, T., Kawamura, Y., & Kanai, A. (in press). *Jōhō monogatariron - Jinkō chinō, ninchi, shakai katei to monogatari seisei* [Informational narratology: Artificial intelligence/cognition/social process and narrative generation]. Tokyo: *Hakutōshobō.*

Ogata, T., & Morita, H. (2001). Story and discourse in narrative: From the viewpoint of narrative as simulation. *Simulation & Gaming, 11*(1), 40–49.

Ogata, T., & Ono, J. (2016). A way for using the verb conceptual dictionary in an integrated narrative generation system: The use of co-occurrence information on verb concepts. *Journal of Robotics. Networking and Artificial Life*, *3*(3), 209–212. doi:10.2991/jrnal.2016.3.3.15

Ogata, T., & Terano, T. (1991). Explanation-based narrative generation using semiotic theory. In *Proceedings of Natural Language Processing Pacific Rim Symposium* (pp. 321-328). Tokyo: Special Interest Group of Natural Language Processing of Information Processing Society of Japan.

Okada, N., & Endo, T. (1992). Story generation based on dynamics of the mind. *Computational Intelligence*, *8*(1), 123–160. doi:10.1111/j.1467-8640.1992.tb00341.x

Ono, J., & Ogata, T. (2015). Selecting words and notation using literary data in the integrated narrative generation system. *Journal of Robotics. Networking and Artificial Life*, *2*(3), 194–199. doi:10.2991/jrnal.2015.2.3.13

Ono, J., & Ogata, T. (2016). A method of story generation for creating "surprise" using "gap techniques": An approach to an automatic narrative generation game based on table-talk role playing games. *Cognitive Studies.*, *24*(3), 410–434.

Ono, J., & Ogata, T. (in press). Surprise-based narrative generation in an automatic narrative generation game. In T. Ogata & S. Asakawa. (Eds.), Content generation through narrative communication and simulation. Hershey, PA: Information Science Reference (IGI Global).

Onodera, K., Akimoto, T., & Ogata, T. (2012). A state-event transformation mechanism for generating micro structures of story in an integrated narrative generation system. In *Proceedings of the 34th Annual Conference of the Cognitive Science Society* (pp. 2150-2155). Tokyo: Japanese Cognitive Science Society.

Pemberton, L. (1989). A modular approach to story generation. In *Proceedings of the Fourth Conference on European Chapter of the Association for Computational Linguistics* (pp. 217-224). The Association for Computational Linguistics. doi:10.3115/976815.976845

Pérez y Pérez, R., & Sharples, M. (2001). MEXICA: A computer model of a cognitive account of creative writing. *Journal of Experimental & Theoretical Artificial Intelligence*, *13*(2), 119–139. doi:10.1080/09528130010029820

Powers, R. (1995). *Galatea 2.2*. Harper Perennial.

Propp, V. Y. (1968). *Morphology of the folktale* (L. Scott, Trans.). Austin, TX: University of Texas Press. (Original work published 1928)

Rumelhart, D. E. (1975). Notes on a schema for stories. In D. G. Bobrow & A. Collins (Eds.), *Representation and understanding: Studies in cognitive science*. Academic Press. doi:10.1016/B978-0-12-108550-6.50013-6

Sarlej, M. (2014). *A lesson learned: Using emotions to generate stories with morals* (Doctoral dissertation). Computer Science and Engineering, University of New South Wales, Sydney, Australia.

Schank, R. C., & Abelson, R. P. (1977). *Scripts, plans, goals, and understanding: An inquiry into human knowledge structures*. Lawrence Erlbaum.

Schank, R. C., & Riesbeck, C. K. (1981). *Inside computer understanding*. Lawrence Erlbaum.

Sharples, M. (1996). An account of writing as creative design. In C. M. Levy & S. Ransdell (Eds.), *The science of writing: Theories, methods, individual difference and applications* (pp. 127–148). Lawrence Erlbaum.

Shklovsky, V. (1990). *Theory of prose* (B. Sher, Trans.). Dalkey Archive Press.

Si, M. (2010). *Thespian: A decision-theoretic framework for interactive narratives* (Doctoral dissertation). Faculty of the USC Graduate School, University of Southern California.

Sutskever, I., Vinyals, O., & Le, Q. V. (2014). Sequence to sequence learning with neural networks. In Z. Ghahramani, M. Welling, C. Cortes, N. Lawrence, & K. Weinberger (Eds.), Advances in Neural Information Processing Systems (Vol. 27, 3104–3112). Montreal, Canada: Academic Press.

Swartjes, I. (2010). *Whose story is it anyway? How improve informs agency and authorship of emergent narrative* (Doctoral dissertation). University of Twente, Enschede, The Netherlands.

Swift, J. (2005). *Gulliver's travels*. Oxford, UK: Oxford University Press. (Original work published 1726)

Tale of the Henike. (2012). (R. Tyler, Trans.). London: Penguin Books. (Original work published the Kamakura era)

Turner, S. R. (1994). *The creative process: A computer model of storytelling and creativity*. Lawrence Erlbaum.

Watanabe, N. (2012). *Nihon shōsetsu gijutsushi* [A history of technologies of Japanese novels]. Tokyo: Shinchōsha.

Wayne, G., & Danihelka, I. (2014). *Neural turing machines*. arXiv:1410.5401

Yılmaz, R. (Ed.). (2017). Narrative advertising models and conceptualization in the digital age. Hershey, PA: Business Science Reference (IGI-Global). doi:10.4018/978-1-5225-2373-4

Yokomitsu, R. (1931). *Kikai* [Machine]. Tokyo: Hakusuisha.

Yoshimoto, T. (1965). *Gengo nitotte bi toha nanika* [What is beauty for language?]. Tokyo: Keisōshobō.

Yoshimoto, T. (1968). *Kyōdō gensō ron* [Communal illusion]. Tokyo: Kawadeshobō-shinsha.

Zhang, Y., Ono, J., & Ogata, T. (2011). An advertising rhetorical mechanism for single event combined with conceptual dictionary in narrative generation system. In *Proceedings of 7th International Conference on Natural Language Processing and Knowledge Engineering* (pp. 340-343). The Institute of Electrical and Electronics Engineers. doi:10.1109/NLPKE.2011.6138221

Zhang, Y., Ono, J., & Ogata, T. (2012). Single event and scenario generation based on advertising rhetorical techniques using the conceptual dictionary in narrative generation system. In *Proceedings of the 4th IEEE International Conference on Digital Game and Intelligent Toy Enhanced Learning* (pp. 162-164). The Institute of Electrical and Electronics Engineers. doi:10.1109/DIGITEL.2012.46

KEY TERMS AND DEFINITIONS

Encoder/Decoder Models: Encoder/decoder models are neural network models for machine translations and short-term conversation. Both encoder and decoder devices consist of recurrent neural networks.

Expanded Literary Theory: A concept for a research field in which narratology and literary theories are organically introduced into computational and cognitive approaches.

***Geino* Information System:** A system model of *geino* production and consumption. GIS has been considered a framework in which various levels of narrative generation processes were driven by authors, receivers, characters, actors, and actresses.

Integrated Narrative Generation System: A synthetic narrative generation system architecture integrating the previous studies by Ogata.

Multiple Narrative Structures: A conceptual model by which a narrative text is multiply constituted and the narrative generation process is also multiply executed.

Narrative Communication: A characteristic of narrative communication is multiplicity. In particular, narrative communication exists on many levels, such as the communication between the narrator and narratee in a narrative world, the communication among characters, as well as the communication between an author and a reader. In addition, there are direct and indirect forms of communication. Thus, a narrative is a multiple and plural collection of such forms of communication.

Narrative Simulation: The authors in this chapter regard conscious performance as narrative generation and simulation by systematically using the analysis results of narrative components and principles of narrative generation and reception as narrative simulation. Computers and artificial intelligence are effective tools for narrative simulation. In addition, automated narrative generation systems are important subjects for narrative simulation.

Variational Autoencoders (VAE): While encoder/decoder models show outperformed achievement, they also possess shortcomings such that the correspondences between source and target information are rigid. VAE models might suggest further varieties of outputs via latent variables that exist between the source and target modules. Thus, VAEs might be candidates for more redundant and complicated story generations.

Section 2
Systems and Models for Narrative Generation and Simulation

Chapter 2
An Integrated Approach to Narrative Generation:
From Mishima and *Kabuki* to Narrative Generation Systems

Takashi Ogata
Iwate Prefectural University, Japan

ABSTRACT

This chapter seeks to undertake a comprehensive structure of the author's narrative generation research. In particular, the chapter compactly shows the whole of the narrative generation studies as an indirect purpose by taking several concrete examples and aims to consider and discuss the respective components as the direct purpose. Through this chapter, the author presents an entire framework of narrative analyses in relation to the integrated narrative generation system and Geinō information system, and conducts the analyses of a novel by Yukio Mishima and several aspects of kabuki. The final part provides directions for partially incorporating the results of the narrative analyses of Mishima and kabuki into the above narrative generation systems. In relation to this book's title, Content Generation Through Narrative Communication and Simulation, this chapter selects "narrative content" as "content" to be generated, conducts the analyses of narrative "communication," structure, and techniques, and attempts narrative "simulation" using the author's narrative generation systems.

INTRODUCTION

The objective of this chapter, as a whole, is to introduce and outlook the composition of the author's narrative generation studies, which incorporates fundamental considerations, narrative research and analysis, system design and development, and narrative generation practice. However, because Ogata (2016a) stated the fundamental considerations in detail, that part is omitted in this chapter. This chapter comprehensively describes the range from the narrative research and analysis to the system design and development as a continuous organically-integrated research. Part of narrative research and analysis corresponds to the study of a kind of narrative communication and, in particular, this theme especially

DOI: 10.4018/978-1-5225-4775-4.ch002

Copyright © 2018, IGI Global. Copying or distributing in print or electronic forms without written permission of IGI Global is prohibited.

researches and analyzes the problems of characters and stories contained in a novel by Yukio Mishima and *kabuki* (Ogata, 2016b). On the other hand, the system design and development corresponds to the study of narrative generation or a kind of narrative simulation and, in this chapter, the author particularly conducts narrative simulations using the Integrated Narrative Generation System (INGS) and the *Geinō* Information System (GIS) explained in Chapter 1. Both narrative communication and narrative simulation are central concepts or terms in this book. Although the author's study in particular aims to practically develop and distribute real narrative works produced by narrative generation systems themselves or the interactions or collaborations in diverse methods between narrative generation systems and humans, this chapter introduces the process up until the phase before the abovementioned final goal by using partial materials.

The central part of this chapter is composed of the "BACKGROUND," five subsequent sections, and finally, the continuation into "FUTURE RESEARCH DIRECTIONS" and "CONCLUSION." The middle five parts are as follows:

In the first section, "NARRATIVE ANALYSES FOR DIVERSE NARRATIVE PHENOMENA AND ELEMENTS: A NARRATIVE GENERATION PERSPECTIVE," the author shows various results acquired through previous narrative analyses and lists future directions. In particular, the main purpose of these narrative analyses is not the reading and interpretation of works. Generally speaking, a main goal of narrative analyses in literary studies has been to read and interpret works, and diverse methods and theories were developed toward correct readings and interpretations, further novel and amazing ones. Narrative analyses sometimes explore the structure and representation of a narrative text themselves and, at other times, study the environment and context surrounding a text. By contrast, a chief purpose of the author's narrative analyses here is not in reading and interpreting the text, but gaining implications for the design of narrative generation mechanisms and the development of systems. Consequently, the results will be related to the design and development of narrative generation systems.

The second section is "AN ANALYSIS OF A NOVEL BY YUKIO MISHIMA: THE NOVEL AS A PLURAL APPARATUS AND A TEXT ANALYSIS BASED ON THE CHARACTERS." In this section, using a medium-length novel, *Gogo no Eikō* [*The Sailor Who Fell from Grace with the Sea*] (1963) by Yukio Mishima (1925-1970), the author researches and analyzes in detail the actions and thoughts of the main characters to make clear that the reality in this novel is created through the actions and thoughts of various characters and the mutual relations. The present step of this research and analysis indicate that, in the story generation mechanism in INGS, the story generation functions created by each character, in addition to the author's story generation function, must be added to the story generation mechanism that has been modeled as the function of author as a whole.

The next section, "MULTIPLE NARRATIVE STRUCTURES OF *KABUKI*: STORIES AND PEOPLE," continues to present the narrative analysis as follows. In particular, with regard to *kabuki*, the author researches and analyzes the characteristics of stories and characters from the viewpoint of a mainly multiplicitous and multiple-narrative-structure model. First, the author re-analyzes a story of a *kabuki* play based on a study that considered complex multiple structures in *kabuki* narratives from the perspective on which the above considerations are applied to the field of narrative generation. Further, the multiple structures of characters are researched and analyzed from various viewpoints. Although these are also undertaken with the goal of application to narrative generation or simulation by the author similar to the above research, as well as to the development of a novel by Mishima, the central objective is to introduce the acquired methods and knowledge in GIS as a system model in which the INGS systems are contained.

In the fourth section, "NARRATIVE GENERATION OR SIMULATION DESIGN BASED ON ANALYSES OF MISHIMA AND *KABUKI*: SIMPLE EXAMPLES," the author aims to conduct, on a small scale, experiments to introduce and implement the analysis results of a novel by Mishima into narrative simulation or generation mechanisms using INGS. Further, the author deals with acquired *kabuki* knowledge, particularly the aspects of person and story, seen from the viewpoint of the multiple narrative structures model in the previous section in order to introduce it into the INGS and GIS systems. The current INGS does not yet have the mechanisms required to fully achieve and implement this purpose, so the narrative simulation (generation) method presented here implies a future direction for extending the INGS architecture.

BACKGROUND

This section introduces the following two backgrounds: Yukio Mishima and *kabuki*. Of course, the direct objectives of this chapter are not to discuss Mishima and *kabuki* themselves. However, they have an important meaning beyond simply being used as material. *Gogo no Eikō* [*The Sailor Who Fell from Grace with the Sea*] by Mishima, along with aspects of *kabuki,* are researched and analyzed with the intention of utilizing the results for narrative simulation or generation mechanisms using INGS and GIS.

Yukio Mishima

Yukio Mishima ("Mishima Yukio," in his Japanese name representation), died, shockingly, when the authorI was 12 years old and in the sixth year of my elementary school (1970 in the Christian Era and Showa 45 in the Japanese Emperors' era). One of the first triggers of the author's narrative study was really this impact made by the death of Mishima. For several years after his death, the author read many of his literary works and continued to feel the large impact by his death. The influence from Mishima further resulted in my strong interest in *kabuki*, *ningyō jōruri,* and Japanese classical literature from boyhood. Although Japan after Mishima produced many excellent literary authors and novelists and their works, including Kōbō Abe (1924-1993) (1973, 1977), Kenzaburō Ōe (1935-) (1973, 2009), Kenji Nakagami (1946-1992) (1977, 1982), Haruki Murakami (1949-) (1985, 1994-1995), Ryū Murakami (1952-) (1980, 1997), for me, literature gained importance after Mishima. This was also true after the Western literary authors and works from the beginning of the 20th century until the mid, starting from the great authors and works including Marcel Proust (1871-1922) (2003), James Joyce (1882-1941) (1922, 1939), Robert Musil (1880-1942) (1930, 1932)), Franz Kafka (1883- 1924) (2009a, 2009b), William Faulkner (1897-1962) (1929, 1936), Earnest Hemingway (1899-1961) (1929, 1940), and such Japanese authors and works as Sōseki Natsume (1867-1916) (1905, 1916), Jun'ichirō Tanizaki (1886-1965) (1924, 1943-1948), Riichi Yokomitsu (1898-1947) (1930, 1931), and Yasunari Kawabata (1899-1972), (1935-37-1947, 1961). Influenced by the above feeling, for approximately thirty subsequent years, the author has been directly away from Mishima or all kinds of worlds of literature itself. For the author, narrative generation systems have been developed as, so to speak, contemporary folktales, rather than aiming at literature. After all, since 2000, I have reread the newest complete works by Yukio Mishima, *Ketteiban Mishima Yukio Zenshū*, published by Shinchosha (2000-2006), from end to end, including many works that I had already read in junior high and high school.

Of course, Mishima was a rare literary person in modern Japanese literature, and even further, throughout the entire history of Japanese literature, in the sense that he influenced and shocked many people. The influence was, in many cases, associated with his dramatic death at forty-five years old, which was at the same time a very comical death in that it did not have real and political effectiveness. However, influence by Michima's literature, which covers a diverse set of literary genres including novels, dramas, essays and critiques, and many dialogues, diaries, letters, as well as many documents that were not recorded in the above works, such as interviews by popular magazines, did not necessarily rely on, so to speak, Avant-garde literary techniques and experiments. In this sense, the literary style of Mishima, unlike previous famous authors, including Sōseki Natsume (1906, 1908), Riichi Yokomitsu (1930, 1931), Jun'ichiro Tanizaki (1933), Yasunari Kawabata (1954), was highly classical and conservative. However, at the same time, his classical features were based on his strategic intention to introduce a classical aesthetic tradition of Western literature, such as ancient Greek literature and French classicism, and furthermore, a conscious adoption of not using Avant-garde and experimental literary techniques in the twentieth century. In this sense, his strategy may actually be Avant-garde, so to speak, in the sense that he went against convention. Mishima's literature may be similar to Mozart's music (1756-1791) in that they contained all of the artist's emotions in classical forms as much as was possible. In this sense, his literature may be also similar to Thomas Mann (1875-1955) (1998, 1999, etc.) and Albert Camus (1913-1960) in the 20th century.

One reason that the influence of his literary works cannot be escaped from his human existence, and further, the extreme style of his death, is considered that classical and neat, as literature, works of novels and dramas by Mishima are closely interacted with, so to speak, his "thought." In a sense, for Mishima's literary works, the side of content can be said to be very essentially important. Thus, although ideological essays regarding his works have continuously been appearing, there have only been a few studies that focused on analyses of his narrative forms and structures. However, as mentioned above, in his literature, Mishima intentionally and strategically made full use of classical styles and forms, and was heavily influenced by Western literature. At the same time, because the works are different from Western classical works, it is possible, and necessary, to create non-ideological analyses focusing on this point or analyzing and studying the works from the viewpoint of the collision between form and thought in novels.

Amongst his many and diverse novels, the short stories contained in his first book, *Hanazakari no Mori* [*Forest in Full Bloom*] (1944), which was published when he was 19 years old, were written using an ornate style that included very elaborate rhetoric to represent narratives, treating the Japanese ancient history and middle ages as source material. The document named *Shibai Nikki* [*Plays Diary*] (1991) written in the same period, was collection of records in theaters, *Kabukiza* and others, in Tokyo, and demonstrated that his literary career originally began under the heavy influence of Japanese classical literature and *kabuki*. This may reflect the fact that Japan at this time was involved in the Pacific War in World War II and Japanese culture and literature were especially admired. Many literary authors who belonged to Mishima's generation frequently saw this war objectively and critically, such as Yutaka Haniya (1909-1997) who wrote a monumental novel, *Shirei* [*Death Spirits*] (1946-1996), or directly supported the war by writing poems and novels of nationalism or admiration of the war, such as *Ryoshu,* [*Loneliness on a Journey*] (1937-1946) by Riichi Yokomitsu. Still others described experiences of directly entering the war as soldiers, such as *Shinkū Chitai* [*Zone of Emptiness*] (1952) by Hiroshi Noma (1915-1991), and *Nobi* [*Fires on the Plain*] (1952) and *Leyte Senki* [*A Record of the Battle of Leyte*] (1971) by Shōhei Ōoka (1909-1988). Many authors of Mishima's generation who were teenagers during the war, including Takaaki Yoshimoto (1924-2012) (1966, 1990, etc.), showed emotional responses toward going into the war. In contrast, in the post-war generation that included Kenzaburō Ōe (1965, etc.) and Jun Etō (1932-1999) (1959, 1970-1999, etc.) (Etō was one of the most famous critics in the post-war generation), some authors admired the American democracy as a positive introduction into the post-war society, while other authors criticized it. Although the directions are different, the actions and thoughts of many literary authors in this generation rotated around an axis of American democracy. Actions, styles, themes, and thoughts of literary authors of Mishima's generation who were emotionally involved in the Pacific war were also considered be a kind of norm for the following generation's literary authors.

After the war, Mishima began to clearly show influences from Western literature and French psychological novels in *Ai no Kawaki* [*Thirst for Love*] (1950) and Greek literature in *Shiosai* [*The Sound of Waves*] (1954). Further, he published gay literature based on the tradition of *kabuki,* the Western tradition of sodomy, and further, his personal preference, such as in the first half of *Kamen no Kokuhaku* [*Confessions of a Mask*] (1949) and in *Kinjiki* [*Forbidden Colors*] (1951-1953). Additionally, after he wrote several unique novels, including *Shizumeru Taki* [*A Sinking Waterfall*] (1955) as a non-love story and many popular novels, which are made up of novellas, including *Natsuko no Bōken* [*An Adventure of Natsuko*] (1951), and *Kōfuku-gō Shuppan* [*Kōfuku-gō Sails*] (1955), he published *Kinkakuji* [*The Temple of Golden Pavilion*] (1956) that was a representative work in the middle period of his literary career. Although Mishima described beautiful boys, girls, and young men in *The Sound of Waves* and *Forbidden Colors*, his favorite characters were rather literally dirty boys and young men who were ugly and had deep-seated body issues. The hero of *The Temple of Golden Pavilion* was just such a character. Although based on the story, this is a mere crime novel in which an ugly young man with nothing to his name sets fire to an old and famous temple in Kyōto that he has decided is a symbol of beauty, this novel had an extraordinary and abnormal power based on the intensity of the hero's selfish philosophy. Such a selfish philosophy was also showcased in later novels including, *Utsukushii Hoshi* [*A Beautiful Star*] (1962), *Gogo no Eikō* [*The Sailor Who Fell from Grace with the Sea*] (1963), and so on.

Kyōko no Ie [*Kyōko's House*] (1959) by Mishima, was generally evaluated as a failed work. This long novel is not certainly interesting to read. The author guesses that one of the reasons it failed was that Mishima attempted to use a different literary form or structure from his previous style. Mishima himself stated that this novel imitated the "merry-go-round method" in *Yukari no Onna* [*A Marginal Woman*] (1919) by the famous and excellent writer Kyōka Izumu (1873-1939). The *kanji* representation of "Kyō (鏡)" in "Kyōka (鏡花)" means "mirror," and "Kyō (鏡)" in "Kyōko (鏡子)" also uses the same kanji. It would be almost impossible to translate his literary works, which are expressed by gorgeous, highly sensory, and poetic words and sentences, into foreign languages.

Actions and stories that are not essentially interacted with by several main characters rotate through the structure of *Kyōko's House*. Through this structure, Mishima excluded the element of an organized and tight entanglement of the plot line, and instead fragmentally described a cross-section of each life through the views of several characters who accidentally came together at a place provided by a central heroine in the novel, Kyoko; in this way, he represented an overall picture of one era in his contemporary Japan. The reason that this was a rare experimental novel for Mishima and why this was judged as a failure (or if it is truly a failure) are issues to be determined in the future.

In addition to the above stories, which can be referred to as novellas as they are made up of both short and long novels, Mishima wrote many short stories that have been frequently judged as interesting and excellent, as opposed to his novellas and novels. For example, *Manatsu no Shi* [*Death in Midsummer*] (1953) was a narrative that answered the question, "why does the death occur in midsummer?" by using only vivid descriptions instead of explanation, and *Hashi-zukushi* [*The Seven Bridges*] (1958), a narrative that used a style for covering several bridges in the city of Tokyo, following the style of Japan's traditional narrative. Further, *Mikumano Mōde* [*Acts of Worship*] (1965) was a short narrative story that used Shinobu Orikuchi (1887-1953), who was a famous and great folklorist, as a model, in order to dissect the problems of Japanese *geinō* or traditional performing arts. In addition, his many and diverse scenarios for dramas have been criticized by many critics and audiences who say that Mishima is a playwright rather than a novelist. Sometimes, I imagine that if Mishima had been born in the Edo era in Japan, he would have been an outstanding *kabuki* writer. In fact, Mishima wrote several *kabuki* scenarios in a pseudoclassical style, including *Iwashiuri Koi no Hikiami* [*The Sardine Seller's Net of Love*] (1954) and *Chinsetsu Yumiharizuki* [*A Wonder Tale: The Moonbow*] (1969), that continue to play currently. In addition, *Kindai Nōgaku-shū* [*Five Modern Nō Plays*] (1956) was a contemporary version of *Nō* dependent upon *Aoi no Ue* [*Lady Aoi*] written by Zeami Motokiyo (1363?-1443?), which was an adaption of a part of *Genji Monogatari* [*The Tale of Genji*] by Murasaki Shikibu. As other examples, Mishima wrote and performed many great scenarios for drama, including *Rokumeikan* (1956), a tragedy in the bizarre era trend of Western Europe set in a Western-style building in the Meiji era, *Sade Kōshaku Fujin* [*Madame de Sade*] (1965), a dialogue drama focusing on a woman who is waiting for her imprisoned husband and finally rejects him when he returns home, and *Raiō no Terrace* [*The Terrace of the Leper King*] (1969), which describes a Cambodian king's dream of building a magnificent temple and his body's collapse. One of the characteristics of Mishima's scenarios is to mix and harmonize both the features of an absolute dialogue drama written by using artificial speech language and introducing the *Shingeki* (a modern drama style in Japan influenced by Western drama), and the theatricality as the fascination of stories or plots that were inherited from *kabuki* and *Nō*. Furthermore, his essays frequently have the style of academic papers, such as in *Chikamatsu Hanji* [*On Chikamatsu Hanji*] (2003) and *Bunka Boei Ron* [*Discussion on the Defense of Culture*] (1969), or take on a kind of poetic prose, such as in *Taiyo to Tetsu* [*Sun and Steel*] (1968). Additionally, letters among Mishima and many people, including Yasunari Kawabata, Donald Keene (1922-), remind us of Mishima's kind and polite personality.

In his last few years, Mishima dedicated his life to writing *Hōjō no Umi* [*The Sea of Fertility*] (1969-1971), a long novel consisting of the following four volumes: *Haru no Yuki* [*Spring Snow*] (1969), *Honba* [Runaway Horses] (1969), *Akatsuki no Tera* [The Temple of Dawn] (1970) and *Tennin Gosui* [The Decay of the Angel] (1971). He also participated in political acts up until the end. Although Mishima previously had chiefly written essays regarding literature and culture in a broad sense, focusing on beautiful subjects, in his final period, essays with political tendencies gradually increased. However, this fact is not due solely to Mishima's personality. The 1960s was an era of politics and evolution worldwide. In Japan, Takaaki Yoshimoto, who was a poet and critic in Mishima's time, wrote political and ideological essays using important keywords, such as *jiritsu* ("self-reliance") (Yoshimoto, 1966) and *kyodō gensō* ("communal illusion") (Yoshimoto, 1968) based on complex emotions that cannot be classified simply as "left-wing," although he did perform left-wing activities. Ichirō Murakami (1920-1975), one of Yoshimoto's writing friends, was an emperor-worshipper who eventually committed suicide using a Japanese sword. Kenzaburō Ōe, who came after Mishima, also wrote essays based on his left-wing ideology and took part in political activities. However, in the case of Ōe, his novels portrayed the dense emotions of the characters that went beyond political ideologies in the narrow sense, such as sentiments and emotions associated with the right-wing and terrorism. Although these works showed the conflict between reason and emotion, it was actually linked to Ōe's contradictory but high literary evaluation. In addition, Kazumi Takahashi (1931-1971) who wrote about right-wing and nationalistic thought and sentiment, published many novels, such as *Jashūmon* [*Heretical Faith*] (1965-1966) and *Nihon no Akuryō* [*Demon of Japan*] (1966-1968), along with essays such as *Waga Kaitai* [*My Dismantling*] (1971), and academic papers regarding Chinese literature, including *Ri Shōin* (1958), along with Ōe, in spite of the left-wing viewpoint of his political ideology.

The Sea of Fertility, composed of the four volumes mentioned above, was Mishima's final and longest novel. The entire work narrates the existence of the character as a bystander, Honda Shigetoshi. In the final volume, Honda was, as a viewer, arrested for peeping at Hibiya Park in Tokyo, and his status and honor as a judge and a lawyer was damaged. In Mishima's works, peeping frequently appear. For example, *The Sailor Who Fell from Grace with the Sea* begins from a scene where a boy, who is actually a hero in this novel, peeps at the sexual act between his mother and her lover, who is another hero, from the room next door. Throughout all the volumes in *The Sea of Fertility*, the narrative progresses by using Honda, who is essentially a viewer, as a kind of subsidiary character. At the same time, though this is generally considered the most important feature of this novel, each character, a hero or a heroine, in the four volumes, is linked to each other through the thread of *rin'ne-tensho* ("reincarnation"). However, the hero in the last volume, Yasunaga Toru in *The Decay of the Angel*, is shown to be cut from this thread. However, each volume develops relatively independent narratives. Volume I, *Spring Snow*, is a love story, volume II, *Runaway Horses*, is a political novel, volume III, *The Temple of Dawn*, is a sexual novel, and volume IX, *The Decay of the Angel*, is a nihilistic novel. The young heroine in *Spring Snow*, Ayakura Satoko, appears again in the last scene of *The Decay of the Angel* as a high-ranking nun in an old temple in Nara to conclude the entire narrative. Satoko, like Mishima's *Madame de Sade*, rejects Matsugae Kiyoaki, who is Satoko's lover from her younger days and the hero in the volume I; in the end of this volume, Satoko rejects Kiyoaki again, using Honda as a substitute, in the final scene of volume IV. The ending of *The Sea of Fertility* is very similar to the last scene of *Forest in Full Bloom*. In addition, the structure of this story reminds us of the fact that Mozart used a hidden melody in his first symphony as the theme composed of four sounds in the final part of his final great symphony. Moreover, the description of this last scene is similar to the last scene in *Yume no Ukihashi* [*The Floating Bridge of Dreams*], which is the last chapter in *Genji Monogatari*. Besides, this four volume work was written using unique Japanese rhetoric with frequent instances of difficult vocabulary specific to Mishima. For instance, the depiction of scenes of Bangkok in Thailand is very beautiful and includes the appearance of printed characters. At the same time, although Mishima's prose has a subtle ornate style when other works than the above novel are included, it is very logical and clear in comparison with the sensory and illogical prose that is seen in the works by Kyōka Izumu and Yasunari Kawabata, and different from the prose by Kenzaburō Ōe that has unique, sensory, and difficult features in spite of the strong influence from Western literature.

Before he turned 40, Mishima was not necessarily highly political. Certainly, when he was in the 10th grade during the Pacific War, he participated in a literary group called *Nihon Roman-ha* ("Japan Romantic School"), and sometimes expressed his political and cultural opinions based on Emperor worship. However, these opinions were made up of a highly sensory psychological tendency that was influenced by the times and not associated with some particular political action. After the war, Mishima brought his non-political aesthetic and literary values to the forefront, and performed colorful and diverse literary and aesthetic activities from his stance that radically disobeyed popular common sense in his era. Basically, he did not have intention or interestingness to actual political actions. For Mishima, who died at 45 in 1970, *Showa 45*, his fourth decade corresponded to the last half of the 1960s during a season of politics, rebellion and Avant-garde in the world. For example, in the 1960s, Miles Davis (1926-1991), who was creating well--featured music after joining a group with Charlie Parker (1920-1955), expressed new and diverse styles in jazz, produced and played intense and, so to speak, ominous music that could not be referred to as simply the introduction of rock & roll or the invention of "fusion"; he then entered into an age of stopping his musical activities as if he had fallen down. After his comeback, Miles Davis returned to the neat well-featured music again, fully dependent upon his earlier special music styles and playing experiences.

In Japan, socially, student movements in universities and other places were very active. Yoshimoto became an ideological leader and Ōe repeated positive political statements based on his standpoint of post-war liberalism. An interesting action by Mishima was that, at the University of Tokyo in 1969, he was invited to a meeting held by *Zenkyōtō* ("All-Campus Joint Struggle League") (Mishima, 1969) to take part in an open discussion in front of a large general audience, mainly university students, and, at the end, said that if the Zenkyōtō would recite *Ten'nō-heika Banzai!* ("Glory be to his majesty the Emperor") at that time, he would be able to join hands with the Zenkyōtō to perform political acts together with them. Although Zenkyōtō rejected his proposition as a matter of course, Mishima's statement showed that Mishima at this age was quite conscious of the practical effectiveness of political acts beyond simple political philosophy. The author considers that one of the largest reasons was his crisis consciousness to socialism and communism. Although the progressives and leftists in this period included people who criticized existing socialism and communism and tried to show new ideas, such as Yoshimoto and Yutaka Haniya, quite a lot of, so to speak, "intellectuals with progressive ideas" of their same period, with the University of Tokyo as one of the largest bases, did not hide their sympathy to socialism and communism and regarded them as ideal social systems.

Such a sense of crisis against socialism and communism existed as the foundation of Mishima's political actions. On the other hand, Mishima's aversion was stirred up by America, which had previously been an enemy of Japan, or by the relationship between Japan and America in the post-war era, or by Japan itself. In particular, Mishima hated that America's influence in all areas including culture had become enormous, Japan had become a vassal state or dependent country of America, and the Japanese people had become slaves of America. Perhaps this crisis of consciousness toward socialism and communism and his aversion to a Japan that was dominated by America became two poles that supported Mishima's political activities in his final years and, in the political season of that moment, Mishima performed nationalistic acts for an absolute emperor system and risked his life to defend the traditional culture of Japan. Moreover, there was a kind of philosophy supporting the above opinions regarding the association between language and reality. In particular, Mishima held an opinion that the language of literary authors and novelists was a mere excrement that is not linked to reality. In contrast, Mishima tried to consciously use language that was closely associated with the real world. An important key word in this situation was "promise." This "promise" indicated and regulated future actions and, in an essay titled *Hatashi-eteinai Yakusoku* [*A Promise That Has Not Played*] (1970), Mishima described how many things promised by himself and others directly after the war had not been fulfilled, and he stated frankly that he was despairing of society and perhaps himself. This essay has frequently been cited as his indication or expectation for Japan's future. Mishima himself frequently, at various times in this final period, said such things as, "I will necessarily do the thing I promised once." and "If I promised to die, I will be dead." Mishima's final dramatic action was a culmination of the above elements. Although it was a ridiculous farce at first glance, the Japanese have been obliged to disentangle the meanings and constructively interpret them since.

Kabuki

In the early 17th century, when an age called *sengoku jidai* (the Age of Provincial Wars) in the Japanese history had ended, and several wars, such as *Ōsaka Fuyu no Jin* (Winter Siege of Ōsaka) (1614), *Ōsaka Natsu no Jin* (Summer Siege of Ōsaka) (1615), and *Shimabara no Ran* (Shimabara Rebellion) (1637-1638), broke out, *Kabuki* was started by a group led by a female dancer called Izumo no O-kuni in Kyōto, a political and cultural center and the biggest city in Japan in this period. "Izumo" was a land in the Chūgoku region and its name is famous because it is of one of the main places in *Kojiki* (1958), a nation-creation myth of Japan. (Introductory and detailed description of *kabuki* and relating *geino* are included in such books as Kawatake (1992, 2003), Leiter (2014), and Watanabe (1989).)

Kabuki was a kind of synthesis of previous diverse *geinōs*, rather than an art created and started from scratch. Tsubouchi Shōyō (1859-1935), who was a novelist, academician of literature and drama, and later, *kabuki* writer, called *kabuki* "chimera" to indicate its synthesized and pragmatic characteristics. In other words, *kabuki* is a synthesized genre of drama or narrative that incorporates a variety of *geinō* (performing arts) genres, such as Japanese dances, *Nō*, *kyōgen*, and *ningyō jōruri* (puppet drama), into a rich form, and also includes various narrative elements. Further, *kabuki*, as opposed to *Nō*, through the history, never evolved toward pure art and continued to introduce other *geinō* and literature genres in both form and content, and mutual influences with other genres. In Japan, *kabuki* as a novel is a kind of "hodgepodge" that can incorporate various genres, and has continued to exist as a kind of synthetic form that enables it to contain diverse forms and contents of *geinō*, arts, and literature. Actually, many repertoires that are currently playing also include, in addition to works fused to forms of *ningyō jōruri*, diverse other fusion forms, such as the fusion of the form of *Nō*, for example *Kanjinchō* [*The Subscription List*] (1840), the fusion of the form of Japanese dance, for example *Kyōganoko Musume Dōjōji* [*The Dapple-patterned Maiden at the Dōjōji Temple*] (1753), and the fusion of contemporary dramas, for example *Genroku Chūshingura* (1982) by Seika Mayama (1878-1948). These are currently played in mixed forms monthly on stages at Kabukiza and other theatres, and the audiences receive all of themes *kabuki* works.

Kabuki, until now, has repeated various frictions between political power and social institutions. It was, from the very beginning, a target of repression by the Edo government, and *Yūjo kabuki* (prostitute *kabuki*) by troupes of young women and *Wakashu kabuki* (young men's *kabuki*) by troupes of boys, were collapsed under the oppression of the Edo government. After all, the tradition of *Yarō kabuki* (Adult men's *kabuki*) by adult men has been communicated to the present-day *kabuki*. Additionally, *kabuki* theaters and environments surrounding them were regarded as *akushos* (dangerous places), along with licensed quarters including Yoshiwara (Edo), Shimabara (Kyōto) and Shinmachi (Ōsaka), which were the representative places, and many places in other local cities. These theaters and the *akushos* surrounding the theaters were often destroyed and forcibly transferred to other places by the Edo government. Furthermore, in the first period of Meiji era, a kind of *kabuki* modernization movement was conducted by the Meiji government and, after the end of the Pacific War, the oppression of *kabuki* by American occupation forces was carried out. Although on television, in novels, and in academic papers in present-day Japan, there are collective and personal regulations regarding "restricted words and phrases in broadcast codes" and "discriminatory terms" and to crucial scenes, discriminatory words and brutal or crucial scenes and events like killing a child, from contemporary viewpoints, frequently appear in the magic cloak of invisibility of traditional *geinō* and classical *geinō* and sometimes wrapped in a comical oblate, on stages of *kabuki* and *ningyō jōruri*.

A main feature of *kabuki* in the first half of the Edo era was a very productive mutual relationship with *ningyō jōruri*. *Ningyō jōruri* is a kind of narrative drama that inherited the tradition and characteristics of *Katarimono* (narrative) from the middle ages in Japan, including *Biwa-hōshi* (biwa-playing minstrel) who narrated *Heike Monogatari* [*The Tale of the Heike*] (1991-1993) and performers who narrated *Sekkyōbushi* [Sermon ballads] [(Sekkyō, 1998), in which the following three elements are fused: the operation of puppets by *ningyō-tsukai* players, the narration by *tayū* players, and the *shamisen* accompaniment by *shamisen* players. *Ningyō jōruri*, peaking in a period of the Edo era called Genroku era, increased in sophistication around two theaters, namely Takemoto-za and Toyotake-za, built in Ōsaka, and many great scenario writers, such as Chikamatsu Monzaemon (1653-1725) and Ki-no Kaion (1663-1742), and experts including Takemoto Gidayū (1651-1714), appeared. Afterwards, through the age of great writers, such as Takeda Izumo I (?- 1747), Takeda Izumo II (1691-1756), Namiki Sōsuke (1695-1751), Miyoshi Shōraku (birth and death unknown), and Chikamatsu Hanji (1725-1783), *ningyō jōruri* and *kabuki* competed with one another to create interesting plays. However, after the period of Chikamatsu Hanji when *ningyō jōruri* was on the decline, *kabuki*-original works took center stage and excellent *kabuki* authors, including Namiki Shōza I (1730-1773), Sakurada Jisuke I (1734-1806), Namiki Gohei I (1747-1808), Tsuruya Namboku IV (1755-1829), and Kawatake Mokuami (1816-1893), appeared.

After the Meiji era, a new age began for *kabuki* with the introduction of Western dramas into Japan. In Japan, after the Meiji era, people had highly illusionary Western images or norms, and a chief social trend was to strongly or violently criticize and condemn the previous (particularly in the Edo era) Japanese politics, social institutions or systems, and cultures. *Kabuki* was also recognized as a relic of the previous generation to be overcome, and became an object of the "theater reform movement." In fact, after this age, in addition to the contents of *kabuki*, many other elements, such as the structure of theaters and the methods for watching plays, were reformed. Although *kabuki* was an almost dramatic genre in the previous age, after this age, new theater genres different from *kabuki* called *shingeki*, *shinpa*, *shinkokugeki,* and so on, were established, and Japan's dramas basically progressed as their coexistence. In the Edo era, the scenarios or scripts of *kabuki* had been originally written by authors working in each theater. In contrast, after the Meiji era, the writing style changed, as *kabuki* writers outside the theaters, including novelists, playwrights and academics, freely wrote scenarios. Their works were frequently called *shin-kabuki* (new *kabuki*s), as opposed to the old *kabuki*s in the Edo era. The new *kabuki*s also provided new narrative characteristics, such as emphasizing human mental processes and realistic human actions instead of the absurd and preposterous story developments seen frequently in previous *kabuki* plays. Many new *kabuki* scenarios were written and played in this way. However, a new event, in which *kabuki* synthetically introduced diverse theatrical styles in the new age to develop as an integrated *kabuki* or a new theatrical genre with a new name, has not come to pass. Audiences who were not satisfied with the reformed drama styles and new *kabuki*, finally and again moved toward the characteristics of old *kabuki*, such as absurdity, a variety of imaginative leaps performed in fixed patterns, the intense fusion of diverse theatrical elements, the unrealistic and unnatural performances and playing styles based on heritage, as elements to defend and inherit, and were enthusiastic in the traditional *kabuki*, with negative recognition that it ought to be dined for new performing arts. After all, *kabuki* had become a kind of traditional *geinō*. At the same time, *kabuki* has been continuing to hold contemporary popularity in spite of a traditional *geinō*. This is a mysterious feature of *kabuki*. Yukio Mishima, who wrote and played in the most contemporary and *shingeki* dramas in a Western style, also made several successful *kabuki* works by using a pseudoclassical style.

The author previously described the main concepts of *kabuki* (Ogata, 2016b), including stages and audiences, pure-*kabuki* and *gidayū-kabuki*, *jidai-mono* and *sewa-mono*, drama and dance, *aragoto* (formal performing style), *wagoto* (realistic performing style), and the synthesis of music. Another important theme is the problem of language in *kabuki*. After the Meiji era, in *kabuki*, the method by which actors are selected according to a scenario written by an author was adopted for the first time. In the previous age, basically, a scenario or script (called *daichō*) was written for specific actors in a theater, and the stage drama was produced by the actors themselves. For this reason, *kabuki* scenarios or scripts could not easily have the characteristics of a drama. (In contrast, *ningyō jōruri* had an actual style wherein a *tayū* read a scenario book in spite of the inheritance of the tradition of *katarimono*, a performing art genre by narration used since the middle ages, and many scenarios were written by many authors.) However, the language of dramas was described in the remaining *daichō*sand, of course, a main element in a *kabuki*'s performance is language. Although such language as a drama itself formed the center of a *kabuki* work, an essential feature in *kabuki* was, at the same time, the language of criticism that has been holding much power and has been produced in large quantities from the beginning until now. In the Edo era, language as a criticism of *kabuki* was mainly published in periodical books called *yakusha-hyōbanki*, which described *kabuki* actors' reputations or opinions and attracted many readers. This tradition of critical language has continued by changing the form. *Yakusha-hyōbanki*s themselves are no longer published. However, the critical tradition and situation of *kabuki*, where many critical and academic texts are produced, has not changed. Although the author has not yet sought to undertake a full-fledged analysis, the author predicts that various seeds for the poetics of dramas and narratives exist in *kabuki-hyōbanki* and critical texts that inherited this tradition.

NARRATIVE ANALYSES FOR DIVERSE NARRATIVE PHENOMENA AND ELEMENTS: A NARRATIVE GENERATION PERSPECTIVE

"Narrative analysis" has been conducted in a variety of academic fields. However, for the author, narrative analysis is not the only essential method for designing and developing narrative generation systems: Various methods can be used. Pure thought is also useful to designing and developing the entire architectures and partial components in narrative generation systems. Methods that are dependent on theories and methodologies related to the narrative and literature are also effective. Concurrently, the author has conducted the design and development of narrative generation systems by using, in parallel, several methods including pure idealistic thoughts, theoretical thoughts, and concrete narrative analyses. Narrative analysis has been adopted as a necessary tool for deciding the entire architectures of narrative generation systems and implementing formal generation methods of each part such as story, narrative discourse, and narrative representation.

However, the author's study, currently, has reached the development stage of an integrated narrative generation system (INGS), which is described in detail in Chapter 1 (Ogata, 2017) of this book and that of Ogata (2016a). Therefore, current necessary and important issues for the author are to introduce concrete knowledge contents into the INGS system, and narrative analyses and knowledge acquisition based on the materials of actual works and texts are important. Thus, through the progression or development of this research, the main goal of narrative analyses also has been changing gradually. Additionally, because previous narrative analyses have not been conducted systematically, more conscious and systematic narrative analyses are required in the future.

The author has analyzed narratives in the following genres to develop individual narrative mechanisms and application systems: (1) Folktale analysis by the narrative theory of Propp (1968), (2) Novel 1: An analysis of the story and plot in a detective story, (3) Novel 2: An analysis of the hyper-text structure in a detective story, (4) Novel 3: An analysis of the mutual cognitive structures of the characters in *The Sailor Who Fell from Grace with the Sea* by Yukio Mishima (1991), (5) Advertisement 1: An analysis of story structures in television commercial films, (6) Advertisement 2: An analysis of rhetorical techniques for introducing a product into a television commercial-like story, (7) Movie 1: An analysis of movie works made by a complicated temporal progression of events, (8) Movie 2: An analysis of the original camerawork in *Tokyo Monogatari* [*Tokyo Story*] (1953) by Yasujirō Ozu (1803-1963), (9) Comic or *manga*: A discourse analysis of a Japanese *manga* (comic) work, *Mezon Ikkoku* (1992-1993) by Rumiko Takahashi (1992-1993), (10) Dream: a kind of narrative discourse analysis for transforming real materials into a story using the dream interpretation theory of Sigmund Freud (1856-1939), and (11) Drama: a story analysis using the story grammar and reinterpretation of an analysis of a tragedy in the poetics by Aristotle (384-322 BC) (1997).

In the following part, the author describes these narrative analyses in the linkage with narrative elements in INGS and the narrative phenomena including INGS.

An Overview of Narrative Analyses From a Narrative Generation Perspective

As stated above, the narrative analysis method has been conducted in a variety of academic fields from humanities. These include literary theories and narratology (the morphology of the folktale by Propp (1968) and the narrative discourse theory by Genette (1972) are respectively based on structural analyses of "Russian fairy tales" and *In Search of Lost Time* by Proust (2003)), marketing, advertising and management science (Fukuda (1990); Kanai, Takai, & Nakanisi (2009)), sociology (Fujii, Hasegawa, Nakano, & Hatori, 2011), psychology and clinical psychology (Morioka, 2002; Bruner, 2002; White, 1980), film theories (Bordwell, 1988; Stam, Burgoyne, & Flitterman-Lewis, 1992), drama theory (Hara, 2013), and informatics such as cognitive science and artificial intelligence (Ogata, 2011). They have a long history. In the West, *Poetics* by Aristotle, based on an analysis of *Oedipus Tyrannus* by Sophokles (497/496-406/407 BC) (1994), is very famous. Also in Japan, the followings works are known as critical texts relating to concrete narrative analyses: the discussion of "comparison between histories and fictions or novels" through a dialogue between two characters in the twenty five chapters (*Firefly*) in *Genji Monogatari* by Murasaki Shikibu (1993-1997), "*kyojitsu-hiniku-ron*" (a theory that the appeal of art lies in the slender margin between real or truth and unreal or fiction) of Chikamatsu Monzaemon in *Naniwa Miyage* [*Naniwa Souvenir*] by Hozumi Ikan (Koretsura) (1692-1769) (1959), the "*haishi shichisoku*" theory (the description of seven types of techniques for writing a novel) shown in *Nansō Satomi Hakkenden* [*The Eight Dog Chronicles*] (1814-1842) by Kyokutei Bakin (1767-1848), who was one of the greatest novelists in Japan (Watanabe (2012) explained the theory in detail), *Bungakuron* by Natsume Sōseki (2009), and *Gengo ni totte Bi toha Nanika* by Takaaki Yoshimoto (1965).

As an overview, the objectives of narrative analyses are divided into a kind of interpretation by pure academic curiosity and pragmatic approaches that aim at the contribution for creating actual works. However, the former enables to contribute to the latter, and the latter frequently has some academic value. In addition, although some studies were not narrative analyses in the narrow sense and truly had other purposes, namely the authors essentially did not intend the works to be narrative analyses, they can be regarded as narrative analyses from the narrative generation perspective by the author. For instance,

Saito and Ogata (1998) reinterpreted the dream interpretation by Freud (1900) as a kind of narrative technique or a series of narrative techniques to transform a person's real experience or experiences into a narrative. In particular, the study by Freud elaborately described an algorithm of a "dream process" through which the mental filtering based on a person's complex operates to the material of a dream to transform and distort it. The above idea by Saito and Ogata treated the above mechanism as a kind of defamiliarization by transforming and substituting the properties in the elements in an event. This idea is of course related to the defamiliarization and effects presented by Schcrovsky (1893-1984) (1990) and Breckt (1898-1956) (1973).

As stated above, for the author, narrative analyses are not necessarily only preconditions for designing and developing narrative generation systems. Various methods can be used for that purpose. Methods that are dependent on theories and methodologies related to the narrative and literature can be a direction as well. Originally, a particular narrative analysis itself, in many cases, already relies on specific methodologies and theories related to literature and the narrative. Thus, previously, the author has conducted the design and development of narrative generation systems by using, in parallel, several methods, including pure idealistic thoughts, theoretical thoughts and concrete narrative analyses. Narrative analyses, as a possibility, have been adopted, according to necessity, for deciding each part of the entire architecture of narrative generation systems and implementing formal generation methods of each of the parts, including story, narrative discourse and narrative representation. However, the author's study is currently reaching the development stage of INGS. Therefore, current necessary and important issues are narrative analyses and narrative knowledge acquisition based on the materials of actual works and texts to introduce concrete narrative knowledge contents into INGS beyond the previous tasks of the design and development of mainly formal composition of the systems (Ogata, 2014; Ogata, Arai, & Ono, 2016). Therefore, through the progression or development of the research, the main goal of narrative analyses also has been changing gradually. Furthermore, because previous narrative analyses necessarily have not been conducted systematically, more conscious and systematic narrative analyses will be required in the future. At the same time, this goal is necessary to be compatible with a direction to the analysis and interpretation that focus on specific narrative works.

The author, here, introduces an overview of INGS's feature for the following explanation. Figure 1 shows the characteristics of the composition. In this figure, the term "formal mechanisms" means fundamental mechanisms for generating narratives using the "knowledge contents" if they exist. On the other hand, the term "content mechanisms" is a collection of knowledge for concretizing the generation in such various levels as the narrative overall structures and partial structures. The "dictionaries" are located in the middle of the above two groups. INGS aims at a versatile or general narrative generation mechanism. However, there is also an opinion that if we emphasize reasons for explaining or justifying narrative genre division, such as folk tales, novels, films, and dramas and further their surface expression forms, the existence of versatile and general narrative mechanisms may be only an illusion. Hasumi

Figure 1. Characteristics of the composition of INGS

Formal Mechanism	***Medieval Mechanism***	***Content Mechanism***
Story Generation Mechanism Narrative Discourse Mechanism Narrative Representation Mechanism	Conceptual Dictionaries Language Notation Dictionaries	Narrative Content Knowledge Base State-Event Transformation Knowledge Base

(2014) posed a serious question regarding novels as an object of narratology. If this kind of thinking is dependent on the consciousness that certain elements deviated from being defined as basic narrative ones by narratology, including the method of event development (i.e., story) and construction method (i.e., narrative discourse) and the communication between the narrator and narratee, and further elements nullifying their division constitute the defining characteristics of a novel, the author also shares awareness of this kind to some extent. At the same time, the author considers that the change in the quality of narratives themselves by changes of the representation styles and media used for them and the transformation of human consciousness according to the above factors is still only partial. Moreover, the author thinks that logics that characterize new narrative genres and styles, including novels and cinemas, are also highly narratological. Certainly, the intentionality of narrative generality and the versatility of narrative generation led by narrative generality tend to be interpreted as representing more narratological faith. Nevertheless, the author will take this position according to the above awareness of the problem.

The main modules of the generation process in INGS are generation mechanisms for a story, narrative discourse, and narrative representation. At the conceptual level, a story is the structure of a temporal sequence of events, whereas the narrative discourse is the structure of construction that a story is edited or processed. The important parts of both story generation and narrative discourse are their narrative technique components, which are divided into story techniques and narrative discourse techniques, and each control component. A narrative technique is a rule-based procedure for extending and transforming a tree form that represents each conceptual structure for a story or narrative discourse. The expansion and transformation correspond to generating each level of a narrative. Branches in a tree structure are related to the dictionaries and other knowledge elements to form a complex network as a whole. A conceptual structure, here, means a kind of internal representation structure before it is concretized by using the corresponding surface representation by language, image, and so on. In the human case, it corresponds to a kind of a formation step to a narrative idea in the human mind. The input information for a story technique is a part in a story's tree structure or the whole, and the story technique returns an extended or transformed tree structure as the output information. This tree structure is also related to the dictionaries and knowledge elements in INGS. On the other hand, the input information for a narrative discourse technique is a part of the tree structure of a story or a part of a narrative discourse itself, and the narrative discourse technique returns a transformed tree structure of the narrative discourse. If associating with dictionaries and knowledge elements is a narrative semantic definition, the same association as the story techniques is basically held in the narrative discourse process. Here, extension or expansion means that elements included in each structure increase, whereas transformation is equivalent to changing the construction without increasing the elements. Thus, the narrative discourse mechanism mainly uses the transformation process.

In principle, in story generation that corresponds to the extension of a structure, the knowledge content is necessary for extending and transforming concretely the tree structure. For instance, when a story technique takes an event in a story's tree structure as the input information and extends it into a lower event sequence, the lower event sequence itself corresponds to the knowledge content that is used by the story technique. Commanding to extend the lower event sequence means a formal mechanism. If many lower event sequences can be applied to a single event in some mechanism, the diversity or possibility of stories to be generated spreads even if only one story technique is used. In addition, as mentioned above, because the role of narrative discourse techniques is to transform formally the structure of a story, this kind of content knowledge is not essentially required. On the other hand, this kind of content knowledge can be prepared for each representation mechanism for language, music, and image. Various mechanisms can be used for extracting, storing, and utilizing the parts in various levels of existing works. The narrative content knowledge bases store the content knowledge. These are divided into the story content knowledge base and others. As extending systematically the design of narrative content knowledge bases is an important goal for the future development of INGS, systematization and organization processes are required for narrative analyses.

Previous narrative analyses by the author have consciously referred to traditional narratology and literary theories in the literary field. However, narrative analyses based on narrative generation frameworks from the fields of informatics and cognitive science that intentionally do not use existing literary studies and narratology will be a possible direction. In fact, in recent AI and cognitive science, there are also analyses of creative processes in artists (Kudo, Okada, & Chen, 2015) and the pursuit of neural technology (Asakawa, 2015). By contrast, the author has intended to adopt literary methods again and apply them. The author has considered that narratology and literary theories show an intensive representation of strong cognitive frameworks that human literary cognition has traditionally cultivated. The author believes that literature and the narrative strongly express a unique and relatively independent aspect or level in human cognition that differs from other levels. This idea may be influenced by Yoshimoto's (1968) hierarchical division of "individual illusion (mental level)-pair illusion (human relationship level)-collective illusion (social and institutional level)." If a new narrative generation method could be developed without the direct relations to narratology and literary theories, the author considers that connecting the method to them is very important for narrative generation research. Of course, it is also necessary to consider the perspectives of narratology and literary theories.

Figure 2 plots previous narratological and literary studies on an overall architecture of the author's narrative generation system (INGS is a current embodiment). This figure sets elements related to narrative generation and reception as the following: (1) to (5) correspond to functions to perform narrative generation or a kind of narrative agents and (6) to (8) are equal to structural types to construct a narrative text.

Figure 2. The entire framework of INGS and the relationships with narratology and literary theories

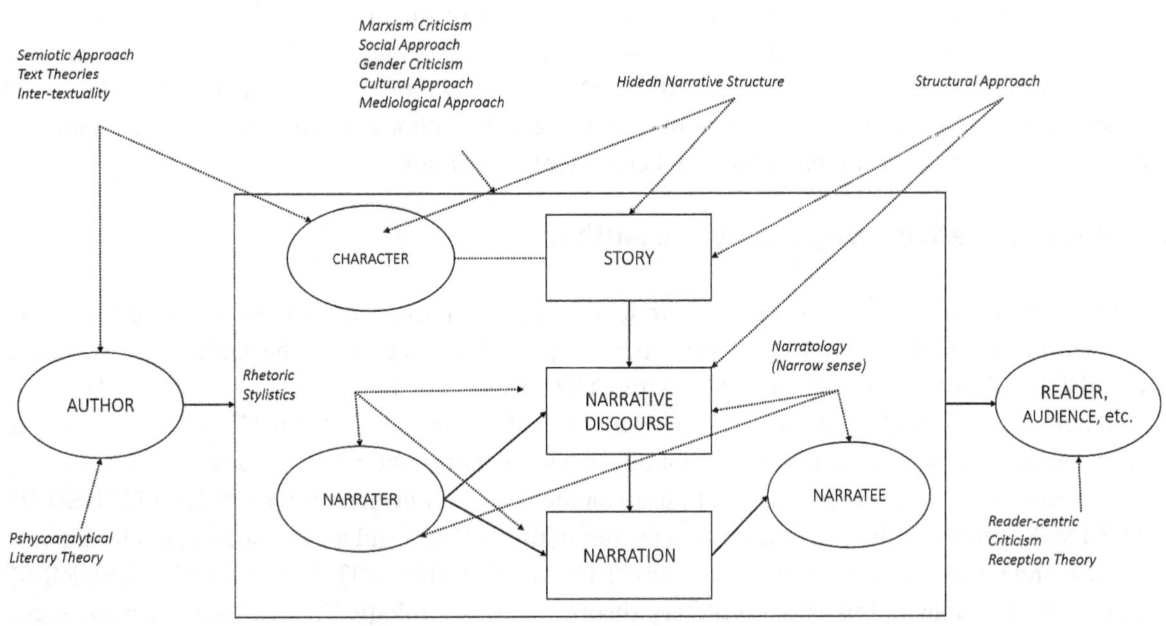

The expanded literary theory described in Ogata (2016a) and Ogata, Kawamura and Kanai (in press) is really a plan to elaborate and integrate previous literary theories into a macro narrative generation and production framework. Incidentally, the author knows that contemporary literary theories disapprove of such systematization that may give a rustic impression and, as it seems, continue to corrode the foundation of literature by being choice dependent on the intention of destroying systematization and institutionalization. However, the author's opinion is that the extremely simplified schematization or description of a system of literature and the narrative are necessary for rescuing literature and the narrative from their institutionally dying state. As another topic, in this figure, both narrative generation and narrative reception are respectively divided into sender/narrator and receiver/narratee. This shows an aspect of the multiple narrative structures model (Ogata, 2016b; Ogata, Kawamura, & Kanai, in press).

The narrative analyses in this chapter are related to the framework of this expanded literary theory in many points. However, the current expanded literary theory focuses on referring to previous literary theories and narratology and using them through computational formalization. For example, the authors have been developing story content grammar for a mechanism in INGS (Imabuchi & Ogata, 2012, 2013, 2014a). This was defined essentially based on the theoretical description by Propp (1968) and exemplars used by Propp himself in this study.

INGS also uses both the narrative discourse theory by Genette (1972) and the reception theory by Jauss (1970). Propp's theory described above was based on an analysis of Russian fairy tales, and similarly the narrative discourse theory by Genette was a study that was the abstraction and generalization of an analysis of *In Search of Lost Time*. In this way, applying narratology and literary theories is frequently employed to indirectly utilize results of narrative analyses. A future direction is to bridge narratology to unique narrative analyses and to introduce its results into the development of narrative generation mechanisms. So far, the author and the research group have acquired a new narrative technique called "multilayered narrative discourse" by applying Genette's theory into a *manga* (comic) analysis (Endo & Ogata, 2003a, 2003b; Endo & Ogata, 2004a, 2004b) and analyzed Japanese folk tales by using the above method by Propp (Ogata & Fujiwara, 2015; Ogata, Fujiwara, & Imabuchi, 2014; Fujiwara & Ogata, 2014). These studies also exemplify pursuits of this kind of direction. A more important way is to link these studies to the invention of a unique narratology or literary theory beyond a collection of both old (previous) narratological theories and literary theories. Although, in INGS, the fact that various narratologies and literary theories that have different origins and thoughts are systematically integrated also seems an embodiment of a new form of narratology, the author aims to develop a narratology or literary theory based on a comprehensive and consistent description.

Previous Narrative Analyses by the Author

The following description shows the narrative text analyses that the authors have conducted so far. In this description, "GENRE" means each narrative group in which an object to be analyzed is contained, and "MEDIUM" is each representation tool through which an analysis object is represented and socially distributed. Next, "OBJECT" shows an actual work or a collection and, by "GOAL" and "RESULT," the author means the object, intention, or aim for an analysis and acquired results. These descriptions may include methods for a way or technique to be used for the analysis. Further, the term "RELATIONSHIPS WITH INGS" corresponds to the future possibilities of use in INGS and may include a simple explanation for a previously introduced part. The term "RELATIONSHIPS WITH LITERARY THEORIES" mentions the relations of this issue to literary theories and narratology. This last issue is also related to the expanded literary theory by the author. Other narrative analyses conducted by the authors were in the following: An analysis of *Oedipus Tyrannus* by Sophokles using *Poetics* by Aristotle (Aruga & Ogata, 1998), narrative analyses of entertainment (*geinō*) performers or their life histories (Amino & Ogata, 2000; Amino, Kawamura, & Ogata, 2002a; Kawamura & Ogata, 2000a, 2000b, 2000c; Ogata, 1997; Ogata & Amino, 2002; Ogata & Kawamura, 1998), a structural analysis of television news stories (Ueda, 2006), an analysis of properties of characters in novels (Fukuda, Kurisawa, & Ogata, 2013; Ishii & Ogata, 2006; Imabuchi & Ogata, 2014b; Kumagai, Ogata, & Oikawa, 2010; Oikawa & Ogata, 2012), and music (jazz) analyses. The *kabuki* study by the author (Ogata, 2016b) is also on the stage of analyses and conceptual considerations for the modeling and systematization for narrative generation.

- **Genre:** Advertisement, **Media:** Television
  - **Object:** About 100 Television commercial films that were broadcasted in Japan in the first half of the 1990s.
  - **Goal:** After verifying that stories in television commercials can be analyzed using the similar methods with folk tales and novels, this study applies the analysis results into an advertising scenario generation system using a developing narrative generation system.
  - **Result:** The authors achieved this goal, as a person (the author) described, using language, the event sequences in television advertising films and represented them using the tree structure form for a story used in a narrative generation system (Ogata & Watanabe, 1995; Ogata, Watanabe, Hori, & Ohsuga, 1993, 1995a, 1995b; Ogata & Kanai, 2010b).
  - **Relationships With INGS:** The formal representation of stories in television advertising films can be stored in the corresponding story content knowledge base as a type of story-relating knowledge content in INGS to expand concrete examples in narratives including fragmentary narrative knowledge.
  - **Relationships With Literary Theories:** The author regards advertising narratives as a kind of "contemporary folk tale." Folk tales do not adhere to narrative realistic norms, and many series of cruel violence and murder as well as surreal incidents and events occur. Further, realistic responses and psychological responses do not occur, and all events are narrated and received as if they were ordinary things. Although a difference from folk tales is that things such as violence and murder ordinarily do not occur, advertising works in contemporary society involve a large number surrealistic events, and the receivers accept them in their ordinary lives without special consciousness in viewing strange or abnormal events and things. Additionally, folktale-like characteristics in contemporary advertisements are shown in the social production phenomena in which advertising works that are dependent on, so to speak, the consciousness of a division of labor by gender role, such as "a woman cooks and a man eats it," gradually decrease according to the intervention that began from mainly intellectuals and a kind of social censoring, and advertisements with the reverse features increase incrementally.
- **Genre:** Advertisement, **Media:** Television
  - **Object:** More than 1,000 television advertising films that were broadcast in Japan from the beginning of the 2000s to about 2010.
  - **Goal:** This study defines the objective of a television commercial as the proposition and appeal of a product (brand) and analyzes the forms of television commercials as "rhetoric or

rhetorical techniques for introducing a product" to develop an experimental system including the above analysis.

- **Result:** This study analyzed the relationships between a product that forms a theme in a television commercial and the event development, the appearance and usage, amongst others, by describing the event development. In particular, this study showed that various types of de-familiarization rhetoric to a product are used as main techniques to extract and classify such techniques. This classification was enabled by what was de-familiarized in an event that represents a product and the usage form (Abe, Ogata, & Hanada, 2008; Zhang, Ono, & Ogata, 2011a). The authors developed an experimental system for performing the product de-familiarization using this result (Ono, Zhang, & Ogata, 2012; Zhang, Ono, & Ogata, 2011b, 2012a, 2012b).
- **Relationships With INGS:** This study is related to the following problems: the change of constraints related to concrete values to be inserted into both verb and noun concepts in the event that constructs a story and a narrative discourse (this is combined with the change of properties that the values of the verb concepts and noun concepts have) and the change of concepts based on the association relationships among concepts that is related to co-occurrence information and metaphor. Concurrently, at first, this analysis result is mainly located on a type of the story techniques in INGS. Moreover, the acquired rhetorical techniques for introducing products, including various techniques in addition to de-familiarization techniques, can be stored into the story content knowledge bases as each type of exemplar knowledge similar to the above case of commercial analysis. In addition, this analysis does not necessarily treat only event sequences in television commercials, which is different from previous commercial analysis. Because this is an analysis regarding the change of elements within each event, it is related to more micro parts and processing, such as the internal structures of an event and the properties of a concept.
- **Relationships With Literary Theories:** This study is highly related to the literary theory of de-familiarization since Schcrovsky (1990) and Breckt (1973). Although the de-familiarization by Schcrovsky originally means a technique for literary language that shows ordinary things as new and strange things, in commercials, an ordinary product appears as a strange thing. The short story in advertising is useful for representing this de-familiarization to the consciousness.

- **Genre:** Short story, **Media:** Book (paper)
  - **Object:** *Maiko Satsujin Jiken* by Yamamura (1988).
  - **Goal:** This study analyzes the methods of mutual transformation between a story and a plot, which is the construction of a work to be represented, using a short detective story by Yamamura Misa, who is a writer of popular fiction in Japan, to introduce the results into the narrative generation systems by the author. A characteristic of detective stories is that the temporal order in a story is variously transformed in the plot. In this story, a preceding murder in the temporal order appears in the last part of the plot, and other plot-making techniques such as omission and imagination, are diversely utilized.
  - **Result:** The author wrote a summary of this fiction as a constructive event sequence, namely a plot, and transformed its description into a temporal event sequence of the story. Additionally, the author extracted methods that enable the temporal order transformation between the story and plot, including methods based on characters' viewpoints to define and

utilize them as the techniques for the part of story-plot transformation in a narrative generation system that the author was developing (Ogata, Hori, & Ohsuga, 1996).

  - **Relationships With INGS:** Ings has not been used to prepare a "narrative discourse knowledge base" thus far. However, the author considers storing the transformation patterns from a story to narrative discourses, by combing narrative discourse techniques (dependent upon a detective story in this case) with methodological patterns for adjusting narrative discourses according to the difference of narrative genres. In synthesizing subsequent narrative generation systems and INGS, the concept of the plot was overlapped with a part of the concept of narrative discourse that introduces the narrative discourse theory by Genette (1972), especially the techniques for temporal order transformation and viewpoint. This transformation method will be able to fuse and re-define the above narrative discourse techniques. Another issue is organizing hierarchically the result of the story analysis to incorporate it into the story content knowledge base.
  - **Relationships With Literary Theories:** Regarding the difference and discrimination between story and plot in novels, there is a famous definition by Forster (1879-1970) (1956). These studies by the author also relied on scenario analysis studies and scenario making books for movie films and television dramas. After that, the term of the plot was changed to the word of narrative discourse, which is a concept comprising the term of the plot more comprehensively by referring to literary theories and narratology such as the narrative discourse theory by Genette. The age when novels employ new narrative and literary methods has already transpired. We may be transitioning to an age of inertia and consumption after innovative artistic concepts and actual works have appeared. However, conversely, the present time may be an age when a variety of techniques and methods developed previously are accumulated as shapes or patterns suitable for the folkloric analysis (and utilization) of literary works. As the study of folktales is not necessarily a literary criticism that deals with excellent works in literary and artistic senses, the narrative analyses for novels and stories in this period, in line with this study's objective, also selected the objects for narrative analysis from the same viewpoint above.
- **Genre:** Short story, **Media:** Book (paper)
  - **Object:** *Mienai Fukushū* [*Revenge Invisible*] (Miyoshi, 1993).
  - **Goal:** This study analyzes (describes) that different stories are produced based on several characters' viewpoints, or more correctly speaking, different stories are generated from a story, from the perspective of a hypertext-like method. This forms a part of considering the narrative discourse mechanism in a narrative generation system by the author.
  - **Result:** This analysis described each story by focusing on all characters' viewpoints or perspectives in a detective story, and constructed and visualized by hyper-text structures respectively in independent events and parts where several characters' routes are combined to consider the structure of a story (Ishii & Ogata, 1998).
  - **Relationships With INGS:** This structural analysis gives implications to the descriptive form of a narrative discourse and a story. These are respectively represented as a tree structure in INGS. The center of the description is an event, and each character is involved in the tree structure. This study will contribute to this mechanism. As shown in Figure 1, so far, because elements called narrative agents were basically treated to be involved in the tree structures and states of an event, a story and a narrative discourse, the definite descrip-

tions and definitions of narrative agents themselves did not exist except for the descriptions of a narrator and a narratee that were set in the narrative discourse mechanism. The next narrative analysis is related to this problem. The fact that different narrative discourses are produced by each character is relied on their thoughts or recognitions in addition to their viewpoints or perspectives. In the cases of a short story, *Yabu no Naka* [*In a Grove*] (1922), by Akutagawa and a movie, *Rashōmon* (1950) by Akira Kurosawa (1910-1998) (Kurosawa and Hashimoto, 1988), the diversity of narrative discourses based on differences of the characters' recognitions, at last, linked to the result that a story proposed remained a mystery in the works. On the other hand, in detective stories, different narrative discourses, which are generated through the reasoning by a detective or detectives and the other characters, construct pseudo-stories or fictional stories in the framework of a fictional story. The role of narrative discourse that produces such pseudo-stories is a part beyond the theoretical range of the narrative discourse theory by Genette. Although Genette also referred to the movie, *Rashōmon*, in relation with the problem of viewpoint or focalization as a type of narrative discourse techniques, his description did not reach the problem of pseudo-stories generation in this discussion.

- **Relationships With Literary Theories:** In addition to hyper-text studies from informatics, in the field of literary theories, this study relates to themes of focalization and viewpoint in the narrative discourse theory as well as other studies including the polyphonic theory by Bakhtin (1984). A main concern of the previous hyper-text studies was the topic of the branching of a simple story. By contrast, the idea presented here was more complicated than narrative hyper-text structures. The viewpoint and focalization in the narrative discourse theory were connected to the problem of selection, whereas using hyper-text structures in which apposition is a basis can shed new light on this problem. The polyphonic theory may also be able to be associated to hyper-text-like representation for coexisting spatially different diverse voices. Beyond introducing directly knowledge and methods by literary theories and narratology into narrative generation systems, setting some unique structure between the theory and the system will be necessary for the future expanded literary theory. Hyper-text is also one possibility toward the problem.

- **Genre:** Novel, **Media:** Book (paper)
    - **Object:** *Gogo no Eikō* [*The Sailor Who Fell from Grace with the Sea*] (1963) by Yukio Mishima. This analysis will be described in detail in AN ANALYSIS OF A NOVEL BY YUKIO MISHIMA [A NOVEL AS A PLURAL APPARATUS AND A TEXT ANALYSIS BASED ON THE CHARACTERS in this chapter.
    - **Goal:** Under the hypothesis that characters of a fiction are constructed through the recognitions of both the characters themselves and the narrator, this study analyzes quantitatively and qualitatively the main characters and the narrator from the perspective of their recognitions about themselves and other characters. This analysis was performed for linking to a developmental consideration for modeling each character defined in narrative generation systems.
    - **Result:** Throughout the entire story, the authors temporarily listed information related to the characters, including himself or herself, for each character and the narrator. Through this information, a narrative world (regarding the characters) was emerged based on the construction by the characters including the narrator. The criteria of the world construction in

this novel involve the viewpoints (perspectives) through which a character sees or perceives events and, furthermore, how a character recognizes events and characters including the character's self. At last, the dramatic and dynamic characteristics in a novel are generated from especially the mutual recognitions among the characters, such as matching and discrepancy. This study bridged the above results to a developmental idea of the narrative generation systems (Oikawa & Ogata, 2012).

  - **Relationships With INGS:** The recognition of each characters and the mutual recognition between two characters in a novel is a problem that can be covered by the current narrative discourse mechanism in the author's research because they are beyond this range. For incorporating them into INGS, at first, such subjects in a novel as the narrator and each character are necessary to model more definitely. In particular, the characters are currently defined as the knowledge elements that form a part of components of an event and a state. The contents are described as property lists. Future necessary works involve extending a character to a model as one of the various components that are developed incrementally through a generation process and adding mental and cognitive elements into the properties. This is related to the revision of narrative knowledge contents and narrative generation mechanisms. If this study is able to make a model of the mutual recognitions among characters and extract the hyper-text structures, they can be stored into the narrative content knowledge bases for story and narrative discourse.
  - **Relationships With Literary Theories:** Overlapping the problem of the above hyper-text structures with literary theories will facilitate further discussion. Although the polyphonic theory by Bakhtin (1984) describes that novels by Leo Tolstoy (1828-1910) (*War and Peace* (2009, 2010), *Resurrection* (1869), etc.) were monophonic novels and, by contrast, novels by Fyodor Dostoyevsky (1821-1881) (*Crime and Punishment* (2014), *Demons* (2008), etc.) were polyphonic novels to divide these novels into two types, the authors can view polyphonic characteristic in all the novels; furthermore, they can imagine a kind of mixed forms such as a polyphonic narrative including monophonic narratives.
- **Genre:** Short story and Novel, **Media:** Book (paper)
  - **Object:** Several short stories and novels by Akutagawa Ryūnosuke (1892-1927), Kenzaburō Ōe, Yukio Mishima, and so on.
  - **Goal:** This study analyzes the Japanese writing method, particularly character notation, in especially novels to utilize these results in a part of the character notation mechanism and the language representation dictionaries in INGS. This is intended, for example, to develop a generation mechanism for making the notation that imitates the visual and visible impressions the character representation of a work by a writer.
  - **Result:** In this study, mainly *kanji, hiragana, katakana* and *romaji* are used as the main character types for narrative language representation to experiment the mechanisms for controlling the representation according to the evaluation criteria including readability or comprehensiveness and difficulty to read, and narrative analyses and the simulation experiments to incorporate a part of the results into INGS for the usage (Kamada & Ogata, 2013a, 2013b).
  - **Relationships With INGS:** In INGS, each concept in the terminal concepts in the noun conceptual dictionary and verb conceptual dictionary used directly by the story generation mechanism is used as the components in an event. In addition, when the sentence transformation mechanism transforms each event to the corresponding sentence or sentences,

specific character notations are selected using the language notation dictionaries developed by Ogata and Ono (2015a). This study is equal to the knowledge and rules for the decision. The basic rules are the ones to use character notations that have high usage frequency in the specific age's range and a specific narrative genre. Imitating a specific writer's character notation pattern is also included in a method based on a relatively narrow range. As the current mechanism in INGS is not still a decided version and the system uses default values in many cases, the authors will continue this study.

- **Relationships With Literary Theories:** The author does not know about any literary theories supporting this kind of narrative analysis. In the field of linguistics, Murakoshi (1998) presented a study focusing on the problem of Japanese character notation. However, the authors' research is necessary to go beyond, in a part, linguistic studies of character representation because it must deal with narrative and literature. Although this is not necessarily related to only novels and stories, the difference of character notation by each work produces different impressions in narrative genres that use Japanese characters. Furthermore, it frequently represents each author's thought itself. In Japanese, in which diverse character types appear, a word has the possibility of many notations and which character for a word is really used can be an important point for narrative creation. For instance, Jun'ichirō Tanizaki, after the age of his "classical returning," adopted a style of character notation that frequently used many *hiragana* characters in *Manji* [*Quicksand*] (1931) and so on to succeed in creating the novel's soft and vague impression. The visible impression of the first half of *The Temple of Dawn* (1970) by Yukio Mishima was very impressive or shocking for the author. The character notations in the novels are also related to the contents of their novels. Additionally, for example, in Sōseki Natsume, the difference between the gorgeous and highbrow impression in his first novels, such as *Kusamakura* [*Grass Pillow*] (1906) and *Gubijinsō* [*Field Poppy*] (1907), and the sober and temporal impression of novels from *Sanshirō* (1909) and *Meian* [*Light and Darkness*] (1917) may be influenced by various literary elements: contents, character notations, and used characters' kinds and tendencies. These problems may be too difficult to be treated in narrative generation formalisms.

- **Genre:** Movie, **Media:** Film (image)
  - **Object:** *Battleship Potemkin* (1925) by Sergei Eisenstein (1898-1948), *The Color of Pomegranates* (1968) by Sergei Parajanof (1924-1990) and several photographs that were taken by the authors (Kanai, Ogata, & Shinohara, 2003).]
  - **Goal:** A point of a film study with Kanai (Kanai & Niwa, 2008; Kanai, 2013) is the problem of non-story's characteristics in films. Through several cooperative research projects, the author also analyzed, for image narratives, rhetoric of works in which temporal progression is complicated and rhetoric for intervening intentionally a story's sequence. This study was also conducted as a part of these studies originally to clearly analyze the characteristics of story recognition by the receivers and introduce the acquired knowledge into narrative generation systems.
  - **Relationships With INGS:** Differing from other narrative analyses by the author, this focuses on the side of the narrative receiver and, instead of analyzing directly structures and representations of a text itself, the authors used a method to analyze clearly aspects of the reception in receivers, who receive texts of a film work and a photograph work through

mainly questionnaire surveys. In particular, this study divided the subjects into the following two groups: the first group who knew the story in a film work and the second one who did not know it. In the results, the authors clearly analyzed that the story cognition may disturb the recognition of non-story elements in the object and acquired an indication that intentionally disturbs the receiver's story recognition by a method, namely a story cutting technique. They are very important for recognizing the value of the rhetoric unique in the film that can be absorbed into the stories. The authors considered that the acquired knowledge has practical effects for appealing an advertising product (brand) and bridged it to propose the following typical advertising scenario flow: "At first, a product is introduced into a story flow, and then, the existence of the product itself is emphasized through the intentional cutting of the story." In addition, the authors linked this knowledge to simulations for cutting stories (Kanai, Ogata, & Shinohara, 2003; Mukouyama & Ogata, 1999, 2001; Mukouyama, Kanai & Ogata, 2001; Ogata & Mukouyama, 2001; Kanai & Ogata, 2004; Mukouyama, Shinohara, Kanai, & Ogata, 2002).

◦ **Relationship With Literary Theories:** The narrative discourse techniques in the current version of INGS use, as a basis, a system that relied on the narrative discourse theory by Genette. The author is trying to incorporate elements and techniques not included in the above techniques, such as narrative discourse techniques for explanation and description for slowing down and stopping the temporal progression of a story by utilizing properties in the components of an event. This analytical study shows that, for cutting a story in the film, techniques for surface representation for music, sound, image, and language can be used as well in addition to the above conceptual level's narrative discourse techniques. Concurrently, the system of narrative discourse techniques must be qualitatively extended from the level of only the application of Genette's theory to a wider unique system. As understood from the above description, this narrative analysis basically influences to extend the aspect of the mechanism of narrative discourse, which is related to the narrative representation mechanism. Additionally, it will be linked to the problem of acquisition of the knowledge contents to be stored in the content knowledge base for narrative discourse, though this mechanism is not included in the current INGS, through collecting the examples of story cutting in actual works of movies and other narratives. Perhaps, this is also related to the problem of defamiliarization of a narrative. This analysis forms a group of defamiliarization related to the narrative discourse techniques for cutting a story, in contrast to a group of defamiliarization that can be defined by changing the properties of the components in a story. Therefore, although there are various levels and techniques for defamiliarization, the framework of narrative generation enables an organic approach for the consideration. As another problem, the author has considered in the relationship with real problems of the film study: Although, in the film, the unique logic and rhetoric certainly exist or can exist for the film that are different from novels and folktales, the film has been acquiring the popularity by combining with narratives. Doubtlessly, this historical fact must not be ignored. One of the most important reasons that the film has not been isolated from the contemporary popular cultures needlessly by becoming an avant-garde art genre was in the narrative. Both anti-narrative and non-narrative must be practiced dependently on this fact, though the author's narrative generation research is also extremely an anti- and non- narrative research.

- **Genre:** Movie, **Media:** Film (image)
  - **Object:** *Tokyo Monogatari* [*Tokyo Story*] (1953) by Ozu Yaujirō.
  - **Goal:** Although a direct goal was to simulate the camerawork of *Tokyo Story* by Ozu using an imaging tool, TVML (NHK Science & Technology Research Laboratories, 2017)_the long term goal was to make a first step for developing the techniques of viewpoint or camerawork for visualizing the image in a movie generation mechanism for narrative generation.
  - **Result:** In this study, the authors divided all parts of this work into the units of shots to be analyzed and described the camerawork of all shots in the relationships with the narrative content described in the film. As a result, the authors showed the basic patterns regarding the techniques of making a motion picture of a character and two characters, and introducing external scenes. Moreover, the authors showed that the violation and deviation, such as a moving shot, from a typical pattern in Ozu were performed in a kind of a climax scene and the point of transition in the story. Thus, this analysis showed the movement form based on the repetition of basic patterns as the majority and very few deviations. Continuously, the authors have tried to simulate this result using the TVML tool and partially developed an image representation mechanism that automatically simulate or imitate the basic pattern of this film in accordance with the arrangement and the context of the prepared image materials. Other remaining issues include comparing this analysis result of *Tokyo Story* to other movies by Ozu, by generalizing the method of the shot analysis (Ogata, Tachibana, & Tomite, 2009; Tachibana & Ogata, 2009).
  - **Relationships With INGS:** In the current INGS, the image expression mechanism has remained a relatively incomplete part, and the result of this Ozu's movie analysis has not been incorporated into the mechanism. In the future research direction, the author aims to generate, in the image expression mechanism in INGS, more symbolic and semiotic, or artistic images, which are relating to the next *manga* (comic) analysis, instead of making realistic animated movie. Although knowledge of camerawork techniques is chiefly related to the mechanism of image expression, if this mechanism can have real images as examples, and not having concrete images of each character or making them variables, this kind of knowledge will be also stored into the content knowledge base for image expression.
  - **Relationships With Literary Theories:** The camerawork in the film is closely related to the problem of the viewpoint in narrative discourse. However, there is also an interesting difference between the viewpoint (perspective) as a narrative discourse technique and the viewpoint (perspective) as camerawork. The viewpoint based on a specific character as a narrative discourse technique defines the things and objects that the character recognizes as the object of discourse. By contrast, the viewpoint that is dependent on the camera in the film is, in an ordinary case, not set as the viewpoint (perspective) of a specific character but as an unidentified viewpoint (perspective) as if it is an omniscient viewpoint (perspective). Furthermore, in the film, although a viewpoint based on a specific character can exist, the faithful representation frequently causes discomfort images like an experimental film. Concurrently, at first, it is necessary to answer a fundamental question about "what is the camera in the film?" In addition, based on this consideration, associating camerawork in the film with narrative discourse techniques will be required.

- **Genre:** *Manga* (Comic), **Media:** Book (paper)
  - **Object:** *Mezon Ikkoku* [Maison Ikkoku] (1992-1993) by Rumiko Takahashi (1957-).
  - **Goal:** Originally, the authors have studied *manga* (comic) in the context in order to develop a "hyper-comic" that represents a *manga* work using the hyper-comic structure (Endo & Ogata, 2003a; Mori & Ogata, 2005; Ogata & Mori, 2005). Based on various interesting knowledge acquired in this process, the authors have continued a series of studies regarding the analyses of *manga* works. Concurrently, these studies have mixed analysis and development.
  - **Result:** The authors called one of the most interesting and exciting methods, for the author's narrative discourse techniques, that is original and unique in *manga* "multilayered narrative discourse." This is a technique through which different narrative discourses are simultaneously represented in a *koma* (frame) in *manga*. For instance, for an event in a *manga* work, various multiple representation techniques are applied including the following: simultaneous representation from different viewpoints in a *koma* (the narrative discourse of focalization), inserting both the past and future of an event into a *koma* (the narrative discourse of temporal order transformation), and arranging both an external action or state and an internal or mental state in a *koma* (the fusion of external focalization and internal focalization). These techniques were also incorporated into the hyper-comic systems developed by the authors (Endo & Ogata, 2003b; Ogata & Endo, 2004; Endo & Ogata, 2004a, 2004b).
  - **Relationships With INGS:** Both the methods of hyper-comic and multilayered narrative discourse have not been incorporated into the current version of INGS. One of these reasons is, as mentioned in the above, that the direction of image expression in INGS has not been decided clearly. Future experimental trials will be able to introduce, especially, the multilayered narrative discourse techniques into a part of INGS, regardless of static or dynamic image. More generally, the authors have aimed to use, as a basis, the image expression methods applying the multilayered characteristics and multiplicity of narrative expression like the multilayered narrative discourse. *Manga* is a very efficient material for considering visual methods of symbolic and semiotic narrative representation.
  - **Relationships With Literary Theories:** The multilayered narrative discourse is a unique technique that is especially adequate in *manga*s (comics) that the narrative is developed on visual display by contrast to novels that the narrative is represented through language. However, this kind of representation in the film, even though the narrative is similarly represented on visual display, will produce very unnatural and experimental impression to the receivers. Movies and television dramas also use a method through which the responses to a same event by different characters are simultaneously represented on divided displays. However, the pleasure of appreciating the film itself is frequently inhibited by such an experimental method. On the other hand, in the case of *manga*, this kind of technique gives more natural and pleasant impression to a receiver. This distinction may rely on the difference between dynamic or moving image and static or stopping image. In the case of a moving image, as the receiver focuses on the next images in a flowing image, the focusing by the receiver on the arrangement itself in a display is frequently inhibited. In contrast, in the case of a static image, the receiver can move freely the viewpoint within a display and consider the relationships among objects that compose the image.

The author will propel this research to the next stage, which will be stated in the next section, after a comprehensive consideration of these fragmental narrative analyses. Otherwise, many narrative analyses can also be utilized in the future, particularly in INGS. For example, there is also a route for using the results of the analyses of television commercial messages as event sequences for stories in INGS. Further, there are many aspects related to hypertext methods, though any hypertext-relating mechanism has not been applied to or used in the narrative generation systems including INGS.

Figure 3 situates the analysis objects or themes, genres and works explained in the above in a macro framework of narrative generation that were shown in Figure 2. The main analysis themes were story, narrative discourse, and characters. On the other hand, the chief analysis objects were television advertisements, novels, movies, and *manga*. However, regarding the television images and *manga*, the authors essentially dealt with symbolized objects instead of the images themselves. The main analysis focus was the structural aspects of the story and narrative discourse. On the other hand, only the partial surface aspects, such as the narrative aspect of a language, were treated. Additionally, many of the analysis works themselves were conducted by hand or manually.

Towards Future Narrative Analyses

The author is starting toward different directions that are dependent on the above results of narrative analyses. The targeted topics are divided into the following two aspects: the processing mechanisms in narrative generation systems and acquiring the content knowledge. The goal of the latter is to acquire elements in the knowledge bases of a story of narrative discourse and narrative expression (for language, music, and image), and the knowledge contents are to be stored in the conceptual dictionaries and language dictionaries from mainly actual data. On the other hand, the former includes the acquisition of knowledge related to the mechanisms to drive generation, the entire architecture of narrative generation in the most macro level, by using the above knowledge contents. Although the former was the central part of previous narrative analyses, a point of future narrative analyses will transit to acquire knowledge contents that correspond to the latter because a current direct issue is to integrate these results into INGS.

Figure 3. A framework of narrative generation and the elements of narrative analysis

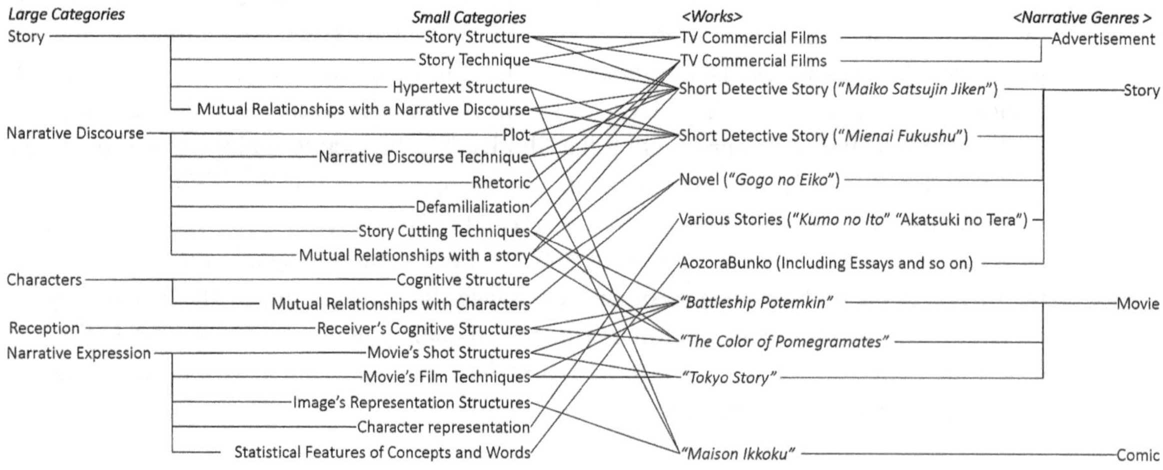

Texts as Objects

The analysis objects with which the authors have dealt covered diverse genres from novel, advertisement, film, *manga*, folk tale, drama, dream to music, *geinō* (performing art), and *kabuki* including the texts that have been merely referred to. In the future, the author intends to consider two directions, namely, a more systematic approach referring to a narrative genre system (Ogata, 1999) and the directions toward a personal and private level's narratives, which will be mentioned in a following section. These two directions, however, appear to contradict each other. Therefore, is the plan to address this is to comprehensively view the genres in a considerably larger range in the narrative genre system and, at the same time, select each work based on the author's personal and private preference to a significant extent. Although the work selection in previous narrative analyses was certainly done arbitrarily so far, the author, in the future, will increase the degree of consciousness in the arbitrary sense that is dependent on the system framework of the narrative genre. The author has preferred to deal with popular narratives such as advertising films and detective stories so far. In general, analyzing the typical or archetypal structures of narratives from popular narratives, such as advertising and detective stories, is rather easy more than from, so to speak, literary or artistic narratives. Such idea or thought may be important when the goal is to acquire narrative knowledge contents. However, the author seeks to undertake in extending the range of objects of narrative analyses in the future toward the works in more literary or artistic and, further, personal levels. In this sense, although the author also aims to approach the area called literary criticism, popular, structural and universal layers in narratives are seized as the basis or foundation of narrative analyses in a persistent manner.

Text Analysis Methods

The analysis methods of target texts can be divided into qualitative and quantitative analysis. Three types of structural, content, and surface analyses are also differentiated by another measure. First, the term "structural," here, means analyzing narrative semantic, conceptual, and deep structures related to story and narrative discourse. Second, the term "content" analysis means the type of analysis that considers various concepts represented in narratives and their mutual relationships. On the other hand, "surface" means the phenomenological analysis at the level of narrative representation media including language and so on. Both structural and content analyses are conducted based on the processing of the information that was acquired as the results of a surface analysis. The qualitative/ quantitative analysis and structural/content/surface analysis form respectively different groups; therefore, their combinations are also possible. Although the structural/content analysis and surface analysis respectively have a tendency to combine with qualitative analysis and quantitative analysis, there are also diverse methods, such as the quantitative consideration of a structural analysis result and the performance of a surface analysis by a qualitative method. However, for example, the quantitative analysis for constructing narrative structures from the result of a statistic language analysis is generally too difficult to perform by present techniques. In the case of structural analysis, typically, it is necessary to transform a surface text into its unique representation to show the meaning once and the degree of the ease of transformation decides the possibility of a quantitative analysis. Machinery and automatic processing that is necessary in quantitative analysis is also possible if the above transformation is mechanically possible. In a structural analysis, this difficulty of automatic transformation causes the difficulty of a quantitative analysis. As an overview, in the fields of artificial intelligence, cognitive science, and natural language processing, in the period from the 1970s to the beginning of the 1990s, many techniques and systems were developed for sentences and narratives in the structural, semantic, and content levels. Narrative generation systems were included in these studies. However, after that time, statistical and quantitative studies for the surface levels of language became a main stream instead of the above types of studies. Treating collectively a certain amount of narrative texts is very difficult using the previous methods for content and semantic understanding of narratives. Of course, it was also too hard to apply narrative analysis methods that were proposed in narratology and literary theories to such studies. Although a clearly essential approach is to add the methods of statistical and quantitative analysis to the methods of previous narrative structural analysis and its semantic analysis, it remains a difficult process.

Classifying Content Knowledge

Knowledge contents to be stored in the story content knowledge base in INGS form various types of units for acquiring and storing of knowledge, such as an event, an event pair (a binomial event sequence), and a polynomial event sequence.

First, in basic terms, an event unit corresponding to a motif of a narrative can be considered. According to Nonaka (2015), motifs mean “concrete things and objects that are repetitively represented in various literary works and are outstanding themes, and they include images, symbols, characters, utterances, actions, events, and situations.” If the author focuses on an event here, the author calls a motif an event that appears in many narratives and plays important roles in the story progression in a narrative. Although it is a concept that has been presented in folktale study, this concept will be applied to narratives rather than folktales, such as modern and contemporary novels and stories. Here, an event is frequently a symbolic and generic event, which in this case, is composed of a collection of many events. This means that a motif described as an event is basically expanded to a polynomial event sequence in actual narrative practices. The next event pairs include narrative knowledge as a causal chain or temporal chain between two events in narratological sense, such as “Prohibition-Violation” and “Battle-Victory (Defeat).” The functional theories by Propp (1968) and Greimas (1966), a successor of Propp’s theory, are known to be constructed by these kinds of many event pairs. Similar to the above, these can also be realized in the association with polynomial event sequences.

The following two types of event sequences are regarded as the last polynomial event sequences: There are two event sequences in the level of human behavior in a relatively micro type, which are called script (Schank & Abelson, 1977) in artificial intelligence and cognitive science, and event sequences for developing and detailing an abstract or generic event in a relatively macro type. The examples include “eating at a restaurant” and “wedding ceremony” that can be interpreted as a scene. However, a scene that is different from an event is not necessarily required. Events such as “eating (at a restaurant)” and “marrying” can be regarded as more abstract events, which is substantially equal to treating them as scenes, instead of understanding them as concrete ones, which have a short temporal range that can be detailed by more concrete events, namely polynomial events. A more macro type is a sequence of events of a summarized structure of an entire story, which includes the functional sequences by Propp (1968). Further, each event in a polynomial event sequence can also be developed or detailed by events of the lower level. Ogata (2008a) presented a basic idea about the concrete development and construction of events. For example, basic actions such as “walking,” “running,” and other concrete actions are combined in order to define actions in the level of “appearing” and “whaling,” and abstract actions such as “kidnaping” can be defined by the above second level. This paper showed the following classification of the hierarchy of actions: (1) a pause as a body's static state, (2) a body movement or an action as a sequence of pauses, (3) the ordering combinations between actions and environmental elements, namely, places and instruments, and (4) a more complex action by the combination of many actions. The above (3) and (4) approximately correspond to the events in INGS. Dependent on the above ideas and the considerations, the author would like to address this problem theoretically and systematically in the future. The story content knowledge base in INGS respectively stores various types of event units of one, pair, and polynomial in various levels through which the story techniques expand and transform them.

As a next topic, several researchers have attempted to apply the morphology of Russian folktales on event sequences by Propp to folktales in other countries and other general narrative texts (Greimas, 1966; Dundes, 1965). The authors have analyzed Japanese folktales using the functional theory by Propp from the perspective of narrative generation that needs elaborated formalization (Ogata & Fujiwara, 2015; Ogata, Fujiwara, & Imabuchi, 2014; Fujiwara & Ogata, 2014). Asano (2016) presented her Propp-based structural analysis of human-animal-marriage folktales in Japan by referring to the extended formalization for story generation by the above papers by Ogata and the group. Although Ogata has defined and implemented the story content grammar by expanding and formalizing the Propp's theory as an important part in INGS, these attempts remain a possibility for future development. A problem is that each "function," which is a central concept in the theory by Propp and the definition for comprehending many concrete events that is used to decide a narrative structure in the genre of Russian fairy tales treated by Propp, is too abstract and comprehensive to specify it in an actual text. Propp himself originally invented the functional theory to avoid the arbitrary in the previous motif analyses in the studies of folktales. However, a text analysis based on this functional theory is too difficult to be conducted as a formal and mechanical method because of its reliance on the interpretation abilities and context understanding abilities of each analyzer.

On the other hand, Propp's theory is not only a functional theory, but also a hierarchical whole which involves the methods in multiple levels for actualizing the functional theory: This includes the level of function (as a single unit), the level of function pair (as two units), the level of function group (as several units), the level of "move" as a sequence of functions (as several units), and the level of the combination or connection of moves. This is an important reason that the author has been focusing on his theory. The levels stated in the above also correspond to such narrative levels. As seen in Propp's theory and, further, in story grammar models, if an entire narrative is a hierarchical structure of components in various levels, which can be called by many names, it is possible to analyze these levels to hold in narrative knowledge. The classification of content knowledge here means this kind of narrative analysis. In addition, the degree of formality makes the difference between the theory by Propp and story grammar. Although the former is a very formal study in the field of literary theories, the degree of formality is weak than story grammar. However, this fact means that Propp's theory occupies the medieval position between formality and knowledge content. It is somewhat regarded as a useful feature from the perspective of narrative generation studies.

Last, the author would like to consider the analysis methods. As mentioned above, the analysis using the functional theory by Propp frequently causes the arbitrary by each analyzer. A point to be considered is that rather the method of motif analysis, though Propp himself originally aimed to avoid the arbitrary to present his functional method, may decrease the arbitrary for extracting the motives of texts because it is an analysis based on the surface characteristics of an event in texts. As a different interesting narrative analysis, a method that utilizes rather positively the arbitrary can also exist. In this sense, the author is interested in a method proposed by Roland Barthes (1915-1980) (1975) that divided a short story, *Sarrasine* by Honore de Balzac (1799-1850) (2017), into 561 reading units, namely, lexis, to create diverse interpretation routes like a network. This can be regarded as a method for making a kind of semantic network according to the various codes and rules from a part in a narrative text as a starting node. *Les mythologiques (Vol.1)* by Claude Levi-Strauss (1964) may have similar characteristic. These are not only narrative analyses, but also the generation of semantic structures from which various narratives can be produced beyond original analysis materials. In this sense, it may be effective to comprehend the functional theory by Propp as a possible framework for generating narratives rather than as a method to aim at narrative analysis itself. If there is a room to extend its theoretical construction, extending the concrete embodiment forms in each function can be shown through "examples" by Propp to the range to be deduced from definitions and rules of a function. If the definition of each function itself also has a kind of the arbitrary, a productive direction will introduce the mechanism that can change flexibly the levels of definition of each function. Definitions with very weak constraints cover many realization forms; in contrast, definitions with very strong constraints have a few realization forms.

Personal and Private Content Knowledge

Another plan on the target texts for narrative analysis is personal and private text analysis by the author himself. This plan organizationally and systematically uses previous texts that the author has read and written as the subject of narrative analyses. If these are stored in the narrative content knowledge bases, narratives by the author himself who is utilizing them can indirectly be generated, although these are certainly a kind of autobiographical narratives albeit as much deconstructed and restructured as possible. In particular, according to Ogata, Kawamura, and Kanai (in press) who described in detail the plan and methods of a narrative generation research in a personal and private level, personal and private knowledge is divided into personal records of reading, personally written texts, various discourses regarding persons in the personal human relations, and other personal level's information. These types of knowledge are stored in various knowledge bases in INGS and GIS through the process of deconstruction and reconstruction and finally utilized as materials for narrative generation in diverse methods. This will be described in other papers.

AN ANALYSIS OF A NOVEL BY YUKIO MISHIMA: THE NOVEL AS A PLURAL APPARATUS AND A TEXT ANALYSIS BASED ON THE CHARACTERS

The next section shows an actual narrative analysis from the perspective of narrative characters in a novel as an aspect of the diverse possibilities of narrative analyses described in the previous section. In this chapter, however, this narrative analysis aims for a simple and experimental narrative simulation using the Integrated Narrative Generation System (INGS) to show actual bridging from a narrative analysis to a narrative simulation; this will be extended to the level of an entire INGS design.

This section is composed of the following sub-sections: First, in "What is Reality in Narratives?" the author considers the problem of reality in narratives as a fundamental consciousness. In particular, an objective of this section is to discuss the problem of multiple narratives' generation by characters through analysis of a novel by Yukio Mishima. Next, in "A Narrative Generation Model as a Mutual Recognition Mechanism Among Characters," the author introduces *The Sailor Who Fell from Grace with the Sea* by Mishima (1963), and lists the basic concepts required for text analysis to make a document called a "questionnaire" that contains the analysis results for the entire text. Each questionnaire is then analyzed from quantitative and qualitative perspectives. In the next section, "A Quantitative Analysis of Cognitive Information," quantitative analyses regarding the characters are performed in order to consider the construction of this novel. In contrast, "A Qualitative Analysis of Cognitive Information and its Development" shows narrative qualitative analyses of this novel from viewpoints based on the above questionnaire. In the first sub-section, "*Semantic Transition of Mutual Cognitive Processes*", the transition of mutual cognitive processes among the characters is plotted to consider various interpretation possibilities for this novel. The next sub-section, "*Generating Narrative Variations Using a Combination of Mutual Relationships of Cognitive Information*," shows that the novel was derived using various mutual relations among the characters' cognitions. Last, in *The Sailor Who Fell from Grace with the Sea* and Folktales, looked at from a different viewpoint, the similarity between the structure of this novel and the structures of several folktales is used to discuss the narrative universality of this novel. Finally, in "Concluding Remarks: What is the Reality in a Narrative, or Toward the Introduction of a Narrative Generation System," the author reconsiders the problem of reality in novels or narratives and shows directions for incorporating knowledge and methods that were acquired from these narrative analyses into a narrative generation system by the author, namely the INGS.

What Is Reality in Narratives?

The author has been considering how reality is constructed through a narrative. The author's basic intention is to explore multiple and multilayered passages to a reality that is different from a kind of nihilism belief that any realities do not exist. This is a basic and fundamental concern that supports the author's narrative generation research and is also related to the multiple narrative structures model by the author.

In this chapter, the author investigates this topic through a concrete narrative analysis rather than discussing it directly or comprehensively. In particular, a novel by Mishima, *The Sailor Who Fell from Grace with the Sea*, is examined to analyze the process or mechanism through which the novel's reality and real images emerge and are constructed from the worldviews of each character and their mutual relationships. This study was conducted to consider the above problem.

In a Grove (1922), by Akutagawa, and *Rashōmon* (1950), by Kurosawa, are examples in which many contradicting events at the story level are described, and they have evoked many discussions and interpretations to date. Ōoka (1996), through his narrative analysis, insisted that this type of narrative in actuality reflected reality. Outside of literary studies, Kanai, Takai, and Nakanishi (2009), researchers in the science management field, selected these narratives as symbolic material to examine the problems of subjective recognition and narrative generation in business administration. In addition, in narrative generation studies using a computer, Bae, Cheong, and Young (2011) presented a system that generated different stories from a group of events based on "internal plural focalization" by Genette (1972) in an attempt to simulate the story of *Rashōmon*. This internal plural focalization is a type of technique of narrative viewpoint, also called perspective by Genette, through which many characters' viewpoints exist in parallel.

However, different from *In a Grove* and *Rashōmon*, the events that occur in the story are very clear in *The Sailor Who Fell from Grace with the Sea*, and the complexity and multiplicity of reality are necessarily represented through special techniques for narrative discourse. Instead, this novel takes a very orthodox, or typical realism, style, and is far from an intentional technical experiment. Therefore, the fact that this novel proposes new ideas regarding relations between the narrative and reality is perhaps not why Mishima wrote this novel. This novel rather naturally represents the plurality of each character's perception in the small narrative world and the relativity of the world's construction in the characters. Representing the plurality and relativity of a world was the role of novels in the age of large narratives (1979) by Jean-François Lyotard (1924-1998). (However, at the same time, this may mean that a similar analysis is possible for any novel and the same conclusion can be reached. Originally, a problem may be a fact that uses as the object Mishima's novel that may perhaps seem to be the most non-multiple. However, the novels by Mishima, by contrast to a kind of strength of the construction by Mishima himself, contain many possibilities for deconstruction and reinterpretation.)

As stated in the previous section, Bakhtin's polyphonic theory (1984) divided novels into two types: a narrative novel in which the narration (voice) is centrally controlled by a meta-level author, and a novel that is concretized through uncontrolled narration (voice) by each character in addition to the narrator. According to the above idea, *The Sailor Who Fell from Grace with the Sea* seems to be a novel that belongs in the former group. A narrator with an evil and ironic figure (voice) frequently appears in this novel. Each character seems at times like a puppet controlled by this narrator and his extraordinary thoughts.

However, a "narrative generation model as a mutual recognition mechanism among characters" presented in this chapter states that all novels, and even more so, all narratives, are at least potentially, or as the possibility of deconstruction polyphonic, plural, and multiple. This chapter takes the first step toward the narrative generation model as a mutual recognition mechanism among characters and deals with an aspect of narrative plurality based on an actual novel by Mishima. When potential possibilities of deconstruction or reconstruction are considered, novels by Tolstoy (from 1865–69, 1899, etc.), which were defined as monophonic novels by Bakhtin, can also be regarded as more dynamic and polyphonic novels. Different from the above strengths of Mishima, the novel by Mishima, *The Sailor Who Fell from Grace with the Sea,* is also supported by a kind of theatrical construction so as to enable stage performance and, in this sense, it has a strongly polyphonic nature. The polyphonic theory by Bakhtin originally indicated in theatrical narratives that the story and narrative discourses progress and are developed through conversation.

A goal in this chapter is to take a step toward fixing such problems, and this chapter specifically deals with only one aspect of polyphony on the formal and technological level. Although it is necessary to, for example, enter each character's inner life to consider this problem more deeply, this is beyond the scope of this chapter.

A Narrative Generation Model as a Mutual Recognition Mechanism Among Characters

Kumagai, Ogata, and Oikawa (2010), and Onodera, Kumagai, and Ogata (2010) addressed how characters are constructed in another novel by Mishima, *Utage no Ato* [*After the Banquet*] (1960). Their objective was to study and analyze how the characters are constructed using knowledge contents, including their external and mental properties, with the goal of introducing them into a narrative generation system (INGS). These studies indicated that one of the dramatic features in the novel was the result of correspondence and contradiction. Each character has a unique worldview, and the actual narrative is formed depending on the various techniques that are used to multiple synthesized narrative materials generated by each character. Introducing knowledge contents into INGS may be too difficult an issue at present. At the same time, Oikawa and Ogata (2010, 2012) used an approach that is directly related to this chapter, and this chapter elaborates and extends the findings from their papers. In particular, this chapter revises several analytic problems and extends and elaborates a quantitative analysis that has not previously been described in detail to consider the concrete and detailed directions for incorporating them into INGS. Additionally, many parts of the following figures and tables expand and revise those from the above papers. In the following sections, according to the main idea of "narrative generation as a mutual recognition mechanism among characters," the author uses *The Sailor Who Fell from Grace with the Sea* to analyze and consider various aspects of acquired concrete knowledge. The important idea is to comprehensively understand information relating to characters as cognitive information. All actions and thoughts from all characters are constructed as mutual cognitive information. Based on the analysis, the author considers some dynamic features and implications for narrative generation. Finally, a rough plan to introduce the result of this analysis into the future design of narrative generation system is laid out.

This novel by Mishima, *The Sailor Who Fell from Grace with the Sea,* consists of "Part 1: Summer," which contains eight chapters from chapter 1 to chapter 8, and "Part 2: Winter," which contains seven chapters from chapter 1 to chapter 7. A very rough synopsis of this novel is shown for the reader's convenience: Noboru, who peeped into the bedroom of a sailor, Ryūji, and his mother, Fusako, believed that Ryūji is a hero and adored him. However, Noboru knew that Ryuji and Fusako loved each other and had decided to marry and further that Ryūji would like to abandon the sea and choose a life on land instead. According to a proposition made by a friend called "the chief," Noboru and his friends (including the chief) decided to kill Ryūji at a hill at Sugita in Yokohama from where the sea can be seen. In the end, they introduce Ryūji to the hill to make him drink poisoned tea and murder him. This is merely a synopsis from Noboru's viewpoint. Further, in the moving scene in the town of Yokohama before reaching the place of the murder, a *michiyuki* to take [*eikō* in Japanese] Ryūji is narrated. (*Michiyuki*, especially in *kabuki* and *ningyō jōruri*, means scenes where characters move from one place to another, over the course of several scenes (Ogata, 2016c)). This towing [*eikō*] is overlapped to the last bitter glory [*eikō*].

Table 1 shows an overview of the events in each chapter and the corresponding characters.

As seen in Table 1, although many characters appear in this novel, considering that there are other sub-characters that may enable more interesting analysis and consideration, this analysis deals with only four characters, Noboru, Ryūji, Fusako, and the chief, along with a narrator who is also recognized as a kind of character. The narrator in this novel perhaps does not intentionally lie and corresponds to the idea of a "reliable narrator" (Booth, 1983).

As a first step in the novel analysis, the author extracted all sentences relating to these four characters and classified them into the following three types: "conversational sentence (spoken sentence)," "thinking sentence," and "descriptive sentence" (Table 2). Conversational or spoken sentences and thinking sentences are used by all characters, including the narrator, and descriptive sentences are used only by the narrator. Figure 4 shows an example.

Next, from all of the sentences in this novel, the author classified all information for expressing thoughts, properties, and actions for all characters, including the narrator, as "cognitive information of characters." The cognitive information of the characters that was extracted from the description sentences was classified as "factual cognitive information," and the cognitive information of characters that was extracted from conversational and inner dialogue sentences was classified as "thinking cognitive information." Additionally, factual cognitive information and thinking cognitive information were further divided into the "actions" of the characters—"internal information," meaning the characters' thoughts, and "external information" involving the properties, appearance, and roles of the characters outside of their thoughts.

Here, behavior that is classified as "actions" can be called "external actions," and in contrast, behavior that is simply "internal information" can be called "internal actions." External and internal actions can

Table 1. Events and characters in The Sailor Who Fell from Grace with the Sea

Chapter1, Part1	Content	Noboru peeks into the room of Fusako and sees Fusako and Ryuji being intimate with each other.										
	Character	Noboru Kuroda	Fusako Kuroda	Ryuji Tsukasaki	Died father	The chief						
Chapter2, Part1	Content	Ryuji wakes up in Fusako's room. Ryuji recalls an event during a sea voyage. Fusako tells Ryuji that Noboru feels something.										
	Character	Noboru Kuroda	Fusako Kuroda	Ryuji Tsukasaki	Crews	The older seaman	Sampan	A woman				
Chapter3, Part1	Content	Fusako is the owner of Rex, a shop selling Western goods. Fusako recalls her encounter with Ryuji the day before yesterday.										
	Character	Noboru Kuroda	Fusako Kuroda	Ryuji Tsukasaki	Four shoppers	Manager Shibuya	Yoriko Kasuga	Shipping executive	Stevedores			
Chapter4, Part1	Content	Ryuji passes time in the park until he is to meet Fusako. Ryuji recalls the conversation he had with Fusako yesterday after their meal. After that, by chance Ryuji meets Noboru and Noboru's friends.										
	Character	Noboru Kuroda	Fusako Kuroda	Ryuji Tsukasaki	Boys	The chief						
Chapter5, Part1	Content	Noboru lies to his mother and goes to meet the chief and the rest of the gang. Noboru insists that Ryuji is a wonderful person, but the chief refutes this. The chief says that murder is necessary to fill the void in the world, and Noboru and his friends kill a cat.										
	Character	Noboru Kuroda	Fusako Kuroda	Ryuji Tsukasaki	The chief	Number one	Number two	Number four	Number five	Teachers	Watchman	Stray cat
Chapter6, Part1	Content	After killing the cat, Noboru meets with Ryuji by chance, and he worries about whether he notices something. After that, the two go home together and talk about life on the sea.										
	Character	Noboru Kuroda	Fusako Kuroda	Ryuji Tsukasaki	The chief	Number one	Number two	Number four	Number five	House keeper		
Chapter7, Part1	Content	Ryuji and Fusako sadly part the following day. Noboru thinks about peeping-in on them when they return home, so he is angry when they stay overnight in a hotel.										
	Character	Noboru Kuroda	Fusako Kuroda	Ryuji Tsukasaki	House keeper							
Chapter8, Part1	Content	The next day, Ryuji boards his ship, says goodbye to Noboru and Fusako, and leaves.										
	Character	Noboru Kuroda	Fusako Kuroda	Ryuji Tsukasaki								
Chapter1, Part2	Content	Ryuji returns from his voyage. Fusako and Ryuji are both happy, but Noboru is angry that he has returned.										
	Character	Noboru Kuroda	Fusako Kuroda	Ryuji Tsukasaki	Old driver	House keeper	The Rakuyo's officers					
Chapter2, Part2	Content	Fusako and Ryuji go to see the first sunrise together on New Year's Eve. There, Ryuji proposes to Fusako, and Fusako accepts.										
	Character	Noboru Kuroda	Fusako Kuroda	Ryuji Tsukasaki	House keeper	Manager Shibuya						
Chapter3, Part2	Content	Ryuji does not board his ship when the day of departure arrives. Yoriko visits Rex, the Western goods store. Yoriko says that Ryuji should be investigated. The results of the investigation showed that there are no problems with Ryuji.										
	Character	Fusako Kuroda	Ryuji Tsukasaki	Yoriko Kasuga	Manager Shibuya							
Chapter4, Part2	Content	Noboru starts junior high school. Noboru, the chief, and the rest of the gang gather and have a meeting. They talk about Ryuji.										
	Character	Noboru Kuroda	Fusako Kuroda	Ryuji Tsukasaki	The chief	Number one	Number two	Number four	Number five			
Chapter5, Part2	Content	Ryuji and Fusako tell Noboru that they are going to get married. Noboru had not thought that deeply that he could actually be his father. One evening, Noboru tries to peek into Fusako's room, but Fusako catches him and scolds him, but as a father figure, Ryuji only gently tells him to be careful.										
	Character	Noboru Kuroda	Fusako Kuroda	Ryuji Tsukasaki								
Chapter6, Part2	Content	Noboru asks the chief to call an urgent meeting. The chief and the rest of the gang are told about the behavior of Ryuji up to that time and decide to execute him.										
	Character	Noboru Kuroda	The chief	Number one	Number two	Number four	Number five					
Chapter7, Part2	Content	Noboru asks Ryuji and he promises to meet with the chief and the others. Noboru and the others take Ryuji to the dry dock and he talks about life on the sea. Ryuji drinks the tea given to him by Noboru that contains sleeping medicine.										
	Character	Noboru Kuroda	Fusako Kuroda	Ryuji Tsukasaki	The chief	Number one	Number two	Number four	Number five	First officer		

Source: Oikawa and Ogata (2012).

Table 2. Three types of sentences

Sentence Type	Meaning	Sender
Conversational Sentence	A sentence to describe the content of conversation by a character corresponding to the following one. ・A sentence to describe the content of conversastion surrounding using " 「」 ". ・A sentence shown using "*kataru* [*narrate1/Talk*]" and "*iu* [*say*]".	Characters except for narrator
Thinking Sentence	A sentence to describe the content of thought by a character corresponding to the following one. ・A sentence surrounding using " 『』 ". ・A sentence shown using "*shiru* [*know*]", "*kanjiru* [*feel*]", "*omou* [*think*]" and "*darō* [*will*]".	Chractrs except for narrator
Descriptive Sentence	A sentence to describe actions of a character except for the above types.	Narrator

Source: Oikawa and Ogata (2012).

Figure 4. Examples of conversational sentence (spoken sentence), thinking sentence, and descriptive sentence
Source: Oikawa and Ogata (2012).

"Sleep well, dear." Noboru's mother closed his bedroom door and locked it. What would she do if there were a fire? (Chapter 1, Part 1)
"Let's not expect too much, dear, until we're certain this letter is what we need." Thinking about it later, Fusako realized that she had felt her heart begin to dance even as they had stood looking up at the ship. *That funny: I'm just as excited as Noboru.* (Chapter 3, Part 1)

Conversational (Spoken) Sentence: ———
Thinking Sentence: ═══
Descriptive Sentence: ～～～

be regarded as dynamic information, and "external information" can be regarded as static information. Further, external actions can be divided into static actions—in other words, events as states, and dynamic actions, or events as nonstates.

When the three types of sentences described above, namely conversational sentences, thinking sentences, and descriptive sentences, are the formal components in a novel, the external actions, internal actions, and external information included in the factual cognitive information and thinking cognitive information correspond to semantic components.

Cognitive information here does not simply refer to the psychological or mental states of characters. Instead, it consists of all the information regarding characters that a character (c) has—namely, all the information regarding c and the other characters. The characters, including the narrator, are the source of all the information in the novel. Although this study limits its scope to a few characters, cognitive information involves all information relating to the world and nature of other characters. Of course, it also involves other characters, including a manager, Shibuya, and Yoriko Kasuga, who does not seem to be related to the main story at a glance. Further, geographical and scenery information from the old town in Yokohama in the age of streetcars is also given to the readers. In sum, an entire novel is a multiple and plural collection of the cognitive information of characters, including the narrator. The world of a novel is constructed from the plural viewpoints of many characters. A temporal and spatial world is also constructed through plural perspectives. A world is created through overlapping viewpoints. As shown in Figure 5, a character, Noboru, is composed of the factual cognitive information of a narrator

Figure 5. Construction of the character Noboru using factual cognitive information and thinking cognitive information
Source: Oikawa and Ogata (2012).

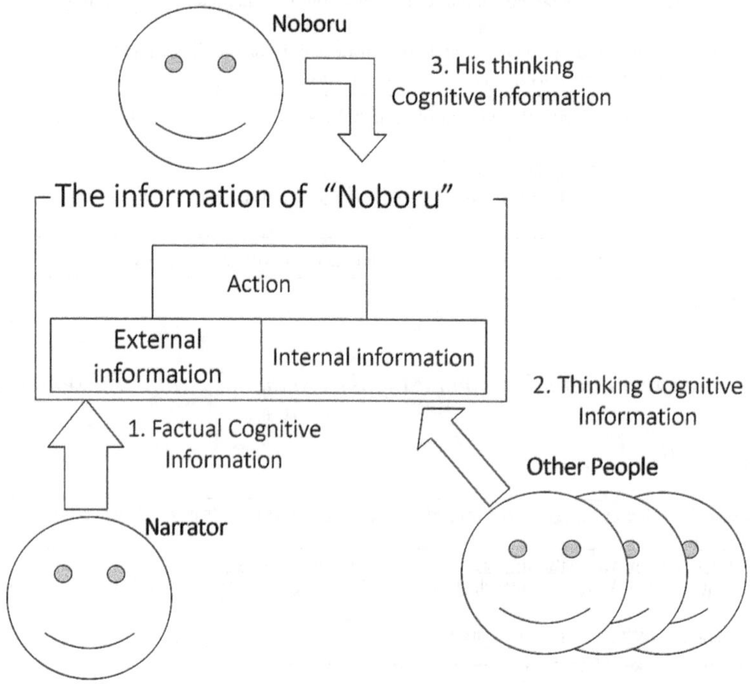

who has three types of information, similar to the thinking cognitive information of each character and, further, the thinking cognitive information of the character himself/herself.

Based on the above model, the author designed a questionnaire to classify the cognitive information for the four main characters to prepare a document for analyzing cognitive information in detail. In particular, for the entire novel, the author divided the sentences relating to the characters into semantic units that basically had a verb, a subject, one or more objects, and other elements. For the questionnaire, the author used the original sentences themselves, divided the sentences, and, further, summarized the sentences. The questionnaire was described as dividing sentences into subjects, objects, actions, internal information, and external information. Figure 6 shows a sample of the actual examples. In the factual cognitive information, the subject is only equal to the narrator, and the objects correspond to the four characters. Actions, internal information, and external information are included under each character as objects. Meanwhile, the subjects and objects in thinking cognitive information are commonly the four characters, and actions, internal information, and external information are set under each character.

For a more detailed analysis of the questionnaire, the author made a program tool, a "character information extraction tool," that conducted information extraction under specific conditions, including the character as a subject and information types. Although a novel has various subjects and objects of information, each character in a narrative world may, so to speak, equally live its individual life. The narrator constructs his/her particular narrative through a particular focus. According to different emphases, diverse narrative flows (stories) will be produced. The actions, internal information, and external information of each character can be selected and represented collectively by utilizing this character

Figure 6. Construction of the questionnaire and its description based on the sentences in the novel
Source: Oikawa and Ogata (2012).

She was only thirty-three and her slender body, shapely from playing tennis every week, was beautiful. Usually, **she got right into bed after touching her flesh with perfumed water**, ...
Chapter 1, Part 1

Fact/Thought	Subject	Object	Kinds	Information	
Factual cognitive information	Narrator	Noboru	Action	in the chest	in the chest
			Internal	The humiliation was enormous.	The humiliation was enormous.
			External	thirteen-year-old	thirteen-year-old
		Fusako	Action	in the room of Fusako	in the room of Fusako
			Internal	Let him out first thing-she had promised herself that	Let him out first thing-she had promised herself that
			External	thirty-three	thirty-three
				playing tennis	playing tennis
				slender, shapely, and beautiful	slender, shapely, and beautiful
					She Got right into bed after touching her flesh with perfumed water
Thinking cognitive information	Noboru	Noboru	Action		
			Internal	He vowed heaver to do anything that might attract the grownups' attention to the chest.	He vowed heaver to do anything that might attract the grownups' attention to the chest.
			External		
		Fusako	Action		
			Internal	What if the wooden door warped in the heat or paint clogged the key hole?	What if the wooden door warped in the heat or paint clogged the key hole?
			External		

information extraction tool. Each set is considered a prototype that shows the above equal lives of the characters. Table 3 shows the results of information extraction. Table 4 and Table 5 show actual examples from the questionnaire.

Further, each character is formalized as a synthesis of cognitive information. When a character is defined, this character is "an object of formation" for the characters, including her/himself, in addition to "a subject of formation" for the characters including her/himself. A narrator, as a subject of formation, formalizes actions, internal information, and external information apart from her/himself through the factual cognitive information. Other characters can be the objects of formation by the narrator and the other characters, in addition to being the subjects of formation for the other characters aside from the narrator. Although all characters except for the narrator can be both the subject and the object for formation, only the narrator cannot be the object for formation by the characters other than the narrator. Figure 7 shows the above relationships. In this figure, character A, as a subject for formation, formalizes actions, internal information, and external information of both character A and character B. At the

Table 3. Information extraction results from the analysis of The Sailor Who Fell from Grace with the Sea

	Action	Internal Information	External Information	Total
Factual Cognitive Information	828	424	312	1564
Thinking Cognitive Information	120	301	219	640

Source: Oikawa and Ogata (2012).

Table 4. An example of the factual cognitive information of the narrator (Chapter 1, Part 1)

Cognitive Type	Subject	Object	Type	Description
Factual Cognitive Information	Narrator	Noboru	Action	in the room of Noboru
				rummaging through his room
				pulling out all the drawers
				in the chest
			Internal	The humiliation was enormous
				He couldn't believe he was looking at his mother's bedroom
			External	thirteen-year-old
				Last name is Kuroda
		Fusako	Action	in the room of Fusako
				touching her flesh with perfumed water
			Internal	Let him out first thing-she had promised herself that
			External	mother
				Last name is kuroda
				His mother loved all kind of handicraft
				to sit completely naked for a few minutes before going to bed
				thirty-three

Source: Oikawa and Ogata (2012).

Table 5. An Example of the factual cognitive information of Ryūji and Fusako (Chapter 2, Part 1)

Cognitive Type	Subject	Object	Type	Description
Thinking cognitive information	Ryuji	Noboru	Action	The boy was still in the house
		Ryuji	Internal	He loued the groves of wine plams
				He hated, the immobility of the land, the eternally unchanging surfaces
				Groly!
				There's just one thing I'm destined for and that's glory
				There must be a special destiny in store for me
		Fusako	Internal	He knew, she was uneasy even while her eyes were closed
		. . .		
	Fusako	Noboru	Internal	Noboru this morning, almost as if he knew
				He seems to like you a lot
			. . .	
		Fusako	Internal	I still don't understand how this could have happend

Source: Oikawa and Ogata (2012).

Figure 7. Mutual relationships of the characters' formation
Source: Oikawa and Ogata (2012).

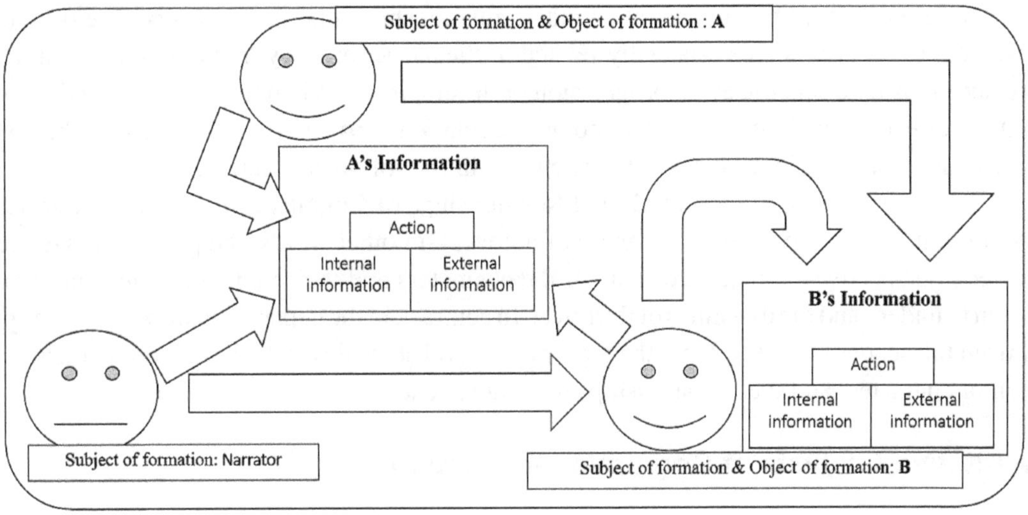

same time, the actions, internal information, and external information of character A are constructed as the object of formation by the narrator and character B. In addition, there are vague points concerning classifying conditions; for example, information that was interpreted as external information sometimes includes information that can be interpreted as actions and internal information. Moreover, when new information was described in the questionnaire, in deciding whether the previous information should be deleted, the author followed everyday sense because, in many cases, explicit descriptions did not exist in the novel. This is related to the problem of the duration time of each information. Another problem is that characters who are not clearly named in a novel cannot be specified in the strict sense. For instance, an explicit description of the chief does not exist in the scene where Ryūji firstly meets him. From the viewpoint of Ryūji in this scene, he is only one of several boys. Strictly speaking, the reader merely guesses that this character is the same character named "the chief" from the descriptions in other scenes. In this analysis, when a character is clearly the same as a character described in other places, the author interpreted that both of the characters are the same.

Mutual cognitive relationships among characters are formed by applying or using the model described above. In particular, as shown in Table 6, the text of a novel is divided into formal and semantic aspects,

Table 6. From text to dynamism in a novel

Making and Using the Text Relating to a Character	Content
Text elements relating to a character	Formal: 1) Dscriptive, 2) Conversational, 3) Thinking Semantic: 1) Action (dynamic), 2) External informtion (static), 3) Internal information (dynamic)
Constitutional elements for making a character	1) The subject to formalize (the person to formalized), 2) The object to be formalized (the object to be formalized)
The dynamism by using the mutual recognition relationships among charaters	1) Commonality/difference, 2) Perception, Recognition/Nonperception, Nonrecognition

and character formation is conducted for both aspects. The dynamics of a novel are formed along the diverse relationships among the characters. The dynamism here means that the development (movement) of a novel is affected by the mutual cognitive relationships among characters. The development and movement of a novel is thus especially related to the aspect of story in the narrative that requires selective decisions for a specific event progression or development. When there are, at one time, several possibilities for event development, mutual cognitive relationships can propel several of the possibilities for selection and decision. This will be discussed in the following section, "Generating Narrative Variations using a Combination of the Mutual Relationships of Cognitive Information." Furthermore, as shown in Figure 8, in the reception process of a novel—in other words, the process as viewed from the receiver's perspective—a reader recognizes the characters and their mutual relationships from text recognition to understand the dynamics of the novel. In contrast, in the generation process—or the process viewed from the sender's perspective—the writer of a novel steps down the logic of dynamism into the formation of characters and their relationships to create a text.

A Quantitative Analysis of Cognitive Information

Characters as subjects of formation and characters as objects of formation are respectively formed both by various types of sentences at a formal level (conversational sentence, thinking sentence, and descriptive sentence) and by actions, internal information, and external information on a semantic level. As shown in Figure 9, the characters as the subject of formation are divided into the narrator and other characters. Each character other than the narrator represents actions, internal information, and external information through the use of conversational sentences or thinking sentences. Meanwhile, the narrator as the subject of formation represents actions, internal information, and external information of the four characters by using descriptive sentences. Conversely, when a character is seen as an object of formation, first, the narrator forms the character using the representation of actions, external information, and internal information by using descriptive sentences; in contrast, other characters form that character using the representation of actions, external information, and internal information by using conversational sentences and thinking sentences.

Figure 8. Generation and reception process of a novel seen from the perspective of this analysis

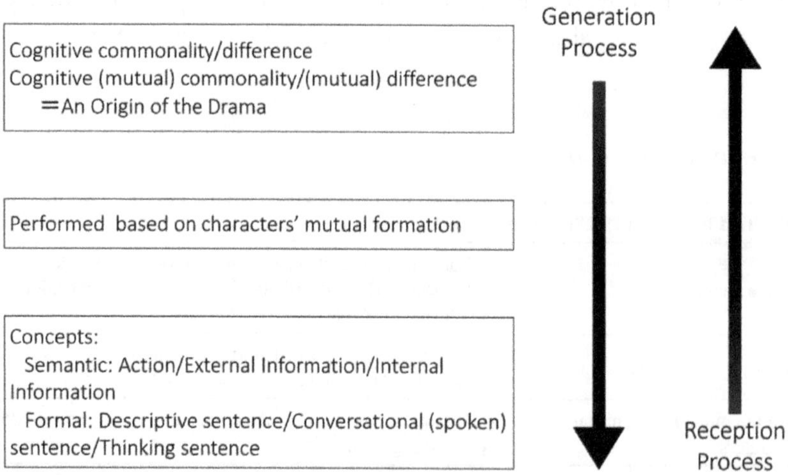

Figure 9. Various formation methods of the characters

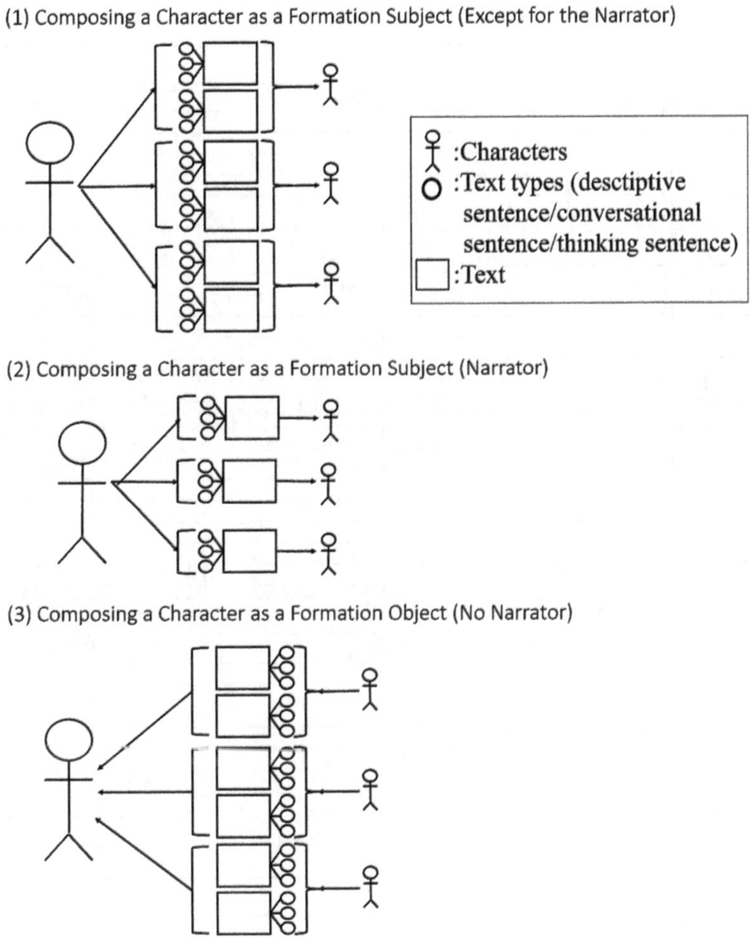

Based on the framework of Figure 9, several graphs can show quantitative information. At first, as a graph corresponding to Figure 9 (1), for each of the four characters, the graph of Figure 10 can be drawn to show the quantitative proportion of the actions, external information, and internal information by the conversational sentences and thinking sentences of the other three characters. Figure 11 corresponds to Figure 9 (2) to show the actions, external information, and internal information based on the descriptive sentences of the narrator. Figure 12 corresponds to Figure 9 (3), showing the quantitative information of how the four characters other than the narrator are formed by themselves and the narrator.

In Figure 10, there is much information regarding the other characters, Ryūji and Fusako, that was introduced by Noboru. By contrast, very little information about the chief is given by Noboru. This indicates that Noboru is one-sidedly defensive in the relationship between the chief and Noboru and that Noboru is a kind of object to be operated on. Regarding Ryūji, much of his information is brought from Ryuji himself and Noboru. However, not much information is given about Fusako by Ryūji, even though Ryūji hopes to marry Fusako. Regarding Fusako, she gives almost the same quantity of information relating to Fusako herself, Ryūji, and Noboru in the entire novel. In the case of the chief, there is a lot of

Figure 10. Quantitative construction of the other characters' formation by subjects of formation except for the narrator

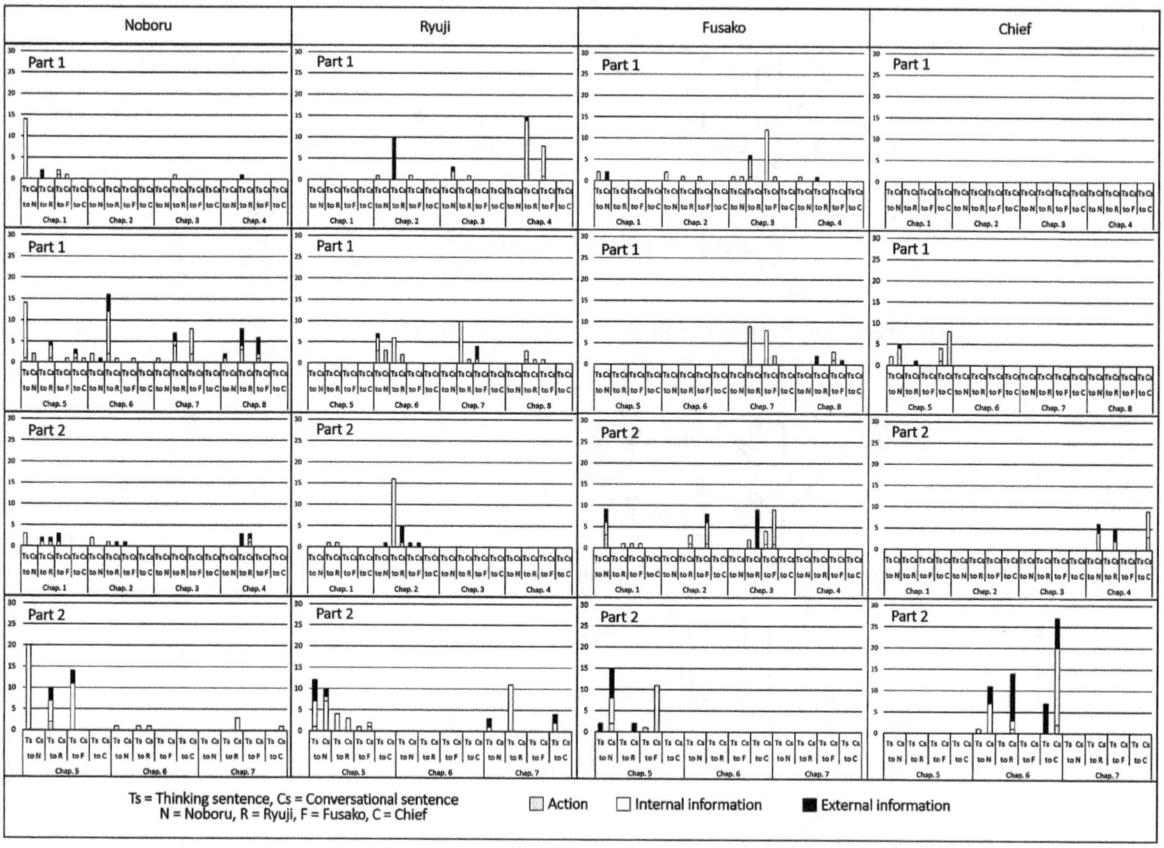

information relating to the chief himself, along with Noboru, and a kind of self-referential information that increases toward the end. The information about Ryūji also increases toward the end of the novel.

Figure 11 shows the descriptive sentences of the narrator. As a whole, although the quantity of actions is higher and some internal information also exists, they are equally distributed among actions, external information, and internal information. This indicates that this novel uses similar techniques as those used in traditional realism novels. Additionally, in Chapter 5 in Part 1, only Noboru and the chief appear and, in the following parts, the chief does not appear in the descriptive sentences until Chapter 6 in Part 2, which is close to the end of this novel. The author of this chapter presumes that Chapter 5, Part 2, is an important section in which an element, che chief, essentially influences the story's progression. In Figure 12, each character as an object to be formed is designed in relatively equal proportion between actions and internal information. Although much information objectifies Noboru and Ryūji throughout the novel, Chapter 5 in Part 1 has a lot of information on the chief, and Chapter 5 in Part 2 includes much information on Fusako.

In the future, it will be possible to discuss the characteristics of *The Sailor Who Fell from Grace with the Sea* using this quantitative information by further elaborating on the above results. At the same time, as an example of narrative generation techniques, the study of narrative simulation will be able to consider that a partial change of information arrangement regarding characters leads to a change in the

Figure 11. Quantitative construction of the other characters' formation by the formation of the subject = narrator

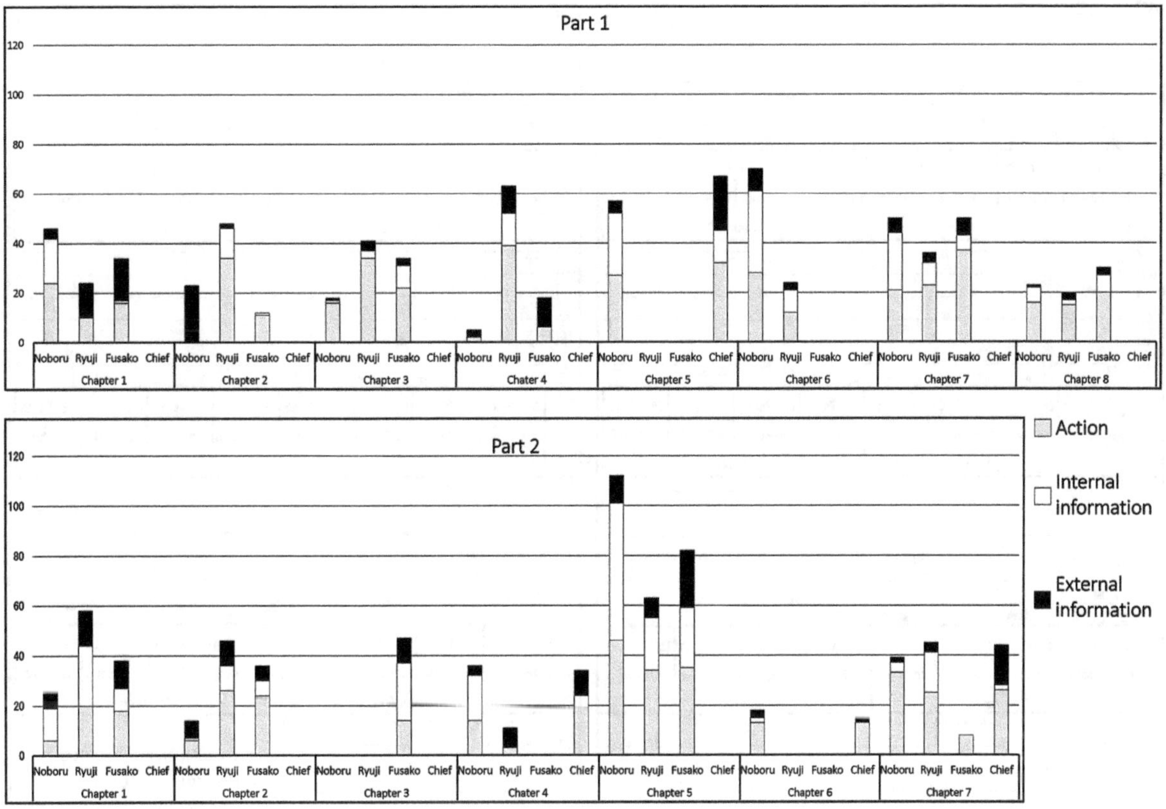

entire structure of the novel. For example, more experimental novels frequently use a technique in which many characters are formed only through actions and external information, and internal information is given only to a selective character (though whether Mishima, who had a strongly classical artistic orientation, was interested in such a direction, is up for discussion). This may also be discussed in relation to the methods that are frequently adopted for remaking or adapting a novel to a movie, for example.

A Qualitative Analysis of Cognitive Information and Its Development

The study and analysis of *The Sailor Who Fell from Grace with the Sea* can be used to understand the semantic problems relating to the dynamics of the development or progression of a narrative.

Semantic Transition of Mutual Cognitive Processes

In this novel, Ryūji and Fusako, after their first meeting, were able to leave each other. They always felt happy when they met again and, they hoped to marry each other in the end. Their cognitive information was gradually increasing with positive commonality. By contrast, the relationship between Ryūji and Noboru deteriorated. Although at first, they both thought that Ryūji is a hero who will someday perform a splendid action (a positive commonality), Ryūji gradually abandoned his vision and dream of becom-

Figure 12. Quantitative construction as subjects of characters' formation

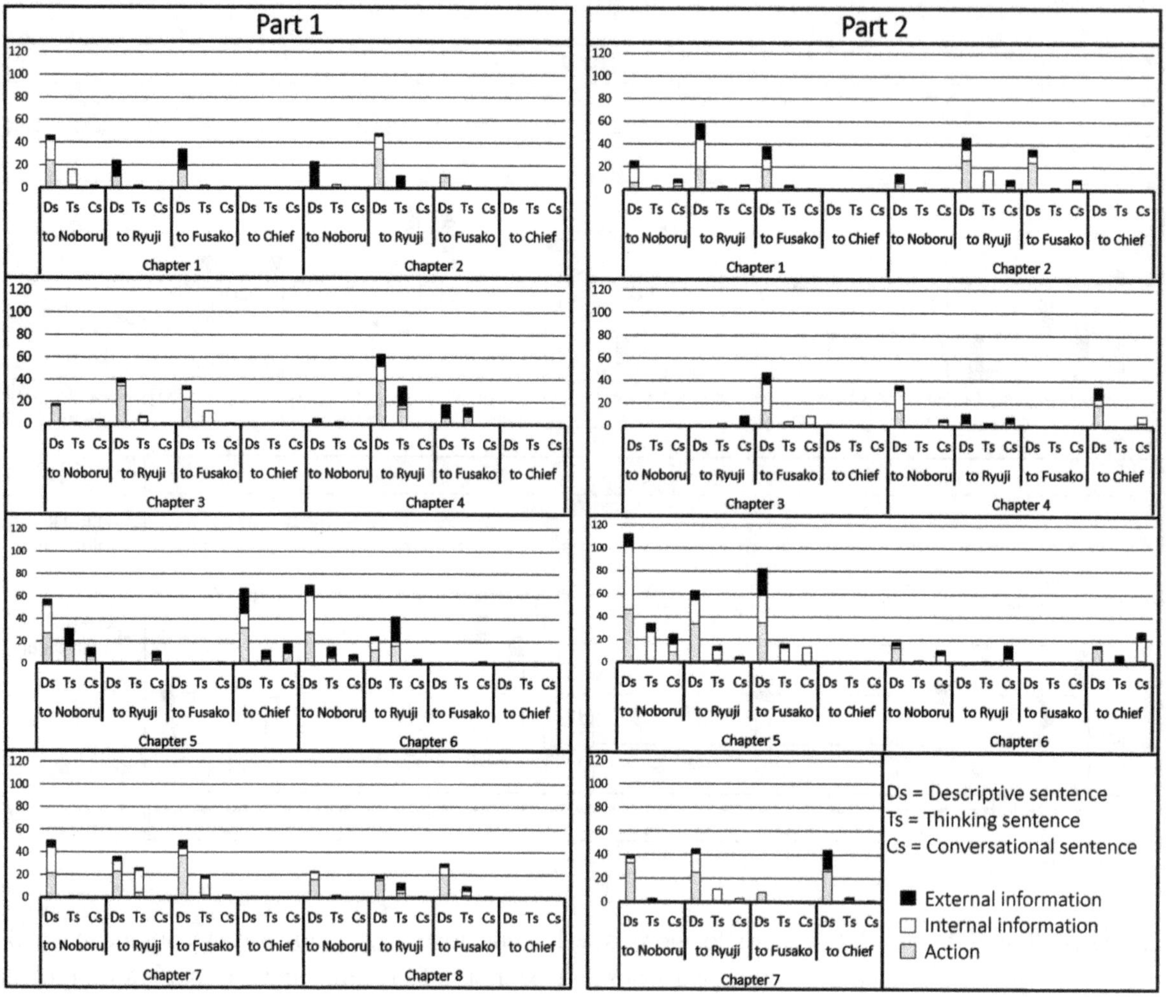

ing a hero and Noboru came to feel disgust for Ryūji (differentiation). Ryūji's feelings toward Noboru basically did not change. However, Noboru's feelings toward Ryūji shifted negatively. In the end, the idea between Noboru and the chief about killing Ryūji matched up (commonality), and the narrative reached a tragic ending. Mutual relationships and changes of cognitive information among the characters produced dynamic characteristics in the story development or progression of the narrative.

As an example of the transition of mutual characters' formation, the author shows the transition of each character's cognitive information toward Ryūji. As shown in Table 7, the entire novel is divided into five parts, and the positions of the mutual cognitive information among the characters is relatively strongly changed.

The author attempted to extract the information using the character information extraction tool to analyze the cognitive information of each character toward Ryūji. This procedure is shown in Table 8, which also includes examples.

Figure 13 shows the transition of cognitive information toward Ryūji by the four characters as acquired through the above procedure. The parts where several characters' rings overlap show the com-

Table 7. Dividing the novel into portions for describing the transition figures of characters' cognitive information

Range	Overview
Part 1: Chapter 1 - 5	Ryuji meets Fusako and Noboru/The existence of Ryuji is informed to the chief
Part 1: Chapter 6 - 8	Conversation between Noboru and Ryuji/Love meetings between Ryuji and Fusako/Departure of Ryuji
Part 2: Chapter 1 - 4	Returning of Ryuji/Ryuji and Fusako decides their marriage
Part 2: Chapter 5	Ryuji and Fusako informe their decision of marriage to Noboru/Peeping of Noboru is known
Part 2: Chapter 6 - 7	Noboru, the chief and other friends dicide to kill Ryuji/Their *michiyuki* to perform his murder

Source: Oikawa and Ogata (2012).

Table 8. Procedure for showing the transition of the cognitive information of characters

<table>
<tr><th>The Overview of Procedure</th><th>Concrete Examples</th></tr>
<tr><td>(1) Extracting the internal and external information from each character to the object to be formed (Ryuji)</td><td rowspan="2">An example of Ryuji himself: ((認知[Cognition] 思考[Thinking]) (部[Part] 1) (章[Chapter] 4) (主体[Subject] 竜二[Ryuji]) (対象[Object] 竜二[Ryuji]) (種類[Kind] 内的[Internal]) (情報[Infomation] 男はいつか全てを捨てて栄光をつかみに行かなければいけない[I'll have to jump out of be and set out alone (for the groly)]))
An example of Noboru: ((認知[Cognition] 思考[Thinking]) (部[Part] 1) (章[Chapter] 5) (主体[Subject] 登[Noboru]) (対象[Object] 竜二[Ryuji]) (種類[Kind] 外的[External]) (情報 [Information] 何かそのうちすばらしいことをやる[I can't exactly, but it'll be something … terrific.]))
An example of Fusako: ((認知[Coginition] 思考[Tinking]) (部[Part] 1) (章[Chapter] 7) (主体[Subject] 房子[Fusako]) (対象[Object] 竜二[Ryuji]) (種類[Kind] 内的[Internal]) (情報 [Information] 夢や幻想にとらわれていない[She was relieved to know that he was not a dreamer]))」
An example of the chief: ((認知[cognition] 思考[Thinking]) (部[Part] 1) (章[Chapter] 5) (主体[Subject] 首領[Chief]) (対象[Object] 竜二[Ryuji]) (種類[Kind] 外的[External]) (情報 [Information] なにもやらない[A guy like that never does anything.]))」</td></tr>
<tr><td>(2) Classifying the above extracting information according to the subject to form</td></tr>
<tr><td rowspan="2">(3) Extracting the information with extraordinary cognitive information and the information with commonality and difference from the above information</td><td>An examples of commonality:
((認知[Cognition] 思考[Thinking]) (部[Part] 1) (章[Chapter] 4) (主体[Subject] 竜二[Ryuji]) (対象[Object] 竜二[Ryuji]) (種類[Kind] 内的[Internal]) (情報[Information] 男はいつか全てを捨てて栄光をつかみに行かなければいけない[I'll have to jump out of be and set out alone (for the groly)]))
((認知[Cognition] 思考[Thinking]) (部[Part] 1) (章[Chapter] 5) (主体[Subject] 登[Noboru]) (対象[Object] 竜二[Ryuji]) (種類[Kind] 外的[External]) (情報[Information] 何かそのうちすばらしいことをやる[I can't exactly, but it'll be something … terrific.]))</td></tr>
<tr><td>An examples of difference:
((認知[Cognition] 思考[Thinking]) (部[Part] 1) (章[Chapter] 5) (主体[Subject] 登[Noboru]) (対象[Object] 竜二[Ryuji]) (種類[Kind] 外的[External]) (情報 何かそのうちすばらしいことをやる[I can't exactly, but it'll be something … terrific.]))
((認知[cognition] 思考[Thinking]) (部[Part] 1) (章[Chapter] 5) (主体[Subject] 首領[Chief]) (対象[Object] 竜二[Ryuji]) (種類[Kind] 外的[External]) (情報[Information] なにもやらない[A guy like that never does anything.]))</td></tr>
</table>

Source: Oikawa and Ogata (2012).

mon cognitive information in the corresponding characters. From these transitions, this novel can be interpreted as a simple narrative of the triangular relationships among Noboru, Ryūji, and Fusako, in which Noboru destroys the real relationship between Ryūji and Fusako to construct an eternal mental relationship between Ryūji and himself.

Figure 13. Transition of each character's cognitive information in his or her relationships with Ryūji
Source: Oikawa and Ogata (2012).

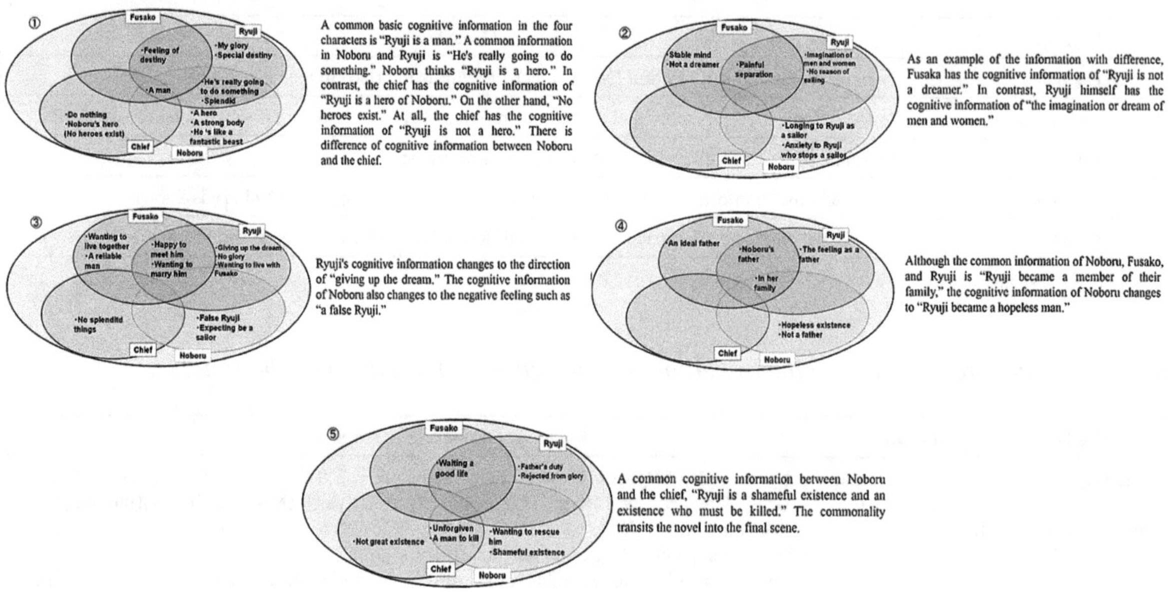

Generating Narrative Variations Using a Combination of the Mutual Relationships of Cognitive Information

Figure 13 showed that the story development in a narrative was driven by the change and transition in commonality and difference in the cognitive information among characters. This figure, at the same time, indicated that such a method can also function as a story generation technique or as one of the technique groups in the narrative generation system. This study was performed on the basis of a plan in which the analytical study is concretely incorporated into the methods of the narrative generation system.

As another issue, in addition to the [commonality/difference] of the cognitive information among the characters shown in the previous section, the author explores a similar but different possibility by adding another constructing element, that is, [recognition/nonrecognition]. "Recognition" means that a character knows the internal information of other characters; in contrast, "nonrecognition" is when a character does not know the internal information of other characters. The contrasting elements of commonality and difference in the previous analysis can also be called [harmony/dissonance]. "Harmony," or commonality, indicates a situation wherein the same internal information is commonly held between two characters. By contrast, "dissonance," or difference, shows a situation wherein the same internal information is not commonly held between two characters. For instance, [A likes B/B likes A] is an example of harmony, but [A likes B/B dislikes A] is an example of dissonance. The form of [A believes B is a hero/B believes A is a hero] can be understood as a transformation of the harmony characteristic. Similarly, [A believes that A is an ordinary person/B believes that A is a hero] is a transformation of the dissonance characteristic. Further, a contrasting element exists in the internal information, [positivity/negativity], but the author does not deal with it here.

By combining the above two kinds of contrasting elements, diverse combinatorial situations can be produced regarding "like/dislike" between A and B: A and B have [harmony] (mutually like or mutually dislike) and mutual [recognition]; A and B have [dissonance] (one likes and the other dislikes) and only A is [recognition]; A and B have [dissonance] and mutual [recognition], A and B have [dissonance] and mutual [nonrecognition]. Such relationships can be a driving power for narrative production and generation and can produce narrative variations. When there are two characters, four combinations of [recognition/nonrecognition] and two combinations of [harmony/dissonance] can be created. There are eight total combinations. Figure 14 shows these cases.

The current author found examples of [recognition/nonrecognition] and [harmony/dissonance] of information in *The Sailor Who Fell from Grace with the Sea*. The right side of Figure 15 shows the thinking cognition information of Noboru and Ryūji in Part 1, Chapter 4 and Chapter 5. Both these parts contain the information that "Ryūji is a splendid person" [harmony], but they respectively do not know it [nonrecognition]. If, at that time, they had mutually recognized [recognition] this information, the ending of this narrative might have been different. Similarly, the left side of Figure 15 shows an example of the [recognition] and [harmony] between Ryūji and Fusako. Additionally, in this case, if the cognitive information had been [nonrecognition] and [dissonance], changes might have occurred in the narrative. Therefore, the author treats the [recognition/nonrecognition] and [harmony/dissonance] in cognitive information as a type of parameter that influences the narrative to produce variations and diversity or developmental possibilities.

Figure 14. Examples of combinations of [recognition/nonrecognition] and [harmony/dissonance] in cognitive information

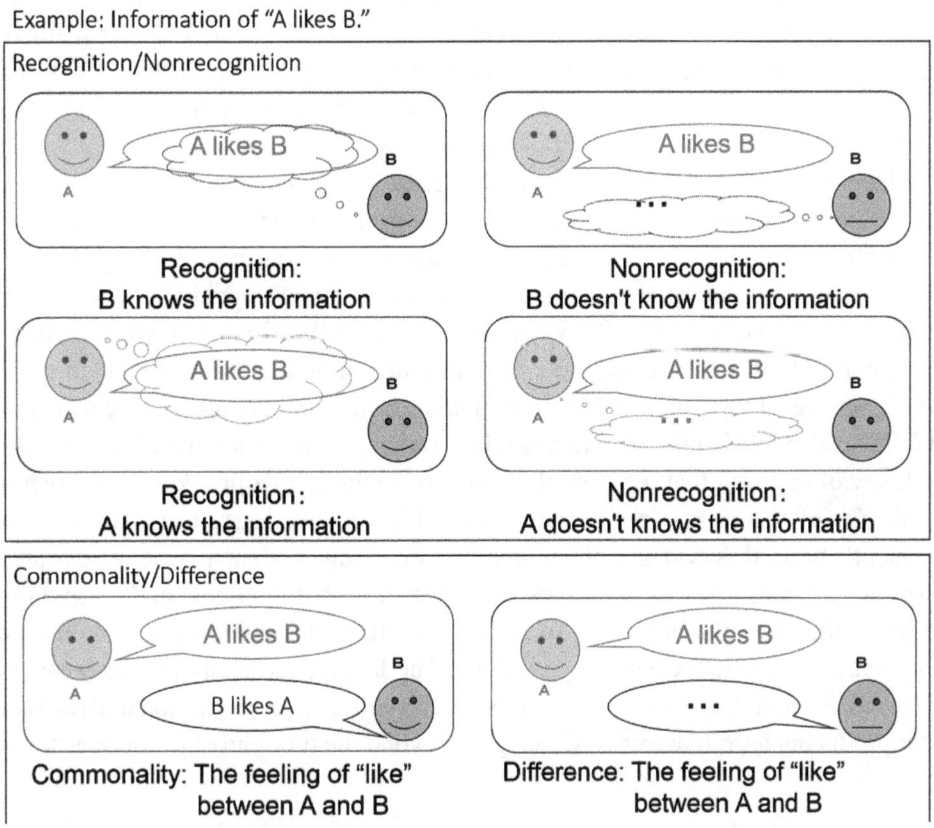

Figure 15. Examples of the cognitive information combinations in The Sailor Who Fell from Grace with the Sea
Source: Oikawa and Ogata (2012).

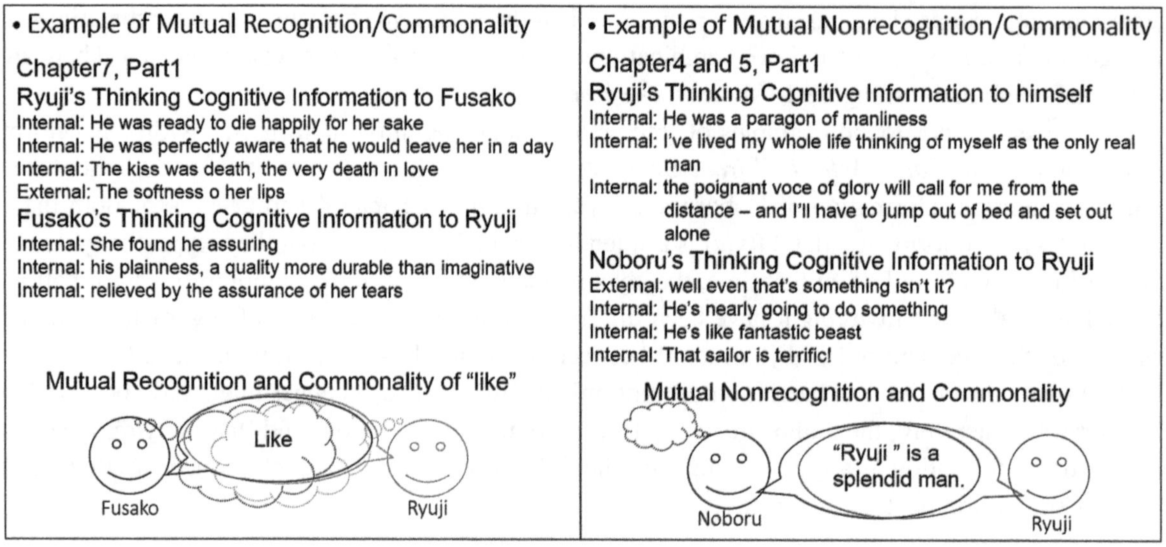

Additionally, as the author will describe in detail in the next section of this chapter, in *kabuki* and *ningyō jōruri*, many works form complicated and, so to speak, strange and extraordinary stories. *Naimaze* ("mixture") (Miura, 2000) is a technique for creating such stories intentionally or methodologically, which basically involves mixing several stories, characters, and places in different works to produce something quite new. For example, Hashimoto (2012) provided a description that included a critique of the incomprehensible and esoteric story of *Honcho Nijushiko* [*Japan's 24 Paragons of Filial Piety*] (1766) by Chikamatsu Hanji (1725-1783), who was a great *ningyō jōruri* writer in Edo era, and his colleagues. Furthermore, complex stories or narrative developments that frequently appear were formed by techniques of mutual recognition between characters and audiences (as mentioned by Oikawa and Ogata [2012]). For instance, in the scenes showing the *seppuku* of Hayano Kanpei in *Kanadehon Chūshingura* [*The Treasury of Loyal Retainers*] (1748) by Namiki Sōsuke (1695-1751) and other writers, the central character, Kampei, did not know about the events that the audiences knew about. In the scene with Kojirō, who is a scapegoat for Taira-no Atsumori in *Ichinotani Futaba Gunki* [*Chronicle of the Battle of Ichinotani*] (1751), also by Namiki Sōsuke and other writers, the story's other characters and the audience do not know of an event that the central characters, including Kojirō, know of. Such bizarre and complex intricacies of a story may not be associated with narrative interest in a simple sense. Rather, they may frequently be used as evidence of low-quality work. However, such stories also provide a unique viewpoint for viewing narratives on stages, especially with regard to *kabuki* and *ningyō jōruri*. There are also readers who rather like such types of stories. Creating such complex or complicated narrative techniques may also stimulate the author's creativity. The fact that so many mysteriously complicated and bizarre narratives exist shows the problems of social, communal, or institutional narrative techniques and norms for producing narrative works, which goes beyond the problem of techniques for simply constructing personal narratives. In any case, these are also the problems relating to narrative multiplicity or the multiple narrative structure model by the author. In this chapter, the author could not discuss the relationship between the form of a narrative and its reception and recognition, that is, audience interest. The discussion of such problems in relationships with narrative multiplicity will be a future research topic.

The Sailor Who Fell from Grace With the Sea and Folktales

Instead of the cognitive mutual relationships among characters, the mechanism in which the stated knowledge, namely the internal information and external information of characters, assimilates a composition or a macro story in *The Sailor Who Fell from Grace with the Sea* can be compared to the structure of folktales on an abstract level. For example, Figure 16 compares *The Sailor Who Fell from Grace with the Sea* to the stories of *The Little Mermaid* (2014) by Hans Christian Andersen (1805-1875), and *Tsuru Nyobo* [*Crane's Return of a Favor*] (2017), a Japanese folktale; all three are narratives. Mishima's novel is simple and similar to folktales and has a beautiful structure like folktales. This fact may be related to the dramatic and theatrical characteristics of this novel.

The next interpretation is frequently possible in folktales: the transition of internal information and external information of the characters in a narrative function used as motivation for an event or action that influences the narrative (story) development or progression. For instance, in *The Little Mermaid*, shown in Figure 17, "a mermaid falls in love with a prince"; the internal information of the mermaid drives events (actions), such as "the mermaid transforms into a human" and "the mermaid walks onto the land." An event (action), "the mermaid disappears in a foam of bubbles," is driven by the external information of the prince, "the prince is marrying a woman different from the mermaid," and internal information of the mermaid, "the mermaid does not want to kill the prince." Similarly, in the case of *The Sailor Who Fell from Grace with the Sea*, as the simplest example, Ryūji's internal information, "Ryūji falls in love with Fusako," drives his action, "Ryūji goes onto the land," as well as Noboru's internal information, "Noboru adores Ryūji, who is a sailor (Noboru falls in love with Ryūji)," and further links to the action, "Noboru tries to kill Ryūji who went onto the land." In this manner, the internal information of a character frequently produces an event (action) and the combination of external information and internal information creates a new event (action). Internal information, external information, and actions in characters operate on each other to drive the story in a narrative.

Figure 16. The similarity of structures between The Sailor Who Fell from Grace with the Sea and folktales
Source: Oikawa and Ogata (2012).

Gogo no Eiko Interpretation (1)	Ryuji came to the land from the sea. Ryuji abandoned his life on the sea. Ryuji no longer seeks only "glory." Ryuji has left the land.	The mermaid surfaces on the sea. The mermaid abandoned her life in the sea. The mermaid refused to return to being a mermaid The mermaid disappeared as foam.	*A Little Mermaid*
Gogo no Eiko Interpretation (2)	Noboru and Ryuji became friends. Noboru wanted Ryuji to be a "hero." Ryuji is no longer a hero. Noboru rejected Ryuji and came to kill Ryuji.	The woman became friends with the elderly couple. The woman said "I do not want you to peek into my room" They broke their promise. The woman became a crane and left the couple.	*Tsuru Nyobo*

Figure 17. Generation of events (actions) from internal information/external information in folktales
Source: Oikawa and Ogata (2012).

The Little Mermaid
[Little Mermaid] Internal information: The mermaid comes to like the prince.
⇒Events: The mermaid loses her voice. The mermaid gains legs. The mermaid goes up onto land.
[Little Mermaid] Internal information: The mermaid does not want to kill the prince.
[Prince] External information: The prince marries a girl who is not the mermaid.
⇒ Events: The mermaid disappears as foam.

Tsuru Nyobo
[Crane] Internal information: The crane wants to return the kindness of the elderly couple.
⇒ Events: The crane turns itself into a young woman and goes to the elderly couple.
[Crane] Internal information: They do not know she is a crane.
[Wife and husband] External information: The elderly couple realize that the young woman is a crane.
⇒ Events: The crane leaves the elderly couple.

Concluding Remarks: What Is the Reality in a Narrative? or Towards the Introduction of a Narrative Generation System

The narrative analysis proposed in this section introduces the problem of inserting the recognition or cognition of characters into a narrative generation system. However, the recognition or cognition here does not refer only to narrow human thoughts but also has a comprehensive meaning relating to the construction of a narrative world, and thoughts and emotions are simply a partial element. In this section, the author presumes that all behaviors generated through a narrative, including the external actions of characters, internal information such as thoughts and emotions, and external information such as names and social characteristics, are the production of the cognitive world of each character, including the narrator, and the story in a narrative is developed from these mutual relationships. In addition, the author believes that the plot construction and language representation for narrative discourse are triggered by the different kind of cognitions by the narrator, which is the cognition directed at the narrative itself and the meta-level cognition for the narrative world. Moreover, a different route, wherein the character's cognition influences the side of narrative discourse too, may be possible. These problems will be considered in future research.

The theme of this section is strongly related to the property information (in particular, property frames) that is held by each character in the mechanism of INGS. In this system's architecture, each noun concept holds the corresponding property frames. In particular, a property frame for a character refers to a set of information that is held at each point on a timeline for defining the information features of a character who appears in the generated narrative—namely, each concrete character. The property frame of a character includes long-term characteristics that are hard to change, such as her/his "name," short-term information that is easy to change, such as "clothing," and intermediate things such as "hobbies" and internal characteristics relating to mentality and emotion. Diverse information, including [recognition/nonrecognition] and [harmony (commonality)/dissonance (difference)], is stored in the property frame of each character to be managed effectively.

At the simplest level, the story corresponds to an image of the world that is viewed through the cognition of a specific character. Of course, this involves cognitive information related to various objects, in addition to the characters, that were not touched on in this section. On a more complex level, the story is a collection where the images of the world, as seen by many characters, including the narrator, are "adjusted" according to various methods. A possible important future issue will contain the following topic: the degree of the above adjustment may decide the range of story processing and narrative discourse processing.

In the extended plan of INGS that was indicated from the analysis and consideration in this section, which is dependent on the cognitive information of characters that is stored and managed in respective property frames, a mechanism that provides for the mutual operation of cognitive information in the property frames of several characters is overlapped onto the above basic strategy. At this level, narrative generation techniques that use various parameters, such as [harmony (commonality)/dissonance (difference)], [recognition/nonrecognition], and [positivity/negativity], are prepared to play an especially important aspect of story generation at the single or combinatorial level.

MULTIPLE NARRATIVE STRUCTURES OF *KABUKI*: STORIES AND PEOPLE

The multiplicity and multilayered characteristics of *kabuki*, as the next section takes up, enable diverse types of reception that are of interest for the various perspectives inherent in the social distribution process. This means that, so to speak, diverse triggers give rise to narrative. The creators, from the viewpoint of distribution strategies including marketing, use various narrative creation mechanisms. The narrative value of multiplicity in *kabuki*, namely the power of imaginative and fictional narrative production, is effective and useful for diverse and differentiated interpretation of its worlds. Further, it enhances the depth of the works.

Although multiplicity or multilayered characteristics may be common in other narrative genres, *kabuki*, which has a long history of over four-hundred years and continues as a living dramatic genre today, is especially multiplicitous due to its synthesis of diverse forms, techniques, and genres. *Kabuki* exists as a concreteness of rich multiplicity.

From a different viewpoint, Fujii (1942-), a poet and researcher of Japanese literature, hypothesized in *Nihon Bungaku Genryū-shi* [*A History of Origins in Japanese Literature*] (2016) that Japanese literature has transitioned from "folktale" to "narrative (in the narrow sense)" and, further, "fantasy." The "folktale," Fujii says, is a form from an era of no character lasting until the beginning of the Nara (710-794) and Heian (794- 1185) eras. The "narrative" is a style originating from the Heian era to the beginning of the Kamakura (1185-1333) and Muromachi eras (1336-1573). "Fantasy" is a form from contemporary society. Although *kabuki* first employed the genre of fantasy, as in old-style-*ningyō jōruri* of the Muromachi era, it also contains elements and styles of earlier folktales and narratives. Fujii has stated that a characteristic of narratives is to indulge within the narration itself and, in contrast, a characteristic of fantasies is to be a narrative that emphasizes structure, development, and conclusion. *Kabuki* certainly emphasizes structure as a dramatic or theatrical art. At the same time, *kabuki*, which partially originated in *katarimono* (narration), is strong in the pleasure of narration itself, which also demonstrates the narrative multiplicity of *kabuki*.

Multiple Narrative Structures in *Kabuki*

As Ogata (2016b) examined its history and characteristics, the author understands *kabuki*, which originated during the beginning of the Edo era, as a rich synthesis of drama and narrative that incorporates a variety of *geinō* (performing arts) genres, such as Japanese dances, *Nō*, *kyōgen* and *ningyō joruri* (puppet drama), and also includes various narrative elements. In the Western tradition, the basis of drama and other narrative forms originated in Aristotle's *Poetics* (1997): that the story or plot ("mythos") manages the other narrative elements such as characters and thoughts. By contrast, in *kabuki*, the story or plot was originally an element that was added to aid comprehension and to help control a collection of performances by an actor or actors. All narrative elements have equal importance in *kabuki*.

According to Kawatake (2003), Shōyō Tsubouchi (1859-1935), a Japanese literary researcher and author of novels and dramas including *kabuki*, compared the non-hierarchical, collective, and comprehensive characteristics of *kabuki* to a "chimera." The author uses this analogy to suggest the "multiplicity" of *kabuki*'s characteristics, applying the model of multiple narrative structures that forms the theoretical basis of the narrative generation study presented here. In particular, *kabuki* uses a variety of *kata*s (forms), which means collections of paternal knowledge relating to the various elements or components in *kabuki*. The typical example is the playing patterns performed by actors in each *kabuki* scene. However, in a wider sense, it includes story patterns and world settings such as characters and narrative stages. The *kata* in *kabuki*, which includes various types as shown above, enables free combination of narrative elements to construct the multiple structures in a work (Watanabe, 2013).

However, it must also be a mistake that Japanese literature is based on different principles from Western literature. For example, discussions concerning differences between narratives and histories were commonly provided by Aristotle (*Poetics*) and Murasaki Shikibu (in the twenty-five chapters (*Firefly*) in *Genji Monogatari*, according to Hikaru Genji). They stated that narratives are means for representing possible truths rather than existing facts and are able to simultaneously express alternative possibilities of representation and interpretation. Likewise, although narratives are often connected to, so to speak, escape, they are frequently associated with the transformation of a reality by showing other realities. Thus, various multiplicities, such as between history and narrative and between fact and truth, are also examples of narrative-related multiplicities.

In addition, the author would like to explain relationships between *kabuki* and narrative in order to avoid some misunderstanding and confusion. In *kabuki*, a narrative means the story or plot in a work in the wider sense of narrative. In contrast, it can also encompass the narration performed by a character on stage, which is a narrower sense of narrative. Both of the narratives form partial elements of an entire *kabuki*. However, the concept of narrative discussed here has wider and more comprehensive meanings, which also includes the level of representation or expression in addition to levels of story and plot. The media for representation or expression include language, music, image and, further, body. From the author's viewpoint, an entire *kabuki* stage corresponds to a narrative. In this sense, the narrative generation of *kabuki* naturally has the meaning of generating the entire performance of a *kabuki* play.

Ogata (2016b) surveyed and analyzed the themes of *kabuki* shown below: (1) Real incident, (2) Work, (3) Genre, (4) Material or topic, (5) Person, (6) Story and plot, (7) Actor and place, (8) Time (era or age), (9) Style (form or pattern), (10) Theatre (stage and seating), (11) Audience, (12) Text, (13) Production of scenario (*daichō*), (14) Direction, and (15) Stage performance. The following description shows these overviews.

1. **Real Incident:** Stories or plots in *kabuki* are frequently constructed based on actual or real incidents. An incident is composed of several events that have several necessary elements, such as characters. They typically use historical sets of events that have been repeatedly introduced and arranged in many *kabuki* works. At the same time, many works were made using contemporary social events in each era as the materials. The relationships between real elements and fiction were not simple.

Frequently, the fictional figure based on a real event or character conversely influenced the actual image of the event or character.

2. **Work:** *Kabuki* work is frequently revised from another work, for the following various reasons: In the Edo era, consciousness of authorship was very weak in *kabuki* creators; a main method of industrial enterprise was based on adapting a work on a case-by-case basis and arbitrarily to characteristics of the actors and theatres (*shibai-goya*). This frequently accompanied the next transboundary of genres.
3. **Genre:** *Kabuki* is a collection of many existing genres and formed as the mixed whole of the next elements: dramas including *Nō, kyōgen* and *ningyō jōruri*; Japanese dances; katarimono (narration) including *Heike Monogatari* (1991-1993) and *sekkyōbushi* (Sekkyō, 1998); Edo novels; musical genres including music for *Nō* and *kyōgen, shamisen* music in the Edo era, and music for *katarimono* including *Gidayūbushi*. Furthermore, recently, new types of *kabuki* are beginning to appear using animation and computer graphics.
4. **Material or Topic:** *Kabuki* frequently uses common materials and themes. This is related to sequential production, such as producing a work based on a material link to the previous work. The editing of the materials is closely related to the editing of the works. The materials here are not necessarily real events. If a material originally relies on a real incident or event, it can also be adapted for efficient narrativity. Such selection of multiple materials depended on the organization of the "world (*sekai*)" that produced *kabuki* rather than the arbitrary preferences of particular authors.
5. **Person:** A "person" in *kabuki* is either an "actor," a "(dramatic) character," or a "real person." The actor performs on stage and the character is part of the narrative of a work. The three types of persons form very large multiplicities themselves and in their relationships to the temporal and spatial levels of the work. The first person, as an actor or performer, plays a dramatic character in the work on the stage. At the same time, the existence of the real actor who has a name also has a large and essential meaning and, further, has a story through the "name" that has been inherited temporarily. On the other hand, the person as a dramatic character is, in many cases, not the person limited to only a work and appears in other *kabuki* works, works in different genres, histories as non-fiction, and so on.
6. **Story and Plot:** A work is frequently composed of a collection of diverse elements and components that are too hard to call one work. A side-story is enlarged to become a large drama and a character who is an original hero becomes a mere subsidiary character to make a series of narratives. In some cases, the mutual relationships among each part seem arbitrary and in other cases the styles of narrative development are very weak.
7. **Actor and Place:** Watanabe (1989) mentioned that a limited number of actors in theatre troupes would have had large repertories of *kabuki*, and so would perform a variety of dramatic characters in diverse narratives. The characters and a stage (place) were covered by the assets of the theatre troupe. The characters are classified into relatively few categories and each character who has a concrete name is of one category. Concurrently, several different characters can also be categorized into a category, and an actor is able to perform them by changing costume and makeup. The place and stage are also based on basic principles and composed in combination with characters according to the dramas to be played. *Kabuki* is a system that enables an actor to play many different character roles using a limited number of costumes, as well as the closely related maquillage and combinatorial composition.

8. **Time (Era or Age):** Different historical times are frequently mixed or overlapped in *kabuki* plays. Regardless of historical setting, features of the Edo era frequently appear, from stage and place, to furnishings, costumes, speech, scenes, and backgrounds.
9. **Style (Form or Pattern):** "Style (form or pattern)" here is used to mean "performing style," in which many *geinō* elements are adopted onstage in *kabuki* plays, such as Japanese dance, music, narration, and other actor styles. There are a variety of patterns of multiplicity and diverse possibilities dependent upon the constraints of the prepared elements and combinations. For instance, the music can include many genres, such as *nagauta*, *kiyomoto*, *tokiwazu*, and others. The historical multiplicities of actor forms are inherited age to age. The narration of *takemoto* has the characteristic of continuity and cutting from *ningyō jōruri*.
10. **Theatre (Stage and Seating):** The traditional dramas of Japan incorporate the theatre itself as a necessary piece of particular genres. The basic principle was not that theatres and stages are universal spaces that exist for performance of various genres. Traditionally, respective theatres and stages for *Nō*, *ningyō jōruri*, and *kabuki*, have existed. An outstanding feature of the theatres of *kabuki* is *hanamichi*, which is used to create appearances, to leave a character, and so on.
11. **Audience:** *Kabuki* is primarily an object to be viewed at the theatre by an audience and is closely, essentially, and mutually bound with the existence of the theatre. As seen in the examples of the *hanamichi* and *kakegoe*, the audience also plays a part in the multiple iterations of *kabuki*.
12. **Text:** Reading (receiving) novels and poems is an experience through which a person interprets the physical characters of movable type in a paper book (or today an electronic book that imitates a paper book). A line of characters themselves is a text. By contrast, receiving a play from the stage is, in the primary sense, to perceive humans' physical actions that the actors perform, as well as the equipment and decor (symbolic stage settings). Unlike a book, an onstage play is not a representation solely based on the enumeration of words, but is also a collection of bodily actions and sometimes the stage itself accompanying these actions. *Kabuki* has a long tradition of essays and criticisms originating with *Yakusha Hyōbanki* ("Actors Reputation Record") in the Edo era (Taguchi, 2011), which was a series of books that mainly commented on *kabuki* actors and their performances. The style has been persistently dependent upon the fact that an audience views a *kabuki* play onstage at a theatre. At the same time, *kabuki* has another type of text on the level corresponding to "scenarios" or "scripts." Unlike the above multiplicity of texts, there are also multiple relationships among different genres, such as the multiplicity of transformational relationships among different genres, like *Nō* and *kabuki*, *kyōgen*, and *ningyō jōruri* and *kabuki*.
13. **Production of Scenario (*Daichō*):** The production of *kabuki* scenarios has historically strengthened collaborative production, from the production of the first works with the characteristics of a freak show and dance, to the systematic production of large-scale and complex. Collaborative production is a method through which the *kabuki* scenario is completed by several writers.
14. **Direction:** The mixed features of "time (era)" and the related "place (stage)" influence the "direction" of the actual stage. Recombining costumes, speech, and music is standard in *kabuki*. Because makeup and costume are made according to each character's paternal form, features such as realistic consistency and naturalness is not considered frequently. This is formal and stylistic characteristic of *kabuki*.
15. **Stage Performance:** Because *kabuki* was contemporary to the Edo era, each performance of a new work was done in the form of *tōshi jōen*, in which an entire play was performed uninterrupted. However, a new play was not always performed in this manner, but according to more complex

rules. A typical performance form was that of a *jidai-mono* or *sewa-mono* work. In contrast, after the Meiji era, many new *kabuki* works, such as *shin-kabuki* (new *kabuki*), were written, because classical Edo *kabuki* had been performed repeatedly and the form of *midori jōen*, which began in Osaka in the Edo era, was generalized. The *midori jōen* is a form in which only a part of a work (a *dan* corresponding to an act, a *ba* corresponding to a scene in a *dan*, or an edited part of several *dans* or *bas*) is played to make a *kabuki* performance through a collection of several parts.

Story in *Kabuki*

The author would like to consider story (scenario) in *kabuki*. Firstly, the multiplicity that is realized in various levels and combinations in the narratives of *kabuki*, in the wide sense that the author has stated, must produce a kind of difficulty in perceiving *kabuki*. In the plays of *kabuki*, there are simple and clear scenarios, such as *Kanjinchō* [*The Subscription List*] (1840), and many plays have rather compressed stories in only a *dan* or a *ba*. This is a reason that a performance of the *midori jōen* is effectively possible. In addition, if a scenario here is seized as a concept similar to a plot, although plot is a wider concept than story, plot can be regarded as similar to story because many scenarios of *kabuki* are constructed according to a story's progression.

However, a story or a scenario of *kabuki*, as a whole, seems to be embraced by mysterious multiplicities. One aspect of these multiplicities is partially presented in "Story or Plot" in the above list. Moreover, the connection among each part often seems arbitrary and the development method is, so to speak, weak in many cases. In a part of a drama, such as a *dan*, there is at a glance a dull and weak progression from the first part to the middle part. However, afterwards, before we know it in many cases, triggered by a kind of metamorphosis of a main character, the story expressively rises to the climax. This metamorphosis is frequently introduced into a play through the pattern of an ordinary character that was "actually" an extraordinary character. Also, as a whole, this creates a necessity or tightness distinct from modern and contemporary literature, as if the components of a composition are simply and arbitrarily connected. A narrative of *kabuki* is not, perhaps, something that is constructed only from the object of performance in a single time and place. It is formed as the whole of a play, including the narrative of the *kabuki* play, and further in the multiple relationships with the diverse elements of the environment that surrounds it. Accordingly, like in the real world, the relationships among events and various other elements may admittedly seem arbitrary. Furthermore, although each part of a play may frequently be rather monotonous, when they multiply connect to the other elements, they appear in an inevitable figure as if other possibilities cannot be imagined. In addition to the heaviness that other possibilities cannot be imagined, a heaviness of selection also links to reality. On the level of a scenario or story, in a part or in the whole, the author thinks that the true pleasure of viewing a *kabuki* play is to experience, in the temporal experience of an actual theatre, the qualitative transformation of a decidedly worldly setting to an inextricably involved and inevitable narrative that is gradually and qualitatively realized in an unexpected form.

For example, in the episodes regarding Okaru and Kanpei in *Kanadehon Chūshingura* [*The Treasury of Loyal Retainers*] (1748), although the complications and changes can be treated as techniques based on a strong characteristic of adaptation, the complexity of this revision must be of a reason that produces a sense of inevitability and existentiality to the audience when the accumulation of contingency from the first part of the story is recognized. As another example, in *Sukeroku Yukari no Edo-zakura* [*Sukeroku: Flower of Edo*] (1733), the tight ending exposes the *Soga-mono*, one of the typical *katas* (patterns) of story, character, and place in revenge tales, which follows radically and dramatically on a monotonic and enumerative introduction of characters. Concerning changes that are not sufficiently realistic to pierce these scenarios and stories, the inevitability and existentiality might be ensured to a considerable extent by the external, environmental, contextual, and situational knowledge of era's generation. However, in the current society in which such environments and contexts have been lost, the complicated features in the stories of *kabuki* remain an essential element of entertainment.

A book by Osamu Inumaru (2005), *Tenpō Jūichinen no Chūshingura: Tsuruya Namboku Kamikakete Sango Taisetsu wo Yomu*, demonstrates the multiplicity of *kabuki*'s stories. This book is a unique effort to restore a book on *kabuki* at Kawarasaki-za (in Edo) in Tenpō 11 (1840), from a total title, *Kibakazari Chūshingura* (1840). "Kibakazari" means "horse ornament." This title refers to an edited whole in which several existing plays are combined. This synthesis was planned by Namiki Gohei III (1789-1855). As a sequence of plays in *Kibakazari Chūshingura*, *Sayogoromo Oshidori no Tsurugiba* (1739) by Namiki Sōsuke (1695-1751) is makes up the first part, and *Tōkaidō Yotsuya Kaidan* [The *Ghost Stories at Yotsuya on the Tōkaidō*] (1825) and *Kamikakete Sango Taisetsu* (1825) by Tsuruya Namboku IV (1755-1829) follow.

Sayogoromo Oshidori no Tsurugiba is a work by a *ningyō jōruri* author, Namiki Sōsuke, who wrote one of the most famous *ningyō jōruri* plays in *Chūshingura-mono*, *Kanadehon Chūshingura*, with Takeda Izumo II (1691-1756) and Miyoshi Shōraku (17th-18th centuries). This play features a largely different character formation and story development in Kō-no Moronao and Enya Hangan, the two main characters in *Kanadehon Chūshingura*, from their images in the following *Chūshingura-mono*. The setting of this play is the world of *Taiheiki* [*Record of the Great Peace*] (1960-1962) in the era of Muromachi, which is directly passed on to *Kanadehon Chūshingura*. On the other hand, *Tōkaidō Yotsuya Kaidan* was the most representative play of the side stories in *Kanadehon Chūshingura*. The hero of this play is Tamiya Iemon, who had been a retainer of the Enya family, from whom he was banished after stealing. The last *Kamikakete Sango Taisetsu* was also a *Chūshingura-mono*, and a side story of *Kanadehon Chūshingura*. This play described a love and crazed revenge by the main character, Fuwa Kazuemon who has another name, Satsuma Gengobei, of a branch of the Enya family. Unlike Tamiya Iemon, Fuwa Kazuemon finally participates to the laid to Kira's residence of the Akō samurais. This last play was also a parody or adaptation of *Godairiki Koi no Fūjime* [*Five Great Powers that Secure Love*] (1794), which was a great work of *kabuki* by Namiki Gohei I (1747-1808).

As mentioned above, the work called *Kibakazari Chūshingura* was not a simple collection of the above narratives but was repeatedly adapted. The following description explains this point: the origin of the narrative of *Sayogoromo Oshidori no Tsurugiba*, the first part of *Kibakazari Chūshingura*, is an episode in *Taiheiki* called *Enya Hangan Zanshi no Koto* (an event of the tragic death of Enya Hangan) (in the Volume 21 of *Taiheiki*). In this episode, Kō-no Moronao, who was a vassal of the Ashikaga family, was attracted by the beauty of the wife of Enya Hangan, who was a daughter of Sanada no Miya. Moronao wanted to get her. However, she rejected him in a *waka* (short poem) in *Shin Kokin Waka Shū* (1959), "*Sanakida ni Omoki ga Ue no Sayogoromo Waga Tsuma Naranu Tsuma na Kasaneso*" (This short poem means "don't have two husbands"). As a result, Moronao slandered Enya Hangan to Ashikaga Takauji (1305-1358), the shogun of the Ashikaga shogunate, and the wife of Enya was killed in a fire along with his whole clan and finally Enya himself, who performed *seppuku*. Namiki Sōsuke, using this episode as material, largely remade the narrative of the one-sided Enya's collapse into a complex narrative around politics and love or *giri* (justice or duty), and *ninjou* (human feeling). In this narrative, both Kō-no Moronao and Enya Hangan are beautiful young men who put their whole heart and soul into their respective loyalties. Moronao's unrequited love of the wife of Enya Hangan, Kahoyo, hides his true intention. In addition, a tragic love story between Moronao and his wife, Taema, is also central to this story. Furthermore, this narrative, which was originally written as a scenario of *ningyō jōruri*, was, in an entire *Kibakazari Chūshingura*, a drama that was seen as a dream by Ōboshi Yuranosuke, who was a hero of *Chūshingura-mono*, including *Kanadeon Chūshingura* as a typical play. According to a tendency in *kabuki* and *ningyō jōruri*, the dream scene is performed behind a *taremaku* (drop curtain) on which a "心" (*kokoro*, mind) is drawn. The setting of *Taiheiki* itself was directly inherited by *Kanadehon Chūshingura* and, therefore, Kira Kōzukenosuke Yoshihisa (1641-1703) in the real history directly became Kōno Moronao and similarly Asano Takuminokami Naganori (1667-1701) also became Enya Hangan. However, as people know, the relationship between both characters in *Kanadehon Chūshingura* is rather similar to *Taiheiki*. In this common scenario, Moronao's one-sided love of Kahoyo causes continuous tragedy and comedy in this long and complicated theatrical narrative. Further, in *Tōkaidō Yotsuya Kaidan*, the setting of *Taiheiki* largely reverted. Tamiya Iemon, the failed Kayano Kanpei, and one other defect to the side of Kō-no Moronao and push him into his last act of destruction, dreaming of a happy life with his wife, Oiwa. However, another and more crazed killer, Satsuma Gengobei, a devil hero in *Kamikakete Sango Taisetsu*, is welcome by the masterless samurai Akō, or Ōboshi Yuranosuke, as their boss or don, and continues his extreme murders and finally transforms in a flash into a justified samurai who majestically returns to the samurai group of Akō for revenge against Kira Kōzukenosuke. This work is also a side story of *Chūshingura* and, at the same time, utilizes a mechanism in which a tragedy is caused by the magic symbol of "五大力 -> 三五大切 (Godairiki -> Sango Taisetsu)," cited from a great *kabuki* play as an extreme love story in the Edo era, *Godairiki Koi no Fūjime*. In this story, Sangorō and his lover, Koman, who deceived a masterless samurai, Satsuma Gengobei, steal money from Gengobei to give to Kazuemon, so that he might get revenge. After all, they were killed by Satsuma Gengobei, who is actually Fuwa Kazuemon. This bizarre story is extremely complex but logical. As described above, the element of story (scenario) does not exist independently, but as multiple relations with other diverse elements as described below:

- **Real Event:** *Taiheiki* has been treated as a historical book, and the events of Akō have also been recognized as historical fact.
- **Work:** The literary sequence from a work to another work and the continuation are seen.
- **Genre:** There are variations on genres, such as *Taiheiki* as a historical narrative, *Sayogoromo Oshidori no Tsurugiba* and *Kanadehon Chūshingura* as *ningyō jōruri* plays, and *Godairiki Koi no Fūjime*, *Tōkaidō Yotsuya Kaidan* and *Kamikakete Sango Taisetsu* originally written as *kabuki* plays.
- **Material or Topic:** For example, *Chūshingura-mono* served as a setting material, and the magic word of *Godairiki* served as a motif used in several works.
- **Person:** In particular, both Kō-no Moronao and Enya Hangan are regarded as actual historical persons. At the same time, in *Kanadehon Chūshingura*, Kira Kōzukenosuke Yoshihisa and Asano Takuminokami Naganori are largely different from their actual historical selves. In addition, this *kabuki* play was, in the Kawarasaki-za in Edo, performed by Ichikawa Ebizō V (previously Ichikawa Danjūrō VII) (1791-1859), Onoe Eizaburō III (later Onoe Kikugorō IV) (1808-1860), Ichikawa Danzaburō V (?-1854), and the other actors.
- **Time (Era):** As an ordinary style of *kabuki*, the Muromachi era (past) and Edo era (now) were dealt with by mixing these sequence of plays.

- **Theatre (Stage and Seats):** Kawarasaki-za in Edo, which was a theatre that had an extraordinary and temporary meaning, was used.
- **Production, Direction, and Stage Play of Scenarios (*Daichōs*):** Larger and comprehensive plays for actual stages were fluidly produced to contain several plays or parts.

Person in *Kabuki*

In *kabuki*, there are various kinds of "persons," such as "actors (or performers)," "(dramatic) characters" and "real persons." These temporally and spatially form and possess multiple existences and relationships.

First, the actor performs a character on a *kabuki* stage. However, the actor him or herself has a very important and essential value as well. In *kabuki*, "an actor plays" sometimes has meaning more important than in universal dramas that focus on characters. Originally, through the Edo era, a *kabuki* scenario (*daichō*) was not written using the characters' names but using the actors' names. In other words, many *kabuki* scenarios were written to emphasize and strengthen the personalities and characteristics of actors or performers.

Although the actor is a human who has a real body, a real person in *kabuki* is further divided into the following two parts: the real actor who is represented by his "stage name," and the real human who is symbolized by his "real name." These correspond to the spatial forms of a person. On the contrary, another unique point is the fact that a stage name, in many cases, has a temporal tradition and a history or a kind of story that is inherited over generations. This means that actors who retain stage names through a variety of different performances exist at each point in continuity with other "real" persons. An actor is located in a temporal and historical continuity. Thus, the existences of various persons and stories can be multiplied in various ways.

On the other hand, a "person" as a character is not limited to a single *kabuki* play. A certain character in a work, for instance, can occasionally appear in other *kabuki* plays, other works in other genres, non-fictional histories, etc. A character is, thus, an existence who represents a particular scenario in relation to the other appearances in the temporal and spatial situations of *kabuki*. A character overlaps with her or his appearances in other *kabuki* plays and other genres.

One great contemporary *kabuki* actor, Bando Tamasaburō V (1950-), has a multiplicitous identity, as seen below:

- He is a man and his real name is Morita Shinichi. He is a son-in-law of Morita Kan'ya VIV (1907-1977).
- He has a history of acting and inherited his name "Bando Tamasaburō" from his adoptive father. His name further links to the past persons (actors) having the same name.
- He is an actor who has performed many different characters in many classical *kabuki* plays.
- He is an innovator and successor of a new tradition who has introduced new dramas from other *kabuki*-related genres, such as *Tenshu Monogatari* [*Castle Tower Story*] based on a play by Izumi Kyōka (1917), into *kabuki* to grow them in the context of *kabuki*.
- He is a director of diverse plays in the *kabuki* genre.
- He is a performer and artist who transcends the boundaries of genres such as Japanese dance, classical Chinese opera, and reading aloud.
- He is a movie director whose works include *Tenshu Monogatari* (Bando, 1995), based on a play by Izumi Kyōka (1917).

- In recent years, he has fulfilled the role of an educator and has trained many *kabuki* actors by performing with them.

Discussing *onnagata* is necessary in order to understand the "person" of *kabuki*. Although *kabuki* originated in *yūjo* ("prostitutes") *kabuki*, the transition from *wakashu* ("boys") *kabuki* to *yarō* ("adult men") *kabuki* transformed it into a drama genre performed by adult men only (Kawatake, 1992, 2003). Real women do not appear on the *kabuki* stage; however, actors, as *onnagata*, further exhibit the multiplicity of *kabuki* by incorporating real men's sexuality. As *onnagata* is considered to be one of the most important and extraordinary elements that contributes to the attractiveness of *kabuki*, it has been the focus of many discussions.

To consider the "person," the transformation of characters according to the motif of *jitsuha* ("actually") (Gunji, 1963; Imao, 1970;) also plays an important role in *kabuki*, which is simultaneously strongly related to the problem of *geinō* styles. Many characters in *kabuki* are multiplexed and present complex images through manipulation of the *jitsuha*. In many cases, the transformation of the *jitsuha* is created by transforming the character of an unknown commoner into a famous and historical character, namely a hero or a heroine. Two contrasting sub-genres in *kabuki*, the *sewa-mono* and *jidai-mono*, are related to this feature. The *sewa-mono* is a comparatively realistic *kabuki* genre where the characters are common people. By contrast, the *jidai-mono* is a relatively formal and stylistic *kabuki* genre based on historical worlds and characters. Concurrently, these are also used as concepts to show the performance styles of *kabuki* actors. The styles of the *sewa-mono* frequently merge with the style of *jidai-mono* to create a unique impression. In the *jidai-mono*, the transformation of a character through the *jitsuha* occasionally triggers movement from a *sewa*-style scene to an original *jidai*-style scene. Further, these concepts, *sewa-mono* and *jidai-mono* or *sewa* and *jidai*, sometimes appear in the micro performances of a character.

For example, in a *sewa-mono kabuki*, a character or an actor occasionally acts and speaks in the *jidai-mono* style. *Sewa-mono* and *jidai-mono* or *sewa* and *jidai* are concepts that show two types of *kabuki* performance styles or forms, namely realism (*sewa*) and formalism (*jidai*). The multiple rhythms through which the formal style is inserted into the realistic style, and the contrary rhythm through which the real style is inserted into the formal style, produces a unique spectacle on the *kabuki* stage.

Moreover, there are two performing styles of actors: actors based on *jidai* and actors dependent on *sewa*. A famous example was Nakamura Kichiemon I (1886-1954), who was based on *jidai*, and Onoe Kikugorō VI (1885-1949), based on *sewa*. They were longtime co-performers and their collaborative performances themselves created a unique rhythm based on the alteration or harmony between *jidai* and *sewa*. Their basic styles and collaborative features as an established tradition have been inherited by the present Nakamura Kichiemon II (1944-) and Onoe Kikugorō VII (1942-).

NARRATIVE GENERATION OR SIMULATION DESIGN BASED ON ANALYSES OF MISHIMA AND *KABUKI*: SIMPLE EXAMPLES

The following section bridges the narrative analyses of Mishima and *kabuki* into concrete narrative simulations using INGS and GIS. The details of INGS were presented in the introduction of Ogata's (2016a) "Computational and Cognitive Approaches to Narratology," while the introduction of this book, as well as this chapter, provides overviews.

INGS is a mechanism that systematizes narrative generation and the reception process. In the author's framework, narrative generation in the wide sense is dealt with in two types of processes: narrative generation and the reception process, as well as narrative production and the consumption process. The former corresponds to narrative generation on the personal level, whereas the latter is equal to narrative generation on the level of social distribution. That is, INGS is equivalent to a narrative generation system that corresponds to the personal level. On the other hand, narrative generation as social distribution is analyzed by another narrative generation system, the *Geino* Information System (GIS), which was explained by Ogata (2016b) as well as in the introduction of this book.

Narrative Simulation Based on the Analysis of a Novel by Mishima: A Simple Example

The author tries to simulate the result of analyzing a novel by Mishima using several functions of INGS to expand this system's architecture. This trial focuses on each character's actions and thoughts to generate a narrative as a whole by combining each character's simulations. In this framework, a story is constructed with a collection of each character's actions and thoughts. Since a story in the current INGS has a hierarchical structure, this new model requires the consideration of an extended form for story representation. Therefore, these attempts at developing extended applications will contribute to the expansion of the INGS architecture. In particular, the author experimentally presents a narrative simulation mechanism to realize a model of narrative reality construction composed of the actions and thoughts of several characters, as well as their mutual relationships as explicit character agents and partial narrative generation functions based on the character agents.

The experimental system inputs characters' internal information to generate short stories or scripts using a knowledge base that stores scripts. This small program admits two characters. The internal information of each character composed of "goal," "desire", "cognition." The "goal" defines each character's final objective and the "desire" shows the desire that each character has. On the other hand, the "cognition" means the degree that a character knows the internal information of the other character and the character himself/herself. In the mechanism of the program, "goal" contributes to select a script as the core of generated stories. In contrast, the "desire" and "cognition" control to select one or more scripts (sub-scripts) that the system uses in the generation process of the program. In addition, in the experimental system, a (sub-)script is not repeatedly used. A script contains a verb concept and the following symbols: "<desc-X>" is used to insert the explanation of a character's internal information; "<sub>" calls a sub-script; "<end>" finishes a generation processing. The descriptive form of each script is if-then form and a rule refers to the information that is stores in the "cognition." The following is the algorithm:

1. Based on the internal information of a character, the system decides a core script.
2. The system sequentially reads the elements of the script to perform the respective adequate procedures including the following types:
    a. *Verb* (a real verb concept): The system generates an event including character A and B.
    b. "<desc-X>": "X" is a variable for character A or B. The system generates the explanation of the corresponding character. Each explanation is transformed into the corresponding sentence.
    c. "<sub>": The system calls a sub-script for recursive processing. (In this experimental program, the desires of A and B are neccearily different and, based on the following four cases of recognition/nonrecognition of the differece, four kinds of sub-scripts are used:

i. A [recognition]/B [nonrecognition] -> ”intentional betrayal” sub-script
ii. A [nonrecognition]/B [recognition] -> “non intentional betrayal and the blocking” sub-script
iii. A [cognition]/B [cognition] -> “intentional betrayal and the blocking” sub-script
iv. A [nonrecognition]/B [nonrecognition] -> “non intentional betrayal” sub-script

d. “<end>”: The system finishes a generation cycle.

3. Finally, the system sequentially outputs all of the generated sentences.

Figure 18 shows input examples and generated or output story sentences in cases of the (3)-a) and c).

GIS or “GIS Including INGS”

The author has been studying *kabuki* in order to introduce the acquired knowledge into the INGS and GIS systems. This means that the author has been studying *kabuki* from the viewpoint of the multiple narrative structures model. The author generally considers a narrative work’s generation and production processes from the perspective of composition through multiple narrative structures. For example, a narrative’s flow comprises the multiple structures of a story in a semantic flow and a plot in a constructive one. A *kabuki* narrative is a particularly rich object for the multiple narrative structures model. For example, the author has analyzed the multiplicity of *kabuki* regarding fifteen kinds of elements or components. One element is “person.” A “person” in *kabuki* can be divided into the following three aspects: the real “person,” who lives in the actual world; the “person” as an actor who has a history of performing roles; and the “person” of one or more *kabuki* characters that appear on the stage. Each person has their own

Figure 18. A simple simulation based on the mental models of two characters

Example (1)
Input:
```
(((ID A) (goal 夏期講習[summer seminar]) (desire リード[lead]) (cognition (B (desire 拮抗[rivalry])))) ((ID B) (goal 夏期講習[summer seminar]) (desire 拮抗[rivalry]) (cognition nil))))
```
Output:
Aの目的は「夏期講習」である。Aは、密かにリードしたいと思っている。AがBを見舞う。BがAを待つ。Bの目的は「夏期講習」である。Bは、密かに拮抗したいと思っている。Bが起き上がる。BがAと夏期講習について話す。Aが嘘をつく。Aが逃げる。BがAを見送る。Aが夏期講習に行く。Bが裏切りを知る[A’s purpose is taking the “summer seminar.” A wants to lead in study. A inquires after B. B waits for A. B’s purpose is taking the “summer seminar.” B wants to rival A. B gets up. B talks to A about the “summer seminar.” A lies to B that A don’t take the “summer seminar.” A escapes from B. A takes the “summer seminar.” B knows that B was betrayed by A.]

Example (2)
Input:
```
(((ID A) (goal 夏期講習[summer seminar]) (desire リード[lead]) (cognition (B (desire 拮抗[rivalry])))) ((ID B) (goal 夏期講習[summer seminar]) (desire 拮抗[rivalry]) (cognition (A (desire リード[lead]))))))
```
Output:
Aの目的は「夏期講習」である。Aは、密かにリードしたいと思っている。AがBを見舞う。BがAを待つ。Bの目的は「夏期講習」である。Bは、密かに拮抗したいと思っている。Bが起き上がる。BがAと夏期講習について話す。Aが嘘をつく。Aが逃げる。BがAを止める。[A’s purpose is taking the “summer seminar.” A wants to lead in study. A inquires after B. B waits for A. B’s purpose is taking the “summer seminar.” B wants to rival A. B gets up. B talks to A about the “summer seminar.” A lies to B that A don’t take lecture. A escapes from B. B keeps A.]

history or story. In the course of this study, knowledge on the analyzed multiple narrative structures in *kabuki* will be introduced into INGS and GIS. In addition, INGS corresponds to the narrative generation reception process at the personal narrative level and, on the other hand, GIS is equivalent to the narrative production consumption process at the social distribution level. Both of these processes construct an entire narrative process or a mechanism. The *kabuki* research and analysis discussed in this paper will be extended to an entire narrative mechanism that includes these two processes.

Simply speaking, specific knowledge in *kabuki* is contained in GIS and the other general knowledge required for narrative generation is stored in INGS. Although narrative generation by INGS concerns narrative generation for each unit of work, narrative generation by GIS means narrative generation at a more complete level, where a sequence of narrative works is generated according to the repetitive use of INGS. The author's basic idea here is that the latter type of narrative generation is also performed by a kind of narrative technique that transcends a mere accidental sequence.

On the other hand, *kabuki* knowledge mechanisms are related to INGS in addition to GIS. Although the author would like to consider in elsewhere the introduction of acquired knowledge into INGS, many elements seem to be contained within range of the work resource in GIS. In particular, *kabuki* knowledge seems to contain 1) Real event, 2) Work, 3) Genre, 4) Material or topic, 6) Story, 7) Place (Stage), 8) Time (Era or Age), 9) *Geinō* style, 12) Text, 13) Production (*Daichō*), 14) Direction, and 15) Stage Performance. However, the works in GIS do not necessarily indicate *geinō*-like artistic or literary works in the narrow sense and include *geinō*-news-like works, life works, and so on. In this sense, they are also related to the *geinōjin* resource and life resource. On the other hand, the elements and mechanisms regarding *geinō* history and receiver were comparatively few as a result. Elements including historical aspects of works and persons (actors) and stage performance are related to *geinō* history. Future issues are the research and analysis of *kabuki* focusing on dynamic aspects of narrative production and consumption themselves, and further the exploration of a route through which *kabuki* analysis is organically designed from the viewpoint of GIS modeling.

In this research plan, these surveys and analyses will be formalized for use in GIS including INGS. As shown in Figure 19, in a generation cycle, INGS receives the above knowledge and additional related knowledge from GIS to generate the narrative conceptual structures for a story as well as a narrative discourse before expressing these structures for narrative representations. The part of narrative expression or representation is conducted on the staging mechanism in GIS. Furthermore, in the business model, there will be a variety of possibilities for the actual distribution: expressing or representing on personal computers and stages, developing and distributing second works through books and other media, etc. However, these matters exceed this chapter's scope.

As mentioned above, the elements of "person" in *kabuki* were, for instance, divided into three aspects: (1) a real "person" who lives in the actual world; (2) a "person" as an actor with a specific name who has a history of performing roles; and (3) a "person" as a specific *kabuki* character that appears onstage. Each person has their own history or story. In the course of this study, knowledge of the analyzed multiple narrative structures in *kabuki* will be introduced into INGS and GIS. This part focuses on the concept of "person" in *kabuki* to consider a design and development plan using INGS and GIS according to concrete modeling by analyses.

The person relating to the above (2) has a stage name and is defined as a part of the *geinōjin* resource in GIS. This *geinōjin* resource contains several *geinōjins* who have the same name, such as Nakamura Kichiemon (I, II). These data describe a set of common personalities of several real actors who have this one name in addition to the different types of personalities each actor possesses. On the other hand,

Figure 19. Generation cycle of kabuki narratives using GIS and INGS

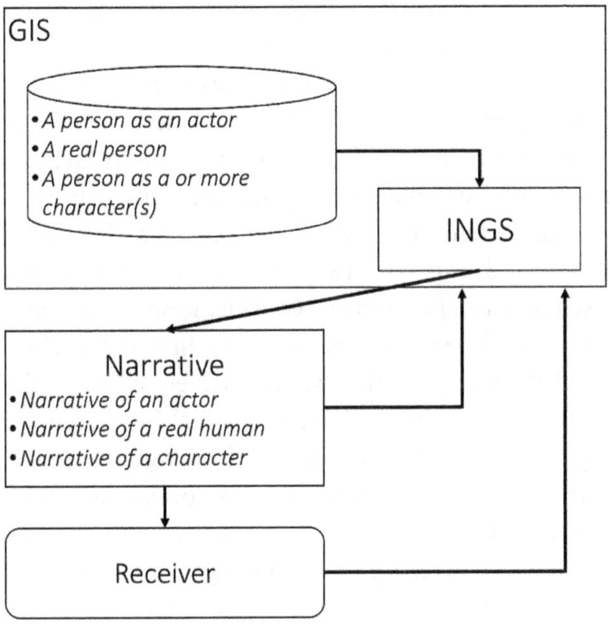

the above (1) concerns a person who has a real name and is living as a real human in the real world. In the *geinōjin* resource, this type of person is continually represented as the first type of person. Similarly, the above (3) relates to a person who should be defined in relation with a specific *kabuki* work in order to form an element of the work resource in GIS. Because this type of person can frequently be used in many *kabuki* plays, it is necessary to store the person as a specific character, not just a character who forms a part of a specific play.

As shown in Figure 19, in order to ensure a concrete execution method during the narrative generation cycle of GIS, when INGS generates a narrative, it receives various information, including the above three types of person-related information, to create the basic narrative structure. At the same time, general information except for the basic information on persons is supplied from the INGS side. Although GIS provides more specific information and knowledge, INGS prepares more general information. Furthermore, through the narrative production-consumption cycle of GIS, various sides of the person continue to produce or distribute narratives in a wider sense. Particularly, the next narrative production in the cycle can be executed by triggering all of the above three types of persons. For instance, the *kabuki* narrative production-consumption system can create a series of stages for the actor. It can also produce a series of stages where a *kabuki* character continuously appears. A primary effect for narrative generation involving the above method is to employ a concrete method with a person setting to strengthen and emphasize the impression of the generated narratives and upgrade the quality. Moreover, this contributes to enlarging diversity in the narrative distribution in GIS, namely the deviation and evolution of narratives. In particular, narrative distribution and expansion proceeds from a variety of narrative parts or sides, including the whole of a narrative and narratives. The above method produces diverse possibilities and provides relatively thick profile information on each character that provides concreteness and depth in the development.

The author shows a generation image. At first, INGS generates an ordinary narrative and, through the linkage with GIS and INGS, in a hyper-text situation in the case of "person," various narratives are generated, including narratives of the persons as characters, narratives of the persons as actors, and narratives of characters as real humans. Of course, narratives regarding each *kabuki* element except for persons are also generated in relation to the original narrative. These narratives are composed of each narrative space. An entire narrative is composed of these multi-layered and multiple collections. According to each perspective and viewpoint of reception and anticipation, each narrative receiver can focus on several types of persons (elements) to elaborate and expand the narrative.

Such a narrative image is related to the next two types of methods of narrative and narrative generation that Ogata (2008b) discussed as a preliminary consideration: branched narrative (generation) and compressed narrative (generation). The former has an image in which various possibilities in narrative generation are radially extended from a situation where a variety of possibilities are concealed. This is the possibility of a story in the most ordinary case and the real image corresponds to one that is fixed in the forms such as gaming books and adventure games. However, the author considers to include different narrative discourses from a same story in addition to stories. The above description means that a narrative can be seen as a diverse possibilities' space, regardless implicit and explicit. If the above is an image of the spatial extension of the diversity of narrative generation, the latter compressed narrative, on the other hand, shows an image of compression of the diversity in narrative generation. If their two types of narratives respectively take the form of a narrative work, the former is a narrative where diverse possibilities are spatially arranged as the possibilities themselves and the reading is entrusted to the freedom of each of the readers within a range. By contrast, in the latter form of narrative, the range of free reading is narrower and a compressed narrative itself can be seen as if a completed narrative work.

However, the extreme narrative image aimed at in this chapter is a little different from the above types of narrative images. The three levels of narratives in this image are the first narrative that corresponds to several groups of texts that compose a hyper-text space, the second level that corresponds to a text collection that is generated and changed through the links from the first narrative, and, furthermore, the third level on which the above two narratives are compressed and changed.

In addition, Amino, Kawamura, and Ogata (2002a, 2002b), in their series of papers, partially showed narrative generation of the lives and life courses of *geinōjin*. The author will expand these previous studies into design and development using INGS and GIS in the future.

Simple Examples Based on Analyses of *Kabuki*

This section presents two mechanisms related to narrative generation based on *kabuki* analyses.

Semi-Automatic Acquisition of Property Information of Ichikawa Ebizō XI

The first example is a semi-automatic acquisition mechanism of a property list of a contemporary *kabuki* actor, Ichikawa Ebizō XI. He is one of the most experienced *kabuki* actors, who inherited the traditions of the Ichikawa Danjūrō family.

Within this framework, a property is the description of the characteristics and features of an object. In INGS, properties are utilized as the knowledge for explaining and describing specific elements, mainly in events, in contrast to events that progress through characters' actions in narratives. The properties are developed for each element of mainly noun conceptual dictionaries in the INGS. Since the noun conceptual dictionary has numerous elements, it is necessary to develop an automatic or semi-automatic property acquisition and structuring mechanism.

The proposed property acquisition technique takes the text in the overview section of a concept's Japanese Wikipedia entry that corresponds to a concept in the noun conceptual dictionary in INGS as input information. The technique outputs the property description by the frame form. In particular, using MeCab (Kudo, 2013), based on postpositional particles and verbs, the technique recursively analyzes the input text to set the parts of verbs or postpositional particles in a sentence as the slot names of properties and the rest of the sentence as values in a property frame.

In this example, the author expanded the object on Wikipedia to be treated to the whole of "Ichikawa Ebizō (Jūichidaime)" except for the "Notes" section to acquire the properties. In particular, as pre-work, the author divided the above text into "*geinōjin* information" and "life information" and, further, classified respective groups into lower categories. Then, the above technique was applied to categorized text groups (Appendix 1). Subsequently, the author acquired a part of the description from his property list and the entire hierarchical structure as shown in Figure 20.

Naimaze: Mixing Narratives Based on Propp's Method

Next, the author presents a method for simulating *naimaze* in *kabuki* using Ogata and Hosaka's study (2004) related to Propp's (1968) folktale theory. Propp presented a way that stories are combined using several patterns of combining "moves." In Propp's narratological theory, the most basic narrative

Figure 20. A property list (a part) and the hierarchical structure (whole) of Ichikawa Ebizō XI

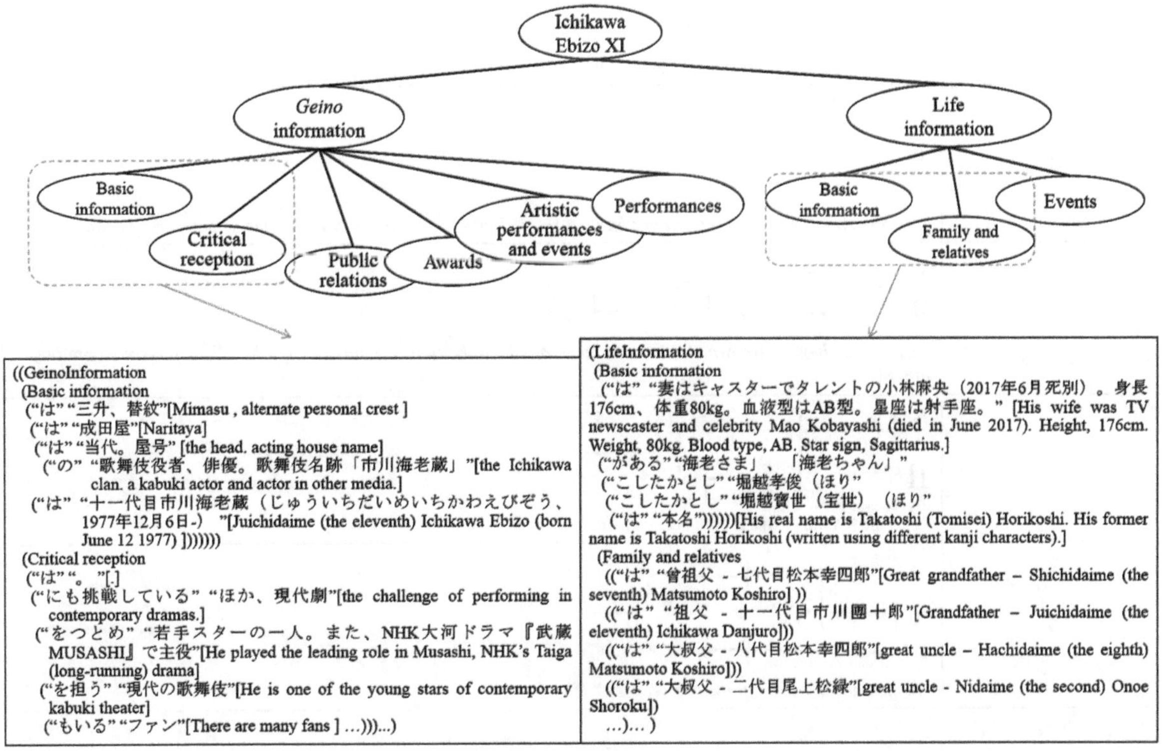

units for folktale-like stories are thirty-one kinds of "functions." A move is composed of the selective sequence of functions and many actual folktales are the combinations of several moves. Table 9 shows examples of the combination patterns of moves as proposed by Propp. The author's idea is to implement the *naimaze* in *kabuki* by using Propp's move method.

Table 10 shows three types of examples of *naimaze* by hand using Propp's method: (1) The first example shows that the folktale story *Sanmai no ofuda* [*The three charms*] (Sanmai no ofuda - Wikipedia) is based on the story of a *kabuki* work, *Narukami* (Japan Actors' Association, & The Organization for the Preservation of Kabuki, 2017), based on the above method 1. The main characters are changed to the characters in *Sanmai no ofuda*; (2) The second is an example in which, using method 2, the story of *Kanjinchō* [*The subscription list*] (Kanjinchō - Wikipedia) is inserted into the first move by the story of *Sanmai no ofuda,* and the main characters in *Kanjinchō*, Benkei and Minamoto no Yoshitsune, appear; (3) The final example deals with the *naimaze* of characters only. In particular, in the story of *Sukeroku* [*Sukeroku: Flower of Edo*] of *kabuki*, the characters of *Sukeroku* are replaced by the main characters in *Gogo no Eiko* [*The Sailor Who Fell from Grace with the Sea*], the chief, Fusako, Ryūji, Noboru, and Yoriko.

Table 9. Move combination patterns

1	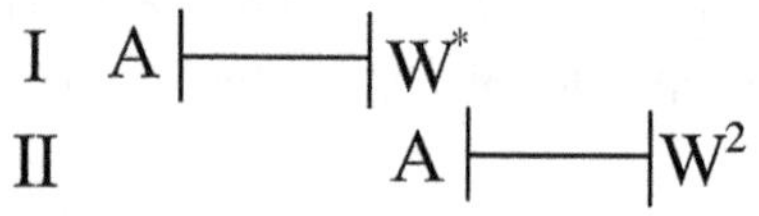 *"One move directly follows another move."*
2	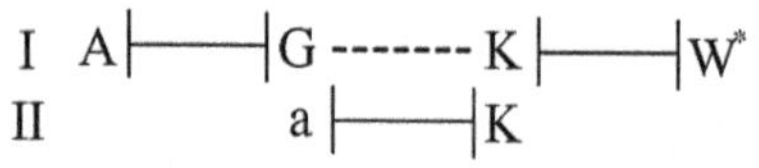 *"A new move begins before the termination of the first one."*
3	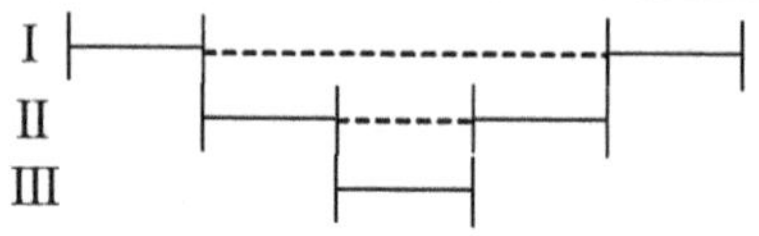 *"An episode may also be interrupted in its turn, and in this case fairly complicated schemes may result."*
4	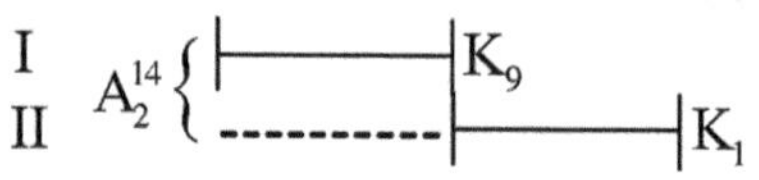 *"A tale may begin with two villainies at once, of which the first one may be liquidated completely before the other is."*
5	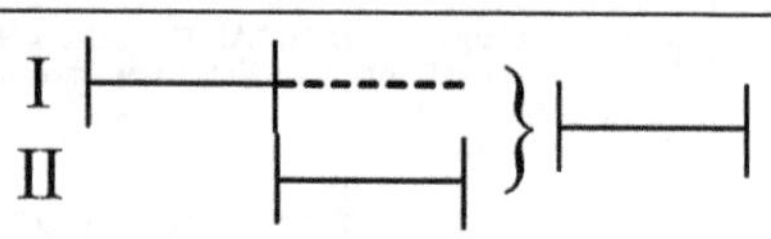 *"Two moves may have a common ending."*
6	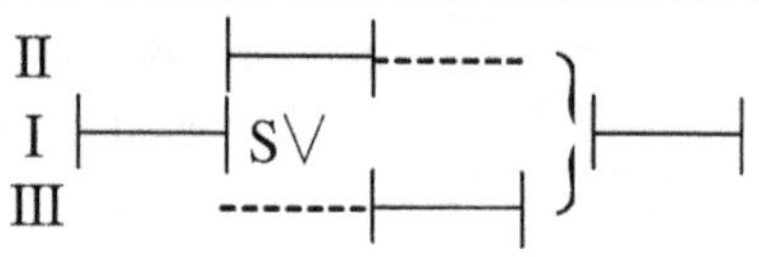 *"Sometimes a tale contains two seekers."*

Source: Ogata and Hosaka (2004).

In this chapter, the author focused on the narrative multiplicity in *kabuki* as a means of considering future directions for narrative generation research. This examination was based on the system development of two mutually related systems, INGS and GIS. In particular, this section demonstrated the various types of persons involved in *kabuki* by discussing *kabuki*'s conceptual design using INGS and GIS. In the future, the author plans to elaborate on designing the persons and other elements of *kabuki* in order to approach an experimental implementation using/involving INGS and GIS.

Table 10. Examples by naimaze of stories and characters

Method	Result
[Method 1] *Narukami → Sanmai no Ofuda*	雨が降らず、国中が日照りに苦しんでいる。鳴神上人が、帝が約束が守らなかったことを恨み、竜神を滝壺に封じ込めてしまったからだ。その上人の北山の庵めざして、一人の妙齢の美女が登って来る。彼女は亡き夫の想いの残った衣を濯ぎたいが水がないので、滝の水を求めてここまで来たと言う。夫とのなれそめ、川を渡って彼のもとへ通う様子を、裾をまくり白い足もあらわに語って見せる女の姿に、上人も思わず身を乗り出す。ふと疑いを持った鳴神上人に、女は一転して、出家し弟子になりたいと言い出す。上人が弟子の白雲坊、黒雲坊を使いにだし二人きりになると、彼女は急に具合が悪くなったふり。驚いた上人は介抱するうちに、彼女の胸に触れてしまう。初めて知る女人の肌の柔らかさに、次第に自分が押さえられなくなる上人。女は夫婦の盃と言って上人を酔いつぶし、傍らの滝に張られた注連縄を切る。封印が解かれた竜神は天にかけ昇る。すると即座に大雨が降りだした。女は上人の行力を破るため遣わされた宮廷一の美女、雲の絶間姫であったのだ。謀られたと知った上人は髪を逆立て炎となって荒れ狂い、止める弟子たちをなぎ倒し投げ飛ばし、六法を踏みながら、姫の後を追って行く。鳴神上人に追い付かれそうになった雲の絶間姫が「大の川、出ろ」と呪って2枚目の札を投げると、なるほど、大の川が出た。だが、鳴神上人はぐびぐびと飲み干した。次は「火の海、出ろ」と呪って最後の札を投げると、火の海が出た。しかし鳴神上人は川の水を吐いて吹き消した。寺に逃げ帰った雲の絶間姫は和尚に助けを求め、真面目に修行に励むことを条件に壺に入れてもらった。和尚は囲炉裏で餅を焼き始める。やがて鳴神上人が寺に入って来て「雲の絶間姫を出せ」と迫る。和尚が「その前にわしと術比べをしよう。山ほどに大きくなれるか」と言うと、鳴神上人は「ああ、出来るとも」と言って、ぐんぐんと大きくなった。和尚が「豆になれるか」と言うと、鳴神上人は「ああ、出来るとも」と言って豆になった。豆になった鳴神上人を和尚は焼けた餅に挟んで食べてしまった。[The rain has stopped falling and the whole country is suffering from a drought. This is because Narukami Shonin (a priest) holds a grudge against the Emperor for not keeping his promise, and has caged the dragon god of rain behind a waterfall. A beautiful young woman appears, heading for Shonin's hermit cave in the northern mountain. She says that she wants to wash the clothes of her dead husband in which her feelings for him linger, but because there is no water, she has come to the waterfall to find the water to wash the clothes. To say farewell to her husband, the woman crosses the river toward Shonin, and lifts up the hem of her skirt to reveal her white legs, and without thinking, Shonin bends forward toward her. To the suspicious Narukami Shonin, the woman turns and says that she wants to become a nun and his disciple. Shonin sends out his two disciples, Hakuunbô (the white cloud bonze) and Kokuunbô (the black cloud bonze) to bring her nun garments, and then the woman suddenly becomes sick. The surprised Shonin attends to her, and while doing so he touches her breast. He has never touched a woman before and he is gradually unable to control his desire due to the softness of her skin. Seizing her chance, the woman brings out to drinking cups and gets Shonin drunk, and in his drunkenness he reveals that he keeps the dragon god imprisoned behind a sacred rope across the waterfall. As Shonin sleeps drunkenly, the woman creeps away and cuts the rope and releases the dragon god, and immediately it begins to rain heavily. The woman was in fact Kumonotaema Hime (Princess), the most beautiful woman at the court, sent by the Emperor to break the power of Narukami. When he revives and becomes aware of what happened, his hair stands on end and he becomes enraged, he turns into flames, he fights and knocks down the disciples who attempt to stop him, and he chases after the princess. The princess, who can see Narukami chasing after her, throws down the second paper charm and says a curse, "Make a big river appear behind me," and sure enough, a big river appears. But Narukami uses his magic powers to swallow the water in the river. Next, the princess uses her final charm and says the curse, "Make a sea of fire appear" and a sea of fire appears. But Narukami uses the water he has swallowed to put out the sea of fire. The princess hurries back to the temple and seeks the help of the priest, who makes her promise to train more seriously after that, and hides her in a large pot. The priest begins baking rice cakes in the hearth. Then Narukami enters the temple and demands that the priest give him the princess. The priest says that before that, let's see which one of us is the best at changing shapes. He asks "Can you make yourself as big as a mountain?" "Yes I can" replies Narukami, and makes himself as big as a mountain. The priest then asks, "Can you make yourself as small as bean?" "I can do that too" Narukami replies, and makes himself as small as a bean. The priest picks up Narukami, who is now the size of a bean, stuffs him in the rice cake he is baking, and eats him.

continued on following page

Table 10. Continued

Method	Result
[Method 2] *Kanjinchō* in *Sanmai no Ofuda*	昔々ある村に、寺があった。そこに、小僧と和尚が住んでいた。ある日、小僧が山へ栗拾いに行きたいと駄々をこねた。和尚は仕方なく3枚の札を出すと、小僧に持たせた。山に来た小僧は栗拾いに夢中になっている内に日が暮れる。すると老婆が現れ小僧を家に泊めてくれた。だが夜にふと目覚めた小僧は、老婆が山姥の本性を現し包丁を研いで小僧を食べる用意をするのを目にする。小僧が「糞がしたい」と言うと、山姥は考え込み、小僧を縄で括って便所へ連れて行った。小僧は1枚目の札を便所の柱に括り、「札さま、何かあったら俺になってけろ」と頼んで窓から逃げた。山姥が「もういいか」と尋ねると、小僧に化けた札が「もうちっと」と繰り返す。山姥が「もういいか」小僧に化けた札「まだまだ」山姥が我慢できず便所をぶち破ると、小僧は跡形もなく消えていて、そこには破れた札があるだけだった。だまされたと知った山姥は小僧を追いかける。山姥に追い付かれそうになった小僧が「大の川、出ろ」と呪って2枚目の札を投げると、なるほど、大の川が出た。だが、山姥はぐびぐびと飲み干した。次は「火の海、出ろ」と呪って最後の札を投げると、火の海が出た。しかし山姥は川の水を吐いて吹き消した。寺に逃げ帰った小僧は和尚に助けを求め、小僧は和尚を先頭に山伏の姿で通り抜けようとする。辿り着いた関で、和尚は焼失した東大寺再建のための勧進を行っていると言う。しかし、関守の富樫左衛門の元には既に小僧が山伏姿であるという情報が届いており、山伏は通行罷りならぬと厳命する。これに憤慨した和尚は仲間と富樫調伏の呪文を唱え、疑いを晴らそうとする。感心した富樫は先の和尚の言葉を思い出し、勧進帳を読んでみるよう命じる。和尚はたまたま持っていた巻物を勧進帳であるかのように装い、朗々と読み上げる。なおも疑う富樫は山伏の心得や秘密の呪文について問い質すが、和尚は淀みなく答える。富樫は通行を許すが、部下の一人が強力に疑いをかけた。和尚は小僧を金剛杖で叩き、その疑いを晴らす。やがて山姥が関に入って来て「小僧を出せ」と迫る。和尚が「その前にわしと術比べをしよう。山ほどに大きくなれるか」と言うと、山姥は「ああ、出来るとも」と言って、ぐんぐんと大きくなった。和尚が「豆になれるか」と言うと、山姥は「ああ、出来るとも」と言って豆になった。豆になった山姥を和尚は焼けた餅に挟んで食べてしまった。[Once upon a time there was a temple in a village, in which lived a young monk and a Buddhist priest. One day the young monk said to the priest that he wanted to go to the mountain to collect chestnuts. The priest takes out three charm cards and gives them to the young monk. The young monk goes to the mountain and becomes so absorbed in collecting chestnuts that he is still on the mountain when the sun goes down. Then, an old woman appears and invites the young monk to stay at her home. But during the night, the boy wakes up and sees the woman in her true form of a mountain witch, sharpening a knife in the kitchen preparing to eat him. The young monk says "I want to use the toilet," so the mountain witch thinks about it, and ties him up with a rope and takes him to the toilet. The young monk attaches one of the paper charms to a pillar in the toilet, and says "Pretend to be me and answer the witch," and he flees out of the window. The witch asks "Are you finished?" and the paper charm replies in the voice of the young monk, "Just a little longer." The witch then asks again, "Are you finished?" and the paper charm again replies in the voice of the young monk, "Just a little longer." Finally the witch cannot stand it any longer and breaks down the door of the toilet, to find that the young monk has disappeared without a trace and there is only the torn paper charm. Realizing she had been tricked, the witch chases after the young monk. The young monk, who can see the witch chasing after him, throws down the second paper charm and says a curse, "Make a big river appear behind me," and sure enough, a big river appears. But the witch uses her magic powers to swallow the water in the river. Next, the young monk uses his final charm and says the curse, "Make a sea of fire appear" and a sea of fire appears. But the witch uses the water she has swallowed to put out the sea of fire. The young monk hurries back to the temple and seeks the help of the priest.The young monk and his party are trying to pass, with the priest taking the lead, wearing the disguises of *yamabushi* mountain priests. The priest says that they are travelling to seek donations for the rebuilding of the destroyed Todaiji Temple. However, already the information has been delivered to the barrier keeper, Saemon Togashi, that the young monk and his party are travelling disguised as mountain priests, and he gives the strict order that no mountain priests are to be allowed to pass. Indignant at this, the priest and his friends chant an esoteric Buddhist prayer to Togashi, to attempt to clear his suspicion. This impresses Togashi and is reminded of the previous words of the priest, and he orders him to read the *kanjincho* (a subscription list of people who have donated). The priest pulls out a blank scroll that he happens to have and spontaneously begins to read it, pretending it is the *kanjincho*. But Togashi is still suspicious, and asks him difficult question about the life of a *yamabushi* disciple and about esoteric prayers, but the priest answers without hesitating. Togashi lets them pass, but still has strong doubts about one of the lower-ranked men in the group, who is actually the young monk. The priest beats his master the young monk with his pilgrim's staff, which clears him of suspicion. The young monk, who had escaped from danger, compliments the priest for his quick thinking, but the priest bursts into tears and apologizes to his master for the rude way he had to save his life. Responding to this, the young monk gently takes the priest by the hand and has him think of the story of the battle in which they pursued Taira together. Then Togashi appears and apologizes for his previous rudeness and offers them sake to drink. The priest drinks the sake and performs a dance. The young monk and his party escape while the priest dances. The priest puts on his *oi* (a wooden box carried on one's back to store items for a pilgrimage) takes his leave of Togashi, and hurries after his master. Then the mountain witch enters the temple and demands that the priest give her the young monk. The priest says that before that, let's see which one of us is the best at changing shapes. He asks "Can you make yourself as big as a mountain?" "Yes I can" replies the witch, and makes herself as big as a mountain. The priest then asks, "Can you make yourself as small as bean?" "I can do that too" the witch replies, and makes herself as small as a bean. The priest picks up the witch, who is now the size of a bean, stuffs her in the rice cake he is baking, and eats her.

continued on following page

Table 10. Continued

Method	Result
[Method3] Characters of *Sukeroku* → Characters of *Gogo no Eiko*	花川戸助六という侠客に姿をやつした首領は、源氏の宝刀「友切丸」を探すため吉原に通っている。様々な男が集まる吉原で、遊客にわざと喧嘩を吹っ掛けて刀を抜かせようというのである。そこに助六を情夫にしている花魁の房子と、房子に言い寄る竜二が登場。竜二が友切丸を持っていると勘づいた助六は刀を抜かせようとするが、なかなかうまくいかない。そこへ白酒売に身をやつした兄の登がやってきて弟に意見するが、助六の真意を知った登は自らも喧嘩を売る稽古を始める。やがて房子が一人の侍を伴って再登場。助六はその侍に喧嘩を売ろうとするが、驚いたことにその侍は、兄弟を心配してやってきた母の依子であった。依子は助六に破れやすい紙子の衣を着せて、激しい喧嘩を戒めると登とともに帰ってゆく。舞台には再び竜二が登場。竜二は実は助六が首領と見抜いており、友切丸を抜いて源氏を裏切ることをそそのかす。助六はもちろん応じず、竜二を斬り、友切丸を取り返して吉原を抜け出す。[Soga no Goro, who appears as a guest named Hanakawado Sukeroku, goes to Yoshiwara (the entertainment district) to search for Genji's treasured sword "Tomokirimaru." In Yoshiwara, which is a place where various men gather, he intentionally tries to start fights with men so that they will draw their swords, revealing if they have the sword he is searching for. Agemaki is a courtesan who is frequented by Sukeroku, and the magnificently bearded Ikyuu also appears with Agemaki. Sukeroku thinks that Ikyuu might have Tomokirimaru and tries to get him to draw his sword, but he is unable to. Sukeroku's older brother, Soga no Juro, than appears as a seller of white sake, and on hearing the opinion of his younger brother, he himself starts trying to pick fights. Soon Agemaki returns to the stage accompanied by a samurai. Sukeroku tries to pick a fight with the samurai, but surprisingly that samurai is his mother, Manko, in disguise, who has come because she is worried about the two brothers. Manko dresses Sukeroku in an easily breakable paper kimono and warns him against a fierce fight, and they return to Juro. Ikyuu once again appears on the stage. Ikyuu sees that Sukeroku is actually Soga no Goro, draws Tomokirimaru and tries to persuade him to betray Genji. Sukeroku of course does not agree to this, cuts-down Ikyuu, retrieves Tomokirimaru, and leaves Yoshiwara.]

FUTURE RESEARCH DIRECTIONS

This section shows future research directions of main themes in this chapter.

- **Narrative Analyses:** The author described the future directions and issues of narrative analysis in the last part of "Previous Narrative Analyses by the Author" and "Towards Future Narrative Analyses." A theme that the author would especially like to undertake in the future is narrative analysis in relation to "*Personal and Private Content Knowledge*" in the latter section. The detailed content of this theme was already shown in Ogata (2010) and Ogata (2017c). In particular, Ogata (2017c) showed a plan of research, development, and production that develops systematic knowledge bases dependent on various kinds of narratives, including an author's chronicle of his life, records of reading and appreciation of novels, life chronicles of persons relating to the author, historical chronicles relating to the author, etc., to spin diverse narratives using INGS and GIS. The author will conduct narrative analyses according to this framework in the future. This work will be expanded by the analyses, in the wide sense, of narratives by the author himself in addition to narrative analyses of Mishima and *kabuki*. Namely, this means analysis and use by the author himself of various genres of documents by the author.
- **Analyses of Yukio Mishima:** Regarding the analyses of Mishima's works, a future direction is to extend the scale in order to treat many works by Mishima. Another direction is to undertake the narratological and structural analyses of his works through which previously ideological studies were preceding. The study will accompany a systematic survey of Mishima's studies. The former topic requires systematic understanding of his many works from the narrative generation and multiple narrative structures model. The analyses of his works dependent on the organized method will continue. The author will focus on the structural and narratological analyses in addi-

tion to the ideological analyses of the work' contents. Regarding the latter topic, Mishima focused on the form of a literary work. However, there are a few formal analyses and, further, structural and narratological analyses. These reasons may include that Mishima did not directly adopt, so to speak, avant-garde and experimental techniques and methods for his novels and plays, in addition to his intense thought. The author will attempt formal, structural, and narratological analyses of Mishima's literary texts dependent on this fact.

- **Analyses of *Kabuki*:** On *kabuki*, the author basically analyzes multiplicities for fifteen elements extracted from the viewpoint of the multiple narrative structures. Through the process, the tentative elements may be changed and the entire composition may be restructured. For example, for "Material or topic," it may be relatively easy to make a list of historical (*jidai*) materials and contemporary (*sewa*) materials to survey how they are utilized in actual works. The author will conduct the first step survey according to each element to elaborate and expand them. Furthermore, another interesting issue is to explore and read critical documents on *kabuki*, from *Yakusha Hyōbanki*s of the Edo era to contemporary *kabuki* criticisms, with a consistent consciousness toward multiple narrative structures.
- **Narrative Simulation or Generation by Mishima and *Kabuki*:** In this chapter, the author showed examples of simple systems based on three models by narrative analyses, the model of dramatic characters and relationships, the models of person and story by *kabuki* analyses. In the future, the author will design and develop them at a level that enables integration into INGS and GIS. Of course, the result of extension of the Mishima analysis and *kabuki* analysis will be reflected in the system design and development of INGS and GIS again. Therefore, narrative analyses (a kind of narrative information decomposition) and narrative generation or simulation (a kind of narrative information composition or synthesis) (Ogata, 2017a, 2017b) are dynamically connected.

CONCLUSION

Showing briefly the whole of the author's narrative generation studies is the indirect purpose of this chapter, using several concrete examples and naturally aiming to discuss the following contents as its direct purpose. In particular, through this chapter, the author showed an entire framework of narrative analyses in relation to narrative generation systems, mainly the Integrated Narrative Generation System (INGS) and *Geinō* Information System (GIS), and analyzed a novel by Yukio Mishima and several aspects of *kabuki* as two examples. Furthermore, the final parts offered directions for partially incorporating the results of these narrative analyses as a kind of narrative simulation into the above narrative generation systems.

Previous natural language processing and narrative generation has progressed in close relation with exploration of semantic structures and mechanisms of linguistic texts. Thus, they have had a deep relationship with previous linguistic, narratological, and literary theories. However, recently, as approaches that focus on the surface features of language and narrative are increasing, their semantic consideration and analysis are decreasing. The author anticipates that studying and analyzing language and narratives based on deep interest in narrative and literature themselves will be necessary for satisfactory progression and development of narrative generation. The author is planning to integrate surface approaches in main language processing into deeper semantic approaches. In fact, the author has already been introducing statistical methods for language processing and learning. At the same time, studies, analyses, and narrative simulations utilizing narratology, literary theories and, further, *kabuki* research are given appropriate value as one of the most important elements of these approaches, as shown in the previous description. Study and analysis of Yukio Mishima and *kabuki* will continue, and the range of introduction of narrative generation systems will extend to the objects of largest literary and narratological interest.

ACKNOWLEDGMENT

The author's research described in this chapter was supported by JSPS KAKENHI Grant Numbers 26330258, Support Center for Advanced Telecommunications Technologies Research Grant (2015-2017), and Kayamori Foundation of Information Science Advancement Research Grant (2017).

REFERENCES

Abe, H., Ogata, T., & Hanada, K. (2008). Televi kōkoku no shot niokeru brand dōnyū rhteoric no bunseki - Kōkoku no monogatari seisei system no ichi kikō no tameni [An analysis of brand introduction rhetoric in a shot in television commercial films: For a mechanism of an advertising narrative generation system]. In *Proceedings of the 16th Meeting of Literature, Cognition, and Computer Rereserch Group II in Japanese Cognitive Science Society* (16G-05). Retrieved from http://www.ogata.soft.iwate-pu.ac.jp/LCC2_Web/LCC(II)Proceedings/Proceedings(16)/2008.11.15AbeOgataHanata.pdf

Abe, K. (1973). *Hako-otoko* [The box man]. Tokyo: Shinchōsha.

Abe, K. (1977). Mikkai. Tokyo: Shinchōsha.

Akutagawa, R. (1922). Yabu no naka [In a grove]. *Shinchō*, 1.

Amino, T., Kawamura, Y., & Ogata, T. (2002a). Hierarchical generation of *geinō*-idol stories: Toward *geinō* information system and narrative marketing. In *Proceedings of 17th Congress of the International Association of Empirical Aesthetics* (pp. 549-552). Rome, Italy: University of Rome Tre.

Amino, T., Kawamura, Y., & Ogata, T. (2002b). Narrative generation of *geinō* characters and digital narrative marketing. In *Proceedings of the 16th Annual Conference of the Japanese Society for Artificial Intelligence* (3f2-10). Tokyo: Japanese Society for Artificial Intelligence.

Amino, T., & Ogata, T. (2000). *Geinōjin* no history bunseki to *geinōjin* simulation model [*Geinōjin* history analysis and a *geinōjin* simulation model]. In *Proceedings of the 7th Meeting of Literature, Cognition, and Computer Rereserch Group II in Japanese Cognitive Science Society*. Kofu, Japan: Yamanashi University.

Andersen, H. C. (2014). *The little mermaid: With original illustrations*. Hythlody Press. (Original work published 1837)

Aristotle, . (1997). *Poetics* (M. Heath, Trans.). London, UK: Penguin Classics.

Aruga, H., & Ogata, T. (1998). Structural analysis of tragic story and formalization of general rules. In *Proceedings of the 12th Annual Conference of the Japanese Society for Artificial Intelligence* (pp. 697-700). Tokyo: Japanese Society for Artificial Intelligence.

Asakawa, S. (2015). Neural network monogatari seisei moderu [A neural network narrative generation model]. In *Proceedings of 49th Special Interest Group on Language Sense Processing Engineering in Japanese Society for Artificial Intelligence* (pp. 15–21). Tokyo: Japanese Society for Artificial Intelligence.

Asano, S. (2016). *Propp riron no kōsatsu - Nihon no irui-kon'intan no bunseki wo rei ni* [A consideration of Propp's theory: Based on examples of Japanese human-animal marriage stories] (Master dissertation). Yamagata University, Yamataga, Japan.

Bae, B. C., Cheong, Y. G., & Young, M. R. (2011). Automated story generation with multiple internal focalization. In *Proceedings of the 2011 IEEE Conference on Computational Intelligence and Games* (pp. 211-218). Institute of Electrical and Electronics Engineers. doi:10.1109/CIG.2011.6032009

Bakhtin, M. (1984). *Problems of Dostoevsky's poetics* (C. Emerson, Trans.). University of Minnesota Press. (Original work published 1963)

Kyokutei Bakin. (2003-2004). *Nansō satomi hakkenden* [The eight dog chronicles] (Vols. 1-12). Tokyo: Shinchōsha. (Original work published 1814-1842)

Balzac, H. D. (2017). *Sarrasine* (C. Bell, Trans.). Projects Gutenberg. Retrieved October 15, 2017, 19:45, from http://onlinebooks.library.upenn.edu/webbin/gutbook/lookup?num=1826

Bando, T. (Director), & Ito, H. (Producer) (1995). *Tenshu monogatari* [Castle tower story] [Motion picture]. Japan: Shochiku.

Barthes, R. (1975). *S/Z: An essay* (R. Miller, Trans.). Hill and Wang. (Original work published 1970)

Booth, W. C. (1983). *The rhetoric of fiction*. Chicago, IL: University of Chicago Press. doi:10.7208/chicago/9780226065595.001.0001

Bordwell, D. (1988). *Ozu and the poetics of cinema*. London, UK: British Film Institute.

Brecht, B. (1973). Engeki no tame no shō shikō genre [A principle for thinking theatre]. In Bertolt Brecht engeki ronshū I [Bertolt Brecht's drama theories collection I] (K. Senda, Trans.). Tokyo: Kawadeshobō-shinsha.

Bruner, J. (2003). *Making stories: Law, literature, life*. Cambridge, MA: Harvard University Press.

Camus, A. (1942). *L'Étranger*. Paris: Gallimard.

Camus, A. (1947). *La peste*. Paris: Gallimard.

Dostoyevsky, F. (2008). *Demons* (R. A. Maguire, Trans.). London, UK: Penguin Books. (Original work published 1873)

Dostoyevsky, F. (2014). *Crime and punishment* (O. Ready, Trans.). London, UK: Penguin Books. (Original work published 1866)

Dundes, A. (1965). *The structure of folklore*. Prentice Hall.

Ebizō, I. (Jūichidaime). (n.d.). Retrieved from the Japanese Wikipedia: https://ja.wikipedia.org/wiki/%E5%B8%82%E5%B7%9D%E6%B5%B7%E8%80%81%E8%94%B5_(11%E4%BB%A3%E7%9B%AE)

Eisenstein, S. (Director) (1925). *Battleship Potemkin* [Motion picture]. Soviet Union.

Endo, Y., & Ogata, T. (2003a). *Manga* no gensetsu gihō wo tōgōsuru wakugumi toshiteno hyper-comic [A hyper-comic as a framework for integrating the discource techniques of *manga*]. *Manga Studies, 4*, 113–132.

Endo, Y., & Ogata, T. (2003b). Narratology of *manga* and application to hyper-comic. In *Proceedings of the 29th Annual Conference of the Japanese Society for Artificial Intelligence* (2G2-03). Tokyo: Japanese Society for Artificial Intelligence.

Endo, Y., & Ogata, T. (2004a). Multilayered discourse in hyper-comic. In *Proceedings of the 9th International Symposium on Artificial Life and Robotics* (Vol. 1, pp. 49-52). Ōita, Japan: Oita University.

Endo, Y., & Ogata, T. (2004b). A rhetorical analysis of a Japanese comic for hyper-comic system. In *Proceedings of 18th Congress of the International Association of Empirical Aesthetics* (pp. 502-508). Rome, Italy: University of Rome Tre.

Etō, J. (1959). *Sakka ha kōdō suru* [Authors act]. Tokyo: Kōdansha.

Etō, J. (1970-1999). *Sōseki to sono jidai* [Sōseki and the age] (Vols. 1-5). Tokyo: Shinchōsha.

Faulkner, W. (1929). *The sound and the fury*. London, UK: Jonathan Cape and Harrison Smith.

Faulkner, W. (1936). *Absalom, absalom!* Random House.

Forster, E. M. (1956). *Aspects of the novel*. Boston, MA: Mariner Books. (Original work published 1927)

Freud, S. (1900). *Die traumdeutung*. Leipzig: Franz Deuticke.

Fujii, S. (2016). *Nihon bungaku genryū-shi* [A history of origins in Japanese literature]. Tokyo: Seidosha.

Fujii, S., Hasegawa, D., Nakano, T., & Hatori, T. (2011). Academic genealogies with respect to narrative in human and social sciences and their implication for public policies. *Journal of Japan Society of Civil Engineers, F5-67*(1), 32-45.

Fujiwara, A., & Ogata, T. (2014). Generalizing and expanding the Propp-based story content grammar using the structural analysis of folktales. In *Proceedings of the 13th Forum Information Technology* (Vol. 2, pp. 331-333). Tokyo: Information Processing Society of Japan.

Fukuda, I., Kurisawa, Y., & Ogata, T. (2013). Roles and the management mechanism of internal states of characters in a narrative generation system. In *Proceeding of the 27th Annual Conference of the Japanese Society for Artificial Intelligence* (2I4-2in). Tokyo: Japanese Society for Artificial Intelligence.

Fukuda, T. (1990). *Monogatari marketing* [Story marketing]. Tokyo: Takeuchishoten-shinsha.

Genette, G. (1972). *Discours du récit, Essai de méthode, Figures III*. Paris: Seuil.

Godairiki koi no fujime. (1794). [Five great powers that secure love] [*Kabuki*]. Namiki Gohei I (Scenario). Kyōto, Japan: Nishi no Shibai (First performance).

Greimas, A. J. (1966). *Sémantique structurrale: Recherché de method*. Paris: Larousse.

Gunji, M. (1963). *Kabuki no bigaku* [Aesthetics *of kabuki*]. Tokyo: Engeki-shuppansha.

Haniya, Y. (2003). Shirei [Death Spirits]. Tokyo: Kōdansha. (Original work published 1946-1995).

Hara, M. (2013). *Chikamatsu jōruri no sakugeki-hō* [The dramaturgy of Chikamatsu's jōruris]. Tokyo: Yagishoten.

Hashimoto, O. (2012). *Jōruri wo yomō* [Let's read jōruri]. Tokyo: Shinchōsha.

Hasumi, S. (2014). *Bovary fujin ron* [A Theory of "Madam Bovary"]. Tokyo: Chikumashobō.

Heike Monogatari. (1991-1993). *Shin nihon koten bungaku taikei* (Vols. 44-45) [New Japanese classic literature collection (Vols. 44-45)]. Tokyo: Iwanamishoten.

Hemingway, E. M. (1929). *A farewell to arms*. Scribner.

Hemingway, E. M. (1940). *For whom the bell tolls*. Scribner.

Honcho Nijushikō. (1766). [Japan's 24 paragons of filial piety] [*Ningyō jōruri*]. Ōsaka, Japan: Takemoto-za (First performance).

Hozumi, I. (1959). Naniwa miyage [Naniwa souvenir] (The first part). In Chikamatsu jōruri shū (vol. 2). Tokyo: Iwanamishoten. (Original work published 1738)

Ichinotani Futaba Gunki. (1751). [Chronicle of the battle of Ichinotani] [*Ningyō jōruri*]. Ōsaka, Japan: Toyotake-za (First performance).

Imabuchi, S., & Ogata, T. (2012). *A story generation system based on Propp theory: As a mechanism in an integrated narrative generation system. In Lecture Notes in Artificial Intelligence* (Vol. 7614, pp. 312–321). Berlin, Germany: Springer.

Imabuchi, S., & Ogata, T. (2013). *Methods for generalizing the Propp-based story generation mechanism*. In Lecture Notes in Computer Science (Vol. 8210, pp. 333–344). Berlin, Germany: Springer. doi:10.1007/978-3-319-02750-0_36

Imabuchi, S., & Ogata, T. (2014a). Integrating the event generation mechanism in the Propp-based story generation mechanism into the integrated narrative generation system. *Journal of Robotics. Networking and Artificial Life*, *1*(2), 164–168. doi:10.2991/jrnal.2014.1.2.14

Imabuchi, S., & Ogata, T. (2014b). Propp ni motozuku story seisei system ni okeru tōjō-jinbutsu no kōsatsu [A consideration of characters in a Propp-based story generation system]. In *Proceedings of the 45th Special Interest Group on Language Sense Processing Engineering in Japanese Artificial Intelligence Society* (pp. 17-25). Tokyo: Japanese Artificial Intelligence Society.

Imao, T. (1970). *Henshin no shisō* [The theory of metamorphosis]. Tokyo: Hōsei University Press.

Inumaru, O. (2005). *Tempō jūichinen no chūshingura: Tsuruya Namboku kamikakete Sango taisetsu wo yomu* [Chushingura at Tempō 11: Reading Tsuruya Namboku's kamikakete Sango taisetsu]. Tokyo: Yūzankaku.

Ishii, K., & Ogata, T. (1998). A study on the methodology of hypertext novels based on a prototyping. In *Proceedings of the 12th Annual Conference of the Japanese Society for Artificial Intelligence* (pp. 701-702). Tokyo: Japanese Society for Artificial Intelligence.

Ishii, R., & Ogata, T. (2006). Making of a narrative network from characters histories and making of tories by the tracing towards the general and automat processing of the hyper-comic system. In *Proceedings of the 20th Annual Conference of the Japanese Society for Artificial Intelligence* (2E3-3). Tokyo: Japanese Society for Artificial Intelligence.

Izumi, K. (1917). *Tenshu monogatari* [Castle tower story]. Shinshōsetsu.

Izumu, K. (1919). *Yukari no onna* [A marginate woman]. Fujingahō.

Japan Actors' Association, & the Organization for the Preservation of Kabuki. (2017). *Narukami - Kabuki enmoku an'nai* [Narukami: Kabuki play guide]. Retrieved October 20, 2017, from http://enmokudb.kabuki.ne.jp/repertoire/502

Jauss, H. R. (1970). Literaturgeschichte als provokation. Frankfurt am Main: Suhrkamp Verlag.

Joyce, J. (1922). *Ulysses*. Paris: Sylvia Beach.

Joyce, J. (1939). *Finnegans wake*. London: Faber and Faber.

Kafka, F. (2009a). *The trial* (M. Michell, Trans.). Oxford, UK: Oxford University Press. (Original work published 1925)

Kafka, F. (2009b). *The castle* (A. Bell, Trans.). Oxford, UK: Oxford University Press. (Original work published 1926)

Kamada, M., & Ogata, T. (2013a). Analysis and imitation of the Japanese letter notation in narrative texts. In *Proceeding of the 27th Annual Conference of the Japanese Society for Artificial Intelligence* (2I4-5in). Tokyo: Japanese Society for Artificial Intelligence.

Kamada, M., & Ogata, T. (2013b). Monogatari seisei system ni okeru bun seisei kikō to moji hyōki kikō [The sentence generation and character representation mechanisms in a narrative generation system]. In *Proceedings of the 19th Annual Conference of the Association of Natural Language Processing* (pp. 698-701). Tokyo: Association of Natural Language Processing.

Kamikakete Sango taisetsu. (1825). [*Kabuki*]. Tsuruya Namboku IV (Scenario). Edo, Japan: Nakamura-za (First performance).

Kanadehon chūshingura. (1748). [The treasury of loyal retainers] [*Ningyō jōruri*]. Namiki Sōsuke, Takeda Izumo II, Miyoshi Shōraku (Scenario). Ōsaka, Japan: Takemoto-za (First performance).

Kanai, A. (2013). Eizō kankyō no monogatari to setsudan niyoru kihan riron: "Wakarinikusa" no ninchi wo megutte [Narratives of image environments and a critic theory by cutting: About the cognition of "incomprehensiveness"]. In *Media kankyō no monogatari to kōkyōken* [Narratives in media environments and public sphere] (pp. 193–229). Tokyo: Hōsei Daigaku Shuppankyoku.

Kanai, A., & Niwa, Y. (2008). *Eizō henshū no riron to jissen* [Theories and practices of image editing]. Tokyo: Hōsei Daigaku Shuppankyoku.

Kanai, A., & Ogata, T. (2004). Aspect of non-story processing and film rhetoric composition in the narrative generation mechanism. In *Proceedings of the 9th International Symposium on Artificial Life and Robotics* (vol. 1, pp. 162-165). Oita: International Society of Artificial Life and Robotics.

Kanai, A., Ogata, T., & Shinohara, K. (2002). Film rhetoric generation system for intensive cognitive system. In *Proceedings of IEEE International Conference on Systems, Man and Cybernetics (CD-ROM)*. The Institute of Electrical and Electronics Engineers.

Kanai, A., Ogata, T., & Shinohara, K. (2003). Identidal and different elements in film rhetoric generation. *Transactions of the Japanese Artificial Intelligence Soceity, 18*(2G), 114–121. doi:10.1527/tjsai.18.114

Kanai, T., Takai, S., & Nakanisi, M. (2009). *Katari to katari no aida: Rashōmon teki genjitsu to ningen no responsibility (taiō, koō, sekinin)* [Between narration and deceiving: Rashomon-like reality and human responsibility (corrensponsdence, response, and responsibility)]. Kyōto, Japan: Nakanishiyashoten.

Kanjinchō. (1840). [The subscription list] [*Kabuki*]. Namiki Gohei III (Scenario). Edo, Japan: Kawarasaki-za (First performance).

Kanjinchō. (n.d.). Retrieved from the Japanese Wikipedia: https://ja.wikipedia.org/wiki/%E5%8B%A7 %E9%80%B2%E5%B8%B3

Kawabata, Y. (1948). Yukiguni. Tokyo: Sōgensha.

Kawabata, Y. (1955). Mizuumi. Tokyo: Shinchōsha.

Kawabata, Y. (1961). Nemureru bijo. Tokyo: Shinchōsha.

Kawamura, Y., & Ogata, T. (2000a). *Geinōjin* image marketing system no tameno *geinōjin* homepage no bunseki [An analysis of *geinōjins*' homepages for a *geinōjin* image marketing system]. *Journal of Advertising Science, 40*, 181–192.

Kawamura, Y., & Ogata, T. (2000b). A conceptual framework on *geinō* organization model for artificial *geinō* performers with lives. In *Proceedings of the 5th International Symposium on Artificial Life and Robotics* (pp. 793-796). Oita, Japan: International Society of Artificial Life and Robotics.

Kawamura, Y., & Ogata, T. (2000c). Kasō geinōjin character no jinsei [Lives of virtual characters]. In Y. kawaramu, S. Hamada & T. Ogata (Eds.). Literature and Cognition/Computer 6: Language and literature. Japanese Cognitive Science Society Technical Report (00-No. 32).

Kawamura, Y., & Ogata, T. (2002). A trial on narrative interpretation of *geinō* information system. In *Proceedings of IEEE, International Conference on Systems, Man and Cybernetics (CD-ROM)*. The Institute of Electrical and Electronics Engineers. doi:10.1109/ICSMC.2002.1175727

Kawamura, Y., Ogata, T., & Kanai, A. (in press). Monogatari no wakugumi. [The framework of narrative] In T. Ogata, Y. Kawamura, & A. Kanai (Eds.), *Jōhō monogatariron - Jinkō chinō, ninchi, shakai katei to monogatari seisei* [Informational narratology: Artificial intelligence/cognition/social process and narrative generation]. Tokyo: Hakutōshobo.

Kawatake, T. (1992). *Kabuki: Its beauty and tradition* (C. Holmes, Trans.). Tokyo: Japan Arts Council.

Kawatake, T. (2003). *Kabuki: Baroque fusion of the arts.* Tokyo: The International House of Japan.

Kibakazari chūshingura. (1840). [Horse ornament Chūshingura] [*Kabuki*]. Namiki Gohei III (Ed.). Edo, Japan: Kawarasaki-za.

Kojiki. (1958). In *Nihon koten bungaku taikei 1* [Japanese classic literature collection 1]. Tokyo: Iwanamishoten.

Kudo, A., Okada, T., & Chen, D. (2015). Writing style and revision of a novelist examined through real-time creative process data. *Cognitive Studies*, *22*(4), 573–590.

Kudo, T. (2013). MeCab: Yet another part-of-speech and morphological analyzer (Version 0.996) [Software]. Available from http://taku910.github.io/mecab/

Kumagai, T., Ogata, T., & Oikawa, H. (2010). The construction of a story based on characters' cognitions: The consideration of an aspect of narrative generation based on an analysis of novels. In *Proceedings of the 17th Annual Conference of the Japanese Society for Artificial Intelligence* (1I2-OS1b-4). Tokyo: Japanese Society for Artificial Intelligence.

Kurosawa, A. (Director), & Minoura, J. (Producer) (1950). *Rashōmon* [Motion picture]. Japan: Daiei.

Kyōganoko musume Dōjōji. (1753). [The dapple-patterned maiden at the Dōjōji temple] [*Kabuki* dance]. Fujimoto Tobun (Lyrics). Edo, Japan: Nakamura-za, (First performance).

Leiter, S. L. (2014). *Historical dictionary of Japanese traditional theatre (2nd ed.).* Lanham, MD: Rowman & Littlefield.

Lévi-Strauss, C. (1964). *Mythologiques 1: Le cru et le cuit*. Paris: PLON.

Lyotard, J-F. (1979). *La condition post moderne*. Paris: Les edition de Minuit.

Mann, T. (1998). *Buddenbrooks* (H. T. L. Porter, Trans.). Vintage Books. (Original work published 1901)

Mann, T. (1999). *Doctor Faustus: The life of the German composer Adrian Leverkuhn as told by friend* (J. E. Woods, Trans.). Vintage Books. (Original work published 1947)

Mayama, S. (1982). *Genroku Chūshingura (1, 2)*. Tokyo: Iwanamishoten. (Original work published 1934-1941).

Mishima, Y. (1944). *Hanazakari no mori* [Forest in full bloom]. Tokyo: Shichijōshoten.

Mishima, Y. (1949). Kamen no kokuhaku. Tokyo: Kawadeshobō.

Mishima, Y. (1950). Ai no kawaki. Tokyo: Shinchōsha.

Mishima, Y. (1951). *Natsuko no bōken* [An adventure of Natsuko]. Tokyo: Asahi-Shimbunsha.

Mishima, Y. (1953). Manatsu no shi [Death in midsummer]. In Manatsu no shi [Death in midsummer]. Tokyo: Sōgensha.

Mishima, Y. (1954). Shiosai. Tokyo: Shinchōsha.

Mishima, Y. (1954). Iwashiuri koi no hikiami [The sardine seller's net of love]. *Engekikai*, 11.

Mishima, Y. (1955). *Shizumeru taki* [A sinking waterfall]. Tokyo: Chūōkōronsha.

Mishima, Y. (1955). *Kōfukugō shuppan* [Kōfukugō sails]. Tokyo: Shinchōsha.

Mishima, Y. (1956). Kinkakuji. Tokyo: Shinchōsha.

Mishima, Y. (1956). Rokumeikan. Tokyo: Tokyo Sōgensha.

Mishima, Y. (1956). Kindai nōgaku shū. Tokyo: Shinchōsha.

Mishima, Y. (1956). Aoi no ue. In Kindai nōgaku shū. Tokyo: Shinchōsha.

Mishima, Y. (1958). Hashi-zukushi. In Hashi-zukushi. Tokyo: Bungeishunjūsha.

Mishima, Y. (1959). *Kyōko no ie* [Kyōko's house]. Tokyo: Shinchōsha.

Mishima, Y. (1960). Utage no ato. Tokyo: Shinchosha.

Mishima, Y. (1962). *Utsukushii hoshi* [A beautiful star]. Tokyo: Shinchosha.

Mishima, Y. (1965). Mikumano mōde. In Mikumano mōde. Tokyo: Shinchōsha.

Mishima, Y. (1965). Sado kōshaku fujin. Tokyo: Kawadeshobō-shinsha.

Mishima, Y. (1968). Taiyō to tetsu. Tokyo: Kōdansha.

Mishima, Y. (1969). *Raiō no terrace* [The terrace of the leper king]. Tokyo: Chūōkōronsha.

Mishima, Y. (1969). *Chinsetsu yumiharizuki* [A wonder tale: The moonbow]. Tokyo: Chūōkōronsha.

Mishima, Y. (1969). *Bunka bōei ron* [Discussion on the defence of culture]. Tokyo: Shinchōsha.

Mishima, Y. (1969). *Tōron Mishima Yukio vs. Zenkyōtō - <Bi to Kyōdōtai to Tōdai Tōsō* [Discussions Mishima Yukio vs. Zenkyōtō: Beauty and community and Tokyo university dispute]. Tokyo: Shinchōsha.

Mishima, Y. (1969). Haru no yuki. Tokyo: Shinchōsha.

Mishima, Y. (1969). Honba. Tokyo: Shinchōsha.

Mishima, Y. (1970). Akatsuki no tera. Tokyo: Shinchōsha.

Mishima, Y. (1970). Hatashi-eteinai yakusoku - Watasi no naka no 25 nen [A promise that has not played: 25 years in me]. *Sankei Shimbun* (Evening edition).

Mishima, Y. (1971). Tennin gosui. Tokyo: Shinchōsha.

Mishima, Y. (1991). Shibai nikki [Plays diary]. Tokyo: Chūōkōronsha. (Original work written 1942-1947)

Mishima, Y. (2003). Chikamatsu Hanji [On Chikamatsu Hanji]. In Mishima Yukio Zenshū 26 [Mishima Yukio Collection 26] (pp. 392-396). Tokyo: Shinchōsha. (Original work written 1943)

Mishima, Y. (1951, 1953). Kinjiki. Tokyo: Shinchōsha.

Mishima, Y. (1969-1971). *Hōjō no umi* [The sea of fertility]. Tokyo: Shinchōsha.

Mishima, Y. (2000-2006). *Ketteiban Mishima Yukio Zenshū* [Complete Mishima Yukio Collection]. Tokyo: Shinchōsha.

Mishsima, Y. (1963). Gogo no eikō. Tokyo: Kōdansha.

Miura, H. (2000). Naimaze [To blend]. In *Shinpan - Kabuki jiten* [New version: Encyclopedia of kabuki] (p. 310). Tokyo: Heibonsha.

Miyoshi, T. (1993). Mienai fukushū [Revenge invisible]. In *Mienai fukushū* [Revenge invisible]. Tokyo: Kōdansha.

Mori, Y., & Ogata, T. (2005). Hyper-comic no kōsō to hyper-link oyobi koma gōsei no jidōka [A plan of hyper-comic and the automatization of hyper-link and frame composition]. In *Proceedings of 19th Special Interest Group on Language Sense Processing Engineering in Japanese Society of Artificial Intelligence* (pp. 1–11). Tokyo: Japanese Society of Artificial Intelligence.

Morioka, M. (2002). *Monogatari toshiteno mensetsu - Mimesis to jiko no hen'yō* [An interview as a narrative: Mimesis and self transformation]. Tokyo: Shin'yōsha.

Mukouyama, K., Kanai, A., & Ogata, T. (2001). An analysis of the rhetoric of the film and an attempt to an editing system. In *Proceeding of the 15th Annual Conference of the Japanese Society for Artificial Intelligence* (1F1-11). Tokyo: Japanese Society of Artificial Intelligence.

Mukouyama, K., & Ogata, T. (1999). Transformation of time-order in narrative: A consideration based on movie films. In *Proceeding of the 13th Annual Conference of the Japanese Society for Artificial Intelligence* (pp. 492-493). Tokyo: Japanese Society of Artificial Intelligence.

Mukouyama, K., & Ogata, T. (2001). Monogatari eizō ni yoru ukete no ninchiteki kōka no bunseki [An analysis of cognitive effects of receivers using narrative moving image]. In *Proceedings of the 13th Annual Conference of the Japan Simulation & Gaming Association* (pp. 5-10). Tokyo: Japan Simulation & Gaming Association.

Mukouyama, K., Shinohara, K., Kanai, A., & Ogata, T. (2002). Rhetorical analysis and automatic editing of the film. In *Proceedings of 17th Congress of the International Association of Empirical Aesthetics* (pp. 571-574). Rome, Italy: University of Rome Tre.

Murakami, H. (1985). Sekai no owari to hard boiled wonderland. Tokyo: Shinchōsha.

Murakami, H. (1994-1995). Nejimakidori chronicle. Tokyo: Shinchōsha.

Murakami, R. (1980). Coin locker babies. Tokyo: Kōdansha.

Murakami, R. (1997). In the miso soup. Tokyo: Yomiuri Shimbunsha.

Murakoshi, Y. (1998). Fukuzatsuka sareta nihongo no moji hyōki - Moji bunkaron [Complicated Japanese character representation: Study on the culture of characters]. *Atomi. English Studies*, *12*, 11–35.

Musil, R. (2017). *The man without qualities* (S. Wilkins, Trans.). Picador. (Original work publishued 1930, 1932)

Nakagami, K. (1977). Karekinada [The sea of withered trees]. Tokyo: Kawadeshobō-shinsha.

Nakagami, K. (1982). Sen'nen no yuraku [A thousand years of pleasure]. Tokyo: Kawadeshobō-shinsha.

Natsume, S. (1906). Kusamakura. *Shinshōsetsu*, 6.

Natsume, S. (1907). *Bungaku ron* [A theory of literature]. Tokyo: Ōkurashoten, Hattorishoten.

Natsume, S. (1907). *Gubijinsō* [Field poppy]. Asahi-shimbun.

Natsume, S. (1908). Kōfu. Asahi-shimbun.

Natsume, S. (1908). Sanshirō. Asahi-shimbun.

Natsume, S. (1916). *Meian.* Asahi-shimbun.

Natsume, S. (1905-1907). Wagahai ha neko dearu. Tokyo: Ōkurashoten & Hattorishoten.

NHK Science & Technology Research Laboratories. (2017*). TVML - TV program making language: TVML toha nanika?* [What's TVML?]. Retrieved October 5, 2017, 11:00, from http://www.nhk.or.jp/strl/tvml/

Noma, H. (1952). *Shinkū chitai* [Zone of emptiness]. Tokyo: Kawadeshobō.

Nonaka, R. (2015). *Bungaku no yōgo* [Terms of literature]. Tokyo: Shōhakusha.

Ōe, K. (1965). *Genshuku na tsunawatari* [Serious ropewalking]. Tokyo: Bungei-shunjū.

Ōe, K. (1973). *Kōzui ha waga tamashii ni oyobi* [The flood invades my spirit]. Tokyo: Shinchōsha.

Ōe, K. (2009). Suishi. Tokyo: Kōdansha.

Ogata, T. (1997). *Geinō* character heno monogatarisei no fuyo - Joron-teki kōsatsu [Giving narrativity to *geinō* characters: An intoruductive consideration]. In *Proceedings of the 28th Annual Conference of the Japanese Academy of Advertising* (pp. 58-61). Tokyo: Japanese Academy of Advertising.

Ogata, T. (1999). Monogatari genre taikei no mōrateki kentō [A comprehensive consideration of a narrative genre system]. In N. Yoshimine, H. Akama, & A. Tokosumi (Eds.), Literature and Cognition/Computer 2: The Expansion of Literature. Japanese Cognitive Science Society Technical Report (00-No. 40).

Ogata, T. (2008a). Monogatari seisei systems ni okeru eizō kosei he mukete [Towards image editing in a narrative generation system]. In A. Kanai & Y. Niwa (Eds.), *Eizō henshu no riron to jissen* [Theories and practices of image editing] (pp. 165–235). Tokyo: Hōsei University Press.

Ogata, T. (2008b). Ryūdō to kotei (2) [Fluidity and fixation (2)]. In *Proceedings of the 15th Meeting of Literature, Cognition, and Computer Rereserch Group II in the Japanese Cognitive Science Society* (15W-05). Retrieved from http://www.ogata.soft.iwate-pu.ac.jp/LCC2_Web/LCC(II)Proceedings/Proceedings(15)/15W-05Ogata.pdf

Ogata, T. (2010). Shōsetsu - Ryūdō to kotei, sakuhin no hō he [Novels: Fluidity and fixation, towards a work]. In T. Ogata & A. Kanai (Eds.), *Monogatariron no jōhōgaku josetsu - Monogatari seisei no shisō to gijutsu wo megutte* [An introduction to informatics of narratology: Towards the thoughts and technologies of narrative generation] (pp. 130–169). Tokyo: Gakubunsha.

Ogata, T. (2011). Narrative generation system as the practice of "informatics of narratology.". *Journal of Japan Society for Fazzy Theory and Intelligent Informatics, 23*(5), 14–24.

Ogata, T. (2014). Form and content in narrative generation: From the viewpoint of the implementation in an integrated narrative generation system. In Information Processing Society of Japan, Technical Reports, Natural Language Processing (2014-NL-217). Tokyo: Information Processing Society of Japan.

Ogata, T. (2016a). Computational and cognitive approaches to narratology from the perspective of narrative generation. In T. Ogata & T. Akimoto (Eds.), Computational and cognitive approaches to narratology (pp. 1-73). Hershey, PA: Information Science Reference (IGI Global). doi:10.4018/978-1-5225-0432-0.ch001

Ogata, T. (2016b). Kabuki as multiple narrative structures. In T. Ogata & T. Akimoto (Eds.), Computational and cognitive approaches to narratology (pp. 400-431). Hershey, PA: Information Science Reference (IGI Global).

Ogata, T. (2016c). Narrative generation of "zukushi": Towards its systematization through surveying *kabuki* and developing a proper noun conceptual dictionary in INGS. In *Proceedings of the 30th Annual Conference of the Japanese Society for Artificial Intelligence* (1K5-OS-06b-2). Tokyo: Japanese Society for Artificial Intelligence.

Ogata, T. (n.d.a). Monogatari to ningen/shakai/kikai – Tajū monogatari kōzō kara ningen/kikai kyōsei-kei he [Narrative and human/society/machine: To human/machine co-existence system from multiple narrative structures]. In Jōhō monogatariron - Jinkō chinō, ninchi, shakai katei to monogatari seisei [Informational narratology: Artificial intelligence/cognition/social process and narrative generation]. Tokyo: Hakutōshobō. (in press)

Ogata, T. (n.d.b). Naibu heno monogatari seisei mataha watakushi monogatari ni mukete [Narrative generation to inside or toward "I" narratives]. In T. Ogata, Y. Kawamura, & A. Kanai (Eds.), Jōhō monogatariron - Jinkō chinō, ninchi, shakai katei to monogatari seisei [Informational narratology: Artificial intelligence/cognition/social process and narrative generation]. Tokyo: Hsakutōshobō.

Ogata, T., & Amino, T. (2002). Tajū monogatari kōzō to *geinō* character no monogatari seisei system [Multiple narrative structures and the narrative generation system of *geinō* characters] In *Proceedings of the 19th Annual Conference of the Japan Cognitive Science Society* (pp. 130-131). Aichi, Japan: Japan Cognitive Science Society.

Ogata, T., Arai, T., & Ono, J. (2016). Using synthetically collected scripts for story generation. In *Proceedings of the 26th International Conference on Computational Linguistics: System Demonstrations* (pp. 253-257). Tokyo: The COLING 2016 Organizing Committee.

Ogata, T., & Endo, Y. (2004). Narrative discourse theory and a hyper-comic system. In *Proceeding of the 18th Annual Conference of the Japanese Society for Artificial Intelligence* (2D2-01). Tokyo: Japanese Society for Artificial Intelligence.

Ogata, T., & Fujiwara, A. (2015). A generalization of the method of specifying each "function": For an expansion of the Propp-based story generation mechanism in an integrated narrative generation system. In *Proceeding of the 29th Annual Conference of the Japanese Society for Artificial Intelligence* (3G4-OS-05b-3). Tokyo: Japanese Society for Artificial Intelligence.

Ogata, T., Fujiwara, A., & Imabuchi, S. (2014). A way to relatively freely define the sequence of "functions" for a story: Generalizing a Propp-based Story Generation System. In *Proceedings of the 28th Annual Conference of the Japanese Society for Artificial Intelligence* (2F5-OS-01b-2in). Tokyo: Japanese Society for Artificial Intelligence.

Ogata, T., Hori, K., & Ohsuga, S. (1996). An analysis of narrative structure and generation process for narrative generation system. *Cognitive Studies, 3*(1), 72–109.

Ogata, T., & Hosaka, Y. (2004). Transformation of story in the story generation system based on narratology. In *Proceedings of the 9th International Symposium on Artificial Life and Robotics* (Vol.2, pp. 593-596). Oita, Japan: Oita University.

Ogata, T., & Kanai, A. (2010a). *Monogatariron no jōhōgaku josetsu - Monogatari seisei no shisō to gijutsu wo megutte* [An introduction to informatics of narratology: Towards the thoughts and technologies of narrative generation]. Tokyo: Gakubunsha.

Ogata, T., & Kanai, A. (2010b). Story to shōhin = brand - Seisei ni muketa kōkoku no bunseki [Stories and products = brands: An analysis of advertisements towards narrative generation]. In T. Ogata & A. Kanai (Eds.), *Monogatariron no jōhōgaku josetsu - Monogatari seisei no shisō to gijutsu wo megutte* [An introduction to informatics of narratology: Towards the thoughts and technologies of narrative generation] (pp. 42–115). Tokyo: Gakubunsha.

Ogata, T., & Kawamura, Y. (1998). *Geinōjin* no monogatari simulation no kihon shisō [A basic theory of the narrative simulation of *geinōjins*]. *Bulletin of Nikkei Advertising Research Institute, 180*, 26–31.

Ogata, T., Kawamura, Y., & Kanai, A. (in press). *Jōhō monogatariron - Jinkō chinō, ninchi, shakai katei to monogatari seisei* [Informational narratology: Artificial intelligence/cognition/social process and narrative generation]. Tokyo: *Hakutōshobō.*

Ogata, T., & Mori, Y. (2005). A systematic view of narrative discourse based on "hyper-comic" system with automatic generation mechanism. In *Proceedings of the 19th Annual Conference of the Japanese Society for Artificial Intelligence* (3D3-01). Tokyo: Japanese Society for Artificial Intelligence.

Ogata, T., & Mukouyama, K. (2001). The discourse analysis of movie film. In *Information Processing Society of Japan, Technical Reports Computers and the Humanities, CH-49*, 9–16.

Ogata, T., & Ono, J. (2015). Language notation dictionaries and the use in an integrated narrative generation system. In IEICE Technical Report of Technical Committee on Natural Language Understanding and Models of Communication (Vol. 115, No. 69, pp. 25-30). Tokyo: Institute of Electronics, Information and Communication Engineers.

Ogata, T., Tachibana, S., & Tomite, S. (2009). Monogatari gainen hyōgen kara no eizō no seisei to jidō camera work - "Tokyo monogatari" no bunseki to simulation [Image genertion from narrative conceptual representation and automatic camerawork: An analysis of "Tokyo story" and the simulation]. In *Proceedings of the 26th Annual Conference of the Japan Cognitive Science Society* (P2-32). Tokyo: Japan Cognitive Science Society.

Ogata, T., & Wanatabe, K. (1995). Jinkō chinō ni yoru kōkoku sakusei shien system no tame no monogatari-gata CF no kōzō bunseki to kōkoku no monogatari seisei katei no kentō [Structural analysis of narrative commercial films for advertising making support system by artificial intelligence and the consideration of the advertising narrative generation process]. *Journal of Advertising Science, 31*, 153–157.

Ogata, T., Wanatabe, K., Hori, K., & Ohsuga, S. (1993). Life style marketing heno monogatari seisei system no oyo [Application of a narrative generation system to life style marketing]. In *Proceedings of the Joint Conference of System Simposium and Intelligent System Simposium of the Society of Instrument and Control Engineers* (pp. 217-224). Tokyo: Society of Instrument and Control Engineers.

Ogata, T., Watanabe, K., Hori, K., & Ohsuga, S. (1995a). A basic framework of the application of narrative generation system for integrated support of marketing/advertisement. *Journal of the Japan Society for Management Information, 4*(1), 19–42.

Ogata, T., Watanabe, K., Hori, K., & Ohsuga, S. (1995b). Monogatari seisei system ni yoru kōkoku sōsaku shien wo mokuteki to shita televicomercial no kōzō bunseki [A structural of television commercial films for advertising creation support by a narrative generation system]. *Journal of Advertising Science, 30*, 1–22.

Oikawa, H., & Ogata, T. (2010). Tōjō jinbutsu no ninchi jōhō wo motta monogari naiyō kikō jitsugen ni mukete - Shōsetsu no bunseki to system no teian [Towards the story generation mechanism with the cognitive information of characters: An analysis of a novel and the system proposition]. In *Proceedings of the 22th Meeting of Literature, Cognition, and Computer Rereserch Group II in Japan Cognitive Science Society* (22W-02). Retrieved from http://www.ogata.soft.iwate-pu.ac.jp/LCC2_Web/LCC(II)Proceedings/Proceedings(22)/22W-02Oikawa&Ogata.pdf

Oikawa, H., & Ogata, T. (2012). Tōjō jinbutsu no sōgo ninshiki kikō tosite no monogatari seisei no kōsatsu [A consideration of narrative generation as the mutual cognition mechanism of characters]. In *Proceedings of the 29th Annual Conference of the Japan Cognitive Science Society* (pp. 540-549). Nagoya, Japan: Japan Cognitive Science Society.

Onodera, K., Kumagai, T., & Ogata, T. (2010). Monogatari naiyō no ichibu toshite no story sekai wo tsukuru system no shisaku to shōsetsu bunseki ni yoru sono kakuchō no kentō [A prototype system to create a story world as a part of a story and a consideration of its expansion by a novel analysis]. In *Proceedings of the 20th Meeting of Literature, Cognition, and Computer Rereserch Group II in Japan Cognitive Science Society* (20W-04). Retrieved from http://www.ogata.soft.iwate-pu.ac.jp/LCC2_Web/LCC(II)Proceedings/Proceedings(20)/20W-04onodera.pdf

Ōoka, S. (1952). Nobi. Tokyo: Sōgensha.

Ōoka, S. (1971). *Leyte senki* [A record of the battle of Leyte]. Tokyo: Chūōkōron-shinsha.

Ōoka, S. (1996). Akutagawa Ryūnosuke wo bengosuru - Jijitsu to shōsetsu no aida [Defending Akutagawa Ryunoske: Between a fact and a story]. In *Ōoka Shōhei Collection 14* (pp. 532–556). Tokyo: Iwanamishoten. (Original work published 1970)

Ozu, Y. (Director), & Yamamoto, T. (Producer) (1953). *Tokyo monogatari* [Tokyo story] [Motion picture]. Japan: Shōchiku.

Parajanof, S. (Director) (1968). *The color of pomegranates* [Motion picture]. Soviet Union (Armenia).

Propp, V. Y. (1968). *Morphology of the folktale* (L. Scott, Trans.). Austin, TX: University of Texas Press. (Original work published 1928)

Proust, M. (2003). In search of lost time (T. Kilmartin, Trans.). Modern Library. (Original work published 1913-1927)

Saito, Y., & Ogata, T. (1998). A consideration of a computational modeling of Freud's dream theory. In *Proceeding of the 12th Annual Conference of the Japanese Society for Artificial Intelligence* (pp. 703-706). Tokyo: Japanese Society for Artificial Intelligence.

Sanmai no ofuda. (n.d.). Retrieved from the Japanese Wikipedia: https://ja.wikipedia.org/wiki/%E4%B8%89%E6%9E%9A%E3%81%AE%E3%81%8A%E6%9C%AD

Sayogoromo oshidori no tsurugiba. (1739). [*Ningyō jōruri*]. Namiki Sōsuke (Scenarios). Ōsaka, Japan: Toyotake-za (First performance).

Schank, R. C., & Abelson, R. P. (1977). *Scripts, plans, goals, and understanding: An inquiry into human knowledge structures*. Lawrence Erlbaum.

Sekkyō. (1998). *Kojōruri sekkyō shū (Shin nihon koten bungaku taikei 90)* [A collection of old jōruris and sekkyōs (New Japanese classic literature collection 90)]. Tokyo: Iwanamishoten.

Murasaki Shikibu (1993-1997). *Genji monogatari (1-5)*. Tokyo: Iwanamishoten.

Shin kokin waka shū. (1959). *Shin kokin waka shū* [The new collection of wakas, past and present]. Tokyo: Iwanamishoten. (Original work published the Kamakura era)

Shklovsky, V. (1990). *Theory of prose* (B. Sher, Trans.). Dalkey Archive Press. (Original work published 1925)

Sophocles. (1994). Oedipus tyrannus. In *Ajax, Electra, Oedipus tyrannus* (H. Lloid-Jones, Trans.). Cambridge, MA: Harvard University Press. (Original work published around 429 BC)

Stam, R., Burgoyne, R., & Flitterman-Lewis, S. (1992). *New vocabularies in film semiotics: Structuralism, post-structuralism and beyond*. London: Routledge.

Sukeroku. (n.d.). Retrieved from the Japanese Wikipedia: https://ja.wikipedia.org/wiki/%E5%8A%A9%E5%85%AD

Sukeroku yukari no Edo-zakura. (1733). [Sukeroku: Flower of Edo] [*Kabuki*]. Edo, Japan: Ichimura-za (First performance).

Tachibana, S., & Ogata, T. (2009). Extracting of rules for cameraworks in "Tokyo story" of Ozu. In *The 69th National Convention of Information Processing Society of Japan* (1ZD-1). Tokyo: Information Processing Society of Japan.

Taguchi, A. (2011). *Kabuki kara Edo wo yominaosu* [Reading again Edo from kabuki]. Tokyo: Yoshikawa-kobunkan.

Taiheiki. (1960-1962). *Nihon koten bungaku taikei 34-36* [Japanese classic literature collection 34-36]. Tokyo: Iwanamishoten. (Original work publishued the Muromachi era)

Takahashi, K. (1958). *Ri Shōin*. Tokyo: Iwanamishoten.

Takahashi, K. (1966). *Jashūmon* [Heretical faith]. Tokyo: Kawadeshobō-shinsha.

Takahashi, K. (1971). *Waga kaitai* [My dismantling]. Tokyo: Kawadeshobō-shinsha.

Takahashi, K. (1980). Nihon no akuryō [Demon of Japan]. Tokyo: Shinchōsha. (Original work published 1966-1968)

Takahashi, R. (1992-1993). *Mezon Ikkoku (1-10)* [Maison Ikkoku (1-10)]. Tokyo: Shōgakkan. (Original work published 1980-1987)

Tanizaki, J. (1925). Chijin no ai. Tokyo: Kaizōsha.

Tanizaki, J. (1931). Manji. Tokyo: Kaizōsha.

Tanizaki, J. (1933). *Shunkinshō* [A portrait of shunkin]. Tokyo: Sōgensha.

Tanizaki, J. (1946-1948). Sasameyuki. Tokyo: Chūōkōronsha.

Tōkaido Yotsuya kaidan. (1825) [*The ghost stories at Yotsuya on the Tōkaido*] [*Kabuki*]. Tsuruya Namboku, et al. (Scenario). Edo, Japan: Nakamiura-za (First performance).

Tolstoy, L. (2009). *Ressurection* (A. Briggs, Trans.). London, UK: Penguin Books. (Original work published 1899)

Tolstoy, L. (2010). War and peace (L. Maude, Trans.). Oxford, UK: Oxford University Press. (Original work published 1865-1869)

Tsuru nyōbō. (2017). [Crane's return of a favor] (Y. Mori & M. Pertseva, Trans.). London, UK: YellowBirdProject.

Ueda, K. (2006). *Hōdō-bangumi-fū scenario jidō seisei no kenkyū* [A study on automatic composition of news-story-like scenarios] (Master dissertation). Yamanashi University, Kofu, Japan.

Watanabe, N. (2012). *Nihon shōsetsu gijutsushi* [A history of technologies of Japanese novels]. Tokyo: Shinchōsha.

Watanabe, T. (1989). *Kabuki - Kajō naru kigō no mori* [Kabuki: The forest of excessive signs]. Tokyo: Shin'yōsha.

Watanabe, T. (2013). *Kabuki - Kata no shinzui* [Kabuki: The essence of kata]. Tokyo: Kadokawa-gakugei-shuppan.

White, H. (1980). The value of narrativity in the representation of reality. In W. J. T. Mitchell (Ed.), *On narrative*. Chicago, IL: The University of Chicago Press. doi:10.1086/448086

Yamamura, M. (1988). Maiko satsujin jiken [A murder of an apprentice geisha]. In *Miyako odori satsujin jiken* [A murder of miyako dance] (pp. 7–53). Shinchōsha.

Yokomitsu, R. (1931). *Kikai* [Machine]. Tokyo: Hakusuisha.

Yokomitsu, R. (1931). Jikan [Time]. Chūōkōron, 4.

Yokomitsu, R. (1932). *Shanghai*. Tokyo: Kaizōsha.

Yokomitsu, R. (1946). *Ryoshū* [Loneliness on a journey]. Tokyo: Kaizōsha.

Yoshimoto, T. (1965). *Gengo ni totte bi toha nanika* [What is beauty for language?]. Tokyo: Keisōshobo.

Yoshimoto, T. (1966). *Jiritsu no shisō-teki kyoten* [An ideological base of self-reliance]. Tokyo: Tokumashoten.

Yoshimoto, T. (1968). *Kyōdō gensō ron* [Communal illusion]. Tokyo: Kawadeshobō-shinsha.

Yoshimoto, T. (1990). *Matthew-sho shiron, tenkōron* [Gospel of Matthew, political conversion]. Tokyo: Kōdansha.

Zhan, Y., Ono, J., & Ogata, T. (2012a). Single event and scenario generation based on movement and constraint in conceptual dictionary. In IEICE Technical Report of Technical Committee on Natural Language Understanding and Models of Communication, NLC2011-60 (Vol. 111, No. 427, pp. 65-70). Tokyo: Institute of Electronics, Information and Communication Engineers.

Zhang, Y., Ono, J., & Ogata, T. (2011a). Defamiliarization rhetoric and scenario generation for events using the constraints in a conceptual system. In *Proceedings of the 26th Annual Conference of the Japanese Society for Artificial Intelligence* (1N1-OS-1a-1). Tokyo: Japanese Society for Artificial Intelligence.

Zhang, Y., Ono, J., & Ogata, T. (2011b). An advertising rhetorical mechanism for single event combined with conceptual dictionary in narrative generation system. In *Proceedings of 7th International Conference on Natural Language Processing and Knowledge Engineering* (pp. 340-343). Institute of Electrical and Electronics Engineers. doi:10.1109/NLPKE.2011.6138221

Zhang, Y., Ono, J., & Ogata, T. (2012b). Single event and scenario generation based on advertising rhetorical techniques using the conceptual dictionary in narrative generation system. In *Proceedings of the Fourth IEEE International Conference on Digital Game and Intelligent Toy Enhanced Learning* (pp. 162-164). The Institute of Electrical and Electronics Engineers. doi:10.1109/DIGITEL.2012.46

KEY TERMS AND DEFINITIONS

Expanded Literary Theory: A concept for a research field in which narratology and literary theories are organically introduced into computational and cognitive approaches.

***Geino* Information System:** A system model of *geino* production and consumption. GIS has been considered a framework in which various levels of narrative generation processes were driven by authors, receivers, characters, actors, and actresses.

Integrated Narrative Generation System: A synthetic narrative generation system architecture integrating the previous studies by the author.

Kabuki: Kabuki is one of the most popular genres of dramas and performing arts that synthesize diverse elements, including scenario, music, performance, and so on. The author (Ogata) has analyzed kabuki from multiple narrative structures to introduce the results into the integrated narrative generation system.

Multiple Narrative Structures (Model): A conceptual model by which a narrative text is multiply constituted and the narrative generation process is also multiply executed.

Narrative Analysis: Narratives have been analyzed in diverse academic genres, such as literature and psychology, because they correspond to an important method for human recognition of worlds. This chapter showed a new approach that comprehensively seizes narrative analyses in various research areas from the perspective of narrative generation.

Yukio Mishima: He is a writer of novels, dramas, and essays, having written many works that mix classical realistic styles and his unique thought and philosophy. Although many previous studies of Mishima have focused on his thought and philosophy, this chapter presents a new approach that concentrates on an aspect of the narrative structures of a novel by Mishima.

APPENDIX: ICHIKAWA EBIZŌ XI'S PROPERTY INFORMATION ACQUIRED FROM JAPANESE WIKIPEDIA

Geinō Information

基礎情報 [Basic Information]

十一代目 市川 海老蔵(じゅういちだいめ いちかわ えびぞう、1977年12月6日 -)は、歌舞伎役者、俳優。歌舞伎名跡「市川海老蔵」の当代。屋号は成田屋。定紋は三升、替紋は杏葉牡丹。愛称に「海老さま」、「海老ちゃん」がある。[Juichidaime (the eleventh) Ichikawa Ebizo (born June 12 1977) is a kabuki actor and actor in other media. His kabuki name is "Ichikawa Ebizo" as the head of the Ichikawa clan. His acting house name is Naritaya. His family crest is Mimasu and his alternate personal crest is Gyoyobotan. He is affectionately known as "Ebi sama and "Ebi chan."]

評価 [Critical Reception]

古典の大役に挑み、初役を多くつとめ、高い評価を得ている。[He has taken on the challenge of the major roles in the kabuki classics and also played many roles for the first time, and his performances have been highly praised.]

「海老さま」と人気のあった十一代目市川團十郎に重ね合わすファンもいる。現代の歌舞伎を担う若手スターの一人。また、NHK大河ドラマ『武蔵 MUSASHI』で主役をつとめたほか、現代劇にも挑戦している。[There are many fans of Ebi sama" who are also fans of the popular Juichidaime Ichikawa Danjuro. He is one of the young stars of contemporary kabuki theater. He played the leading role in Musashi, NHK's Taiga (long-running) drama, and also taken on the challenge of performing in contemporary dramas.]

父・團十郎が健在であった当時、海外公演などで一緒に舞台に上がった時には演出のことで揉めたことがよくあった。團十郎が海老蔵の意見を聞き入れて許してくるときもあったが、そういうときの家庭内の空気はよくなかったという。だが、反発していたときにずっと優しく見守ってくれていた團十郎に常々感謝の言葉を述べている。[At the time his father, Danjuro was alive, they frequently came into conflict when they performed together on stage, such as during overseas performances. There were times when Danjuro listed to and accepted Ebizo's opinion, but the atmosphere within their home at that time was not good. However, Ebizo has frequently expressed his gratitude to Danjuro, who always watched kindly over him even when they were in conflict.]

婚外子(非嫡出子)が発覚した際に寛大な態度を見せていた父・團十郎も、2007年に海老蔵が風呂場でケガをして歌舞伎公演を降板した時はさすがに激怒し「公演に穴を空けたんだから、自己管理がなっていない。今回は同情できん」とコメントしていた。2010年に発生した暴行事件の被害を受けた際にも再度激怒し「(予定されていた京都南座での顔見世興行の)けいこに入れないのではないか。(事件に巻き込まれたとは言え、その事件の原因を作ったと言う)責任の上では、出演すべきではないと思っている」と前置きし「大変失礼な行動で、当人の自覚のなさがなせるわざ。憤りを感じている」と海老蔵を突き放していた。[While his father Danjuro had shown a tolerant attitude when it was discovered that Ebizo had a child born outside of marriage (an illegitimate child), he was furious with Ebizo in 2007 when his son was injured in a bathroom and his kabuki performances has to be cancelled, commenting that "He has made this absence in his public performances, so he has no self-control. I cannot forgive him this time." He was furious again when he was injured during a violent incident that occurred in 2010, and he commented that "Will he be able to join (the performance with star cast scheduled to take place at the Kyoto Minami-za Theater)? (While Ebizo was caught up in the incident, it was said that it occurred because of his behavior) As it was his responsibility, I think he should not perform," and he harshly criticized Ebizo, saying "His actions were extremely rude and he must take a strong look at himself. I feel angry."]

10代の頃の海老蔵は幼少時から続く厳しい稽古と家柄・伝統の重責に耐え切れず反発を繰り返していたという。そんな彼を立ち直らせたのは、偶然フィルムで見た『勧進帳』の弁慶をつとめる祖父・十一代目市川團十郎の芸の美しさと勇姿に感動したからと語っている。祖父を目標に掲げているが、その理想を追うがゆえに苦しみ、現在も、もがき続けているという。[When Ebizo was in his teens, he repeatedly rebelled against the rigorous training that he had undergone continually since early childhood and also the heavy responsibility of his family name and tradition. It is said that what made him reform his attitude was when he was greatly moved by the beauty and the courage of a performance by his grandfather, Juichidaime Ichikawa Danjuro, playing the role of Benkei in Kanjincho, which he saw by chance on film. With his grandfather's performance as his goal, he has suffered in his pursuit of this ideal and even today continues to struggle to achieve it.]

以前は舞台に上がることが苦痛であったが、歌舞伎に真剣に打ち込むようになった今はプライベートの方が苦痛に感じるという。これが異様なことかと悩んで五代目坂東玉三郎に相談したところ、「あら、それは当たり前よ」と返され、安心したと述べている。また、坂東玉三郎とそういったことを共感できたことを嬉しく思ったとも語っている。[In the past he found it difficult to appear on stage, but today, when he is devoting himself diligently to kabuki, he feels it is more difficult to be a private person. He was worrying about the strangeness of this and discussed it with Bandoutama Saburou V, who told Ebizo that "It is natural you feel that way," after which he became more relaxed about it. He also said that he was very happy that Bandoutama Saburou was able to empathize with him about his concerns.]

本格的な筋力トレーニングやヨガを行っており、雑誌『ターザン』などの表紙を飾ったこともある。[He engages in full-scale strength training and yoga and has appeared on the front of magazines, such as Tarzan.]

成田屋のお家芸「歌舞伎十八番」のうち、今日ではあまり上演されなくなった演目の復活上演を積極的に行っている。[The Naritaya acting house of artists are actively reviving and performing those works in the Kabuki Jūhachiban (the repertoire of 18 major kabuki plays) that today are not frequently performed.]

芸歴・出来事 [Artistic Performances and Events]

- 1977年12月6日 - 東京都に生まれる。父・十二代目市川團十郎と母・希実子(旧姓・庄司)の長男。祖父は「海老さま」こと十一代目市川團十郎。[December 6, 1977 – Born in Tokyo. The eldest son of his father Junidaimei (the twelfth) Ichikawa Danjuro and his mother Kimiko (maiden name, Shoji). His grandfather was "Ebi sama," the Juichidaime Ichikawa Danjuro.]
- 1983年5月 - 歌舞伎座『源氏物語』の春宮で初お目見得。[May 1983 – His gave his first public performance as Togu in *The Tale of Genji* kabuki play]

- 1985年5月 - 歌舞伎座『外郎売』の貴甘坊で七代目市川新之助を襲名。[May 1985 - He assumed the name of shichidaime (the seventh) Ichikawa Shinnosuke for the performance of Kikanbo in the *Uiro Uri* kabuki play]
- 1996年3月 - 幼稚園・初等部・中等部・高等部まで青山学院で過ごし、高等部から堀越高等学校に転校。[March 1996 – After attending the kindergarten, primary, secondary, and high school departments of Aoyama Gakuin, he transferred to Horikoshi High School]
- 1997年3月 - 堀越高等学校を卒業。[March 1997 – He graduated from Horikoshi High School]
- 2000年 歌舞伎座『源氏物語』の光君をつとめ、会場は連日満員、チケットは発売初日に完売するほどの人気を得る。五代目尾上菊之助、二代目尾上辰之助とともに「平成の三之助」と呼ばれ、新たな歌舞伎ブームを起こす。[2000 – He played the role of Hikaru Kimi in *The Tale of Genji* kabuki play, and the venue was full on each night and the tickets were so popular as to be sold out on the first day they went on sales. Together with Godaime (the fifth) Onoe Kikunosuke and Nidaime (the second) Onoe Tatsunosuke, he became of the "Heisei no san Suke" (the three "Sukes" of the Heisei period) and helped create a new boom in kabuki.]
- 2003年2月 - 日置明子との間に非嫡出子(女児、当時1歳)がいることが判明。子は認知して養育費を支払っていることを会見で説明。[February 2003 – It was discovered that he had an illegitimate child with Akiko Hioki (a girl, 1 year old at that time)."At a press conference, he explained that he recognized the child was his and was paying child support.]
- 2004年4月4日 - 成田山新勝寺で襲名披露、奉告のお練り。京成本線京成上野駅 - 京成成田駅間で運行された列車「海老蔵号」に乗車した(京成AE100形電車を使用)。[April 4 2004 – He gave the performance for the succession of his stage name at the Naritasan Shinshoji Temple and the parade for the report to the deity was held. A train named "Ebizo" began operations between the Keisei Main Line Keisei Ueno Station and Keisei Narita Station (a Keisei AE 100-type train was used).]
- 2004年5月 歌舞伎座『助六由縁江戸桜』の花川戸助六、『暫』の鎌倉権五郎ほかで十一代目市川海老蔵を襲名。[May 2004 – He assumed the name Juichidaime Ichikawa Ebizo on performing various kabuki roles including Hanakawado Sukeroku in *Sukeroku Yukari no Edozakura* and Kamakuranogongorou in *Shibaraku*.]
- 2004年6月30日 - 成田山大阪別院明王院で襲名披露奉告。京阪本線天満橋駅 - 香里園駅間で列車「海老蔵号」が運行(京阪8000系電車を使用)。[June 30, 2004 – he gave the performance for the assumption of the name and the notification ceremony was held at the Myoo-in Temple of Naritasan Osaka Betsui. The train "Ebizo" began operations between the Keihan Main Line Tanmabashi Station and Kariyosen Station (a Keihan 8000 series train was used).]
- 2004年10月 - フランス・パリのシャイヨ宮劇場で「市川新之助改メ十一代目市川海老蔵襲名披露フランス公演」。同国政財界のトップも観劇し、『ル・モンド』紙が一面全面を使って「17世紀末以来の日本の伝統的演劇の中で名をとどろかせてきた一族の出身」「26歳のスター」「若く美男で特に『必殺の視線』を持っている」となどと報じ、現地でも大きな話題を呼ぶ。[October 2004 – At the Palais de Chaillot Theater in Paris France, he gave a public performance of the performance he gave when his name was changed from Ichikawa Shinnosuke to Juichidaime Ichikawa Ebizo. The performance was attended by leading members of the political and business worlds, and the newspaper Le Monde gave an entire page for its coverage of the performance, reporting that "he is a member of family that has been distinguishing itself in traditional Japanese theater since the end of the 17th century," that "he is a

star at 26 years old," and that he is "a young and handsome man who in particular possesses 'the gaze of death'"(the *nirami* glare used in kabuki), and his performance attracted a lot of attention locally.]

- 2006年9月7日 - 映画『出口のない海』の宣伝も兼ねて、『クイズ$ミリオネア』(フジテレビ)に出演。[September 7 2006 –While promoting the movie *Deguchi no nai Umi* (The Sea with No Exit), he appeared in the *Quiz $ Millionaire* (Fuji Television).]
- 2007年3月 - パリ・オペラ座で初の歌舞伎公演を父とともに実現。『勧進帳』の弁慶で「紅葉狩」の舞いを披露し、パリの絶賛を浴びる。引っ込みの飛び六方を花道に見立てた中央通路で行って観客を驚かせる。[March 2007 – He performed with this father for the first ever kabuki performance at the Theatre National de l'Opera de Paris. He performed the *Momijigari* dance of Benkei in *Kanjincho*, and earned the praise of Paris. He surprised the audience by jumping into the central aisle to perform the Tobiroppo (the flying exit) along the *hanamichi* (the flower road) passage from the stage.]
- 2007年7月13日 - 楽屋の風呂場で転倒し、割れた戸のガラスで右足の裏を切る大けがを負い、大阪松竹座「七月大歌舞伎」を降板。[July 13 2007 – He fell over in the bathroom of a dressing room and suffered a serious injury, cutting the back of his right foot on broken door glass, and he had to withdraw from the July Great Kabuki at Osaka Shochiku-za Theater.]
- 2009年 - 2007年10月14日に放送された海老蔵に密着したドキュメンタリー番組『名門に生まれるということ…〜市川海老蔵・宿命と苦悩の物語〜』(フジテレビ系)が、ニューヨークフェスティバルのアート部門で金賞を受賞。[2009 – October 14 2007, a documentary on the life of Ebizo was broadcast "Born into fame; the story of the fate and struggles of Ichikawa Ebizo" (Fuji Television-affiliated) and it received the Gold Award in the Arts Section of the New York Festival.]
- 2009年5月23日 - TBSの連続テレビドラマ『MR.BRAIN』に出演。初の民放の連続ドラマ出演であり、初の現代劇出演となる。[May 23, 2009 – He appeared in BS's serialized drama *MR.BRAIN*. It was the first time he had appeared in a commercial serialized drama and it was his first appearance in a contemporary drama.]
- 2010年11月25日早朝、西麻布の飲食店で暴行を受け、頭部、顔面を負傷(11代目市川海老蔵暴行事件)。帰宅後に妻の麻央が救急と警察に通報し虎の門病院に緊急搬送される。歌舞伎俳優の仲間らと飲食後、数人のグループと海老蔵だけが合流、その後、先に帰った数人のグループとは別の数人のグループとトラブルになり殴られたとみられ、警視庁目黒署は傷害事件として捜査を開始。しかし、海老蔵は11月25日午後に予定されていた「初春花形歌舞伎」(2011年1月公演、東京・ル テアトル銀座)の記者会見を体調不良を理由にキャンセルしたにもかかわらず、11月24日夜から飲みに出ていたことが発覚。11月25日夜、成田屋後援会主催の「後援会の集い」開催後に急遽、父・團十郎が記者会見を開き「本人の自覚のなさに怒りを感じる」と謝罪した。怪我のため、11月30日から出演予定だった京都・南座「吉例顔見世興行 東西合同大歌舞伎」を降板した。海老蔵本人が12月7日、都内のホテルで記者会見を行い「日ごろの自分のおごりが招いたことだと思います」と謝罪した。また、会見に同席した松竹の社長が、海老蔵の歌舞伎出演を無期限で自粛することを発表した。無期限謹慎に伴い、「初春花形歌舞伎」は中止となり、名古屋・御園座「二月大歌舞伎」(2011年2月公演)を降板となった。[Early in the morning of November 25, 2010, he injured his head and face in an assault incident in a restaurant in Nishi-Azabu (the Juichidaime Ichikawa Ebizo assault incident). After

returning home, his wife, Mao, reported the incident to the emergency services and to the police, and he was rushed to Toranomon Hospital. It seems that after eating and drinking with his friends, who were kabuki actors, a group of a few people joined with Ebizo, and when they want home, he was assaulted by a stranger whose group he had joined, and the Metropolitan Tokyo Meguro Police Station started an investigation into the incident in which he was injured. However, there was criticism of Ebizo when it was discovered that he went out drinking on the night of November 24, even though he had earlier cancelled a press conference, citing ill health, for the Early Spring Flower Kabuki (to be performed in January 2011 at Le Theater Ginza, Tokyo) that was scheduled to be held in the afternoon of November 25. On the evening of November 25, after the Naritaya acting house hurriedly convened a meeting of the supporters' association, his father, Danjuro, held a press conference and criticized him, saying "I feel angry at his lack of self-awareness." Due to his injuries, he had to withdraw from the festive *kaomise* performance of the Tozaigodo Kabuki, which was scheduled to be held from November 30 at the Minzami-za Theater, Kyoto. Ebizo himself gave a press conference at a hotel in Tokyo on December 7, and apologized that "I think my daily behavior invited this incident." In addition, the Shochiku Theater Company President, who attended the press conference, announced that Ebizo would not be appearing in any productions for an indefinite period. Alongside this punishment for an indefinite period, the Early Spring Flower Kabuki was cancelled, and he withdrew from the February Great Kabuki to be performed at the Misono-za Theater, Nagoya (in February 2011).]

- 2011年7月2日、謹慎を解かれて新橋演舞場「七月大歌舞伎」で舞台復帰。「お客様から温かい声援を頂戴し、身の引き締まる思い。こうして舞台に立たせていただけることに感謝し、日々の舞台に全身全霊で挑んでまいります」とのコメントを発表した。[July 2, 2011 – His punishment was ended and he returned to the stage for the July Great Kabuki at Shinbashi Enbujō. He released a comment that "the warm cheers and applause from the audience inspired me. I am grateful for being able to return to the stage and every day, I will take on the challenge of performing with all of my heart and soul."]
- 2013年正月、14年ぶりに出演する「新春浅草歌舞伎」の初日を迎え、開演前に東京・浅草公会堂前で共演者らと鏡開きを行った。[New Year 2013 – On the first day of the New Year Asakusa Kabuki, in which he was performing for the first time in 14 years, prior to this performance, he held a mirror opening together with his co-starts in front of the Asakusa Public Hall, Tokyo.]
- 2014年1月30日、自身の公式ホームページを作成予定とブログで発表。[January 30, 2014 – He announced on his blog that he plans to create his own official website.]
- 2015年7月29日、千葉県成田市の観光大使「御案内人」に就任。[July 29, 2015 – He was appointed as the "tour guide" tourism ambassador of Narita City, Chiba Prefecture.]
- 2015年11月、「吉例顔見世大歌舞伎　11世市川団十郎五十年祭」(歌舞伎座)の『江戸花成田面影』で長男・観玄が初お目見え。[November 2015– The first performance of his eldest son Kangen in *Edo no Hana Narita no Omokage* in the festive *kaomise* Performance of the Great Kabuki in the 11th Generation Ichikawa Danjuro Fifteenth Festival (Kabuki theater).]
- 2015年より成田市御案内人を務めている。[He has served as the ambassadorial 'tour guide' of Narita City since 2015.]

広報 [Public Relations]

- 2013年4月9日にブログを開始しているが、1日に10回以上更新するほど更新頻度が高い。アメーバMVBを受賞した。[He started a blog on April 9, 2013, and he updates it very frequently, sometimes more than 10 times a day. He received the Ameba MVB award.]
- 2009年、父・市川團十郎とフランス広報大使に就任。[In 2009, His father, Ichikawa Danjuro, was appointed public relations ambassador to France.]
- 2013年正月、新春浅草歌舞伎において、市川海老蔵の睨みを見れば、無病息災とのアナウンスを行った。[New Year 2013. It was announced that if Ichikawa Ebizo glared at you in the New Year Asakusa Kabuki, you would enjoy good health.]

受賞歴 [Awards]

- 1995年 『仮名屋小梅』の濱本清で眞山青果賞新人賞 [1995 Best newcomer at the Mayama Seika Awards for his role of Kiyoshi Hamamoto in *Kanayakome]*
- 1995年 『鏡獅子』で松竹会長賞 [1995 Shochiku Chairman's Award for his performance in *Kagamijishi]*
- 1997年 『吉原雀』で松竹会長賞 [1997 Shochiku Chairman's Award for his performance in *Yoshiwarasuzume*]
- 2000年 『勧進帳』の弁慶、『天守物語』の図書之助で読売演劇大賞杉村春子賞 [2000 Yomiuri Theatrical Grand Awards Haruko Sugimura Award for Benkei in *Kanjincho* and for Zusho Nosuke in *Tenshu Monogatari*]
- 2001年 松尾芸能賞新人賞、芸術選奨文部科学大臣新人賞受賞 [2001 Best newcomer prize in the Matsuo Prize of Entertainment. Best newcomer award in the Minister of Education Award for Fine Arts]
- 2007年 フランス芸術文化勲章(L'Ordre des Arts et des lettre)のシュヴァリエ(Chevalier)受章 [2007 Bestowed the title of Chevalier of the L'Ordre des Arts et des letter by France]
- 2007年 ベストドレッサー賞特別賞 [2007 Special award in the Best Dressed Awards]
- 2014年 第37回日本アカデミー賞 優秀主演男優賞を受賞 [2014 Best actor award in the 37th Japan Academy Awards]
- 2014年 Yahoo!検索大賞 2014・俳優部門 [2014 Yahoo! Search Grand Prize 2014 in the actor category]

出演作品 [Performances]

歌舞伎*[Kabuki]*

天衣紛上野初花「雪暮夜入谷畦道」(三千歳と直侍)の片岡直次郎,鳴神の鳴神上人,源氏物語の光君,助六由縁江戸桜の花川戸助六,鏡獅子の小姓弥生後に獅子の精,勧進帳の弁慶、富樫左衛門 [Naojiro Kataoka in Kumo ni Magou Ueno no Hatsuhana *Yukinoyubeiiriyanoazemich* (3,000 years old and Naozamurai),Narukami Shonin in *Narukami*,Hikaru Kimi in *The Tale of Genji*,Hanakawado Sukeroku in *Sukeroku Yukari no Edozakura*,the spirit of a lion after Kosho Yayoi in *Kagamijishi*,Benkei in *Kanjincho*, Saemon Togashi]

海外公演*[Overseas Performances]*

十一代目市川海老蔵襲名披露　歌舞伎パリ公演(パリ・国立シャイヨー劇場)(2004年10月),訪欧歌舞伎公演(ロンドン・サドラーズ・ウェルズ劇場、アムステルダム・スタッツスハウブルフ劇場)(2006年5月、6月),パリ　オペラ座　松竹大歌舞伎(パリ・オペラ座　ガルニエ宮)(2007年3月),松竹大歌舞伎　モナコ公演(モナコ・オペラ座　サル・ガルニエ)(2009年9月),松竹大歌舞伎　ロンドン公演(ロンドン・サドラーズ・ウェルズ劇場)(2010年6月),松竹大歌舞伎　ローマ公演　Shochiku Grand Kabuki featuring Ebizo Ichikawa XI(ローマ・アルジェンティーナ劇場)(2010年6月),市川海老蔵 シンガポール公演「古典への誘い(いざない)」JAPAN THEATER "Produced and headlined by EBIZO ICHIKAWA XI(シンガポール・マリーナベイ・サンズマスターカードシアター)(2014年11月),EBIZO ICHIKAWA XI's JAPAN THEATER 2015(シンガポール・マリーナベイ・サンズグランドシアター)(2015年10月),市川海老蔵　GRAND JAPAN THEATER　フジャイラ公演(フジャイラ・ミラマール・アルアッカビーチリゾート)(2016年2月),市川海老蔵　GRAND JAPAN THEATER　ニューヨーク公演(ニューヨーク・カーネギー・ホール)(2016年3月) [Kabuki performance in Paris of the performance he gave on the assumption of his name of Juichidaime Ichikawa Ebizo (the National Palais de Chaillot Theater, Paris) (October 2004),Kabuki performances in a tour of Europe (at the Saddlers Wells Theater, London, and the Stadsschouwburg Theater, Amsterdam) (May and June 2006),the Theatre National de l'Opera de Paris Shochiku Great Kabuki (the Theatre National de l'Opera de Paris, Palais Garnier) (March 2007),Shochiku Great Kabuki Monaco performance (the Opéra de Monte-Carlo, Salle Garnier) (September 2009),Shochiku Great Kabuki London performance (the Saddlers Wells Theater, London) (June 2010),Shochiku Great Kabuki Rome performance Shochiku Grand Kabuki featuring Ebizo Ichikawa XI (Teatro-Argentina, Rome) (June 2010),Ichikawa Ebizo Singapore performance "Invitation to the Classics (Izana)" JAPAN THEATER "Produced and headlined by EBIZO ICHIKAWA XI (Marina Bay Sands MasterCard Theater, Singapore) (November 2014),EBIZO ICHIKAWA XI's JAPAN THEATER 2015(Marina Bay Sands Grand Theater, Singapore) (October 2015), Ichikawa Ebizo GRAND JAPAN THEATER Fujairah performance (Fujairah Miramar, the Al-Acka Beach Resort) (February 2016), Ichikawa Ebizo GRAND JAPAN THEATER New York performance (Carnegie Hall, New York) (March 2016)]

テレビドラマ*[TV Dramas]*

大河ドラマ(NHK)[*Taiga* drama (NHK)]

花の乱(1994年) - 足利義政(青年時代) 役,武蔵 MUSASHI(2003年) - 主演・宮本武蔵 役,おんな城主 直虎(2017年) - 織田信長 役,12時間超ワイドドラマ(テレビ東京),豊臣秀吉 天下を獲る!(1995年) - 吉法師 役,炎の奉行 大岡越前守(1997年) - 大岡市十郎 役,第8回時代小説大賞スペシャル「仲蔵狂乱」(朝日放送) - 中村仲蔵 役 [*Hanna no Ran* (1994) – role of Ashikaga Yoshimasa (in his youth),MUSASHI (2003) – lead role of Miyamoto Musashi,*Onna Joshu Naotora* (2017) – the role of Oda Nobunaga,*12-jikan Cho-wide Drama* (TV Tokyo),*Toyotomi Hideyoshi Unifier of a Country!* (1995) – role of Kipposhi,*Honoo no Bugyou Ookaechizennokami* (1997) – role of Oka Ichijuro, *The 8th Era Novel Grand Prix Special "Nakazo Kyouran"* (Asahi Broadcasting) – role of Nakamura Nakazo]

MR.BRAIN 第1話・第7話・第8話(2009年、TBS) - 武井公平 役 [*MR.BRAIN* episodes 1, 7, and 8 (2009, TBS) – role of Kohei Takei]

生誕100年記念松本清張ドラマスペシャル「霧の旗」(2010年、日本テレビ) - 主演・大塚欽也 役 [*Drama Special on the 100 year anniversary of the birth of Matsumoto Seichou, "Kiri no Hata"* (2010, Nippon Television) – lead role of Kinya Otsuka]

金曜プレステージ「長谷川町子物語～サザエさんが生まれた日～」(2013年、フジテレビ) - 9代目市川海老蔵 役 [*Friday Prestige "Hasegawa Machiko Monogatari – the day that Sazae san was born -"* (2013, Fuji Television) –role of the 9th Ichikawa Ebizo]

土曜ドラマ「弱くても勝てます ～青志先生とへっぽこ高校球児の野望～」(2014年、日本テレビ) - 谷内田健太郎 役 [*Saturday Drama "Yowakutemo Katemasu: Aoshi Sensei to Heppoko Kōkō Kyūji no Yabō"* (2014, Nippon Television) – role of Kentaro Yachida]

石川五右衛門(2016年、テレビ東京) - 主演・石川五右衛門 役 [*Ishikawa Gouemon* (2016, TV Tokyo) – lead role of Ishikawa Gouemon]

テレビアニメ*[TV Animation]*

名探偵コナン コナンと海老蔵歌舞伎十八番ミステリー(2016年1月9日・16日、読売テレビ) - 市川海老蔵(本人) 役 [*Detective Conan Conan and the Ebizo Kabuki Jūhachiban Mystery* (January 9 to 16, 2016 Yomiuri Television) – role of Ichikawa Ebizo (himself)]

吹き替え*[Voice Over Performances]*

オール・イズ・ロスト ～最後の手紙～(2014年) - 我らの男 役(ロバート・レッドフォード) [*All is Lost – the Last Letter* (2014) – Role of 'our man" (Robert Redford)]

映画*[Movies]*

出口のない海(2006年) - 主演・並木浩二 役,一命(2011年) - 主演・津雲半四郎 役,利休にたずねよ(2013年) - 主演・千利休 役,喰女-クイメ-(2014年) - 主演・長谷川浩介 役,無限の住人(2017年) - 閑馬永空 役 [*The Sea with No Exit* (2006) – lead role of Koji Namiki,*Harakiri: Death of a Samurai* (2011) – lead role of Hanshirô Tsugumo, *Ask This of Rikyu* (2013) – the lead role of Sen no Rikyu, *Over Your Dead Body* (2014) – lead role of Kousuke Hasegawa, *Blade of the Immortal* (2017) – role of Eiku Shizuma]

その他の舞台*[Other Stage Performances]*

ライル(1990年) - ジョッシュ役,スタンド・バイ・ミー(1991年) - 主演・クリス役,天守物語(1999年) - 図書之助 役(五代目坂東玉三郎、宮沢りえと共演),海神別荘 - 公子 役(坂東玉三郎と共演),疾風のごとく(2002年) - 鈴木猪平 役,宮本武蔵(2003年) - 主演・宮本武蔵 役,信長(2006年) - 主演・織田信長役,天守物語(2006年) - 図書之助役(坂東玉三郎、二代目市川春猿と共演),海神別荘(2006年) - 公子 役(坂東玉三郎と共演),ドラクル(2007年)- 主演・レイ 役(宮沢りえと共演) [Lyle (1990) – role of Josh, *Stand by Me* (1991) – lead role of Chris,*Tenshu Monogatari* (1999) – role of Zusho Nosuke (Bandoutama Saburou V, joint performance with Rie Miyazawa),*Kaijin Besso* – role of young nobleman (joint performance with Bandoutama Saburou),*On the Wings of the Wind* (2002) – role of Suzuki Inohira,*Miyamoto Musashi* (2003) – the lead role of Miyamoto Musashi, *Nobunaga* (2006) - the lead role of Oda Nobunaga, *Tenshu Monogatari* (2006) – the role of Zusho Nosuke (joint performance with Bandoutama Saburou, Nidaime (the second) Junen Ichikawa,*Kaijin Besso* (2006) – role of young nobleman (joint performance with Bandoutama Saburou),*Dracula* (2007)- the lead role of Ray (joint performance with Rie Miyazawa))

CM [Commercials]

伊藤園「お〜いお茶」(2000年 -),ヤマキ(2000年 - 2010年),明治製菓「ショコラクール」(1995年),三井生命(1998年),NEC「Expressワークステーション」(1998年),ミズノ「スーパースター」(2003年),TSUTAYA DISCAS (2009年8月 -)テレビショッピング番組の司会者役,飯田グループホールディングス(2014年-),ライオン「贅沢Care」(2015年),ジェイテクト(2016年) [Itoen *O–Io-Cha* (2000 -),Yamaki (2000 - 2010),Meiji Seika *Chocolate Cool* (1995),Mitsui Life Insurance (1998),NEC *Express Workstation* (1998),Mizuno *Superstar* (2003),TSUTAYA DISCAS (August 2009 -) moderator role in a TV shopping program, Iida Group Holdings (2014 -),Lion *Luxury Care* (2015),JTEKT (2016)]

Life Information

基本情報 [Basic Information]

本名は堀越 寶世(宝世)(ほりこし たかとし)。旧名は堀越 孝俊(ほりこし たかとし)。[His real name is Takatoshi (Tomisei) Horikoshi. His former name is Takatoshi Horikoshi (written using different *kanji* characters).]

妻はキャスターでタレントの小林麻央(2017年6月 死別)。身長176cm、体重80kg。血液型はAB型。星座は射手座。[His wife was TV newscaster and celebrity Mao Kobayashi (died in June 2017). Height, 176cm. Weight, 80kg. Blood type, AB. Star sign, Sagittarius.]

趣味・嗜好*[Hobbies and Likes]*

特技はバスケットボール、趣味は相撲鑑賞。 学生時代はバスケットボール部に所属していた。スタジオジブリのアニメ作品の大ファン。「おしゃれイズム」に出演した際に、『崖の上のポニョ』の非売品の人形と宮崎駿が同作を制作する際に使用した鉛筆をプレゼントされ、涙ぐんで喜んでいた。宮崎本人と対談したこともあり、その際に自身が実践しているタワシで体をなでる健康法を宮崎も行っていることがわかり、共通点があったことに感動したという。以前は寿司を月50回食べに行ったり、タバコを1日4箱分吸ったり、酒をあびるように飲むなど不健康な生活をしていたが、心境の変化でタバコは2004年の海老蔵襲名時にやめ、「歌舞伎をやるとき、神様に捧げることも意識しなくちゃいけないかなと。だから、心と体を清くしなくちゃ」という思いから不規則な食生活や酒、肉、魚も2008年11月頃からやめていたが、麻央との結婚後に酒、肉、魚は再開している。[He plays basketball and was a member of the basketball club when a student. He enjoys watching sumo. His is a big fan of the anime movies of Studio Ghibli. When he appeared in the program *Oshareism*, he was presented with a figure from *Ponyo* that was not available for sale and the pen that Miyazaki Hayao had used to draw this anime, which moved him to tears of joy. He also talked with Mr. Miyazaki, and he learned that Mr. Miyazaki also practices a health technique using a brush on the body that he himself practices, and he was moved by this point in common between them. He had previously lived an unhealthy life, eating sushi up to 50 times a month, smoking 4 packets of cigarettes a day, and drinking until he was drunk. But he had a change of heart and gave up cigarettes in 2004 when he assumed the name of Ebizo, saying that “When I perform kabuki, I think I must be aware of giving praise to God.” Therefore, from the idea of “purifying his mind and body,” from around November 2008 he gave up his irregular eating habits, and also gave up alcohol, meat, and fish. But he began to again drink alcohol and eat meat and fish after his marriage to Mao]

論文[Articles]

国立情報学研究所収録論文 国立情報学研究所 [National Institute of Informatics' Collection of Articles, National Institute of Informatics]

五代目尾上菊之助とは幼馴染で同級生。小学生の頃、彼の家の別荘に招かれたときにいたずらをしようとしたら菊之助の母である富司純子に叱られたが、これが家族以外の人に叱られた初めての経験だったという。[He was a childhood friend and classmate of Godaime (the fifth) Onoe Kikunosuke. When he was an elementary school student, he was invited to his friend's residential villa, and he was scolded by Junko Fujimoto, the mother of Kikunosuke, for being mischievous. This was his first experience of being scolded by someone outside of his family.]

再従兄弟に四代目尾上松緑、七代目市川染五郎が、再従姉妹には松本紀保(七代目染五郎の姉)・松たか子(同妹)がいる。

伊藤英明とは親友で、お互いを「英明」、「孝俊(本名の堀越孝俊)」と呼び合う仲。[His second cousins (male) include Dainime (the second) Onoe Shoroku, Shichidaime (the seventh) Ichikawa Somegorō, and his second cousins (female) are Matsumo Tokio (the sister of Shichidaime Somegorō) and Matsu Takako (the same). He is close friends with Hideaki Ito and they call each other "Hideaki" and "Takatoshi" (his real name is Takatoshi Horikoshi).]

出来事 [Events]

- 2009年11月19日 - フリーキャスターの小林麻央との交際が『日刊スポーツ』で報じられる。同日中に連名で、結婚を前提に交際し婚約することをファックスで発表。年が明けた2010年1月29日に正式に婚約発表の記者会見を執り行った。同年3月3日婚姻届を提出し、7月29日に結婚式並びに披露宴を執り行った。[November 19, 2009 – It was reported in *Nikkan Sports* that he was dating the TV newscaster Mao Kobayashi. On the same day, it was announced by fax that they had been dating on the premise of marriage toward them becoming engaged. After the New Year, on January 29, 2010, they held a press conference in which they officially announced their engagement. They submitted the marriage notification on March of the same year, and the wedding ceremony and reception took place on July 29.]
- 2010年11月25日早朝、西麻布の飲食店で暴行を受け、頭部、顔面を負傷(11代目市川海老蔵暴行事件)。帰宅後に妻の麻央が救急と警察に通報し虎の門病院に緊急搬送される。歌舞伎俳優の仲間らと飲食後、数人のグループと海老蔵だけが合流、その後、先に帰った数人のグループとは別の数人のグループとトラブルになり殴られたとみられ、警視庁目黒署は傷害事件として捜査を開始。しかし、海老蔵は11月25日午後に予定されていた「初春花形歌舞伎」(2011年1月公演、東京・ル テアトル銀座)の記者会見を体調不良を理由にキャンセルしたにもかかわらず、11月24日夜から飲みに出ていたことが発覚。11月25日夜、成田屋後援会主催の「後援会の集い」開催後に急遽、父・團十郎が記者会見を開き「本人の自覚のなさに怒りを感じる」と謝罪した。怪我のため、11月30日から出演予定だった京都・南座「吉例顔見世興行　東西合同大歌舞伎」を降板した。海老蔵本人が12月7日、都内のホテルで記者会見を行い「日ごろの自分のおごりが招いたことだと思います」と謝罪した。また、会見に同席した松竹の社長が、海老蔵の歌舞伎出演を無期限で自粛することを発表した。無期限謹慎に伴い、「初春花形歌舞伎」は中止となり、名古屋・御園座「二月大歌舞伎」(2011年2月公演)を降板となった。[November 25, 2010 Early in the morning he injured his head and face in an assault incident

in a restaurant in Nishi-Azabu (the Juichidaime Ichikawa Ebizo assault incident).After returning home, his wife, Mao, reported the incident to the emergency services and to the police, and he was rushed to Toranomon Hospital. It seems that after eating and drinking with his friends, who were kabuki actors, a group of a few people joined with Ebizo, and when they want home, he was assaulted by a stranger whose group he had joined, and the Metropolitan Tokyo Meguro Police Station started an investigation into the incident in which he was injured. However, there was criticism of Ebizo when it was discovered that he went out drinking on the night of November 24, even though he had earlier cancelled a press conference, citing ill health, for the Early Spring Flower Kabuki (to be performed in January 2011 at Le Theater Ginza, Tokyo) that was scheduled to be held in the afternoon of November 25. On the evening of November 25, after the Naritaya acting house hurriedly convened a meeting of the supporters' association, his father, Danjuro, held a press conference and criticized him, saying "I feel angry at his lack of self-awareness." Due to his injuries, he had to withdraw from the festive *kaomise* performance of the Tozaigodo Kabuki, which was scheduled to be held from November 30 at the Minzami-za Theater, Kyoto. Ebizo himself gave a press conference at a hotel within Tokyo on December 7, and apologized that "I think my daily behavior invited this incident." In addition, the Shochiku Theater Company President, who attended the press conference, announced that Ebizo would not be appearing in any productions for an indefinite period. Alongside this punishment for an indefinite period, the Early Spring Flower Kabuki was cancelled, and he withdrew from the February Great Kabuki to be performed at the Misono-za Theater, Nagoya (in February 2011).]

- 2011年7月25日、妻・麻央との第1子となる長女・麗禾(れいか)が誕生。[July 25, 2011, Reika, his eldest daughter and his first child with his wife Mao, is born.]
- 2013年2月3日、父・12世團十郎が死去。市川宗家当主の家督を引き継ぐ。[February 3, His father Danjuro XII, dies. He inherits from his father the title of the head of the Ichikawa clan.]
- 2013年3月22日、妻・麻央との第2子となる長男・勸玄(かんげん)が誕生。[March 22, 2013, Kangen, his eldest son and second child with his wife, Mao is born]
- 2015年2月4日、本名を堀越孝俊から、堀越寶世(宝世)と改名したことを、ブログで発表。[February 4, 2015, He announces on his blog that he has changed his real name from Takatoshi Horikoshi to Takatoshi Horikoshi (Tomisei) (written with different kanji characters).]
- 2016年6月9日、妻・麻央が乳がんを患っていることを公表した。[June 9, 2016, It is announced that his wife Mao is suffering from breast cancer.]
- 2017年6月22日、妻・麻央が死去。翌日の緊急会見で妻の死を公表した。[June 22, 2017 His wife, Mao, dies. Her death is announced in a special press conference the following day.]

家族・親族 [Family and Relatives]

曾祖父 - 七代目松本幸四郎,祖父 - 十一代目市川團十郎,大叔父 - 八代目松本幸四郎,大叔父 - 二代目尾上松緑,父 - 十二代目市川團十郎,叔母 - 二代目市川紅梅,妹 - 三代目市川ぼたん,妻 - 小林麻央,義姉 - 小林麻耶 [Great grandfather – Shichidaime Matsumoto Koshiro,Grandfather – Juichidaime Ichikawa Danjuro, great uncle – Hachidaime (the eighth) Matsumoto Koshiro,great uncle - Nidaime (the second) Onoe Shoroku,father – Junidaime Ichikawa Danjuro, aunt – Nidaime (the second) Ichikawa Kobai,sister – Sandaimei (the third) Ichikawa Botan,wife - Mao Kobayashi, sister-in-law - Maya Kobayashi]

- 2010年1月29日、フリーアナウンサーの小林麻央と婚約発表会見を行った。その後3月3日に婚姻届を提出し、結婚披露宴を行った。[January 29, 2010, He holds a press conference to announce his engagement to freelance TV announcer Mao Kobayashi. After that, they submitted the wedding notification on March 3 and held the wedding ceremony.]
- 2011年7月25日、第一子となる長女・麗禾が誕生。[July 25, 2011 His eldest and first child, Reika, is born]
- 2013年3月22日、第二子となる長男・勸玄が誕生。[March 22, 2013, His second child and eldest son, Kangen, is born]
- 2016年6月9日、麻央が乳がんを患っていることを記者会見にて明らかにした。[June 9 2016, It is announced at a press conference that Mao is suffering from breast cancer.]
- 2017年6月23日、自身のブログで「人生で一番泣いた日です」と麻央の死をほのめかす文面を公表した。同日、舞台終演後の14時30分に緊急記者会見を行い麻央が前日の6月22日夜に自宅で死去したことを報告した。麻央の死去当日、海老蔵は舞台の稽古中で、自身の携帯電話に麻央の危篤を知らせるLINEのメッセージがあったことから急遽帰宅し、義姉の小林麻耶らとともに最期を看取った。麻央の最期の言葉は「愛してる」だった。[June 23, 2017, On his own blog, he posts that this is "the day I have cried the most in my life," implying Mao's death. On the same day, after a stage performance at 2.30pm, he holds a press conference and reports that Mao died at home on the evening of the previous day, June 22. On the day of Mao's death, Ebizo was rehearsing on stage, and he returned home suddenly upon receiving a LINE message on his mobile phone informing him that Mao's condition had deteriorated. Together with his sister-in-law Maya Kobayashi, they spent the final moments together with Mao. Mao's final words were "I love you."]

Chapter 3
Narrative Simulation for Film Rhetoric Composition With or Without Story and Nostalgia Effects

Akihito Kanai
Hosei University, Japan

ABSTRACT

In addition to the determinacy created by the stories' or characters' goal-directed actions, the indeterminacy created by the non-story and nostalgia aspects of rhetoric is an essential issue of narrative simulation for non-story film rhetoric composition. The narrative simulation can test cognitive effects created through the interaction between the cognitive process, story, discourse, and the rhetoric of a film. Non-story film editing can be classified according to the categories of rhythm and nostalgia, and can be used for narrative film rhetoric simulation. Nostalgia may emerge with the determinacy of the place and time and the indeterminacy of non-story aspects of rhetoric. Non-nostalgia narrative may emerge with the indeterminacy of the place and time and can be simulated by the use of the non-story editing regarding the rhythm categories.

INTRODUCTION

Narrative simulation is a process of composing and designing various kinds of narrative rhetoric and of testing the cognitive effects of that narrative. Many cognitive effects of narrative are caused by the effect of the determinacy and the indeterminacy on the interaction between cognitive process, story, discourse, and rhetoric themselves. For example, the indeterminacy emergent from the cutting techniques for narrative space and time on the narrative film can cause a viewer to experience cognitive transition and intensive cognitive effects. Based on the cutting techniques used to generate the indeterminacy with regards to time, space, or characters in continuous shots, a viewer or a reader can feel less constrained with regards to story comprehension and can reset the viewpoint to subtle elements, such as individual

DOI: 10.4018/978-1-5225-4775-4.ch003

Copyright © 2018, IGI Global. Copying or distributing in print or electronic forms without written permission of IGI Global is prohibited.

shots. The cognitive transition caused by the indeterminacy of narrative film rhetoric can cause cognitive effects, such as reality or nostalgia effects. The reality of, or the nostalgia effects of, the narrative film can be enhanced or reduced by controlling the determinacy of its story and by controlling the indeterminacy of non-story aspects of rhetoric. This chapter is specially focused on the topic of narrative simulation for non-story film rhetoric composition.

Generally, based on various narrative simulations, one single narrative is produced. However, using computer technology, the diversity and the fluidity of the world of narrative content can itself also be one narrative work. Kanai (2016) argued that computational narrative film rhetoric composition system, in particular with regards to the specific place with or without story and nostalgia effects. Many kinds of nostalgia can be actualized using a strategy that employs both story and non-story cognitive and aspects of rhetoric by the system, by which various kinds of film rhetoric can be composed from the same shots or stories. Thus, the nature of nostalgia and narrative can be studied. The various kinds of computational narrative film rhetoric composition can be considered as being a narrative simulation by which the cognitive effects created through the interaction can be designed and tested. In this chapter, using the film rhetoric composition system, the author provides special analyses of the two types of narrative simulation and the cognitive effects of various edited films as they relate to the indeterminacy and the determinacy from the rhetoric of the film editing and from the three kinds of nostalgia.

The film-editing-based determinacy and indeterminacy can be a key concept for narrative simulation. There are two different aspects of rhetoric in film editing. The difference is very important in terms of the design determinacy and indeterminacy of film cognition and composition: narrative simulation. First, one is a dialectic aspect, in which the totality and the determinacy of the story concepts are important (Eisenstein, 1949). The other one is an irrational cutting aspect, in which the subtle non-story elements, such as editing technique itself are important. In addition to the determinacy created by the stories' or characters' goal-directed actions, the indeterminacy created by the non-story elements of rhetoric, and the nostalgia aspects of rhetoric are essential issues of narrative simulation for film rhetoric composition. Based on the indeterminacy, the narrative simulation mechanism can emphasize the non-story rhetorical aspects of films. The aspects of rhetoric can cause cognitive effects that do not arise through comprehending a story but which instead arise through the audiovisual situation itself.

The author classified the editing into 16 rhythm editing categories based on Eisenstein's four methods of montage theory (metric montage, rhythmic montage, tonal montage, and overtonal montage) regarding the indeterminacy. Next, the author designed 10 kinds of 52-second films using 90-second sequences of 18 shots each from *The Passion of Joan of Arc* (1928) directed by Carl Th. Dreyer, for narrative simulation. Then, the author analyzed the cognitive effects of the edited films.

Other than by the categories of rhythm, editing can alternatively be classified based on nostalgia. Nostalgia can emerge from various different types of non-story film rhetoric. Non-story-based nostalgia does not always follow comfortable cognition. Some nostalgia is evoked from the loss of a place's good past. Other nostalgia is evoked from the unforgettably bad past of a place. Furthermore, nostalgia without story may emerge suddenly with the determinacy of the place and the time, and the indeterminacy of non-story rhetorical elements such as irrational shots. For these reasons, to simulate narrative film rhetoric, the rhythm editing categories and nostalgia found in non-story narratives must be examined.

In this chapter, the focus is on the narrative film simulation for non-story narrative rhythm and nostalgia in order to discuss and explore the entire narrative concept.

BACKGROUND

When making a narrative film, generally, a director makes some kind of structure. According to Chatman (1990), the following four elements of the techniques when making the structure of a film are these: events, editing, photography, and recording. Based on Chatman (1990), the author decided to define the rhetoric of the film; doing so because a director combines the above techniques with certain purposes. Generally, the rhetoric of the film is accomplished by the purpose of telling some story from explicit or implicit events. Previous studies of film cognition also showed how viewers have understood the contents of stories. However, a film is not always created with the purpose of representing the story's contents: the rhetoric of the film may have a purpose that is not to represent a discourse-based story about the events. Philosopher Deleuze (1990) said that after World War II, films had stopped being "movement-images" and instead had become "time-images." Some filmmakers aimed to construct relationships by using irrational cutting and the absence of common measuring within their films. There are films for which it is necessary to realize the film structure is independent from the story's contents. For example, a film might intentionally be edited to include a shot generally considered to be an editing error. In such a film, a purely audiovisual situation emerges; and the point where force is applied is placed in the description itself, in addition to the actions of the characters. Here, a film does not always have an overall meaning; and the subtle element of each shot becomes important. With regards to the purpose of the rhetoric of the film, there is a difference between the movement-image and the time-image, as Deleuze (1990) said. Then, the parts where emphasis is placed on the elements of the film structure are different. Deleuze (1985) argued that irrational cuts in the film are related to the time-image. Although the time-image concept was not argued as narrative simulation, the concept bears a close relationship with narrative simulation based on the cutting technique.

The author defines the cutting technique as a technique of creating irrational cuts in a film. Cutting techniques are used to generate an irrational relationship or an unfamiliar situation in the film and to create an alienation effect (Brecht & Willett, 1964). Narrative simulation for film rhetoric composition, using various editing strategies, relates to the cutting technique; and the indeterminacy can emphasize the subtle elements of each shots.

Narrative Simulation, Montage Theory, and Cutting Techniques

One famous film theory shared by a film director is the montage theory of Eisenstein (1942). The montage theory can be used as a tool of narrative simulation. He says that taking Cut A from a theme and Cut B from the same theme and placing the two juxtaposed cuts in contrast to each other can provide one clear image of the contents of the theme. The emphasis of the theory is on the overall meaning of the film.

Eisenstein (1949) analyzed the four rhythm editing categories from the dialectic aspect of rhetoric.

1. Metric montage is based on the absolute lengths of pieces.
2. Rhythmic montage is based on the lengths of pieces using visual compositions of the shots.
3. Tonal montage is based on the emotional meaning of the shots.
4. Overtonal montage is based on the collective calculation of each piece's appeal.

In this chapter, we expand the four categories of montage theory, based on the indeterminacy from the irrational cutting aspect of rhetoric.

There are two different purposes in the rhetoric of the film (Kanai, 2002). The first purpose is to tell some story. However, "the rhetoric of the film with the purpose of telling a consistent story" (S-type rhetoric) is only one possibility; and "the rhetoric of the film with a purpose other than telling a consistent story" (NS-type rhetoric) exists, too. S-type rhetoric can be created using dialectic editing. Also, NS-type rhetoric can be created using irrational cutting.

Dialectic continuity is used in S-type rhetoric. For example, spatial continuity ensures that a viewer can understand the characters' relative locations – even when they are not in the same frame. Moreover, continuity editing allows for temporal manipulation (Bordwell & Thompson, 1997). A viewer tends to recognize the rhetoric of a film as rhetoric for understanding the story (Cowen, 1988; Avrahami and Kareev, 1994; Schwan, Hesse, and Garsoffky, 1998). This tendency interacts with determinacy from a dialectic aspect of film editing. When the rhetoric is structured to tell a consistent story, the viewer's constraint regarding the wish to understand a consistent story fits the rhetoric of the film; that is, the film is related to (and falls within) the viewer's constraint. In contrast, discontinuity must be emphasized to make NS-type rhetoric. Here, based on the destabilization and the indeterminacy created by the discontinuity, the viewer sometimes cannot establish a consistent story from the images. Consequently, attention to the rhetoric itself is enhanced.

Based on the cutting to make the indeterminacy from the irrational relationships of time or character in continuous shots, a viewer or a reader can relax the constraint about story comprehension and reset the viewpoint to better view subtle elements, such as individual shots.

Eisenstein's four methods of montage are based mainly on the dialectic S-type rhetoric. The four methods can be expanded based on three irrational relationships, 1) time, 2) character, and 3) time and character to simulate various narratives using the cutting techniques.

The cutting techniques for narrative space and time in the film can cause the viewer's cognitive transition from story-driven determinacy to non-story rhetoric-driven indeterminacy. Based on the cognitive transition, cognitive effects such as intensive reality effects can emerge.

Narrative Simulation and Nostalgia

Nostalgia-based narrative film rhetoric generation can be a tool of narrative simulation, too. Using images of the past in cuts according to the cutting techniques for generating nostalgia effects, several narrative simulations for both story-type and non-story type film rhetoric composition can be done.

Nostalgia has mainly been argued by researchers like Stern (1992) as a longing for a good but lost personal and historical past. In general, nostalgia refers to a longing for the past. Holbrook and Schindler (1991) defined it as being a preference toward objects (people, places, or things) that were more common when one was younger. By contrast, Davis (1979) argued that there are three kinds of nostalgia: simple nostalgia, reflexive nostalgia, and interpreted nostalgia. Simple nostalgia emerges from the good past. Reflexive nostalgia can emerge from both the good and bad past. Interpreted nostalgia can emerge from the reality or the indeterminacy regarding the past.

Computational narrative simulation can be argued as being the choice of a type of rhetoric used as a strategy in order for the viewer's cognitive processes to relate to various kinds of nostalgia. In Kanai (2016), using a cognitive and computational model, the rhetoric of the film was classified into four kinds of nostalgia – including non-nostalgia. Kanai (2016) focuses on three kinds of nostalgias regarding a certain place, as suggested by Davis (1979): "simple nostalgia" "reflexive nostalgia" and "interpreted nostalgia." Simple nostalgia emerges from the good past without cognitive transition and de-familiarization. Reflexive nostalgia emerges from both the good and bad past, with cognitive transition and de-familiarization. Interpreted nostalgia emerges from the reality or the uncertainty of the past with cognitive transition and de-familiarization.

Simple nostalgia emerges from affection for the past of a place. By contrasts, reflexive and interpreted nostalgia emerge from the reality and the uncertainty about the past of a place as related to unfamiliar situations, with cognitive transition and alienation effects based on the cutting techniques. A computerized classification can be used to simulate rhetoric and films for various kinds of nostalgia. The generated films can reveal both the narrow story and the broad non-story aspects of the rhetoric, narrative, and cognition of the past and the film. Without using story structures and goal-oriented characters, nostalgia-based visual narrative rhetoric could be simulated.

FILM RHETORIC COMPOSITION AND NARRATIVE SIMULATION

In general, film creation requires choosing and mixing types of rhetoric – whether S-type or NS-type – according to a director's strategy based on the constraints of story comprehension. When the constraint is relaxed, an irrational cut of NS-type rhetoric may cause a "resetting of one's viewpoint" and "affect, which does not arise through comprehending a story, but rather through the audiovisual situations" themselves (Kanai, 2001b). A resetting of one's viewpoint indicates that the viewer's viewpoint shifts from the need for determinacy in a story-based narrative to acceptance of the indeterminacy of the non-story narrative. This reflects the object associations within the film and the "mood" or the details of the film. "Affect, which does not arise through comprehending a story, but rather through the audiovisual situation" is caused by the audiovisual situation that emerges from the mood and the object associations of the film.

In NS-type rhetoric, the editing, recording, and photography of a film are not always subordinate to the determinacy of the overall story. As stated above, the focus is on non-story narrative, the mood and the object associations, or the reality related to the unfamiliar situations; rather than on the events in the story. The determinacy of such associations and situations causes cognitive effects that do not arise in the process of comprehending a story. Kanai (2001a) indicated that when a viewer is able to relax his or her constraint with regard to the need to comprehend a story, this strengthens those cognitive effects, which do not arise in the process of comprehending the story.

The indeterminacy derived from non-story rhetorical elements creates new realities, nostalgia effects, or meanings related to unknown memories and affects that do not arise through story comprehension alone. The indeterminacy can emerge through the sudden appearance of a section of NS-type rhetoric. In this case, a viewer sometimes cannot apply the determinacy from the consistent story. Therefore, attention to the audio-visual situation itself or the subtle elements is enhanced. This occurs because the indeterminacy generates new cognitive effects related to unknown memories and affects that do not arise through story comprehension.

NS-type rhetoric is created through cutting techniques used to create indeterminacy between 1) the rhetorical elements of two shots; 2) events and images; or 3) sounds and images (Kanai & Ogata, 2004b). The indeterminacy created through the cutting techniques described above is used in many artistic films, television advertisements, and music videos.

On the contrary, continuity – which is used in many S-type rhetoric films – means that the flow from shot to shot in film is smooth. Thanks to spatial continuity, a viewer can understand the characters' locations. Moreover, continuity editing supports and sustains temporal manipulation as well. Continuity-based determinacy can be created by identical elements in continuous shots. But, to cause intensive cognitive effects using NS-type rhetoric, the discontinuity of events must be emphasized in the rhetoric. A mix of identical and different elements in continuous shots is important source of the cognitive effects of the rhetoric of the film.

NS-type rhetoric may also have different kinds of discontinuity, such as discontinuity between the actor, object, sound, or tone of the photography. The interplay between continuity and discontinuity is important.

The author had proposed a film rhetoric composition system (Kanai & Ogata, 2004b). The system can be used for narrative simulation. The film rhetoric composition system for NS-Narrative includes three parts:

1. A mechanism for the retrieval of shots based on the rhetorical techniques utilized by each;
2. A database of shots;
3. A mechanism for the combination of shots

The user can decide which approaches to use for making discontinuities. The system then retrieves the shots from the database that fits the chosen strategy. The shots are edited as a sequence of shots and outputted. By using this computational approach, we could make many different films from the same shots and use them to study the nature of NS-type rhetoric.

For example, from a database of pinhole camera shots, Kanai & Morohoshi (2005) simulated NS-Narrative work performed by the system. In NS-Narrative Work 1, the tone of the background shot by the pinhole camera is not changed, but the object in the foreground is changed. In the outputted film, the discontinuity is created based on the relationship between rhetorical elements such as the foreground object of the two shots and can cause intensive cognitive effects among viewers. Moreover, in NS-Narrative Work 1, an irrational relationship between sounds and images is also used.

Narrative simulation with the film rhetoric composition system can make use of the "strategic identical element," which makes determinacy continuous, and the "strategic differential element," which makes indeterminacy discontinuous in simulating film rhetoric. For example, a person or an object in one shot is retained in the next two shots as a "strategic identical element." Comparatively, the location is changed from one shot to the next two shots; the location serves as a "strategic differential element." If there is a "strategic differential element," the viewer's attention towards the strategic identical elements is enhanced as the viewer tries to understand the relationship between the shots. For example, the tone of the photography is a "strategic differential element" in many advertising films. The elements cause intensive cognitive effects.

Kanai, Ogata, & Shinohara (2002) simulated eight films for psychological experiments from the same story. The runtime of each film is 15 seconds in six shots. The simulation used location, object, and tone of photography as "strategic differential elements" in each film. For example, one film – by using tone of photography as "strategic differential elements" – can make viewers cause a resetting of their viewpoint and an affect, which does not arise through comprehending a story, but rather through the audiovisual situations.

FILM-EDITING-BASED NARRATIVE SIMULATION

The montage theory of Eisenstein (1942) can be used as a tool for more controlled and expanded narrative simulation for S-type and NS-type film rhetoric. Kanai & Kodama (2010) improved the film rhetoric composition system using the 16 rhythm editing categories to simulate S-type and NS-type rhetoric using Eisenstein's four methods of montage. The system can simulate different types of rhetoric from the same visual elements according to a strategy for intensifying cognitive effects. The details of the 16 categories which together constitute elements of those four methods are listed below: 1) Dialectic metric, 2) Dialectic rhythmic, 3) Dialectic tonal, 4) Dialectic overtonal, 5) Time-cutting metric, 6) Time-cutting rhythmic, 7) Time-cutting tonal, 8) Time-cutting overtonal, 9) Character-cutting metric, 10) Character-cutting rhythmic, 11) Character-cutting tonal, 12) Character-cutting overtonal, 13) Time- and character-cutting metric, 14) Time- and character-cutting rhythmic, 15) Time- and character-cutting tonal, and 16) Time- and character-cutting overtonal.

Kanai & Kodama created 16 kinds of one-minute films using 90-second sequences of 18 shots each from *The Passion of Joan of Arc* directed by Carl Th. Dreyer, using the narrative simulation mechanism; and investigated the difference between the dialectic aspect and the cutting aspect in the films by use of a psychological experiment. *The Passion of Joan of Arc* is one of the most famous of art films containing no spoken dialogue. The shots from *The Passion of Joan of Arc* are famous for their usage of close-up visuals; so that quality makes them suitable for serving as the source of narrative simulation in the study. In this case, the dialectic editing films from the sequence are based on the continuity for the determinacy of the character (Joan) and the location (the cell). By contrast, the irrationally-cut films from the sequence are based on the discontinuity for the indeterminacy of the various characters or the various locations.

Kanai & Kodama conducted the experiment based on the hypothesis "the cutting aspect can enhance the viewpoint diversity of the viewer" and "the dialectic aspect can enhance the viewer's immersion into the story, and the viewer's impression of character." Particularly, Kanai & Kodama (2010) used 10 films from 16 categories (1~8, 13, and 14). In the experiment, 322 subjects (undergraduate students)

Figure 1. The Passion of Joan of Arc

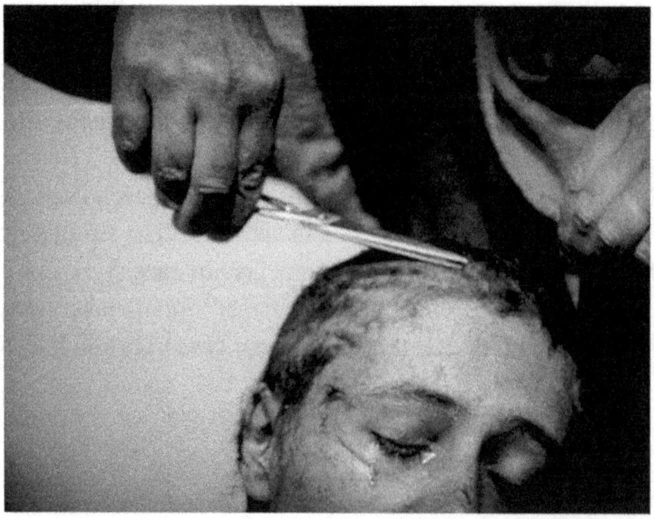

were tested. Subjects were divided into two groups. The first group (177 subjects) was tested for films 1, 6, 3, 8, and 13. The other group (145 subjects) was tested for films 5, 2, 7, 4, and 14. The films were projected to the subjects by means of a video projector. Kanai & Kodama paid extra attention to the subjects' seven-level evaluation of their level of the immersion of the story, their impression of the character, and their viewpoint diversity as being indicative of the cognitive effects of the film. Kanai & Kodama examined the relationships between these evaluations and the editing methods. Also, the table included an open-ended question: "Where was your attention focused?" The results somewhat proved the hypothesis, especially in relation to the metric and the rhythmic montage. The cutting aspect for the indeterminacy-based metric and rhythmic montage can enhance the viewpoint diversity of viewer. Additionally, the dialectic aspect for the determinacy-based metric and rhythmic montage can enhance the viewer's immersion into the story. Also, the results of the overtonal montage also suggest that the overtonal montage has an irrational cutting aspect, even when the film had been based on dialectic-story-type rhetoric.

NOSTALGIA-BASED NARRATIVE SIMULATION

However, the editing structure of the sequence from *The Passion of Joan of Arc* may not evoke any kind of nostalgia in the viewer. Although nostalgia NS-type rhetoric is an important issue in film rhetoric narrative simulation, the strong indeterminacy regarding the time and place of the sequence structure from *The Passion of Joan of Arc* may mean that (for some viewers) nostalgia effects cannot emerge. However, nostalgia effects may emerge from some other editing structure. The type of nostalgia is determined by the cognitive processes generated through the determinacy of the rhetorical elements with regard to time and place. For example, from the film's presentation of certain narrative information for time and space by the use of captions can emerge simple nostalgia (Kanai, 2016).

Narrative simulation, including the strategy for nostalgia, can broaden the potential for narrative composition – especially from the perspective of non-story narratives – without using the story grammar and characters' goal-directed actions. Although story-based plots and characters' goal-directed actions are essential for visual narrative cognition and generation, stories can also constrain this. Because the connections to the past, the memories, and the present always involve indeterminacy regarding the event and determinacy regarding the place and time, non-story narratives and nostalgia effects are more closely related to each other. Past images in a film not associated with a specific story, set of words, or an event can evoke many kinds of nostalgia based on the viewer's cognition. The past images and the cutting techniques, which can relax constraint with regards to the story, can be the main components of visual narrative simulation.

Nostalgia-based narrative rhetoric simulation can include both a story approach and non-story narrative approach. Nostalgia effects may also arise from the indeterminacy from the audiovisual situation. The indeterminacy can cause de-familiarization (Shklovsky, 1966). If the viewer's cognitive processes are transited by de-familiarization from situations of indeterminacy, simple nostalgia for a good past – as well as reflexive or interpreted nostalgia for a bad past – is enhanced by the rhetoric of the film. Because the focus of simulated NS-type rhetoric is on the relationships between rhetorical elements rather than on the events of a past story, the identical elements regarding the time and place in individual shots can generate reality effects for reflexive or interpreted nostalgia.

Simple nostalgia rhetoric can be simulated by presenting consistent narratives such as 'place' images of the past based on continuity editing using explanatory captions in order to secure determinacy of the place and time.

Reflexive nostalgia rhetoric with regards to the timeline of the narrative can be simulated using cutting techniques. In this case, the timeline of a composed visual narrative is not generated through a real time series. The cutting techniques for the timeline create the indeterminacy for the time.

Interpreted nostalgia rhetoric can be simulated by presenting other present period pictures as an irrational cutting after presenting place images of the past. The irrational cutting techniques can produce intensive indeterminacy for the place and time.

Non-nostalgia rhetoric can be simulated by images without explanatory captions for which, there is no specifiable information regarding the place and time to make the determinacy similar to the sequence from *The Passion of Joan of Arc*.

Nostalgia effects are essential for narrative simulation about the past with or without story. The film was shot in a prior age; so because of that, it has a closer relationship with the past. Furthermore, the nature of NS-type film rhetoric can be analyzed as to whether or not nostalgia effects emerge. As previously discussed, NS-type film rhetoric can be simulated through the determinacy and the indeterminacy of events or settings.

The topic of non-nostalgia NS-type rhetoric is also an important issue in film rhetoric narrative simulation. Nostalgia can emerge from any film. Nonetheless, some film directors whose purpose is to create timeless films located in indeterminate places do not want to generate nostalgia effects in viewers. Non-nostalgia-based narratives can be simulated using the strategy for rhythmical editing. Moreover, every film not only has past aspects of rhetoric but also present aspects of rhetoric, as the film may be viewed in the present time. To emphasize and simulate the present aspects of films, the strategy for the non-nostalgia cognitive effects must be involved. With the indeterminacy of the cognition related to the past and place, non-nostalgia cognitive effects are emphasized.

DISCUSSION AND FUTURE RESEARCH DIRECTIONS

In this chapter, only two types of editing-based narrative simulations for film rhetoric composition are discussed. More detailed research on the editing for narrative simulation, and other techniques for non-story narrative film rhetoric such as photography and recording, are needed. Moreover, the whole narrative generation mechanism (e.g., Ogata & Kanai, 2010) includes aspects of both story and non-story processing. Many narrative films have both aspects of rhetoric. Generally, a story and its cognition are factors important to narratives. Consequently, research on story grammar has been the primary computational and cognitive approach to narratives (e.g., Rumelhart, 1975; Thorndyke, 1977). In addition to the stories' or characters' goal-directed actions, the non-story narrative and nostalgia aspects of rhetoric are important issues for narrative simulation. Non-story visual narrative editing and nostalgia effects should be the focus of research on narrative simulation for the visual narrative structure (e.g., Cohn, 2013, 2014). Although non-story processing aspects of rhetoric are emphasized in this chapter, the narrative simulation mechanism can also include aspects of story processing. For example, with regards to story processing as part of the narrative simulation mechanism, Propp's (1968) theory can be used to create a timeline of events; and the theory of consistent paralipsis and paralepsis can be used to generate story discourse (Genette, 1972). The theory of Genette consisted of tense, mood, and voice. The narrative simulation mechanism can place special focus on mood (Kanai & Ogata, 2004a). Mood is defined as being the control of narrative information such as distance, perspective, and alteration. Thanks to mood, the viewer can focus not only on the character but also on the background situation or object of a film. Narrative simulation mechanism can use alterations such as paralipsis and paralepsis to control narrative information. For example, the rhetorical elements of the film such as color, brightness, speed, the number of screens, frequency, and sound can be reduced or expanded from the original film by using the mechanism. The former case is the paralipsis. The latter case is the paralepsis. Based on consistent paralipsis or paralepsis, complicated continuity can be created in a film.

Narrative simulation mechanism can also focus on the theory of parametric narration in fiction film (Bordwell, 1985). Bordwell showed two approaches – the 'ascetic' and 'replete' approaches – to making intrinsic norms in a film. Paralipsis corresponds to the 'fascetic approach, and paralepsis corresponds to the 'replete' approach. Bordwell argued asceticism as the strategy, in which the film limits its norm to a narrower range of procedures than are codified in other extrinsic norms, and replete as the strategy, which can creates an inventory of paradigmatic options. In our narrative simulation mechanism, the extrinsic norms depend on the original film.

In this chapter, narrative simulation for film rhetoric composition is discussed. The narrative simulation mechanism can also be used in the fields of advertising, video abstracting, trailer making, and so on. For example, in advertising, making brand knowledge structures (brand processing) is important. To do so, the advertising rhetoric must be able to reset the viewpoint of the viewer. Useful advertising is done by producing intensive cognitive effects, not only by the ads story being comprehended but also by the rhetoric itself—such as irrational relationships for the indeterminacy existing between two events; an event and an image; or an image and sound. The narrative simulation mechanism can make films by using one or more NS-type rhetoric approaches (discontinuity) through which the user can see all the possibilities of rhetoric creation. To make a viewer process a brand, not only must the determinacy from the events be emphasized, but so too do elements relating to the brand. For example, in a makeup Foundation 1 advertisement analyzed in Kanai & Kato (2001), the character's actions do not associate with one event. Space, time, and action are changed every time the shot changes. But there are associations between the brand character and the brand product. In this case, a viewer who cannot understand consistent story and story processing can be retrained. So, attention to the character herself is enhanced; and character processing is done to promote brand processing. Moreover, the tone of the photography is changed every time from the sixth to ninth shot with the shot changes in this ad. The changes and the indeterminacy cause mood processing and promote brand processing. The narrative simulation mechanism can be the tool of choice for designing this kind of brand processing. To compose and design various kinds of narrative rhetoric, the user can see the possibility of mixing the determinacy-based story processing and the indeterminacy-based brand processing.

CONCLUSION

In this chapter, the focus is on the narrative simulation for non-story narrative regarding rhythm editing and nostalgia effects—in order to discuss and explore the entire narrative concept.

By using a narrative simulation approach, the user can make many different films from the same shots or story, and can study the nature of NS- and S-type rhetoric. Because the intensity of viewer's cognitive effects differs according to the types of the rhetoric, the diversity and the fluidity of simulation-based narrative content itself can also be one narrative work. The nostalgia effects can be enhanced or reduced by controlling the interaction between the narrative cognition processes and the determinacy and the indeterminacy caused by the narrative. Simple nostalgia rhetoric can be simulated by presenting consistent narratives such as place images of the past based on continuity editing in order to secure strong determinacy of the place and time. If the viewer's cognitive processes are transited based on a non-story narrative using the cutting techniques for the few amount of indeterminacy of the place and time, reflexive or interpreted nostalgia effects of non-story-type rhetoric of the film will emerge. Also, the cutting aspect for creating massive indeterminacy of place and time in non-nostalgia rhythmic rhetoric can enhance the viewpoint diversity of the viewer.

In summary, the non-story film editing can be classified by according to the categories of rhythm and nostalgia, and be used for narrative film rhetoric simulation. Nostalgia may emerge with the determinacy of a place and a time and with the indeterminacy of non-story aspects of rhetoric. Non-nostalgia narrative may emerge with the indeterminacy of a place and a time and can be simulated with non-story editing regarding the categories of rhythm.

REFERENCES

Avrahami, J., & Kareev, Y. (1994). The emergence of events. *Cognition*, *53*(3), 239–261. doi:10.1016/0010-0277(94)90050-7 PMID:7842635

Bordwell, D. (1985). *Narration in the fiction film*. Madison, WI: University of Wisconsin Press.

Boym, S. (2001). *The future of nostalgia*. New York, NY: Basic Books.

Brecht, B., & Willett, J. (1964). *Brecht on theatre: The development of an aesthetic*. New York, NY: Hill and Wang.

Chatman, S. (1990). *Coming to terms: The rhetoric of narrative in fiction and film*. Ithaca, NY: Cornell University Press.

Cohn, N. (2013). Visual narrative structure. *Cognitive Science*, *34*(3), 413–452. doi:10.1111/cogs.12016 PMID:23163777

Cohn, N. (2014). You're a good structure, Charlie Brown: The distribution of narrative categories in comic strips. *Cognitive Science*, *38*(7), 1317–1359. doi:10.1111/cogs.12116 PMID:24646175

Cutting, J. E., Brunick, K. L., & Canden, A. (2012). Perceiving event dynamics and parsing Hollywood films. *Journal of Experimental Psychology*, *38*(6), 1476–1490. PMID:22449126

Cutting, J. E., & Iricinschi, C. (2014). Re-presentations of space in Hollywood movies: An event-indexing analysis. *Cognitive Science*, *35*, 1–23. PMID:25087776

Davis, F. (1979). *Yearning for yesterday: A sociology of nostalgia*. New York: Free Press.

Deleuze, G. (1985). *L' Image-temps*. Paris, France: Les Editions de Minuit.

Deleuze, G. (1990). *Pourparlers*. Paris, France: Les Editions de Minuit.

Eisenstein, S. M. (1942). *The film sense* (J. Leyda, Trans.). New York, NY: Harcourt Brace.

Eisenstein, S. M. (1949). *Film form* (J. Leyda, Trans.). New York, NY: Harcourt Brace.

Genette, G. (1972). Discourse du recit: Essai de method [Narrative discourse: An essay in method]. In *Figures III*. Paris: Seuil.

Higson, A. (2014). Nostalgia is not what it used to be: Heritage films, nostalgia websites and contemporary consumers. *Consumption Markets & Culture*, *17*(2), 120–142. doi:10.1080/10253866.2013.776305

Holbrook, M. B., & Schindler, R. M. (1991). Echoes of the dear departed past: Some work in progress on nostalgia. In R. H. Holman & M. R. Solomon (Eds.), *Advances in Consumer Research, 18* (pp. 330–333). Provo, UT: Association for Consumer Research.

Jhale, A., & Young, M. R. (2010). Cinematic visual discourse: Representation, generation, and evaluation. *IEEE Transactions on Computational Intelligence and AI in Games*, *2*(2), 69–81. doi:10.1109/TCIAIG.2010.2046486

Kanai, A. (2001a). The story as a constraint on film. In *Proceedings of the Third International Conference on Cognitive Science* (pp. 503-506). Beijing, China: Academic Press.

Kanai, A. (2001b). Cognitive process model toward the rhetoric of the film. *Cognitive Studies*, *8*(2), 139–150.

Kanai, A. (2002). Film rhetoric and cognition. In *Proceedings of 17th Congress of the International Association of Empirical Aesthetics* (pp. 209-212). Takarazuka, Japan: Academic Press.

Kanai, A. (2003). Non-story type film rhetoric and cognitive effects. In *Proceedings of the Fourth International Conference on Cognitive Science* (pp. 259-264). Sydney, Australia: Academic Press.

Kanai, A. (2006). Reality of unfamiliar situations on moving image. In *Proceedings of 19th Congress of the International Association of Empirical Aesthetics* (pp. 800-803). Avignon, France: Academic Press.

Kanai, A. (2016). Non-story, nostalgia, and film cognition: Nostalgia-based narrative rhetoric composition. In T. Ogata & T. Akimoto (Eds.), *Computational and Cognitive Approaches to Narratology* (pp. 376–390). IGI Global. doi:10.4018/978-1-5225-0432-0.ch015

Kanai, A., & Kato, Y. (2001). Effect of advertising rhetoric on viewer's cognitive Process. *Journal of Advertising Science*, *42*, 87–100.

Kanai, A., & Kodama, K. (2010). Film edit design: Story and irrational cutting. *Cognitive Studies*, *17*(3), 444–458.

Kanai, A., & Morohoshi, C. (2005). NS-narrative and film rhetoric composition system. In *Proceedings of Ninth International Conference on Information Visualisation* (pp.926-927). London: Academic Press. doi:10.1109/IV.2005.91

Kanai, A., & Ogata, T. (2004a). Aspect of non-story processing and film rhetoric composition in the narrative generation mechanism. In *Proceedings of The Ninth International Symposium on Artificial Life And Robotics (AROB 9th '04)* (pp.162-165). Beppu, Japan: Academic Press.

Kanai, A., & Ogata, T. (2004b). Non-story processing on the film rhetoric composition system. In *Proceedings of 18th Congress of the International Association of Empirical Aesthetics* (pp. 433-436). Lisbon, Portugal: Academic Press.

Kanai, A., Ogata, T., & Shinohara, K. (2002). Film rhetoric generation system for intensive cognitive effects. In *Proceedings of 2002 IEEE International Conference on Systems, Man and Cybernetics*. Hammamet, Tunisia: IEEE.

Ogata, T., & Kanai, A. (2010). *Monogatariron no jyohogaku jyosetsu: Monogatariseisei no shiso to gijyutsu wo megutte [An introduction to informatics of narratology: Towards the thoughts and technologies of narrative generation]*. Tokyo, Japan: Gakubun-sha.

Propp, V. (1968). *Morphology of the Folktale*. University of Texas Press.

Rooney, R., Benson, C., & Hennessy, E. (2012). The apparent reality of movies and emotional arousal: A study using physiological and self-report measures. *Poetics*, *40*(5), 405–422. doi:10.1016/j.poetic.2012.07.004

Rumelhart, D. E. (1975). Notes on a schema for stories. In D. G. Bobrow & A. Collins (Eds.), *Representation and understanding: Studies in cognitive science* (pp. 211–236). New York, NY: Academic Press. doi:10.1016/B978-0-12-108550-6.50013-6

Shklovsky, V. (1965). Art as technique. In *Russian formalist criticism: Four essays* (L. T. Lemon & M. J. Reis, Trans. & Eds.). Lincoln, NE: University of Nebraska Press. (Original work published 1917)

Stern, B. B. (1992). Historical and personal nostalgia in advertising text: The fin de siècle effect. *Journal of Advertising*, *21*(4), 11–22. doi:10.1080/00913367.1992.10673382

Thorndyke, P. W. (1977). Cognitive structures in comprehension and memory of narrative discourse. *Cognitive Psychology*, *9*(1), 77–110. doi:10.1016/0010-0285(77)90005-6

Visch, V. T., & Tan, E. S. (2009). Categorizing moving objects into film genres: The effect of animacy attribution, emotional response, and the deviation from non-fiction. *Cognition*, *110*(2), 265–272. doi:10.1016/j.cognition.2008.10.018 PMID:19118823

KEY TERMS AND DEFINITIONS

Cognitive Transition: The cognitive processing of a narrative transition, especially the transition from story-based to non-story-based forms of narrative.

Cutting Technique: A technique used to irrationally cut film with the intent of creating an irrational relationship between adjacent segments.

Indeterminacy: The irrational relationships between time and character or between place and time within continuous shots.

Montage Theory: Film editing theory in which the cut A and the cut B illustrating the same theme are placed in contrast to give a clear representation of the contents of that theme.

Narrative Simulation: A process of composing various kinds of narrative rhetoric and of testing the cognitive effects of narrative.

Non-Story Narrative: A collection of elements (including images or texts) without a consistent story or specific event.

Nostalgia: The emotions that arise from the rise and fall of other times in the place.

Chapter 4
Surprise-Based Narrative Generation in an Automatic Narrative Generation Game

Jumpei Ono
Iwate Prefectural University, Japan

Takashi Ogata
Iwate Prefectural University, Japan

ABSTRACT

The authors have been developing an automatic narrative generation game using the method of table-talk role playing game (TRPG) that is an analog game based on the interactive process by real humans. This system progresses by repeating of the interaction between a game master (GM) and players (PLs). Although the GM prepares a story as a basis of the process, the PLs can detail and change the story. A basic idea in this chapter is that a gap created through the interaction between the GM and the PLs, namely the gap between the original story by the GM and the changed story, gives various impressive effects for an interesting story or narrative, especially a kind of surprise. Based on the above basic idea, in a previous research the authors studied the relationships between gap and surprise, narrative or story techniques producing surprise, and so on using short stories really generated by the authors' narrative generation system.

INTRODUCTION

A Table-talk Role Playing Game (TRPG)[1] is an analog game for which the story changes upon playing the game. Cooperation and opposition drive this process. TRPG generates narratives in such a way that each campaign can be different from another. All participants contribute to the narration within a game as they assume the roles of characters in a story. Changing a story is large in scale because the flow of a story runs off a prepared story framework. The Integrated Narrative Generation System (INGS) developed by the Authors is a system (Ogata, 2016) that generates the conceptual structure of a story or discourse and of its surface expression. During story generation, the INGS uses input parameters that

DOI: 10.4018/978-1-5225-4775-4.ch004

Copyright © 2018, IGI Global. Copying or distributing in print or electronic forms without written permission of IGI Global is prohibited.

represent the structure of a story, and it generates a story with values similar to the parameters given. The discourse mechanism also has a function that generates structure by input parameters. Furthermore, a generation strategy is employed by means of a narrator in the discourse mechanism. However, the story generation mechanism does not operate strategically in the manner that the discourse mechanism does. Therefore, the authors provide a method for more strategic story generation by introducing a story generation model in TRPGs.

One characteristic of the story generation method of TRPG is that participants act as characters in the story. Participants generate motivation as the role of a game participant operating outside of the story and motivation in the role of a character inside of the story, while the goal being to finish the story. Difference between the outside of the motivation and the inside of it generates an unexpected story.

The Authors developed the TRPG-based Automatic Narrative Generation Game (ANGG) (Ono & Ogata, 2016a, 2016b), which uses the existing story generation mechanism in INGS. The Authors intend to develop a new story generation model in which the result is fed back to the INGS. In this work, the Authors focus on a generation model based upon the narrator-and-listener mutual relationship between the Game Master (GM) and Player (PL) for the INGS. In the result, the authors focused on story generation mechanisms and developed its mechanisms. In concretely, Overview of the ANGG and story generation model in TRPG shown, a story generation mechanism by communication between GM and PL was developed, and story generation using Non-Player Character (NPC) was proposed.

Based on the aforementioned result, the authors suggest a story generation model using "surprise" in this report. In TRPG, PL lets a story progress based on the framework of the story that the GM prepared for. The story may drift away from the frame that the GM initially gave for the story. This difference, referred to herein as "gap," evokes surprise in the GM and changes the frame that the GM has initially prepared, changing the story into a different one. The authors define these series of flows as surprise-based narrative generation.

BACKGROUND

Table-Top Role-Playing Game

TRPG is an analog game, usually played with dices, paper, and writing instruments utensils and mainly. To be it is often sometimes called referred to as a Role-Playing Game (RPG), but traditional TRPGs are referred to as such in Japan in order to distinguish it them from the RPG video role-playing game genre that is one of the genres in the digital game in current Japan; called TRPG (Nakagawa, 2016). One such TRPG is Dungeons & Dragons (D&D), a pioneering achievement in the TRPG genre created by is the plays that Gygax[2] (Witwer, 2015). RPG originates in learning means called role playing[3]; it is added a rule to judge the right or wrong of things.

TRPG is handled as a subject of the studies of the communication (Kato & Fujino, 2015). In another study that focuses on the story-creation process of TRPG, an immersive storytelling model is suggested as the model in which the participant of the story participates as one of the characters. An interviewer shares story space with a narrator, and examples controlling the progress of the story interactively include TRPG. There is the study that focuses on the propensity of a person making a story in TRPG and analyzes three kinds of games with an example (Bergström, 2012). Creativity was the scrutinized factor in this study, but the development of the system using a TRPG-based model is not realized.

TRPG is a game that is played by 4 or 5 people. Among the participants, one participant becomes GM, while the remaining participants become PLs. The basic tools that the participants use in a TRPG, are writing implements and some dices. The PLs use the writing implements for recording information about the characters that they act as. Dices are used for deciding the act that the characters perform.

When the participants play a TRPG,

1. The GM either describes the state of a scene as a narrator, or performs the characters.
2. The PLs select an action based on the scene that the GM expressed.
3. The GM expresses a change of scene based on the PL's reaction.

The TRPG proceeds with several cycles of the above exchange of responses.

For example, in a story about a murder case, the game proceeds with the following conversation among participants.

GM: *You, who opened the door, saw these things. There is a person who has fallen down on the floor and the door of the back entrance is half-open. What do you do?*
PL A: *I want to confirm the person's condition.*
PL B: *I want to run after the person who probably escaped from the back entrance.*
GM: *I see. First, I will solve the suggestion of PL A. You approached the person. Then, you notice that a knife is stuck in that person's back. What do you do?*

Other than the decision of actions in a certain scene, the exchanges decide the macro-level of the story.

GM: *The murdered person seems to have fought with another person.*
PL A: *Should we interrogate the person about the murder case?*
PL B: *We need evidence. Therefore, I want a scene from which we can gather information about that person in this town.*
PL A: *Sure, it's a wonderful idea.*
GM: *Well, I accept the suggestion of PL B. The next scene is a scene in which you gather information.*

As stated above, a TRPG has not only simple discussion but also exchanges between the GM and PLs. In addition, the important element is to act as the characters of a story. This is an element of story generation, having a form different from the game given in the next section.

Narrative Generation in Games

Today, the RPG is popular genre in digital games. In the conventional digital games, a player will usually experience a scripted story, according to Matsunaga (2015), a story that not has an outline and is appeared by each playing a game has begun attracting attention, and demand for a story that a developer did not prepare beforehand has increased. The existing game includes making a story. Table 1 shows examples of games that involve making a story. In addition, there have been many studies on automatic story generation for a game. Table 2 shows examples of such studies.

The work involved in making TRPG a digital game has been announced in various media. These brought how to play in TRPG close to a conventional digital game, and PL representing the user of the

Table 1. Games that create a narrative

Name	Media	Feature	Comparison
Once Upon a Time	Card	• Game in which play proceeds by impromptu stories created by the user. • The purpose of the player is to derive a story from the content written down until the end-story card. • The talk around improvising using the card that a person, a thing, a place, an event was written down for the instruction method. • The difficulty that knowledge of children's story in itself of a sense and the motif of the making of some stories is required.	• Resemble TRPG at story generation point by many people. • Because INGS makes up for lack, PLs can suggest an action freely to some extent, and the design system is simple.
Roly Dice	Dice	• Players make a story with a picture drawn on nine dice. • A knowledge and idea power is found more in comparison with Once Upon a Time.	Resembles TRPG at story generation point by many people.
Elegy For a Dead World	Personal Computer	• Game for "writing a story." • Players take a trip to a certain planet on which life became extinct and write a story based on the scenery stimulated by their senses. • Players can read each other's stories shown on a network. • Two stories made from even the same scenery may differ.	• The acquirement of knowledge of the design system of this report aims at the phenomenon that a certain story becomes the materials of other stories. • For a human being making all of it, the design system is automatic in many parts.

Table 2. Studies of narrative generation in games

Name	Content
OPIATE system	• Story generation model about the world of the game. • Character (Non Player Character:) whom a user does not operate directly users give an action purpose to NPC, and the event of the story follows thus. • The story development uses the structured model of the story by the prop, and 31 "functions" and type of seven kinds of characters are used.
Using Social Relationships to Control Narrative Generation	It is a system generating a story, such as the medical drama from the relationship of characters in the healthcare setting, particularly medical case education materials.
Integrating Research in Interactive Storytelling	The user employs a narrative planner. A drama manager produces the outline of the scenario with suspense characteristics and a mental model of the speculation / greed / interest.
Scheherazade	The system that one story is completed by continuing choosing one among a choice displayed in sequence.
Toward Supporting Stories with Procedurally Generated Game Worlds	A user builds the world of the story from an input story (regardless of inputs by a computer or inputs by a person). In addition, users make the game space that a player character can go back and forth freely.
Deep Learning-Based Goal Recognition in Open-Ended Digital Games	It is non-linear and, in the games of the scenario with a plural arrival target, determines the final arrival target from the action of the player through a deep-learning technique.

game, the GM representing the computer (game console) are thought about mainly. However, the game that the authors propose in this paper is closed to game progress in TRPG. In extreme cases, the game user assumes the roles of PL and GM itself, or the game user can become an existence that only starts a game system.

In the digital game industry, the fact that a story is made in a player's head from the events that was experienced in the game accidentally attracted the attention of a developer. The developer calls this phenomenon as "narrative" (Matsunaga, 2015).

As for the story in TRPG, there is a story as a framework that GM prepares first, a story in the progress process of the game and a finished story to appear at the stage when a game was finished. For the narratology by Genette (1972), narrative is an act to talk about contents and it that are talked about contents. In the story in TRPG, the relations of an author (GM) and the reader (PL) exist. However, the relations may become vague temporarily in the process of the game. The authors consider that how to make of a new story exists there.

Gap and Surprise in This Study

As mentioned above, the PLs may suggest the scene that was off the framework of the story that the GM prepared, or they may overturn the framework. Such a suggestion gives various types of surprise for the GM, and it is possible that the GM could change a story.

The study about surprise already many exists. Descartes (1649) stated that passions came in six basic emotions or feelings, and said "surprise is the first of all the passions." Descartes described surprise as "a sudden surprise of the soul." Descartes asserted that when people encounter new things that evoke surprise, it drives a person to acquire knowledge. When the surprise was momentary and anticipatory, Yamane (2005) describes the surprise to which Descartes alludes. As for the surprise, even fiction (Hotta, 2013) is adopted, and the work is regarded as a use in entertainment (Muto, 2016), education again. Similarly, in the game, surprising utilization affects the width of a number, the kind of a generated story. About the surprising durability and the effect, Hotta (2013) said, the suspense was brought about by feeling of strain to continue about a certain fact and the surprise is momentary awareness that is concealed fact by the relations of surprise and suspense that Hitchcock asserted (Trafaut, 1966). The human being who appreciated a story by disclosing information was assimilated into a character, and Hitchcock (Trafaut, 1966) stated that feeling of strain (suspense) that lasted by participating in a story was born. When "telling about a fact to the audience if possible raises suspense except the case that an unexpected ending becomes the top of the story," Hitchcock (Trafaut, 1966) prefers suspense to momentary surprise.

In this study, the authors focus on surprise that change a story GM prepared.

Integrated Narrative Generation System

The Integrated Narrative Generation System (INGS) (Ogata, 2016) is constructed of three mechanisms, various dictionaries, and a knowledge base (Figure 1) and generates the concept structure of an event. The ANGG uses a story mechanism that creates the contents of a story and a knowledge mechanism (in particular, conceptual dictionaries (Ogata, 2015)) in generating an event included in a certain scene.

A conceptual dictionary is a dictionary that systematically stores meaning about vocabularies (concepts), such as verbs, nouns, modifiers, and so on. The Automatic Narrative Generation Game (ANGG) in this research utilizes a verb conceptual dictionary and a noun conceptual dictionary. Figure 2 shows

Figure 1. Overview of an INGS architecture

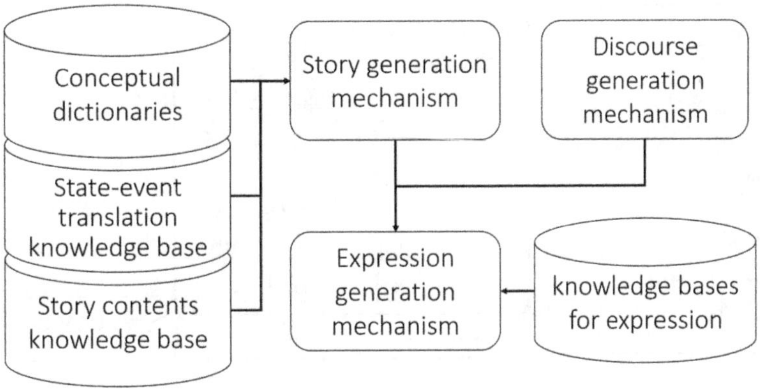

a part of the constitution of the both conceptual dictionaries. A verb concept that is a former terminal element has case structures, a limitation condition about cases, and a sentence pattern. The case structure is required for verb-concept cases, and each case has a limitation condition based on the middle concept of the noun conceptual dictionary. The noun conceptual dictionary has the middle concept; that is, a category to bundle up a terminal concept to appear in a story. In generating an event, the specific range of the noun concept dictionary is determined by a limitation condition, and a concrete factor (character, object, location, etc.) is generated by a chosen terminal concept (Figure 3).

AN AUTOMATIC NARRATIVE GENERATION GAME BASED ON TRPG

Outline of an Automatic Narrative Generation Game

The ANGG has two mechanisms, GM and PL, assuming their correlated roles. The authors mention a combination of users and the computer regarding the GM and PL roles. Table 3 illustrates combination patterns of these. Currently, the authors have developed an ANGG of category C. In category C, the role of a user is to input information about the framework of a story, judging the appropriateness of proposal of PL mechanism at story generation. Common Lisp was used in the development of ANGG.

Figure 2. Structures of verb conceptual dictionary and noun conceptual dictionary in the INGS

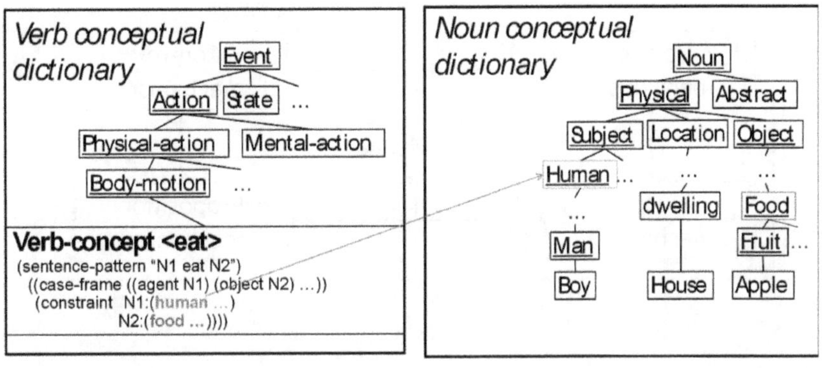

Figure 3. An event generation

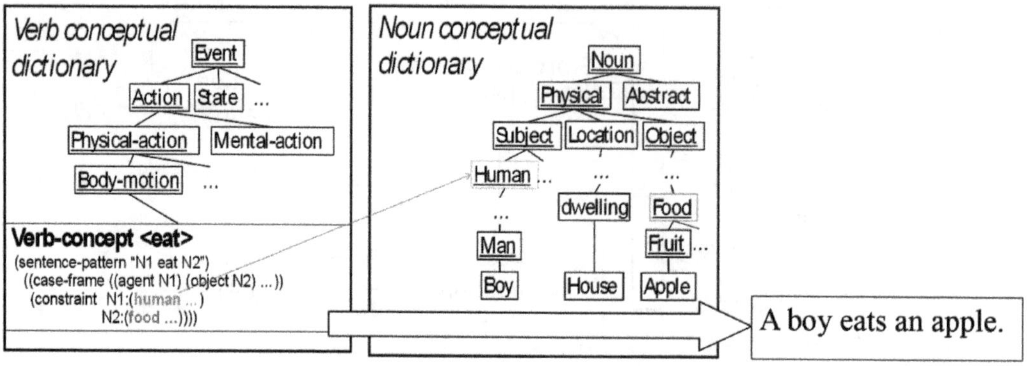

Table 3. Combination patterns of user and computer in the ANGG

		PL Mechanism	
		User	**Computer**
GM Mechanism	**User**	**Category-A** Standard combination in TRPGs.	**Category-C** User inputs a framework of a story; the computer expands the framework.
	Computer	**Category-B** Combination in general RPG at digital game.	**Category-D** Automatic story generation mechanism that combines category-B and category-C.

Figure 4 represents the architecture of the story generation mechanism in the ANGG. The ANGG consists of the GM and PL mechanisms. Each mechanism has a knowledge base about the expansion of a story. In ANGG, data is stored, which is comprised of a set of elements, such as characters, objects, locations, and points in time within a story and their limitations. This data is collectively called the "world setting." The "scene sequence" represents the framework of story that the GM mechanism makes and a generated story from that framework (Figure 5).

Figure 4. Architecture of a story generation mechanism in ANGG

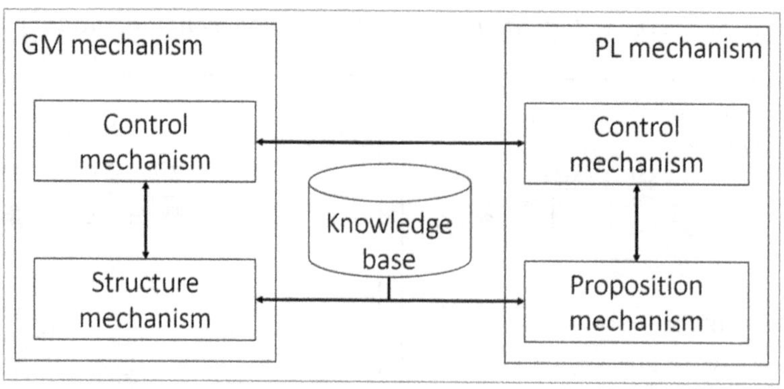

Figure 5. Example of a structure of a scene sequence

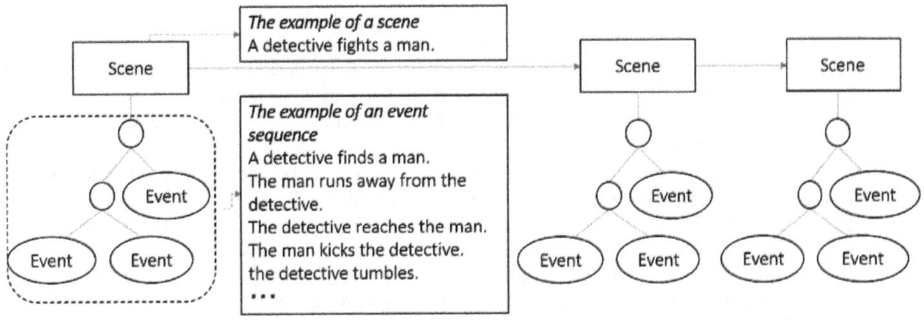

Story Generation by a Method Communication Between GM and PL

Figure 6 is shown the story generation process in the ANGG. The GM mechanism prepares the world setting and early scene sequence (Ono & Ogata, 2016f). The world setting is prepared by combining the same elements or editing an existing world setting. The NPCs are included in the prepared world setting. An early scene sequence is constructed of three or more scenes, based on the prepared world setting. Afterward, the GM mechanism gives a termination condition for story generation to the PL mechanism directly or indirectly. The PL mechanism decides a number of PLMs and structures. Each PLM generates a PC based on the world setting and each PLM's proposal policy (Ono & Ogata, 2016g).

The story generation in this game deals with the insertion of one scene into the scene chain and the development of an event line of a scene (Figure 7). In the case of story generation, the GM system grasps the whole aspect of the framework of story, and the PL system only has the information disclosed by the GM mechanism adversely. The PL mechanism puts together the information that was disclosed about the progress of the story and the knowledge of PLM and suggests a scene. The authors next gather up preparations for story generation, a procedure of the development to a phenomenon line of the scene.

In Table 5, the authors show the data structure of the world setting, scene sequence, and PLM. The data used in the experiment include the co-occurrence information of noun concept and verb concept that was gathered by analyzing works resisted "Aozora Bunko."[4]

Figure 6. The story generation process in the ANGG

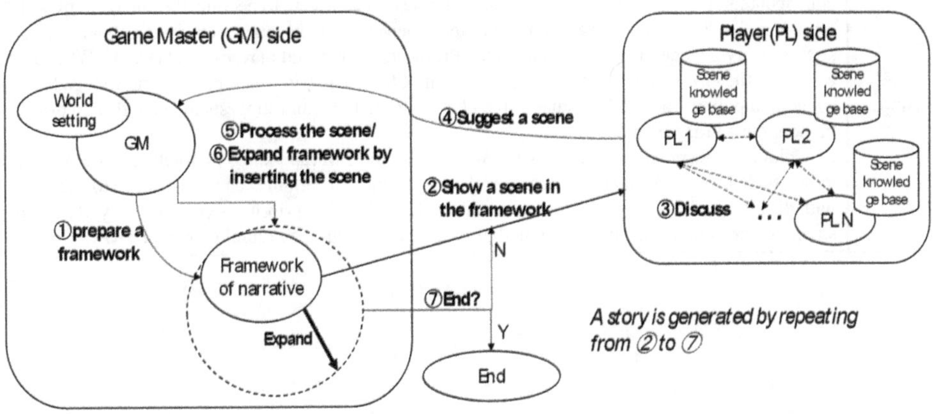

Table 4. Terms in the ANGG

Term	Content
World setting (Ono & Ogata, 2016e, 2016h)	World setting is the setting of components of a story and is restricted to it. Components are characters, objects, locations, and times. It is limited by the components that may come up in a story and it expresses the condition of the kind of world that a generated story exhibits, whether closely mirroring the real world according to our common sense or a fantasy children's world in which a scarecrow can come to life. The PL mechanism is in charge of the Player Character (PC) and of the Non Player Character (NPC) except among components. The PC has a one-to-one relation with the PL mechanism, and the Author does not participate at all, or the GM mechanism participates in NPC where is higher than one adversely. • **Characters:** Elements that actively perform in a story • **Objects:** Elements without characters • **Locations:** Space in which characters and objects exist in a story • **Times:** Temporal flow in a story NPCs can be classified in this game roughly into the following categories: (A) Few people are concerned with the summary of the story: It is the character whom GM operates and is an individual with a name. The attribute information that this NPC has, is the almost same as the attribute information that a PC has; when it returns a reaction to a PC or to act originally, according to the attribute information that it has, GM decides an action. (B) The majority of people who constitute the world: It is the character who does not have any individual name. This type of NPC has a role such as an environment of story rather than a specific person in comparison with the type (A) NPC. With attribute information simplified in comparison with a PC of every individual, this type of NPC can be assumed as plural people in mass as one group. For example, this type of NPC is the group such as "nations of a country", or "youths of a group". The GM manages it, but the action obeys not only the attribute information of the individual but also attribute information (rule) to spread in a group. The attribute information to spread is the influence that PL (or a PC) to NPC give.
Scene sequence	A scene sequence is a passage of story constructed in plural scenes. The scene is one shared figure unit in a story in terms of time and spatiality and is comprised of one or more events. Furthermore, the scene has a purpose and a precondition. The purpose shows contents accomplished by PL mechanism to GM mechanism. For example, a user can describe it using abstract concepts such as "the scenes where a main character fights against an antagonist". This purpose is presented through the exchanges of the GM mechanism and the PL mechanism to the line of a more concrete event. For example, "a chief character invades in a house. An antagonist appears. An antagonist attacks the chief character". A precondition is a condition for a certain scene to perform occurrence. It describes any states about characters, objects locations, and times. When a story progressed, if correspond states are appeared, the GM mechanism judges that a precondition was achieved. In addition, the scene sequence has the end condition that GM system establishes. As for the end, condition describes characters, objects, locations and times, and story generation is finished when this is met.
Game master mechanism	The game master in TRPG manages the preparation and the progress of the story of the framework of the story. The GM mechanism plays the role in the story in the automatic generation game. The GM mechanism controls preparations, such as the story generation of the initial state of world setting and the scene sequence. The preparations for the initial state of world setting and the scene sequence are carried out before story generation. The world setting is prepared for when formed from the beginning by adjusting an arbitrary world setting stored by the knowledge base that GM mechanism has. The GM mechanism uses the existing scene sequence that the scene sequence of the initial state is formed in along the limitation of the world setting from the beginning.
Player mechanism	The player has a role to let a story progress by playing a character in a prepared story. The PL system corresponding to a player suggests an event or scene to lead a state to become the end condition of the scene sequence. The PL mechanism sets up one or more players with the suggestion policy about a scene and the event at every story generation. PL that is included PL mechanism called player model (PLM). When PLM suggests a scene to the GM system, PLM suggests the plan of the scene with reference to a knowledge base based on the suggestion policy. Each PLM evaluates the plan suggested to it and suggests the plan that an evaluation is the highest toward the GM mechanism. In addition, in every scene, priority is given from GM to PLM (appointed by rotation). When this is a standard to be decided, as to which person becomes the viewpoint in a certain scene and a scene to suggest is not fixed with the difference of the evaluation, an opinion of PLM having priority is given priority. By the aforementioned structure, the authors introduce a method of the story generation by plural people in TRPG.

Figure 7. Flow of story generation

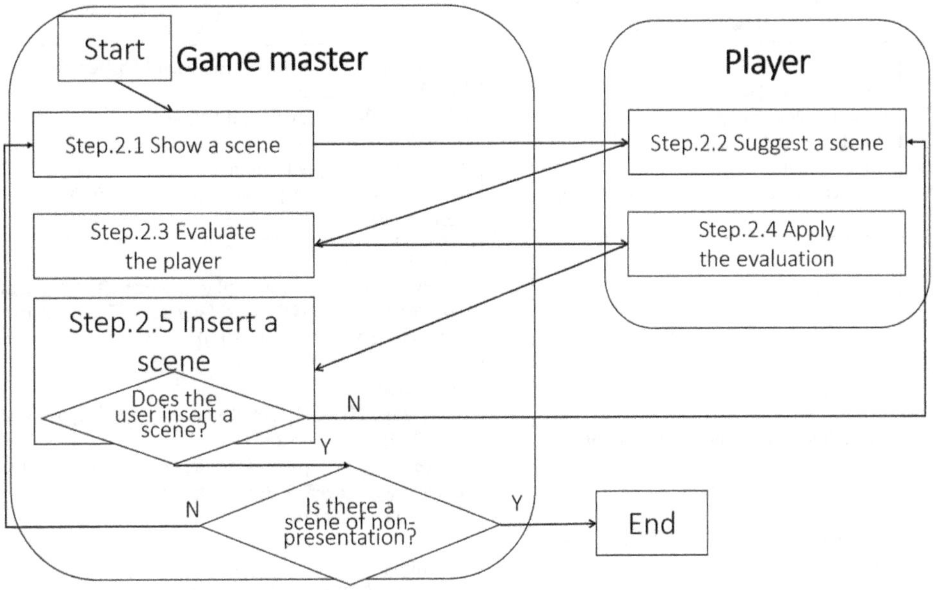

The world setting is described using a conceptual dictionary. Early existing elements are described by noun concepts without restriction. Restrict is described that noun concepts impossible are appeared in a story and changing constraint in verb concepts.

Scenes that are constructed with a pair of occurrence conditions and content describe early scene sequences. The contents are as-yet unrealized scenes. In the case of the realization of the scene, an event is inserted to explain those verb concepts more concretely. Finally, a line structure (Figure 5) comprised of plural structure trees representing one or more events is formed sequentially.

The PL system has a suggestion policy about the generation and knowledge about the realization of the suggestion of the scene. The knowledge uses the collocation information of noun concepts and verb concepts. That are acquired by analysis of existing novels. The information of the collocation of noun concepts and verb concepts in each novel is the knowledge about each novel that each PLM has. For simplification, the authors assume it the knowledge, which is the scene of the phenomenon in this article. In addition, the authors decide that PLM's policy is aiming at the end condition of the story generation in this paper simply. PLM supposes a scene connected to the scene where an end condition was disclosed as a goal between goals and suggests the scene.

Scene Expansion

Figure 8 shows a procedure for the development a scene to an event line. In the case of story generation, the GM system grasps the whole aspect of the framework of a story, and the PL system has only the information disclosed by the GM mechanism adversely. The PL mechanism draws upon information disclosed to the progress of the story and knowledge along with the PLM together and suggests a scene. The scene that GM prepares for story generation is a procedure of the development to an event line of the scene.

Table 5. Forms of data and examples

<table>
<tr><th>Item</th><th>Description Form</th><th>Example</th></tr>
<tr><td>World setting</td><td>((agents <noun>…)
(objects <noun>…)
(locations <noun>…)
(times <noun> …)
(restrict <noun>|<verb>|<constrict>|nil …))</td><td>((agents 探偵[detective] 学生[student] OL[female office worker] 男 [man] 老人[old man])
(objects 証拠物件[evidence] 飯[meal])
(locations 大通り[avenue] 家屋[house] 放送局[broadcast station] 酒屋[liquor store] 駅[station])
(times朝[morning] 昼[noon] 夕[evening] 夜[night])
(restrict nil))</td></tr>
<tr><td>Scene sequence</td><td>(((condition <Precondition for starting a scene>)
(<Contents in a scene>))
・・・
(last-condition <conditions for completion of generation>))</td><td>(((condition nil)
(event 誘拐する1[kidnap] (agent age%学生#1[age%student#1]) (counter-agent age%OL#1[age%female office worker#1]) (location loc%大通り#1[loc%avenue#1]))
)
((condition
(age%探偵#1[age%detective#1] (所持[possession] obj%証拠物件#1[ojb%evidence#1])))
(event 争う2[dispute] (agent age%探偵#1[age%detective#1]) (counter-agent age%学生#1[age%student#1]) (location loc%家屋#1[loc%house#1]))
)
((condition
(age%OL#1 (location obj%安心#1[obj%ease#1])))
(event 助かる1[be saved] (agent age%OL#1[age%female office worker#1]) (location loc%家屋#1[loc%house#1]))
)
(last-condition
(age%OL#1[age%female office worker#1] (location nil)))
)</td></tr>
<tr><td>PLM in a PL mechanism</td><td>(<Player ID>
(Motivation <generation policy>)
(knowledge
(event
(<Verb> (<Verb> <the degree of relationship>) …) …)
(scene
(<Verb> (<Verb><the degree of relationship>)…) …)))</td><td>(0
(Motivation nil)
(knowledge
(event nil)
(scene
(食べる[eat]
(つかまる[be caught] 132.086) (馴染む[adapt oneself] 132.086) …) …)))</td></tr>
</table>

Figure 8. Example of a structure of a scene sequence

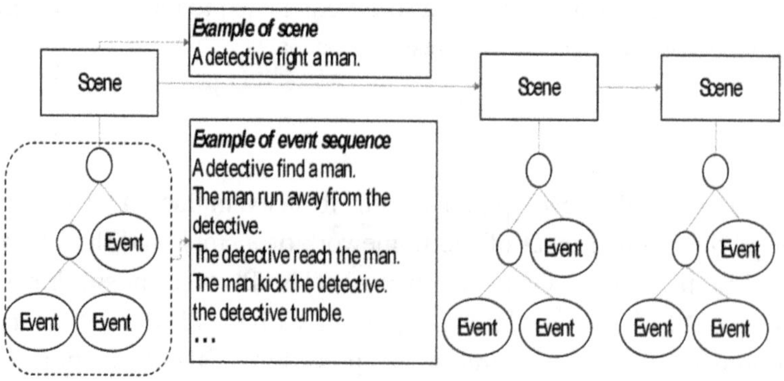

Role of Non-Player Character

The authors intend to treat non-player characters as done in the ANGG. Other studies that treat automatic characters in games or narrative generation (Kamozaki, Ohno, & Thawonmas, 2008). However, the authors treat NPCs as if they had a function in a social group. Concretely, authors introduce the NPC model that Nagaoka (1999a, 1999b) proposed for ANGG, and consider a method of expression for the world that change dynamically in a story. Characters that are included the world setting are called PC or NPC. The former are characters operated by PL or PLM, and the latter are characters that the GM manage without player intervention. In particular, NPCs perform motivational roles or present problems to be solved by the PL or PC, such as an opponent, a supporter, a victim, and so on. Moreover, the PC and NPC have a role-like interface for expanding a scene to events. When a scene is extended to one or more events, at first, the GM as a narrator describes a scene, and next, the PL and GM communicate as the PC and NPC respectively.

The authors consider the effects to ANGG by introducing the NPC that Nagaoka (1999a, 1999b) defined (2016d). The concept in Nagaoka's works is about features like "storing information", an "action base on each judgment criterion" and "changing a judgment criterion through contact with others". A story in a game changes dynamically through the communication between the PC and NPC.

The NPCs mentioned have seven kinds of parameters (Table 6). In addition, there are six kinds of actions that arise from those parameters.

- **Attack:** A directly hostile act.
- **Steal:** A directly hostile act.
- **Giving Gift:** A directly friendly act.
- **Starting Bad Rumor:** An indirectly hostile act.
- **Starting Good Rumor:** An indirectly friendly act.
- **No Action:** A neutral or unconcerned act.

On the assumption that ANGG generates a scene that policeman (policewoman) researches a criminal's address, the authors simulate a work of NPC in ANGG. This assumes a detective PC, and the purpose

Table 6. NPC's parameters

Parameter	Description
Value of feeling	Value that shows how much friendly to same character.
Amount of change to friendly act	Amount of change of "value of feeling" for a character that does friendly act.
Amount of change to hostile act	Amount of change of "value of feeling" for a character that does hostile act.
Reason	Threshold that whether perform a directly hostile act or not perform it.
Value of act	Threshold that whether perform the act.
Health	Value that is affected "attack."
Property	Value that is effected "Giving gift" or "Steal."

of the scene shall be accomplished by obtaining constant numerical "witness information". Here, the authors assume "steal" is to "offer the witness false information" and "giving a gift" is to "offer the witness true information", and suppose that the witness information that the PC possesses increases or decreases. Furthermore, NPCs share a rumor between NPC's group. The NPC's reaction to PC is dull or antagonistic and becomes gathering witness information into difficulties when NPC's group is a village possessing strong suspicions about an outsider. At first, PCs need to conciliate NPCs through some method to gather useful witness information. In other words, this NPC functions as one trial in a story. On the contrary, PCs can collect witness information relatively easily when NPCs consist of cooperative people.

SURPRISE-BASED STORY GENERATION BY USING GAP TECHNIQUE

About Gap Technique

With the surprise in this study, the authors point to the change to be borne in GM by the differences that GM assumed between a story and the story that was actually generated. The authors call the difference of two stories a gap.

When a gap is included in a story, the authors suppose that GM receives surprise from a story. The technique that generates a scene that has a gap is called gap technique. The gap technique quoted defamiliarization technique (Ono & Ogata, 2012) and cutting technique (Kanai, 2010). Those techniques are summarized in Table 7.

In the gap technique, the following methods are considered. The rhetoric of the authors spoke at the top, catabolizing quoted the cutting technique for shortening and extension of the structure for the change of a component and contents.

Table 7. Techniques are referred to gap techniques

Technique	Content
Cutting technique	The cutting technique cuts a story in a consecutive scene of a certain film by lacking in the continuity of the time connection and person, and there is work to strengthen the impression of an arbitrary element. For example, a scene becomes the long silence and a scene where context is unclear is inserted, the scene is cut down by a story, and strengthens the impression (Kanai, 2008). In a definition of the cutting technique by Kanai (2010), the parts to be related to in this article are as follows. Emphasize the editing itself by disturbing the continuity of the phenomenon, and making a difference (non-continuity) between factors between consecutive shots. Repeating the same object and photograph it, and image itself is emphasized by making a phenomenon and the relations of the image irrationality (break).
Defamiliarization technique	Either it is a property of A, or the rhetoric of catabolizing strengthens an impression of element A in itself about any element A of stories by substituting an element in conjunction with A for anything different, which became estranged from the common sense of the guard to daily life. For example, in a car commercial, there is an example which emphasizing the pleasure of home life scenery of the family in the car by showing a scene running in the bottom of the sea.
Discourse technique	Even story verbal explanation mechanisms (Ogata, 2016) that INGS has transforms the structure of the story. The story verbal explanation mechanism transforms the time structure of the story using a recollection structure and replaces the turn of a phenomenon shown by a reader.

- **Shortening of the Structure:** A method to be as short as possible structure that suggests or a flow of the scene in the frame that GM prepared-- (1) a generated event line of abbreviation, (2) replacement of structure, (3) an event line of the abbreviation, (4) replacing an event line.
- **Extension of the Structure:** A method of extension of structure that suggests a flow of the scene in the frame which GM prepared and generated event line to make a detour as much as possible-- (1) extension of structure and (2) an extension of the event line.
- **The Change of Contents:** A method of achieving the purpose of the scene by scene or event where is different from a scene or an event that GM showed-- (1) change of a scene or (2) change of an event.
- **The Change of the Component:** A method of suggesting a scene or an event including an element with or without an association is an element with a scene or an event that GM showed-- (1) change of a character (2) change of an object (3) change of a location, (4) change of a time.

This section shows the generation method of the story to give surprise for GM. With the surprise in this article, the authors point to the change from the differences that GM assumed between the story and the story that was really generated by the GM. The authors call the difference of two stories of this time a gap. When a gap is included in a story, the authors suppose that GM receives surprise from a story. The authors call technique to produce a scene to have a gap toward gap technique (Table 8).

In addition, timing to apply gap technique based on a suggestion policy of PLM. In actual TRPG, it is decided by the tendency of the way of thinking of the player mainly (For example, preference about development, such as the hero's intention and the intention that it is ruin-oriented, and become stable, the intention of the offender for pleasure and so on). However, the Author can apply the gap technique using a random number to periodic timing if it is PLM.

Table 8. Gap techniques

Technique	Method	Procedure
(1) Using an impressive verb or noun	Impressive verb	Generate an event using a verb concept with the big change that is in a state
	Impressive noun	Generate an event using a noun concept that was off a restriction to have of a verb concept
(2) Event generation	Change a verb	Change a verb concept included in it by any method, after having generated an event
	Change a noun	Change a noun concept included in it by any method, after having generated an event
(3) Expand scene sequence	Repetition event	Insert event like targeted event
	New event	Insert event having a strong collocation verb concept included in a target event
	An event by cutting technique	Insert event having a poor collocation verb concept included in a target event
(4) Conversion of a scene	Goal achievement by different method	Change a scene to new scene that can achieve a goal
(5) Reduction of scene structure	Delete a scene	Omit any a scene

Surprise-Based Story Generation

This section mentions a method of story generation that gives surprise to the GM. When the PL mechanism suggests one scene, it applies one or more gap techniques. When the PL mechanism does not apply gap technique. The GM mechanism knows the whole of the story. The GM mechanism gradually shown according to the progress condition of the story to PL mechanism. The PL mechanism refers to characters, objects locations and times from the adopted scene.

In addition, the authors show the below limitations of the implementation for simplification.

- A random number determines an application timing of the technique and the technique to apply.
- GM suggests the first scene of a generated story.
- One scene is presented to one event.
- When the Authors do not use the gap technique, the PLM suggests the scene that assumes an end condition as a goal.
- When the PC of which the PLM is in charge dies, the Authors finish the story generation.
- The end condition of the story generation is given to the PL system directly.

A Calculation Method for Gaps

Collocation information of a noun concept and verb concept (Ono & Ogata, 2015; 2016c) shows relations between nouns, relations between verbs, and relations between nouns and verbs using numbers, wherein larger numbers correspond to stronger relations. An experiment by the authors demonstrated that two elements weakly collocated had the tendency to give a sense of incongruity to a reader (Ono & Ogata, 2015; 2016c). Therefore, the authors suppose that sense of incongruity to be determined by the gap between two elements and suggest a method to calculate a gap value.

The Authors assessed the gap level between a given story (Sa) and stories (Sb) that differed from Sa by calculating it in the next expression (1). The number to subtract from 1 then is a degree of resemblance between Sa and any Sb. The gap parameter accepts decimal numbers from 0.00 to 1.00, where a larger gap value approaches 1.00. The denominator of expression (1) is the greater of the two scene values Sa and Sb. This is to express the influence of the change in the structure level of the scene sequence.

In addition, the Authors calculated a resemblance degree in which Sa perfectly matched Sb which did not have a gap at all.

$$A\ value\ of\ gap = 1 - \frac{a\ sum\ of\ resemblance\ degree\ in\ each\ scene}{Max\left(a\ numer\ of\ scene\ in\ Sa, a\ number\ of\ scene\ in\ Sb\right)} \tag{1}$$

The similar degree between a scene in Sa and a scene in Sb is calculated from the total of the resemblance degrees between all events included in each scene. The resemblance degree between events is shown in expression (2).

$$The\ resemblance\ degree = resemblance\ degrees\ of\ nouns + resemblance\ degrees\ of\ verbs \tag{2}$$

Two scenes that the GM mechanism prepared are compared. Next, scenes that the PL mechanism suggested are compared in the interval in between the scenes that the GM mechanism prepared. If the content of the cases completely matched, the resemblance degree between scenes is assumed collocation information infinity (on the program 999). Comparing two events is comparable to comparing the scene itself. A case having a longer Sb than Sa, generated depending on the gap technique, may be short. For example, two scenes exist at Sa, and a scene exists at Sb in the interval between scenes that the GM mechanism prepared. Expression (1) is given by "1 - α", and the gap value is increased by making a part of α small. Specifically, the first scene in Sa is compared with the first scene in Sb, and the second scene in Sa is a scene for which there was no target for comparison (resemblance degree 0). The authors supposed that changing a structure greatly changes the whole story, and thereby increases the gap.

Experiment and Result

In this section, the amount of surprise that correlates to a gap in a story using the gap technique is validated. This experiment looks at relations between gaps and the tendency toward surprise. Because surprise is of great importance to a story, this experiment assessed whether there was any surprise with an evaluation index. Table 9 shows an experiment summary and Table 10 shows the category of surprise based on the result of this experiment.

Table 9. Summarize experiment

	Content
Subjects	20 (10 TRPG-inexperienced people aged 20-29; 20 TRPG-inexperienced people aged 60-69; 8 TRPG-experienced people aged 20-29)
Samples	10 stories generated using the gap technique
Method	ANGG generated a story (Sb1 - Sb10) using a story (Sa) and the technique without the technique based on the same scene sequence (Sa and Sb1 - Sb10). In addition, the following gap technique was used in the generation of each story, where instructions were handed to a subject before the evaluation (appendix 2), and were instructed as follows: "watch two stories ten times in turn from now on". Story A to show earlier is common every cycle, and story B to show later is different every cycle. Please remember the image in your headfirst because you project story A for 40 seconds. The experimenter project story A for 15 seconds from the next cycle. The experimenter project story B according to length for 40 seconds from 20 seconds. The subject evaluated Sb10 afterwards from Sb1. Firstly, in any time for figure, Sa set the time of 15 seconds after the second for 40 seconds, and the Sb set the time for 40 seconds according to the length of the story from 20 seconds. Procedure of the experiment 1. The experimenter projects "a story (Sa) without the gap technique" on any time, screen 2. The experimenter deletes the story that the experimenter projected on the screen 3. The experimenter projects "a story (Sb) using the gap technique" on any time, screen 4. The experimenter deletes the story that experimenter projected on the screen 5. The experimenter has a subject write in an evaluation in the time of 30 seconds 6. The experimenter returns to 1 after an interval of 5 seconds
Evaluation	For one story, the experimenter printed two answer columns on paper (appendix 3). It is stronger in line and "○" in the point surprised at and, in answer column A, it touches it line and "◎" in the point surprised at for a story printed on paper. In answer column B, subjects was surprised through the whole scenario how for a scale line on printed under answer column A or touch "○" on the scale of the position to correspond to. Lastly, subjects performed a 5-minute freedom description.

Table 10. Results of surprise

Category	Contents
Category-A. Single verb	In the single verb "murdered" gave much surprise. "Murdered" give two times numerical surprise than other verbs, indicating much strong surprise. The second, "made" gives much surprise. The free description of four subjects revealed that "murdered" gives big surprise. The authors know that "made" brought about surprise in a thing related to "an exhibit" from a free description of subject E. In addition, the authors can suppose the surprise was born by many events including "the exhibit".
Category-B. Single event	When comparing the surprise of the whole story, it is thought that "murdered" had a big influence. However, "made" does not give big surprise in comparison with the others. By this experiment, the difference that the latter half of the story in particular gave a lot of surprise to a subject. When the authors think that surprise is momentary as Yamane (2005) described it, it is thought that the impression at the stage when subjects confirmed a story until the last became the surprising evaluation of the completely same story.
Category-C. Replace event	"Fight" in Sb6 and "to get sick" in Sb10 repeat itself. As for the former, as for approximately 80%, the latter, about half of subjects felt surprise when they judged it when they felt surprise for an event to repeat a case around both these events to repeat or to surround the second event. However, as a result of having performed a multiple regression analysis of Sb10 by the method like the case of a surprising evaluation average of the whole story being smaller than other samples and the single verb concept for having only the gap by the event that Sb6 repeats, it is thought that the repetition gives a subject local surprise because the influence of the event to repeat is smaller than other events.
Category-D. Event that expand a story	If the story is long, the aforementioned subject sees an increase in surprise and an impact of the whole story. Therefore, the authors compared the numerical difference of the event included in Sa, and Sb1 to Sb10 and the average of the whole evaluation of the story And, it seems to quite influence surprise when a story becomes long.
Category-E. Event that cuts a flow of a story	The surprise by "the destruction of the continuity of events" is read by a free description. Subject H mentioned, "an opposite poles-like event was described just after that, for the above sentence, was surprised at a change of the development". The event that is not has context or reverses flow of a story given subject surprise. In addition, the authors believe surprise occurred at the point at which a gap was produced for a prospective event from "a part added in comparison with story A" that subject J described. However, it may not be so when it greatly raises surprise within the whole story to realize a prospective flow. The group of single event or pears of events including "eat" such as "eating a chestnut" gave an element of surprise, but the story (Sb8, Sb9) including them is moderately surprising in the evaluation average of the story itself.

A Degree of Surprise Based on a Number of Applied Gap Techniques

In this section, the authors consider results from various points of view. This experiment checks the influence that the number of times that applied gap technique to a story gives for surprise of the whole story.

For the measurement of the ratio of the gap, the authors used a story B, with a gap and another story A, without a gap in an event unit, and calculated the ratio of difference between the two by using the number of elements in story that were different from those story B. For example, the authors calculated a gap ratio of 1:2 when five events were found to have changed in a story consisting of 10 events. The authors prepared 36 samples using four patterns of gap techniques: with gaps of 25%, 50%, 75%, and 100% of the entire story. The authors prepare one story that did not use the gap technique in addition to these to calculate rate of application of the gap. A subject evaluated surprise in five phases of evaluation. Figure 4 shows the reply space used. There were five indices: "No surprised" at the left edge, "Surprised" at the center, and "Very surprised" at the right edge. In the evaluation, the subject marked any one of the indices from five indices consisting of above-mentioned three indices and two indices that there are between three indices. Table 11 shows an average surprising value every technique and slope by linear regression of the graph.

Table 11. Average of surprise and slope in each gap techniques

Method	Average of Surprise	Slope
Impressive verb	3.82	0.27
Impressive noun	3.55	0.09
Change a verb	2.88	0.54
Change a noun	2.87	0.24
Repetition event	1.80	0.35
New event	3.10	0.49
An event by cutting technique	3.17	0.31
Goal achievement by different way	1.60	0.15
Delete a scene	2.43	0.76

- **About Degree of Surprise in Each Gap Technique:** At first, each technique, there is greatly a difference in average of surprising strength. Because it is the technique that used an impressive verb, and a story comes to appear through a shocking verb, "killing", as for the technique that surprise is the strongest in, it is thought that many subjects received strong surprise. It faces each other, and the lowest technique is technique converting the scene, and, as for the expression, it is thought that the authors did not receive much surprise without a big gap being felt for a subject to be different, but to have the same achievement contents. In addition, it is thought that the authors can control surprise at a category level because it becomes the value that surprising average resembled except a part as for the technique in the same category. Because the repeated event is not given strong surprise by the simple repetition, the system need a special control method.
- **About Slope in Each Gap Technique:** The authors explain slope by linear regression of the graph in Table 11. The technique that a difference leaves this place every technique particularly a lurch is sudden is deletion of the scenes. It is thought that this was visible as the change that the numerical decrease in extreme scene is outstanding than other technique. On the contrary, the authors are extremely amazed to learn that the numbers of the event increase and know what the authors do not influence because the technique to gain the number of scenes became the degree of leaning that is moderate than other technique. On the contrary, the technique that a lurch was the slowest is the use of an impressive noun that is, as for this technique, it may be said that it is technique to bring about surprise at the same level when there is many it when there is little application number of times.
- **About "Weariness":** When similar stimulation continues, the stimulation bores a subject. The point of the gap increased to only it, and the story that applied a lot of same technique this time thought that the evaluation that the authors were amazed to learn might decrease in what a subject could be surprised. However, the authors can watch a tendency to give strong surprise so that there is much number of times that applied technique in most technique from a degree of leaning in result and Table 11.

FUTURE RESEARCH DIRECTIONS

At first, this section summarizes the consideration from the aforementioned "Category-A" to "Category-F" in Table 10. In "Category-A", the case is confirmed that a word gave surprise and the relation of the plural words included a certain event give it. "Category-B" often include instances in "Category-A", and the surprise of "Category-B" is similar to that of "Category-A". Influences to the story by the surprise of "Category-C" is small. "Category-D" is almost related to surprise of the whole story, while "Category-E", and gives a big surprise to a subject itself.

In this article, the authors considered a surprise effect from the two viewpoints. One is the surprise effect based on the target scale, such as words, events, and scenes, and the other is the effect by the position of surprise in the flow of the story. In the future, the authors will expand the gap technique based on the aforementioned surprise effect. For example, usage, such as using the gap technique to bring about the strong words of the impression in the latter half of the story is considered while using the gap technique to cut context in the middle stage of the story when the PL mechanism gives the GM mechanism a big surprise and wants to greatly change the flow of the story.

In addition, the authors suggest a control method of story generation based on surprise instead of a generation experiment and consider the following two points as a future experiment policy.

- Expansion of the number of people of the subject
- Comparison (age group, game group) of the group of subjects

About a comparison of the group layer, the authors performed an experiment including both inexperienced persons and experienced persons in TRPGs, but they did not compare the difference. Because the number of people in the study is small, the authors want to try an experiment to compare experienced persons with the inexperienced persons in TRPGs in the future.

CONCLUSION

The authors paid attention to the surprise of GM as hypothesized from the assumption in the story generation process of TRPG as it related to change in the story and tried an implementation of the gap technique to use surprise as one factor of the ANGG for the things mentioned above. The authors compared the evaluation of surprise with the calculation result of the gap obtained from a story using the gap technique and showed that two almost correlated proportionally. Furthermore, the authors performed a classification of surprise and an analysis produced by gap technique, clarifying the impact of surprise based on the structural scale of the gap in one story, the effect of surprise by the kind of the gap, and the impact of surprise from the position of the gap. The authors implemented the gap technique based on the aforementioned knowledge and will arrange the gap technique from two sides of the effect of surprise based on the target scale and the effect of surprise produced by the position in the flow of the story in future research. Furthermore, the authors can include the suggestion of the method to give the GM mechanism a strategic surprise element, and to control story generation.

The result of the surprise-based story generation using the above-mentioned gap technique is fed back to the INGS. INGS is the system that integrates various mechanisms of story generation, and it lays the foundation of different plural applied systems. INGS increases the knowledge that is obtained in this study, and makes the knowledge that is obtained in other studies available for this study. INGS has a generation cycle based on the sufficiency of expectation of a reader and the deviation from that expectation. The knowledge that is obtained in this study is available for the generation cycle.

REFERENCES

Bergström, K. (2012). Creativity rules: How rules impact player creativity in three tabletop role-playing games. *International Journal of Role-Playing, 3*, 4–17.

Caillois, R. (1958). *Les jeux et les hommes: Le masque et le vertige*. Paris: Gallimard.

Descartes, R. (1649). *Les passions de l'ame*. Paris: Henry Le Gras.

Genette, G. (1972). *Narrative discourse: An essay in method* (J. E. Lewin, Trans.). Cornell University Press. (Original work published 1972)

Hotta, T. (2013). The trick of information manipulation: surprise. *The Ryukoku Journal of Humanities and Sciences, 34*(2), 193-204.

Kamozaki, M., Ohno, Y., & Thawonmas, R. (2008). Casting method considering emotions towards actions in a story generation system. *Journal of Digital Games Research, 2*(1), 36–41.

Kanai, A. (2008). Eizo hensyu no ninchi kagaku [Cognitive science of film editing]. In A. Kanai & Y. Niwa (Eds.), *Eizo hensyu no riron to jissen* [Theory and practice of film editing] (pp. 13–38). Tokyo: Housei University Press.

Kanai, A., & Kodama, K. (2010). Film Edit Design: Story and Irrational Cutting. *Cognitive Science, 17*(3), 444–458.

Kato, K., & Fujino, H. (2015). A narrative analysis of a university student from the table talk role-playing game circle: From the viewpoint of communication support. *Bulletin of Tokyo Gakugei University. Education in Science, 66*(2), 333–339.

Matsunaga, S. (2015). Narachibu wo bunkaisuru: Bideo gemu no naratoroji [Dissecting a narrative: A narratology for video games]. *Workshop of "Analytic Philosophy and Art", "Narrative of Game / Narrative of Music"*.

Muto, T. (2016). Attitude of "surprise" in the Noh theory of Zeami. *International Cultural Studies, 22*, 59–72.

Nagaoka, C., & Ogata, T. (1999a). A method of computer game with NPCs that dynamically change. In *Proc. of the 13th Annual Conference of the Japan Society of Artificial Intelligence*, (pp. 165-166). Academic Press.

Nagaoka, C., & Ogata, T. (1999b). About a method of computer game based on autonomous NPC. In *Proc. of the 11th conference of Japan Association of Simulation & Gaming* (pp. 80-83). Academic Press.

Nakagawa, D. (2016). *Gendai game zenshi: Bunmei no yuugi shi kan kara* [Complete history of modern games: From a view of play history in a civilization]. Tokyo: Hayakawa Publishing.

Nomura, K. (2014). *Stori sekai no tukurikata* [How to making a story world]. Tokyo: Shinkigensha.

Ogata, T. (2015). Building conceptual dictionaries for an integrated narrative generation system. *Journal of Robotics, Networking and Artificial Life,* 270-284.

Ogata, T. (2016). Computational and cognitive approaches to narratology from the perspective of narrative generation. In T. Ogata & T. Akimoto (Eds.), *Computational and cognitive approaches to narratology* (pp. 1–74). Hershey, PA: IGI Global. doi:10.4018/978-1-5225-0432-0.ch001

Ogata, T., & Kanai, A. (2010). *An introduction to informatics of narratology: Towards the thoughts and technologies of narrative generation.* Tokyo: Gakubunsha.

Ono, J., & Ogata, T. (2016a). Architecture of a narrative generation system based on a TRPG model: The use of an integrated narrative generation system for knowledge acquisition (Preliminary version). *Bulletin of Networking, Computing. Systems & Software*, *5*(1), 40–48.

Ono, J., & Ogata, T. (2016b). A design plan of a game system including an automatic narrative generation mechanism: The entire structure and the world settings. In *Proceeding of the 2016 International Conference on Artificial Life and Robotics* (pp. 433-436). Academic Press. doi:10.2991/jrnal.2016.2.4.9

Ono, J., & Ogata, T. (2016c). Automatic generation mechanisms for games: For development of an automatic narrative generation game. In *Proc. of the 33rd Annual Meeting of the Japanese Cognitive Science Society* (pp. 175-180). Academic Press.

Ono, J., & Ogata, T. (2016d). Roles of non-player characters in an automatic narrative generation game using an integrated narrative generation system. In *Proc. of Forum on Information Technology 2016* (pp. 131-132). Academic Press.

Ono, J., & Ogata, T. (2016e). Generating stories by changing a world setting. In *Proc. of DiGRA Japan Annual Conference 2016* (pp. 63-66). Academic Press.

Ono, J., & Ogata, T. (2016f). A prototype system of a scene sequence expansion mechanism in an automatic narrative generation game based on TRPG method. In *Proc. of the 30th Annual Conference of the Japan Society of Artificial Intelligence* (1K4-OS-06a-6). Academic Press.

Ono, J., & Ogata, T. (2016g). Implementation of a scene expansion mechanism using an event sequence: As a mechanism in an automatic narrative generation game. *International Journal of Knowledge Engineering.*, *2*(4), 165–169. doi:10.18178/ijke.2016.2.4.073

Ono, J., & Ogata, T. (2016h). A design plan of a game system including an automatic narrative generation mechanism: The entire structure and the world settings. *Journal of Robotics, Networking and Artificial Life*, *2*(4), 243–246. doi:10.2991/jrnal.2016.2.4.9

Ono, J., & Ogata, T. (2017a). Attribute information acquisition in a conceptual dictionary by using Wikipedia and the use in an automatic narrative generation game. In *Proc. of the 31th Annual Conference of the Japan Society of Artificial Intelligence*, (1D3-OS-29b-2in2). Academic Press.

Ono, J., & Ogata, T. (2017b). Changing and transforming a story for a framework of an automatic narrative generation game. *Proc. of the 2017 international conference on artificial life and robotics.* doi:10.2991/jrnal.2017.4.1.16

Ono, J., Tyo, I., & Ogata, T. (2012). Defamiliarization rhetoric and scenario generation for events using the constraints in conceptual system. In *Proc. of the 26th Annual Conference of the Japan Society of Artificial Intelligence*, (1N1-OS-1a-1). Academic Press.

Porteous, J., Charles, F., & Cavazza, M. (2015). Using social relationships to control narrative generation. In *Proceedings of the 29th AAAI Conference on Artificial Intelligence (AAAI), Virtual Agents Demos.* Austin TX: AAAI.

Sawyer, S., & Tapia, A. (2005). The sociotechnical nature of mobile computing work: Evidence from a study of policing in the United States. *International Journal of Technology and Human Interaction, 1*(3), 1–14. doi:10.4018/jthi.2005070101

Truffaut, F. (1966). *Le cinema selon Alfred Hichicock.* Paris: Robert Laffont Editions.

Witwer, M. (2015). *Empire of imagination: Gary Gygax and the birth of Dungeons & Dragons.* London: Bloomsbury Publishing.

Yamane, I. (2005). Phenomenology of surprise. *Journal of Sugiyama Jogakuen University. Humanities, 36*, 13–28.

KEY TERMS AND DEFINITIONS

Automatic Narrative Generation Game: This game is a story generation mechanism. The game has two mechanisms: GM mechanism and PL mechanism based on table-talk role playing game.

Gap: A difference of two stories. The differences that GM assumed between a story and the story that actually generated.

Gap Technique: A kind of story generation technique. The technique generates a gap in a story.

Scene Sequence: A scene sequence is a passage of story constructed in plural scenes. The scene is one shared figure unit in a story in terms of time and spatiality and is comprised of one or more events.

Surprise: An element changes a story in this study.

Table-Talk Role Playing Game: TRPG is an analog game, usually played with dices, paper, and writing instruments.

World Setting: World setting is the setting of components of a story and is restricted to it. Components are characters, objects, locations, and times. It is limited by the components that may come up in a story.

ENDNOTES

1. Japanese English. Role Playing Game (RPG) in foreign countries often points at this analog game. The RPG is called Computer RPG in the digital game. It is called Table-Top Role Playing Game also.
2. A method to do simulated experience in the example by performing in people concerned in a certain example.
3. Gary Gygax (1938-2008) is a well-known game designer of the United States of America. The details to Empire of Imagination (Witwer, 2015) or Wikipedia (https://en.wikipedia.org/wiki/Gary_Gygax).
4. The Web page that shows the literary works that a copyright expired in Japan. The address is "http://www.aozora.gr.jp/".

APPENDIX

Table 12. Generated stories (Sa is not used gap techniques; Sb1 is used gap techniques)

ID	Story
Sa	学生の鈴木がOLの文香を大通りで誘拐する。 探偵が鈴木を大通りで調査する。 探偵が鈴木と家屋で争う。 探偵が文香を家屋で救助する。 文香が家屋で助かる。 [Suzuki who is a student kidnaped Fumika who is a female office worker in an avenue. A detective examined Suzuki in the avenue. The detective and Suzuki disputed in a house. The detective rescued Fumika. Fumika is saved.]
Sb1	学生の鈴木がOLの文香を大通りで誘拐する。 探偵が証拠物件を手紙に大通りで書く。 探偵が鈴木と家屋で争う。 探偵が崖に転がる。 探偵が鈴木と崖で争う。 探偵が崖から家屋に移動する。 探偵が文香を家屋で救助する。 文香が家屋で助かる。 [Suzuki who is a student kidnaped Fumika who is a female office worker in an avenue. A detective wrote evidence to a letter in the avenue. The detective and Suzuki disputed in a house. The detective lies down on a cliff. The detective and Suzuki disputed in the cliff. The detective move from the cliff into the house. The detective rescued Fumika. Fumika is saved.]

Section 3

Computational and Cognitive Modeling to Narrative Communication and Simulation

Chapter 5
Narratology and Creativity

Akinori Abe
Chiba University, Japan

ABSTRACT

In previous studies, the author discussed the creativity in IMDJ. The author discussed it from the perspective of abduction. In addition, the author discussed the role of comfortable communication in the creative situation as well as usual situation. In this chapter, the author discusses the role of narratology in the creative task.

INTRODUCTION

In this chapter, the author will discuss the role of narratology or story telling in the creative task. Narratology was regarded as a concept in story telling or generation. For instance, literary works generation can be achieved by the concept of narratology (Abe, 2016; Ogata, 2016). Previously the author discussed the possibility of the literary works generation by computer (Abe, 2016). Also Rolf Jensen showed the importance of story in selling products (Jensen, 1999). These can be regarded as creative tasks and by the story or narrative, the creativity enhanced in several situations. Thus story or narratology is very important in creativity.

For the conversation activation with a robot, Yamaguchi, Neguri and Otake showed very interesting results (Yamaguchi, Nergui, & Otake, 2014). They conducted experiments in two types of conversation. One was with all human and another was with a robot. The robot presented the reproduced interesting stories. They analyzed the data by the frequency of evoked laughter in each topic and in all participants. The reproduced stories presented by the robot created more laughter than the original stories presented by human. Thus, the robot successfully elicited more laughter than the human participants. Accordingly, they concluded that the robot successfully enlivened group conversation through evoking laughter. In fact, their application is the coimagination sessions for the elder persons. And the activity situation was evaluated by the frequency of laughter. The frequency of laughter will not be connected with the creativity. However, this result show us the possibility of the introducing of proper robot for the activation of conversation which will cause us to the better creativity.

DOI: 10.4018/978-1-5225-4775-4.ch005

Copyright © 2018, IGI Global. Copying or distributing in print or electronic forms without written permission of IGI Global is prohibited.

Therefore, the authors also discuss this type of conversation with a robot. Of course the conversation can be discussed in the context of narratology and storytelling.

BACKGROUND

Narratology in Literature

Narratology is very important in several situation. Especially it is discussed in the field of the computational literary works generation. The author discussed the possibility of the literary works generation by computer (Abe, 2016). Where the author showed several applications such as the automatic waka generation. The author utilized the feature of intertextuality (shown below) to generate literary works. One-hundred waka, included in the Hyakuninisshyu (a waka anthology), were divided into several parts and then rebuilt to generate new waka. Then one-hundred new waka were generated. In fact these waka were generated by combining several phrases from the existing waka. They were not fluently composed, and different seasons were included.

Ogata proposed Computational Narratology (Ogata, 1998; Ogata, 2016). His method is based on the narratology of Propp (1987) and Genette (1972). Based on these theories, the system automatically generates a story such as a legend from nothing. Moreover, he developed the system to automatically generate image works (films, etc.). He is still developing a story-generation system. Currently, it can generate a story outline after setting characters in the story.

Usually several techniques are used in the computational literary works generation. In fact, one of the special feature can be used in the computational literary works generation is the "intertextuality" proposed by J. Kristiva (1980).

Intertextuality

The word's status is thus defined horizontally (the word in the text belongs to both writing subject and addressee) as well as vertically (the word in the text is oriented towards an anterior or synchronic literary corpus)... each word (text) is an intersection of words (texts) where at least one other word (text) can be read... any text is constructed as a mosaic of quotations; any text is the absorption and transformation of another.

This is a very promising feature. Because computers are good at such searching and combination of small materials. Of course the above applications applied this type of feature in literary works generation.

Geravás et al. discussed the Story Generator Project. In their paper, they reviewed many story-generation systems based on artificial intelligence (AI) as follows:

Neither the under-defined nor the over-specific concepts developed in literary theory and Narratology seem good choices for the AI formalization. In the same vein, the limited scope of predominantly descriptive linguistic models renders these unsatisfactory. Conversely, Artificial Intelligence approaches in Story Generation are generally based on a highly reductionist concept of 'story,' which ignores the Humanities `disciplines' insights into the complexity and dynamics of narrative....

In our view, a methodological combination of description, analysis, and generation-in other words: an inter-disciplinary approach-holds the potential for a mutually beneficial qualitative breakthrough in research on Story Generation, and on narrative models in general. This inter-disciplinary approach might start by identifying those existing narrative models in the Humanities whose set of ontological commitments is better suited for the Story Generation task, and by searching for (or producing) computationally oriented implementations of these models (Gervás et al., 2006).

Ryan and Thon replaced "narrative" with "storyworld" and pointed out that "Nowadays, we have not only multimodal representations of storyworlds that combine various types of signs, and virtual online worlds that wait to be filled with stories by their player citizens, but also serial storyworlds that span multiple installments, and transmedial storyworlds that are deployed simultaneously across multiple media platforms, resulting in a media landscape in which creators and fans alike constantly expand, revise, and even parody them (Ryan, & Thon, 2014)." In the future, such media-conscious narratologies can be considered to create better literary works. Since "storyworld" is an extension of "narrative." Anyway, narratology plays a significant role in literary works generation.

Story Telling (Narratology) in Advertisement

Rolf Jensen showed the importance of story in selling products (Jensen, 1999). For instance, an article in (http://cifs.dk/publications/books/rolf-jensen-the-dream-society/the-dream-society/) shows that "The huge increase in material wealth owes much to science and technology, but, in the future, attention will turn away from science toward nonmaterialistic and nonscientific values. The highest-paid person in the first half of the next century will be the "storyteller." The value of products will depend on the story they tell. Nike and many other global companies are already mainly storytellers. That is where the money is - even today. The corporate strategy sessions are increasingly about storytelling - not manufacturing. Our heroes at the Olympic Games in Atlanta will be those telling magnificent stories - and they'll be getting well paid later." That is, the highest-paid person in the first half of the next century will be the "storyteller." In fact, as we can see the situation in CM in Japan (Sapporo? beer), they try to show the background story of the birth of the product. In addition, Sapporo beer's CM film in 2007 entitled "Nai mono hatsukuru shika nai (We must produce necessary products.)[1]" is very famous. It is a musical type advertisement where the story of the beer product procedure is played. Thus, products should have a story inside.

In London, we can enjoy the Restaurant Story[2]. In their dinner course, they provide several chapters as a story. The name of the dinner is "Full Story." It consists of Forward (snacks), Chapter I (Childhood), Chapter II (Sea), Chapter III (Land), and Chapter IV (The End (deserts)). In fact, dinner will be a story. We eat several foods according to the chef's story. In the restaurant, from the menu, we can enjoy the story. Like the advertisement shown above, activities which have story will be fantastic for us. A story is important for our life.

The Role of Narratology in Creativity

Several applications and activities of narratology and storytelling are shown above. In fact, narratology and storytelling are for literary works. In addition, recently they have been applied to medical interview and therapies. In the applications, of course literary works can be generated. As shown in the facts in product selling and advertisements, by the story an additional value can be added to the products. During the dinner in the Restaurant Story, we can enjoy the story as well as the taste of the food. The story might be regarded as an atmosphere, but it can also be regarded as an additional value. We can say more that without story no product can have value inside. Thus, story or narratology is very important in creativity. By the story or narratology, the creativity enhanced in several situations.

ABDUCTION AS STORY GENERATOR

Philosophical Abduction

Peirce classified abduction from a philosophical point of view as the operation of adopting an explanatory hypothesis and characterized its form Peirce (1955).

1. The surprising fact, C, is observed;
2. But if A were true, C would be a matter of course,
3. Hence, there is reason to suspect that A is true.

Then Peirce illustrated abduction as follows:

...abduction is an operation for adopting an explanatory hypothesis, which is subject to certain conditions, and that in pure abduction, there can never be justification for accepting the hypothesis other than through interrogation.

Computational Abduction

The important keyword of the definition is, explanatory hypothesis. That is, abduction is performed as an explanation of something. Peirce would not assume the performance of computational abduction, but several years ago several abduction systems such as Theorist (Poole, Goebel, & Aleliunas, 1987) and ALP (Abductive Logic Programming) (Kakas, Kowalski, & Toni, 1992) are proposed.

Theorist is considered as a computational hypothetical reasoning system. A hypothetical reasoning which is an explanatory reasoning generates (collects, selects) a consistent hypothesis set from hypothesis candidates to explain the given observation. The generated hypothesis set can be regarded as an answer (solution) which can explain the observation. The inference mechanism of Theorist is described as follows:

$F \nvdash O$. (O cannot be explained only by F.) (1)

$F \cup h \vdash O$. (O can be explained by F and h.) (2)

$F \cup h \nvdash \Box$. (F and h are consistent.) (3)

where F is called fact which is always true. On the other hand, h is called hypothesis which is not always true and included in the hypothesis set H ($h \subseteq H$). O is an observation to be explained. $\square$ is an empty set. When $F \cup h \vdash \square$, F and h are not consistent. In the knowledge base, inconsistent information is also included.

Clause Management System (CMS)

Clause Management System (CMS) (Reiter, & de Kleer, 1987) proposed by Reiter and de Kleer is a framework for the database management. The management framework can be regarded as abduction. Since CMS shows missing and necessary minimal clauses for explanation of a certain situation. That is, if we use CMS as abduction, it is possible to generate missing knowledge for a certain inference.

An abductive reasoning in CMS is conducted as follows:

When

$$\sum \nvDash C, \tag{4}$$

(C (observation) cannot be explained only by $\sum$)

CMS will generate a minimal clauses set S to $\sum$ for satisfying the following formulae.

$$\sum \vDash S \vee C, \tag{5}$$

$$\sum \nvDash S. \tag{6}$$

($\neg S$ is not included in $\sum$.)

S is called minimal support clause. And $\neg S$ can be considered as a missing hypothesis set to explain C in the world (knowledge base) of clause set. Accordingly $\neg S$ can be considered as an abductive hypothesis set. For the hypothesis reasoning, it is necessary to prepare a candidate hypothesis set. However, for CMS it is not necessary to prepare such a set. However, the generated hypothesis set cannot always be correct and sometimes it is too minimal. Then if CMS is introduced, it is necessary to be careful in the hypothesis set selection.

Abductive Analogical Reasoning (AAR)

As shown above, CMS generates only the minimal hypothesis set. Thus it is not always the case we can obtain the sufficient hypothesis set. Accordingly the author proposed Abductive Analogical Reasoning (AAR) (Abe, 2000) that logically and analogically generates missing hypotheses. Its generation mechanism is similar to CMS's. Structures of generated knowledge sets are analogous to the known knowledge sets. In the framework of AAR, not completely unknown but rather unknown hypotheses can be generated. In addition, by the introduction of analogical mapping, the new hypothesis evaluation criteria other than Occam's Razor (for instance, criteria such as explanatory coherence (Thagard, 1989)) can be adopted. The inference mechanism is briefly illustrated as follows (for notations, see Abe (2000)):

When

$$\sum \nvDash O, \text{(O cannot only be explained by } \sum.\text{)} \tag{7}$$

$\sum$ (background knowledge) lacks a certain set of clauses to explain O. Consequently, AAR returns a set of minimal clauses S such that

$$\sum \vDash S \vee O, \tag{8}$$

$$\neg S \notin \sum . \tag{9}$$

The result is the same as CMS's. This is not always a guaranteed hypothesis set. To guarantee the hypothesis set, the authors introduced analogical mapping from known knowledge sets.

$$S \mid\!\rightsquigarrow S', \text{(S' is analogically transformed from S.)} \tag{10}$$

$$\neg S' \in \sum, \tag{11}$$

$$S' \mid\!\rightsquigarrow S'', \tag{12}$$

$$\sum \vDash S'' \vee O, \tag{13}$$

$$\neg S'' \notin \sum. \tag{14}$$

O is then explained by $\neg S''$ as a hypotheses set. Thus a new hypothesis set that is logically abduced whose structure is similar to authorized (well-known) knowledge sets can be generated.

Abduction for the Computational Narratology

Thus an abduction performs as the combination of the consistent hypothesis set. Accordingly it can be used several applications such as conversation generation and literary work generation.

For the literary work generation, the author introduced the concept of "intertextuality." Its feature of text as a mosaic of quotations construction and absorption and transformation of another text is easily achieved by abduction. That is, a randomized generation is quite easy but not so interesting. However a logical generation can be achieved by abduction. For instance, if the final goal or result is known, for the explanation of the final goal or result, several quotations which can be regarded as hypotheses are abduced. This type of inference can be applied to the natural language processing. For instance, several natural language processing systems using abduction have been proposed (Stickel, 1988, 1989; Hobbs, Stickel, Appelt, & Martin, 1993; McRoy & Hirst, 1993, 1995). They are systems for natural language interpretation, understanding, or repair of speech act misunderstandings. For example, Hobbs' abductive interpretation is based on the notion that the interpretation of a text is the minimal explanation of why the text should be true. The text interpretation process is performed by abductively proving that it is coherent. However, a more interesting field for abduction in natural language processing is discourse generation. Lascarides and Oberlander (1992) proposed a method of abductive generation for laconic discourse. The method proposed by Lascarides performs interpretation discourse by deductively using defeasible rules and discourse generation by nonmonotonic deductive check and abduction.

For the conversation generation, previously the author proposed a natural language generation framework with examples of an AAR application (Abe, 1997). In addition, the author applied abduction to a simple discourse generation which includes humour (Abe, 1998). In this framework, the structure of the previous conversation[3] is referred to to generate a new conversation. In addition, a humourous conversation is generated by AAR.

The conversation generation process is shown by a simple example. This first example is an abductive explanation of an observation. There is no previous referential conversation. Let the knowledge base include the following clauses.

¬danger_baby:- make_sleep_baby.
Danger_baby:- swallow_baby_pen.
¬pen:- swallow_baby_pen.
Write_letter:- pen.
pencil.

When an observation is ¬danger_baby, one of the hypotheses generated by AAR (CMS) is make sleep baby. However, if the current context[4] (now it is medical treatment) changes to writing, an observation will change[5] to write letter. Then, a hypothesis abduced from AAR becomes write letter:- pencil. This is because there is no pens, and pen is similar to pencil. A new hypothesis write letter:- pencil is generated by AAR.

Actually, the above inference is a sample of a humourous conversation between Mr. A and a doctor as follows:

Mr. A: "Doctor, please come as soon as possible. My baby has swallowed a pen."
Doc.: "I see, I'll be there soon. Do you know what to do before I get there?"
Mr. A: "I'll use a pencil."

If the above result is known, another humourous conversation will be generated by AAR regarding the previous conversation.

Let another knowledge base include the following clauses.

¬ache_B:- stop_bleeding_B.
Ache_B:- penetrate_B_nail.
¬nail:- penetrate_B_nail.
Task_B_carpentry:- nail.
screw.

In this case, under the usual context (it is also medical treatment), if an observation is ¬ache_B, then one of the hypotheses generated by AAR (CMS) is stop_bleeding_B. Since we have the previous conversation example, a context change can be done by referring to it. If the context changes to carpentry, an observation will change to task_B_carpentry, and the hypothesis abduced from AAR is task_B_carpentry:- screw. This is because there is no nails, however, nail is similar to screw. This conversation between Mr. B and a doctor can be expressed as follows.

Mr. B: "Doctor, please come as soon as possible. A nail has penetrated my hand."
Doc.: "I see, I'll be there soon. Do you know what to do before I get there?"
Mr. B: "I'll use a screw."

The discourse generation procedure consists of three inferences.

1. **Deduction:** This is a previous conversation. The current context should be acquired before abduction, that is, during this deduction the current context should be acquired. In this paper, an acquisition of the current context is out of focus. This type of task will be achieved by learning (or induction).
2. **Abduction (AAR):** In this phase an answer to a question is obtained. An observation corresponds to a question and the answer corresponds to hypotheses. Abduction is performed under the above context to return an answer. This process is quite natural for an abductive generation.
3. **Abduction (AAR):** This is another abduction under another context. This is a situation other than the previous situation, therefore, the knowledge base should lack the necessary knowledge. AAR will play a significant role in this situation.

This application was developed for the conversation with joke generation. This type of application was developed for the activation of conversation. This procedure can be applied to the normal conversation as well. Of course an additional emotion can be added to the conversation by this method. In addition, the above application is based on situational inference change. A suitable situation change can lead our thinking in the better direction. Accordingly, if we use this type of situation change not only for making joke but also for giving a certain stimulation, innovative activities can be encouraged.

IMDJ PROCEDURE

Innovation Marketplace on Data Jacket (IMDJ) is called as Innovation Game. The Innovation Game seems a game where a new production will be obtained during the combination of various techniques, materials and previous products.

Usually the game adopt an analogous game system. It uses a large paper. KeyGraph's output is printed on a large paper (game board: Figure 1). For instance as shown in Figure 1, techniques and their abstract explanations are printed. In addition, techniques are linked by the links generated by KeyGraph.

The mechanism of KeyGraph generation was illustrated in Ohsawa, Benson, and Yachida (1998). So the author will not give detailed illustration of the generation of the links. Participants place yellow cards (showing their requirements) and blue cards (their proposal) on the game board. By the above activities, several requirements and proposals are shown. For the game that the author took part in, techniques other than those printed on could be used. Such techniques can be searched by the computer software. They are used in the previous games. Participants generate several proposal by combining techniques on the game board and additional techniques. Then several applications which will satisfy requirements are proposed.

Figure 1. A game board in Innovation Marketplace on Data Jacket

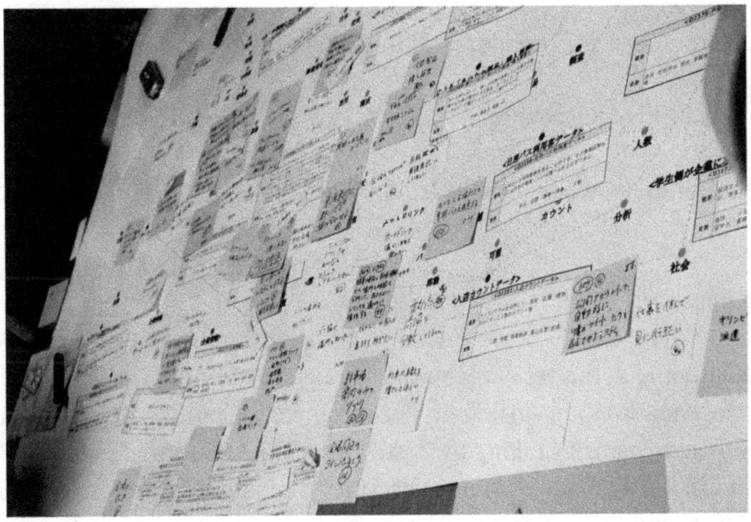

While the game participants buy proposals according to their sense of value (How their requirements are satisfied and the proposal is good.). In addition, proposals are valued by the all participants. The best proposal can obtain money. The winner is a participant who can obtain the biggest money. One of the strategy in this game is to obtain as many money as a participant can. This fact can be regarded as an economic game. For that it is necessary to produce the best and unique proposal that can satisfy one or more requirements. This can be regarded as the best design and requirement satisfaction problem. That is a type of constraint solving problem (CSP) which can be solved by abduction. The author will discuss the production strategy not from the economic viewpoint but from the abductive viewpoint.

To summarize the game, when a requirement (yellow card) is given, a proposal (blue card) will be generated accordingly. Even if the proper techniques are not on the game board, techniques which were used in the previous game can be searched and used. In this sense, the strategy used in this game can be regarded as abduction. The detailed illustration of abduction will be given in the next section. Here, the author will show the brief strategy of the Innovation Game. In the Innovation Game participants do their best to explain the certain requirement by generating or collecting a set of hypothesis (in this case, a set of techniques) in the current environment. Many creative activities can be performed as a case of abduction. This type of inference strategy can be considered as abduction. Of course, if the current environment changes, the inference strategy has the characteristic of non-monotonic reasoning.

ABDUCTION IN IMDJ

In this section, the author will discuss the above strategy in the context of abduction. For the easy understanding, in the illustration, the author will use very simple example as shown in Figure 1 (in the previous section).

A strategy "generating or collecting a set of hypothesis (in this case, a set of techniques) to explain a certain requirement." can be formalized as hypothetical reasoning as follows:

$$\text{Environment} \nvdash \text{requirement}. \tag{15}$$

(In the current environment, it is not possible to explain the requirement.)

$$\text{environment} \cup \text{techniques} \vdash \text{requirement}. \tag{16}$$

(In the current environment, when a set of techniques can be generated, it is possible to explain the requirement.)

$$\text{environment} \cup \text{techniques} \nvdash \square. \tag{17}$$

(In the current environment, the set of techniques are consistent.)

Logically the above equations are sufficient. For instance, we can see requirements such as "I would like to go to see the Olympic game by taking the rest." in the right bottom of Figure 1. The proposal given here is "A fake tweet can be shown in the open account." Techniques to achieve the above proposal are "shop arrival count data" and something (it is not possible to recognize in the figure). The theme in the game was how to make the 2020 Olympic game successful. The original techniques are extracted from the application to solve problems in university lives. Thus game was conducted by using techniques from the rather different theme and field. A participant who proposed this interpreted the requirement as "going to see the Olympic game by pretending his/her place." Then he/she generates a technique satisfying the requirements to pretend his/her place and to make use of tweet technique (perhaps of the Olympic game) by manipulating "shop arrival count data" rather differently from the original usage.

That is, according to the following formula, it is possible to generate a technique set to satisfy the requirements.

$$\text{knowledge of the place the Olympic game is held} \cup$$

$$\{\text{show a different place} \cup \text{perform tweet}\} \vdash \text{pretend his/her place}. \tag{18}$$

Basically in a hypothetical reasoning, the inference is performed by the selection of the existing hypothesis set from the hypothesis base or unification of variables in the hypothesis set. However, in the above example, techniques are not used as they are as well as the requirement is interpreted differently. A hypothetical reasoning basically use hypotheses as they are for the inference. For instance, for the LSI circuit design, the design is conducted by using existing parts. Of course, it will be sufficient to use the existing parts for the design of the LSI circuit. It will not be possible to design the LSI circuit by using non-existing parts. However, if we consider the better design, it will not be sufficient in the limited situation. Accordingly if we would like to produce what we want to really have, it is sometimes impossible to use only the existing techniques to make a brand new product. The above example shows the similar situation. When we make a brand new product, we naturally extend the possible techniques. The situation can be illustrated by the framework of abduction.

In the previous section, CMS is illustrated, that can generate a hypothesis set which is necessary for the inference but missing from the hypothesis base. In addition, AAR is illustrated that is an extension of CMS, which introduces a similar hypothesis set generation.

By using CMS and AAR, the above strategy can be explained. For instance, in the above example, suppose we do not have a technique "perform tweet." Then

knowledge of the place the Olympic game is held

$\cup$ {show a different place} $\nvdash$ pretend his/her place. (19)

If we follow CMS,

knowledge of the place the Olympic game is held $\nvDash$

{$\neg$ show a different place}$\vee$ pretend his/her place. (20)

can be obtained. In order to satisfy the requirement, it is necessary to find minimal S supporting the following formula.

knowledge of the place the Olympic game is held $\vDash$

S $\vee$ {$\neg$show a different place}$\vee$ pretend his/her place. (21)

If S = $\neg$tell can be obtained, the above formula can be satisfied.

knowledge of the place the Olympic game is held $\vDash$

{$\neg$tell $\vee$ $\neg$show a different place} $\vee$pretend his/her place. (22)

As for the clause "show a different place," a technique such as "shop arrival count data" can be used to achieve it [6] . The most difficult problem is how to generate a clause "tell." It will be possible by the introduction of AAR to generate a clause "tell."

When the following formula is obtained;

knowledge of the place the Olympic game is held $\vDash$

{$\neg$tell $\vee$ $\neg$shop arrival count data} $\vee$ pretend his/her place. (23)

It will be necessary to search or generate a technique similar to "tell."' For instance, if we interpret "tell" as "communicate his/her voice," "broadcast'" ("tell $\approx$ broadcast'") can be searched from the knowledge base in the other context or newly generated. In addition, if we interpret "tell" as "communicate phrase (including characters)," "perform tweet" ("tell $\approx$ perform tweet'") can be searched from the knowledge base in the other context or generated newly. The selection of hypothesis set is determined considering if the hypothesis set is consistent with "the place the Olympic game is held" and other techniques, and if it can be used in the context. If it is not consistent, it is necessary to produce new techniques or to replace with the other techniques. This is a non-monotonic aspect of this reasoning. In this case, if the personal information is "broadcast" in "the place the Olympic game is held," it will reveal the personal information. Therefore "broadcast" is not consistent in the situation.

"Perform tweet" has a rather publication feature, but it may not be so bad compared with "broadcast." Accordingly, "perform tweet" can be adopted as a similar technique as "tell." The proposal shown in Figure 1 is determined, because the proposer thought "perform tweet" was enough to keep the privacy of the individual. If it is not still insufficient, it will be necessary to adopt another technique that can keep the individual better, for instance, "send a message via FB (facebook)" ("tell ≈ send a message via FB"). This type of non-monotonic hypothesis selection continues until a consistent hypothesis set can be generated. In addition, when the generated hypothesis set cannot be used as it is, an analogical mapping is introduced to generate new and usable hypothesis set in the situation.

Knowledge of the place the Olympic game is held $|\approx$ {¬send a message via FB ∨

¬shop arrival count data} ∨ pretend his/her place. (24)

AAR can generate more complex hypothesis set than the minimal hypothesis set. Accordingly, the obtained hypothesis set can be more reasonable hypothesis set by referring to the other existing techniques. Of course, during an analogical mapping, the consistency of hypothesis set should be considered. In this chapter, the author used a very simple example to explain the strategies in IMDJ. Furthermore, if all results obtained in IMDJ can be data-based in a logical form, even computers can take part in the IMDJ to generate a new product. As shown above, human participants seem to make an abductive inference in IMDJ. In fact, when the author took part in the IMDJ, if the author could not find any best technique, the author extend functions of the existing techniques to produce the better proposal. That is, based on the existing techniques, new techniques are produced. This production can be considered as an inference of AAR.

In the above, the author explained an example of game performance "...to make use of tweet technique (perhaps of the Olympic game) by manipulating "shop arrival count data" rather differently from the original usage" as abduction. Of course this type of activity can be considered as AAR.

Thus when we make an inference in IMDJ, we basically search or generate techniques by abduction and combine the consistent techniques to produce our proposal that can satisfy the requirements. This type of inference can be regarded as a creative inference. In addition, when we cannot find proper techniques to satisfy the requirements, we perform an analogical mapping from techniques in other context to those in the current context. Then we can generate a proper hypothesis set (techniques) to create proposal as a combination of consistent techniques.

THE ROLE OF NARRATOLOGY IN IMDJ

IMDJ Procedure

In the previous section, the possibility of computational narratology was shown. In addition, in several papers such as Abe (2015), the author pointed out the role of abduction in IMDJ. Innovation Marketplace on Data Jacket (IMDJ) is called as Innovation Game. The Innovation Game seems a game where a new production will be obtained during the combination of various techniques, materials and previous products. During the game participants buy proposals according to their sense of value (How their requirements are satisfied and the proposal is good.). In addition, proposals are valued by the all participants. As shown above, when a requirement is given, a proposal will be generated accordingly. Even if the proper techniques are not shown, techniques which were used in the previous game can be searched and used. In this sense, the strategy used in this game can be regarded as abduction. Thus the IMDJ procedure is regarded as an abductive procedure in the product generation (creativity). Of course products can be generated to explain the requirement. In addition, as shown in Ohsawa, Benson and Yachida (1998), the effect of communication among participants is plays a significant role in creativity. A communication among users is very important to reorganize or improve their thinking. In addition, sometimes even new idea might appear.

Creativity

In this section the author will review several description for the creativity.

Carl Rogers defined creative process as follows (Rogers, 1959).

The creative process is the emergence in action of a novel relational product, growing out of the uniqueness of the individual on the one hand, and the materials, events, people, or circumstances of his life on the other.

Also, in DynaGloss (2002), collective creativity is defined as follows:

A term describing the phenomenon where concepts emerge in people's mind through interacting with knowledge in the world | external representations, with other people, or with computer systems. Designers evolve artifacts by externalizing such concepts and by sharing them with other people. Though creative individuals are often thought of working in isolation, the role of interaction and collaboration with other individuals is also critical. Thus, creative activity grows out of the relationship between an individual and the world of his or her work, and out of the ties between an individual and other human beings[7].

Referring to the above definitions, the author defined creative work as follows (Abe, 2002):

Creative means novel and creative work comes from nothing or from something relative but whose relation to the work was hidden. Actually, for creativity, a sort of intuition or special sense will be necessary. An intuition or special sense will emerge with some stimulus like information (background knowledge). In emergence, knowledge will work as a catalyst.

Thus for creativity, the importance of "action of a novel relational product" and "the role of interaction and collaboration with other individuals" are pointed out. These types of creativity can be achieved by a simple abduction. Accordingly, the abductive process shown in the above can include creativity. However, for the more attractive creativity, a "storytelling" will be necessary. In addition, as pointed out in the previous section, the value of products will depend on the story they tell. Thus narratology is also the important factor in creativity. In the above, it is pointed out that "creative individuals are often thought of working in isolation, the role of interaction and collaboration with other individuals is also critical." During collaboration, it is more necessary to consider the existence of a storyteller. Abduction can have a role of the collaboration between participants and storytellers. Thus by abduction a certain story can be generated as well as a combination of several techniques to explain a requirement.

Communication (in IMDJ)

As pointed out in Abe (2016), during the game, conversation among the participants is very important. Accordingly it will be necessary to design a proper robot for activation of the conversation in IMDJ. In addition, the authors pointed out the importance of emotion in the communication robot. That is, for the better and comfortable conversation, using sympathizing phrase will be important. Especially when persons are depressed they need such sympathizing words. Since they are depressed, they cannot feel self-affirmation. The authors can find a certain tendency in our feeling in conversations. In fact, by the experiments using the several types of communication robots, the authors could find out the pattern as shown below:

The Conversation Introduction Type Robot (Type-2) and the Humour Type Robot (Type-6) Obtain a High Evaluation as Enjoyable

For the type 2 robot, though it is mostly a listener type, participants evaluate it as pleasure instead of boredom. For the type 6 robot, as the authors expected, the evaluation as boredom is low and the evaluation as pleasure is high. For the type 4 robot, it is evaluated as both boredom and irritation.

In the experiments, the type 2 robot functions as a conversation introduction type, that is many introductions to conversations are given. The type 4 robot functions as a non-sympathy type that is, blame and non-sympathy words are given. And the type 6 robot functions as a humour type, that is, more playful and context is not considered. Actually, the authors prepared 6 types of robots, the detailed robot type from which information can be obtained in Abe (2016). When the authors conduct the additional experiments, the authors found that participants asked the computer's opinion and personality. That is, they tend to evaluate low when the computer's interest to them is low. In addition, if participants can find a certain personality in the computer, some of them could enjoy the personality. Unpredictability of the computer sometimes can be regarded as a certain personality to enjoy the conversation. In fact, the comfort situation only helps the creativity, but such situations offer a certain possibility in creativity. Actually, both robots can tell a story and participants can generate, follow and enjoy the story during conversations.

As shown in Introduction, the reproduced stories presented by the robot created more laughter than the original stories presented by human. Thus, the robot successfully elicited more laughter than the human participants. The frequency of laughter will not be connected with the creativity. However, this result shows us the possibility of introducing the proper robot for the activation of conversation, which will cause us to better the creativity. As shown, a communication among participants is very important to reorganize or improve their thinking. In addition, sometimes even new idea might appear. Thus, from the viewpoint of an activated communication, a certain story telling (narratology) will cause the better creativity.

The Role of Narratology in IMDJ

In the above, the author discussed the proposal generation procedure in IMDJ. An abductive procedure will be performed in the product generation (creativity) in IMDJ. Where the possible products can be generated as explaining the requirement. This is a very intellectual procedure and mainly conducted individually. In addition in the above section, the author show the effect of the communication robots in conversations. According to my definition, for the creativity, a sort of intuition or special sense will be necessary. An intuition or special sense will emerge with some stimulus such as information (background knowledge). In emergence, knowledge will function as a catalyst. The catalyst can be obtained during conversation or listening to the story told by the other participants.

That is, the effect of communication among participants plays a significant role in creativity. A communication among users is very important to reorganize or improve their thinking. In addition, sometimes even new idea might appear. The authors can discuss this communication from the perspective of narratology or story-telling. As discussed in the previous section, narratology is a very important concept in valuable activities as well as literary works generation. It is necessary to consider the effect of narratology even during a technical discussion. For instance, for a technical discussion, there should be a certain story. Moderators or communication robots (if applicable) should produce a certain story during the discussion. If they can properly generate or add a story to the technical discussion, participants can generate the better products.

CONCLUSION

In this chapter, the author mainly discusses the effect of narratology or story telling in IMDJ. The author briefly introduced the feature of narratology and several applications based on narratology. Recently, it has been discussed the importance of narratology or story telling in several applications such as an advertisement and intellectual tasks.

In Abe (2015), the author discussed and formalized the role of abduction in the product generation. Abduction can also have a role of the collaboration between participants and storytellers. Thus, by abduction a certain story can be generated as well as a combination of several techniques to explain a requirement.

In Kubo and Abe (2014), the authors discussed the critical points or words where conversations can be activated. In Abe and Hayashi (2016b), the authors discussed what type of communication tool can encourage user's communication and make users feel enjoyable and comfortable. In Abe and Hayashi (2016a), the authors discussed, especially in IMDJ, what types of communication tools encourage user's communication and make users feel enjoyable and comfortable.

Accordingly, for the better product generation in IMDJ the importance of narratology or story telling can be considered.

REFERENCES

Abe, A. (1997). A criterion for hypotheses in abduction. In *Proc. of the 55th. Annual Conf. of IPSJ*, (*Vol. 2*, 6AH-4, pp. 573-574). Academic Press. (in Japanese)

Abe, A. (1998). Applications of abduction. In *Proc. of ECAI98 Workshop on Abduction and Induction in AI* (pp. 12-19). Academic Press.

Abe, A. (2000). Abductive analogical reasoning. *Systems and Computers in Japan, 31*(1), 11–19. doi:10.1002/(SICI)1520-684X(200001)31:1<11::AID-SCJ2>3.0.CO;2-E

Abe, A. (2002). User's interests change as chance discovery. In *Proc. of KES2002* (pp. 1291-1295). Academic Press.

Abe, A. (2015). The role of abduction in IMDJ. In *Proc. of IJCAI2015 International Workshop on Chance Discovery, Data Synthesis and Data Market* (pp. 59-64). Academic Press.

Abe, A. (2016). The possibility of the generation of literary works by computer. In T. Ogata & T. Akiomoto (Eds.), Computational and Cognitive Approaches to Narratology (pp. 75–89). Academic Press. doi:10.4018/978-1-5225-0432-0.ch002

Abe, A., & Hayashi, M. (2016a). On communication assistance via bots ---towards IMDJ. In *Proc. KES2016, Procedia Computer Science* (pp. 1657-1665). Academic Press. doi:10.1016/j.procs.2016.08.213

Abe, A., & Hayashi, M. (2016b). On communication via bots for the computational therapy. In *Proc. of Int'l Workshop on Language Sense on Computer in IJCAI2016* (pp. 61-66). Academic Press.

DynaGloss. (2002). Retrieved May, 2002, from http://Seed.cs.colorado.edu/

Fischer, G. (2000). Social creativity, symmetry of ignorance and meta-design. *International Journal Knowledge-Based Systems, 13*(7-8), 527-537.

Fischer, G. (2004). Social creativity: Turning barriers into opportunities for collaborative design. In *Proc. of the Participatory Design Conference (Pdc'04)* (pp. 152-161). Academic Press. doi:10.1145/1011870.1011889

Genette, G. (1972). *Discours du recit, essai de methode, Figures III.* Paris: Seuil.

Gervás, P., Lönneker-Rodman, B., Meister, J. C., & Peinado, F. (2006). Narrative models: narratology meets artificial intelligence. In *Proceedings of International Conference on Language Resources and Evaluation*, (pp. 44-51). Academic Press.

Hobbs, J. R., Stickel, M. E., Appelt, D. E., & Martin, P. (1993). Interpretation as abduction. *Artificial Intelligence, 63*(1-2), 69–142. doi:10.1016/0004-3702(93)90015-4

Jensen, R. (1999). *The dream society: How the coming shift from information to imagination will transform your business.* McGraw Hill.

Kakas, A. C., Kowalski, R. A., & Toni, F. (1992). Abductive logic programming. *Journal of Logic and Computation, 2*(6), 719–770. doi:10.1093/logcom/2.6.719

Kristeva, J. (1980). *Desire in language: A semiotic approach to literature and art.* Columbia University Press.

Kubo, M., & Abe, A. (2014). Critical points in conversations from the perspective of chance discovery. In *Proc. of KES2014* (pp. 969-978). Academic Press. doi:10.1016/j.procs.2014.08.178

Lascarides, A., & Oberlander, J. (1992). Abducing temporal discourse. In *Proc. of 6th. Int'l Workshop on Natural Language Generation (LNAI-587)* (pp. 167-182). Academic Press.

McRoy, S. W., & Hirst, G. (1993). Abductive explanation of dialogue misunderstandings. In *Proc. of EACL93* (pp. 277-286). Academic Press.

McRoy, S. W., & Hirst, G. (1995). The repair of speech act misunderstandings by abductive inference. *Computational Linguistics*, *21*(4), 435–478.

Ogata, T. (1998). Proposal of computational narratology. *PSJ SIGNotes Computer and Humanities Abstract*, No.041 – 008. (in Japanese)

Ogata, T. (2016). Computational and cognitive approaches to narratology from the perspective of narrative generation. In T. Ogata & T. Akiomoto (Eds.), Computational and cognitive approaches to narratology (pp. 1–74). Academic Press. doi:10.4018/978-1-5225-0432-0

Ohsawa, Y., Benson, N. E., & Yachida, M. (1998). KeyGraph: Automatic indexing by co-occurrence graph based on building construction metaphor. In *Proc. Advanced Digital Library Conference (IEEE ADL'98)* (pp. 12-18). Academic Press. doi:10.1109/ADL.1998.670375

Ohsawa, Y., Kido, H., Hayashi, T., Liu, C., & Komoda, K. (2015). Innovation Marketplace on Data Jackets, for Valuating, Sharing, and Synthesizing Data, Knowledge-based Information. *Systems Practice*, *30*, 83–97.

Ohsawa, Y., & Nishihara, Y. (Eds.). (2012). *Innovators' marketplace*. Springer Verlag. doi:10.1007/978-3-642-25480-2

Peirce, C. S. (1955). *Philosophical writings of Peirce*. Dover.

Poole, D., Goebel, R., & Aleliunas, R. (1987). Theorist: A logical reasoning system for defaults and diagnosis. In The Knowledge Frontier: Essays in the Representation of Knowledge (pp. 331-352). Springer-Verlag.

Propp, V. Y. (1968). *Morphology of the folktale* (2nd ed.; L. A. Wagner, Trans.). University of Texas Press.

Reiter, R., & de Kleer, J. (1987). Foundation of assumption-based truth maintenance systems: Preliminary report. In *Proc. of AAAI87* (pp.183-188). AAAI.

Rogers, C. (1959). *Toward a theory of creativity, in creativity and its cultivation* (H. Anderson, Ed.). Harper & Row.

Ryan, M.-L., & Thon, J.-N. (Eds.). (2014). *Storyworlds across media*. University of Nebraska Press.

Stickel, M. E. (1988). A prolog-like system for computing minimum-cost abductive explanations in natural-language interpretation. In *Proc. of Int'l Computer Science Conf.* (pp. 343-350). Academic Press.

Stickel, M. E. (1989). Rationale and methods for abductive reasoning in natural language interpretation. In *Proc. of INt'l Scientific Symp. "Natural Language and Logic" (LNAI-459)* (pp. 233-252). Springer.

Thagard, P. (1989). Explanatory coherence. *Behavioral and Brain Sciences*, *12*(03), 435–502. doi:10.1017/S0140525X00057046

Yamaguchi, K., Nergui, M., & Otake, M. (2014). A robot presenting reproduced stories among older adults in group conversation. In H. J. Patthi Bin Hussain & Y. Zhu (Eds.), *Applied Mechanics and Materials* (Vol. 541–542, pp. 1120–1126). Murthy Rallapalli and Jamaluddin Mahmud. doi:10.4028/www.scientific.net/AMM.541-542.1120

KEY TERMS AND DEFINITIONS

Abduction: Abduction is an operation for adopting an explanatory hypothesis, which is subject to certain conditions, and that in pure abduction, there can never be justification for accepting the hypothesis other than through interrogation.

Abductive Analogical Reasoning (AAR): The combination of abduction and analogical mapping. AAR can abductively generate a missing hypothesis set which is necessary to explain the observation. The generated hypothesis set can be guaranteed by the existing similar knowledge set.

Creativity: An intuition or special sense will emerge with some stimulus such as information (background knowledge). In emergence, knowledge will function as a catalyst.

IMDJ: Innovation marketplace on data jacket (IMDJ) is called an innovation game. The innovation game is a game where a new production will be obtained during the combination of various techniques, materials, and previous products. Usually the game adopts an analogous game system. It uses a large paper.

Narratology: Dominated by structuralist approaches at its beginning, narratology has developed into a variety of theories, concepts, and analytic procedures. Its concepts and models are widely used as heuristic tools, and narratological theorems play a central role in the exploration and modeling of our ability to produce and process narratives in a multitude of forms, media, contexts, and communicative practices.

ENDNOTES

1 http://www.dailymotion.com/video/x32ov53

2 http://www.restaurantstory.co.uk/

3 For simplification in the example, clauses are simply saved in the knowledge base. Actually, they do not have a structural feature.

4 The current context cannot be automatically acquired by the current AAR framework.

5 Unfortunately, this operation cannot be achieved by the current AAR framework.

6 It is necessary to provide a background knowledge about this knowledge to perform this.

7 This description seems to have already disappeared. However, a paper by Fischer (2000) and the concept of social creativity by Fischer (2004) can be referred to.

Chapter 6
Literary Psychology-Modeling Figure-Ground Structures in Narrative Stories:
Towards a Narrative Content Generation

Eugene Schneider Kitamura
Kobe University, Japan

ABSTRACT

Today more than ever, narrative content generation has become important. This is due to the advances and accessibility of computational devices. As these devices become more familiar to people and easier to handle, there will be greater expectations for autonomous functioning and desires for a natural communication with the users. To achieve such demands, computational devices need to process and generate higher levels of meanings such as context and abstraction of topics. This chapter gives a background on topics that have been developed so far in content analysis and content generation, but focuses mainly on the figure-ground impression model, for both analysis and generating narrative context. By focusing on the characters and their attributes in the text, not only is this model able to represent the figure-ground impressions qualitatively, but also quantitatively. Such a feature may be useful to execute in computational devices such as artificial intelligence.

INTRODUCTION

This chapter focuses on the method to model figure-ground impressions of characters on the readers based on the information provided in the text. Over the years, various methodologies for abstracting narrative text have been introduced. Today, such models and research are relevant more than ever due to the accelerating research, development, and industrial applications of artificial intelligence. For such applications to assimilate into society and into the lives of individuals smoothly, it is critical that they have capabilities for narrative communication that feel natural, ideally to the extent of autonomously generating meaningful contents. So far in academic research, there have been efforts made for creating

DOI: 10.4018/978-1-5225-4775-4.ch006

Copyright © 2018, IGI Global. Copying or distributing in print or electronic forms without written permission of IGI Global is prohibited.

systems for content generation, and text analysis techniques go further back. Yet their results rarely reach the levels of industrial applications. Various difficulties may be blocking the way, such as required computational power, the complexity of processing and generating natural languages, and the difficulty of computationally executing cognitive models. The objective of this chapter is to demonstrate the analysis of narrative story by using a figure-ground impression model, a mathematically developed model based on algebra and logic, then in turn, apply this in reverse for content generation.

BACKGROUND

Some of the early formal efforts of creating stories with computers are TALE-SPIN by Meehan (1976), MINSTREL by Turner (1993), and BRUTUS by Bringsjord and Ferrucci (2000). They were developed with different focus and approaches. TALE-SPIN generates its stories based on a character's goals and properties. A story unfolds as believable characters with unique traits interact with each other. Since the driving force of the story was the individual characters' traits and motives, it may realize short term events, but the overall story may not be coherent or dramatic. MINSTREL was designed based on the idea that story generation is a series of incidental problem solving. Solutions are created by combining already existing solutions that are stored in an already existing set or gained from past experiences. This program allows authors to include their intent, giving an overall theme or a moral message to the plot (Swartjes, Vromen, & Bloom, 2007; Kybartas & Bidarra, 2017). BRUTUS is a system that generates complex stories, but limited to plots based on a betrayal situation. The program is designed to follow the logic of betrayal events as it generates stories. Although the stories include figurative language and dialogues, this program is basically reverse- engineered from an already existing story. The creator's objective was to see how closely the original story can be regenerated (Gervás, 2012; Kybartas & Bidarra, 2017). Although the use of computer programs to generate stories has been around for a while, scholarly efforts of abstracting stories or the use of mathematical methods to model plots go back further. Propp published a book titled *Morphology of the Folktale* in 1928 (Propp, 1928). He analyzed a large number of Russian folktales and broke them down into smaller story units and organized these subunits according to two categories: *functions* and *characters*. There are 31 functions which are story patterns such as "absentation," "interdiction," etc. and 8 character types such as "villain," "hero," etc. This work is significant in that it abstracted stories into universal patterns that can be applied to construct other stories.

In the 1960's and 70's, the Romanian school produced logical-mathematical models to describe literary texts or theatrical works. Marcus (1970) and Dinu (1968, 1970, 1977) attempt to quantify characters' behaviors and relationships mainly, by using statistical methods, graph theory and game theory. Their methods were studied further by Brainerd and Neufeldt (1974) and Mihnea (1977). Marcus' models, initially applied to Romanian plays, have been applied to Shakespearian plays by Brainerd, to ancient Greek drama by Mihnea and to comparisons of Greek and Roman ancient comedies by Hubka (1984). To describe the presence of characters on stage, they use a matrix with the correspondence of characters and scenes in which they appear as seen in Figure 1 and Figure 2.

Based on this information of characters and scenes, they calculated the character density of the scenes, the scenic distance between two characters (the number of scenes between the scenes of encounter of the same two characters), the scenic diameter (the maximum scenic distance between the two characters), the encounter number (the number of scenes in which two characters appear together), character-scene frequency (the fraction of the number of scenes in which a character appears and the entire number of

Figure 1. A character-scene matrix used by Brainerd and Neufeldt (1974). If a character x_j appears in a scene s_i, the intersection of the i-th row (scene) and the j-th column (character) is assigned a 1. Otherwise the intersection is zero.
Adapted from Brainerd and Neufeldt (1974).

$$\xleftrightarrow{\text{characters}}$$
$$\text{scenes}\updownarrow\begin{pmatrix} a_{11}a_{12}\ldots a_{1m} \\ a_{21}a_{22}\ldots a_{2m} \\ \ldots \\ a_{n1}a_{n1}\cdots a_{nm} \end{pmatrix}$$

Figure 2. A character-scene relation table used by Mihnea (1977) in the application for the Greek play Antigona. Note that the character and scene orientation is opposite from Figure 1.
Adapted from Mihnea (1977).

	S_1	S_2	S_3	S_4	S_5	S_6	S_7	S_8	S_9	S_{10}	S_{11}	S_{12}
Antigona	1	0	0	0	0	1	1	1	1	0	0	0
Ismena	1	0	0	0	0	0	0	0	1	0	0	0
Creon	0	0	1	1	0	0	1	1	1	0	1	1
Hemon	0	0	0	0	0	0	0	0	0	0	1	0
Tiresias	0	0	0	0	0	0	0	0	0	0	0	0
Euridice	0	0	0	0	0	0	0	0	0	0	0	0
Coryphaeus	0	1	1	1	1	1	1	1	1	1	1	1
Chorus	0	1	1	1	1	1	1	1	1	1	1	1
The Guard	0	0	0	1	0	1	1	0	0	0	0	0
The Herald	0	0	0	0	0	0	0	0	0	0	0	0
The Auxiliary attendants	0	0	1	1	0	0	0	0	1	0	1	0

scenes), etc. They prioritize characters according to the frequency of appearance of characters or based on the frequency of lines or the number of lines spoken by characters during the theatrical play.

Another attempt to numerically represent the evolution of a play is the use of graph theory to describe the tensions among the characters in the play (Steriadi-Bogdan, 1977). They use each character in a scene as a vertex of a graph. When a social relation is established between two characters, they assign an arc between those two vertices, either a "positive" arc if the social relationship is cooperative or a "negative" arc if the relationship is adverse. Then a stable cycle is defined as the existence of a common opponent that will encourage cooperation between two characters. For example, if there are three characters *A*, *B*, and *C*, and if *A* is in an adversity relation with *B* and *C*, and assuming that *B* and *C* are in a cooperative relationship, then the relationship with *A*, *B*, and *C* is considered stable. Thus whenever there is a pair of adversities or an even number of adversities, it is a sign of a stable situation (Figure 3 (a)). Any other cooperative or adverse relation arrangements are considered as unstable. An *elementary cycle* of a graph is a closed path where no vertices appear more than once in it, except for the initial and terminal vertices of the cycle (Figure 3 (b)). The equilibrium *m* of a graph *S* is computed as $m(S)=b^+/b$, where b^+ is the number of elementary stable cycles and *b* is the number of all elementary cycles of *S*. A negative sign is assigned to the resulting *m(S)* if the social tension of the characters in the scene is bad.

In Figure 3, there are $b^+=3$ positive stable elementary cycles possessing two adversary relationships and $b=6$ elementary cycles. Therefore $m(S) = b^+/b = 3/6 = 0.5$. When such calculation is made in every stage scene, Figure 4 is obtained. The negative sign is assigned in scenes where the relationship is so bad that it leads to a murder or some such attempt by a character.

Mathematical models that use algebra, probability, graph theory, or game theory can reveal the character appearance frequency, appearance duration, character interaction frequency, the change of appearance status, etc. to rank characters according to their appearances or involvement in activities. These methods are useful in characterizing plays and prioritizing characters according to their importance or impact. However, since the characters are mainly evaluated according to their appearances, the methods do not consider the qualitative similarities and differences of characters portrayed while on stage or in the literary works. The qualitative contrast of characters in the scenes is not preserved, therefore it makes no difference whether the characters stand out or blend into the background. The focus of this chapter is not only on the presence of characters on stage but also on the attributes assigned to the characters by the text. The author believes that in theater or literary text, there is more to be said about the characters than the number of appearances in scenes or the number of lines uttered by each character.

Figure 3. (a) Definition of a stable cycle. (b) A graph with 6 characters from A to E. The bold, colored dotted lines are positive stable elementary cycles. The narrow, black dotted lines are adversary relationships. The elementary cycles are the colored cycles.
Adapted from Kitamura (2011a).

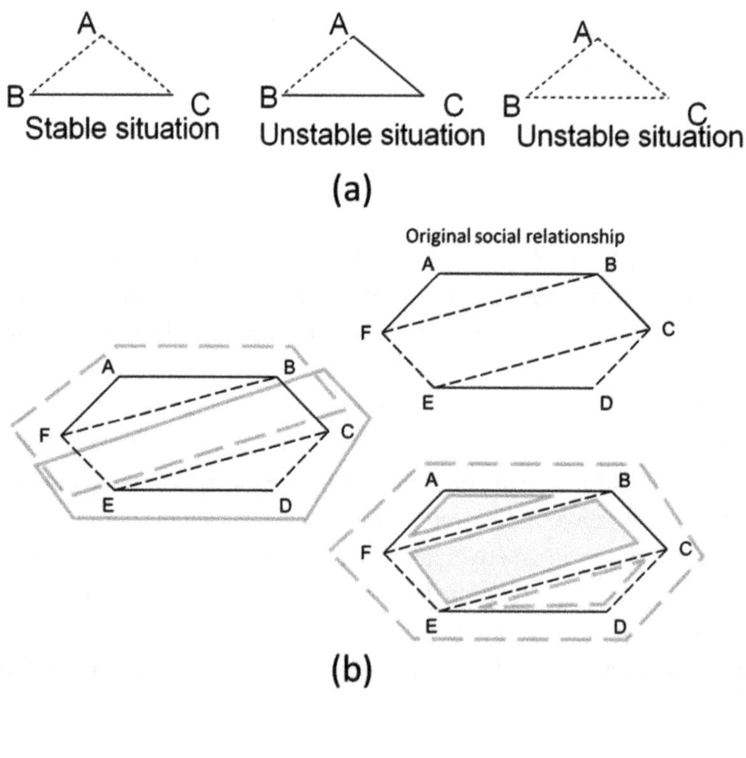

Figure 4. How the tension of a play changes in every scene as the time progresses. The y-values are m(S), the equivalence of the graph. Major conflict points are assigned a negative sign.
Adapted from Steriadi-Bogdan (1977).

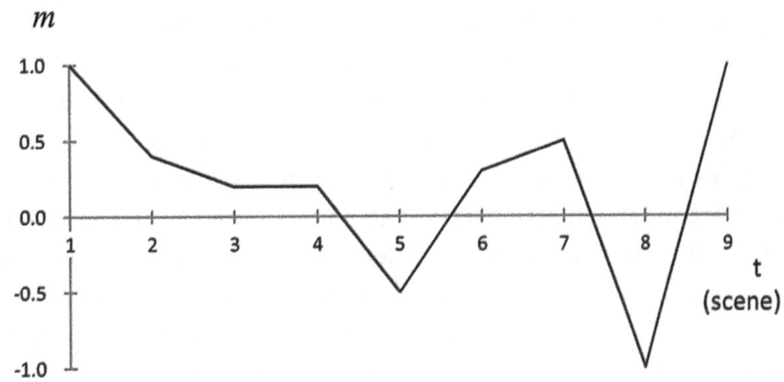

Figure-Ground Gestalt Psychology and Literary Psychology

The foundational concept of gestalt psychology (Koffka, 1935) is the contrast in perception between an object which is the target of attention, known as the figure, and the rest of the perception field known as the ground, forming a figure-ground impression. When the figure-ground status of an object changes, the event is called a figure-ground reversal. Figure-ground reversal is often the trick in illusionary images (Figure 5).

The concept of figure-ground relation continues to find applications inside and outside of gestalt psychology: optical illusion in popular art (Figure 5) (Rubin, 1915; Hoffman, 1983), perception (Palmer, Davis, Nelson, & Rock, 2008; L. Huang & Pashler, 2009; Christman, Sontam, & Jasper, 2009), symmetry patterns in nature recreated by computer (Gershoni & Kobayashi, 2008), human or computer vision for

Figure 5. An example of clear figure-ground impression, Rubin's vase. In this example, the image is recognized even when the figure-ground status is reversed (figure-ground reversal between a white vase and black profile of two faces) (File:Rubin2.jpg).

engineering applications (K.-C. Huang, 2008; Loss, Bebis, Nicolescu, & Skurikhin, 2009), treatment of focus of attention and consciousness as a figure against the ground of lacking consciousness (Forti, 2008; Werner & Strauss, 1941; Siegenthaler & Goldstein, 1967), biological matter vs. abiotic matter in the environment (Rajaniemi & Allison, 2009; Granek & Ruttenberg, 2008), music (Meyer, 1956; Cooper & Meyer, 1960), literature or poetry (Herrnstein-Smith, 1968; Tsur, 2009).

There have been several attempts to investigate figure-ground relations in literature: to treat assumed information as figure and the unconsidered information as the ground (Tsur, 2009; Veale, 2009); to regard subjects of active verbs as figure and state-describing nominal sentences as ground (Labov, 1972); to associate dialogue text as a figure and the narrative text as a ground (Hamada, 2001). Applications of psychological principles to literary text to better understand how readers perceive a literary character's disposition is discussed by Culpeper (1996). In this research Culpeper introduces attribution theory (Jones & Davis, 1965; Kelley, 1967) from psychology and foregrounding theory (Jakobson, 1960; Leech, 1969; Mukařovský, 1970) from literary analysis. Emphasis is on observing the regularity or irregularity in the behavior of characters (attribution theory) and in literary or phonetic patterns (foregrounding theory).

This chapter assumes that gestalt psychology, originally intended for understanding consciousness and perception of the environment, can also be applied to the imaginary world created by a text to analyze the figure-ground relations of characters and events in a story.

OBJECTIVE

In this chapter the author analyzes the figure-ground relations of characters in literary text based on the concept of gestalt psychology and subject-attribute information supplied in the text. While the mind recognizes visual images of objects by distinguishing their forms with the background, the author hypothesizes that such a notion can be applied to characters in stories. The character which the reader pays attention can be considered the figure and the rest of the characters can be considered the ground. The author calls such contrast of character impressions as the figure-ground relations of characters. Depending on what events are taking place in a story or what actions are performed by the characters, the noticeable characters would change. Such changes are called changes in figure-ground relation of characters.

The method introduced in this chapter is able to construct a logical structure that is adaptable to changes that reflect the figure-ground relation of the inputs based on two separate categories of information. To model the figure-ground relation of characters, naturally one category is the characters. The other category can be attributes of the characters. The attributes used in this chapter are the actions of characters or verbs, since the character actions were the most evident changes in the story of the examples used in this chapter. Although the two categories are not restricted to the characters and verbs, it is a natural choice to follow the subject and their predicates since that is the foundation of narratives.

The author uses words attributed to characters in sentences and these attributes are treated as the "same" or "different" among the characters. When the attributes of characters are the same, the characters are treated as "concomitant" characters as in the model discussed by Marcus (1970) and Brainerd and Neufeldt (1974).

By focusing on the characters and their attributes, this chapter has gone beyond the binomial 0 or 1 appearance of characters or organizing the qualitative attribution of characters for ranking purposes. It constructs qualitative figure-ground relations in the scenes and accommodates concepts such as figure-ground reversal of characters or expresses these figure-ground logical structures quantitatively, by directly using words in the text as the source of information.

The focus of attention of which character is a figure and which character is the ground is up to the reader, however, the potential for a figure-ground relationship is already supplied in the text. This is analogous to the visual illusion where the figure and the ground focus can be selected by the viewer of Figure 5, but the figure-ground structure is objectively already present. The method introduced in this chapter mechanically derives the structure of such figure-ground relation of characters based on the information in the text. Although the input text material can be chosen subjectively, once the input text is chosen, the resulting figure-ground relational structure of characters is objective. Which character is considered to be figure or ground again is a subjective matter, since even within the same person the choice for figure and ground can change with figure-ground reversal as in optical illusion. However, the mathematical model provides an objective structure that represents the input from a story situation.

This method provides a way to extract figure-ground relations of characters in a story that would otherwise not be possible with statistical or character-disposition interpretive methods. Naturally, if the amount of information processed is limited, the figure-ground impression may be intuitive. However, as the subject-attribute relations increase, the logical structures effectively extract the figure-ground relations in a scene.

To summarize how the system functions in this chapter, the characters and their attributes are selected from the text and they are organized into a relation table. The system constructs a rough set derived lattice. The complement relations in the constructed lattices can be interpreted as figure-ground relations of characters. Additionally, the complement relations in the lattices can be quantified by complementarity and non-distributivity, allowing quantitative discussions of narratives.

METHODOLOGY

The attribute commonalities and differences of character subjects are preliminarily processed through a double approximation method called rough set theory. Fixed points result from the subject and its attribute information from a scene in the text.

This subject-attribute information is used to construct a lattice structure based on the rough-set derived lattice method. A lattice structure is a convenient device since it is constructed based on qualitative information and provides quantitative results. The quantitative information comes from values such as complementarity, non-distributivity, and the number of N_5's and M_3's. The combination of lattice theory and rough set theory provides diverse lattice structures. The lattice structures are adaptive to various scene settings. The author has used lattice structures to describe the change in the lattice structure in the progression of a story. When there is a difference in attributes between the characters, complements can occur in the lattice which is interpreted as a figure-ground relation. This will be explained more in detail.

Rough Set Theory

Rough set is an approximation method (Figure 6). If there is a target of interest X, it can be approximated as a collection of elements that belong to the target with certainty and those that partly belong to the target. The set of elements certainly related is called the lower approximation, denoted as $R_*(X)$, and

Figure 6. A diagram of the upper and lower approximation method of rough set theory
Adapted from Kitamura and Gunji (2012a).

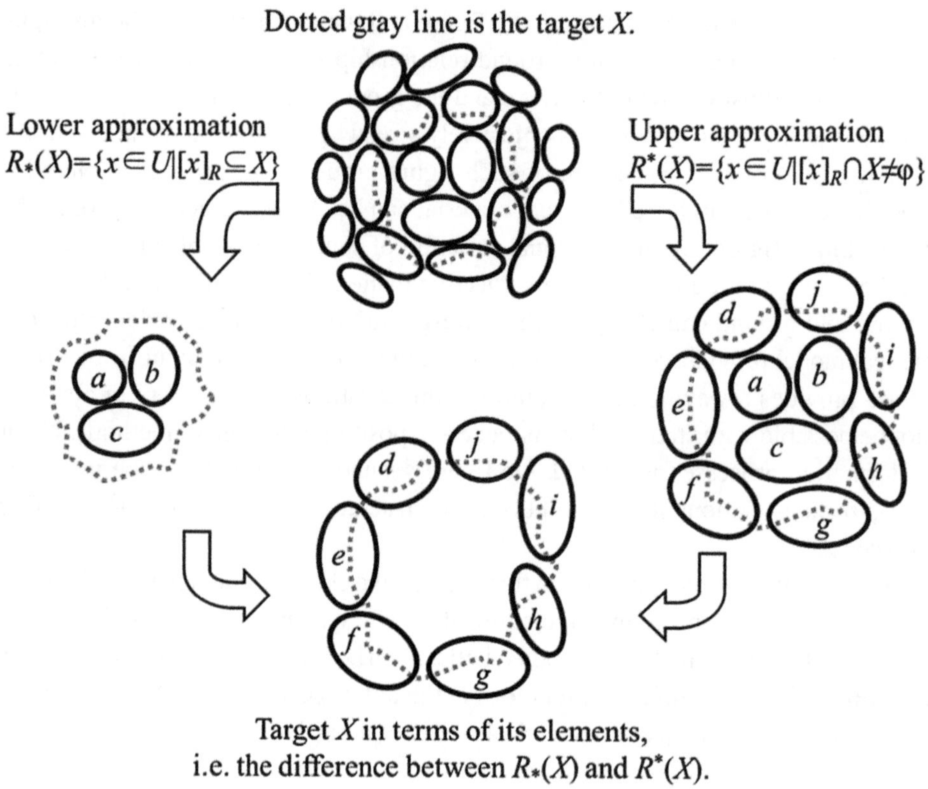

the set of elements partially related is called an upper approximation, denoted as $R^*(X)$ (Pawlak, 1981; Pawlak, 1982). If there is no difference between the lower and upper approximations, the set X is called a crisp set. This means there is no ambiguity about the target.

Rough set theory is founded on the idea that the elements in a set are indistinguishable (because if they were distinguishable and each element could be evaluated, a "rough set" approximation would not be necessary). The indistinguishable elements are said to have an equivalence relation with each other and belong to the same equivalence class. Let $x, y\in U$ be elements of a universal set U and f be a transformation function. If $f(x)=f(y)$, then x and y are defined to have an equivalence relation, i.e. xRy. Express the equivalence relation as R. Then equivalence class (Figure 7 (a)) is expressed as $[x]_R=\{y\in U|xRy\}$. Thus the lower approximation of X is formally defined as,

$$R_*(X)=\{x\in U|[x]_R\subseteq X\},$$

and the upper approximation as,

$$R^*(X)=\{x\in U|[x]_R\cap X\neq\varphi\},$$

where φ represents an empty set (Figure 7 (b)).

Figure 7. (a) Diagram of an equivalence class. $[a]_R=\{a, b\}$, $[c]_R=\{c\}$, $[d]_R=\{d, e, f\}$. *(b) Diagram of a rough set approximation of X. The lower approximation is* $R_*(X)=[c]_R=\{c\}$ *and the upper approximation is* $R^*(X)=[c]_R\cup[d]_R=\{c, d, e, f\}$
Adapted from Kitamura and Gunji (2012a).

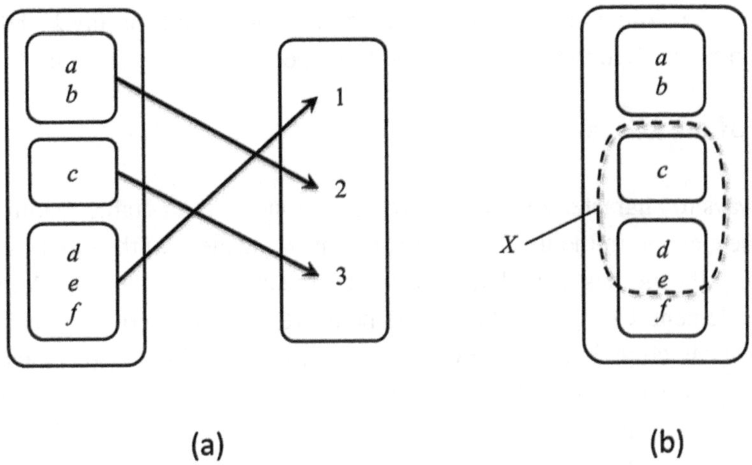

Galois Connection

In a theory of partially ordered set, a Galois connection leads to a complete lattice. Given two partially ordered sets P and Q, a pair of maps (F, G) with $F:P\rightarrow Q$ and $G:Q\rightarrow P$ is called a Galois connection, if $F(x)\leqq y \Leftrightarrow x\leqq G(y)$ for any $x\in P$ and $y\in Q$. A closure operator $C:=FG:P\rightarrow P$ can be constructed from a Galois connection such that, for any $x, y\in P$, (i) $x\leqq C(x)$; (ii) $x\leqq y\Rightarrow C(x)\leqq C(y)$; (iii) $CC(x)=C(x)$. This means that the closure operator is a good and natural operator to take a stable structure in a partially ordered set with respect to F and G. Overall it results in a (complete) lattice $L_T=\{x\in P|C(x)=x\}$.

In the context of a rough set, given a universal set U, the R^* and R_* transition of the power set of U ($R^*:P(U)\rightarrow P(U)$ and $R_*:P(U)\rightarrow P(U)$) constitute a Galois connection. Actually, for any $X, Y\subseteq U$, $R^*(X)\leqq Y\Leftrightarrow X\leqq R_*(Y)$. Thus $C=R_*R^*$ is defined as a closure operator and $L_C=\{X\in U|C(X)=X\}$ is a complete lattice. This lattice, however, is too trivial to observe the structure, since it is destined to be a set lattice. Thus for any $A\in L_C$, complement of A is defined as $A^c=U\text{-}A$. In the figure diagrams, complements are pairs which are indicated by the relative location of the small circles within the elements.

If there are two kinds of binary relations R and S on a universal set U and two kinds of operations R^* and S_* (or R_* and S^*), a pair of operations do not constitute a Galois connection. Indeed, if an operator $T=R_*S^*$ is introduced, T is not a closure operator since it satisfies only (ii) $X\subseteq Y\Rightarrow T(X)\subseteq T(Y)$ and (iii) $TT(X)=T(X)$ for $X, Y\subseteq U$. The author calls this operator pseudo-closure. If fixed points with respect to pseudo-closure are collected by $L_T=\{X\in U|T(X)=X\}$, L_T is a lattice but not a set lattice. Inversely, it can be verified that any lattice is expressed in the form of L_T by determining adequate equivalence relations S and R, which can be utilized to analyze literary texts.

Lattice Theory

Lattice is an algebraic structure where any two elements of a partially ordered set have a unique least upper bound (join or $\vee$) and a greatest lower bound (meet or $\wedge$) (Birkhoff, 1967; Davey & Priestley, 2002). As mentioned before, given two kinds of equivalence relation R and S on a universal set U, a lattice can be constructed by $<L_T; \subseteq>$ with $L_T=\{X\subseteq U | T(X)=X\}$ where $T=R_*S^*$. Actually, an element of L_T is a subset of the universal set, and order is defined by inclusion $\subseteq$. If all subsets of U are collected, L_T is a power set, and is a set lattice in which join and meet are defined by union $\cup$ and intersection $\cap$, respectively. In general, $L_T \neq P(U)$, thus join and meet are defined by the following: for any X, $Y \in L_T$, $X \wedge Y=T(X\cap Y)$, $X \vee Y=T(X\cup Y)$. It can be verified that L_T is closed with respect to $\vee$ and $\wedge$ and that L_T is a lattice.

Characteristic of a Lattice

There are several ways to characterize a lattice structure. One of the notable features of a lattice is an atom. An atom is the element immediately above (directly connected to) the empty set element. For example, in Figure 8 (a), the atom is U, and in Figure 8 (b), the atoms are A and A'. Another characteristic of a lattice is a complement. Complement of an element, $A\in L_T$, is defined as A^c such that $A\vee A^c=U$ and $A\wedge A^c=\varphi$. Note that $A\vee A^c\neq A\cup A^c$ and $A\wedge A^c\neq A\cap A^c$. For example, in Figure 8 (a), a pair of complements are$\varphi$and U, and in Figure 8 (c), φ- U, A-A', B-B', C-C' are complement pairs. Complement pairs are a key to describing figure-ground relations, which together constitute the whole (U). A Boolean lattice is a lattice structure that is distributive, where every element in the lattice has a unique complement, and is closed under the binary operations $\vee$ and$\wedge$ (Figure 8 (a) to (d)). Non-Boolean distributive lattices have some elements with no complements (element A in Figure 9 (a), elements A, B, and C in Figure 9 (b), and elements B and C in Figure 9 (c)). Non-Boolean lattices that do not hold the distributive law are N_5 and M_3 lattices (Figure 9 (d) and (e) respectively) which will be explained in detail in the following sections. These lattices have elements with non-unique complements (A, A', and A'').

Modular and Distributive Lattices

Definitions

If a lattice L satisfies the modular law, L is said to be a modular lattice. The modular law is,

Figure 8. Examples of Boolean lattices. Complement pairs are elements with letters and their corresponding dashed letters.
Adapted from Kitamura and Gunji (2012a).

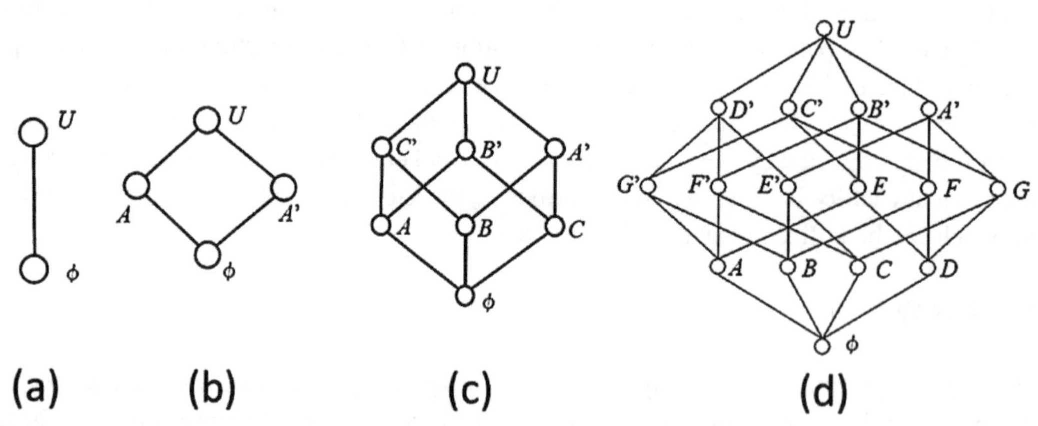

Figure 9. Examples of non-Boolean lattices. Complements are elements with letters and their corresponding dashed letters.
Adapted from Kitamura and Gunji (2012a).

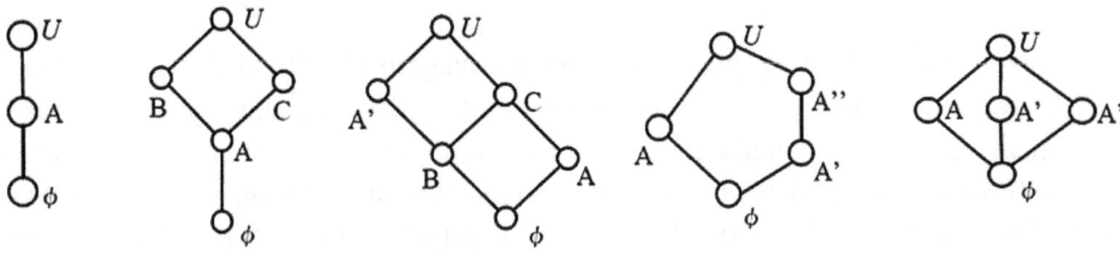

(a) (b) (c) (d) (e)

$$\left(\forall a,b,c \in L\right) a \geq c \Rightarrow a \wedge \left(b \vee c\right) = \left(a \wedge b\right) \vee c$$

As stated earlier in section 2.4, if a lattice L satisfies the distributive law, L is said to be a distributive lattice. The distributive law is

$$\left(\forall a,b,c \in L\right) a \wedge \left(b \vee c\right) \Rightarrow \left(a \wedge b\right) \vee \left(a \wedge c\right)$$

Let L and K be lattices. A map $f{:}L{\rightarrow}K$ is said to be a lattice homomorphism, or simply a homomorphism, if f preserves join and meet, or

$$f\left(a \vee b\right) = f\left(a\right) \vee f\left(b\right) \text{and } f\left(a \wedge b\right) = f\left(a\right) \wedge f\left(b\right).$$

A lattice isomorphism, or simply isomorphism, is a bijective homomorphism. To be bijective means that the elements are one-to-one and onto. As lattice structure, the order structure is preserved. Therefore, a sublattice $f(L)$ of K is isomorphic to L, and f is called an embedding of L into K.

M_3 and N_5 Lattices

Assume that P and Q are disjoint ordered sets. The disjoint union $P \dot{\cup} Q$ of P and Q is the ordered set formed by defining $x \leqq y$ in $P \dot{\cup} Q$ if and only if either $x, y \in P$ and $x \leqq y$ in P or $x, y \in Q$ and $x \leqq y$ in Q. The linear sum is obtained by the following order relation on $P \cup Q$:

$x \leqq y$ if and only if

$x, y \in P$ and $x \leqq y$ in P,

or

$x, y \in Q$ and $x \leqq y$ in Q,

or

$x \in P$ and $y \in Q$.

A diagram for $P \dot{\cup} Q$ is created by placing side-by-side diagrams for P and Q. A diagram for $P \oplus Q$ when P and Q are finite is obtained by placing a diagram for Q directly above a diagram for P. Then add a line segment from each maximal element of P to each minimal element of Q. M_n is defined as the sum $1 \oplus \bar{n} \oplus 1$ (Figure 10 (a)), where **1** represents a single element in the diagram. M_3, which will be seen often in this chapter, will be defined as $1 \oplus 3 \oplus 1$ (Figure 10 (b)). Similarly, N_5 is written as $1 \oplus \left(1 \dot{\cup} 2\right) \oplus 1$ (Figure 10 (c) and (d)).

The M_3-N_5 Theorem

1. Lattice L is non-modular if and only if L has a sublattice isomorphic to the lattice N_5.
2. Lattice L is non-distributive if and only if L has a sublattice isomorphic to the lattice N_5 or to the lattice M_3.

A distributive lattice does not permit the presence of N_5 and M_3 sublattices within its lattice structure. A modular lattice does not permit the presence of N_5 sublattices. Figure 11 shows the correspondence between the various laws and some possible lattices.

Constructing a Rough Set Derived Lattice

If we construct a lattice from a universal set U with only one equivalence relation R, this will always return a Boolean lattice. The atoms of this Boolean lattice, the first elements above the empty set φ, will be the equivalence class of the universal set created by the equivalence relation R. The other elements in this lattice will be a combination of the atom elements, until we have the universal set at the top. Since it is a Boolean lattice, its structure will be determined by the number of atoms or the number of equivalence classes. This is not terribly informative as a tool.

If we introduce two equivalence relations and apply them to the universal set U, we get two sets of equivalence classes. Instead of building a lattice based on only one equivalence relation, which will always result in a Boolean lattice, we can build a latticed based on two equivalence classes. The elements represent one of the two equivalence relations and we need to check the validity of each element for both

Figure 10. Examples of lattice structures and corresponding notations used in the main text

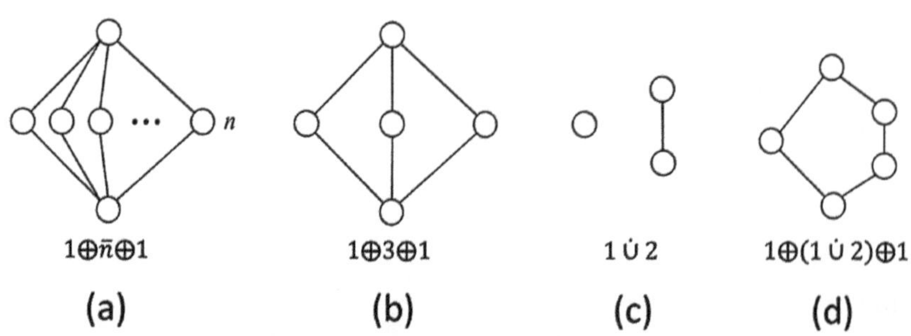

Figure 11. A diagram showing the relationship among the various types of lattices
Adapted from Kitamura (2011).

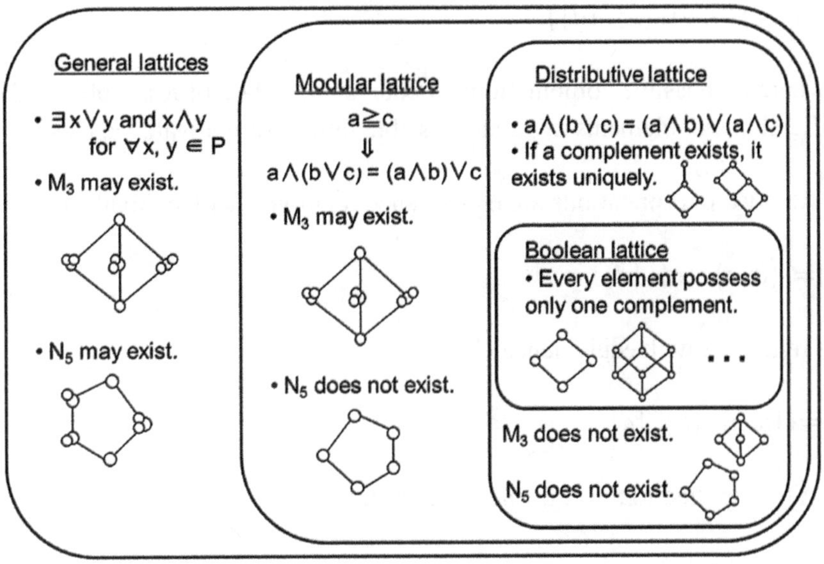

equivalence relations. In order to check this validity, we use a closure operator. Equivalence classes that form a fixed point will be used to construct a lattice.

If we use the same equivalence relation for the closure operator, $R_*(R^*(X))$, we will always get a fixed point $R_*(R^*(X))=X$ and the lattice constructed will always form a Boolean lattice (Fig. 1). If we use two different equivalence relations R and S, then $R_*(S^*(X))$ will not always result in a fixed point. Lattices constructed from the fixed points $R_*(S^*(X))=X$ may result in a Boolean or a non-Boolean lattice.

When a lattice of fixed points is constructed from one equivalence relation, $R_*(R^*(X))=X$, only a set lattice is obtained. A set lattice has two important properties in lattice theory such as distributivity

$$A\wedge(B\vee C)=(A\wedge B)\vee(A\wedge C)$$

for A, B, $C\subseteq U$, and complementarity of which for any $X\subseteq U$ there exists $Y\subseteq U$ such that $X\vee Y=U$ and $X\wedge Y=\varphi$. A distributive complemented lattice is called a Boolean lattice. Note that U and$\varphi$are the greatest and least elements in the lattice L_T. For a set lattice as in Figure 12 (a), elements $\{a, b\}$ and $\{c, d\}$ are complements, since $\{a, b\}\vee\{c, d\}=U$ and $\{a, b\}\wedge\{c, d\}=\varphi$. However, when a lattice of fixed points is constructed from two equivalence relations, $R_*(S^*(X))=X$, the resulting lattice can be either a Boolean lattice or a non-Boolean lattice. This is a result of two equivalence classes fully or partially overlapping each other.

The difference between a lattice of

$$L_C=\{X\subseteq U|C(X)=X\}$$

and

$$L_T=\{X\subseteq U|T(X)=X\}$$

with $C=R_*R^*$ and $T=R_*S^*$ is illustrated in Figure 12. In the case of L_C, when

$$W=\{[a]_R, [c]_R, [d]_R\}=\{\{a, b\}, \{c\}, \{d\}\},$$

then $L_C=P(W)$ where all possible combinations of equivalence class of R are obtained (Figure 12 (a)). By contrast, in L_T, although elements of L_T are possible unions of equivalence class R, some elements are missing (Figure 12 (b)).

In Figure 12, the two interpretations are equivalence relation R with equivalence class

$$\{[a]_R, [c]_R, [d]_R\}=\{\{a, b\}, \{c\}, \{d\}\}$$

and equivalence relation S with equivalence class

$$\{[a]_S, [b]_S, [d]_S\}=\{\{a, c\}, \{b\}, \{d\}\}.$$

When $R_*(S^*(X))$ is applied to the equivalence class $[a]_R$, then

$$R_*(S^*(\{[a]_R\}))= R_*(S^*(\{a, b\}))$$

is obtained. The upper approximation S^* of $\{a, b\}$ in terms of the equivalence relation S is $\{a, b, c\}$ (all elements that intersect $\{a, b\}$). Therefore $R_*(\{a, b, c\})$ is obtained. Next, take the lower approximation R_* of $\{a, b, c\}$ in terms of the equivalence relation R. Then $\{a, b, c\}$ (all elements within $\{\{a, c\}, \{b\}\}$) is obtained. The author started with $X=\{a, b\}$ and finished with

$$\{a, b, c\}\neq R_*(S^*(\{a, b\})).$$

Therefore, $R_*(S^*(\{[a]_R\}))$ is not a fixed point and thus $\{[a]_R\}$ is not an element of the lattice.

Now, check whether $\{[a]_R, [c]_R\}$ is a fixed point, by evaluating $R_*(S^*(\{[a]_R, [c]_R\}))= R_*(S^*(\{a, b, c\}))$. Note that $\{[a]_R, [c]_R\}$ is a compound of two equivalence classes. The upper approximation S^* of $\{a, b, c\}$ in terms of the equivalence relation S is $\{a, b, c\}$ (all elements that intersect $\{a, b, c\}$). Therefore $R_*(\{a, b, c\})$ is obtained. Next, take the lower approximation R_* of $\{a, b, c\}$ in terms of the equivalence relation R. Then $\{a, b, c\}$ (all elements within $\{\{a, c\}, \{b\}\}$) is obtained. The author started with $X=\{a, b, c\}$ and finished with

$$\{a, b, c\}=R_*(S^*(\{a, b, c\})).$$

$R_*(S^*(\{[a]_R, [c]_R\}))$ is a fixed point and thus $\{[a]_R, [c]_R\}$ is an element of the lattice. This process is used for all equivalence classes and their combinations, from the empty set φ to the universal set $U=\{a, b, c, d\}$.

Due to the loss of information, an obtained lattice can be constructed as a non-Boolean lattice. The ambiguity in the interpretation of the original universal set U allows the construction of diverse lattice structures. The resulting lattice is called a rough set derived lattice (Gunji & Haruna, 2010).

Relation Table

The relationship between the equivalence classes grouped by the two interpretations R and S are organized with a relation table shown in Tables 1 through 3. It shows the relationship between the elements of the equivalence relations R and S used in the construction of the lattice in Figure 12. The 1's denote the presence of a relationship and the 0's denote the absence of a relationship. For instance, the trivial example is, in Figure 12 (a) the equivalence class $\{a, b\}$ of R overlaps with $\{a, b\}$ of S, therefore it is marked with 1's in Table 1. On the other hand, since $\{a, b\}$ has no contact with $\{c\}$, it is marked with a 0. In Figure 12 (b), the equivalence class $\{a, b\}$ of R overlaps with $\{a, c\}$ and $\{b\}$ of S, therefore it is marked with 1's in Table 2 and Table 3. However, since $\{c\}$ has no contact with $\{b\}$, it is marked with a 0. Repetitious rows or columns may be united as in Table 3 and still result in the same lattice structure. In subsequent sections, the author will refer to such relation tables. This chapter uses such tables to organize the information and to find fixed points to construct rough set derived lattices as explained in the previous section.

Figure 12. (a) The lattice shown here is a Boolean lattice. Only Boolean lattices result when using fixed points from a single equivalence relation. (b) The lattice shown here is a non-Boolean lattice. Elements {a, b} and {a, b, d} from (a) are missing in (b). Boolean as well as non-Boolean lattices result when using fixed points from double equivalence relation. The ambiguity in the interpretation of the target set causes diverse results. Complement pairs are indicated by the relative location of small circles within the elements.
Adapted from Kitamura and Gunji (2012b).

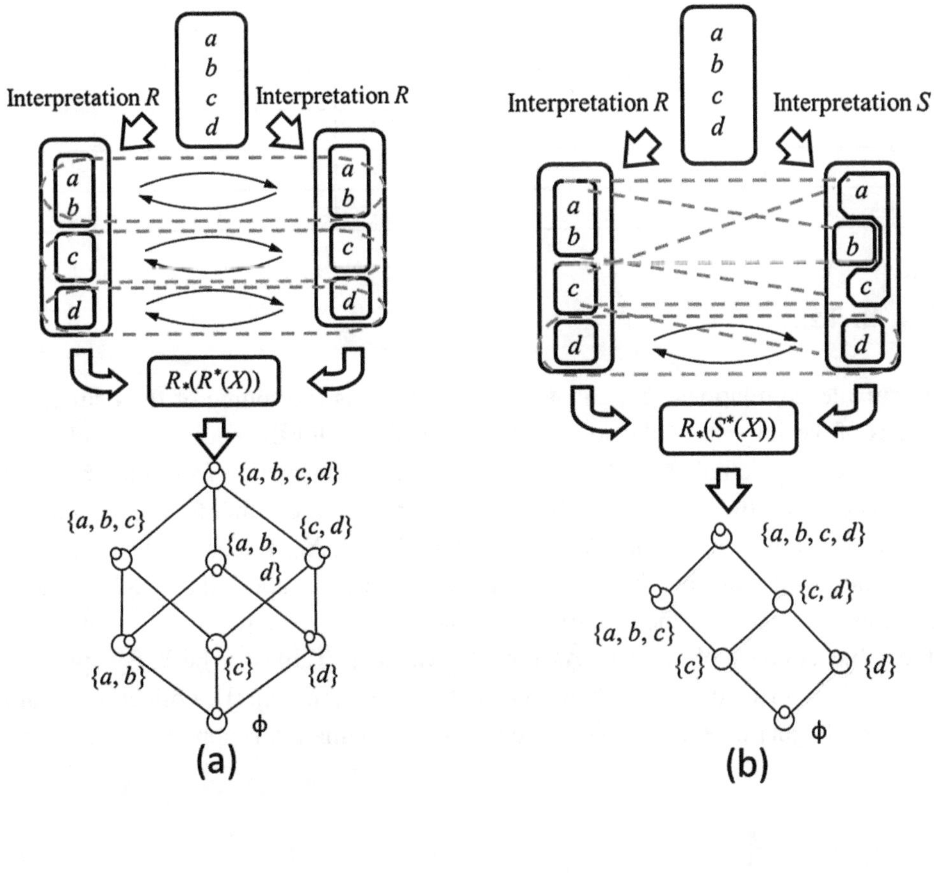

Table 1. A relation table showing the relations between R and R according to the elements, based on Figure 12 (a)

		R		
		$\{a, b\}$	$\{c\}$	$\{d\}$
R	$\{a, b\}$	1	0	0
	$\{c\}$	0	1	0
	$\{d\}$	0	0	1

Table 2. A relation table showing the relations between R and S according to the elements, based on Figure 12 (b)

		S			
		$\{a\}$	$\{b\}$	$\{c\}$	$\{d\}$
R	$\{a, b\}$	1	1	1	0
	$\{c\}$	1	0	1	0
	$\{d\}$	0	0	0	1

Table 3. A relation table showing the relations between R and S according to the elements, based on Figure 12 (b). Unifying repetitive rows or columns gives the same results. Columns {a} and {c} in Table 2 can be unified, although in this example they can be unified from the beginning of the table formation process since they are in the same equivalence class, {a, c}.

		S		
		$\{a, c\}$	$\{b\}$	$\{d\}$
R	$\{a, b\}$	1	1	0
	$\{c\}$	1	0	0
	$\{d\}$	0	0	1

Application to Text

For the two equivalence relations, this chapter uses subjects as the source of the equivalence relation R and predicates of the subjects as the source of their attributes for the equivalence relation S. Subject pronouns are replaced by actual character names. In general, information from the predicates can be a noun, verb, or adjective for the subject's attributes. In this chapter, the author focuses mainly on the verbs, using *Romeo and Juliet* by Shakespeare (Yates-Glandorf, 1985), Act 1 Scene 1. The author is interested in building a lattice with elements that consist of subject sets. To apply the rough set derived lattice method, the author examines whether a subject or subject set is a fixed point, resulting in $R_*(S^*(X))=X$, where X is the subject or a set of subjects. Assume "servants" in Table 4 to be X. By applying the upper approximation of X in terms of the attribute interpretation $S^*(\{\text{servants}\})$, collecting all attributes related to "servants", {fight} is obtained. Then the lower approximation is applied in terms of the subject

Table 4. A relation table showing the relationship between subjects and attributes for Table 3, the lattice in Figure 12 (b), and Figure 13 using Romeo and Juliet, Act 1 Scene 1 as a model

		Attribute (Verb)		
		{enter, swing weapons}	{speak}	{fight}
Subject	{Benvolio, Tybalt }	1	1	0
	{citizens}	1	0	0
	{servants}	0	0	1

interpretation and subjects are collected that "fit" within the collection of attributes obtained earlier, as $R_*(S^*(X))$ implies. Since {servants} is the only subject that "fits" within the attribute {fight}, {servants} is returned. Since $R_*(S^*(\{\text{servants}\}))=\{\text{servants}\}$ is obtained, "servants" is a fixed point and therefore an element in a lattice as seen in Figure 13. Now assume "Benvolio, Tybalt" in Table 4 to be X. Apply the upper approximation in terms of the attribute interpretation $S^*(\{\text{Benvolio, Tybalt}\})$, then {enter, swing weapons, speak} is obtained. Next the lower approximation is applied in terms of the subject interpretation and subjects are collected that belong to the attribute condition, $R_*(\{\text{enter, swing weapons, speak}\})$. Since subjects Benvolio, Tybalt, and citizens have the attribute *enter, swing weapons*, and *speak*, those subjects are returned, as $R_*(S^*(\{\text{Benvolio, Tybalt}\}))=\{\text{Benvolio, Tybalt, citizens}\}$. Since $R_*(S^*(X))\neq X$, {Benvolio, Tybalt} is not a fixed point and therefore not an element in the lattice of Figure 13.

Complements

Complements are two elements $i, j\in U$ that result in the top universal element U when using the join ($i\vee j=U$) and result in the bottom element φ when using the meet ($i\wedge j=\varphi$). Complement is defined as a unary operation or as an element indicated by such an operation using join and meet. Complements are suited for describing the conceptual gestalt impression of figure and ground, since when two elements are put together, they constitute the whole (U) and when the two elements are taken away, they result in emptiness (φ). Boolean lattices are complemented distributive lattices. This means all elements in a Boolean lattice have only one complement. Distributive lattices obeys the distributive law $a\wedge(b\vee c)=(a\wedge b)\vee(a\wedge c)$ for a, b, $c\subseteq U$, but there are elements without complements. There are other lattices such as modular lattices that have elements with more than one complement. In such cases where an element is missing

Figure 13. Lattice structure resulting from Table 4

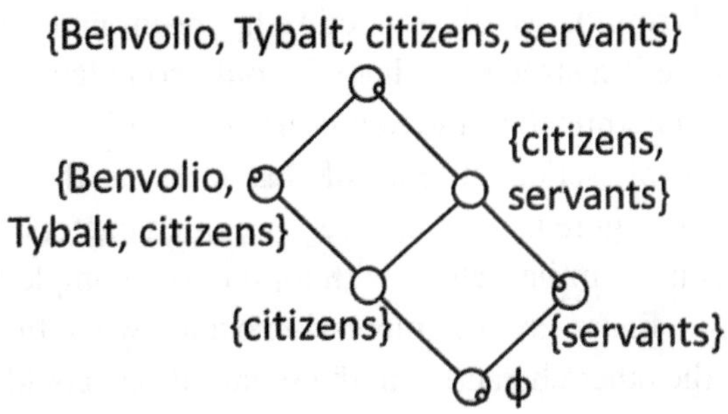

a complement or if an element has more than one complement, the author considers such elements not providing a figure-ground relation, since the complement relation cannot be singularly isolated.

A lattice is quantified by the rate of elements without complements (existence rate) and by the rate of elements with more than one complement (possession rate) (Kitamura and Gunji (2011b)),

$$Complementarity = \frac{Number\ of\ elements\ with\ complements}{Number\ of\ elements\ in\ the\ lattice}.$$

$$Non\text{-}Distributivity = \frac{\left\{ \begin{matrix} Number\ of\ elements\ with\ complement\ incidences \\ (double\ of\ the\ complement\ pairs) \end{matrix} \right\}}{Number\ of\ elements\ with\ complements}.$$

Figure 14 shows examples of relation tables of characters and their attributes, the lattices created from the relation table, and their complementarity (C) and non-distributivity (ND).

The Figure-Ground Interpretations of Lattices

There can be different types of figure-ground situations depending on the resulting lattice structures built from the subject-attribute relationships.

- **Clear Figure-Ground:** A clear figure-ground relation represented by a Boolean lattice is a structure where the elements possess only one complement pair in a lattice (Figure 14 (a)). Every character is contrasted against the rest of the characters, providing a figure-ground impression for every character or set of characters in the scene. This means every character has a clear role or an attribute and possibly the scene is stable and the story progresses with a steady rhythm. A Boolean lattice is a result of a relation table where each character or character groups has/have their own, unshared unique attribute.
- **Limited Clear Figure-Ground:** A limited clear figure-ground relation represented by a non-Boolean distributive lattice is a structure where some elements have a single complement pair, other elements have no complement pairs, and there are no elements with multiple complements (Figure 14 (b)). Not all element characters have complements. Therefore, the figure-ground impression is limited in the scene. Such elements without complements occur because their attributes are included in the attributes of other characters and do not stand out.
- **All or Nothing Figure-Ground:** An all or nothing figure-ground relation represented by a non-Boolean distributive lattice is a structure where the only complement pair is the top-bottom elements. This scene can be interpreted as the figure-ground relation constructed by the universal set as the figure against the empty set or "absence of characters" as the ground. The alternative is the absence of characters as the figure against the presence of characters as the ground (figure-ground reversal). One would obtain a similar lattice with top-bottom complement pair when dealing with only one character. Such a figure-ground impression occurs when there is a character that has all attributes possessed by the other characters in the scene. If one could ignor the character that has

Figure 14. Relation table, lattice, C and ND of different relationships
Adapted from Kitamura (2017).

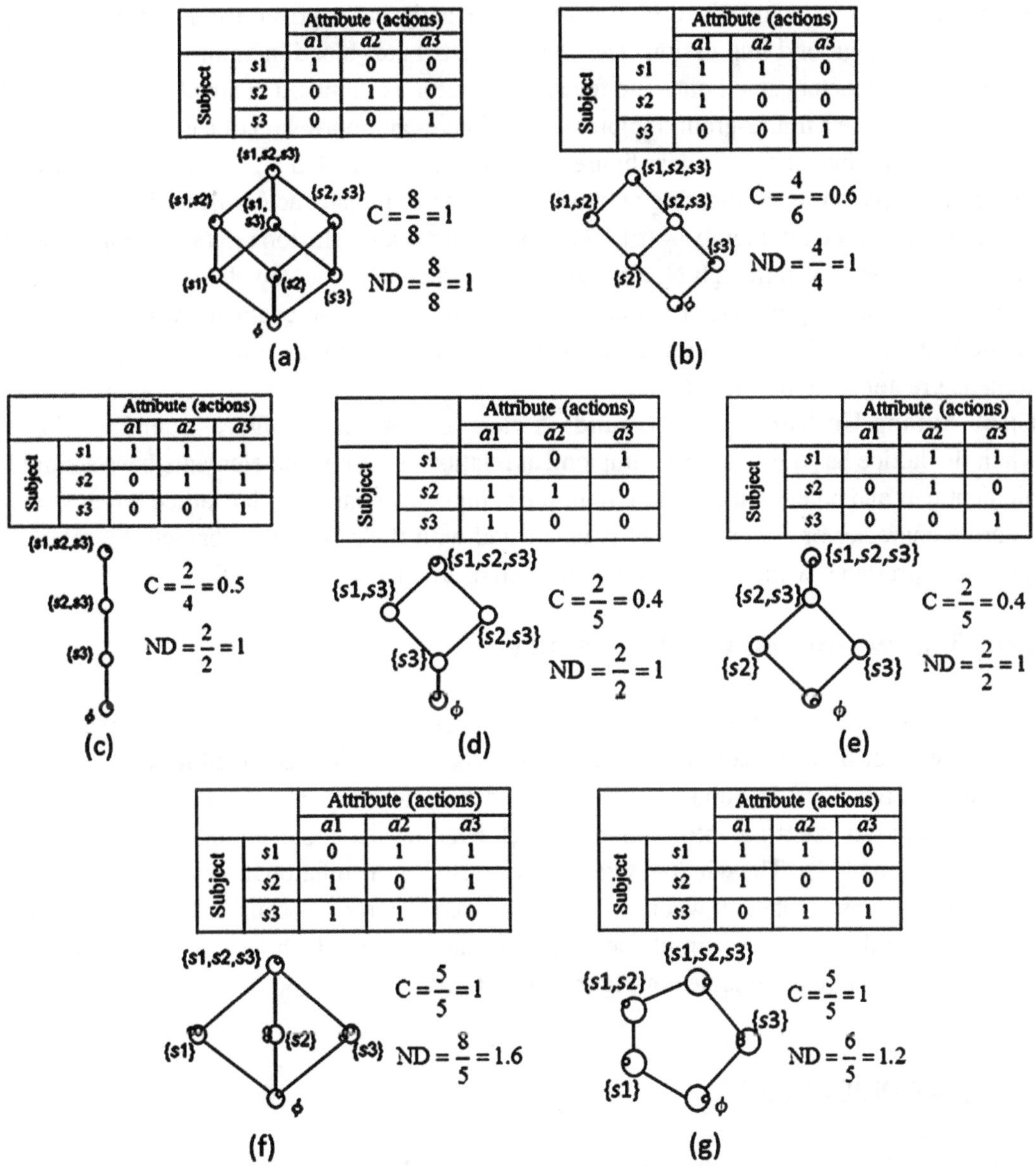

all of the attributes, one can identify substructures of other relationships within the scene (Figure 14 (c), (d), and (e)).

- **Unclear Figure-Ground:** An unclear figure-ground relation represented by a modular or a general lattice is a structure where some elements have multiple complement pairs. Since the top-bottom complement pair will always possess only one complement pair and is present in all lattice structures, it will be ignored in this discussion. In the 1-0 patterns of the relation table presented in Figure 14 (f), the character attributes partly overlap with each other. None of the characters have their own unique attributes. Every subject has two attributes, but no attribute is held commonly by all subjects. Every atom has complements with all of the other atoms. The lattice in Figure 14 (f) is called an M_3 lattice. M_3 is known for each element having more than one complement. Note that the pattern of 1's and 0's in Figure 14 (f) is exactly the opposite from that of Figure 14 (a), the clear figure-ground impression. The character attributes blend in among each other, therefore none of the characters stand out. The focus of attention is scattered. Thus the M_3 lattice is insufficient to describe a figure-ground impression and gives an impression of a chaotic scene. Another lattice structure that has an unclear figure-ground relation is called N_5 (Figure 14 (g)). This lattice structure is created by eliminating an attribute of one of the characters from the relation table in Figure 14 (f), as seen in Figure 14 (g). Therefore, there is an inclusion relationship in the attributes of the characters. Even though N_5 also represents a chaotic scene, the character with an inclusion relation gives an impression of a sidekick or a wingman of the character with more attributes. While both M_3 and N_5 lattices represent unclear figure-ground impressions, the non-distributivity value is greater with the M_3 lattice.

- **Clear Among Unclear Figure-Ground:** A clear among unclear figure-ground relation occurs when the lattice has a mixture of complement relations where some elements have a single complement pair and other elements have multiple complement pairs. Such a lattice represents a scene where a character or a character set is contrasted with the rest of the characters, a clear figure-ground impression, while the rest of the characters are in a chaotic situation.

Sliding Windows for Temporal Dynamics

To capture the change in the lattice structure as the story progresses, the author used a method to consider a fixed number of sentences or lines at a time. When a new line is added in the direction of the story progression, the oldest line under consideration is discarded. Figure 15 shows how the body of text (Figure 15 (a)) is used to extract information for each window size representing a time step or a scene (Figure 15 (b), (c), and (d)). The window size used to construct the relation tables in Figure 15 (b) to (d) is 5 lines (or time steps). Note that when two actions are considered to occur at the same time, they are treated at the same time step as a simultaneous occurrence. Figure 16 shows the transitioning process of lattices based on the relation tables of Figure 15 (b) to (d).

EXAMPLE APPLICATION

As an example, this chapter uses the modern translation of *Romeo and Juliet* by Shakespeare (Yates-Glandorf, 1985), Act 1 Scene 1. The subjects used were the drama characters. The attributes used were the verbs explicitly written as a narration and the lines by each character (the act of *speak*). Other actions implied in the conversations but not explicitly stated as a narration were not used in order to minimize subjective interpretations of the text. This reduced the attributes down to *enter*, *speak*, *strike down their swords*, *fight*, *stay*, *pause*, and *exit*. The ending of the action fight was chosen to be at the arrival (*enter*) of the prince, before the prince started speaking. The attribute *pause* by Romeo in the modern translation acknowledges the verbal zero-signs (Teodorescu-Brinzeu, 1984). Additionally, the attribute "no reference" was used to label subjects who were present on stage but were not assigned actions within the considered window size. To simplify the information processing, repeated conversations between the same characters (for example, conversations between Sampson and Gregory in the opening and between

Figure 15. (a) Tables showing the original body of text. (b) A relation table constructed from lines 1 to 5 of the main text. (c) A relation table constructed from lines 2 to 6 of the main text. (d) A relation table constructed from lines 3 to 7 of the main text.
Adapted from Kitamura (2011).

(a)

Line Number	Subject	Action	Line from the Text
1	Benvolio	*enter*	Enter Benvolio.
2	Gregory	*speak*	"You should say 'better.' Here comes one of my master's relatives."
3	Sampson	*speak*	"My master is better, sir."
4	Abraham	*speak*	"Your're a liar."
5	Sampson	*speak*	"Draw your swords, if you're real men. Gregory, give him your crushing blow."
6	Sampson, Gregory, Abraham, Balthasar	*fight*	They fight.
7	Benvolio	*speak, strike down their swords*	"Stop it, you fools! Put your swards away. You don't know what you're doing." He strikes down their swords.

(b)

Line 1 to 5		Action		
		enter	speak	no reference
Subject	Sampson, Gregory, Abraham	0	1	0
	Balthasar	0	0	1
	Benvolio	1	0	0

(c)

Line 2 to 6		Action		
		fight	speak	no reference
Subject	Sampson, Gregory, Abraham	1	1	0
	Balthasar	1	0	0
	Benvolio	0	0	1

(d)

Line 3 to 7		Action		
		fight	strike down their swords	no reference
Subject	Sampson, Abraham	1	0	1
	Gregory, Balthasar	1	0	0
	Benvolio	0	1	1

Benvolio and Romeo toward the ending of Scene 1) were abbreviated. This reduced the number of actions in the story (performed lines and narrations) from about 110 lines to about 80 lines.

The attribute *nr* or *no reference* is used for characters that do not have any actions within the considered window range. Characters that are explicitly assigned verb attributes are actively engaged in some action in contrast to characters that are not assigned attributes, resulting in the assignment of *no reference*. Since *no reference* is used only for characters that have no attribute within a window frame, if the window size is large and the characters possess an attribute, *no reference* is eliminated and specific attributes are assigned. Therefore, *no reference* has a lower priority compared to the other attributes.

A simplified diagram of the order of events from *Romeo and Juliet* Act 1 Scene 1 is portrayed in Figure 17 as a reference. The author obtained a time evolution of lattices as the story progressed (Figure 18). The complementarity and non-distributivity are plotted as the number of story steps advanced from 1 to 77. Along with the complementarity and non-distributivity, the number of characters and attributes (verbs) in the lattices are also plotted, as well as the appearance duration of each character. For analysis the author took a span of 16 action lines or steps for the source window and incremented this fixed win-

Figure 16. Lattices in this figure are constructed from the relation tables in Figure 15 and it also shows the transition process. (a) A lattice based on relation Figure 15 (b). (b) A lattice showing elements with an X mark that are eliminated as it transitions from Figure 15 (b) to (c). (c) A lattice based on Figure 15 (c). (d) A lattice showing elements with an X mark that are eliminated as it transitions from Figure 15 (c) to (d). (e) A lattice based on Figure 15 (d). The matching color and orientation of the smaller circles relative to the larger circles indicate the complement pairs.
Abbreviations are S=Sampson, G=Gregory, A=Abraham, Bl=Balthasar, Bn= Benvolio, T= Tybalt, O=officers & citizens, C=Capulet, LC=Lady Capulet, M=Montague, LM=Lady Montague, Pr=Prince Escalus, Pf=Prince's followers.
Adapted from Kitamura and Gunji (2010b).

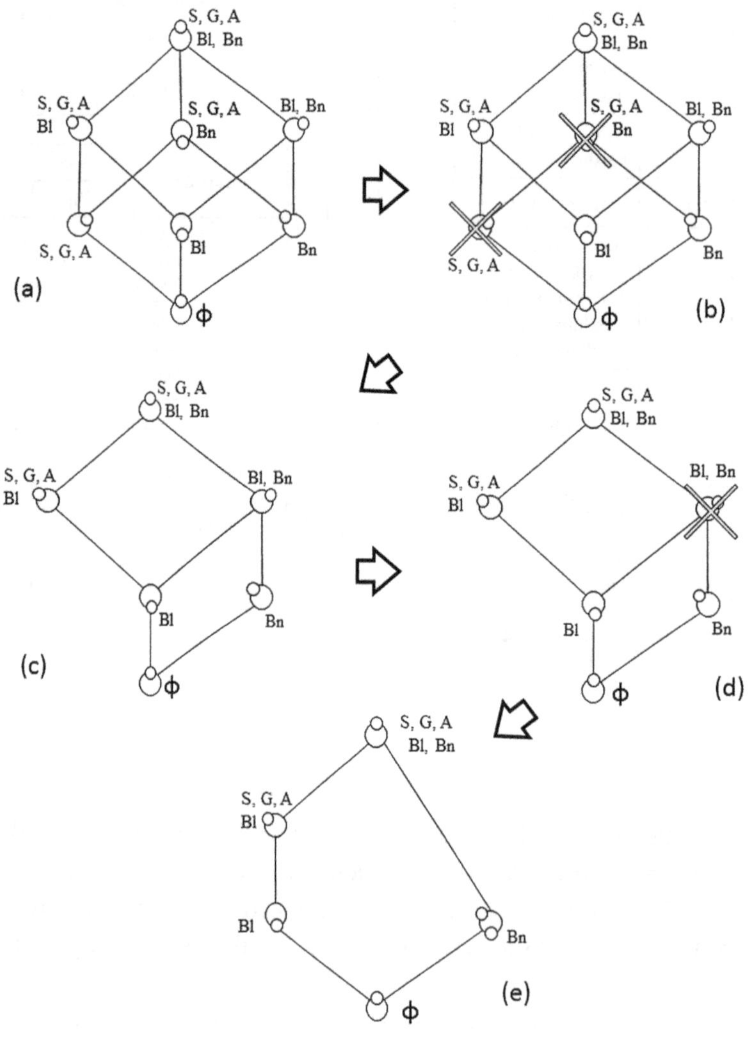

dow size downward step by step. The window span of 16 steps was chosen to include more than three subjects and three attributes as often as possible to obtain an informative lattice. The results obtained from the first 15 steps and the last 15 steps will not be candidates for consideration due to the incremental increase and decrease in the window size (from size 1 to 15 or 15 to 1) from step 1 to 15 and step 62 to 77 in Figure 18. The types of resulting lattices were quantitatively measured by their complementarity

Figure 17. A rough order of events from Romeo and Juliet, Act 1 Scene 1
Adapted from Kitamura (2011).

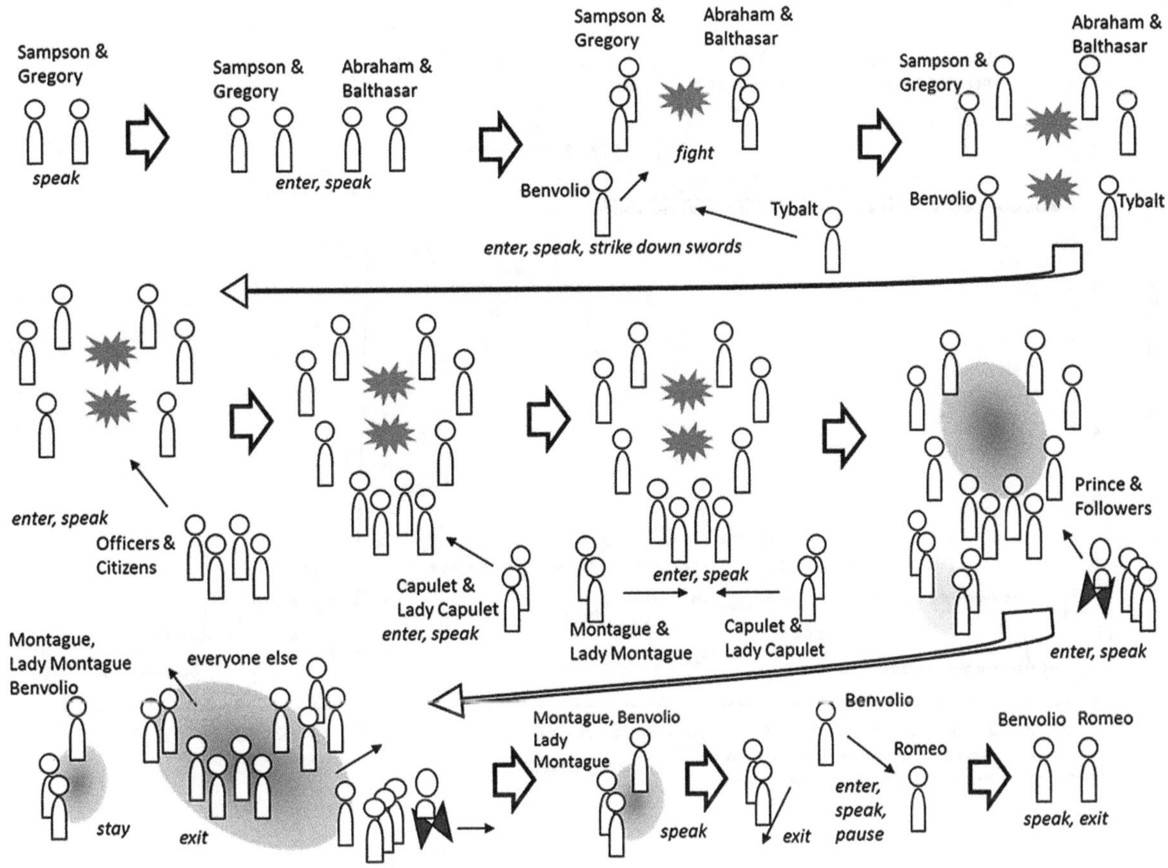

and non-distributivity. The graph of number of characters and attributes in lattices drag longer than the actual presence of characters on stage. This is due to the length of window size (16), where a character or its attribute would not exit the lattice unless the window passes over their attributes. Therefore, the presence of characters and attributes in lattices would be prolonged compared to their actual appearances.

Results of Evolving Lattices

The most notable feature of the graph is the sharp jump of the non-distributivity that coincides with the "All leave except Montague, Lady Montague, and Benvolio" at story step 41. The non-distributivity increases from 1.33 to 3.38. This suggests the strong presence of elements with unclear figure-ground impression during this scene.

From the beginning of the story, the lattice structures are a Boolean lattice and the attribute relations are simple, therefore the figure-ground impression of the story is mostly clear (Figure 19, Clear f-g.). The attributes of characters present are *speak*, *enter*, or *no reference*. The complementarity value is 1 and the non-distributivity value is 1. When the attribute *fight* becomes part of the characters and a fight breaks out in the scene, Benvolio is a witness. Then the figure-ground impression becomes unclear

Figure 18. A plot of complementarity, non-distributivity, the number of characters and attributes in lattice, and the appearance duration of characters on stage
Adapted from Kitamura and Gunji (2010a).

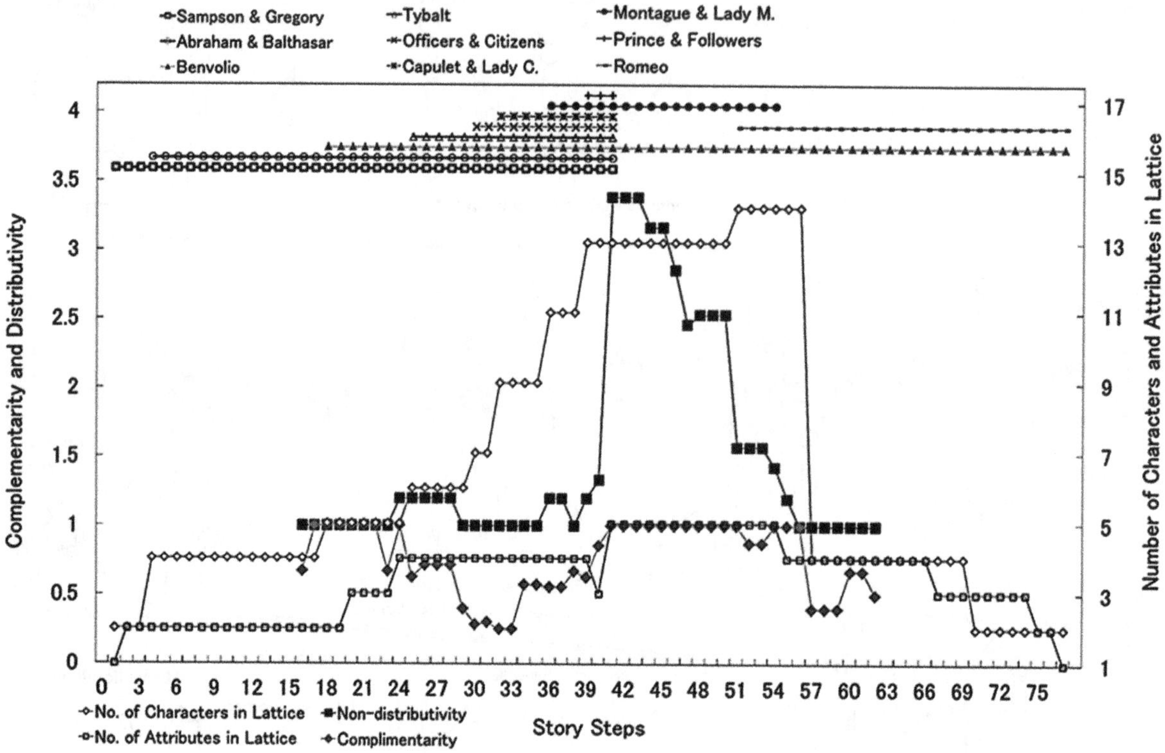

(Figure 19, Unclear f-g.). Until Prince Escalus arrives at step 39 into the scene of a gradually escalated fight, the attributes used to construct the lattices were *enter*, *speak*, and *fight*. The lattice structure is typically an "All or nothing" figure-ground structure (Figure 19, "All or nothing" f-g.). This suggests that there is a character that has all attributes and all other characters' attributes fit within that domineering character's attributes. Even though the number of characters rises steadily between story steps 18 to 39, the non-distributivity does not increase in a like manner. It is as though the figure-ground impression is kept uninteresting while the plot is developing.

After the prince 'spoke' his words, two more attributes are added at step 41, *leave* (or *exit*) and *stay*. The resulting lattices drastically change, raising the non-distributivity value from 1.33 to 3.38. The change is due to the shift in common and non-common attribute patterns of the characters. The attributes *leave* and *stay* induce cavities in the clusters, disrupting the relatively uniform 1-0 structure. Such shifts in the attributes of characters make the figure-ground impression of the scene unclear (Figure 19, Unclear f-g.). In the previous scenes, the figure-ground impression was rather unclear in that there was a domineering character with all attributes in the relation table. After Prince Escalus' speech, the figure-ground impression becomes unclear and chaotic, as the some characters stay and other characters leave the stage. The change in the non-distributivity in these scenes may suggest that the author prepared a dramatic scene by increasing the number of characters and when the potential for tension is at its highest, the attribute relations are shifted to release the tension.

Figure 19. Story line and lattices showing the relation tables and resulting lattice structures from Romeo and Juliet Act 1 Scene 1. As the story progresses, the lattice structures display different types of figure-ground profiles. If a lattice is a Boolean lattice, it is called a clear figure-ground impression since there is a single complement for all elements, even if it possesses multiple characters per element. The figure-ground profile starts with a Boolean lattice representing clear figure-ground impression, then unclear figure-ground impression, "all or nothing" figure-ground impression, unclear figure-ground impression, clear figure-ground impression among unclear figure-ground impression, clear figure-ground impression, and limited clear figure-ground impression (with elements without complements). When the attribute fight appears, the lattice becomes an unclear figure-ground relation (N_5 lattice).
Adapted from Kitamura (2011).

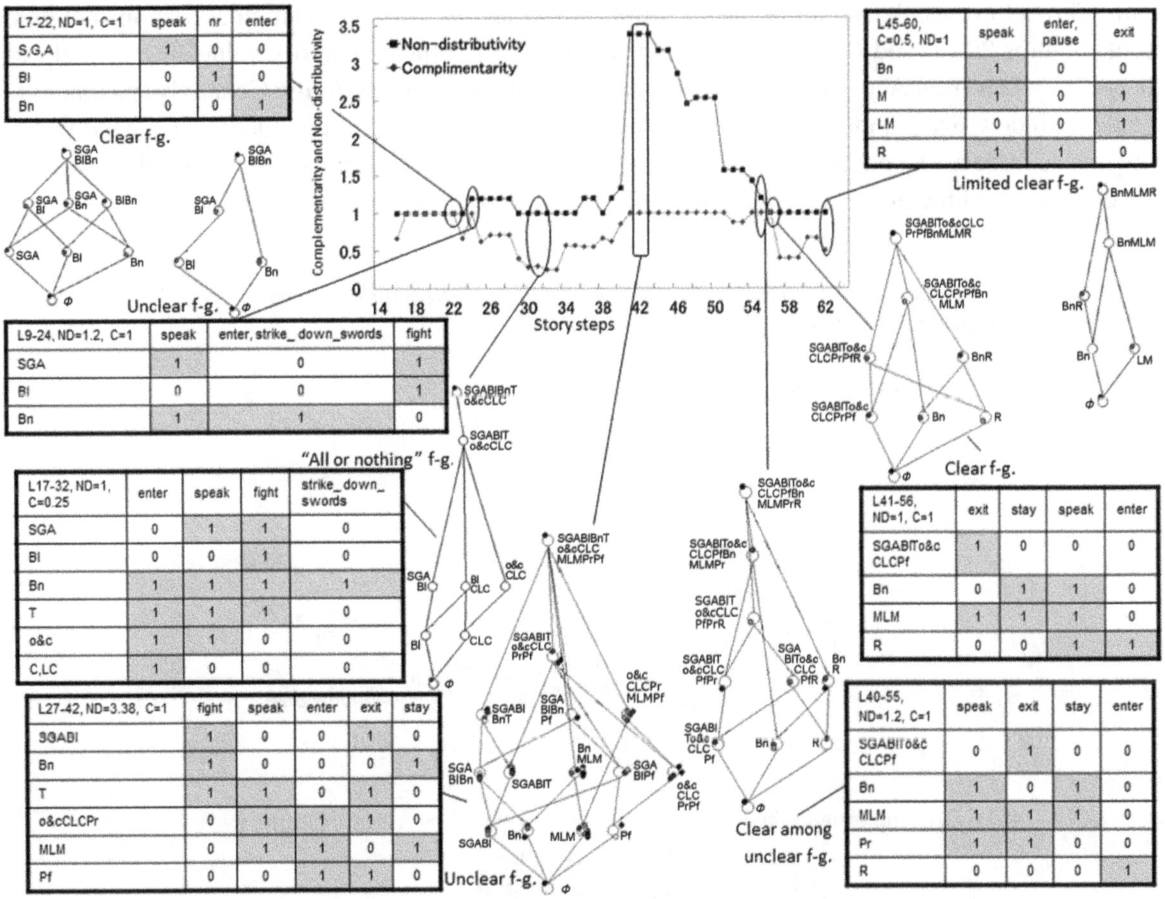

L7-22, ND=1, C=1	speak	nr	enter
S,G,A	1	0	0
Bl	0	1	0
Bn	0	0	1

L9-24, ND=1.2, C=1	speak	enter, strike_down_swords	fight
SGA	1	0	1
Bl	0	0	1
Bn	1	1	0

L17-32, ND=1, C=0.25	enter	speak	fight	strike_down_swords
SGA	0	1	1	0
Bl	0	0	1	0
Bn	1	1	1	1
T	1	1	1	0
o&c	1	1	0	0
C,LC	1	0	0	0

L27-42, ND=3.38, C=1	fight	speak	enter	exit	stay
SGABl	1	0	0	1	0
Bn	1	0	0	0	1
T	1	1	0	1	0
o&cCLCPr	0	1	1	1	0
MLM	0	1	1	0	1
Pf	0	0	1	1	0

L45-60, C=0.5, ND=1	speak	enter, pause	exit
Bn	1	0	0
M	1	0	1
LM	0	0	1
R	1	1	0

L41-56, ND=1, C=1	exit	stay	speak	enter
SGABlTo&c CLCPf	1	0	0	0
Bn	0	1	1	0
MLM	1	1	1	0
R	0	0	1	1

L40-55, ND=1.2, C=1	speak	exit	stay	enter
SGABlTo&c CLCPf	0	1	0	0
Bn	1	0	1	0
MLM	1	1	1	0
Pr	1	1	0	0
R	0	0	0	1

As the characters exit the scene and Romeo enters, the lattice structure becomes simpler. The lattice structure reflects the remaining characters' *stay* and *exit*, contrasted to Romeo's *enter*. This is contrasted in the figure-ground impression of Clear among unclear f-g. in Figure 19. As this chapter approaches the end, a clear and limited figure-ground impression of the characters is seen.

The recurring minor dips in the complementarity correspond to the entry of additional characters on stage (story steps 25, 30, 32, 36, 39). Newly appearing characters typically provide only the attribute *enter*. This attribute usually already existed in the relation table. Consequently a new character would be included in the attributes of another character. The new character would not have a complement of its own, reducing the value of complementarity. This is also seen towards the end of Act 1, Scene 1 where the dialogue is carried out by Montague and Benvolio or by Romeo and Benvolio. The figure-ground impression is clearer.

Graphs for All Window Sizes

In general, it is difficult to determine the "correct" window size for analysis. Typically, a minimum of three subjects is preferred in a window to obtain a lattice structure that would show diverse structures. A window is defined to be the range of events that are considered at a time. Assuming that a story is a time flow of events, the author defines a set of subject and its attribute relation at each instant of an event. Figures 20 (a) and (b) are the non-distributivity and complementarity values respectively for all window sizes from Act 1 Scene 1 of the theatrical work *Romeo and Juliet*. Generally speaking, the smallest window size (window size 2) and the largest window size (the last window size, a window size which is as large as the number of story steps) are not very informative because the smallest window size contains too little information and the largest window size contains too much information.

Figure 20. (a) Non-distributivity and (b) Complementarity for all window sizes
Adapted from Kitamura and Gunji (2014).

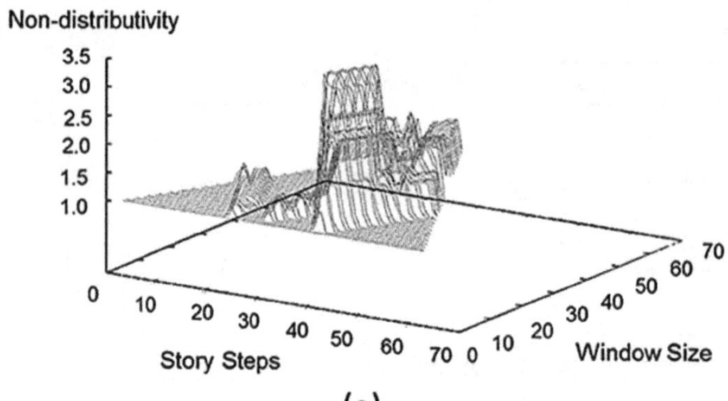

(a)

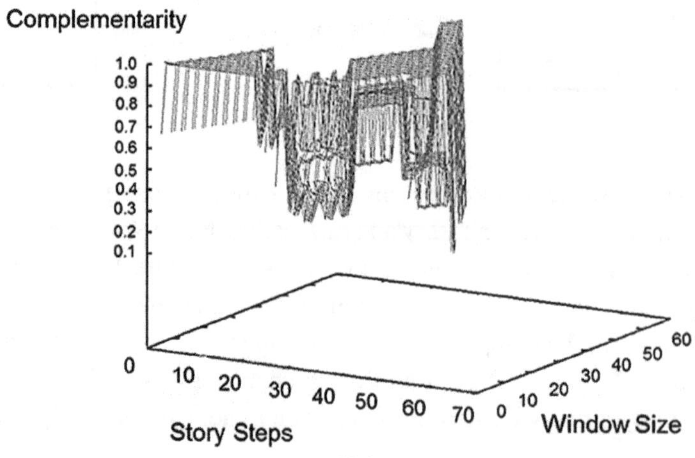

(b)

In Figure 20 (a), the non-distributivity peak (non-distributivity value of 3.38462) occurs at the relatively same location around the window sizes 15 to 25, although the peak shifts slightly towards the end of the story as the window size becomes larger. Since non-distributivity is high for subject-attribute relations with greater partial overlap among all subjects such as M_3, it can be said that the attributes of Figure 20 (a) partially overlap for many of the characters. In Figure 20 (b), the graph for complementarity, is similar to the non-distributivity in that the lower value of complementarity also shifts as the window size becomes larger. The lower value of complementarity suggests that the attributes of some characters are included in the attributes of the other characters in the subject-attribute relation table.

NARRATIVE CREATION

As seen in previous sections, the figure-ground properties of characters in stories can be modeled based on their attributes and expressed numerically. One can use this information in reverse as a guideline to generate stories. One can start with a numerical graph, assign desired lattice structures, label the lattice structures with appropriate characters and attributes, and lead to a story.

Here the author has created an example numerical story line in Figure 21. This will be the approximate outlook of what the story line will be like, so the values do not have to be followed exactly. The graph is roughly modeled after *Romeo and Juliet*, Act 1 Scene 1.

The author has learned from text analysis that a scene with multiple attribute overlaps of different subjects can cause a chaotic scene. This, numerically, can be expressed as lattices with high non-distributivity. It was learned that non-distributivity was associated with the figure-ground relation becoming unclear. A rapid transition would create a dramatic shift in the impression of the subject relations on the reader. This occurs when the tension is developing in the scene among multiple actions taking place. This tends to happen in certain circumstances that involve a group such as *fight*. The tension of the scene is released when the figure-ground property becomes clear after the unclear figure-ground situation. After a scene with multiple attribute overlaps, if the overlaps dissipate and the lattice has lesser complement overlaps per element, then the non-distributivity becomes lower and the chaos will be less, or the figure-ground relations become clearer.

Figure 21. Target figure-ground narrative graph

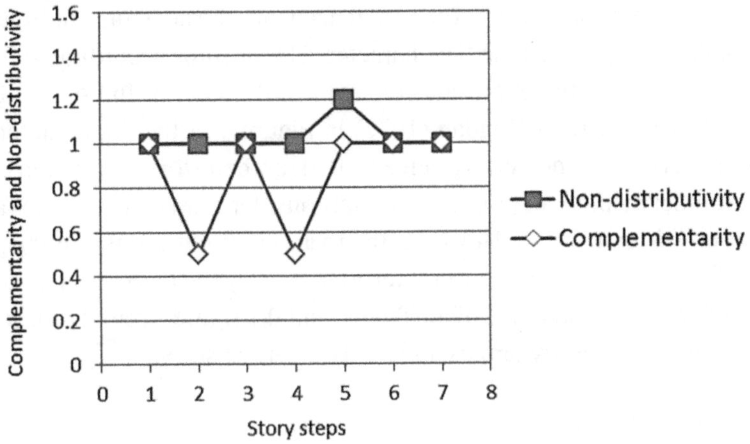

With respect to the complementarity, it would represent an inclusion relation among the characters, weakening the overall figure-ground profile of characters. If subtle characters are desired, the characters can have completely overlapping attributes with other characters such that their attributes would not stand out. This lowers the complementarity where the elements do not have complements. This could be a good way to keep the character profile low. (One could also argue that within the lattice structure, it could have important meaning, especially when the character is an atom on the structure, since the character with that element has fewer attributes, which can be contrasted with other characters with more attributes.) Such shifts in the figure-ground relation or lattice structure can be a hint for generating narratives.

Some lattice structures that would follow closely to the complementarity and non-distributivity values are shown in Figure 22. From the relation table in Figure 22, we can assign subjects and attributes, or characters and their actions, as building blocks to construct a story as in Figure 23.

As an example, based on Figures 22, and 23 generated from the graph in Figure 21, the following story can be created.

Step 1: Alice and Ben were walking along the street downtown, chatting away.

Step 2: As Alice and Ben were walking and talking, they saw Alice's friends, Cindy and Dave, also chatting and taking a walk.

Step 3: Alice and Ben saw Cindy and Dave enter a store. Alice and Ben debated what to do, whether to go greet them immediately or to surprise them at the right moment.

Step 4: Cindy and Dave walked into a department store. They were looked at bags. Alice and Ben decided to look at bags as well, but at the opposite end of the bag section so that they would not be noticed by Cindy and Dave. Ben, who didn't know Cindy and Dave directly, kept an eye on them for Alice as she watched Ben's movements.

Step 5: Now Cindy and Dave started looking at sofas in the furniture section. Alice also looked at sofas, as she watched Cindy and Dave, waiting for the right moment to greet them. Ben watched Alice, Cindy, and Dave to see how things would unfold.

Step 6: Alice surprised Cindy and Dave from behind, as Cindy and Dave were trying out the sofas. They were delightfully surprised to see an unexpected friend.

Step 7: They all merrily chatted as Alice and Ben recounted their story of how they encountered Cindy and Dave, and they all catch up with each other's recent news.

This approach is not a complete content generation device nor does it generate natural sentences. Also note that the verbs have been converted to past tense from the attributes in Figure 23. However, it could be used as a guide to help determine the character relationships according to their attributes. The approach of having a target graph that represents the flow of the story as in Figure 21 may be similar to that of tension of the play by Steriadi-Bogdan (1977) in Figure 4 or the dramatic tension of a story by Pérez y Pérez and Sharples (2001) and Pérez y Pérez (2014) for their story generation program MEXICA. Additionally, there are other methods of plot analysis that consider character attributes as an interpretation of the character's actions (Murai, 2014). However, the method introduced in this chapter uses attributes from the story more directly that involves fewer interpretations by the observer. For generating contents, one can choose a set of characters and a set of attributes, and the figure-ground profiles can be generated to provide a guide for the character dynamics and the flow of the story.

Figure 22. Table showing the steps, lattices, complementarity and non-distributivity and relation table that can form the narrative graph shown in Figure 20

<table>
<tr><th>Steps</th><th>Lattices</th><th>Complementarity & Non-distributivity</th><th>Relation Table</th></tr>
<tr><td>Step 1</td><td>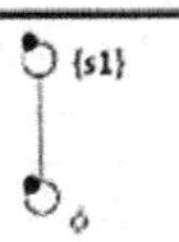</td><td>$C = \frac{2}{2} = 1$
$ND = \frac{2}{2} = 1$</td><td><table><tr><td></td><td>a1</td></tr><tr><td>s1</td><td>1</td></tr></table></td></tr>
<tr><td>Step 2</td><td>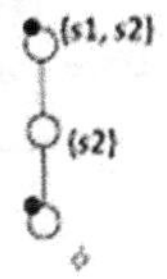</td><td>$C = \frac{2}{3} = 0.6$
$ND = \frac{2}{2} = 1$</td><td><table><tr><td></td><td>a1</td><td>a2</td></tr><tr><td>s1</td><td>1</td><td>1</td></tr><tr><td>s2</td><td>1</td><td>0</td></tr></table></td></tr>
<tr><td>Step 3</td><td>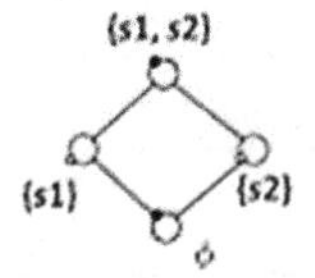</td><td>$C = \frac{4}{4} = 1$
$ND = \frac{4}{4} = 1$</td><td><table><tr><td></td><td>a1</td><td>a2</td></tr><tr><td>s1</td><td>1</td><td>0</td></tr><tr><td>s2</td><td>0</td><td>1</td></tr></table></td></tr>
<tr><td>Step 4</td><td>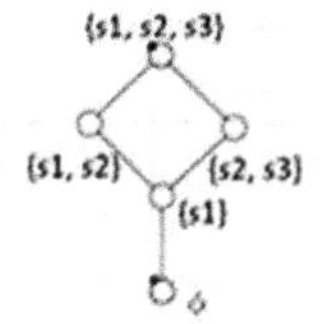</td><td>$C = \frac{2}{5} = 0.4$
$ND = \frac{2}{2} = 1$</td><td><table><tr><td></td><td>a1</td><td>a2</td><td>a3</td></tr><tr><td>s1</td><td>1</td><td>0</td><td>0</td></tr><tr><td>s2</td><td>1</td><td>1</td><td>0</td></tr><tr><td>s3</td><td>1</td><td>0</td><td>1</td></tr></table></td></tr>
<tr><td>Step 5</td><td>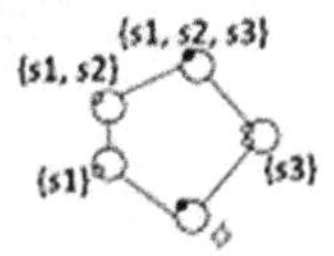</td><td>$C = \frac{5}{5} = 1$
$ND = \frac{6}{5} = 1.2$</td><td><table><tr><td></td><td>a1</td><td>a2</td><td>a3</td></tr><tr><td>s1</td><td>1</td><td>0</td><td>0</td></tr><tr><td>s2</td><td>1</td><td>1</td><td>0</td></tr><tr><td>s3</td><td>0</td><td>1</td><td>1</td></tr></table></td></tr>
<tr><td>Step 6</td><td>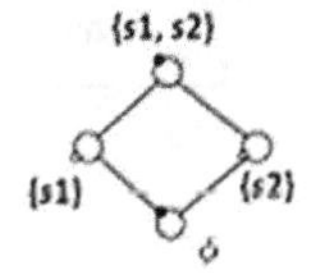</td><td>$C = \frac{4}{4} = 1$
$ND = \frac{4}{4} = 1$</td><td><table><tr><td></td><td>a1</td><td>a2</td></tr><tr><td>s1</td><td>1</td><td>0</td></tr><tr><td>s2</td><td>0</td><td>1</td></tr></table></td></tr>
<tr><td>Step 7</td><td>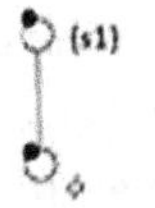</td><td>$C = \frac{2}{2} = 1$
$ND = \frac{2}{2} = 1$</td><td><table><tr><td></td><td>a1</td></tr><tr><td>s1</td><td>1</td></tr></table></td></tr>
</table>

FUTURE RESEARCH DIRECTIONS

The rough set derived lattice applied to story analysis and story generation is still early in its development. There are topics that need to be studied such as the appropriate window sizes, definitions of figure-ground impressions in narratives, and the different combinations for the two equivalence relations.

If the window size is too big or too small, the information considered at a single instance will be too much or too little to be informative. Using the same window size during the story is also questionable,

Figure 23. Table showing the steps, relation table, and subject and attributes that can form the narrative graph shown in Figure 20

Steps | **Relation Table** | **Subjects and Attributes**

Step 1

	speak, walk
Alice, Ben	1

Subject	Attribute
Alice, Ben	speak, walk

Step 2

	speak, walk	see, follow
Alice, Ben	1	1
Cindy, Dave	1	0

Subject	Attribute
Alice, Ben	speak, walk, see & follow (C&D)
Cindy, Dave	speak, walk

Step 3

Subject	enter a store	debate what to do
Alice, Ben	0	1
Cindy, Dave	1	0

Subject	Attribute
Alice, Ben	debate what to do
Cindy, Dave	enter a store

Step 4

	look at bags	watch B	watch C&D
Alice	1	1	0
Ben	1	0	1
Cindy, Dave	1	0	0

Subject	Attribute
Alice	look at bags, watch B
Ben	look at bags, watch C&D
Cindy, Dave	look at bags

Step 5

	look at sofa	watch A	watch C&D
Alice	1	0	1
Ben	0	1	1
Cindy, Dave	1	0	0

Subject	Attribute
Alice	look at sofa, watch C&D
Ben	watch A&C&D
Cindy, Dave	look at sofa

Step 6

	surprises C&D	surprised
Alice, Ben	1	0
Cindy, Dave	0	1

Subject	Attribute
Alice, Ben	surprises C&D
Cindy, Dave	surprised

Step 7

	talk together
Alice, Ben, Cindy, Dave	1

Subject	Attribute
Alice, Ben, Cindy, Dave	talk together

since it is possible that a reader would perceive a story with different window sizes during different intervals separated by different incidences in the story. In fact, in the example for the narrative content generation towards the end of this chapter, the concept of window size was not used explicitly, although at each step considered, there are different a number of lines (quantitatively different amounts of information) considered.

The interpretation of the figure-ground relations from the lattice structure is still open to discussion. For example, although human psychology constantly switches from figure and ground, gestalt psychology suggests that movements are more noticeable as a figure in contrast to the static landscape as a ground or irregularity as a figure in contrast to repetitiveness as a ground. Therefore, the presence of the description of action can be considered as a figure and the lack of such description as a ground. Elements grouped together under *no reference* can be considered as a ground, and characters may go in and out of such attribute category depending on their attribute status. Additionally, an atom can be interpreted as a figure more often than a ground, since an atom by definition will have fewer character members in its set compared to other elements higher in its hierarchy.

In this chapter the author used character subjects as one equivalence relation and the character attributes for the other. Character attributes may be nouns, verbs, etc. There can be other combinations of pairs of equivalence classes that could provide different insights into stories.

With respect to content generation, the rough set derived lattice method, starting with the numerical values of complementarity and non-distributivity, leading to lattice structures and figure-ground profiles of characters, can prove to be a useful guide for story generation, game industrial purpose, or advertisement purposes. The notion of figure-ground perceptions from gestalt psychology is helpful in identifying priorities in the focus of attention. It is imagined that such concepts and models will become important in constructing artificial intelligence devices through visual, auditory, or narrative mediums.

CONCLUSION

This chapter introduced a rough set derived lattice to model the figure-ground impressions of characters on the readers. The source of information comes strictly from the text. Later, this method was applied as a guide for generating narrative contents.

The transition of the complementarity and non-distributivity of the resulting lattices reveal particular shifts in the relations of the attributes of the characters, also seen in the relation tables. It is observed that certain actions were used to change the figure-ground status of the scenes. One typical word was *fight*. Such words are used to change the rhythm or dynamics of the figure-ground profile of the story.

Overall it can be seen that when the figure-ground relation of scenes becomes unclear, there is typically an action that makes the scenes unclear. In previous research by the author, other such verbs were recognized such as *fight* and *laugh*. This happens because when there is a fight, there is usually a witness, and the witness gets involved in the fighting situation by trying to stop the fight or by asking what the fight is about. Similarly with *laugh*, there are people who make a comment and as a result some are laughing and others are laughed at. When such actions are finished, the scene returns to a clear figure-ground relation. Therefore, it can be presumed that certain verbs are used under certain conditions to change the figure-ground profile of a story and possibly cause a sense of drama or thrill to the reader.

Analyzing the figure-ground profile in a story may be useful in characterizing the style of the author or it may help authors create a story with such figure-ground impressions in mind. Just as the author's descriptive style alters the impression on the reader, variations in the input or interpretation of text also alter the resulting lattices. Such shifts of characters' attributes may be suggestive of a writer's technique for assigning character attributes to manage the figure-ground impressions and drama of the stories.

There have been other mathematical methods to abstract narratives in the past. Although they were analytical and novel at the time, the investigations were more academic in motive. Such methodology did not find many applications other than, perhaps, the statistical methods that analyze the use of vocabulary in a literary work with an unknown author to identify the creator. However, today with the advances in high power computing, availability of narratives from social networking services and the internet, and the demand to analyze them for commercial purposes, there are industrial needs to consider alternative methods to extract meaningful information from the constantly flowing big data.

The results of rough set derived lattice model for figure-ground impressions have received comments that they are at risk of being subjective, that is, the results may vary according to the analyst. However, such is the nature of literary works that involve human cognition (with the exception of scientific reports and instruction manuals) and it is wonderful that literary art work is open to multiple interpretations that could go beyond the original intentions of the writer, reflecting the diverse cognitive state of the readers. In this sense, the rough set derived lattice model for figure-ground impressions is an excellent tool, reflecting the nature of human cognitive interaction with narrative text. This may be a trait that is needed for developing artificial intelligence with a closer cognitive mechanism to humans that is capable of generating coherent narrative content through communication.

REFERENCES

Birkhoff, G. (1967). *Lattice theory*. Providence, RI: Colloquium Publications, XXV, American Mathematical Society.

Brainerd, B., & Neufeldt, V. (1974). On Marcus' methods for the analysis of the strategy of a play. *Poetics*, *3*(2), 31–74. doi:10.1016/0304-422X(74)90013-8

Bringsjord, S., & Ferrucci, D. A. (2000). *Artificial intelligence and literary creativity*. Mahwah, NJ: Lawrence Erlbaum Associates, Inc. Publishers.

Christman, S. D., Sontam, V., & Jasper, J. D. (2009). Individual differences in ambiguous-figure perception: Degree of handedness and interhemispheric interaction. *Perception*, *38*(8), 1183–1198. doi:10.1068/p6131 PMID:19817151

Cooper, C. W., & Meyer, L. B. (1960). *The rhythmic structure of music*. Chicago, IL: Chicago UP.

Culpeper, J. (1996). Inferring character from texts: Attribution theory and foregrounding theory. *Poetics*, *23*(5), 335–361. doi:10.1016/0304-422X(95)00005-5

Davey, B. A., & Priestley, H. A. (2002). *Introduction to Lattice and Order* (2nd ed.). Cambridge, UK: Cambridge University Press. doi:10.1017/CBO9780511809088

Dinu, M. (1968). Structures linguistiques probabilistes issues de l'étude du theatre [Probabilistic linguistic structures of theater studies]. *Cahiers de Linguistique Théorique et Appliquée*, *5*, 29–46.

Dinu, M. (1970). Contributions à l'étude mathématique du theatre [Contributions to the mathematical study of theatre]. *Revue Roumaine de Mathématiques Pures et Appliquées*, *15*, 521–543.

Dinu, M. (1977). How to estimate the weight of stage relations. *Poetics*, *6*(3-4), 209–227. doi:10.1016/0304-422X(77)90006-7

File:Rubin2.jpg. (2016, October 8). *Wikimedia Commons, the free media repository*. Retrieved September 29, 2017, from https://commons.wikimedia.org/w/index.php?title=File:Rubin2.jpg&oldid=209158772

Forti, B. (2008). How could phenomenal consciousness be involved in mental function? *New Ideas in Psychology*, *27*(3), 312–325. doi:10.1016/j.newideapsych.2008.10.001

Gershoni, S., & Kobayashi, H. (2005). Symmetry and complementarity- a discussion and a qualitative demonstration with computer generated infinite patterns of natural scenes. In *Proceedings of The First International Workshop on Kansei* (vol. 68, pp. 89-90). The Society of Photographic Science and Technology of Japan.

Gervás, P. (2012). Story Generator Algorithms. In P. Hühn et al. (Eds.), *The living handbook of narratology*. Hamburg, Germany: Hamburg University Press.

Granek, E., & Ruttenberg, B. I. (2008). Changes in biotic and abiotic processes following mangrove clearing. *Estuarine, Coastal and Shelf Science*, *80*(4), 555–562. doi:10.1016/j.ecss.2008.09.012

Gunji, Y. P., & Haruna, T. (2010). A non-boolean lattice derived by double indiscernibility. *Lecture Notes in Computer Science*, *6190*, 211–225. doi:10.1007/978-3-642-14467-7_11

Hamada, S. (2001). Four-layer structure of narratives. *Cognitive Studies: Bulletin of the Japanese Cognitive Science Society, 8*, 319-326.

Herrnstein-Smith, B. (1968). *Poetic closure*. Chicago, IL: Chicago UP.

Hoffman, D. D. (1983). The interpretation of visual illusions. *Scientific American*, *249*(6), 154–162. doi:10.1038/scientificamerican1283-154

Huang, K. C. (2008). Effects of computer icons and figure/background area ratios and color combinations on visual search performance on an LCD monitor. *Displays*, *29*(3), 237–242. doi:10.1016/j.displa.2007.08.005

Huang, L., & Pashler, H. (2009). Reversing the attention effect in figure-ground perception. *Psychological Science*, *20*(10), 1199–1201. doi:10.1111/j.1467-9280.2009.02424.x PMID:19686294

Hubka, K. (1984). The dramatic syllables and hyper-syllables of Menander's 'Samia' and Plautus' 'Mercator'. *Poetics*, *13*(1-2), 83–100. doi:10.1016/0304-422X(84)90032-9

Jakobson, R. (1960). Linguistics and poetics. In T. A. Sebeok (Ed.), *Style in language* (pp. 350–377). Cambridge, MA: MIT Press.

Jones, E. E., & Davis, K. E. (1965). From acts to dispositions; The attribution process in person perception. In L. Berkowitz (Ed.), Advances in experimental social psychology (Vol. 2, pp. 219–266). Academic Press. doi:10.1016/S0065-2601(08)60107-0

Kelley, H. H. (1967). Attribution theory in social psychology. In D. Levine (Ed.), Nebraska symposium on motivation (pp. 192-238). Lincoln, NE: University of Nebraska Press.

Kitamura, E. S. (2011). *Literature analysis with rough set derived lattice* (Unpublished doctoral dissertation). Kobe University, Kobe, Japan.

Kitamura, E. S. (2017). Time flow in character figure-ground relations in literary text--towards story generation. In *Proceedings of the Symposium on Reversible Time, Retardation and Anticipation in Quantum Physics, Biology and Cybernetics held as part of the 29th International Conference on System Research, Informatics & Cybernetics* (vol. 1, pp. 97-102). Tecumseh, Canada: The International Institute for Advanced Studies.

Kitamura, E. S., & Gunji, Y. P. (2010a). Evolving lattices for analyzing behavioral dynamics of characters in literary text. In *The 4th International Conference on the Foundations of Information Science*. tripleC-Cognition, Communication, Co-operation. Retrieved from http://triple-c.at/index.php/tripleC

Kitamura, E. S., & Gunji, Y. P. (2010b). Figure-ground analysis of characters in literary text. In *The 27th Annual Meeting of the Japanese Cognitive Science Society*. Nagoya, Japan: JCSS. Retrieved from http://www.jcss.gr.jp/meetings/jcss2010/proceedings.html

Kitamura, E. S., & Gunji, Y. P. (2011). Expressing implicit figure-ground character information from explicit literary text information. In *2011 IEEE/SICE International Symposium on System Integration (SII)* (pp. 946-950). Piscataway, NJ: IEEE Publication. doi:10.1109/SII.2011.6147576

Kitamura, E. S., & Gunji, Y. P. (2012a). Figure-ground symmetry analysis of characters in literature. Symmetry: Culture and Science, 23(1), 67-96.

Kitamura, E. S., & Gunji, Y. P. (2012b). Figure-ground characteristic of detective mystery The Murders in the Rue Morgue by Edgar Allan Poe. *International Journal of Advancements in Computing Technology*, *4*(22), 291–299. doi:10.4156/ijact.vol4.issue22.32

Kitamura, E. S., & Gunji, Y. P. (2014). Model of figure-ground cognition in literary text. *International Journal of Computing Anticipatory Systems*, *29*, 17–28.

Koffka, K. (1935). *Principles of gestalt psychology*. London, UK: Routledge & Kegan Paul.

Kybartas, B., & Bidarra, R. (2017). A survey on story generation techniques for authoring computational narratives. *IEEE Transactions on Computational Intelligence and AI in Games*, *9*(3), 239–253. doi:10.1109/TCIAIG.2016.2546063

Labov, W. (1972). *Language in the inner city: Studies in the Black English vernacular*. Philadelphia, PA: University of Pennsylvania Press.

Leech, G. N. (1969). *A linguistic guide to English poetry*. London, UK: Longman.

Loss, L., Bebis, G., Nicolescu, M., & Skurikhin, A. (2009). An iterative multi-scale tensor voting scheme for perceptual grouping of natural shapes in cluttered backgrounds. *Computer Vision and Image Understanding*, *113*(1), 126–149. doi:10.1016/j.cviu.2008.07.011

Marcus, S. (1970). *Poetica matematica* [Mathematical poetics, in Romanian]. Bucuresti, Romania: Editura Academiei R.S.R.

Meehan, J. (1981). TAIL-SPIN. In R. Schank & K. Riesbeck (Eds.), *Inside computer understanding: Five programs plus miniatures* (pp. 197–226). Mahwah, NJ: Psychology Press.

Meyer, L. B. (1956). *Emotion and meaning in music*. Chicago, IL: Chicago UP.

Mihnea, T. (1977). Combinatorics and dynamics of characters in drama. *Poetics*, *6*(3-4), 229–254. doi:10.1016/0304-422X(77)90007-9

Mukařovský, J. (1970). Standard language and poetic language. In D. C. Freeman (Ed.), *Linguistics and literary style* (P. L. Garvin, Trans.; pp. 40–57). New York, NY: Holt, Rinehart and Winston.

Murai, H. (2014). Plot analysis for describing punch line functions in Shinichi Hoshi's microfiction. In *Proceedings of the 5th Workshop on Computational Models of Narrative (CMN'14)* (121-129). Dagstuhl, Germany: Schloss Dagstuhl--Leibniz-Zentrum fuer Informatik.

Palmer, S., Davis, J., Nelson, R., & Rock, I. (2008). Figure-ground effects on shape memory for objects versus holes. *Perception, 37*(10), 1569–1586. doi:10.1068/p5838 PMID:19065859

Pawlak, Z. (1981). Information systems-theoretical foundations. *Information Systems, 6*(3), 205–218. doi:10.1016/0306-4379(81)90023-5

Pawlak, Z. (1982). Rough sets. *International Journal of Computer and Information Science, 11*(5), 341–356. doi:10.1007/BF01001956

Pérez y Pérez, R. (2014). The three layers evaluation model for computer-generated plots. In *Proceedings of the Fifth International Conference on Computational Creativity (ICCC 2014)* (220-229). Ljublijana, Slovenia: Jožef Stefan Institute.

Pérez y Pérez, R., & Sharples, M. (2001). MEXICA: A computer model of a cognitive account of creative writing. *Journal of Experimental & Theoretical Artificial Intelligence, 13*(2), 119–139. doi:10.1080/09528130010029820

Propp, V. (1968). *Morphology of the folktale* (2nd ed.; L. Scott, Trans.). Austin, TX: University of Texas Press.

Rajaniemi, T. K., & Allison, V. J. (2009). Abiotic conditions and plant cover differentially affect microbial biomass and community composition on dune gradients. *Soil Biology & Biochemistry, 41*(1), 102–109. doi:10.1016/j.soilbio.2008.10.001

Rubin, E. (1915). *Synsoplevede Figurer* [Visual Figures]. Retrieved July, 2010, from http://en.wikipedia.org/wiki/Rubin_vase

Siegenthaler, B. M., & Goldstein, J. (1967). Auditory and visual figure-background perception by adult aphasics. *Journal of Communication Disorders, 1*(2), 152–158. doi:10.1016/0021-9924(67)90004-4

Steriadi-Bogdan, M. (1977). The evolution of the plot and problems of strategy in a detective play. *Poetics, 6*(3-4), 375–382. doi:10.1016/0304-422X(77)90014-6

Swartjes, I. M. T., Vromen, J., & Bloom, N. (2007). Narrative inspiration: using case based problem solving for emergent story generation. In A. Cardoso, & G. A. Wiggins (Eds.), *Proceedings of the Fourth International Joint Workshop on Computational Creativity* (pp. 21-28). London, UK: Goldsmiths, University of London.

Teodorescu-Brinzeu, P. (1984). The verbal zero-sign in theater. *Poetics, 13*(1-2), 47–56. doi:10.1016/0304-422X(84)90029-9

Tsur, R. (2009). Metaphor and figure-ground relationship: comparisons from poetry, music, and the visual arts. In G. Brône & J. Vandaele (Eds.), *Cognitive Poetics: Goals, Gains and Gaps* (pp. 237–277). Berlin, Germany: Mouton de Gruyter.

Turner, S. R. (1994). *The creative process: A computer model of storytelling and creativity*. Mahwah, NJ: Psychology Press.

Veale, T. (2009). Hiding in plain sight: figure-ground reversals in humour (commentary to Tsur). In G. Brône & J. Vandaele (Eds.), *Cognitive Poetics: Goals, Gains and Gaps* (pp. 279–288). Berlin, Germany: Mouton de Gruyter.

Werner, H., & Strauss, A. A. (1941). Pathology of figure-background relation in the child. *Journal of Abnormal and Social Psychology, 36*(2), 238–248. doi:10.1037/h0058060

Yates-Glandorf, J. B. (Ed.). (1985). *Shakespeare's Romeo and Juliet. In the original and modern English. A parallel text edition*. Logan, IA: Perfection Learning Corporation.

KEY TERMS AND DEFINITIONS

Attribute: A characteristic that is assigned to a character in a story. It can be a noun, verb, adjective, etc.

Complement Pair: A pair of lattice elements that together form a universal set (the entire set of elements, or everything) and without the pair results in an empty set (nothingness).

Complementarity: The existence rate of complement pairs among all elements in a lattice.

Element: A factor in a set that represents something, whether it is a character, attribute, etc. It is one of the building blocks of a lattice.

Figure-Ground: A way to identify the target of attention (figure), contrasted with the rest of background (ground).

Gestalt: Originally a German word that represents shape or form, it is used in story analysis for recognizing characters.

Lattice: A logical structure with elements in an inclusion relation. It is closed at the top with a universal set and closed at the bottom with an empty set.

Non-Distributivity: The possession rate of elements with more than one complement pairs.

Rough Set: An approximation method that uses a collection of elements that certainly belong to the target (lower approximation) and those that partly belong to the target (upper approximation).

Window Size: The number of lines, actions, or events considered at a single instance in a story.

Chapter 7
Narratives of an Artificial Agent:
Mental World and Narrating

Taisuke Akimoto
Kyushu Institute of Technology, Japan

ABSTRACT

In this chapter, the author develops a computational model of the narrative ability for artificial agents. To illustrate an overview of this study, the author addresses an architectural and conceptual systematization of the narrative ability. The proposed model consists of two essential elements: the "mental world" as the internal representation of the world that is formed from many stories, and the mechanism of "narrating" as the act of expressing part of the mental world. In this chapter, the basic concepts and system frameworks of the narrative ability, mental world, and narrating are presented.

INTRODUCTION

Narrative is a crucial aspect for the development of the intelligence of artificial agents. The significance of narrative in the domain of artificial intelligence (AI) is explained from the following two perspectives. First, a narrative is a universal mode of interpersonal communication. In a broad sense, a narrative refers to an expression of events in a real or a fictional world based on a language or other sign systems (Prince, 2003). For example, humans communicate everyday experiences to their family members in a narrative form. Humans acquire and share knowledge of the current status of their societies from narratives in mass communications, e.g., television and newspaper reports. Historical narratives distribute the knowledge of the distant past beyond the time scale of human life. Furthermore, humans cultivate richer worldviews through fictional narratives such as folk tales, fairy tales, picture books, and literary narratives. Second, a narrative or story is thought of as the general form of the representation of a memory of events in the world. In other words, a human mind can organize past experiences in the form of a narrative or story. This type of memory is known as episodic memory (Tulving, 1983) in psychology. The formation of expectations or plans for future events is similar to narrative composition.

In modern society, artificial agents based on AI technologies work, play, or live with humans in real and virtual environments. For example, a humanoid robot Pepper developed by Softbank (n.d.) can

DOI: 10.4018/978-1-5225-4775-4.ch007

Copyright © 2018, IGI Global. Copying or distributing in print or electronic forms without written permission of IGI Global is prohibited.

perform quasi-affective interactions with humans. Several researchers have been addressing the development of computational models of robotic agents who autonomously learn languages or symbols through interaction with the environment (Taniguchi, 2010). However, very few studies have tried to address the computational modeling of the narrative ability as a core element of the intelligence of an agent. The narrative ability of an agent will be an essential element for building a deep relationship with humans. For example, if an agent who lives as a member of a family has the ability to memorize and recount daily experiences, the agent will become an irreplaceable part of the family.

In this chapter, the primary objective is to explore a computational model of the *narrative ability*—a mental system of manipulating narratives—as the foundational element of the intelligence of an artificial agent. The author uses the term *narrative agent* to refer to an agent who possesses the narrative ability. The author assumes that the narrative ability is developed by the following two essential elements:

- **Mental World:** In this study, "mental world" refers to the representation of the world inside the "mind" of an agent, in contrast to the physical world. It is formed from many stories constructed by narrative-based cognitive activities, including interpretations of experiences, interpretations of narratives, and one's imagination.
- **Narrating:** Narrating is the act of expressing a story in the mental world in the form of a narrative that is based on a language or other sign systems.

Throughout this chapter, the author addresses the systematization of the narrative ability. The chapter is organized as follows: In the "BACKGROUND" section, the conceptual and theoretical background of this study will be presented. In the "STRUCTURE OF NARRATIVE" section, the basic structure of a narrative as the basis of modeling the narrative ability will be formalized. In the "BASIC CONCEPT OF THE NARRATIVE AGENT" section, the author will develop a macroscopic architecture of the narrative ability. In the "MENTAL WORLD" and the "NARRATING" sections, the conceptual systematizations of the structure of the mental world and the cognitive process of narrating will be addressed, respectively. Finally, in the "FUTURE RESEARCH DIRECTIONS" section, several future issues will be discussed and in the "CONCLUSION" section, concluding remarks will be presented.

BACKGROUND

In this section, previous AI studies relevant to the narrative ability will be described.

Narrative as Memory and Knowledge

AI Studies by Schank and His Colleagues

From the early years of AI, the relationship between the intelligence and a narrative or a story has been explored by Schank and his colleagues. They proposed several AI theories of narrativity-based models of knowledge representation, including script knowledge, episode memory or story knowledge, and dynamic memory (Schank & Abelson, 1977; Schank, 1982). In addition, they formulated the concept of case-based reasoning (Riesbeck & Schank, 1989) as a model for solving a new problem by using a previous similar episode (a case and its solution). Script knowledge is a well-known knowledge model corresponding to a pattern of a normal flow of events in a specific cultural situation, such as "eating in a restaurant." On the other hand, the dynamic memory model provided a theory for the organization of episodic stories. A key concept of this model is known as a memory organization packet (MOP). According to Schank, a MOP is defined as follows: "A MOP consists of a set of scenes directed towards the achievement of a goal. A MOP always has one major scene whose goal is the essence of purpose of the events organized by the MOP." (Schank, 1982, p. 97). A scene, which is a key element of a MOP, is defined as: "A memory structure that groups together actions with a shared goal, that occurred at the same time. It provides a sequence of general actions. Specific memories are stored in scenes, indexed with respect to how they differ from general action in the scene." (Schank, 1982, p. 95). In a memory system, a MOP corresponds to a high-level structure that associates analogous stories. Based on this knowledge model, Schank discussed the cognitive mechanism for the flexible reminding of stories in various situations.

Episodic Memory and Story Knowledge in Cognitive Architectures

In several recent studies on cognitive architecture, the psychological concept of episodic memory (Tulving, 1983), which refers to the memory of one's past experiences, has been adopted in cognitive architectures. In particular, the Soar cognitive architecture (Laird, 2012) includes episodic memory as one of the knowledge elements (Nuxoll & Laird, 2004, 2007). Although the Soar episodic memory is only a snapshot of the virtual environment at each time step, the knowledge representation of episodic memory is discussed in terms of a narrative or a story (Anderson, 2015; León, 2016; Szilas, 2015). For example, León (2016) proposed a graph-based knowledge representation of a narrative-form memory, including episodic and procedural memories. In addition, León modeled the production of an episodic narrative as a type of narrative discourse generation based on an episodic memory.

On the other hand, in a previous study by Akimoto (2016), stories are classified into the following three types:

- **Experience-Based Stories:** A story constructed based on one's own experiences in the real or the virtual world (i.e., the physical world). This is similar to the episodic memory.
- **Narrative-Mediated Stories:** A story acquired from a narrative (e.g., a novel, a news report, a conversation); as a human learns many stories from narratives that are beyond one's own experiences. This type of story includes factual and fictional stories.
- **Internally Generated Stories:** These are stories generated inside the system of an agent, which include future, imaginary, and generalized stories.

Stories in Common Sense Knowledge Resources

Story or script-like knowledge is also considered as a type of knowledge element in several studies on common sense knowledge resources (Singh, Barry, & Liu, 2004; Chambers & Jurafsky, 2010). Such knowledge corresponds to a socialized knowledge, whereas the aforementioned knowledge models are positioned as a core element in a mental system. For example, Singh, Barry, and Liu (2004) proposed an integration framework for ConceptNet, LifeNet, and StoryNet. ConceptNet is a large-scale semantic network of concepts. A concept corresponds to a word or a phrase, and its semantic knowledge is represented based on its relations to other concepts. StoryNet corresponds to a database of small stories.

A story is stored as simple sentences representing a sequence of events. In the integration framework, ConceptNet and StoryNet are connected in a type of a complementary relationship. More specifically, on the one hand, a story in StoryNet forms a concretely contextualized knowledge on events. On the other hand, concepts in ConceptNet are linked to stories that provide abstract and general semantic knowledge.

Computational Approaches to Narrative Generation

The computational modeling of narrative generation has long been a challenging problem in the field of AI (Gervás, 2009; Ogata, 2016). In this subsection, the author will present an overview of previous studies on computational narrative generation by using the narratological terminologies of dividing the content and expression planes of a narrative, i.e., a "story" and a "discourse" (Prince, 2003).

Story Generation

In a broad sense, story generation refers to the task of composing a chronological development of events to be recounted in a narrative. This task includes the composition of the story world as the background of events. Three major approaches to story generation are the following.

- **Character-Centered Approach:** This approach models the story generation in the form of goal-oriented actions of characters in a preliminarily modeled world. It is rooted in the planning method in AI. Example studies include those of Meehan (1980), Okada and Endo (1992), and Riedl and Young (2010).
- **Structure-Centered Approach:** This approach models the structure of a story or a narrative from an outside perspective to a story, in contrast to the character-centered approach, which assumes an inside perspective to a story. From such a perspective, several researchers attempted to formulations of generative rules or schematic knowledge for producing story structures. Example studies include those of Pemberton (1989), Ogata and Terano (1991), Lang (1999), Bringsjord and Ferrucci (1999), Imabuchi and Ogata (2012), and Gervás (2015).
- **Case-Based Approach:** This approach formalizes story generation as the transformation or adaptation of previous stories based on the concept of case-based reasoning. Example studies include those of Turner (1994), Peinado and Gervás (2005), and Swanson and Gordon (2012).

Narrative Discourse Generation

The task of narrative discourse generation is to compose a structure for a narrative expression, including the generation of a surface expression using natural language or imagery. Several studies have applied the narrative discourse theory of Genette (1980) to the modeling of narrative discourse generation. In his theory, Genette presented a systematic categorization of the structural aspects of narrative discourse based on an analysis of a literary work. Based on his categorization, the narrative issues in the computational task of narrative discourse generation can be organized into three major categories: the "tense," which is relevant to the relationship between the time of the story and the time of discourse, the "mood," which is relevant to the modality of regulating narrative information, and the "voice," which is relevant to the relationship among the narrating, the story, and the discourse.

For example, Ogata (2004, 2016) has proposed a computational theory aimed at developing an integrated system of the Genette-based discourse generation techniques. Based on that theory, Ogata and his colleagues proposed several computer programs for narrative discourse generation as well (e.g., Mukouyama, Shinohara, Kanai, & Ogata, 2002; Akimoto & Ogata, 2015). Montfort (2007) presented an interactive fiction system, in which the progression of a story could be managed through natural language-based interaction with the user. This interaction contains functions to produce Genette-based variations within the discourse. Bae, Cheong, and Young (2011) proposed a narrative generation system that focused on the discourse variation based on the focalization, which is a subcategory of mood in the Genette theory. In this system, different narratives are generated from a given world model based on planning algorithms that involve the viewpoints of the characters toward the same events.

Conceptual Reorganization Toward a Computational Narrative Ability

The aforementioned previous studies provided several essential ideas in formalizing the computational model of the narrative ability. Models and theories of knowledge representation described in "Narrative as Memory and Knowledge" are applicable to the mental world. The dynamic memory model by Schank (1982) suggests an organizational structure of many stories with high-level knowledge elements. The narrative memory model of León (2016) provides the relationship between an episodic memory and a narrative in a cognitive architecture. The manner in which story knowledge in StoryNet and conceptual knowledge in ConceptNet are connected (Singh, Barry, & Liu, 2004) can be applied to the knowledge organization in the mental world. On the other hand, methods of computational narrative generation are applicable to the mechanisms of both the mental world construction and narrating. In particular, story generation is an essential task in constructing the mental world, and discourse generation is similar to the process of narrating.

STRUCTURE OF NARRATIVE: A COMPUTATIONAL MODEL

Before addressing the systematization of the narrative ability, as a basis for the study, this section describes a computational model of a narrative structure proposed by Akimoto (2017). The primary feature of the model is to represent a narrative as a complex arrangement of multidimensional hierarchical graph structures. The following subsections summarize the model according to Akimoto (2017).

Multidimensional Structure of a Narrative

A narrative is a complex object that involves various structural elements. Based on the previous studies in narratology (Chatman, 1978; Prince, 2003) and computational narrative generation (Ogata, 2016), Akimoto (2017) reorganized the structural and surface aspects of a narrative into four dimensions:

- **Story World:** The background world structure, containing information about entities (e.g., characters, objects, and places).
- **Story:** The structure of chronologically organized events.
- **Discourse:** The structure of how a story is organized into a surface expression.
- **Expression:** The surface narrative expression based on language, image, or other sign systems.

These dimensions are combined by using a nested structure, as shown in Figure 1. In particular, a story contains a story world as the background, and a discourse includes a story as the content. An expression is generated based on the discourse. Each of the three structural dimensions—story world, story, and discourse—is a symbolic representation, whereas the expression is a surface media representation.

Hierarchical Graph Model

Each structural dimension described above is represented by a hierarchical graph structure, which organizes various types of structural elements by hierarchical grouping and network-like linkage. A hierarchical graph consists of three types of structural components: a semantic element (SE), a group, and a link:

- **Semantic Element (SE):** The SE contains semantic information for the basic unit in each structural dimension of a narrative.
- **Group:** The group integrates any number of nodes (SEs and/or groups) into a broader unit. This function is similar to the linguistic abstraction or categorization of the member nodes. A group itself contains semantic information as well, in the form of a comprehensive meaning that binds or abstracts the member nodes.
- **Link:** The link connects any two nodes with a relation or a set of connective attributes.

Figure 2 shows an abstracted example of the structure with the three aforementioned components. Although the components are commonly used in any structural dimensions, the content of each type is different in each dimension (Tables 1–3).

In the Appendix, the author provides a set of example representations of a narrative structure, including the story world, the story, the discourse, and the expression. It is based on a simplified fictional version of the Olympic Games presented in Akimoto (2017).

BASIC CONCEPT OF THE NARRATIVE AGENT

In this section, the architecture and the basic concept of the narrative ability will be described. Figure 3 shows the macroscopic architecture of the narrative ability. It consists of the mental world and the two major mechanisms of the reception and generation of narratives or physical events. The function of

Figure 1. Three structural dimensions of a narrative
Source: Akimoto (2017).

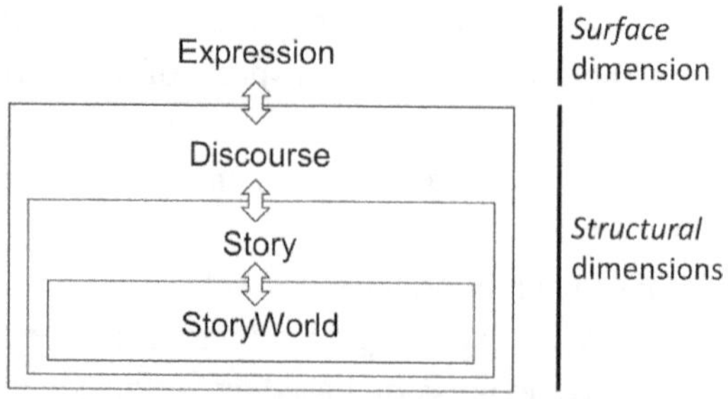

Figure 2. Diagram of the hierarchical graph model
Source: Akimoto (2017).

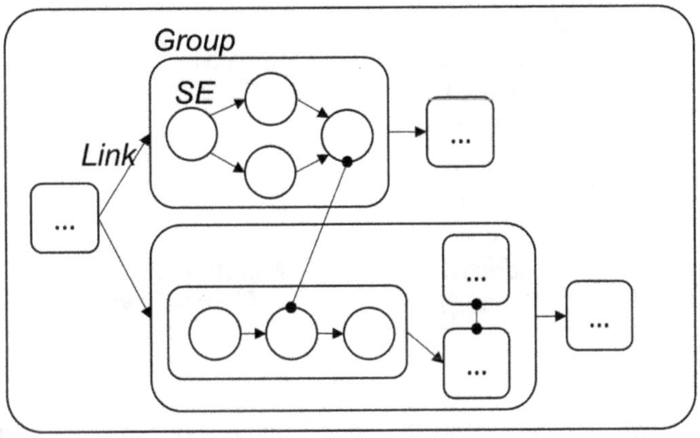

Table 1. Components of a story world structure

Entity (SE)	An individual existence; for example, a human, an object, and a place.
wGroup	An aggregation of entities/wGroups, such as a human group, a spatial unit, and a functional kinship.
wLink	A relation between two nodes; for example, interpersonal relations and spatial relations.

Table 2. Components of a story structure

Event (SE)	An action or a happening.
sGroup	An aggregation of events/sGroups, such as a scene or a broader unit.
tLink	A tLink is a relative temporal relation between two nodes to chronologically organize a story; for example, "before" and "equal."
cLink	A cLink is a causal relation between two nodes.

Table 3. Components of a discourse structure

Discourse Unit or DU (SE)	A minimum segment of a discourse.
dGroup	A broader unit of DUs/dGroups as a semantic or formal segment of a discourse.
dLink	A dLink is a pathway between two nodes with connective logic. The threads of a narrative are composed using dLinks, thus defining the order in which the DUs are expressed.

narrating is included in the generation mechanism. A physical event refers to a change or movement of the physical world based on the perception of the agent. The physical world refers to the external environment in which the agent exists, whereas the mental world is inside the agent. For a virtual agent, the virtual world is viewed as the physical world. The type of the embodiment or hardware configuration the agent has is outside the scope of the study.

Figure 3. The macroscopic architecture of a narrative ability

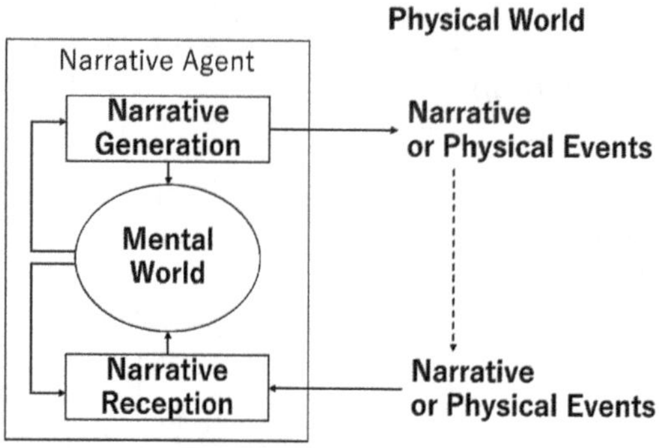

The reception mechanism interprets a narrative or a sequence of physical events in the form of a narrative. It results in a change in or a formation of the mental world. The generation mechanism includes both the functions of the internal construction of the mental world and those of the narrating process. The act of narrating is modeled as the composition of a narrative that expresses a story in the mental world. Moreover, the mental world is the foundational knowledge for the receptive and the generative narrative processing.

The following two subsections describe key notions of the narrative ability.

Narrative-Based Reception and Generation of Physical Events

The reception of physical events refers to an interpretative construction of a story from the perceived events. This thought is based on an assumption that the interpretation of physical events involves a similar cognitive process with the reception of a narrative like a novel or a film, whereas a narrative is primarily composed of a sign system. For example, while reading a novel, readers construct a story inside their minds by interpreting the sentences. In the case of a film as well, an individual constructs a story as the interpretation of moving images and sounds. In a similar manner, a human symbolizes and integrates perceived physical events into the form of a story. Here, the interpretations of similar sequences of physical events are partially different from each other. This cognitive mechanism will be discussed in further detail in the following sections.

On the other hand, the generation of physical events is similar to the construction of a plan for the future based on a goal, schema, or other thought styles. In the narrative agent, this process is viewed as the performance of a story that has been constructed in the mental world. It may include the online reconstruction of the performing story. The result of the acts is reflected in a story of past experience. A difference or conflict between a plan and the result, e.g., a failure of a plan and a deviation from a script, will be a key factor in forming a meaningful story and narrative. An example story involving such a conflict is the following: "A few days ago, I walked into a famous book store to look for an interesting book. But I immediately left the store because a member of the store staff forced me to sing a song loudly."

Narrative Communication

From a communicative perspective, sending and receiving a narrative between agents corresponds to the generation and the interpretation of a narrative, respectively. In this context, the narrative generation (i.e., narrating) is formulated as a narrative discourse generation based on a story remembered from the mental world. On the other hand, the narrative interpretation is formulated as the construction of a story into the mental world. The above idea is illustrated by using a simple framework of communication (Figure 4). A narrative serves as the vehicle for distributing a story that has no materiality. Essentially, the interpretation of a narrative involves multiplicity, i.e., the story that has been composed as an interpretation of the narrative will partially differ from one recipient to another.

MENTAL WORLD

In this section, the representational structure of the mental world will be presented.

Basic Structure

In this study, it was assumed that a mental world is formed as a complex network of various types of mental objects.

Classification of the Mental Object

A mental object is the basic element of the mental world. It is classified into four subclasses, which fall under two major divisions of mental objects, namely, the concrete and the abstract (Figure 5).

A concrete mental object represents a unique object that includes the following two subclasses.

- **Mental Image:** A verbal or visual image corresponding to a story in the mental world.
- **Story:** A unit of temporally and semantically organized events, which forms a cognitively manipulatable fragment of the world.

Figure 4. Simple diagram of the narrative communication

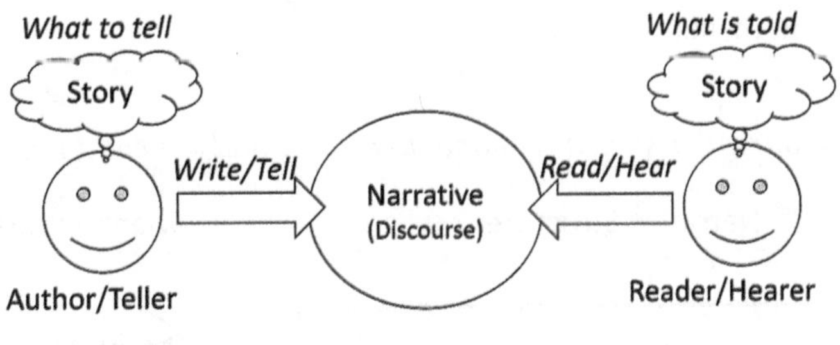

Figure 5. Basic classification of mental objects

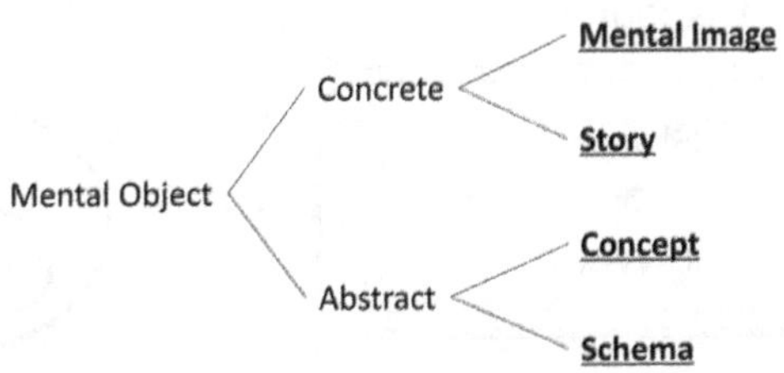

A mental image is internally formed while generating a narrative or while interpreting a narrative or physical event. The relationship between a mental image and a story is similar to the one between the content and the expression planes of a narrative. Hence, the aforementioned multidimensional structure of a narrative (Akimoto, 2017) is translated to the representations of a story and a mental image in the mental world, as illustrated in Figure 6. In particular, the representational structure of a story that involves a story world in the narrative structure model is applied to a story in the mental world model. Expression and discourse are a set in the narrative structure model, which is applied to the representation of a mental image in the mental world model.

An abstract mental object represents conceptual or structural knowledge. It has no direct correspondence to a unique object. The following two subclasses are included in this type:

- **Concept:** A primitive element that constructs the meanings of objects and the events in stories.
- **Schema:** A schema is a structured composition of two or more concepts or (sub-) schemata. The schemata underpin the structuring of stories and mental images. In addition, a schema itself has a compositional meaning.

Organization of Mental Objects

Mental objects are organized into a network structure in the form of a weighted graph. More specifically, an edge represents the strength of the relatedness between two mental objects. Figure 7 shows the overall organization of a mental world. According to the aforementioned classification of mental objects, the mental world is divided into the concrete and abstract layers. The concrete layer consists of two sub-areas for mental images and stories, and the abstract layer consists of two sub-areas for concepts and schemata. The basic role of the abstract layer is to underpin the conceptual and the structural construction and organization of the concrete mental objects.

The basic structure of each subarea is explained below:

- **Area of Concepts:** This area is similar to a semantic network of concepts. More specifically, each edge represents a semantic relation. Moreover, concepts are connected to relevant elements in schemata, stories, and mental images.

Figure 6. Translating the narrative structure model to a story and a mental image in the mental world

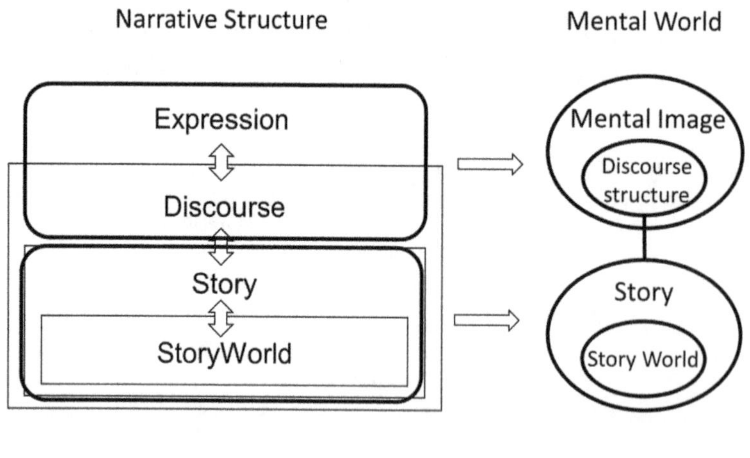

Figure 7. An overall mental world structure

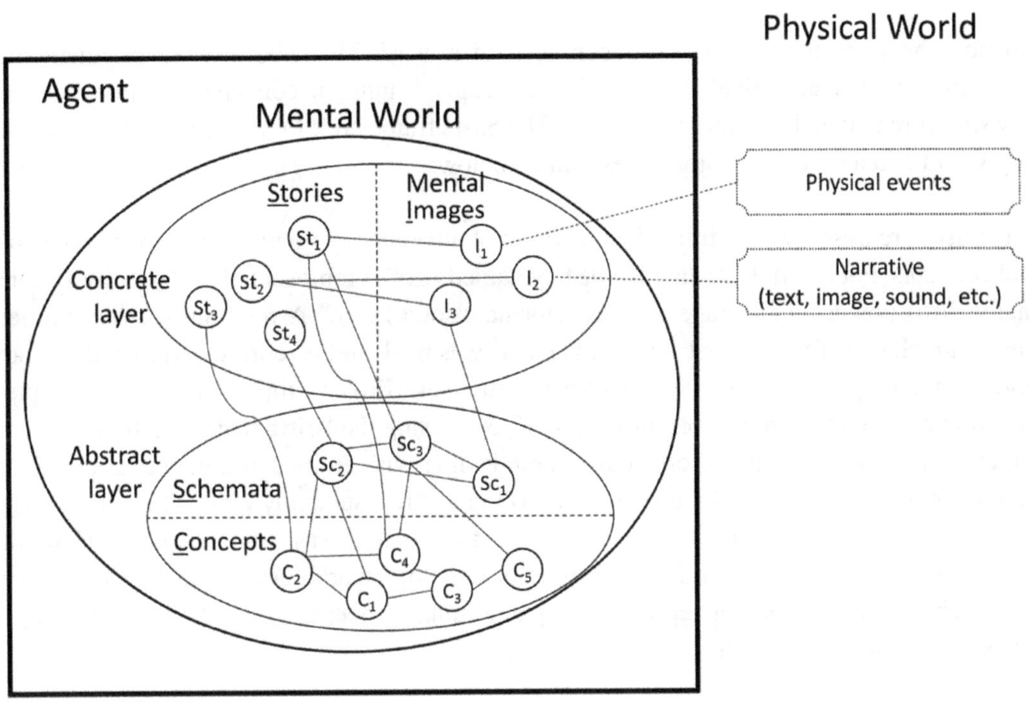

- **Area of Schemata:** Schemata are mutually connected based on their relatedness and semantic relation. This area is similar to a semantic network as well. Additionally, schemata are connected to relevant elements in schemata, stories, and mental images.
- **Area of Stories:** There is no direct connection among stories. Stories are organized based on the connections to the abstract mental objects, which provide high-level meanings and structures to stories. In other words, mutual relations among stories, e.g., the similarity and the derived relations among stories, are formed via abstract mental objects. In addition, each story is connected to zero or more mental images.
- **Area of Mental Images:** There is no direct connection among mental images. A mental image has connections to zero or more stories. In addition, the discourse structure accompanying a mental image is connected to schemata or concepts.

In the following subsections, the structure of the mental world will be presented from several perspectives. First, the basic classification of concepts will be defined. Second, the notion and role of the schemata will be described. Third, the relationship among the physical world (or physical events), mental images, and stories will be explained. Fourth, the structure of time, an essential aspect of the organization of stories in the mental world, will be modeled. Finally, a preliminary consideration on the dynamic aspect of the mental world will be presented.

Classification of Concepts

In the mental world, concepts are divided into two categories: linguistic and ontological concepts.

Linguistic Concepts

A linguistic concept corresponds to the meaning(s) of a word. The subclasses of linguistic concepts include nominal, verbal, adjectival, and adverbial concepts. Linguistic concepts are atomic constituents of a story structure that includes the story world. The basic framework for the representation of an entity in a story world and an event in a story is explained below:

- An entity is represented in a frame format (a set of attributes) with nominal, adjectival, and adverbial concepts. For example, "a handsome boy named Jiro" is represented as: "((entity-type human) (name Jiro) (gender male) (age 11) (exterior handsome) ...)." A relation to other entities is an important element for the construction of an entity as well, and is represented by links to other entities. For example, the semantic structure described as "Jiro's birthplace is Kyoto" is represented by a link between the entities of "Jiro" and "Kyoto" using the "birthplace" relation.
- An event is represented based on a case frame format with entities and verbal, nominal, and adverbial concepts. For example, an event described as "Jiro suddenly kicked his mother, Hanako" is represented as "(Kick (adverb suddenly) (agent Jiro) (counter-agent Hanako))." Here, the case values "Jiro" and "Hanako" refer to entities in the story world. An abstract or non-entity concept such as "blue" (color) is represented by a nominal concept, e.g., "(Paint (agent Jiro) (object House) (in [complement] blue))."

Ontological Concepts

An ontological concept represents an identical entity over multiple stories in a mental world. In many cases, an identical entity is referred to by a proper name, such as "Mt. Fuji," and "Jiro Suzuki." The author provides an example scenario to explain the notion of the ontological concept. In the mental world of an agent named K, K oneself appears in many stories of one's past experiences (e.g., episodes of "climbing Mt. Fuji" and "playing tennis with Jiro"). In each of these stories, K is separately stored as a partially different entity in attributes such as "age," "hairstyle," and "body shape." However, K should know that these different entities of K are the same entity, the self. This identification is underpinned by the connection to the ontological concept "K" or "self." Thus, on the one hand, the concrete knowledge on entities is separately contained in each story; on the other hand, ontological concepts serve as pointers to determine the sameness of entities over different stories.

The basic subclasses of ontological concepts are listed below:

- **Self:** The agent oneself.
- **Other:** A human or an artificial agent other than the self.
- **Time:** A conceptualized time in a mental world. This is an essential element of the mental world as the basis of the temporal organization of stories. A model of time structure in the mental world will be presented later.
- **Space:** A place in which an agent can exist and act.
- **Natural Thing:** This type includes animals, plants, and other natural objects.
- **Artifact:** This type includes instruments, machines, art works, narratives, and other objects made by humans or agents.

Schema of Narratives

In a broad sense, a schema refers to a structured knowledge or a framework of thinking. Various types of schematic knowledge have been proposed and used in studies of computational and cognitive models of both generative and interpretive narrative processing. For example, the script theory (Schank & Abelson, 1977) is applied to several narrative generation and interpretation programs (Schank & the Yale A.I. Project, 1975; McIntyre & Lapata, 2009). The concept of story grammar (Rumelhart, 1975), a grammatical knowledge that frames the development of narrative sentences, is used as the basis of the cognitive and computational processing of narratives (Thorndyke, 1977; Pemberton, 1989; Lang, 1999; Bringsjord & Ferrucci, 1999; Imabuchi & Ogata, 2012). A MOP in the dynamic memory model of Schank (1982), which provides a high-level structure of stories, is viewed as a type of schematic knowledge as well.

Based on the aforementioned background, this study considers a schema as constructive knowledge for the generative and interpretive processing of a story, a mental image, a narrative, and a physical event. A schema provides a composite structure or a pattern of organizing concepts, whereas a concept is an atomic semantic knowledge. A schema is formed through a generalization or abstraction of one or more concrete narrative structures. Hence, although the knowledge representation of a schema has not yet been modeled, a schema will be represented as a structure that is analogous to the hierarchical-graph-based representation of a narrative structure (see "STRUCTURE OF THE NARRATIVE"). Namely, a schema is organized based on hierarchical grouping and network-like linkage of concepts.

Relationship Among the Physical World, Mental Images, and Stories

Next, the author describes the notion of the concrete mental objects. As previously described, in the mental world of an agent, perceived physical events are represented and memorized in the forms of stories and mental images. To clarify this notion, the author describes the relationship among the physical world, mental images, and stories according to an example scenario illustrated in Figure 8. This example assumes a physical world situation that is linguistically expressed as: "An agent is in a park in which many children, including Saburo, are moving. Saburo is a human partner of the agent. The agent is seeing this scene." The cognitive processes of constructing mental images and stories in this situation are explained below.

1. **Visual Mental Image:** The agent constructs a visual mental image focusing on the motion of Saburo.
2. **Story:** The agent constructs a story based on an interpretation of that image. For example, when the agent saw a sequence of movements that is linguistically expressed as "Saburo was messing around with another child named Goro, and then Saburo started to cry," there exist several potential interpretations, such as "while Saburo was playing with Goro, Saburo suddenly started to cry" and "Saburo fought with Goro, and lost." These different stories may exist simultaneously in the mental world and may be reconstructed when the agent hears the reason why Saburo was crying (e.g., "Saburo got stung by a bee when he was playing with Goro").
3. **Story World:** The constructed story is accompanied by the story world that consists of only the relevant information around the story. For example, in the story presented above, the information about places other than the park and children other than Saburo and Goro will be eliminated from the story world.

Figure 8. Construction of the mental images and stories

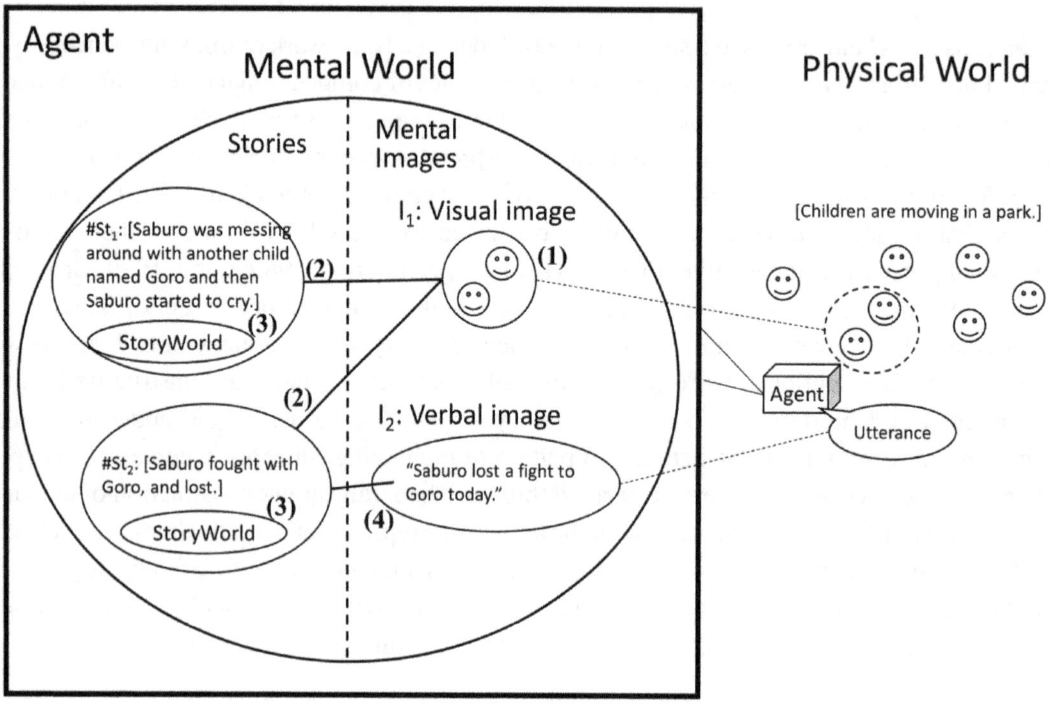

4. **Verbal Mental Image:** When the agent reports the story to Saburo's mother, a verbal mental image for communicating the story is composed in the form of sentences (e.g., "Saburo lost a battle to Goro today."). It is then provided as output, as an utterance.

Although the above example simulated a case of experience-based processes, stories and mental images can be composed from imagination and a narrative interpretation as well.

Time Structure of the Mental World

Time is an essential aspect of the memory (Tulving, 1983; Sato, Ochi, & Shimojima, 2008). In addition, time is a traditional philosophical question and the close relationship between (mental) time and the narrative has been pondered by philosophers, e.g., Ricoeur (1983–1985), Omori (1996), and Nobuhara (2017). In this study, the author postulates that the mental structure of time is formed as the temporal organization of stories. Time as a subclass of an ontological concept serves as the basis of the temporal organization of stories. In considering the time structure, the author distinguishes the following three modes of temporal organization:

- Anteroposterior relation between events.
- Linguistically conceptualized index that corresponds to a specific time segment.
- Artificial time units, including year, month, day, hour, minute, and second.

The anteroposterior relation between events is a fundamental element, particularly for the organization of the internal structure of a story. It corresponds to tLink in the narrative structure model of Akimoto (2017) (see Table 2). The notion of tLink is rooted in the classification of temporal relations between events that has been proposed by Allen (1984). On the other hand, indices for the temporal position of each story (i.e., "when") seem important in the organization of many stories and reasonable for reminding stories. Thus, the author assumes that the temporal organization of stories is primarily underpinned by conceptualized indices that correspond to time segments. In addition, artificial time units are important for the time orientation of such indices. Based on the above thought, the author introduces the following two conceptual elements for the time structure.

- **Time Segment:** A linguistically conceptualized index that corresponds to a specific time segment, e.g., "high school years," "July 1999," "last summer," "today," "now," and "near future."
- **Time Axis:** The cognitive tool for recognizing the chronological time based on the artificial time units including year, month, day, hour, minute, and second.

(This time-structure model has been partially inspired by the philosophical time theory by Omori (1996).)

Figure 9 illustrates the time structure of the mental world based on the above elements. A story is connected to a time segment. A time segment is anchored on a specific range on the time axis. For example, in Figure 9, $story_a$ is linked to the time segment "high-school years." This time segment is anchored to [1996–1999] on the time axis. A time unit can also be used in the name of a time segment (e.g., "1999s"). Time segments are hierarchically organized by the whole-part relationship. In Figure 9, for example, "first summer holiday" is positioned as part of "high school years." Time segments that are

Figure 9. Time structure of the mental world

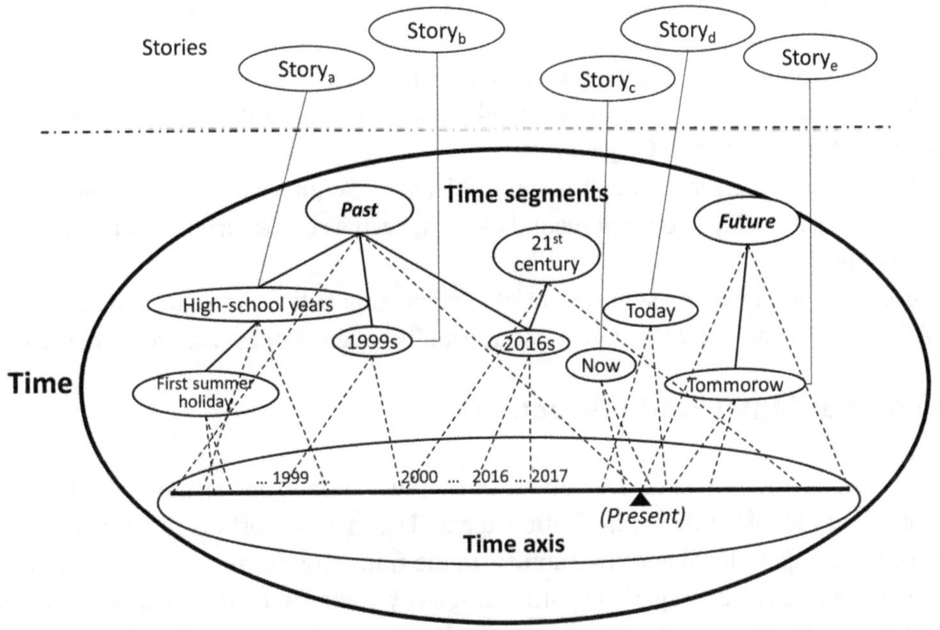

recognized as past and future are positioned under the time segments "past" and "future," respectively. A time segment involving the present, such as "now" and "today," is neither "past" nor "future." In addition, a fictional story may be connected to a specific time segment as a setting of time, e.g., "modern age," "primitive age," and "nineteenth century."

The time structure helps the agent remember a story. For example, if the agent were asked by a human to tell an episode from "last summer," the agent will be reminded of one of the stories connected to the time segment "last summer." Even if such time segment does not exist, the agent may be able to retrieve an alternative time segment by referring to [July–August, 2016] on the time axis.

It should be noted that past and future stories are essentially changeable objects, which are reconstructed interpretatively or imaginatively from the present point of view. For example, a boy has a dream to become a fictional hero, such as "Ultraman;" such a fantastic dream will change to a more realistic vision when he becomes an adult. In addition, a memory of a childhood experience changes over time, including the memory being forgotten.

Formation of the Mental World

In this study, it is assumed that the mental world is essentially a dynamic knowledge system that is formed through various experiences in the "life" of an agent. Although the author has no clear idea for the development of such a dynamic system yet, the formation process of a mental world will be modeled as bottom-up and distributed activities of various formational actions of the mental objects. These actions are driven by the generation and reception mechanisms. Several conceivable formational actions are listed below.

- **Formation of a Mental Object:**
  - Story formation by narrative interpretation, physical event interpretation, one's imagination, and reconstruction of an existing story.
  - Mental image formation by narrative perception, physical event perception, and internal generation based on a story.
  - Schema formation by structural generalization of stories or mental images.
  - Concept formation by semantic generalization of stories or the partial structures.
- **Connection Among Mental Objects:**
  - Making a connection between mental objects or adding weight to a connection based on various relationships between mental objects, such as co-occurrence, succession, similarity, and opposition.
  - Disconnection or decreasing weight of a connection between mental objects.
  - Adding a semantic relation into a connection between concepts and/or schemata.

Summary of the Mental World Structure

In this section, the author constructed a holistic conceptual framework of the mental world, the representation of the world inside the "mind" of an agent. The mental world is the central element of the architecture of the computational narrative ability. In the framework of the mental world, the world for an agent is represented as an aggregation of stories. A story contains the information of concrete events and things. These stories are semantically and temporally organized based on the relationships to abstract mental objects including concepts and schemata. In addition, the correspondence between a story and the physical world is intermediated by the mental images.

NARRATING

In the previous section, the author described the representational structure and the basic concepts of the mental world. In this section, the author addresses the formulation of narrating, i.e., the act of expressing a story in the mental world. This mechanism is the second essential element of the narrative ability.

Situations and Functions of Narrating

Acts of narrating can be set in various situations. The author classifies the situations of narrating from the perspective of communication structure.

- **Figure 10(a):** Unidirectional or bidirectional communications with one or a few humans/agents, e.g., mail, dialogue, and chat.
- **Figure 10(b):** Unidirectional or bidirectional communications with several and unspecified humans/agents, e.g., broadcasting, social networking service, blog, and microblog.
- **Figure 10(c):** Solo narrating, such as a monologue, a diary, and the process of producing a work (e.g., novel, film scenario, and comic).

In addition, acts of narrating have various functions across the aforementioned situations. Four main functions are listed below.

- **Distribution of Stories:** A narrative is a vehicle for distributing stories among humans. Stories, such as personal daily experiences and socially significant events, will provide valuable information to humans and artificial agents that live in human societies.
- **Self-Expression:** Essentially, a narrative reflects the world-view of the teller. In this sense, narrating is a type of self-expression.
- **Reconstruction of Stories:** Narrating will be a process of reconstructing a story in the mental world as well. In cases of humans, for example, a human concretizes a dim memory into a clear story through narrating it and recomposes his/her past life stories through narrating them.

Figure 10. Situations of narrating from the perspective of communication structure

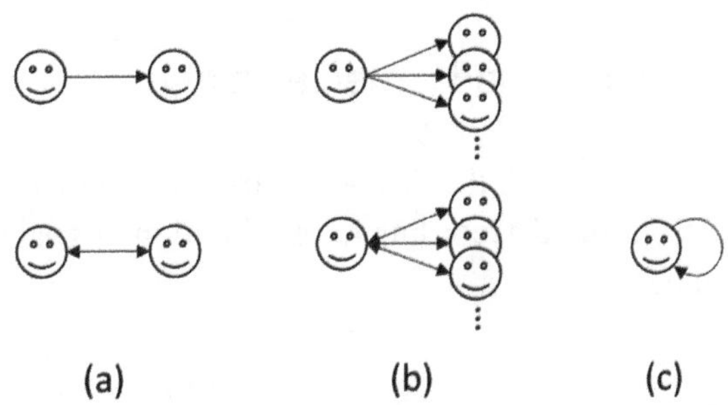

- **Creative Activity:** The creation of a narrative work is an aspect of narrating as well. This type of activity will play a significant role in the development of richer mental worlds for both the creator and the recipients.

Mechanism of Narrating

The cognitive mechanism of narrating is modeled as a type of narrative discourse generation. This process is similar to the task of generating a discourse structure and sentences in previous computational models of narrative generation, e.g., the discourse and the expression generation phases in the integrated narrative generation system of Ogata (2016) and the narrator module in the interactive fiction system of Montfort (2007). The architecture of narrative memory proposed by León (2016) positions the production of an episodic narrative as a type of narrative discourse generation.

However, the primary feature of this study is to model the mechanism of narrating in connection to the proposed mental world model. The mechanism consists of two major processes: 1) remembering a story in the mental world and 2) composing a discourse structure and mental image to express the story.

The Remembering of a Story

In this process, a story to be told is recalled in the mental world. Which story is required and the manner of remembering it differ depending on the situation and the context of the narrating. For example, in a dialogue with a human, when the agent is asked by the human to talk about a childhood episode, the agent should be reminded of a story relevant to one's childhood experiences. In this case, the time segment referred to as "childhood" in the mental world will be used for the remembering of an appropriate story. On the other hand, when the agent wants to take an overseas trip, stories of one's or others' past experiences of overseas trips (e.g., good experiences and failures in foreign countries) will be helpful in planning the trip well.

However, this study provides a basic model for the remembrance of a story. The basic idea is to position abstract mental objects (i.e., concepts and schemata) as the basis of the remembering of an appropriate story. The process of remembering is modeled on the activation of mental objects and the propagation of the activation level along the connections among mental objects. In a mental world, each mental object always has an activation level. These activation levels are changed by external or internal stimuli. External stimuli include a narrative being currently received, perceiving physical events, a story or a topic questioned by others in a dialogic situation, etc. Mental objects relevant to such stimuli are activated. Internal stimuli include the propagation of activation levels from other mental objects. Overall, the activation levels of abstract mental objects are propagated to stories, and an agent will be reminded of a story with a high activation level.

Composing a Discourse Structure and a Mental Image

This process generates a mental image with the discourse structure from a remembered story. The manner of telling a story should be controlled according to the situation or goal of the narrating, as a human tells an episode in various manners.

As mentioned in the "BACKGROUND" section, Genette (1980) presented the basic aspects in the structural variation of narrative discourses. This theory has been applied to the computational modeling of narrative discourse generation (e.g., Montfort, 2007; Ogata, 2016). Such computational models can be adopted in the mechanism of narrating. According to the categories of Genette, the present author presents several example techniques for creating a structural variation in the narration of a story.

- **Temporal Order:** The agent changes the order of recounting events in a story. For example, the agent starts a narrative from the tail end of the story for a rhetorical purpose.
- **Hiding:** The agent omits events in a story. For example, the agent omits events that are uncomfortable to talk about.
- **Summary and Stretch:** The agent controls the detail level of the narrated story for efficient communication.
- **Commentary and Description:** The agent describes events, as well as commentaries or descriptions of humans, places, or other entities in a story. For example, the agent first explains the key persons in a story to facilitate the reader in understanding the story.
- **First-Person:** In agent's narratives, the agent oneself is designated as the first-person.

FUTURE RESEARCH DIRECTIONS

This chapter presented an overview of a computational narrative ability model for a narrative agent. Because this study involves several difficult issues, in the future, the proposed model will be divided into several sub-issues corresponding to each subsection in the preceding two sections. More specifically, the priority of the present author is to concretize the representational structure of the mental world.

For example, modeling the detailed structure of the semantic and temporal organization of stories in a mental world will be a major subject. Psychological studies on the episodic or autobiographical memory (Tulving, 1983; Sato, Ochi, & Shimojima, 2008) will provide a scientific basis for modeling the organizational structure of stories. Another crucial issue is to develop a combined model of the representation, usage, and formation of schemata for the basis of structural manipulation of a narrative.

In addition, although the dynamic nature of the mental world through the "life" of a narrative agent was not extensively discussed in the chapter, modeling its mechanism, i.e., the dynamic formations and changes of the mental objects and the organization thereof, is an even more challenging issue.

CONCLUSION

In this chapter, the author developed the starting point for a computational and constructive approach to intelligence by focusing on the generality of the abilities to manipulate narratives in human intelligence. The author addressed an architectural and conceptual formulation of the narrative ability of an artificial agent. The basic concepts of the two essential elements of the narrative ability, i.e., the mental world constructed from stories and the mechanism of narrating as the act of expressing part of the mental world, were presented.

The main contributions of this chapter are summarized below.

- The author proposed a novel concept for developing agent intelligence, i.e., the architecture of an AI system centered on the story-based world representation.
- The holistic structure of the system was systematically described. Several elemental issues that have a close relationship to essential AI problems were organized into the proposed architecture.

ACKNOWLEDGMENT

This research was supported by The Telecommunications Advancement Foundation (Japan).

REFERENCES

Akimoto, T. (2016). Exploratory approach to the computational modeling of narrative ability for artificial intelligence. *International Journal of Knowledge Engineering*, *2*(4), 170–176. doi:10.18178/ijke.2016.2.4.074

Akimoto, T. (2017). Computational modeling of narrative structure: A hierarchical graph model for multidimensional narrative structure. *International Journal of Computational Linguistics Research*, *8*(3), 92–108.

Akimoto, T., & Ogata, T. (2015). Experimental development of a focalization mechanism in an integrated narrative generation system. *Journal of Artificial Intelligence and Soft Computing Research*, *5*(3), 177–188. doi:10.1515/jaiscr-2015-0027

Allen, J. F. (1984). Towards a general theory of action and time. *Artificial Intelligence*, *23*(2), 123–154. doi:10.1016/0004-3702(84)90008-0

Anderson, T. S. (2015). From episodic memory to narrative in a cognitive architecture. In *Proceedings of 6th Workshop on Computational Models of Narrative* (pp. 2-11). Academic Press.

Bae, B. C., Cheong, Y. G., & Young, M. R. (2011). Automated story generation with multiple internal focalization. In *Proceedings of 2011 IEEE Conference on Computational Intelligence and Games* (pp. 211-218), Seoul, South Korea: IEEE. doi:10.1109/CIG.2011.6032009

Bringsjord, S., & Ferrucci, D. A. (1999). *Artificial intelligence and literary creativity: Inside the mind of BRUTUS, a storytelling machine*. Mahwah, NJ: Lawrence Erlbaum.

Chambers, N., & Jurafsky, D. (2010). A database of narrative schemas. In *Proceedings of Seventh International Conference on Language Resources and Evaluation* (pp. 1614-1618). Academic Press.

Chatman, S. (1978). *Story and discourse: Narrative structure in fiction and film*. Ithaca, NY: Cornell University Press.

Genette, G. (1980). *Narrative discourse: An essay in method* (J. E. Lewin, Trans.). Ithaca, NY: Cornell University Press. (Original work published 1972)

Gervás, P. (2009). Computational approaches to storytelling and creativity. *AI Magazine*, *30*(3), 49–62. doi:10.1609/aimag.v30i3.2250

Gervás, P. (2015). Computational drafting of plot structures for Russian folk tales. *Cognitive Computation*. doi:10.1007/s12559-015-9338-8 PMID:27642369

Imabuchi, S., & Ogata, T. (2012). A story generation system based on Propp theory: As a mechanism in an integrated narrative generation system. In H. Isahara & K. Kanzaki (Eds.), *Advances in Natural Language Processing: Proceedings of the 8th International Conference on Natural Language Processing (LNAI)* (*vol. 7614*, pp. 312-321). Berlin, Germany: Springer. doi:10.1007/978-3-642-33983-7_31

Laird, J. E. (2012). *The Soar cognitive architecture*. Cambdidge, MA: The MIT Press.

Lang, R. R. (1999). A declarative model for simple narratives. In *Narrative Intelligence: Papers from the 1999 AAAI Fall Symposium* (Technical Report FS-99-01, pp. 134-141). North Falmouth, MA: AAAI.

León, C. (2016). An architecture of narrative memory. *Biologically Inspired Cognitive Architectures*, *16*, 19–33. doi:10.1016/j.bica.2016.04.002

McIntyre, N., & Lapata, M. (2009). Learning to tell tales: A data-driven approach to story generation. In *Proceedings of Joint Conference of the 47th Annual Meeting of the Association for Computational Linguistics and the 4th International Joint Conference on Natural Language Processing of the Asian Federation of Natural Language Processing* (pp. 217-225). Suntec, Singapore: Academic Press. doi:10.3115/1687878.1687910

Meehan, J. R. (1980). *The metanovel: Writing stories by computer*. New York, NY: Garland Publishing.

Montfort, N. (2007). *Generating narrative variation in interactive fiction* (Doctoral dissertation). Available from ProQuest. (AAI3271851)

Mukouyama, K., Shinohara, K., Kanai, A., & Ogata, T. (2002). Rhetorical analysis and automatic editing of the film. In *Proceedings of 17th Congress of the International Association of Empirical Aesthetics* (pp. 571-574). Academic Press.

Nobuhara, Y. (Ed.), *Jikan, jiko, monogatari* [Time, self, and narrative]. Tokyo, Japan: Shunjusha.

Nuxoll, A. M., & Laird, J. E. (2004). A cognitive model of episodic memory integrated with a general cognitive architecture. In *Proceedings of International Conference on Cognitive Modeling* (pp. 220-225). Academic Press.

Nuxoll, A. M., & Laird, J. E. (2007). Extending cognitive architecture with episodic memory. In *Proceedings of the 22nd National Conference on Artificial Intelligence* (pp. 1560-1565). Academic Press.

Ogata, T. (2004b). Toward the consistent simulation of narrative discourse based on narratology. In *Proceedings of the Ninth International Symposium on Artificial Life and Robotics* (*Vol. 2*, pp. 579-584). Oita, Japan: Academic Press.

Ogata, T. (2016). Computational and cognitive approaches to narratology from the perspective of narrative generation. In T. Ogata & T. Akimoto (Eds.), *Computational and cognitive approaches to narratology*. Hershey, PA: IGI Global. doi:10.4018/978-1-5225-0432-0.ch001

Ogata, T., & Terano, T. (1991). Explanation-based narrative generation using semiotic theory. In *Proceedings of Natural Language Processing Pacific Rim Symposium 1991* (pp. 321-328). Academic Press.

Okada, N., & Endo, T. (1992). Story generation based on dynamics of the mind. *Computational Intelligence, 8*(1), 123–160. doi:10.1111/j.1467-8640.1992.tb00341.x

Omori, S. (1996). *Toki ha nagarezu* [Time does not flow]. Tokyo, Japan: Seidosha.

Peinado, F., & Gervás, P. (2005). Creativity issues in plot generation. In *Workshop on Computational Creativity, Working Notes, 19th International Joint Conference on A.I.* (pp. 45-52). Academic Press.

Pemberton, L. (1989). A modular approach to story generation. In *Proceedings of the Fourth Conference on European Chapter of the Association for Computational Linguistics* (pp. 217-224). Academic Press. doi:10.3115/976815.976845

Prince, G. (2003). *A dictionary of narratology* (Revised Ed.). Lincoln, NE: University of Nebraska Press.

Ricoeur, P. (1983–1985). *Temps et récit (Tome I–III)*. Paris, France: Seuil.

Riedl, M. O., & Young, R. M. (2010). Narrative planning: Balancing plot and character. *Journal of Artificial Intelligence Research, 39*, 217–267.

Riesbeck, C. K., & Schank, R. C. (1989). *Inside case-based reasoning*. Mahwah, NJ: Lawrence Erlbaum.

Rumelhart, D. E. (1975). Notes on a schema for stories. In D. G. Bobrow & A. Collins (Eds.), *Representation and understanding: Studies in cognitive science*. Waltham, MA: Academic Press. doi:10.1016/B978-0-12-108550-6.50013-6

Sato, K., Ochi, K., & Shimojima, Y. (2008). *Jidenteki kioku no shinrigaku* [Psychology of autobiographical memory]. Kyoto, Japan: Kitaohji shobo.

Schank, R. C., & The Yale A.I. Project. (1975). *SAM: A story understander*. Research Report #43, Yale University, Department of Computer Science.

Schank, R. C. (1982). *Dynamic memory: A theory of reminding and learning in computers and people*. New York, NY: Cambridge University Press.

Schank, R. C., & Abelson, R. P. (1977). *Scripts, plans, goals, and understanding: An inquiry into human knowledge structures*. Mahwah, NJ: Lawrence Erlbaum.

Singh, P., Barry, B., & Liu, H. (2004). Teaching machines about everyday life. *BT Technology Journal, 22*(4), 227–240. doi:10.1023/B:BTTJ.0000047601.53388.74

Softbank. (n.d.). *Robot*. Retrieved from https://www.softbank.jp/en/robot/

Swanson, R., & Gordon, A. S. (2012). Say Anything: Using textual case-based reasoning to enable open-domain interactive storytelling. *ACM Transactions on Interactive Intelligent Systems, 2*(3), 16. doi:10.1145/2362394.2362398

Szilas, N. (2015). Towards narrative-based knowledge representation in cognitive systems. In *Proceedings of 6th Workshop on Computational Models of Narrative* (pp. 133-141). Academic Press.

Taniguchi, T. (2010). *Komyunikeishon suru robotto wa tsukureruka* [Constructive Approach towards Symbol Emergence System]. Tokyo, Japan: NTT Publishing.

Thorndyke, P. W. (1977). Cognitive structures in comprehension and memory of narrative discourse. *Cognitive Psychology*, *9*(1), 77–110. doi:10.1016/0010-0285(77)90005-6

Tulving, E. (1983). *Elements of episodic memory*. Oxford, UK: Oxford University Press.

Turner, S. R. (1994). *The creative process: A computer model of storytelling and creativity*. Mahwah, NJ: Lawrence Erlbaum.

KEY TERMS AND DEFINITIONS

Concept (Mental Object): The primitive element of constructing the meanings of things and events in stories.

Mental Image (Mental Object): A verbal or visual image corresponding to a story in the mental world.

Mental Object: The basic element of the mental world, which includes a mental image, a story, a concept, and a schema.

Mental World: The representation of the world inside the "mind" of an agent, in contrast to the physical world. It is formed as a complex network of various mental objects, including stories.

Narrating: The act of expressing a story in the mental world in the form of a narrative based on a language or other sign systems.

Narrative Ability: The mental system that manipulates narratives. It includes two essential elements: the mental world and the mechanism of narrating.

Narrative Agent: An artificial agent who has a narrative ability.

Physical World: The external environment an agent exists in. For a virtual agent, the virtual world is viewed as the physical world.

Schema (Mental Object): A structured composition of two or more concepts or (sub-) schemata.

Story (Mental Object): A unit of temporally and semantically organized events. A story forms a cognitively manipulatable fragment of the world.

APPENDIX

Figure 11. An example representation of a simple narrative structure
Source: Adapted from Akimoto (2017).

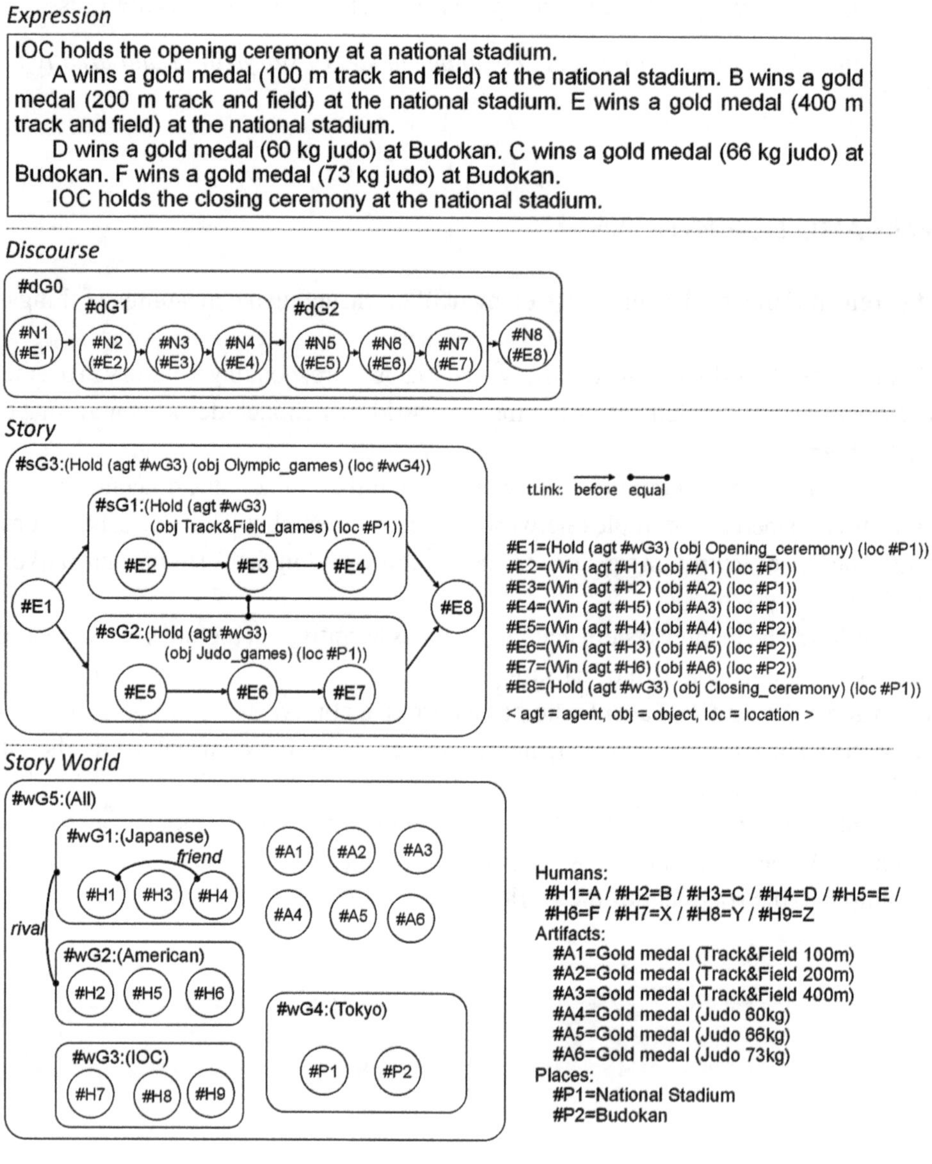

Chapter 8
A Phenomenological Model For Generating the Tasting Description of Japanese Sake

Hiroki Fukushima
Kyushu Women's University, Japan

ABSTRACT

In this chapter, the author proposes a multifaceted representation model for the sensory domain of taste, especially the taste of sake. The author aims to bridge the domain of taste and the domain of words and, on the basis of the findings of the first-person-singular study, proposes that the pictorial description, together with the verbal description, can achieve the aim. As the results of the study, the author finds the difference between the manner of description of the PTG (primary taste group for sake: sweetness, umami, and acidity) and the STG (stimulus taste group: astringency and dryness). The PTG tends to be described in curvy shapes; in contrast, the STG tends to be represented in linear patterns.

INTRODUCTION

The description process (typically by sommeliers) of tastes and odors is widely thought to involve the following assumptions:

1. The wine has some flavors,
2. The taster detects the flavors via olfactory receptors,
3. The taster selects one of the flavors,
4. The taster identifies the exact word for the flavor.

This can be called "a binomial model of the sense and the expressions," which leads to a myth: There would be a "right perception" and a "right expression." However, in actual situations, our perceptual representations of taste or smell are often vague, and a set of verbal expressions is not given. In this paper, we adopt a phenomenological model that claims that the taste of the *sake* does not exist in the

DOI: 10.4018/978-1-5225-4775-4.ch008

Copyright © 2018, IGI Global. Copying or distributing in print or electronic forms without written permission of IGI Global is prohibited.

sake itself: It *appears* or *arises* between *sake* and the subject (taster) as a personal image. In other words, the object (in this case, the taste of *sake* in the real world) cannot exist independently of the subject (the taster). In this paper, the author tries to deal with not the object itself, but the "experienced representation of the object" from a first-person point of view, which highlights "my tasting experiences" as "I taste something." This paper seeks to develop a multi-faceted model for generating tasting representations.

BACKGROUND

The studies of the narrative are expanding toward various neighboring domains. shows the expanding structure of the narratology as "A comprehensive framework for research in narrative generation." In the framework, Ogata classifies the research into four phases; the Narrative generation systems, Interdisciplinary narratology, Narratological approaches to various fields, and Related studies in the broadest sense.

This study is an attempt and an illustration of the analyzation of the multi-faceted narratological description of the sensory information. More specifically, the aim of this study is to show the relationships between the two modes of description – the verbal description and the pictorial description – of the sense of taste. This study would be classified into the "Narratological approaches to various fields" in the Ogata's framework.

Among the inter-disciplinal domain of narratology, one of the most living areas would be the cognitive narratology. A series of cognitive scientific studies by Kanai et al. (Kanai & Kodama, 2010; Kanai & Ogata, 2004a, 2004b) has tried to reveal the relationships among story, non-story, or discourse, especially in films.

The author's study can be lined up in these cognitive narratological studies. Yet, the study presented in this chapter deals with rather lower – sensory level– cognition.

A natural language is generally an audiovisual-dominant symbol system. It categorizes the world into words: Cats are differentiated from dogs, which, in turn, are differentiated from wolves. Cats, dogs, and wolves are grouped together as a category of animals, which is different from fruit, which includes apples and oranges. Thus, a language operates according to the principle of differentiation. The principle works strongly or weakly in different domains because each domain has its intrinsic discriminable power. The discriminability of the sensory perception of taste is considerably weak, and thus, the number of words that name tastes directly is limited to not more than 10 words in the case of Japanese; these are the words for the *five basic tastes*, *astringency*, and *dryness,* plus a few words for complex tastes like *koku* (or '*rich taste*').

It can be said that producing the representations of taste has two difficulties: the lack of discriminability or differentiation and the lack of expressions for the domain of taste. However, the door to the verbal expression of the taste is not completely shut.

Majid and Burenhult (2014) did a study with speakers of Jahai (a language spoken by hunter-gatherers in the Malay Peninsula) and suggested that the long-held assumption that people are bad at naming smells is not universally true. Jahai has a dozen different words to describe smells of different qualities. In a comparative study, Majid and Burenhult found that Jahai speakers were better able to name odors differentially and concisely than their English-speaking counterparts. On the basis of the results, they claim that odors are expressible in language, as long as one "speaks the right language." What is, then, "the right language" to describe the sensory perception of taste?

The ability to verbalize taste is not exclusive to sommeliers and other professionals, but the question is: How do people bridge the gap between the sense of taste and the language they use? In other words, what kind of strategies do they employ to express something hard to verbalize?

When people describe tastes, it is a common strategy to say "taste *like a* banana." This strategy, even used by specialists like sommeliers, suggests that we tend to turn to a different source ("banana" in this case) (Wilson & Stevenson, 2006). Seto et al. (2003) collected a vast amount of expressions used to describe the perception of taste and smell, and showed that the number of expressions describing those perceptions directly is very limited, and that the metaphorical expressions are pervasively used instead.

In studies investigating the relationship between sensory perceptions and linguistic expressions, the notion of metaphor has been used in a broad sense, including similes (e.g., taste like a banana), the onomatopoeias or sound symbolic expressions (e.g., crispy), shapes expressing non-shape targets (e.g., a "round" taste), synesthetic expressions (e.g., smooth taste), or other expressions based on other sensory domains. The important function of metaphors is using the information or knowledge of the other domain (the source domain) for understanding the target domain.

It seems that metaphor-based studies thus far have tended to focus on the relationship between the inter-sensory domains (e.g., the relationship between the olfactory domain and the tactile domain). In this study, the author is interested in a more holistic multi-faceted representation of taste, which combines both verbal and nonverbal representations. The combined representation takes the form of pictures.

MAIN FOCUS OF THE CHAPTER

Taste is not a set of elements. When we taste something, we taste it as a whole. There are some salient characteristics in the taste, and people detect them as the defining features of the taste. When we say "Something is sweet and sour," sweetness and sourness come to us as salient tastes. However, sweetness and sourness do not exhaust the taste we experience. In this paper, the author proposes a multi-faceted model for generating the tasting descriptions of *sake*.

The cognitive process of taste is embedded in the higher cognitive functions. Hence, the model includes not only the sensory domain, but also various other domains such as the verbal domain, the non-verbal domain, the instrumental domain as the extension of the body, and so on (see Figure 1).

In Figure 1, the domains are described separately. Yet, taste is something one experiences as a whole. Thus, one cannot be able to say that one domain is superordinate or subordinate to the other. Neither can one say that domain A includes domain B as a subset. In describing the taste of *sake*, we cannot resort only to sound symbolism characteristics of the auditory domain. The author argues that pictorial descriptions, complemented by verbal descriptions, can embrace the multi-faceted nature of *sake* tasting. A salient tasting feature is easily detected when one drinks a *sake*. For example, acidity may stand out in a certain *sake*. In that case, one may draw a picture with a thorn (or a *thorn* pictorial) along with some verbal explanations. The multi-faceted nature of *sake* tasting assumes that there can be multiple salient features or dots occurring simultaneously when one drinks a *sake*. A *thorn* pictorial is an intuitive representation of the experience of drinking a given *sake*. If the *thorn* representation has a structure, it is not a tree structure, but rather, it is a "semilattice structure" (Alexander, 1966). Alexander (1966) illustrates the difference as in Figure 2.

Figure 1. The multi-faceted model for the tasting description

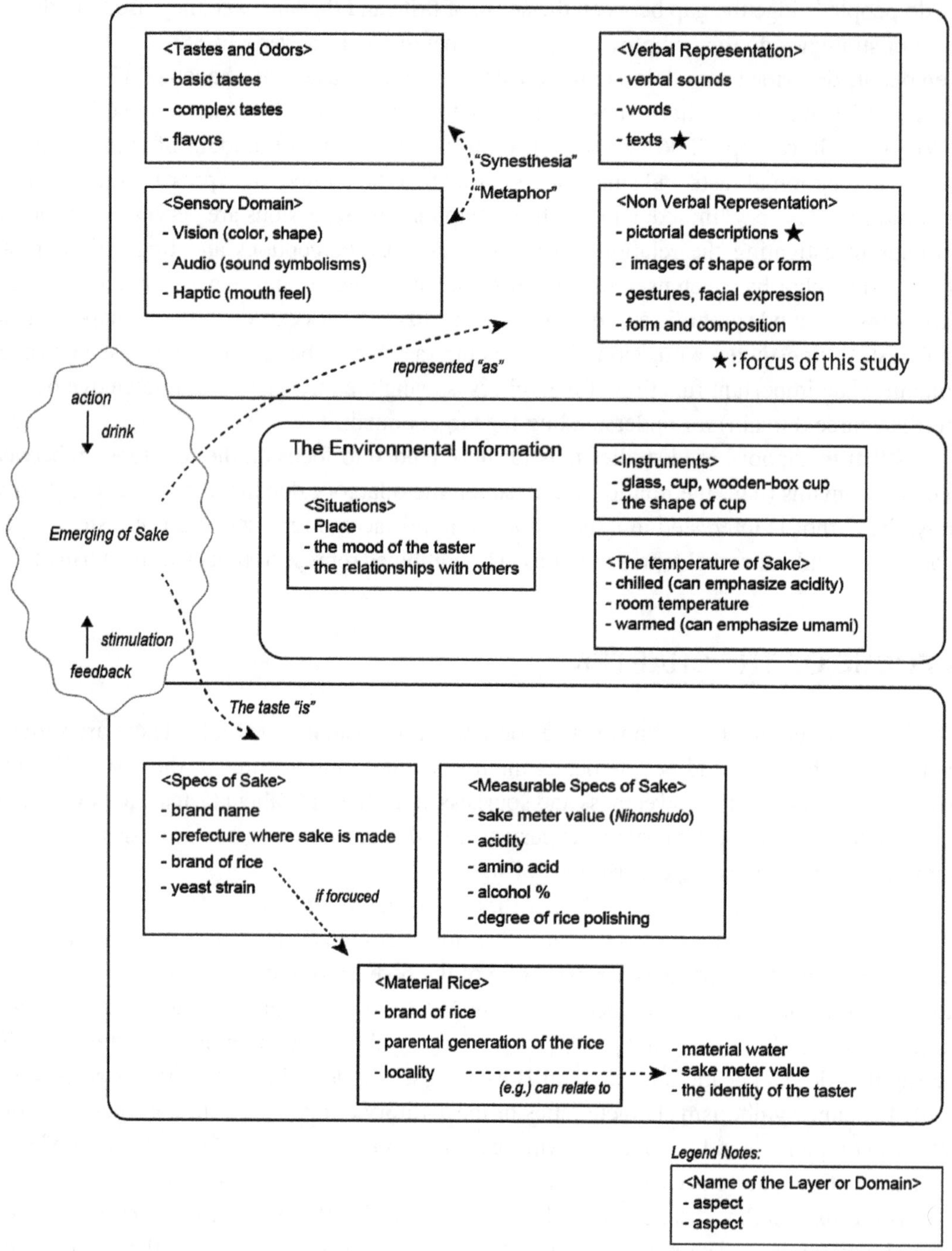

In Figure 2, the one on the left is a semilattice structure, in which there are no a priori links between dots, but there are only *potential possibilities* to link. The relationships *appear, arise or emerge* as the result of the action (i.e., the tasting of a *sake*).

Figure 2. The tree structure and the semilattice structure
Alexander, 1966.

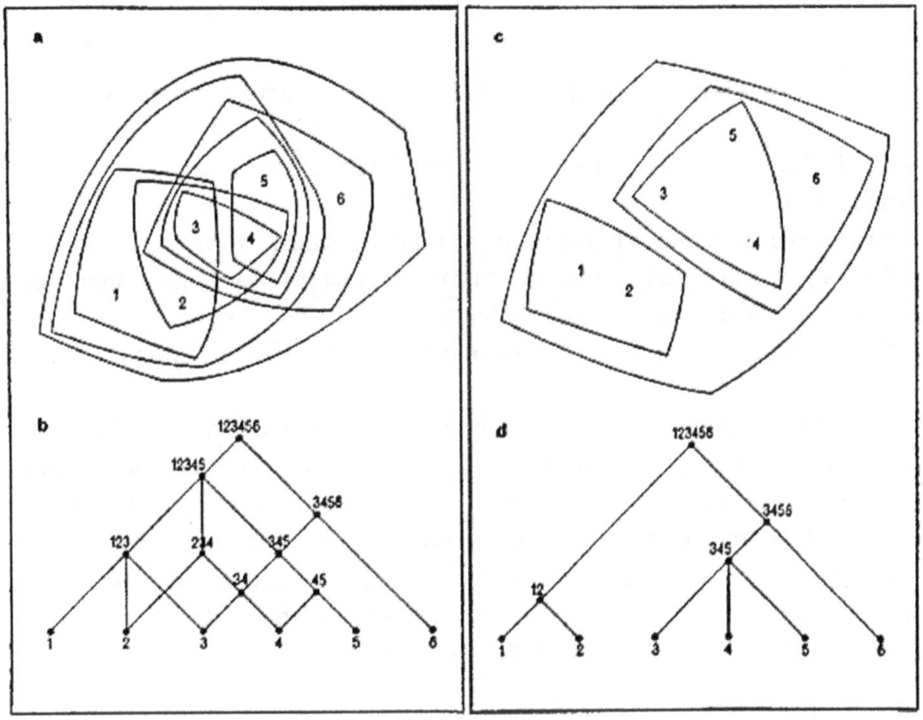

The Pictorial Representations and the Verbal Representations

In this section, the author offers a way of generating the tasting descriptions of Japanese *sake*. In order to capture the multi-faceted nature of tasting, verbal representations alone do not suffice. Our proposal is that the primary way of describing taste should be pictorial representations. The representations dealt with in this study are not objective or static ones that can be measured through sensory techniques. Tasting a *sake* is a subjective experience, and describing the taste should be subjective, accordingly. This is why we call this approach "the first person singular approach." The act of describing the taste of *sake* requires the aggregate of the descriptions of the dynamic process—our sense-making process of every cup of *sake* that changes its face every time we drink.

In the following experimental study, the author himself became the participant or informant, and the analyst of the data produced by the participant. The informant produced a drawing or what we call "pictorial representation" and verbal descriptions every time he drank a *sake* of a different kind. The drawing and the accompanying words (verbal descriptions) together represented the experienced taste of *sake* on the part of the informant. Drawings are not conventionalized codes and may look quite arbitrary to a third person. There are no rules about how to analyze them. In other words, the informant has to become the analyst in order to make sense of the representation produced by the informant. This first-person-singular approach is appropriate when the top-down cognitive process is dominant, and the individual differences in terms of the conditions of tasting (i.e., the capacity of the oral cavity, or the way of moving tongues, etc.) influence the sensation of taste.

Methodology

Procedure

More specifically, the multifaceted descriptions of the taste of *sake* were given in the following steps:

Step 1: To write the basic data [brand name, the date of drinking] of *sake*.
Step 2: To taste a brand.
Step 3-a: To write some verbal description of the taste impressions.
Step 3-b: To draw a pictorial description(s) of the taste impressions (Some notes are added to the drawing to clarify the intended meaning of the drawing).
Step 4: To write additional data (e.g., the degree of confidence of the description).

Figure 3 is an example of the multifaceted description of the perceived taste of a *sake*.

This pictorial description itself is unintelligible to a third person. For one thing, words are given in Japanese. In this paper, the author translates Japanese descriptors (within the pictorial description) into English when needed. Another, more serious, reason is that the drawing(s) are open to interpretation. As shown in the following section, a post-hoc analysis of drawings showed that there were certain elements identifiable in the drawings produced to describe the tastes of different *sakes*. With those elements, the author-analyst is able to minimize the arbitrariness of interpretation.

The Elements of the Pictorial Descriptions

Table 1 shows a summary of the elements of the pictorial descriptions the author-informant produced.

Figure 3. An example of the multifaceted description of the taste of a sake (the brand = Tedorigawa; the date = March 3, 2017)

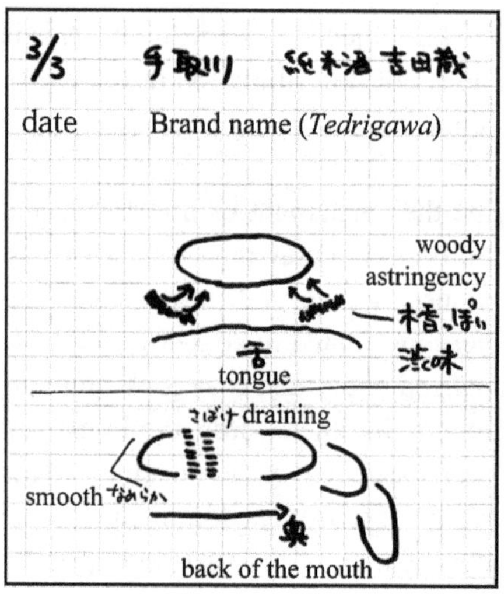

VERBAL DESCRIPTION

Coming in smoothly, but the water drains in the middle and feels even weak.

Getting back the smoothness and the slippy outline toward the finish, then slips into the throat.

Feel woody astringent flavor that spreads in the nose; the astringency lifts the smooth taste on the center of the tongue from both sides of the tongue.

Table 1. The elements of pictorial descriptions

Element	Property	Example
Line	Straight	line segment angle straight arrow
	Curve	wave line free line curved arrow
Shape (2D)		circle oval free liner shape free curve shape solid arrow thorn
Form (3D)		sphere curve form cloud
Pattern		dots lines scribble chevron curve filled in

The descriptions can be generally classified into Line, Shape, Form and Pattern as shown in the right-most column of Table 1. Lines can be either straight or curved, where straight lines include line segment, angle, and straight arrow, and curved lines are classified into wave lines, free curves, and curved arrows.

The classification of shape is for the 2D figures including circle, oval, free liner shape, free curve shape, solid arrow, and thorn shape. For 3D figures, the author set a class of form, which includes sphere, curvy 3D form, and form of cloud. In addition, there are some descriptions as patterns: the pattern with dots, the pattern with lines, the pattern with curves, the pattern with scribbles, the pattern with chevrons, and the pattern filled in by a color.

The Semantic Features of the Pictorial Description

If there is a set of elements in the pictorial descriptions, then what does each element mean? As regards this question, the author found three major types of semantic features:

- Element of taste
- Symbolic description of taste
- Outline of taste

These features basically represent the expressions of the perceived tastes of *sake* in terms of the possible shapes of the mouth. Some semantic features describing additional information (not the taste itself) were also found. Those features are related to:

- Direction
- Axis
- Timeline
- Movement
- Power
- Part of the body
- Indication
- Point of view

Let us illustrate with the drawings of *Tedorigawa* (a brand name of *sake*) in Figure 4. As shown in the figure, we can identify seven elements: shape (oval), line (curved arrow), pattern (scribble), part of the body (line showing the tongue), pattern (pattern with lines), movement (movement to the throat [line]), and axis (front-to-back movement in the mouth [arrow]).

The semantic features that the author offered here would contribute to answering the question of "what is described by an element." For example, the oval shape within the drawing represents the nature of taste, and the scribbles show a taste of "woody astringency."

The Roles of the Pictorial Descriptions and the Verbal Descriptions

In the preceding section, the author proposed a set of elements and semantic features for analyzing the pictorial descriptions. Verbal descriptions are also important indicators of the taste of a *sake*. In this section, as a step toward the analysis of the relationships of the multiple representations, the author analyzes the relationships between the pictorial descriptions and the verbal descriptions. The relationships that the author focus on here address the following question: What is described verbally, and what is described pictorially?

Descriptions of the taste of *sake* can be made a) pictorially and verbally, b) only pictorially, or c) only verbally. Table 2 shows four possible cases of descriptions. A is a case where verbal descriptions are also shown pictorially; there is a correspondence between a verbal descriptor and its pictorial draw-

Figure 4. Example of the elements of the pictorial descriptions (the brand = Tedorigawa)

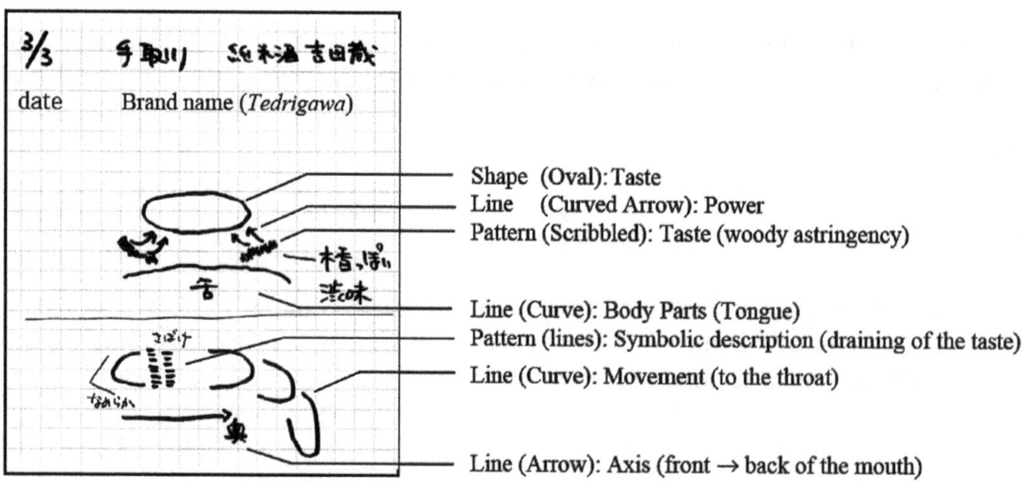

Table 2. The relationships between pictorial description and verbal description

		Verbal Description	
		Described	Not Described
Pictorial Description	Described	A	C
	Not Described	B	D

ing. B is a case where verbal descriptions are not expressed in the pictorial representation given by the informant, while C is a case where only pictorial descriptions are given and there are no corresponding verbal descriptions. D contains neither drawings nor verbal descriptions, and is irrelevant here. In this paper, the author compares A and B.

In order to examine the differences and the characteristics of A and B, the author divided all the verbal descriptions manually into two parts (see Table 3). The dividing process is based on the one-to-one correspondence of a word to an element of the picture. Thus, the extracted sentences are not complete sentences; hence, the "Number of Sentences" of case A and case B are blanked in Table 3.

In this study, the characteristic words of the two cases were determined using the Jaccard coefficient method. The Jaccard coefficient measures the similarity between finite sample sets and is defined as the size of the intersection divided by the size of the union of the sample sets:

Jaccard Coefficient: $(X \cap Y) / (X \cup Y)$
X: The frequency of the word "X"
Y: The frequency of the word "Y"

The Jaccard index takes a value range from 0 to 1 (0% to 100%): The higher percentage, the more similar the two word sets. For data analysis, the author used the KH Coder (Higuchi, 2004) as a coding and calculating tool.

General Tendency

In this section, referring to the Jaccard index, the author examines the general tendency of the characteristic words in case A and case B. In this study, the words that take over 0.075 of Jaccard index are regarded as characteristic words. Table 4 and Table 5 list the characteristic words in case A and case B, respectively.

Table 3. The verbal descriptions in cases A and B

	All Data	Case A	Case B
Tokens	5,551	2,558	2,918
Types	1,053	597	745
Number of Sentences	125	-	-
Number of Brands of *Sake*	58	58	58
Average Frequency	2.80	2.33	2.13
Frequency SD	5.87	4.11	3.78

Table 4. The characteristic words in (case A)

	Words (Japanese)	PoS	Total Freq.	Freq. in (A)	Jaccard Index
1	tongue (shita)	noun	55	37	0.446
2	spread (hirogaru)	verb	18	15	0.221
3	last (saigo)	noun	24	15	0.203
4	back (oku)	noun	21	14	0.194
5	surface (hyomen)	noun	13	12	0.171
6	mouth (kuchi)	noun	17	12	0.157
7	center (chushin)	noun	16	11	0.134
8	tip of tongue (shitasaki)	noun	11	9	0.129
9	Alcohol (arukooru)	noun	14	9	0.123
10	Nose (hana)	noun	17	9	0.119
11	come in (hairu)	noun	10	8	0.119
12	astringency (shibumi)	noun	10	8	0.114
13	throat (nodo)	noun	13	8	0.113
14	acid (san)	noun	14	8	0.113
15	astringent (shibu)	noun	14	8	0.108
16	entrance of the throat (nodomoto)	noun	7	7	0.105
17	shape, form (katachi)	noun	9	7	0.105
18	space (kuukan)	noun	7	6	0.091
19	expand (nobiru)	verb	8	6	0.090
20	mid point (man-naka)	noun	6	5	0.076
21	round (marui)	adj	6	5	0.076
22	wave (yureru)	verb	6	5	0.076
23	hard (katai)	adj	6	5	0.076
24	keep (tamotsu)	verb	6	5	0.076
25	go up (agaru)	verb	6	5	0.076

Note.[1]

In these tables, words are classified according to their parts of speech: nouns, verbs, and adjectives. In the below, the author takes a closer look at the function of nouns and verbs.

Nouns for Taste

A main function of nouns in the tasting descriptions can be thought as pointing out the element of the tastes of a *sake*. Beside the verbal descriptions, the element of taste is described in the pictorial descriptions. A comparison of Table 4 and Table 5 shows that there are clear differences between the high frequency words in the two cases. The following is the list of the salient words for taste drawn from Table 4 and Table 5.

Table 5. The characteristic words in (case B)

	Words	PoS	Total Freq.	Freq. in (B)	Jaccard Index
1	taste (aji)	noun	56	29	0.341
2	feel (kanjiru)	verb	29	16	0.225
3	acidity (san)	noun	24	13	0.188
4	umami (umami)	noun	25	13	0.186
5	feeling (kanji)	noun	11	10	0.170
6	swallow (nomikomu)	verb	11	9	0.150
7	sweetness (amami)	noun	17	9	0.136
8	think (omou)	verb	9	8	0.136
9	stay (nokoru)	verb	8	7	0.119
10	outline (rinkaku)	noun	14	7	0.108
11	drink (nomu)	verb	6	6	0.103
12	feeling (inshou)	noun	7	6	0.102
13	sake (sake)	noun	8	6	0.100
14	clean (kirei)	adj	8	6	0.100
15	sweet (amai)	adj	8	6	0.100
16	rice (kome)	noun	8	6	0.100
17	little (sukoshi)	adv	9	6	0.098
18	umamiful (umai)	adj	10	6	0.097
19	fizzy (happou)	noun	11	6	0.095
20	upper side (ue)	noun	12	6	0.094
21	tranceparency (toumei)	adj	12	6	0.094
22	flavor (kaori)	noun	12	6	0.094
23	dence (koi)	adj	6	5	0.085
24	thought as (omoeru)	verb	6	5	0.085
25	go through (nukeru)	verb	8	5	0.082
26	light (karui)	adj	9	5	0.081

Note.[2]

Case A: *Alcohol, Astringency, Acid, Astringent*
Case B: *Taste, Acidity, Umami, Sweetness, Flavor*

In the tasting descriptions of *sake*, the feeling of "alcohol" can be interpreted as "dry taste." In the case of wine, the taste of *astringency* (*tannic taste*) is one of the most important tastes that gives wines some "*body*." As for *sake*, on the other hand, the *astringency* is basically an undesirable taste, and it has traditionally been thought of as one of the "off-flavors." Recently, especially the past 10 years or so, a little bit of *astringency* in *sake* has become welcomed by *sake* fans, for it can make the *outline* of *sake* clearer.

From the comparison of the salient words as mentioned above, it can be inferred that the elements of taste that are described both pictorially and verbally (case A) do not refer to the fundamental taste of *sake*. On the other hand, the elements described only verbally (case B) directly refer to the primary elements for the taste of *sake*. *Sake* is made of rice, and hence, the *sweetness* of the sugar of rice and the *umami* from fermented rice is the primary elements of the taste of *sake*. Both sweetness and umami appeared in case B.

The *astringency* and *alcohol* (*dry taste*) are not included in the basic five tastes (sweet, sour, salty, bitter and umami); rather, they are "mouth feelings" or stimuli in the mouth. Those characteristics are often described along with a pattern with *lines* (see Figure 5). The words "acid" and "acidity" are semantically related, and yet, there is a difference in describing the taste of *sake*: The word *acid* in case A describes "acid as the perceived stimulation," and *acidity* in case B means "the acidity as the experienced taste."

It is not common or possible to draw pictures about the nature of taste when one tastes sweetness or umami. As shown in Figure 6, the taste of sweetness or umami is described verbally, and the drawing only shows the position or movement or shape of the taste.

The author draws a tentative conclusion that the taste itself is conceptualized verbally rather than pictorially, and that the mouth feels, or the stimulating tastes can be described, pictorially along with verbal descriptions.

Figure 5. Tasting descriptions of Fukumitsuya

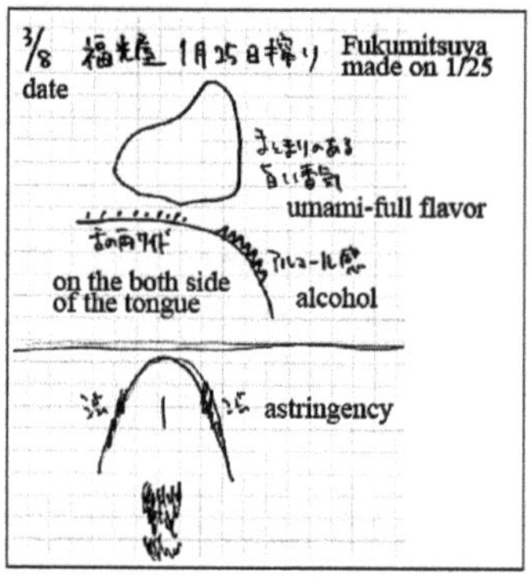

VERBAL DESCRIPTION

Coming in smoothly, yet the white astringency
on both sides of the tongue is felt as "Sabu-Sabu" [sound symbolism].

The throat-burning alcohol realizes the dense air
huddling on the center-upper side of the tongue.

Figure 6. Tasting descriptions of Sohgen

VERBAL DESCRIPTION

Umami-full initial flavor, like the center of bread or well-cooked rice.
The mouth feel is dense and highly viscous.

It surges ahead in three waves: sweetness, umami, and complex taste.
The third wave is the melting pot of the taste.
Yet I feel a bitter taste next to the back teeth.

Nouns for Space and Body Parts

Of the words used to describe the taste of *sake*, let us take a look at the words of high frequency relating to space and the body part. Here again, a comparison is made between the two cases A and B.

Case A: Tongue, Back of-, Surface, Mouth, Center, Tip of tongue, Nose, Throat, Entrance of throat, Middle point
Case B: *Upper side*

These words are often used together as in "I feel white astringency on the *surface of the tongue,*" and "The sweet flavor spreads into the *back of the nose.*"

Some descriptions consisted of only the figure of taste, and others included the body parts independently of the figure of taste. Thus, the body parts can be described both verbally and pictorially. Still, there are some differences in the method of description. The pictorial descriptions intuitively show the point or position of the mouth.

For example, in the pictorial description of Figure 7, the midpoint of the *tongue* and the *throat* is covered with the *patterns of lines.* The verbal description corresponding to this was "around the back side of the root of the tongue." The author has identified more than 100 expressions (such as *tongue, back of the tongue, middle point of the tongue…*) for indicating body parts (especially points in the mouth and nose) in the verbal descriptions.

Verbs

The characteristic verbs for each case (A and B) are the following:

Case A: *Spread, Expand, Wave, Keep, Going up*
Case B: *Feel, Swallow, Think, Stay, Drink, Thought as, Go through*

The number of verbs is limited, but one can identify some tendencies in their function. In case A, the characteristic verbs (e.g., spread, going up) represent the "movement" of the taste in the mouth. In contrast, the characteristic verbs (e.g., swallow, drink) of case B represent the "action" of the body or

Figure 7. Tasting descriptions of Kaga no Tsuki

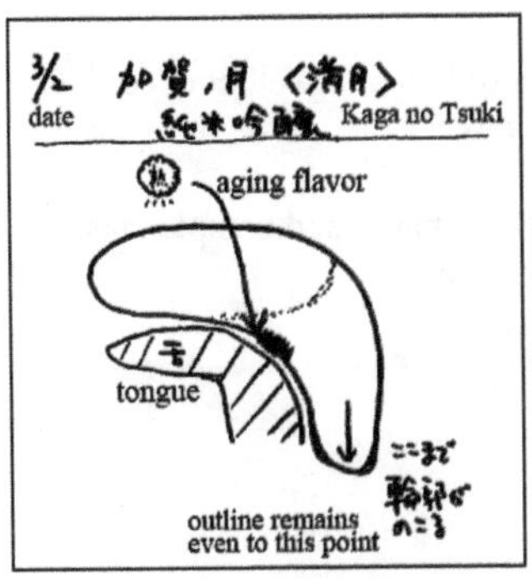

VERBAL DESCRIPTION

Dense, yet smooth attack. Subtle aging flavor passes the nose.

Round-shaped outline from the smooth attack is the characteristic of this sake.

Mature-aged flavor gradually changes its face to the astringency, and it is felt in the back of the mouth.

The outline remains even in the throat.

the impression of the taste. The movement of the taste can refer to the changing process of tasting in time and space.

The author suggests that sound symbolic expressions are also used for modifying the changing process (Fukushima et al., 2016). For example, Japanese "fuwatto," which roughly means "softly," is a highly symbolic word that goes with "hirogaru" ("spread"), thus saying "fuwatto hirogaru" (spread softly).

Thus, these findings suggest that the multiple descriptions (i.e., sound symbolism, drawings, verbal descriptions) can be strategically applied in order to represent rather abstract referents such as movements or changing processes of the taste.

The Multiple Descriptions of Taste

On the basis of the preceding discussion, the author examines the detailed relationships between the verbal description and the pictorial description in more detail in this section.

In order to show the relationships between the two descriptions, the author examined the correspondence of the element of taste and the element of the picture (i.e., what element of taste is described as what element of the picture). In Figure 8, acidity goes with E1 (circle shape), "sweetness" goes with E2 and E3 (circle shape and pattern with lines), and "astringency" goes with E4 (scribbled pattern).

Note that, as illustrated in Figure 8, one taste can be described by multiple elements (i.e., E2, E3); thus, the number of elements is more than that of the element of taste.

In total, 175 pictorial elements for taste were detected. The tastes were classified into *sweetness, umami, acidity, astringency, dry, salty, bitter, fizzy, aging, flavor, fruity*, and *roast*. Here, the synonyms or inflection word types are integrated into one cover term (e.g., *dry*, alcohol to "*dry*")[13]. Figure 9 shows the correspondence matrix between the elements of pictorial description and the words of taste.

From the matrix in Figure 9, the tastes of *sweetness, umami*, and *acidity* seem to have common patterns. The tastes of astringency and dryness also seems to share the patterns. Thus, the author identifies the two groups; PTG (the Primary Taste Group) for *sweetness, umami*, and *acidity* and STG (the Stimulating Taste Group) for astringency and dryness. Words describing other tastes were rarely used, and hence, they are excluded from the grouping.

The composition rates (%) of each group are shown in Figure 10. The two graphs here show contrasting differences in the elements of Shape and Pattern. The difference can be summarized as follows:

Figure 8. An example of the multiple elements (brand: Ibuki)

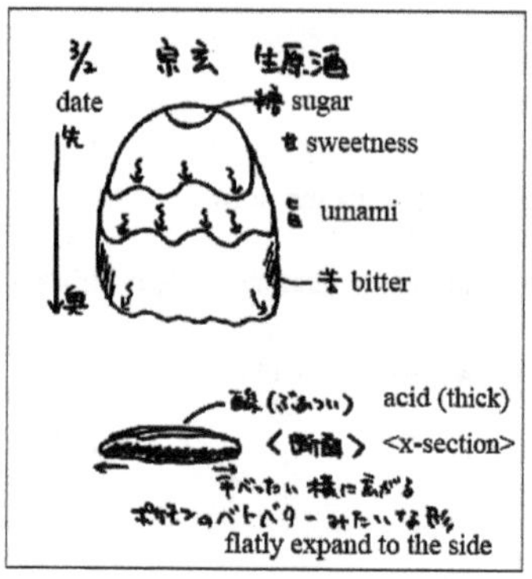

VERBAL DESCRIPTION

Umami-full initial flavor, like the center of bread or well-cooked rice.
The mouth feel is dense and highly viscous.

It surges ahead in three waves: sweetness, umami, and complex taste.
The third wave is the melting pot of the taste.
Yet I feel a bitter taste next to the back teeth.

Figure 9. Matrix of the frequency of the taste and the elements of the drawings

		LINE			CURVE			SHAPE (2D)						FORM (3D)			Pattern					
		line	angle	arrow	weave	curve	curve arrow	circle	oval	free linear	free curve	solid arrow	thorn	sphere	curve form	cloud	dots	lines	scribble	chevron	curve	filled in
PTG	sweet			1		2	3	4	7	1	12	2					1	2	2	1		
PTG	umami	1		1		2	2	1		1	8	2	1		1	1	1	1	3			1
PTG	acidity			3		3	2	2	5	1	11			1	2			1	4	1		1
STG	astringency		1	1		2	1		1		2		1				1	5	5		1	1
STG	dry			1			1					1	4			1		3	3	2	1	1
	salty						3				3							1				
	bitter										1							1				
	fizzy				1	1											1	1		1		
	aging	1						1		1	2					1		1				
	flavor							2									2					
	fruity	1									1										1	
	roasty					1	1									2			1			

Figure 10. The composition rates of the elements of the PTG and STG

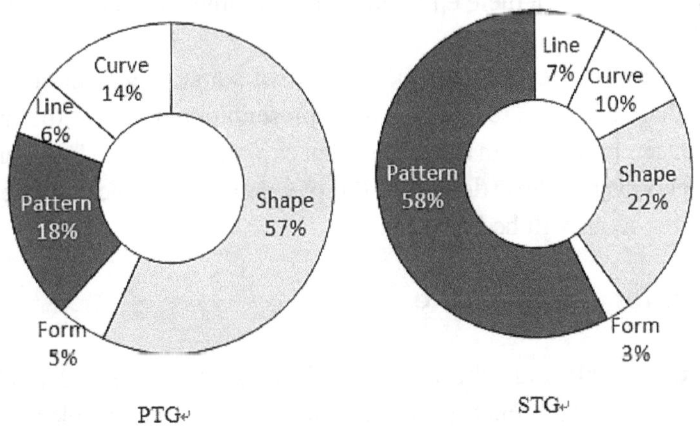

1. **PTG:**
   a. *Shape (57%)*, especially in *free-curve* shape, is mostly frequently used.
   b. *Sweetness* and *acidity* are often represented as *ovals.*
   c. Other frequent shapes include *curve*, *curved arrow*, and *scribbled* pattern.
   d. Curvy figures tend to be preferred.
2. **STG:**
   a. *Pattern* (58%), especially the *line pattern* and *scribbled* pattern, is most frequently used.
   b. *Dry* is described mainly in the *thorn* shape, *line* pattern, and *scribbled* pattern.
   c. Linear shape tends to be preferred.

FUTURE RESEARCH DIRECTIONS: APPLICATION

As an application of this study, the author is interested in the narratological domain of human creativity aid. Some fundamental studies on the method and the theory of narrative generation model applying human creativity aid (Hori 1994, 2004, 2007). In this section, the author attempts to offer a creativity aiding strategy for generating the descriptions of the sense of taste.

We express what we experience. Some experiences are easy to describe and some are otherwise. The author assumes that tasting is a difficult area to describe. One is satisfied with what one tastes, feeling that one does not need to put the experience in words. However, there is an interplay of experience and expression: Expression can enhance experience, and vice versa. This suggests that learning how to express increases the discriminating power when one tastes something. If so, it is worthwhile to devise a way of expressing one's taste.

In the training for sommeliers, the most basic practice is to name the flavors of the various objects. Using a real object or a set of flavor chips, sommeliers practice pointing out the correspondence of the flavors and names. As for the language system, this flavor-identification process corresponds to the categorical function of the noun. However, even if a sommelier can name all of the elements of the taste with a full set of nouns, that sommelier cannot explain the events occurring in his or her mouth. In order to give an account of the taste as events, the verbs are indispensable.

One of the most important functions of verbs is to describe the changings of an object in time and space. Additionally, verbs have a role of describing the relationships of objects. Without these functions, the descriptions for taste would be a mere enumeration of comments, such as "there are tastes of…," or "I feel the taste of…."

Yet, how to use verbs to help people describe the taste of something is an open question. In this paper, the author argues that drawings are an effective representational tool of the taste of *sake*. Pictorial descriptions were produced intuitively in the experiment explained above. However, the author was able to extract a set of elements even in those drawings. If those elements are incorporated into the production of more refined icons, the icons will be beneficial.

Verb-Oriented Tool for Tasting Sake

As pragmatic implications of this study, the author developed a "verb-oriented tool for tasting *sake*" (see Figure 11) with which one can discriminate the taste of *sake*. The tool was developed in the following way.

First, the author listed the verbs for tasting descriptions for *sake*, using the *sake* tasting corpus of the listed verbs; the following words were excluded from analysis: words of low frequency (under four times), and functional verbs[4]. As a result, 86 verbs were extracted (see lower half of Figure 11).

Next, the author manually organized the verbs into some clusters, based on the similarity of the meaning of verbs. In this process, the hierarchical clustering method in KH Coder and the affinity diagram were referred to. From this clustering, 24 verb clusters were given.

In order to link the sense of taste and the corresponding verb, the author drew a picture that represented the common image of the verbs within a cluster.

The picture consists of two color elements. The abstract figures in the charts stand for the elements of the taste. The two colors give a difference of the "main taste" and the "sub taste." Here, the figure of dot pattern shows the main taste. The user will substitute an element of taste for a figure. In this way, the author produced pictures for all the clusters (Figure 11).

Figure 11. Sake tasting chart (a verb-oriented tool for tasting sake)

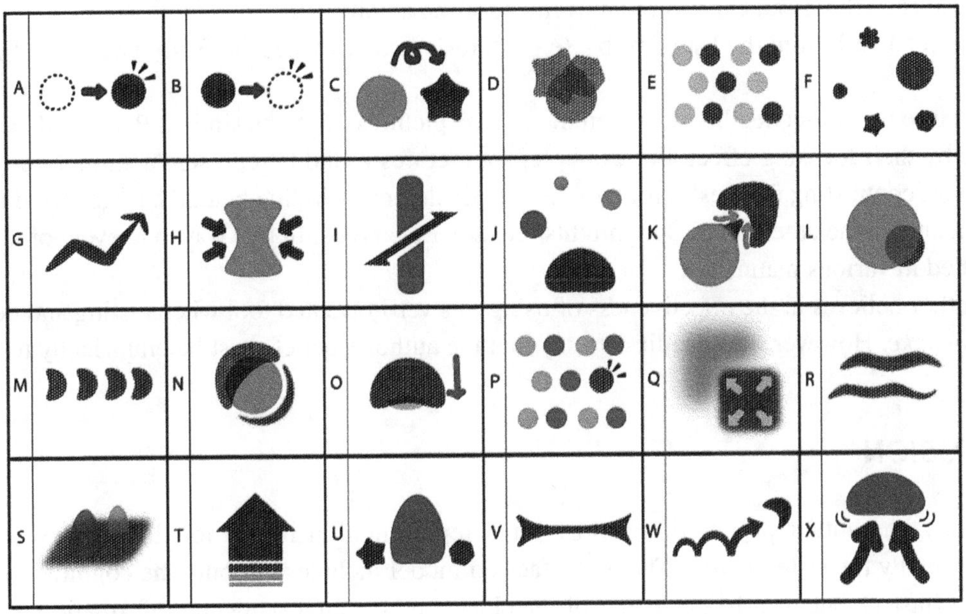

A	appear arise open bloom show up	B	disappear vanish fade out	C	change turn alter	D	mix intermix cross	E	repeat cluster	F	scatter popping enliven spread
G	run run through pierce	H	fasten make firm tighten	I	cut slash cruck	J	settling sink lie	K	take out absorb lead derive	L	hide glimpse
M	keep remain sustain	N	encircle cover enfold tuck rim	O	blank occupied lap over guard	P	stand out show up	Q	take position spread open	R	wave float drift flow
S	take root deep-root drop anchor	T	increase raise add spice enhance	U	unite equip partake	V	tense stretch	W	jump spring	X	move up lift uprise surge

Each drawing or icon is intuitively easy to understand even without lengthy explanations. To use this tool or chart, the standard procedures involve the following steps:

Step 1: Taste a *sake* and describe the elements of the taste and flavor verbally. (e.g., "I can see fresh acidity and fruity sweetness.")

Step 2: Choose the main taste to describe. (e.g., "I feel strong sweetness, but I instead want to express the acidity.")

Step 3: Select a picture, and put the main taste into the figure of dots (e.g., "H or U seem good... I'll choose H so that I can express the movement of the acidity.")
Step 4: Select a verb from the list of verbs. (e.g., "Fresh acidity makes the fruity sweetness firm.")

The picture is color-coded because even though the pictures might be similar, the verbal expressions can differ by their focusing effect. For example, the pictures L and O represent a similar composition, but they have contrasting focuses: L focuses on a small element—hiding behind a large element—as the main element. On the other hand, O highlights the larger elements. In this way, one event of tasting can be described in various manners.

The author believes in the effectiveness of using this verb-oriented tool when tasting and describing the taste of *sake*. However, it is needless to say that the author's belief must be empirically tested.

CONCLUSION

In this study, the author proposed a multi-faceted representation model for the sensory domain of taste—especially the taste of *sake*. The multi-faceted model includes not only the cognitive process of the subject (taster), but also the properties of the object and the environmental information.

The starting point of the model is not the information of the object. Rather, from the phenomenological stance, or more specifically from the viewpoint of the first-person-singular study, we set the emergence of the sensory experience as the origination of the model. In this model, the sensory experience emerges, appears, or arises as the aggregate of the dynamic process within the subject, the object, and the environment.

Yet, revealing the whole multi-faceted structure of a cup of *sake* would be impossible, for the "all elements of the whole structure" cannot be defined a priori. Thus, a study of multi-faceted structure needs some focusing point. In this study, the author focused on the relationships between the verbal descriptions and non-verbal descriptions.

The author discovered the following general tendencies based upon analysis of the parts of speech:

1. The sensation of taste itself is conceptualized verbally rather than pictorially.
2. The mouth feels, or the stimulating tastes can be described, pictorially as the symbolic descriptions.
3. The body parts can be described both verbally and pictorially. In particular, the pictorial descriptions intuitively show the point or position of the mouth.
4. The movement of the taste tends to described both pictorially and verbally. In contrast, the movement of the body parts tends to be described only verbally.

Further, as the results of the examination of the relationships between the pictorial elements and the words of verbal description, the author found the following differences between the manner of description of the PTG (Primary Taste Group: *sweetness*, *umami*, and *acidity*) and the STG (Stimulus Taste Group: *astringency* and *dryness*):

1. **PTG:**
    a. *Shape (57%)*, especially in *free-curve* shape, is mostly frequently used.
    b. *Sweetness* and *acidity* are often represented as *ovals.*

c. Other frequent shapes include *curve*, *curved arrow*, and *scribbled* pattern.
d. Curvy figures tend to be preferred.

2. **STG:**
a. *Pattern* (58%), especially the *line pattern* and *scribbled* pattern, is most frequently used.
b. *Dry* is described mainly in thc *thorn* shape, *line* pattern, and *scribbled* pattern.
c. Linear shape tends to be preferred.

Verbal expression is limited when it comes to describing the area of the sensory perception of taste. The author sought to bridge the domain of taste and the domain of words, and, on the basis of the findings of the first-person-singular study, proposed that the pictorial description, together with the verbal description, can achieve the aim. Because of the nature of the study, it is not possible to generalize, and yet, if the first-person-singular studies are accumulated, one will be able to compare and contrast the data to see if there are generalizable tendencies when people describe the taste of *sake*, for example.

In this study, in order to reveal the coverage area of the verbal descriptions and the pictorial descriptions, the author examined the correspondence of the verbally described element of taste and the element of the picture (i.e., what element of taste is described as what element of the picture).

This kind of interpretation seems valid only for drawings in which the elements are identical. In many cases, however, the pictorial tasting descriptions are more complex, and the elements of the drawing do not correspond to the elements of the verbal descriptions on a one-to-one basis. In this case, the pictorial representation should be interpreted holistically, with the use of the available pictorial and verbal description.

This study proposed a multi-faceted model, focusing on the verbal description domain and non-verbal description domain. The model would contribute to opening the gate to studies of the multiple representations, in contrast to the former studies of literal metaphors. Other questions worthy of future research are how the verbal representation relates to other non-verbal representations (i.e., gestures or facial expressions) and how the environmental information (i.e., circumstances or instruments for drinking) interacts with the representation of *sake*. This study is a first step in steering the research of taste toward taste as human-experience.

ACKNOWLEDGMENT

This research was supported by the Graduate School Doctoral Student Grant-in-Aid Program of Keio University (2015-2017).

REFERENCES

Alexander, C. (1966). A city is not a tree. *Design*, 46–55.

Fukushima, H., Mutsumi, I., & Shigenori, T. (in press). The usage mechanism of Japanese ideophones in the description of taste: Morphological and co-occurrence analysis of the description words of wines and sakes. *International Journal of Computational Linguistics Research.*

Higuchi, K. (2004). Quantitative analysis of textual data: Differentiaiton and coordination of two approches. *Sociological Theory and Methods*, *19*(1), 101–115.

Hinton, L., Nichols, J., & Ohala, J. J. (2006). *Sound symbolism*. Cambridge, UK: Cambridge University Press.

Hori, K. (1994). A system for aiding creative concept formation. *IEEE Transactions on Systems, Man, and Cybernetics*, *24*(6), 882–894. doi:10.1109/21.293507

Hori, K. (2004). Do knowledge assets really exist in the world and can we access such knowledge?: Knowledge evolves through a cycle of knowledge liquidization and crystallization. LNAI, 3359, 1–13.

Hori, K. (2007). *Sozo katsudo shien no riron to oyo* [Theories and applications of creativity support]. Tokyo: Ohmsha.

Kanai, A., & Kodama, K. (2010). Film edit design: Story and irrational cutting. *Cognitive Studies*, *17*(3), 444–458.

Kanai, A., & Ogata, T. (2004a). Aspect of non-story processing and film rhetoric composition in the narrative generation mechanism. In *Proceedings of The Ninth International Symposium on Artificial Life and Robotics* (*Vol. 1*, pp. 162–165). Academic Press.

Kanai, A., & Ogata, T. (2004b). Non-story processing on the film rhetoric composition system. In *Proceedings of 18th Congress of the International Association of Empirical Aesthetics* (pp. 433–436). Academic Press.

Peirce, C. S. (1974). *Collected papers of Charles Sanders Peirce*. Cambridge, MA: Harvard University Press.

Seto, K. (2003). *Kotoba wa aji wo koeru [Words excel the taste]*. Tokyo: Kaimeisha.

Shigenori, T., & Masahiro, F. (1998). *Imizukeron> no tenkai [The evolution of the <sense-making theory>]*. Tokyo: Kinokuniya.

Shinohara, K., Yamauchi, N., Kawahara, S., & Tanaka, H. (2016). Takete and Maluma in action: A cross-modal relationship between gestures and sounds. *PLoS One*, *11*(9), e0163525. doi:10.1371/journal.pone.0163525 PMID:27682989

Wilson, D. A., & Stevenson, R. J. (2006). *Learning to smell*. Baltimore, MD: Johns Hopkins UP.

Real Wine Guide. (2007–2009). *RWG* (vol. 19–26). Academic Press.

Hasegawa, K. (2015). *Nihonshu techo* [Sake handbook]. Gakken Publishing.

Kimishima, S. (2011). *Nihonshu kanzen guide* [Perfect sake guide]. Ikeda.

Matsuzaki, H. (2000). *Nihonshu guide book* [Sake guide book]. Shibata.

SSI. (2010). *Nihonshu techo* [Sake handbook]. Tokyo: Shoseki.

Yamamoto, Y. (2014). *Gensen nihonshu techo* [Selected sake handbook]. Sekai Bunka-sya.

KEY TERMS AND DEFINITIONS

Multi-Faceted Representation: A manner of representation proposed in this study. It consists of multiple representations, such as sensory representation, verbal representation, and non-verbal representation.

PTG (The Primary Taste Group): An operational taste group for sweetness, umami, and acidity. These tastes are primaly elements of the taste of sake.

Sake: An alcoholic beverage (so-called "Japanese rice wine") made by fermenting rice. The primary tastes of sake are sweetness, umami, and acidity. The flavor is fine and thin; the high-class sake "Ginjohshu" has a fruity flavor like a banana, a melon, or an apple.

STG (The Stimulating Taste Group): An operational taste group for astringency and dryness. These tastes are thought as supplemental taste for sake. A sutable amount of astringency gives sake the outline of the taste. And dryness is an important factor of the afterflavor. However, too much astringency or dryness would spoil the taste of sake.

ENDNOTES

1. Table 4. *Note.* The classification of words according to the part of speech is made on the basis of original Japanese expressions.
2. Table 5. *Note.* The classification of words according to the part of speech is made on the basis of original Japanese expressions.
3. The integrated synonym list is: "dry" (dry, alcohol), "acidity" (acid, acidity, the taste of acid).
4. "Suru," "naru," or "aru" in Japanese, which correspond to "do" or "be" in English.

Chapter 9
Haiku-Like Aesthetic Sentence Composition Through the Narrative Process

Yoshihiko Nitta
Nihon University, Japan

ABSTRACT

Aesthetic sentences often behave freely from ordinary grammatical constraints; nevertheless, they maintain rich message transmitting power. This is apparently a mysterious language phenomenon, which dexterously gives full play to its strong narrative power on the reader's soul. In this chapter, the author takes haiku, classical Japanese short poetic sentence, as a model of aesthetic sentence. By using the concept of functional grammar and season-word ontology, the author tries to approach the secret of taciturn beauty in poetic sentences. The beauty of haiku exists in ellipses, suggestions, and eloquent mutism of 5-7-5 syllable short sentences. In this chapter, the author introduces the functional grammar as a device for explaining the meaning and construction of haiku. The functional grammar claims that every sentence is composed of two categories: kernel sentence and meta-sentence. The author tries to reveal the secrets of the aesthetic beauty of the ultimately simple sentence, haiku.

INTRODUCTION

Aesthetic sentences often behave freely from grammatical constraints. Poetic sentences, such as Haiku, in particular are often far beyond grammatical completeness while bringing an incredibly attractive power to human being's linguistic sensitivity.

Thus, the author can expect to obtain techniques for composing impressive sentences or delivering persuasive talks through a study on poetic sentence constructions. Though there are many genres or styles in poetic sentences, in this paper, the author takes haiku, classical Japanese short poetic sentence, as a typical example of a beautiful persuasive sentence. By using the functional grammar concept, the author tries to elucidate the secret of simple sentential beauty. The essence of the beauty of haiku often exists

DOI: 10.4018/978-1-5225-4775-4.ch009

Copyright © 2018, IGI Global. Copying or distributing in print or electronic forms without written permission of IGI Global is prohibited.

in ellipses, abbreviations, and suggestions: eloquent mutism. Various events and situations that tacitly suggest the deep emotions and feelings of writers are embedded in a very short and simple sentence, which is composed of 5-7-5 letters words or phrases.

Usually haiku never talks directly about the emotions or declarations of the writer's mind; it only suggests them by using simple words that describe the weather, plants, animal, climate, or scenic beauty. Haiku is always expecting and inviting readers' conjecture or imagination (Nitta, 2013).

Haiku is now moving out from the classical region of Japanese culture or literary arts and becoming an international model of sentential beauty. On these grounds, the author has taken haiku and its English translations as a poetic sentence corpus, which is using functional grammar to investigate the secret of beautiful and simple sentence constructions.

The main point of functional grammar is that it regards every sentence as composed of two types of sentences: kernel sentence and meta-sentence. Meta-sentences can be understood as a sentence structuring operator, while kernel sentences are simple structured, mono-predicate sentences. Kernel sentences have obvious translations of canonical forms, while meta-sentences represent the logical-semantic structure of sentences, which take kernel sentence(s) as their dominating variable(s). From meta-sentences, the author can draw a lot of useful semantic information.

The author shows typical examples of meta-sentences obtained from the haiku corpus. The author expects that through meta-sentences, the essence of the simple beauty of haiku can clearly extracted. This extracted essence will provide some hints for composing beautiful sentences together with fundamental language teaching methods.

BACKGROUND

Basics of Haiku

Haiku, the classical Japanese literary art, is now very popular among people of various classes and educational backgrounds. Lots of culture books provide guidelines for beginners composing Haiku. They provide some hints and lots of examples talking about mental snapshots, suggesting some deep and wide ideas by treating small parts of things, events, natural beauty, weather, etc. However, their explanations and discussion cannot go further than suggesting only some deep and fascinating features of Haiku. In many cases, some sense of frustration is left behind.

Herein, the author would like to present a very conscious informal introduction to Haiku. The origin of Haiku may be found in the Hokku ("発句") of Renga ("連歌").The representative author is Basho ("芭蕉") in the mid-Edo era. In the Meiji era, Masaoka Shiki ("正岡子規") completed the formal style and established the Haiku as an authoritative literary art. The definition is very simple, such as 5-7-5 phonetic character construction, usage of segmenting word ("切れ字" Kireji), and season word ("季語" Kigo). The candidate for the season word is given by Saijiki ("歳時記"), which is a kind of ontology describing human beings' ordinary lives in the coordinates of four seasons—a poetic date scale. Haiku and Tanka form two big parts of the mainstream of Japanese short poems.

People who live outside of Japan's ordinary circumstances may find it difficult to interpret and write Haiku. The author advises them to just neglect the formal definition of Haiku. Using three to five English phrases, you can write Haiku as short poetry. Let us try some Haiku.

In the shadow of sunflower, I see the time past.
Himawari no Kage ni hisomu-ya Sugita Hibi
("向日葵の陰に潜むや過ぎた日々") Toushu ("透舟")
Winter morning, strong taste of coffee, delight and energy for today's work.
Fuyu-no Asa Tsuyoki Koh-hi-ni Yaruki Waku
("冬の朝強き珈琲にやる気湧く") Toushu ("透舟")

The above two Haiku are kind of awkward, but ignore their clumsiness. The essential point is that the readers should enjoy and feel appreciation for poetry or enter the poetic mind-set ("詩心" Shigokoro). Since ancient times, Japanese people have enjoyed writing Haiku and reading Haiku for expressing and interpreting some deep and moderate emotions, which are often flavored with elegant humor.

The season word is primarily used to indicate the time or date concerning the Haiku, but actually, it represents so much information about a writer's mind and circumstances. It is a kind of language magic that only one word can convey so much rich information. On this account, the readers are highly advised to read Haiku Saijiki [Haiku Ontology] with real appreciation, in which they will find lots of secret jewels of human life.

In this chapter, the author plans to present a new and computational view of Haiku composition that will resolve people's frustration.

The main idea is to view Haiku as a kind of fragmental sentence composed of kernel sentences and meta-words. Kernel sentences are basic sentences that may be understood easily. Meta-sentences define the relation between kernel sentences.

In this chapter, the author provides lots of illustrative and attractive Haiku examples.

In opposition to the author's Haiku view, as expected, there are many refutations that say that Haiku is not a scientific sentence and that is impossible to treat it from a computational viewpoint. In this chapter, the author will not develop counterarguments against these refutations. Instead, the author would like to spend more energy on displaying more persuasive and attractive Haiku composition examples.

Aesthetics of Haiku

Let us take a look at the aesthetic behavior of Haiku reflected in only one character change. In the previous Haiku, let us make a change from "ageru (あげる)" to "agaru (あがる)":

空の青引き寄せむとて凧あがる 透舟 (H'j)
H'j = Sora-no Ao Hiki-yose-mu tote Tako Agaru Toushu

Thus, only one character is changed from "e" to "a." However, this microscopic change leads to a very big meaning change.

(Hj) 凧あげる———— Tako Ageru: using Transitive Verb

The Haiku writer is flying a kite so as to draw the blue sky to his hand. Under a clear and open sky, he is full of energy and wants to fetch the blue sky. A refreshed and magnanimous feeling is expressed in the Haiku.

(H'j) 凧あがる——— Tako Agaru: using Intransitive Verb

In this case, the kite seems to have its own will and ability to control its flight. It is this kite that tries to fetch the blue sky.

Which of the two versions is more feasible or beautiful depends on the reviewer's sense of beauty and poetic mind.

The point of this section is that in poetic sentences like Haiku, very small portions of words or letter may drastically affect the aesthetics of the Haiku. This is why Haiku is difficult to understand and yet deeply meaningful.

META-SENTENCE AND FRAGMENTAL SENTENCE

Let us show a simple and easily understandable example of haiku and its associated meta-sentences together with an English translation.

空の青引き寄せむとて凧あげる　　　新田透舟 (Hj)
Hj = Sora-no Ao Hiki-yose-mu tote Tako Ageru Nitta Toushu
He = Flying the kite ----- makes me feel like drawing the blue sky with kite-string.
Mj(Kj1,Kj2, Kj3) = Kj1, Kj2, tote Kj3
Kj1= Sora-no Ao
Kj2= Hiki-yose-mu
Kj3= Tako Ageru

Haru-no sumi-kitta aozora-ni Tako-wo ageteiru-to, naiyara sora-no ao-saga Tako-to issho-ni hikiyose-rareru youda. Haru-no Aozora-wa kokoro-ga ookiku hiraku-youda.

(In an azure sky I am flying a kite while feeling that I can draw the blue sky by pulling the kite string. Oh what a nice and blue spring sky it is! It makes my mind broad and open.)

He(Ke1, Ke3, Ke2) = Ke3 Ke2 Ke1
Ke1 = "Blue Sky"
Ke2 (=Vt N feel like Ving) = "makes me feel like drawing"
Ke3= "flying a kite"

Reference and association are important to feel appreciation for the spring blue sky, which makes people minds open wide.

R (K1, K2, K3) = {Time=Spring, Cold winter was over, Place=maybe a park or an open square where people are gathering and talking.}

Now the author claims that every sentence is composed of two categories: kernel sentence K and meta-sentence M(). Let us denote K as a kernel sentence and M() as a meta-sentence (Nitta, 2012c). The meta-sentence behaves like a function over the kernel sentence, and so the author can write

$S = M(K)$

Here, S denotes a sentence. If the author would like to emphasize that sentence S is written by language j or language e, then the author would write,

$Sj = Mj\ (Kj)$ or $Se = Me\ (Ke)$

where Mj means the meta-sentence in language j, and Ke means kernel sentence in language e.

If the author denotes the translation between language j and language e as Tran,

$Tran: Sj \rightarrow Se$

Then, at the same time,

$Tran: Mj() \rightarrow Me()$

represents the bilingual alignment between language j and e, whose concrete example will be shown later.

1. Explanation About Kernel Sentence K

The "kernel" designates the kernel of sentential meaning and the kernel of translation. Roughly, the kernel sentence has a simple predicate-and-argument structure, that is, one verb and dominating noun(s). A kernel sentence can be a form of no verb(-phrase), that is, of a noun(-phrase) only.

The kernel sentence usually has an obvious translation of a canonical form and has a high possibility of pseudo-symmetrical translation property.

If sentence K has a symmetrical translation property, then

$Tran(K) = K'$ and $Tran^{-1}(K') = K$

In the case of pseudo-symmetrical translation property,

$Tran^{-1}(K') = K$

The antonym of "symmetrical translation property" is "directional translation property," that is, $Tran^{-1}(Tran(S)) \neq S$.

If sentence S has a symmetrical translation property, then this sentence is easily translatable and has an obvious translation. Thus, these kinds of sentences are expected to form some baseline for overall translation.

2. Explanation About Meta-Sentence M()

A meta-sentence is a kind of hyper-sentence that operates over kernel sentence(s). This operation is viewed as a sentence constructing operation that makes actual surface sentences using kernel sentence(s) as its component. The essential part of a meta-sentence depends on function words in Japanese and prepositions and connection words in English.

Now let us see a concrete example of fragmental syntax in haiku, which still maintains a strong message-passing ability. Haiku is composed of only 17 phonetic characters, which nevertheless have strong appealing power to readers. In compensation for this stylish conciseness, Haiku is often obliged to transcend the ordinary sentential syntax. It may lack a main verb, subject, and/or object, but it still maintains a strong message-passing ability. Let us see a typical example.

***Furuike-ya kawazu tobi-komu mizu-no oto Bashou

("古池や蛙飛び込む水の音　　　芭蕉")
Furuike = old pond = Noun
ya = Function Word
kawazu = frog = Noun
tobi-komu = jump into = Verb Phrase
mizu = water = Noun
no = Postpositional Particle (designating "belonging")
*Translation (Interpretation):
***Kanjaku-nari Furuike-no katawara / Aogaeru Tobi-komu Mizu-no-naka / Mizu-utu
Oto Hitotsu-Ari (Literal reading of Kanpei (Chinese Haiku)
("閑寂なり古池の傍ら/青蛙飛び込む水の中/水打つ音一つあり　　　中国語俳句の逐語訳")
***An old pond-----/A frog dives into / with a quiet splash Translated by Nitta Toushu
***An old quiet pond---- / A frog jumps into the pond / plash! Silence again. Harry Behn

The syntactic structure of an original Haiku is

Subj(N) + F + Subj(N) + Vi + Subj(NP)

which is fragmental. Nevertheless, the sequence of Noun or Noun Phrase plus Function Word brings about a deep poetic meaning.

To clarify the deep poetic meaning, it is useful to apply the notion of kernel sentence and meta-sentence. Let H be an original Haiku, and then meta-sentence M() and kernel sentences K1 and K2 of H make a formula:

H = M(K1, R, K2)
K1 = Furuike-ga aru=There is an old pond.
K2 = kaeru-ga Mizu-ni tobi-kon-de oto-wo tate-ta=A frog jumped into water with a splash.
R = Scene-event relation

In Haiku H, the first noun old pond (Furuike) has no verb and stands alone. Some imaginary association with the noun, old pond, derives the kernel sentence K1 and relation R.

This example suggests that even one isolated noun can convey lots of information if the noun is chosen carefully.

From Chinese sentences to English or Japanese sentences, the author can relatively easily obtain direct word-by-word translations. These word-by-word translations are usually of fragmental syntax but can still transfer substantial messages. Let us see another example.

C = (Literal reading of Chinese) = Kotoshi okonau-wo ezu-tomo mata myounen ari / furui-okoseya yaruki-wo!
("今年行うを得ずとも　また明年あり/奮い起こせや　やる気を!")

A direct translation of C to English may be:

Tran(C) = this year not done, again exists next year, encourage sprits!

If the author denotes Sj as the source language sentence, Se as the target (=translated) sentence, and Tran as the translator between Sj and Se, then the author will write

Tran(Sj) = Se

For the translation between language j and language e.

The author proposes that each sentence S be composed of two categories: kernel sentence(s) K and meta-sentence M(). A meta-sentence is a sentence structuring operator.

S=M(K),

Tran(S) = Tran(M(K)) = Tran(M) (Tran(K)).

Roughly, kernel sentence K represents simple structured, mono-predicate sentences that have obvious translations of canonical forms, while meta-sentence M() represents the logical-semantic structure of sentence, which take K as the dominating variable and shows a relationship among kernel sentences.

INTERPRETATION OF HAIKU BY META-SENTENCE

Haiku has reached the limit of simplification in its sentential form while preserving the potential of rich message-passing ability to readers. It depends on the imaginary association potential of component words and phrases, especially the season words that the author will treat later. This situation can be formalized in a somewhat naive intuitive style as follows:

H = K + R
H: Haiku sentence (very short simple concise (pseudo-)sentence
K: Kernel Sentence (that has canonical meaning)
R: References to outer world (Association, Conjecture); especially the reference to Haiku Ontology

R naturally depends on H.

R = f(H) or R = f(H, K)

f is a function that has H and K as its objective variables. F is a meta-sentence that exists at the base of haiku H. The successfulness of semantic interpretation by meta-sentences will be confirmed through the translation of Japanese haiku into English haiku.

Paying attention to the form:

H - K = R

The author would like to extract R (from H) as the reference to outer world (or circumstance) knowledge that is often stored accumulatively in Haiku Ontology. R depends on H. The author can write:

R = f(H) or R = f (H, K)

Thus, later, the author will identify R(・) with Haiku Ontology.

The function f() can be interpreted as a meta-sentence that exists at the base of haiku H. Note that for notational simplicity, the author uses $M = f^{-1}$. From now, on the author treats M() as meta-sentence instead of F().

In the following, the author will show concrete examples of Haiku interpretation by meta-sentence formation and references to Haiku Ontology (for details, see the next chapter).

*** 梅咲くや何が降っても春は春　　　加賀千代女
Hj = Ume saku-ya nani-ga futte-mo haru wa haru Kaga Chiyojo
He = flowering plum----/ even if rain or snow falls / spring is spring

translated by P. Donegan (Yamane, 1996)

Hj = K1 dearu-kara+tatoeK2 demo + zettai-ni K3
K1 = Ume-ga saku = plum is flowering
K2 = Nanika-ga furu = something falls
K3 = Haru de-aru = it is sprib now
Hj= M(K1, K2, K3)

Tran(Hj) = As plum is flowering, even if rain or snow falls, it is already and definitely spring.
The reference to Haiku Ontology may give us circumstance information as follows:
Ume-saku (梅咲く) plum is flowering

∈ Time (early spring)
∈ Event (taking a stroll)
∈ Location (a garden)
∈ Weather (spring drizzle)
∈ Participant (maybe an aged writer)
∈ Situation (Relaxing and welcoming the arrival of spring)
*** 陽炎(かぎろい)や人も立木もゆらゆらと　　　新田透舟

Hj = Kagiroi ya Hito mo Tachiki mo Yura-yura to Nitta Toushu
He = Heat haze shakes gently ----- both people and clump of trees.
Mj(Kj1, Kj2, Kj3) = Kj1 ya Kj2, Kj3
Kj1 = Kageroi
Kj2 = Hito mo Tachiki mo
Kj3 = Yura Yura Yureru

Haru-no nodokas-tp nukumori-wa, hitobito-no kinchou-wo toite hotto-shita kibun-ni saseru. nagaku samui fuyu-ga owari atatakai kisetsu-ga tourai-shita-koto-wo, sasayaka-ni yorokobu kimochu-ga sunao-ni yomi-komare-te-iru.

(A calm and quiet atmosphere of spring season is described in a frank and strait fashion together with the delightful relieved feeling of welcoming warm spring arrival.)

He(Ke1,Ke3, Ke2) =Ke1 Ke3(=Vt Adv) Ke2
Ke1 = "Heat haze"
Ke3(=Vt Adv) = "shakes gently"
Ke2= "both people and clump of trees"

Reference and association are important to get the both heart-and-body-warming atmosphere

R (K1, K2, K3) = {Time=Spring, Cold winter was over, Place=maybe park or grassland where people are gathering against a background of grove.}

Referring to Haiku Ontology the author may get,

Kagiroi(陽炎) Heat haze

∈ Time (midst of spring)
∈ Event (taking a stroll)
∈ Location (maybe a natural park or garden)
∈ Weather (Heat Haze, Mist)
∈ Participant (writer)
∈ Situation (Enjoying a short time recess)
*** 梅が香や鳥は寝させて夜もすがら 千代女
Hj = Ume-ga ka-ya tori-wa ne-sasete yo-mo sugara K. Chiyojo
He = the plum's fragrance / makes the birds sleep-----/ the night falls translated by P. Donegan (Yamane, 1996)
Hj = K1 wa K2-saseru Adv
K1 = Ume-no kaori = plum's fragrance
K2 = Tori-wo ne-saseru = makes the birds sleep
Adv = hito-ban-jyuu = all night long
Hj= M(K1,K2,Adv)

Tran(Hj) = The plum's fragrance makes the birds sleep all night long.

Corresponding Local Haiku Ontology:

Ume-ga-Ka(梅が香) Plum's fragrance

∈ Time (midst of spring, night)
∈ Event (taking a night rest)
∈ Location (her garden)
∈ Weather (Heat Haze, Mist)
∈ Participant (writer)
∈ Situation (Enjoying an atmosphere of spring night)
*** 梅が香や殊に月夜のおもしろし　　　千代女
Hj = Ume-ga ka-ya koto-ni tsukiyo-no omoshiro-shi K. Chiyojo
He = the plum's fragrance / makes it interesting-----/ especially that the moonlight night
Hj = K1 wa K2 wo tokubetsu-ni K3 ni-suru
K1 = Ume-no kaori = plum's fragrance
K2 = Tsukiyo = moonlight night
K3 = omoshiroi = interesting

Tran(Hj) = The plum's fragrance makes especially the moonlight night interesting.

*** 我が我を置き忘れたる暑さかな　　　千代女
Hj = Wa-ga ware-wo oki-wasure-taru atsusa-kana
He = I forget / where to put myself-----/ so hot today translatede by Nitta Toushu
K1 = Kyou-no atsu-sa = hot day today
K2 = Watashi = myself
K3 = Watashi-no mi-wo dokoka-ni oku-koto = to put myself
K4 = wasureru = forget

Tran(hJ) = Today is so hot that I forget where to put myself.

*** 木枯らしやすぐに落ち着く水の月　　　千代女
Hj = Kogarashi-ya sugu-ni ochituku muzu-no tsuki K. Chiyojo
He = chilly wind----/ the moon's reflection / soon becomes calm translated by P. Donegan (Yamane, 1996)
Hj = K1 ga K2 wo V shite-iru-ga sugu-ni notV ni-naru
K1 = Kogarashi = chilly wind
K2 = Mizu-ni utsuru tsuki-kage = the reflection of the moonlight on the water surface
V = midasu = to make rumple
notV = midare-te inai, ochitsui-te iru = be not stirred, be calm
Tran(Hj) = The chilly wind makes the reflection of the moonlight rumple but soon it becomes calm.
*** おそるべき君等の乳房夏来(きた)る　　　西東三鬼
Hj6 = Osoru-beki kimi-ra-no chibusa natsu ki-taru Saitou Sanki
He6 = shocking to see / your glamorous breasts----/ summar has come
translated by N. Toushu
Hj6 = K1 ga K2 shita-ga K3 wo shirase-te kure-ta.
K1 = Osoroshi-hodo-ni kan-nou-teki-na kimira-no chibusa =your threateningly voluptuous breasts
K2 = I am shocked by
K3 = summer has come

Tran(Hj6) = The voluptuously exposed breasts of yours makes me shocked but at the same time realize that summer has come.

Osoru-beki Chibusa(おそるべき乳房) Shockingly voluptuously built breasts

∈ Time (midst of hot summer)
∈ Event (taking a night rest)
∈ Location (seaside shore, swimming pool bench)
∈ Weather (Fine)
∈ Participant (middle aged dirty-minded man, writer)
∈ Situation (Enjoying the arrival of hot summer)
*** 花冷えのちがふ乳房に逢ひにゆく 眞鍋呉夫

- K1 =花冷え(桜が咲いたが寒い)
- K2 =私は別の女に逢いにゆく
- m(" 乳房 ")= " 女 "," 愛人 "
- 省略=理由,気分(罪悪感と期待感(?)),

状況,全体的に暗い倦怠感,など

- M(K1,K2)= K1の頃,K2という事象(行動)が発生した

花冷えのちがふ乳房
∈ Time (early spring, occasionally cold day)
∈ Event (a secret meeting, tryst)
∈ Location (some love hotel or woman's house)
∈ Weather (maybe cloudy)
∈ Participant (man and woman not married)
∈ Situation (Going to enjoy a secret immoral love)
*** 密会の窓より高し梅雨の駅. 眞鍋呉夫

- K1 =私は女と密会している
- K2 =(宿泊しているホテルの)窓よりも駅が高いところにある
- K3 =梅雨時である
- M = K1 そして K2 に気づいた,時はK3
- 省略(不言): なぜ駅の高さが気になるのか? 全体的心情.状況

梅雨の駅
∈ Time (early summer, rainy season)
∈ Event (a secret meeting, tryst)
∈ Location (some love hotel just adjacent to the railway station)
∈ Weather (Rainy)
∈ Participant (man and woman committing adultery)
∈ Situation (Enjoying a secret immoral love)
*** 墓洗ふ汝(なれ)の隣は父の座ぞ 角川源義
Hj = Haka arau nare-no tonari-wa chichi-no za-zo
Kadokawa Genyoshi who survives his son.
He = Washing the gravestone of my son-----/ soon I will go / to your next. translated by N. Toushu
Hj = K1 shite-iru-ga K2 de-aru (K3 seyo)
K1 = haka-wo arau = Washing the gravestone

K2 = Omae-no tonari-wa chichi-no za-de-aru = your next is my position
K3 = Sabishi-garazu-ni matte ina-sai = Don't be lonesome and wait me for a short time
Tran(Hj) = I am washing your gravestone where I will visit soon, so don't feel lonely and wait my arrival.

Corresponding Local Haiku Ontology:
Haka-Arai(墓洗ひ) Washing the gravestone

∈ Time (autumn)
∈ Event (Visiting his son's grave)
∈ Location (graveyard)
∈ Weather (maybe cloudy)
∈ Participant (writer, survived father)
∈ Situation (Thinking of the early death of his son, Loneliness)
*** 死ぬときは箸を置くやうに草の花 小川軽舟
Hj = Shinu-Toki-wa Hasi-wo Oku-youni Kusa-no Hana Ogawa Keishuu
Hj = K1 suru-toki-wa K2 suru-youni K3
K1 = shinu = Dying
K2 = hashi-wo-oku = finish eating
K3 = Kusa-no-hana = Nmeless grass flowers
Tran(Hj) = He =The way of man's dying should resemble the way to finish eating; Look withered un-named grass flowers.

Corresponding Local Haiku Ontology

Shinu-Toki(死ぬとき) The tome of death

∈ Time (autumn)
∈ Event (Person's Passing away)
∈Location (garden, field, or his humble house)
∈Weather (maybe cloudy)
∈Participant (aged lonely male writer)
∈Situation (Thinking of one's last moment calmly)
*** 実のあるカツサンドなり冬の雲 小川軽舟

The author will show only the corresponding part of Haiku Ontology.
katsu-sando(カツサンド) Cutlet Sandwich

∈ Time (winter)
∈ Event (Person's Passing away)
∈Location (some local restaurant, serving rather simple foods usually)
∈Weather (cloudy)
∈Participant (aged lonely male writer)
∈Situation (eating a frugal meal)

SEASON WORD ONTOLOGY FOR HAIKU

To make and enjoy Haiku, it is necessary to use SAIJIKI, a glossary of seasonal words. Usually, Saijiki is a structureless plain lists of seasonal words that is often accompanied by illustrative verses and some concise explanations. Saijiki is often read as a life-course guide for daily lifestyles, events, foods, customs, manners etc.

These seasonal words or phrases are mutually related and deeply bound to everyone's daily life. In this sense, Saijiki has an ontological property. In the following, the author will illustrate a typical example of Saijiki as a poetic ontology and show how Saijiki is useful to understand and discern the beauty of Haiku.

In this section, the author will treat Haiku-Saijiki as an Ontology of human beings' daily life. First, the author must explain and/or define the ontology.

Originally, an ontology was a philosophical concept of old German investigating the essential nature of existence of all the things in this world. For the highly computerized modern world of today, Tom Gruber expanded the concept of ontology to construct a universal knowledge describing system (Gruber, 1993).

Following his idea, the author can view an ontology as a kind of meta-program specification language to describe new knowledge. From our standpoint, "knowledge" means a "new machine or device manipulation knowledge." In his ontology, the fundamental knowledge specification categories include entity (individual item, object, class, set), property, relation, condition, constraint, rule (if-then formulae), or event.

The author also has to explain and introduce the concept of "upper ontology." The upper ontology is defined to be the sub-ontology located at the top position among all other ontologies that can thus command the entire domain of involved ontologies. The upper ontology is sometimes called upper-level ontology, top-level ontology, general ontology, or general purpose ontology (Takeda, 2004; Bateman, Henschel, & Rinaldi, 1995; Jurisica, Mylopoulos, & Yu, 1999). The concept of ontology can be expanded from the information theory (Guarino, 1998).

The author claims that upper ontology for human beings' daily life should directly reflect the intuitive understanding, natural association, and common sense of ordinary people. If this Haiku upper ontology could have a natural linkage to the common Saijiki, it would provide a good guide for understanding the aesthetics of poetic sentences, especially Haiku.

Next, the author would like to construct an upper ontology of Haiku Saijiki by referring to classical Saijiki such as Ohno and Haiku-Bungakukan (1994) and Mizuhara (2005).

Figure 1. Upper Ontology of Haiku Saijiki

- *Upper Ontology of Haiku Saijiki (The Glossary of Seasonal Words)*
  ∋ Time x Space x Event x Weather x Participant x Situation
- *Time ∋ Month, Season, esp. the end of the year, New Year, January, the Bon, the Festival of the Dead, Summer Vacation, the Tanabata, the Festival of the Weaver Star and the Cowherd Star, the Dry Season,*
- *Space ∋ Location, Places of scenic beauty and historical interest, Remains and ruins, Historical building, Temple, Shrine, School, etc. Houses, Seashore, Mountain, Lake, Valley,*
- *Event ∋ Festival, Ceremony, Various activities of the school year,*
- *Weather ∋ Rain, Shower, light rain, drizzle, pouring rain, the typhoon brought torrential rains, drenching rains, misty rain, drizzle, fine rain, summer afternoon shower, spring rain, spring drizzle, freezing rain, cloudy weather, haze, mist,*
- *Participant ∋ Human, Animal, Abstract Thing, Machine, Vehicle,*
- *Situation ∋ Mood, Atmosphere, Happy Occasion, Congratulation, Appreciation, Solemn Atmosphere, Serious Situation, Mysterious Situation, Fanny Situation, Heart-warming Situation, Smile-provoking Situation, Sad Situation, Gloom-, Depression-, Despondency-, Miserable-, Melancholy-, Puzzling-, Fascinating-, Irritating-, Angry-,-Situation,*

Beneath the items given in the above Upper Ontology of Haiku, there are a lot of keywords.

Usually, the top category of the keyword's location assignment is arranged, not by alphabetical order, but by Time and Date, that is, Month (∋The Beginning of the Year, January, February, March, April, May, June, July, August, September, August, November, December (= Shiwasu, Teacher Running), the End of the Year, or the Four Seasons (∋ early spring, middle spring, late spring, early summer, midsummer, late summer, early autumn, middle autumn, the harvest season, late autumn, early winter, midwinter, severe winter, late winter)

Thus, each keyword inevitably has a lot of seasonal information and the potential to indicate a fixed time point on the calendar. For this reason, each keyword is called a seasonal word or phrase.

Every seasonal word carries lots of information and messages about human beings' daily life activities and social events in a corresponding time-point; thus, the Haiku, in spite of its ultimately short and concise 5-7-5 style, can convey very fruitful and imaginative messages to readers.

The guideline for successfully understanding or interpreting any Haiku that you may encounter is to have your own rich Haiku Ontology or Saijiki in mind. Haiku Ontology is a well-established and profound knowledge base covering a massive range of human activities.

Next, let us try to expand our profound knowledge about human beings' ordinary life activities, which will give you a kind of mental consolation or feeling of nostalgia.

COMPOSITION OF HAIKU-LIKE SENTENCES AS A NARRATIVE PROCESS

Haiku has achieved the limit of simplification; nevertheless, it maintains its message-passing ability. It depends on the imaginary association potentials of component words and phrases. This situation can be formalized in a somewhat naive intuitive style (Nitta, 2012d) as follows:

$H = K + R$

H: Haiku sentence (very short simple concise (pseudo-)sentence)

K: Kernel Sentence (that has canonical meaning)

R: References to outer world (Association, Conjecture)

R naturally depends on H.

$R = f(H)$ or $R = f(H, K)$

f is a function that has H and K as its objective variables. F is a meta-sentence that exists at the base of haiku H. The successfulness of semantic interpretation by meta-sentences will be confirmed through the translation of Japanese haiku into English haiku.

Figure 2. A Part of Haiku Ontology around the Season Word "Flying Kite"

Tako-age(凧あげ)flying a kite ∈ Time (early spring)
∈ Event (playing for rest)
∈ Location (an open space or field)
∈ Weather (fine weather with blue sky, but maybe with a breeze)
∈ Participant (maybe a young naughty boy of mischievous age)
∈ Situation (Relaxing and Refreshed, lively, sprightly)

Pay attention to the form:

H - K = R

The author would like to extract R, reference to the outer knowledge world. R depends on H. The author can write,

R = f (H) or R = f (H, K)

The function f() can be interpreted as a meta-sentence that exists at the base of haiku H. Note that for notational simplicity, the author uses $M = f^{-1}$. From now on, the author treats M() as meta-sentence instead of F().

Let us see some examples.

★Hc4: 月亮代表我的心　你問我愛你有多深
He 4: Blight moon light----
represents
our hearts clearly
then I'd like to ask the moon-----
still my sweetheart's love continues
as deep as before
Hj 4: 明月我が心を映す　いざ問わん汝は未だ我を思うや
K1 = 月亮代表
K2 = 我的心
K3 = 你問
K4 = 忘我愛你
K5 = 有多深
Tran(Hc4) = 月の光は私の心を表す　あなたは私に愛の深さを尋ねる
日 没 牛 群 山 風 涼
Sun set cows gather on hill wind cool
無人 街 灯 対 愁 眠

No man street light match with sorrow sleep

- 良好的治安秩序
  Sound Social Order
- 盛世中国
  Prosperous China
- 天下大治
  is going ahead the right track.
- ・・・穏定的社会美杯
  harmonious social care
- 如沐春風。
  just like a spring breeze.

In this chapter, the author can not treat the classical beauty of Chinese poems such as in (Yoshikawa & Miyoshi, 1952) owing to limited space.

COMPUTATIONAL ASPECT OF HAIKU-LIKE SENTENCE GENERATION

In this section, the author would like to refer to an early work of pseudo-Haiku generation by Mizutani (1979a, 1979b). His work was done using insufficient computational resources that were not yet equipped with enough ability to treat Japanese characters.

In the following, the author shows some examples of generated Haiku.

From Mizutani (1979a) and English translation by N. Toushu:

- Hana Akari Hito-no Yukusue Tsuku-duku-to
  花明り人の行末つくづくと
  [In the dim light of cherry blossom, I think of the future life over and over.]
- Naga Haka-wo Otonai-kite Shinobu Aki-no Tsuki
  汝が墓を訪ひ来て偲ぶ秋の月
  [Under the Autumn moon, I visited your grave and thought your time.]
- Waga Koi-wa Sora-no Hate-naru Shirayuri-ka
  わが恋は空の果てなる白百合か
  [My love may be something like a white lily in bloom over the sky.]
  From Mizutani (1979b) and English translation by N. Toushu:
- Fuyu-no Tsuki Ikyou-ni Sumite Haya Yo-nen
  冬の月異郷に住みてはや四年
  [Winter moon, already four years have passed since I lived in this foreign country.]
- Aki-kusa-ya Hito-no Ykusue Tsukuduku-to
  秋草や人の行く末つくづくと
  [Autumn grass makes me think deeply of our future.]
- Aki-no Hi-ni Kinou-no Gotoku Kyou-mo Mata
  秋の日に昨日のごとく今日もまた
  [In Autumn, I live today just as same as yesterday.]

The basic mechanism of the Haiku generator program is a kind of naïve coupling work between upper phrases (5-character-length Japanese phrase) and lower phrases (7+5 = 12-character-length Japanese phrase). Very simple phrase matching tests such as part-of-speech adequacy, verb-noun connection, and Kireji [special Japanese character to indicate phrasal emphasis] judgement are done.

Reading the Haiku above, the reader may feel that they are understandable enough as full-fledged Haiku. However, this Haiku generator program (Mizutani, 1979a, 1979b) was not equipped with any natural language understanding power. Thus, the apparent plausibility of the generated Haiku can be attributed to luck and good-quality phrases (Nitta, 2015). Some formal treatment of semantics of haiku is argued in (Nitta, 2012b).

Haiku-like sentences can easily be manipulated as a kind of regular language (Saraki & Nitta, 2005).

Fragmental sentence patterns like

Kj1 ya Kj2, Kj3
N no N
N mo N
N ga VP mo
(in Japanese Haiku)
NP VP ----N and N
NP ---- NP VP ---- NP VP
(in English Haiku)

can be treated as a kind of pattern matching by some appropriate finite state machine (Kinyon, 2001; Saraki & Nitta, 2008).

TRANSLATION USING FUNCTIONAL GRAMMAR

Some translation may be necessary for nonnative Japanese language people to understand haiku written in Japanese. The idea and methodology of meta-sentences in functional grammar are useful for this translation. In this chapter, the author has used a little bit simplified notion of functional grammar. The fully equipped standard version of functional grammar can be seen in (Dik, 1997)

Basics of Meta-Sentence

Readers should recall that every sentence is composed of two categories: kernel sentence K and meta-sentence. M() Let us denote K as kernel sentence and M() as meta-sentence. Meta-sentences behave like a function over the kernel sentence, and so the author can write

$$S = M(K)$$

Here, S denotes a sentence. If the author would like to emphasize that sentence S is written by language j or language e, then the author would write

$$Sj = Mj\ (Kj)$$

or

$$Se = Me\ (Ke)$$

where, Mj means the meta-sentence in language j, and Ke means the kernel sentence in language e.

If the author denotes the translation between language j and language e as Tran,

$$Tran: Sj \rightarrow Se$$

Then at the same time,

Tran: Mj()→ Me()

represents the bilingual alignment between language j and e, whose concrete example will be shown later.

Translation Through Meta-Sentences

First, let us show concrete examples.

- **Surface sentences:**
  S1: Shbai gara kare-wa kane nokoto-niha nukeme-ga nai.
  (商売がら彼は金のことには抜け目がない。)
  S2: shoubai-wo shite-iru-node kare-wa kane-niha binkan de-aru.
  (商売をしているので彼は金には敏感である。)
  S3: Because of the nature of his business, he is sharp about money.
  S4: His business makes him sensitive about
- **Kernel sentences:**
  K1 = "Kare-wa kane-niwa nukeme-ga nai"
  ("彼は金には抜け目がない")
  K2 = "kare-wa kane-niwa binkan de-aru"
  ("彼は金には敏感である")
  K3 = "he is sharp about money."
  K4 = "he is sensitive about money"
- **Meta-sentences:**
  M1(N,Sent) = N gara(がら) Sent
  M2(N,Sent) = N shite-iru-node(しているので) Sent
  M3(N,Sent) = Because of N, Sent
  M4(N,Sent) = N make Sent

Here, N and Sent are meta-symbols (syntactic variables) as usual.
Later, the author will use simplified expressions such as

M1 = ~ gara …
M3 = Because of ~, …

Eventually, translation is the functional mapping of Tran() over kernel sentence K and/or meta-sentence M(). Bilingual alignments are the outcomes from Tran().

Tran: K1 → K3 or Tran(K1) = K3
Tran: M1()→ M3() or Tran(M1()) = M3()
M1(N, K1) = M1("Shoubai", "Kare-wa kane-niwa nukeme-ga nai")
= "Shoubai gara Kare-wa kane-niwa nukeme-ga nai"
Tran(M1) (Tran("Shoubai"), Tran("Kare-wa kane-niwa nukeme-ga nai"))
= M3(Tran("Shoubai"), Tran("Kare-wa kane-niwa nukeme-ga nai"))

= M3(“Business”, “he is sharp about money. ”
= “Because of the nature of his business, he is sharp about money.”

For each meta-sentence M(), its mapped image Tran(M()) is essentially dependent on the value of its dominant variable(s) K. Typical evidence of this dependency is illustrated in the following examples.

In the above, N = “Shoubai” and K = “Kare-wa kane-niwa nukeme-ga nai.”

Now, if the author puts N = “Sensei toiu shoubai” (“先生という商売”)and K = “Watashi-wa okonai-wo tsutsusinde-iru.” (“私は行いを慎んでいる”)

Then,

$$\text{Tran (M1(N, K))} \neq \text{M3 (Tran(N), Tran(K))}$$

but

$$\text{Tran (M1(N, K))} = \text{M5 (Tran(N), Tran(K))}$$

or

$$\text{Tran: M1(N, K)} \rightarrow \text{M5 (Tran(N), Tran(K)}$$

Here M5 (N, K) = As N, K

Finally,

M5 (Tran(N), Tran(K)) = “As Tran(N), Tran(K).”

= “As a teacher, I try to be careful of my behavior.”.

Collected Examples of Meta-Sentences

First the author has to note the directionality of translation.

Tran^{-1} (Tran(S)) ≠ S for almost all translations Tran and sentences S.

The notion of directionality or unsymmetrical property has been studied pragmatically in translation theory (Munday, 2009; Nitta, 1986, 2001, 2002, 2012a) in opposition to the notion of natural translation.

Thus, translations of meta-sentence M() and bilingual alignment inevitably have directionality or unsymmetrical property, Tran^{-1} (Tran(M())) ≠ M()

This is the main reason for the overall difficulty of translation. Here “j” stands for Japanese language and “e” stands for English language.

To collect meta-sentences useful for j-to-e directional translation, the author can use some effective trigger word or phrases as follows.

- ~shite…suru [~して…する]
- ~de-aru-ga-yue-ni …de-aru (da) [~であるがゆえに　…である(だ)]
- ~shita-node… [~したので…]
- ~da-kara… [~だから…]

These kinds of trigger-word oriented meta-sentences can be obtained relatively easily from a well-designed bilingual corpus by using regular expression based-text mining technique. Character class switching from Kanji to Hiragana gives a good clue for effective mining (Saraki & Nitta, 2008).

Typical Japanese meta-sentences generally have the following structure:

M(K1, K2) = "K1 shite K2 shita"
= "K1 shite K2 ni-natta"
="K1 [da]kara K2 shita"
Here K1 = kernel sentence representing cause or reason,
K2 = consequence, result, event
The translated meta-sentence generally has the following style:
Me(Tran(K2), Tran(K1)) = Sent2 +Sent1
= Sent2 + Conjunction + Sent1
= Sent2 + VPing1
= Sent2 + Preposition + VPing1
= Sent2 + to + VPinfinitive1
Here, Sent2 = Tran(K2), VP1 = Tran(K1).

(1) K1 ∈ cause, reason K2 ∈ involuntary event occurrences

Mj(K1, K2) = "Sono hako-wo mochi-age you-**to-shite** Umeko wa kata-no suji-wo tigae-ta."
[その箱を持ち上げよう として 梅子は肩の筋を違えた。]
Me(tran(K2), tran(K1)) = Umeko strained her shoulder **lifting** the box.
Me() = Sent2 + VP**ing**1

(2) K1 ∈ origin, cause) K2 ∈effect, reward

Mj(K1, K2) = "Kare-wa shingou-wo mushi-**shite** omoi batsu-wo uke-**ta**."
[彼は信号無視を して 重い罰を受けた。]
Me(tran(K2), tran(K1)) = He was severely punished **for** runn**ing** a red light.
Me() = Sent2 + for + VP**ing**1

If a bilingual corpus is equipped with semantic role code annotations, the meta-sentence extracting processing will be much more powerful. A somewhat similar idea can be seen in (Bateman, Henschel & Rinaldi, 1995). Currently, the author is using the following codes:

FUTURE RESEARCH DIRECTIONS

The next step is to construct a more powerful program to extract and manipulate meta-sentences and to make an extensive experiment to investigate the aesthetics of Haiku-like poetic sentences. The construction of substantial Haiku Ontology is also the author's next goal.

The author and the readers live in an aggressively expanding artificial intelligence era. Various kinds of automatic sentence and/or text generators for practical language usage will soon emerge. Haiku has a highly intelligent and creative human-oriented aesthetics that will create a strong seawall to prevent the invasion of the automatic artificial intelligence tide. However, the author cannot be indifferent to this trend. The author has a plan to construct a kind of Haiku-making agent that can range over Haiku-

Table 1. Table of Semantic Role Marker (Nitta, 2012d)

Semantic Role	Examples
A (Agent)	The policeman caught a thief. She has a dream that her son ･･･
O (Object)	･･･produces a current of air･･･ ･･･make sounds by sending air
C (Complement)	He is the mayor of our city. Having to do with France ･･･
R (Relating)	According to the radio news, today's weather is partly rainy･･･
I (Instrument)	･･･taking pleasure in giving pain to others ･･･destroys with an explosion･･･
S (Source)	The spy came from the cold country. They make cheese out of milk.
G (Goal)	make angry, go to bed, a ground prepared for plants
L (Location)	a small vessel for traveling on water ･･･being on the inside
T (Time)	We will stay this hotel for six weeks. get up at 6 a.m. sharp
P (Purpose)	travel by boat for pleasure They stopped to smoke.
X (Situation, Event)	a man who is rough and rude in speech and manner We all are in the same situation.
D (Degree, Mode)	Take it as much as possible. You can hit me, if I am wrong, but very gently.
M (Modification, Constraint)	You must report here tomorrow at seven sharp. His teacher was an irresistibly attractive lady.
W (Wake (わけ)) (Cause, Reason)	Bring my umbrella, as the weather is threatening. Please treat me to a lunch; today, I am short of money.
K (Kekka (結果) (Consequence, Result)	The robbery shot a clerk to death. He lived his life in virtuous penury and finally starved to death.

ontology from corner to corner with some strong emotion and can compose a Haiku-like shot sentence. The purpose of this agent construction is to reveal the difference between: creative Haiku writing by humans and mimic Haiku writing by artificial intelligence.

CONCLUSION

The author viewed Japanese poetic sentences, especially a group of Haiku, through two kinds of semantic devices. One device was functional grammar, and the other was Haiku Ontology or Haiku Upper Ontology.

Thanks to the effective power of these devices, the author successfully revealed the secret of the "concise beauty" of Haiku to some extent. Haiku is an extremely simple Japanese poetic sentence, which is now a worldwide compositional model of beautiful sentences.

The most vital feature in functional grammar is the notion of meta-sentences, a kind of operator for surface sentence formation. Meta-sentences work over the domain of kernel sentences. The kernel sentence behaves like a fundamental element in language translation, which has canonical forms of translation correspondence in target language and bi-directional (symmetrical) translation properties. Thus, kernel sentence has a simple structure, is easily translatable, and forms the baseline of overall translation.

Here, the author should note that translation can be read as a version of semantic interpretation if the author gives a semantic form to the translated target.

The author also introduced the notion of Haiku Ontology or Haiku Upper Ontology and then gave a demonstration of the construction of a small version of Haiku-Upper-Ontology by using several classical Saijiki as the referencing corpus. Haiku Ontology gives us profound knowledge about keywords/key phrases that compose the kernel of Haiku. The superficial mission of this keyword/key phrase is providing temporal or seasonal information, but actually, the amount of provided information is far more than that. This is the reason that an ultimately concise sentence like a Haiku can represent or carry such a rich and fruitful message in it.

Currently, meta-sentences have been extracted and collected semi-automatically using naive pattern-matching programs based on regular expressions (Kinyon, 2001; Saraki & Nitta, 2008). The author expects some novel meta-sentences can be extracted from parallel text analysis (Bentivogli & Pianta, 2005; Church, Dagan, Gale, Fung, Helfman, & Satish, 1993; Macklovitch & Marie-Louise, 1996; Mihalcea & Simard, 2005).

REFERENCES

Bateman, J., Henschel, R., & Rinaldi, F. (1995). *The generalized upper model 2.0.* Retrieved from http://www.darmstadt.gmd.de/publish/komet/gen-um/newUM.html

Bentivogli, L., & Pianta, E. (2005). Exploiting parallel texts in the creation of multilingual semantically annotated resources: The MultiSemiCor Corpus. *Natural Language Engineering*, *11*(3), 247–261. doi:10.1017/S1351324905003839

Church, K., Dagan, I., Gale, W., Fung, P. N., Helfman, J., & Satish, B. (1993). Aligning parallel texts: Do methods developed for English-French generalize to Asian languages? In *Proceedings of the Pacific Asia Conference on Formal and Computational Linguistics* (pp.1-12). Taipei: Academica Sinica.

Dik, S. C. (1997). The theory of functional grammar (Vols. 1-2). Berlin: Mouton de Gruyter.

Gruber, T. R. (1993). A translation approach to portable ontology specifications. *Knowledge Acquisition*, *5*(2), 199–220. doi:10.1006/knac.1993.1008

Guarino, N. (1998). Formal ontology and information systems. In N. Guarino (Ed.), *Formal Ontology in Information Systems. Proceedings of FOIS'98* (pp. 3-15). Amsterdam: IOS Press.

Jurisica, I., Mylopoulos, J., & Yu, E. (1999). Using ontologies for knowledge management: An information systems perspective. In *Proceedings of Annual Conference of the American Society for Information Science* (pp. 380-401). Washington, DC: American Society for Information Science.

Kinyon, A. (2001). A language-independent shallow-parser compiler. In *Proceedings of the 39th ACL Annual Meeting (European Chapter)* (pp.322-329). Association for Computational Linguistics.

Macklovitch, E., & Marie-Louise, H. (1996). Line 'em up: Advances in alignment technology and their impact on translation support tools. In *Proceedings of the 1996 AMTA* (pp. 145-156). The Association for Machine Translation in the Americas.

Mihalcea, R., & Simard, M. (2005). Parallel texts. *Natural Language Engineering, 11*(3), 239–246. doi:10.1017/S1351324905003827

Mizuhara, S. (Ed.). (2005). *Shinso-ban - Haiku sho saijiki* [Remodeled version: Handy glossary of seasonal words for haiku]. Tokyo, Japan: Ohizumi-shoten.

Mizutani, S. (1979a). Haiku-wo tsukuru keisanki [A computer program for generating haikus]. *Tokyo Joshi Daigaku Ronshu, 52,* 85-97. Retrieved from http://opac.library.twcu.ac.jp/opac/repository/1/4744/

Mizutani, S. (1979b). Futatabi haiku-wo tsukuru keisanki [One more a computer program for generating haikus]. *Tokyo Joshi Daigaku Ronshu, 63,* 106-103. Retrieved from http://opac.library.twcu.ac.jp/opac/repository/1/4833/

Munday, J. (2009). *Introducing translation studies.* Abingdon, UK: Taylor & Francis Group.

Nitta, Y. (1986). Idiosyncratic gap: A tough problem to machine translation. In *Proceedings of the Computational Linguistics (COLING' 86)* (pp. 107-111). The Association for Computational Linguistics. doi:10.3115/991365.991394

Nitta, Y. (2001). The utility and problem of insufficient machine translation. *Economic Review of Nihon University, 80*(4), 1–54.

Nitta, Y. (2002). Problems of machine translation: From a viewpoint of logical semantics. *Economic Review of Nihon University, 72*(2), 23–42.

Nitta, Y. (2012a). *Kikai hon'yaku no Genri to Katsuyoho - Kotenteki kikai hon'yaku saihyoka no kokoromi* [Principle of machine translation and its practical usage: An attempt to reassess the value of classical transfer-based machine translation]. Tokyo, Japan: Akashi-shoten.

Nitta, Y. (2012b). HAIKU no imi no keisiki teki kaishaku no kokoromi [An essay on a formal interpretation of HAIKU]. In *Proceedings of A-13-5 Thought and Language Session, IEICE Conference at Okayama University* (p. 215). Tokyo, Japan: The Institute of Electronics, Information and Communication Engineers.

Nitta, Y. (2012c). An approach to linguistic aesthetics by functional grammar. In *Proceedings of the 22nd Biennial Congress of the International Association of Empirical AESTHETICS (IAEA) 2012 Aug* (pp. 22-25). Rome, Italy: University of Rome Tre.

Nitta, Y. (2012d). Aesthetic sentence generation by functional grammar. *Economic Review of Nihon University, 82*(3), 9-17.

Nitta, Y. (2013). Silence of beautiful sentences - The mechanism of omission in HAIKU. In *Proceedings of the IEICE Conference on Study of Thought and Language. Meiji University., International General Research Laboratory* (*Vol. 114*, No. 442, pp. 73-78). Tokyo, Japan: The Institute of Electronics, Information and Communication Engineers.

Nitta, Y. (2015). On the formal generation of Haiku. In Technical Report of IEICE (2015-3) (Vol. 114, No. 465, pp. 23-26). Tokyo, Japan: The Institute of Electronics, Information and Communication Engineers.

Ohno, R. (Supervisory Editor) & Haiku-Bungakukan (Ed.). (1994). Handy-version introductory haiku saijiki. Tokyo: Kadokawa-shoten.

Saraki, M. (Ed.). (2008). Seiki-Hyougen-to Text Mining [Regular expression and text mining]. Tokyo, Japan: Akashi-shoten.

Saraki, M., & Nitta, Y. (2005). The semantic classification of verb conjunction in the "Shite" Form. *Proceedings of Spring IECEI Conference* (A-13-3). Tokyo: The Institute of Electronics, Information and Communication Engineers.

Takeda, H. (2004). Upper Ontology. *Journal of Artificial Intelligence Japan, 19*(2), 172–186.

Yamane, T. (1996). *Chiyo-Jo's haiku seasons* (Y. Ishibashi & P. Donegan, Trans.). Matto City Publishing.

Yoshikawa, K., & Miyoshi, T. (1952). *Shin-Toshi-sen* [Selected collection of new Tang-era Chinese poetries]. Tokyo, Japan: Iwanami-shoten.

KEY TERMS AND DEFINITIONS

Functional Grammar: Grammar formalism that regards sentential meaning as a mathematical function, where its arguments are kernel sentences. Its functional behavior is determined by meta-sentences.

Haiku: Japanese short poem that has seventeen syllables in 5-7-5 form. Its origin is the head poem of Renga (linked verse). It has a rule involving the special functional character Kireji and season words.

Kernel Sentence: A unitary simple sentence that has a self-explanatory meaning.

Meta-Ontology: A higher concept of ontology that typically defines its structure.

Meta-Sentence: A framework for defining a basic sentence that represents the meaning of said Haiku.

Seasonal Word Ontology (Saijiki, Haiku Ontology): A book or database that is composed of season word and its definitions and explanations on actual usage together with associated environmental information. Every person perhaps may have his/her own ontology in his/her mind.

Chapter 10
Literary Metaphor Comprehension and Production:
A Unified View

Akira Utsumi
The University of Electro-Communications, Japan

ABSTRACT

This chapter addresses literary metaphors, which are used in literary works to enrich the meanings and evoke aesthetic effects. The aim of this chapter is to provide a unified view that can explain how literary metaphors are understood and generated. The chapter authors argue that comprehension of various types of literary metaphors involves a process of direct or indirect categorization by integrating and extending existing metaphor theories and empirical findings, in particular the author's metaphor research such as the interpretive diversity theory of nominal metaphors and the indirect categorization theory of predicative metaphors. The chapter authors also apply the unified view of literary metaphor comprehension to metaphor production, and discuss how people generate literary metaphors.

INTRODUCTION

Metaphor is one of the most important rhetorical devices that enrich narrative discourse or literary work. This chapter particularly focuses on *literary metaphors*, which are primarily used for evoking aesthetic or poetic effects on readers/hearers, rather than explanatory metaphors used for clarifying what writers/speakers want to convey. In his "*Rhetoric*," for example, Aristotle listed three functions of metaphors by stating that "metaphor especially has clarity and sweetness and strangeness." Literary metaphors are associated with sweetness and strangeness, while explanatory metaphors are associated with clarity.

Literary metaphors often convey a variety of meanings. For example, consider a famous literary metaphor in Shakespeare's play "Romeo and Juliet."

(1) But, soft! What light through yonder window breaks? It is the east, and Juliet is the sun!

DOI: 10.4018/978-1-5225-4775-4.ch010

Copyright © 2018, IGI Global. Copying or distributing in print or electronic forms without written permission of IGI Global is prohibited.

The metaphor "Juliet is the sun" in (1) can express a variety of meanings such as that Juliet appears above Romeo, bringing him hope and gladness, and he cannot live without her. These rich meanings cannot be conveyed effectively by literal language. More importantly, if these meanings are literally expressed, his words lose aesthetic or poetic effects on the audience. Existing empirical findings support the richness of interpretation as the characteristic feature of literary or poetic metaphors. Utsumi (2005) demonstrated that poeticality rating of metaphors was positively correlated with the richness of interpretation (or interpretive diversity) and richer interpretations of metaphors involved more emergent meanings. Roncero & de Almeida (2015) reported that interpretive diversity was negatively correlated with metaphor conventionality. These findings suggest that literary metaphors tend to be novel or creative in nature.

The question that arises here is how literary metaphors are processed. This chapter addresses this question, and provides a unified view of literary metaphor comprehension and production by reference to the author's previous studies on metaphors. The central argument of the unified view is that literary metaphor comprehension and production can be explained as *categorization*, the process by which distinct entities are treated as equivalent. In the rest of this chapter, how categorization is essentially involved in metaphor comprehension and production will be described in detail.

BACKGROUND

The Structure of Metaphors

Metaphor is a figurative expression in which a certain concept is described in terms of another unlike concept. *The tenor* of a metaphor is the concept described by the metaphor, and *the vehicle* is the concept employed to describe the tenor. For example, the metaphor (2) has the tenor "my love" and the vehicle "a red rose," and the metaphor (3) has the tenor "that man" and the vehicle "a wolf."

(2) My love is a red rose.
(3) That man is a wolf.

Metaphors are classified into two types, namely *nominal metaphor* and *predicative metaphor*. Nominal metaphors and predicative metaphors differ in what is being processed metaphorically; some specific things such as living creatures and objects referred to by a noun (or a noun phrase) are figuratively described by nominal metaphors, while actions, events, or properties are described figuratively using predicative metaphors. In other words, the tenor and vehicle are noun concepts in the case of nominal metaphors, and predicates in the case of predicative metaphors. The above metaphors (2) and (3) are typical examples of nominal metaphors, while the following expressions are examples of predicative metaphors.

(4) Public anger boils over.
(5) Anna ate up the whole story.
(6) deep red laugh

Predicative metaphors can be further classified into *verb metaphors* and *adjective metaphors* depending on whether verbs or adjectives are used metaphorically.

For nominal metaphors of the type "A is B," both tenor and vehicle are explicitly expressed as in the case of (2) and (3). Some nominal metaphors, however, do not involve an explicit reference to the tenor. For example, metaphoric referential expressions such as (7b) refer to the tenor in terms of the vehicle without explicitly expressing the tenor.

(7) a. That man is aggressive and fierce.
b. *The wolf* is attacking me in a wild frenzy.

Note that the tenor of "A is B" metaphor such as (2) and (3) is also a topic, but the tenor of referential metaphors such as "that man" in (7b) cannot be the topic of that sentence. The vehicle "wolf" is the topic of the sentence (7b).

On the other hand, in the case of predicative metaphors, only the vehicles are verbalized in the metaphorical expressions. This is because the tenor of predicative metaphors cannot be verbalized; this motivates the metaphorical use of verbs or adjectives. For example, the vehicle of the verbal metaphor (4) is the state of *boiling over* and the tenor is the state described metaphorically by *boiling over*. More concretely, predicative metaphors (4) and (5) have the following structure:

(4') Public anger's state of α-ing is something γ's state of boiling over.
(5') Anna's action of α-ing the story is her action of eating up something γ.

The tenor of these predicative metaphors is an unexpressed state or action α. Adjective metaphors such as (6) also have the same structure.

(6') Laugh's property of being α is something γ's property of being deep red.

This structure of predicative metaphors has not been discussed clearly in the existing literature. Sometimes the terms "tenor" and "topic" are used confusingly for predicative metaphors. For example, the subject "public anger" of the metaphor (4) is not a tenor, but the topic of the metaphor. Note also that, as I will explain in the next section, comprehension of predicative metaphors involves identification of an entity γ that literally expressed by the vehicle (i.e., boiling over or being deep red).

Review of Existing Studies on Metaphor Comprehension and Production

Most of the existing studies on metaphor have addressed comprehension of nominal metaphors (e.g., Bowdle & Gentner, 2005; Glucksberg & Keysar, 1990). In contrast, only a few attempts have been made at exploring comprehension of predicative metaphors and production of metaphors.

Comprehension of Nominal Metaphor

Psychological or cognitive studies on nominal metaphor have found that nominal metaphor comprehension involves two different processes, namely, *comparison* and *categorization*. The comparison view (Gentner, 1983) argues that metaphors (and analogies) are processed as comparisons consisting of a process of structural alignment between representations of the tenor and the vehicle followed by a process of projection of aligned features or relations into the tenor. For example, in comprehending the metaphor "A rumor is a virus," the tenor "rumor" and the vehicle "virus" are aligned, salient alignments such as ones about contagion, infection prevention, or sanitary habits are found, and features and relations inferred from such alignments are projected into the tenor. Note that the initial alignment process is symmetric (i.e., the products of the process do not change even if the tenor and the vehicle are reversed), while the subsequent projection process is asymmetric (i.e., directional). Hence, the intuition that the reversed metaphor "A virus is a rumor" seems meaningless can be attributed to the projection process, not to the alignment process. On the other hand, the categorization view (Glucksberg, 2001; Glucksberg & Keysar, 1990) claims that metaphors are regarded as categorization (i.e., class-inclusion) statements expressing that the tenor is a member of an abstract superordinate category exemplified by the vehicle. For example, the metaphor "My job is a jail" is comprehended so that the tenor "my job" is categorized as an ad hoc category like "unpleasant and confining things" to which the vehicle "jail" typically belongs. Note that the tenor also plays an important role in metaphor comprehension; it constrains dimensions by which it can be characterized. In the case of the above metaphor, "my job" facilitates attribution of features related to tasks and jobs, while blocking out irrelevant features such as ones related to jail building.

Recent studies have attempted to reconcile these two opposite views of metaphor comprehension into a coherent metaphor theory. They have explored the metaphor property that determines the choice of comprehension strategy between categorization and comparison and proposed three different views: the conventionality view (Bowdle & Gentner, 2005), aptness view (Glucksberg & Haught, 2006b, 2006a; Jones & Estes, 2006), and interpretive diversity view (Utsumi, 2007). Bowdle & Gentner (2005) have claimed that it is vehicle conventionality that determines the choice; their career of metaphor theory argues that although metaphors are initially processed as comparisons, conventional metaphors are processed as categorizations by accessing the stored metaphoric categories that are conventionalized by repeated figurative use of the vehicle term. Against the conventionality view, Jones & Estes (2005, 2006) and Glucksberg & Haught (2006b) have advocated that metaphor aptness mediates both the processes. This view argues that while metaphors are initially processed as categorizations, less apt metaphors are processed as comparisons. Against these views, Utsumi (2007) has argued that *interpretive diversity* determines whether metaphors are processed as comparisons or categorizations. Interpretive diversity refers to the semantic richness of metaphors and depends on the following two factors: the number of features or interpretations that constitute the figurative meaning, and the uniformity of the salience distribution of those features. A higher value of interpretive diversity means that the metaphor has a larger number of meanings (or interpretations) and that the salience of those meanings is more uniformly distributed. The interpretive diversity view then argues that although metaphors are initially processed as comparisons, diverse metaphors (in particular, literary metaphors) fail to be processed as comparisons and must be reinterpreted as categorizations, because categorization is often expected to attribute many features of a category to the members of that category.

Comprehension of Predicative Metaphor

Glucksberg (2001) and Torreano, Cacciari, & Glucksberg (2005) claim that the categorization view of nominal metaphors can be applied to comprehension of predicative metaphors. Just as nominal metaphors use noun vehicles that epitomize certain categories of objects or situations, predicative metaphors use verbs that epitomize certain metaphoric categories of actions. For example, in the following metaphors, the verb "fly" evokes the abstract category of speedy travel because flying can be considered a prototypical action in that category.

(8) John hopped on his bike and flew home.
(9) The rumor flew through the office.

The conceptual metaphor theory (Lakoff & Johnson, 1980, 1999) explains that metaphorical expressions, in particular predicative metaphors, are interpreted as verbal instantiations of *conceptual metaphors*. Conceptual metaphors are preexisting cross-domain analogical mappings that are grounded in embodied experiences, and our conceptual system is structured by conceptual metaphors. For example, the following predicative metaphors can be understood on the basis of the conceptual metaphor ARGUMENT IS WAR.

(10) a. He shot down all of my arguments.
b. I demolished his argument.
c. Your claims are indefensible.

The vehicles "shoot down," "demolish," and "indefensible," which are terms for describing physical battle, are used metaphorically to express verbal battle.

Metaphor Production

As compared to metaphor comprehension, only a few studies have addressed the process of metaphor production, possibly because a production process is generally difficult to examine by psychological experiments.

Previous studies on metaphor production did not directly address the process of metaphor production; rather they analyzed the products of metaphor production in terms of the qualitative dimensions of metaphors or individual differences. For the qualitative dimensions of metaphor products, Fainsilber and Ortony (1987) found that descriptions of emotional states contained more metaphorical language than did descriptions of actions. Katz (1989) examined the properties of metaphor vehicles by asking participants to choose, from a set of alternatives, a vehicle that completes a given sentence frame (e.g., Chemistry is the ____ of science) as comprehensible and apt metaphors. The result was that participants were likely to choose the vehicles that were moderately distant from the tenor and referred to concrete domains. For individual differences, Hussey and Katz (2006) examined whether metaphor production in online conversation is affected by gender and friendship status. They found that men produced more metaphors than woman, but the amount of metaphor produced did not differ between conversations with a friend and a stranger. In contrast, it was found that women produced more metaphors when chatting with a friend than with a stranger. Chiappe & Chiappe (2007) demonstrated that people with high working memory capacity produced more apt metaphors than low capacity individuals. Other studies also reported that the quantity and quality of metaphor products were affected by individual differences such as writing experience (experienced or novice) (Williams-Whitney et al. 1992) and reasoning and imagery ability (Katz 1989).

METAPHOR COMPREHENSION

Metaphor comprehension is a process of deriving an interpretation I from a metaphor M given in the context C.

$$I = f\left(M;C\right)$$

The context or situation C refers to extrasentential (or extra-metaphorical) factors, which are divided into verbal and nonverbal factors. It is well known that contextual or situational factors affect metaphor comprehension and production, but it is nevertheless beyond the scope of this chapter.

According to the structure of metaphors explained in the last section, it is obvious that the comprehension process $f\left(M\right)$ differs between nominal and predicative metaphors. In the rest of this chapter, the tenor and vehicle of a metaphor are denoted by α and β, respectively. The topic of the metaphorical expression is denoted by δ. In the case of predicative metaphors, an implicit topic (or intermediate entity) literally expressed by the vehicle is denoted by γ.

For a nominal metaphor of the type "α is β," some properties and relations $p(\alpha)$ of the tenor highlighted by the vehicle constitute an interpretation I of that metaphor. Metaphor comprehension is thus the process of deriving properties of the tenor $p(\alpha)$ that are similar to some salient properties $q(\beta)$ of the vehicle, which is formalized as follows:

$$\mathrm{BE}(\alpha, \beta) \rightarrow \exists p\, \exists q\, \mathrm{SIM}(p(\alpha), q(\beta)), \tag{11}$$

where $\mathrm{SIM}(p, q)$ denotes that properties p and q are associated with or similar to each other. For example, in the case of the metaphor (2), the properties of being beautiful and graceful correspond to p and q.

For a predicative metaphor, its interpretation I is the tenor $\alpha(\delta)$ (i.e., states, actions, events that are concerned with the topic δ) and comprehension can be regarded as a process of finding α.

$$\beta(\delta) \rightarrow \exists \alpha\, \exists \gamma\, \mathrm{SIM}(\alpha(\delta), \beta(\gamma)) \tag{12}$$

where the notations $\alpha(\delta)$ and $\beta(\gamma)$ indicate that the tenor and vehicle are predicates that respectively take δ and γ as an argument. Comprehension of predicative metaphors involves identification of γ, although it does not necessarily constitute an interpretation.

From these formalizations, we can see that metaphor comprehension is a similarity discovery process in which readers attempt to find or discover the similarity between the topic and vehicle of a given metaphor that constitutes the intended meanings of the metaphor. When a metaphor is conventional or explanatory, the similarity is easy to find; the metaphorical meaning can be accessed directly from the lexical meaning of the vehicle, or only a few salient features are obviously shared by the topic and vehicle. On the other hand, when a metaphor is novel or literary, the similarity is not easy to find and readers struggle to discover a variety of potential similarities enough for the metaphor to make sense. Through this effortful process, rich metaphorical interpretations are obtained and such semantic richness evokes poetic or aesthetic effects on readers. In the following sections, I explain in details that the similarity discovery is the process of ad hoc or improvised categorization.

Comprehension of Nominal Metaphors

In this chapter, we argue that the cognitive mechanism governing the similarity discovery process for comprehending literary nominal metaphors is ad hoc categorization. According to the categorization view (Glucksberg, 2001; Glucksberg & Keysar, 1990), nominal metaphor comprehension consists of the following two steps:

1. A category C is exemplified by the vehicle β, which is a prototypical member of that category.
2. The tenor α is treated as a member of the category C. The interpretation of the metaphor is a set of prototypical or salient properties and relations in that category.

For a conventional metaphor, the category C may preexist and the vehicle β may be a conventional name of that category. The preexisting category is accessed at Step 1 and the tenor is interpreted as a member of that category. For example, the vehicle "creampuff" in the following metaphor has a lexical meaning of "an ineffectual person" and thus creampuff is a conventional name of the category of an ineffectual person.

(13) He is a creampuff.

For a literary or novel metaphor, a new category C is created on the spot. An ad hoc category is determined primarily by the vehicle, but the tenor α may impose constraints on the properties by which it can be characterized. For example, in the case of the metaphor (3), an improvised category of fierce and dangerous living things is created by the vehicle "wolf," and the metaphor is interpreted as a class inclusion assertion that the tenor "that man" is a member of the created category, as shown in Figure 1(a).

Why are literary nominal metaphors comprehended as categorizations, not as comparisons? How is the argument of literary metaphor comprehension as categorization consistent with the existing metaphor views described in the review section? Before providing an answer to these questions, we note one empirical finding that motivates this argument. As mentioned before, three metaphor properties, namely, vehicle conventionality, metaphor aptness, and interpretive diversity, have been proposed to determine the choice between categorization and comparison. Utsumi (2011) has attempted to answer the question regarding which of these three properties best affect the choice by using cognitive modeling and computer simulation based on a distributional semantic model. The result was that both interpretive diversity and vehicle conventionality affected the choice between the two processes, but metaphor aptness did not affect this choice.

Following this finding, we can provide a whole picture of nominal metaphor comprehension as follows:

1. A conventional metaphor such as (13) is easily comprehended by a categorization process, in which the static metaphoric category (or metaphorical meaning) lexically encoded in the vehicle is retrieved from the mental lexicon and attributed to the tenor, as argued by the conventionality view (Bowdle & Gentner, 2005).
2. If a given metaphor is not conventional, it is initially attempted to be comprehended by a comparison process. When the tenor and vehicle have a few highly salient similarities enough to yield a plausible interpretation of the metaphor (i.e., a less diverse interpretation suffices for comprehension), the comprehension process succeeds.
3. The ad hoc categorization process is invoked when the initial comparison between the tenor and vehicle does not succeed, because it cannot yield any salient similarities, as argued by the interpretive diversity view (Utsumi, 2007).

Figure 1. Direct categorization versus indirect categorization for predicative metaphors. Entities derived during comprehension are indicated by boldface.

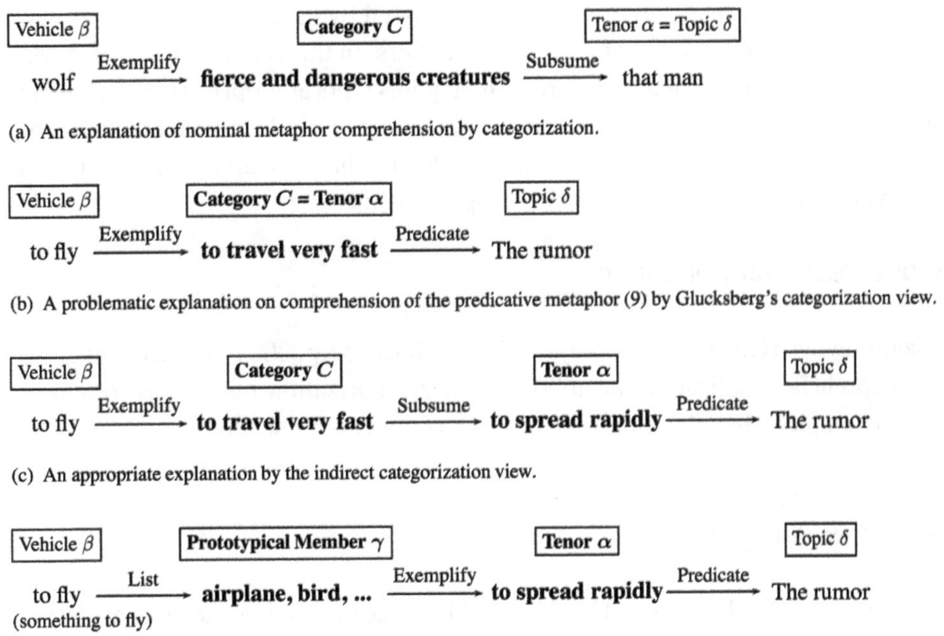

(a) An explanation of nominal metaphor comprehension by categorization.

(b) A problematic explanation on comprehension of the predicative metaphor (9) by Glucksberg's categorization view.

(c) An appropriate explanation by the indirect categorization view.

(d) More appropriate explanation by the indirect categorization view.

Literary metaphors are comprehended via a categorization process (i.e., Step 3 above) because they are likely to convey diverse meanings so that they achieve aesthetic or poetic effects. The comparison process is not appropriate for literary metaphor comprehension because diverse and creative interpretations are unlikely to be yielded by simply comparing the tenor and vehicle. The initial alignment is primarily derived from the known similarity and thus a derived interpretation tends to be less creative and less diverse. Given that a literary metaphor serves as an efficient way of describing the tenor from a novel perspective, the process of metaphor comprehension should be able to derive a metaphorical interpretation primarily from the vehicle. In other words, comprehension of literary metaphors requires a process of similarity creation rather than similarity identification.

Note also that one related limitation of the comparison process is that it suffers from a serious problem of dealing with unspecified tenors (e.g., Glucksberg, McGlone, & Manfredi, 1997). When hearers are unfamiliar with the tenor, they cannot align the tenor with the vehicle, and thus, cannot derive similarities sufficient to yield a proper interpretation. For example, in comprehending the metaphor (14)

(14) That supermodel is a rail.

people employ the stereotypical knowledge about supermodel to compare "that supermodel" with "a rail," and easily recognize that they share the property of being thin. However, when more general words are used as a tenor such as "That woman is a rail" or "That person is a rail," it is difficult to find common properties by comparing the tenor and vehicle. Categorization is thus required for interpreting these metaphors with unspecified tenors.

Comprehension of Predicative Metaphors

We also argue that predicative metaphors are comprehended by categorization, but its comprehension process is more complicated than that of nominal metaphors. In this section, we explain why the simple categorization process for comprehending nominal metaphors is not appropriate for predicative metaphors, and propose indirect or two-stage categorization as a process of predicative metaphor comprehension. Note that predicative metaphors cannot be comprehended by the comparison process because the tenor of predicative metaphors is unspecified before comprehension.

Problems of Direct Categorization

The categorization view (Glucksberg & Keysar, 1990; Glucksberg, 2001; Torreano et al., 2005) argues that people comprehend predicative metaphors via a categorization process as they do for nominal metaphors. For example, when the following metaphors are comprehended,

(8) John hopped on his bike and flew home.
(9) The rumor flew through the office.

the category of "speedy travel" is evoked by the verb "fly" because flying can be considered a prototypical action in that category.

This explanation seems to be valid, in particular for this example. However, it is not sufficient for a full-fledged account of predicative metaphor comprehension for two reasons. One reason is that many verbs are less likely to evoke such superordinate categories. For example, consider the verb *boil* in the metaphor (4) "Public anger boils over." What superordinate categories can be exemplified by the verb *boil*? It is very difficult to imagine any abstract categories that include the state of boiling as a prototypical member and can be attributed to the topic *anger*. A number of empirical findings have supported the validity of this difficulty; event categories are represented by fewer levels (generally two) and with fewer distinctions at the superordinate level than object categories (Vigliocco & Vinson, 2007). This difficulty is more serious for adjective metaphors. Adjectives have no hierarchical structures and it is impossible to think of properties at a more abstract level than the meaning of adjectives. For example, we cannot imagine any superordinate properties of the adjective *red* in the adjective metaphor (6).

Another reason for the insufficiency of the direct categorization account is that it cannot explain the structural difference between predicative and nominal metaphors. Glucksberg's categorization view has assumed the abstract category exemplified by the vehicle as the tenor (and thus the interpretation of metaphors). In the case of the metaphor (9), for example, the category C of *fast travel* is regarded as the tenor α, as shown in Figure 1(b). However, this explanation is apparently inconsistent with the metaphor structure (9').

(9) The rumor flew through the office.

(9') The rumor (δ)'s action of α-ing ($\approx$ spreading rapidly) is γ's action of flying (β).

The intended action of rumor expressed figuratively by the vehicle of flying is not an abstract category C of fast travel, but a specific action of rumor such as "spreading rapidly and disappearing soon," as shown in Figure 1(c). In other words, both tenor and vehicle of predicative metaphors are prototypical members of the abstract category *C*, just as in the case of nominal metaphors. Furthermore, this "category-as-tenor" assumption cannot explain the richness of the metaphorical meanings expressed by literary predicative metaphors. For example, people can derive more meanings from the metaphor (9) than supposed in the categorization theory (e.g., to travel fast); the rumor spreads rapidly and suddenly, the rumor is dispersed or disseminated, the rumor disappears or is forgotten very soon, and so on. These rich interpretations are unlikely to be derived directly from the verb *fly*, given that the semantic structure of verbs is hierarchically less rich.

Indirect Categorization

The two problems posed by the direct categorization view can be overcome by the indirect categorization view proposed by Utsumi and Sakamoto (Utsumi & Sakamoto, 2011, 2007a, 2007b, 2010).

The intuitive idea behind indirect categorization is that a correspondence between the actions or events literally expressed by the verb or adjective and the actions or events to be attributed to the topic would be indirect and mediated by an intermediate entity, rather than direct as predicted by the categorization theory. As illustrated in Figure 1 (c), in the case of the "fly" metaphor, the verb *fly* first evokes an abstract category *C* as an intermediate entity, and then its prototypical member "to spread rapidly and soon disappear" is chosen for the tenor and attributed to the topic "rumor" being described. This explanation is consistent with the structure of predicative metaphors (9') in that the tenor α ("to spread rapidly and soon disappear") is a specific action of the topic *rumor* (δ), not the abstract *C*.

However, this explanation cannot resolve the main problem that many verbs and almost all adjectives are unable to evoke any abstract categories. The indirect categorization view explains that an intermediate entity is assumed to be a set of things that are likely to fill the arguments of the vehicle predicate β, namely, the subject and direct object of a verb or the modificand of an adjective. This type of an intermediate entity corresponds to γ in the comprehension structure of predicate metaphors expressed by Equation (12).

(5) Anna ate up the whole story.

Figure 2. Predicative metaphor comprehension by indirect categorization without an abstract category. Entities derived during comprehension are indicated by boldface.

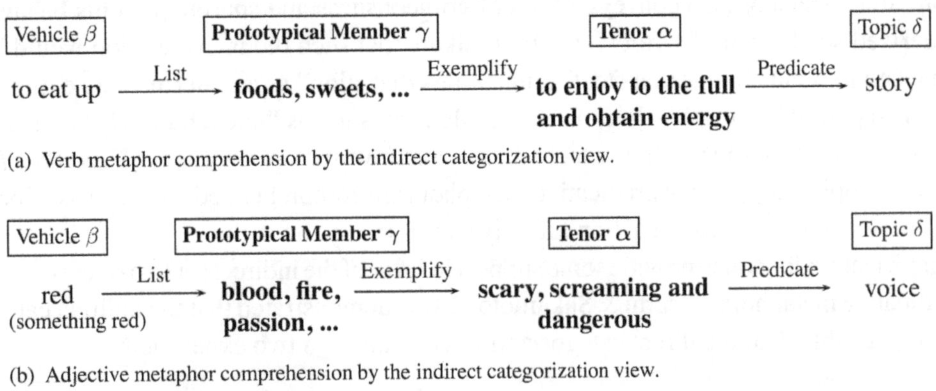

For example, the metaphor (5) may be comprehended as shown in Figure 2(a). First, people unconsciously think of a variety of salient members involved in the category "something to eat up" literally expressed by the vehicle β of predicative metaphors. This association or enumeration process is followed by the categorization process in which some members relevant to the explicit topic "story" are abstracted into an improvised category such as "an action of enjoying something to the full and obtaining energy for living one's daily life," resulting in the interpretation that Anna enjoyed the whole story to the full, from which she obtained energy for living her daily life. Note that this comprehension process is also applied to explain the "fly" metaphor (9), as shown in Figure 1(d). The tenor α of spreading rapidly and soon disappearing can be exemplified by a set of prototypical members γ (e.g., airplane, birds) of the category "something to fly."

Adjective metaphors are more likely to be comprehended in this way because one cannot imagine any abstract category that subsumes the vehicle adjective β as a prototypical member. For example, in comprehending the metaphor (15), some members such as "blood" and "fire" of the category "red things" referred to by the adjective "red" are enumerated, as shown in Figure 2(b).

(15) red voice (One's voice is red)

From these intermediate entities γ, exemplars relevant to the topic "voice" are selected and then evoke an abstract category of being scary, screaming and dangerous, which is regarded as the tenor α of the metaphor.

The validity of intermediate entities γ for predicative metaphor comprehension can be justified by the observation that predicative metaphors are more comprehensible when the intermediate entity γ is explicitly expressed using a phrase "like a γ."

(16) The rumor flew through the office like a jet.
(17) I float like a butterfly, sting like a bee.
(18) One's voice is red like a fire.

For example, the expression (17) is the words of Muhammad Ali, a famous American boxer who won World Heavyweight Champion three times. This sentence is a predicative metaphor that expresses Ali's boxing style by describing his swift footwork as *to float* and his lightning-quick punch as *to sting*. These metaphorical meanings are not likely to be evoked directly by these verbs. For example, it is difficult to imagine that the action of moving to evade a punch is derived through the abstraction of the verb *float*. Furthermore, this metaphor also conveys a kind of gorgeousness and sharpness in his behavior, which cannot be derived solely from the verbs. It is more likely that such the interpretation would be derived when people call to mind "things that float" and "things that sting" as an intermediate entity, and in the case of this metaphor they are verbalized in the simile form such as "like a butterfly" and "like a bee." Simile phrases such as these are often attached to predicative metaphors (e.g., "*Time flies like an arrow*"). These examples suggest that predicative metaphors are comprehended on the basis of prototypical entities that perform or undergo the action literally expressed by the verb.

Some empirical findings also provide some support in favor of the indirect (or two-stage) categorization view of predicative metaphors. Utsumi & Sakamoto (2011) demonstrated that the indirect categorization view is more plausible than the direct categorization view through two experiments.

- In the offline comprehension experiment, participants were asked to write down interpretations (i.e., the tenor α) of 40 predicative metaphors, and those interpretations were examined as to whether they were derived directly from the verb or indirectly associated with the verb. The result was that significantly more interpretations (38%) were associated indirectly with the verb than those (19%) derived directly from the verb ($p < .001$). This difference was observed independent of metaphor aptness and vehicle conventionality.
- In the online comprehension experiment, a priming paradigm was used to assess the online availability of intermediate entities. A predicative metaphor was presented as a prime and its effect on the speed of lexical decision about a subsequent target word was measured. As a result, the target word associated with the intermediate category (800.3ms) was significantly faster to judge than the target word unrelated to the metaphor (843.1ms) and marginally significantly faster than the target directly associated with the verb (828.5ms).

Some computational methods for recognizing predicative metaphors in natural language processing have employed an idea similar to the indirect categorization view. Li, Zhu, & Wang (2013) have proposed a method for recognizing predicative metaphors by comparing the degree of selectional preferences of the vehicle verb β between literally and metaphorically related arguments. In the case of the metaphor (5), some hypernyms (e.g., fiction, message, literary work) of the direct object *story* are compared with metaphorically related entities of *story* in terms of the selectional preference of the verb *eat up*. Metaphorically related entities are chosen from the metaphor database they constructed. For example, *foods* and *sweets* are selected as metaphorically related entities when the metaphor database contains *Stories are foods* and *Stories are sweets*. These metaphorically related entities can be regarded as intermediate entities γ, although they are not chosen from the category of things that can be eaten up. Nevertheless, the effectiveness of Li et al.'s (2013) method lends some support to the indirect categorization view.

The conceptual metaphor theory argues that predicative metaphors are understood by conceptual metaphors. For example, the implicit topic γ (e.g., enemies) of the metaphor "He shot down all of my arguments" can be perceived from the conceptual metaphor ARGUMENT IS WAR. Hence, the conceptual metaphor theory has in common with the indirect categorization view in this respect. The difference between the indirect categorization view and the conceptual metaphor theory lies in the conventionality of the relationship between the explicit and implicit topic. The conceptual metaphor theory focuses on the preexisting metaphorical mapping acquired through experiential correlation, while the indirect categorization view emphasizes creation of metaphorical mappings between the implicit topic γ (or the tenor α) and the explicit topic δ.

METAPHOR PRODUCTION

Metaphor production can be viewed as a vehicle discovery process in which appropriate vehicle words are searched for so that the generated metaphor can convey the intended meaning.

For nominal metaphors, the vehicle β with the properties q is determined from the tenor α and its properties $p(\alpha)$ that are intended to convey by this metaphor.

$$p(\alpha) \rightarrow \exists\beta\ \exists q\ \mathrm{SIM}(p(\alpha), q(\beta)) \tag{19}$$

For example, consider the case in which one want to express "A plan does not always go as scheduled" by a nominal metaphor with the tenor "plan." According to the categorization view of metaphors, this process can be modeled as searching for members of the intended category *C* of "something that does not always go as scheduled," as shown in Figure 3(a).

For a generated metaphor to be literary or innovative, it is preferable that its vehicle is a coherent but unexpected member of the category and some other similarities can be created by the metaphor. It follows that less prototypical members of the category are likely to be searched as a vehicle for producing literary metaphors, as compared to the production of explanatory or nonliterary metaphors. For example, the category of something that does not always go as scheduled includes "love" and "management" as prototypical members, but less prototypical members such as "weather" and "shopping" are also considered as a potential vehicle.

Utsumi & Sakamoto (2015) provided empirical evidence in favor of the categorization view of literary metaphor production.

- In the offline production experiment, participants generated 20 metaphors for explanatory or literary purposes by answering appropriate vehicles given a tenor and its property to convey. As a result, less prototypical members of the category (i.e., property) to be attributed to the tenor were chosen as a vehicle for literary metaphors than for explanatory metaphors. In addition, it was found that generated literary metaphors were more novel and had less tenor-vehicle similarity than explanatory metaphors. These findings are consistent with the above view of literary metaphor production.
- In the online priming experiment, participants were presented with a sentence frame consisting of a tenor and a property as a prime, and asked to consider an appropriate vehicle word. Afterwards, they were presented with a target stimulus, either of high-prototypical word, low-prototypical word, unrelated word, and nonword, and asked to make a lexical decision about the target. The result was that both prototypical and less prototypical members were activated in producing literary metaphors, while neither members were activated in the production of explanatory metaphors.

Figure 3. Nominal and predicative metaphor production. Entities derived during comprehension are indicated by boldface.

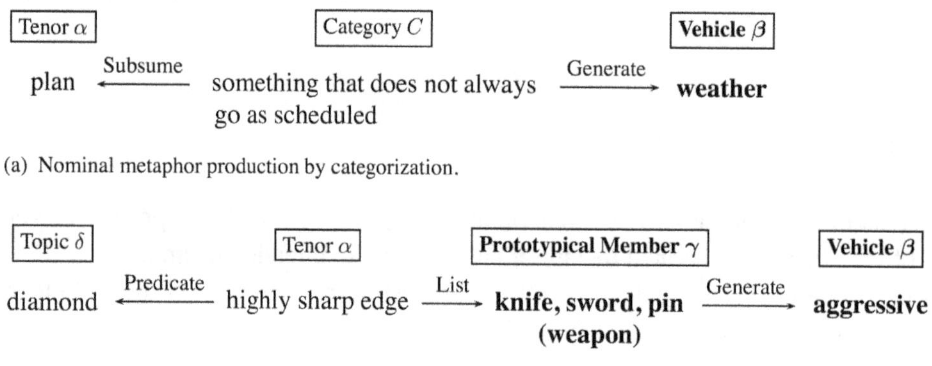

(a) Nominal metaphor production by categorization.

(b) Predicative metaphor production by indirect categorization.

Production of predicative metaphors also involves the discovery of vehicles that are expressed by verbs or adjectives. According to the indirect categorization view, people would attempt to discover an appropriate vehicle (i.e., a verb or adjective) that figuratively describes the topic by searching potential intermediate entities γ that can be the argument of a vehicle verb or the modificand of a vehicle adjective.

$$\alpha(\delta) \rightarrow \exists\beta\ \exists\gamma\ \mathrm{SIM}(\alpha(\delta), \beta(\gamma)) \tag{20}$$

For example, when generating a predicative metaphor to express the high sharpness (α) of cut edges of a diamond (δ), people have to consider intermediate entities γ that belong to the category of being sharp, as shown in Figure 3(b). If they include knife, sword, pin and other things that can be used as a weapon, people are likely to think of the adjective "aggressive" as a vehicle β, thus generating a metaphor "That diamond is aggressive" or "aggressive diamonds." No empirical studies have been made on production of predicative metaphors, and thus it is unclear whether the proposed view of predicative metaphor production is psychologically plausible, which awaits further research.

A UNIFIED VIEW OF METAPHOR COMPREHENSION AND PRODUCTION

Following the discussion in the preceding sections, we can summarize a unified view of literary metaphor comprehension and production in Figure 4. Both metaphor comprehension and production involve categorization as a mechanism of establishing a figurative correspondence between tenor and vehicle, as shown in Figure 4. A nominal metaphor is a class-inclusion statement expressing that the tenor is a member of an abstract category exemplified by the vehicle. Therefore, people have to discover an appropriate abstract category to comprehend a nominal metaphor, while people have to discover an appropriate vehicle that can exemplify the abstract category to produce a nominal metaphor. A predicative metaphor is a statement in which the tenor predicate is related to the vehicle predicate in terms of some prototypical members of their evoked categories. It follows that predicative metaphor comprehension

Figure 4. A unified view of metaphor comprehension and production by categorization.

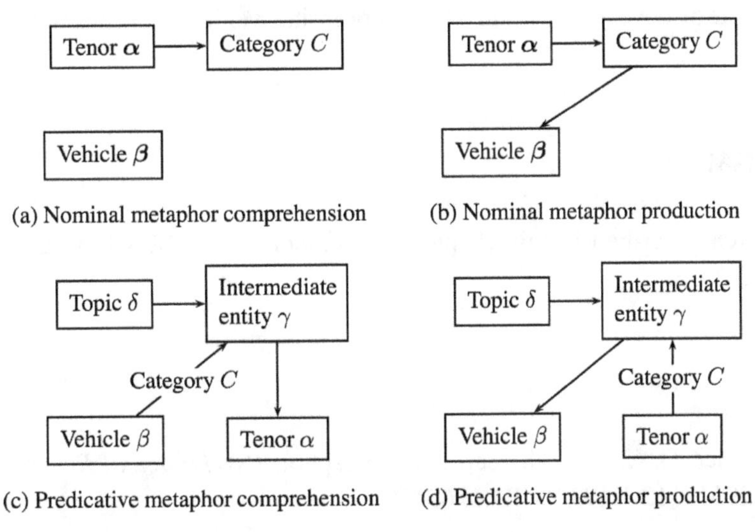

involves search for some prototypical members (i.e., intermediate entities) of the category expressed by the vehicle predicate and categorization of those prototypical members. On the other hand, predicative metaphor production involves search for some prototypical members of the tenor category and categorization of those prototypical members.

FUTURE RESEARCH DIRECTIONS

The psychological validity of the unified view of literary metaphor comprehension and production should be justified further by empirical studies. In particular, future empirical studies must address predicative metaphor comprehension and metaphor production.

Another important research direction would be the development of computational model for literary metaphors. In the field of natural language processing, automatic metaphor identification recently becomes a hot research topic and a number of computational methods have been proposed (e.g., Shutova, 2015; Veale, Shutova, & Beigman Klebanov, 2016). However, very few studies in NLP have tackled metaphor comprehension and production. Although in cognitive science some computational studies have addressed nominal metaphor comprehension (e.g., Kintsch, 2000; Utsumi, 2011), no studies have been made on predicative metaphor comprehension and metaphor production. Therefore, it is interesting and vital for further research to explore computational models of metaphor processing, especially models for literary metaphor processing, on the basis of the unified view of metaphor comprehension and production proposed in this chapter. Furthermore, I believe that developing a computational model of metaphor comprehension and production is crucial to narrative generation and human-computer interaction.

CONCLUSION

In this chapter, we provided a unified view of literary metaphor comprehension and production. As explained in this chapter, both comprehension and production involve the process of categorization. Comprehension is a similarity creation process in which the similarity is created or discovered between the tenor and vehicle of a given metaphor, and categorization is used as a way of similarity creation. Production is a vehicle discovery process in which appropriate vehicles are chosen from among members of the category.

ACKNOWLEDGMENT

The author's research described in this chapter was supported by JSPS KAKENHI Grant Numbers 23300098 and 15K12045.

REFERENCES

Bowdle, B., & Gentner, D. (2005). The career of metaphor. *Psychological Review*, *112*(1), 193–216. doi:10.1037/0033-295X.112.1.193 PMID:15631593

Chiappe, D., & Chiappe, P. (2007). The role of working memory in metaphor production and comprehension. *Journal of Memory and Language*, *56*(2), 172–188. doi:10.1016/j.jml.2006.11.006

Fainsilber, L., & Ortony, A. (1987). Metaphorical uses of language in the expression of emotions. *Metaphor and Symbolic Activity*, *2*(4), 239–250. doi:10.1207/s15327868ms0204_2

Gentner, D. (1983). Structure mapping: A theoretical framework for analogy. *Cognitive Science*, *7*(2), 155–170. doi:10.1207/s15516709cog0702_3

Glucksberg, S. (2001). *Understanding Figurative Language: From Metaphors to Idioms*. Oxford University Press. doi:10.1093/acprof:oso/9780195111095.001.0001

Glucksberg, S., & Haught, C. (2006a). Can Florida become *like* the next Florida? When metaphoric comparisons fail. *Psychological Science*, *17*(11), 935–938. doi:10.1111/j.1467-9280.2006.01807.x PMID:17176422

Glucksberg, S., & Haught, C. (2006b). On the relation between metaphor and simile: When comparison fails. *Mind & Language*, *21*(3), 360–378. doi:10.1111/j.1468-0017.2006.00282.x

Glucksberg, S., & Keysar, B. (1990). Understanding metaphorical comparisons: Beyond similarity. *Psychological Review*, *97*(1), 3–18. doi:10.1037/0033-295X.97.1.3

Glucksberg, S., McGlone, M., & Manfredi, D. (1997). Property attribution in metaphor comprehension. *Journal of Memory and Language*, *36*(1), 50–67. doi:10.1006/jmla.1996.2479

Hussey, K. A., & Katz, A. N. (2006). Metaphor production in online conversation: Gender and friendship status. *Discourse Processes*, *42*(1), 75–98. doi:10.1207/s15326950dp4201_3

Jones, L., & Estes, Z. (2005). Metaphor comprehension as attributive categorization. *Journal of Memory and Language*, *53*(1), 110–124. doi:10.1016/j.jml.2005.01.016

Jones, L., & Estes, Z. (2006). Roosters, robins, and alarm clocks: Aptness and conventionality in metaphor comprehension. *Journal of Memory and Language*, *55*(1), 18–32. doi:10.1016/j.jml.2006.02.004

Katz, A. (1989). On choosing the vehicles of metaphors: Referential concreteness, semantic distances, and individual differences. *Journal of Memory and Language*, *28*(4), 486–499. doi:10.1016/0749-596X(89)90023-5

Kintsch, W. (2000). Metaphor comprehension: A computational theory. *Psychonomic Bulletin & Review*, *7*(2), 257–266. doi:10.3758/BF03212981 PMID:10909133

Lakoff, G., & Johnson, M. (1980). *Metaphors We Live By*. The University of Chicago Press.

Lakoff, G., & Johnson, M. (1999). *Philosophy in the Flesh: The Embodied Mind and Its Challenge to Western Thought*. Basic Books.

Li, H., Zhu, K. Q., & Wang, H. (2013). Data-driven metaphor recognition and explanation. *Transactions of the Association for Computational Linguistics*, *1*, 379–390.

Roncero, C., & de Almeida, R. G. (2015). Semantic properties, aptness, familiarity, conventionality, and interpretive diversity scores for 84 metaphors and similes. *Behavior Research Methods*, *47*(3), 800–812. doi:10.3758/s13428-014-0502-y PMID:25007859

Shutova, E. (2015). Design and evaluation of metaphor processing systems. *Computational Linguistics*, *41*(4), 579–623. doi:10.1162/COLI_a_00233

Torreano, L., Cacciari, C., & Glucksberg, S. (2005). When dogs can fly: Level of abstraction as a cue to metaphorical use of verbs. *Metaphor and Symbol*, *20*(4), 259–274. doi:10.1207/s15327868ms2004_2

Utsumi, A. (2005). The role of feature emergence in metaphor appreciation. *Metaphor and Symbol*, *20*(3), 151–172. doi:10.1207/s15327868ms2003_1

Utsumi, A. (2007). Interpretive diversity explains metaphor-simile distinction. *Metaphor and Symbol*, *22*(4), 291–312. doi:10.1080/10926480701528071

Utsumi, A. (2011). Computational exploration of metaphor comprehension processes using a semantic space model. *Cognitive Science*, *35*(2), 251–296. doi:10.1111/j.1551-6709.2010.01144.x PMID:21429000

Utsumi, A., & Sakamoto, M. (2007a). Computational evidence for two-stage categorization as a process of adjective metaphor comprehension. *Proceedings of the Second European Cognitive Science Conference (EuroCogSci2007)*, 77–82.

Utsumi, A., & Sakamoto, M. (2007b). Predicative metaphors are understood as two-stage categorization: Computational evidence by latent semantic analysis. *Proceedings of the 29th Annual Meeting of the Cognitive Science Society (CogSci2007)*, 1587–1592.

Utsumi, A., & Sakamoto, M. (2010). Predicative metaphor comprehension as indirect categorization. *Proceedings of the 32nd Annual Meeting of the Cognitive Science Society (CogSci2010)*, 1034–1039.

Utsumi, A., & Sakamoto, M. (2011). Indirect categorization as a process of predicative metaphor comprehension. *Metaphor and Symbol*, *26*(4), 299–313. doi:10.1080/10926488.2011.609120

Utsumi, A., & Sakamoto, M. (2015). Discourse goals affect the process and product of nominal metaphor production. *Journal of Psycholinguistic Research*, *44*(5), 555–569. doi:10.1007/s10936-014-9305-7 PMID:24924472

Veale, T., Shutova, E., & Beigman Klebanov, B. (2016). *Metaphor: A Computational Perspective*. Morgan & Claypool Publishers.

Vigliocco, G., & Vinson, D. P. (2007). Semantic representation. In M. G. Gaskell (Ed.), *The Oxford Handbook of Psycholinguistics* (pp. 217–234). Oxford University Press.

Williams-Whitney, D., Mio, J., & Whitney, P. (1992). Metaphor production in creative writing. *Journal of Psycholinguistic Research*, *21*(6), 497–509.

KEY TERMS AND DEFINITIONS

Categorization: A cognitive process by which distinct entities—vehicle and tenor in the case of metaphor processing—are treated as equivalent.

Intermediate Entity: A concept that connects the vehicle to the tenor indirectly in the process of comprehending predicative metaphors.

Literary Metaphor: A metaphor used in literary works to evoke aesthetic or poetic effects on readers.

Metaphor: A figurative expression in which a certain concept is described in terms of another unlike concept.

Nominal Metaphor: A metaphor by which some specific things such as living creatures and objects referred to by a noun are described figuratively.

Predicative Metaphor: A metaphor by which actions, events, or properties are described figuratively.

Tenor: A word or phrase that refers to the concept described figuratively in a metaphor (e.g., "Juliet" in the metaphor "Juliet is the sun").

Vehicle: A word or phrase used to describe a tenor metaphorically (e.g., "the sun" in the metaphor "Juliet is the sun").

Chapter 11
Logic as a Narrative

Koji Sawa
International Christian University, Japan

ABSTRACT

In this chapter, the authors present an argument which can be called "logic as a narrative." First, they consider two different types of systems concerning logic. One is formal logic, which is ordinarily called mere logic. Another one is a collective of knowledge that we may not regard as logic at first glance. The argument of "logic as a narrative" starts with a comparison between two types of logical systems. Formal logic, which is often handled as mathematical logic nowadays, can be regarded as one of the mathematics, as the name itself indicates. As well as the other mathematical systems, formal logic is formalized and schematized by axioms; hence, it is also an axiomatic system. All the propositions are described axiomatically; thus, axioms and application rules of axioms precede propositions. Outside situations that are not supposed in an axiomatic system cannot be naturally represented by the system. The expressive power depends on each system. As a result, the description by mathematical logic becomes static and the system itself is regarded as a non-dynamic one.

INTRODUCTION

It is being considered that logic is a packed powerful system. By using logic, things or matters are classified into some groups. In a similar way, accumulated situation is applied into another unexperienced situation. Each specific experience is transformed into a general law through already approved logic. Formal logic is one of the most sophisticated such ones. Meanwhile, logic is ineffective for completely unknown situations. At the periphery of logic, things are examined whether they are incorporable to logic or not, and logic itself is updated.

In this chapter, above features are focused on as intrinsic and important functions of logic. The features can be summarized as soundness on each instant, and updatability of a logical system. A system satisfying the soundness and the updatability is a useful logical system, and called such a logical system a *Logic as a Narrative* (LaaN) in this chapter. A proposal of LaaN is as follows. First, two different types of systems concerning logic are considered. One is formal logic, which is ordinarily called merely as logic. Another one is a collective of knowledge that may not be regarded as logic at the first glance. The argument of LaaN starts with a comparison between such two types of structures.

DOI: 10.4018/978-1-5225-4775-4.ch011

Copyright © 2018, IGI Global. Copying or distributing in print or electronic forms without written permission of IGI Global is prohibited.

Formal logic, which is often handled as mathematical logic nowadays, can be regarded as one of the mathematics, as the name itself indicated. As well as the other mathematical systems, formal logic is formalized and schematized by axioms, hence it is also an axiomatic system. All the propositions are described axiomatically, thus axioms and rules of the application of axioms precede propositions. Outer situations that are not supposed in an axiomatic system cannot be naturally represented by the system. The expressive power of the system depends on each system. As a result, the description by mathematical logic becomes static and the system itself is regarded as a non-dynamic one.

It is sometimes difficult that a non-dynamic system responds to indeterminate situations properly, because all the situations of the indeterminate world cannot be described preliminarily (McCarthy & Hayes, 1969). In fact, this is an inevitable feature of the indeterminate one by its definition. For example, logical inclusive relation is ensured by definitions of both antecedent and consequent. The definitions of objects and relations among objects precede detailed observations of objects that are applied in the system. One of the purposes of formal logic is an abstract description of relations among objects under eliminations of features of each object.

What are more practical logical systems? One direction to the solution is a basis-free construction. Here, the basis means an axiom or a definition. In addition, the basis also indicates other ones: Top and Bottom elements. In general, the definition of complement of an element needs Top and Bottom elements. Top and Bottom elements are representations of the whole and the empty of the world, respectively. Adopting Top and Bottom elements is a decision of the range influenced by the system. In this sense, the Top and Bottom elements are bases of the logical system, which determines the act of the system. Practical logical systems may include variable Top and Bottom elements. For example, consider subsets of $\{a, b\}$. The Top and Bottom elements are $\{a, b\}$ and $\{\}$, respectively. However, when subsets of $\{a, b, c\}$ is considered, the Top and Bottom elements become $\{a, b, c\}$ and $\{\}$. Note that the former Bottom element is represented by to either $\{c\}$ or $\{\}$ in the latter system, thus the former and latter do not necessarily correspond to each other. The former system is a subsystem of the latter one.

These basis-free features can enable the system to have a potential to be connected to both change of situations in the system itself and new situations in other systems. Though such system acts as a consistent logical system in a current moment, at the same time, it has an ability to change in order to adapt a new situation. It is important to satisfy concurrently these two aspects: consistency and adaptability. When a system has these two aspects, the system is regarded as a useful logical system.

This chapter is organized as follows: in the first subsection of the second section, some different aspects of logic are discussed when logic is treated as a formal system. To group the aspects into some pairs helps us to understand. In the second subsection of the second section, a narrative is introduced as a theoretical apparatus of an integration of the divided logics. This subsection is a theoretical description of the project of LaaN. In the third section, a concrete network model representing LaaN is developed. The model is a simple but strong network model, similar to the BA model (Barabási & Albert, 1999). This part is based on a preprint (Sawa, 2015). In the fourth section, some meanings, implications and future possibilities to be evoked from LaaN and the model are presented. In sum, this chapter is a proposal that logic becomes more useful when it is treated as one with a narrative or a narrative itself.

BACKGROUND

Some Dichotomies Around Logic

There are some pairs of opposite matters around the context of logic, except the most popular pair, syntax and semantics. One is the type-token distinction (Gunji et al., 2010). Type is a generalized concept rising from each thing, while token is each particular thing itself. For example, when you see a car, the car itself is a token. On the other hand, a concept of cars like "not bicycle but car" is a type. A type of the car is deviated from a token of the car. A car becomes a type when it is compared to other sort of vehicles or considered with inclusive relations. Meanwhile, it becomes a token when its specific situation of the car is focused on. As above, there are not strict difference between type and token, but only relative and ambiguous labeling. In traditional formal logic, it seems that only type-like features are focused. Indeed the strategy is appropriate and useful in order to consider formal relations among well-known things. However, in order to construct a new proposition about unknown and/or novel ones, the token-ness is important; it demands careful observations on them. Formal logic with consideration more about token is akin to embodied mathematics (Lakoff & Núñez, 2000). Mathematics is formalized as well as formal logic. However, both are based on observations and acts as proofs. They inevitably need the token-ness while the emergence and/or accumulation of knowledge are considered.

The second dichotomy is presented around logic and proverbs. In general, all proverbs do not have logical validness. However, proverbs are occasionally accepted as true facts. What is the difference between logic and proverbs? In other words, can a proverb be changed to a logical fact smoothly?

The meaning of a Japanese proverb "Kaze ga fukeba okeya ga moukaru" is that "if the wind blows the bucket makers prosper." The proverb can be divided to several relations between two objects. That is, if the wind blows then dust rises, and if dust rises then it gets into eyes, and so on. There are some independent relations that are seemed to be logically correct, however, the whole sequence is more incorrect than each relation. The difference between proverbs and logic is connected to a problem of the scope of logic. There are some variations of systems of formal logic. This fact indicates that there are no universal and final representations of logic. A system of logic is chosen as appropriate according to each standpoint. The logical correctness of an assertion, for example a proverb, may change according to circumstances, time, and/or standpoints. Time is one-dimensional, therefore, variations of the logical correctness according to time can be considered as a sequential one. Here, a logic with time variations is regarded as LaaN, under the assumption that time is a driving factor of a narrative.

The third dichotomy is a global versus a local property. There is not the final global logic; a complete observation of the whole world is impossible and perspectives are restricted. Therefore, each standpoint inevitably becomes local. The truth value of an assertion depends on a system which the assertion belongs to. That is, it can be said as "it is true for me that …" or "false at that time" etc. The former is restricted to an individual, and the latter is restricted to a moment. It is important that the transition and/or concatenation of local logics are considered while the absence of the final global logic is postulated. The gap between local and global logic itself may become a representation of the driving power of new discoveries or concepts.

Narrative as a Mediator

There are some situations enforced to choose a formal one or an actual one exclusively. This alternative makes our attitudes discrete. That is, for example, in this situation a systematical act is better, on the other hand in that situation, the influence from the actual life is more important. Each body and/or consciousness plays a role as an integrator of the divided attitudes physically and/or mentally. A narrative is one of the other theoretical apparatuses for the integration. It works as a mediator like body or consciousness within the narrative world itself.

A narrative as a mediator does not need the outside of the narrative. This is the reason why a narrative is occasionally regarded as an autonomous one. The outer reality is enclosed in the narrative. The matters to be referred are not on the outside but on the inside of the narrative. A logical narrative is consistent in a moment, and also may be inconsistent in a time series at the same time. The utility of logic in a real life coincides with the evolvability in a time series. Logic becomes more consistent by means of considerations of variations with time. In this way, logic can obtain a dynamic property by virtue of the narrative nature of logic, holding a consistency that eventually leads to the utility.

From this point of view, LaaN is different from traditional formal logic. Traditional formal logic is either an atemporal one, or one with time which is extrapolated (temporal logic: Pnueli, 1977). LaaN that has already obtained dynamic features is also different from static systems by definition. On the other hand, LaaN is similar to living matters and AI (artificial intelligence) due to its non-deductive property. Living matters do not exist axiomatically, and AI is static as a system but has adaptive abilities. It is remarkable that the non-deductive properties of living matters and AI have different foundations; they are rather totally opposite of each other. Embodied mathematics (Lakoff & Núñez, 2000) is a study that tries to propose another basis of mathematics that is intrinsically deductive and systematically represented. It can be regarded that the embodied mathematics changes the rule-based manner of the proof and/or the development of mathematics to a rule-like-based manner. Note that, in general, this argument between a rule-based manner versus a rule-like-based one is essential and important in order to address the problem of a development or an emergence.

LaaN is also similar to a Project called Non-Axiomatic Reasoning System: NARS (Wang, 2007). The NARS proposed a system constructing a reasoning method in a non-axiomatic way. Instead of axioms, the NARS needs a database-like knowledge. This axiom versus database scheme easily implies a dichotomy between deduction and induction, which can be as a rule-based and fact-based way, respectively. The NARS is designed to be both a current consistency composed of an internal structure and an acquisition of new knowledge from an external environment.

Outline of Logic as a Narrative

The approach to LaaN is a model-composing one. A logical connective, implication is naturally represented by a directed edge, thus a network composed of directed edges can be regarded as a logical system. Adding nodes and edges represents acquirements of experience. When logical connective implications are represented by directed edges, the resulting set of directed edges can be regarded as a complex network of logic. In this chapter, a network model that represents a deductive-logic-like structure composed of implications is presented. The proposed network model grows like the BA model reported by Barabási and Albert (1999). Though the BA model references the whole of the existing network when a node is added, the proposed model references only part of the existing network. In this view, the proposed model is more realistic than the BA model. However, it also exhibits power law characteristics.

The driving force of the model is the transitivity of the implication. The transitivity is one of the fundamental features of logic, which is expressed as "if $A \supset B$ and $B \supset C$, then $A \supset C$." It can be illustrated by the inclusive relation, hence it is very acceptable. As the model construction, the objective of this study is an emergence of complex-networks-like features when logic is regarded as a network. It is only premised on the fundamental logical feature: the transitivity, and some transformations without global perspectives.

LOGIC AS A COMPLEX NETWORK

The implicational relation "if A then C" is an ordered binary relation in formal logic. Therefore, it may be represented by a directed edge, such as "$A \rightarrow C$," instead of the frequently used representation "$A \supset C$." Thus, a real-world set composed of a huge number of implicational relations, such as "if X is a crow then X is a bird" or "if X is a kitten then X is a cat," can be regarded as a directed complex network. Though there are some formal representations of logic, as in mathematical logic (Shoenfield, 1967), proof theory (Troelstra & Schwichtenberg, 2000), and lattice theory (Davey & Priestley, 2002), these representations mainly focus on algebraic structure. On the contrary, in this chapter, the network-like features of logic are presented.

The pioneering models of complex networks are the ER model (Erdős & Rényi, 1960), WS model (Watts & Strogatz, 1998), and BA model (Barabási & Albert, 1999). Of these, the model proposed in this article is most similar to the BA model, proposed by Barabási and Albert. The BA model consists of two main features: growth and preferential attachment. Growth represents the step-wise evolution of a network by adding nodes and directed edges. The preferential attachment rule is employed when a new node is added to an existing network. This rule determines the probability of a new edge being formed between the new node and existing nodes according to their number of attached edges. Thus, nodes with many attached edges acquire more edges, whereas those with fewer edges struggle to acquire new edges. As a result of this preferential attachment, the BA model exhibits power law characteristics in terms of its degree distribution. The power law is sometimes referred to as being scale-free, and is a universal phenomenon displayed in the metabolic networks of organisms (Albert et al., 2000), topology of the Internet (Faloutsos et al., 1999), directed graphs on the Web (Broder et al., 2000), and so on. The fact that the BA model demonstrates the power law implies that it is as universal as these other networks.

In general, there are two inferences in logic: deduction and induction. In this chapter, only deductive inference which presents fewer problems than induction is treated. One famous representation of deduction is: "All men are mortal. Socrates is a man. Therefore, Socrates is mortal." That is, deduction is broadly reasonable to most people. At first, the process of deduction is formulated, then transformed into a network of logic based on deductive inference.

In the BA model, all information about the entire existing network is referenced when a new node is added. This is not a problem when there are few nodes or edges. However, if thousands of nodes or edges exist, this reference to the whole of the network becomes too strong and idealistic. In fact, there are some modified models that limit their reference to a local, finite part of the network (Broder et al., 2000; Gomez-Gardenes & Moreno, 2004; Wang et al., 2009). In the proposed model, the reference and transformation also remain local; thus, the proposed model is more realistic than the BA model. Despite this restriction, the proposed model also exhibits the power law in terms of degree distribution. This new result adds deductive logic (to be precise, local deductive logic that does not assume the wholeness of the network) to the collection of networks that exhibit the power law.

The proposed model is constructed as below. First, deduction is formulated into a scheme. For a set B, consider a tautological binary relation $B \rightarrow B$. In logic, this binary relation is called the reflexive law; under normal conditions, there is generally no argument with this relation. Next, bring up a subset A of B on the left of "→,"and a set C whose subset is B on the right of "→." Thus, a new binary relation $A \rightarrow C$ is formed. This binary relation is ensured by the inclusive relation of sets or the transitive law in logic. The validity of this implicational binary relation $A \rightarrow C$ is easy to understand by substituting the sets of "cats," "kittens," and "animals" for B, A, and C, respectively (see Figure 1). Roughly speaking, the transformation is a manipulation akin to "collapsing the left and expanding the right." This newly-formed binary relation is not novel, but is sound. In addition, the transformation exactly coincides with the "Socrates" example described above, where A, B, and C are regarded as "Socrates", "men", and "mortals," respectively. Thus, this transformation is a schematic representation of deduction.

The BA model network grows in a step-by-step manner as nodes are added. At each step, the number of edges of every node (i.e., the complete network) is checked. That is, in the BA model, it is assumed there is some viewpoint that can overlook the whole of the network, even as the network becomes huge. This assumption is not quite realistic when real-world networks are considered. Therefore, this assumption is not adopted and instead introduce a local network transformation into the model as the network grows. This local transformation proceeds as follows:

Figure 1. Forming implicational relations. This transformation is represented as "collapsing the left and expanding the right" from the tautological binary relation "cats → cats."

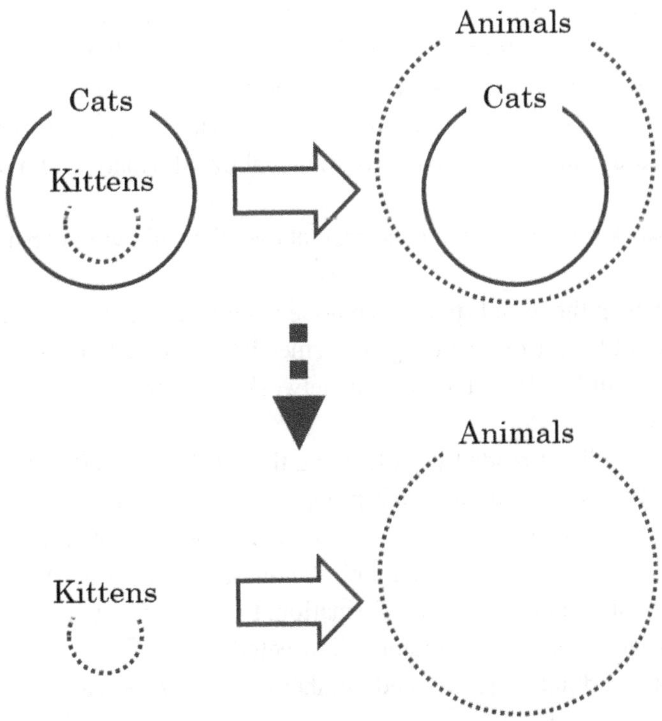

Step 1: Choose a node p from an existing network.

Step 2: Prepare a node p' that is a copy of p and a directed edge between p and p'. The direction of the directed edge is determined at random with a probability of 0.5. Regardless of its direction, the new directed edge (either $p \rightarrow p'$ or $p' \rightarrow p$) represents a tautological binary relation at this moment, because p and p' have the same representation.

Step 3: Transform the new directed edge by the deductive transformation described above, i.e., "collapsing the left and expanding the right."

Step 4: The set of nodes that have a directed edge to or from p are called the *adjacent set*. Check whether p' and each node in the adjacent set have an implicational relation "→" (details are described later). If p' and a member of the adjacent set have an implicational relation "→," form a directed edge between p' and that node in the natural direction.

Step 5: Recheck the implicational relations "→" between p and each node of the adjacent set. If p retains any such relations, the directed edge between p and the node is maintained. Otherwise, remove the directed edge.

Steps 4 and 5 illustrate why the transformation is called "local," as only those directed edges to nodes in the adjacent set are checked. Nodes outside the adjacent set are not examined.

The manipulation of "collapsing the left and expanding the right" is implemented using bit strings. A binary relation "→" between two bit strings $a_1\, a_2\, a_3 \ldots a_n$ and $c_1\, c_2\, c_3 \ldots c_n$ is defined as follows:

Definition $a_1\, a_2\, a_3 \ldots a_n \rightarrow c_1\, c_2\, c_3 \ldots c_n$ iff $a_i \leq c_i\ \forall i$, where a_i and c_i are either 0 or 1.

For example, the 4-bit strings 0110 → 0111 and 0101 → 1111 satisfy this definition. However, 0110 does not have a binary relation with 1101, because the third bit does not satisfy the definition. This binary relation is formed from the reflexive law of "→" by "collapsing the left and expanding the right." For example, 0101 → 1111 can be formed from 0111 → 0111 by "collapsing the left" to give 0101 → 0111 and "expanding the right" as 0111 → 1111. The former binary relation 0111 → 0111 is validated by the reflexive law of "→." This representation by bit strings also gives a representation of the deductive transformation. Figure 2 shows an example of the local transformation of a network represented by bit strings.

Using the local network transformation described above, the following construction is proposed:

Step 1: Consider m nodes in the initial state. Each node is represented by an n-bit string. If each pair of nodes is in the state of "→," a directed edge is formed between them in the corresponding direction.

Step 2: Choose a node at random from the existing network, and conduct the local network transformation around this node.

Step 3: In the new node, each bit made by "collapsing the left" is set to 0 if its former value is 0; otherwise, it is set to 0 or 1 at random with a probability of 0.5. Each bit of the new node made by "expanding the right" is set to 1 if its former value is 1; otherwise, it is set to 0 or 1 at random with a probability of 0.5. This step is repeated until the left and right nodes become different.

Step 4: If, in the process of local network transformation, two nodes that are the same are formed, then they are linked to each other by two reciprocal directed edges.

Step 5: Steps 2–4 are iterated until a predefined number of nodes N is reached.

Figure 2. An example of local network transformation represented by bit strings. From the initial network (upper left), a node p = 1100 is randomly chosen and copied as p'. Thus, a tautological binary relation is formed (upper right). The tautological binary relation is transformed by the deductive transformation of "collapsing the left and expanding the right" (lower left). The relations between either p = 0100 or p' = 1110, and the existing nodes 0000 and 1101 that have the relation "→" with p are checked. If two nodes are related by "→," a directed edge is added/retained; otherwise, the edge is removed/not added (lower right). By this local network transformation, the existing relation 1110 → 1101 is removed. The node 1111 is not completely referenced by this local network transformation. This explains the meaning of the "local" network transformation.

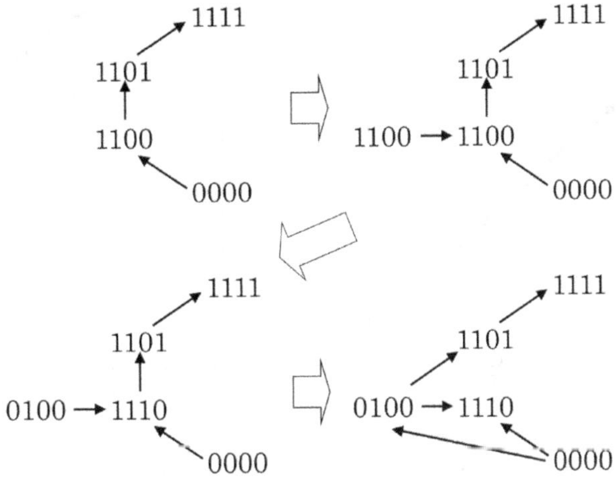

Trials with $m = 2$, $N = 10000$, and 14-bit strings are conducted. The initial nodes are $p_1 = 00000001111111$ and $p_2 = 00000001111111$; thus, there are two reciprocal directed edges $p_1 \to p_2$ and $p_2 \to p_1$. As shown in Figure 3, both the out-degree and in-degree exhibit power-law distributions of the node degree. Figure 4 shows the evolution of the clustering coefficient and average path length with respect to N. The clustering coefficient remains constantly high, and the average path length is proportional to log(N). Note that the edge directions are ignored in calculating the clustering coefficient and average path length; that is, the networks are regarded as undirected networks.

These results show that, like many other networks, deductive logic has universal structure. As logic is used by every healthy subject, this would appear to be valid. That is, logic is one of the most abstract computational models to have been formulated from the real world. If logic is not universal, it would never have become so popular.

The network in the model is updated step by step, including existing nodes and directed edges. At first, the change in the representation of a node (the change in its bit string) may be unexplainable, as may the addition or elimination of a directed edge. However, these aspects of the model correspond to a reconsideration of our recognition of the real world. The change of representation of a node and the addition/elimination of a directed edge represent drastic change of views of the world that are sometimes occurred. Logic that has already been formalized is static and does not vary. However, the logical judgment in the real world is dynamic and pliable. The model in this chapter is a representation of the latter. Such a reconsideration has been argued in the area of artificial general intelligence (Goertzel, 2007). The most important aspect of the proposed model is the sustainment of the power law, no matter how the network is updated.

Figure 3. Distributions of node degrees. (a) Out-degree and (b) in-degree. Each graph shows the relation between the degree (vertical axis) and the rank ordered by the degree (horizontal axis). Both graphs are double logarithmic plots.

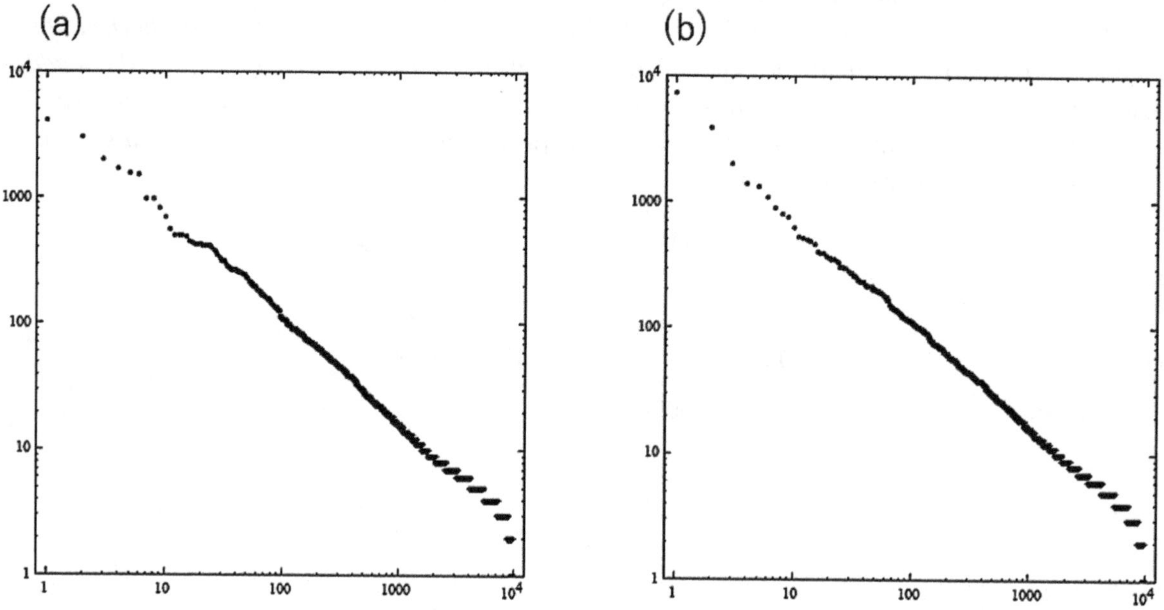

Figure 4. (a) Evolution of clustering coefficient with respect to N for values of N = 10, 20, ..., 100, 200, ..., 1000, 1500, 2000, ..., and 5000. The straight line is positioned at 0.77. (b) Evolution of average path length with respect to N for the same values of N. The curved line is the plot of (4 $\log_{10}N$)/5.

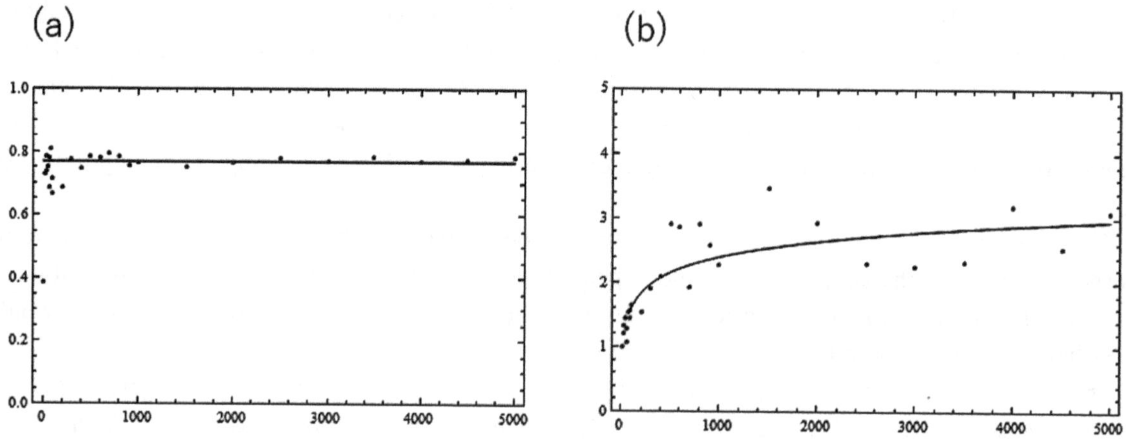

UPDATABLE LOGICAL WORLD AND INVARIANT META-STRUCTURE

One remarkable feature invoked from the model is replacements of the elements that have the most numbers of edges. This feature is never observed in the BA model. The element that has the most value of out-degree (in-degree) is Bottom (Top) element in the context of logic. Figure 5 shows a change of

Top element as time proceeds. Top and Bottom element are representations of "whole" and "empty" respectively. For example, as seen in the definition of the negation, Top and Bottom elements are very fundamental components in each logic. The fundamentality of Top and Bottom can be confirmed in the definition of the negation: "B is the negation of A" is defined as "B AND A" is Bottom, and "B OR A" is Top. Therefore, the replacements of the Top and Bottom elements are an update of the logical world itself. This representation of the update of logical world itself is difficult for traditional formal logic.

However at the same time, the model presents the power law in spite of the updates of logical world. This fact implies an existence of a consistency through different logics. This consistency itself of logics is so critical, that it invokes the power law as one of natural matters. The power law of logics is evidence of the naturalness of logic, and the narrativity of logic is a presentation of bonds of logic.

FUTURE RESEARCH DIRECTIONS

The strengths of the project of LaaN are (1) a novel representation of logic, and (2) a presentation of a simple, strong, and fundamental network model. Inference modeled here is also very simple and reasonable. On the other hand, the weaknesses of LaaN are (3) a lack of some comparisons with other representations of logic, for example, distributive lattice (Davey & Priestley, 2002), and (4) a lack of applications to other narratives. However, one of the insights of LaaN is a possibility to be a representation of "gaps" in a narrative (Ono & Ogata, 2017). The network model in this chapter is so simple that it is applicable to various areas.

Figure 5. Transitions of Top element. The identification number of nodes (vertical axis) and time (horizontal axis).

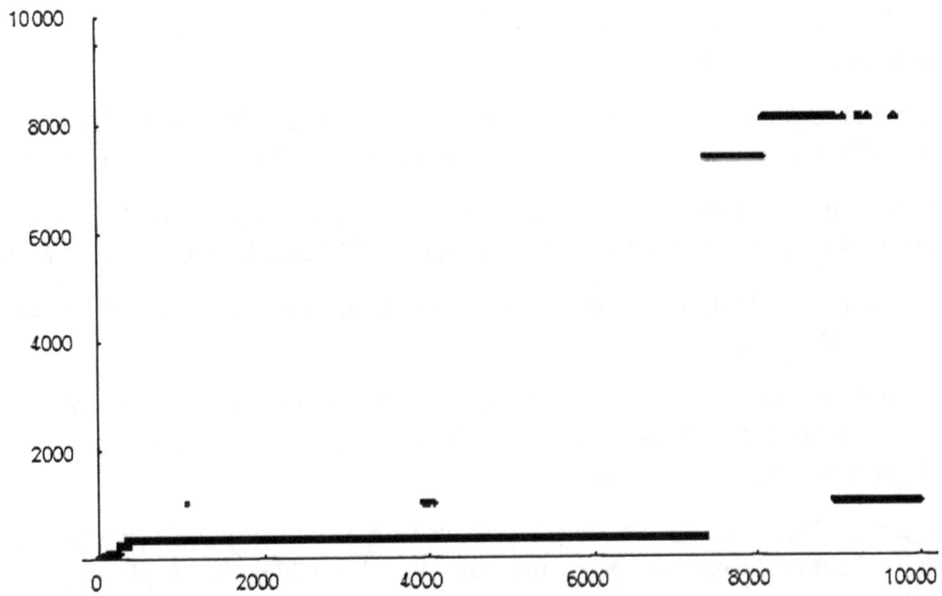

CONCLUSION

In this chapter, a project Logic as a Narrative was proposed. The project is mainly composed of two parts: considerations about logic and its transformation, and its realization as a model like complex networks. A driving force of both the transformation and the integration of logic can be regarded as a narrative, therefore the conceptual method of the project is applicable to various other areas. The model showed universal features as a complex network, in this means, it is also useful and applicable.

REFERENCES

Albert, R., Oltvai, Z. N., Barabasi, A. L., Jeong, H., & Tombor, B. (2000). The large-scale organization of metabolic networks. *Nature*, *407*(6804), 651–654. doi:10.1038/35036627 PMID:11034217

Barabási, A. L., & Albert, R. (1999). Emergence of scaling in random networks. *Science*, *286*(5439), 509–512. doi:10.1126/science.286.5439.509 PMID:10521342

Broder, A., Kumar, R., Maghoul, F., Raghavan, P., Rajagopalan, S., Stata, R., & Wiener, J. et al. (2000). Graph structure in the web. *Computer Networks*, *33*(1), 309–320. doi:10.1016/S1389-1286(00)00083-9

Davey, B. A., & Priestley, H. A. (2002). *Introduction to lattices and order*. Cambridge, UK: Cambridge University Press. doi:10.1017/CBO9780511809088

Erdős, P., & Rényi, A. (1960). On the evolution of random graphs. *Publication of the Mathematical Institute of the Hungarian Academy of Sciences*, *5*(1), 17–60.

Faloutsos, M., Faloutsos, P., & Faloutsos, C. (1999). On power-law relationships of the Internet topology. *Computer Communication Review*, *29*(4), 251–262. doi:10.1145/316194.316229

Goertzel, B., & Pennachin, C. (Eds.). (2007). *Artificial General Intelligence. Cognitive Technologies*. Berlin: Springer. doi:10.1007/978-3-540-68677-4

Gomez-Gardenes, J., & Moreno, Y. (2004). Local versus global knowledge in the Barabási-Albert scale-free network model. *Physical Review. E*, *69*(3), 037103. doi:10.1103/PhysRevE.69.037103 PMID:15089443

Gunji, Y. P., Niizato, T., Murakami, H., & Tani, I. (2010). Typ-Ken (an amalgam of type and token) drives Infosphere. *Knowledge, Technology & Policy*, *23*(1-2), 227–251. doi:10.1007/s12130-010-9107-7

Lakoff, G., & Núñez, R. (2000). *Where mathematics come from: How the embodied mind brings mathematics into being*. Basic Books.

McCarthy, J., & Hayes, P. J. (1969). Some philosophical problems from the standpoint of artificial intelligence. In B. L. Webber & N. J. Nillson (Eds.), *Readings in artificial intelligence, 4* (pp. 431–450). Los Altos, CA: Morgan Kaufmann Publishers.

Ono, J., & Ogata, T. (2017). A method of story generation for creating "surprise" using "gap techniques": An approach to an automatic narrative generation game based on table-talk role playing games. *Cognitive Studies*, *24*(3), 410–434.

Pnueli, A. (1977). The temporal logic of programs. *Proceedings of the 18th IEEE Annual Symposium on Foundations of Computer Science*, (pp. 46-57). The Institute of Electrical and Electronics Engineers, Inc.

Sawa, K. (2015). *Logic as a complex network.* arXiv:1507.00840

Shoenfield, J. R. (1967). *Mathematical logic* (Vol. 21). Reading, MA: Addison-Wesley.

Troelstra, A. S., & Schwichtenberg, H. (2000). *Basic proof theory* (Vol. 43). Cambridge, UK: Cambridge University Press. doi:10.1017/CBO9781139168717

Wang, L. N., Guo, J. L., Yang, H. X., & Zhou, T. (2009). Local preferential attachment model for hierarchical networks. *Physica A*, *388*(8), 1713–1720. doi:10.1016/j.physa.2008.12.028

Wang, P. (2007). The Logic of Intelligence. In B. Goertzel & C. Pennachin (Eds.), *Artificial General Intelligence. Cognitive Technologies* (pp. 31–62). Berlin: Springer. doi:10.1007/978-3-540-68677-4_2

Watts, D. J., & Strogatz, S. H. (1998). Collective dynamics of'small-world'networks. *Nature*, *393*(6684), 440–442. doi:10.1038/30918 PMID:9623998

KEY TERMS AND DEFINITIONS

BA Model: A pioneering model of complex networks. It is mainly composed of two concepts, growth and preferential attachment.

Complex Network: A graph (network) with non-trivial topological features. Most of the research objects have many nodes and edges.

Degree: The number of edges incident to each node.

Implication: A logical connective which represents the relation of “if...then....”

Local Network Transformation: A way of transformation of a graph in the proposed model. The “local” means that only adjacent edges are checked.

Logic as a Narrative (LaaN): A research project representing developments of logic. A narrative is a name of the driving force of the developments.

Power Law: A widely observed feature between two quantities. An index representing universal nature.

Section 4

Analyses, Models, and Systems for Social Narratives

Chapter 12
Narrative Analysis of Employment Support for Students With Developmental Disabilities:
Using an Objective Analysis of Free-Expression Answers

Kai Seino
National Institute of Vocational Rehabilitation, Japan & Toyo University, Japan

Yoko Enomoto
National Institute of Vocational Rehabilitation, Japan

Shiho Miyazawa
National Institute of Vocational Rehabilitation, Japan

ABSTRACT

The text data regarding the free-expression answers on the employment support provided to students with developmental disabilities (unsure students are included) were defined as the narrative. The aim of this research was to obtain suggestions regarding business solutions that could be used to provide employment support for students with developmental disabilities by conducting text mining and narrative theory analysis. Furthermore, the "narrative generation system" is advocated as a comprehensive framework which organically unifies the whole "narrative phenomenon" from various sides. Furthermore, these researches apply the knowledge of other fields, such as pedagogy on developmental disability, personal support, text mining, and a narratology; psychology; engineering; and literature. Therefore, the authors believe that this research corresponds to "narrative generation system" theory research. Thus, it may be possible for suggestions regarding narrative generation to be produced as a secondary result of this chapter's process of analysis.

DOI: 10.4018/978-1-5225-4775-4.ch012

Copyright © 2018, IGI Global. Copying or distributing in print or electronic forms without written permission of IGI Global is prohibited.

INTRODUCTION

This study clarifies the following by analyzing qualitative data from the viewpoint of a narrative: (1) employment support for students with developmental disabilities in Japan and (2) the application possibility of narrative generation by computers. With regard to employment support for students with developmental disabilities, the authors defined free-expression answers by support workers as narratives and analyzed them. As for the application possibility of narrative generation, the authors attempted to apply narrative generation to real students with disabilities who required support.

In recent years, employment support for students with developmental disabilities has become socially important in Japan. Today, the percentage of students going from high school to university in Japan is about 50% (The Ministry of Education, Culture, Sports, Science and Technology, 2017). Moreover, there are 5,436 students who have been diagnosed with developmental disabilities (or students who are suspected to have developmental disabilities and have received special consideration) in universities (Japan Student Services Organization, 2017). This number has increased by 567 since the last fiscal year. Moreover, students diagnosed with developmental disabilities before college admission and who are the targets of special support education are increasing in number. However, after graduating from university, some students experience failure when they enter the working world and notice a developmental disease. In the cases of those who fall in the latter category, it is not easy for youths who have gone on to university to understand their own disabilities and to choose employment suitable for persons with disabilities. In other words, it is not easy for a student to understand and accept his or her own disabilities. Under these circumstances, it is thought that giving dedicated employment support to students with developmental disabilities (or those who are suspected of having such disabilities) is important from the time such students enroll in university.

In addition, for students with developmental disabilities, "the shift from education to work" poses a problem. Specifically, the prognosis of a student diagnosed with a developmental disease is as follows. A total of 34% of highest annual students do not graduate. Moreover, 30% of those who graduate and cannot pursue higher education do not enroll in an institute of higher learning or do not take up posts that fall under regular employment. Thus, it is necessary for employment support that is focused on developmental diseases to be emphasized at the university level. However, such employment support is rarely provided at present. Specifically, "Dissemination of information pertaining to employment support and introduction of a support organization" is 35.2% and "Exploitation of the company to employ and support of job hunting" is 28% (Japan Student Services Organization 2017). In addition, even when a university wishes to provide such support, there are few support workers with "professional expertise in employment support for persons with disabilities." Therefore, when job assistance is offered to a student with developmental disabilities (or a student who is suspected to have such a disability), they are anxious about support workers in university being anxious. The authors named this category V "difficulty of cooperation with the organs concerned outside a university."

However, reports surveying the difficulties experienced by university employment support staff members engaged in the support of students with developmental disabilities (or students suspected of having such disabilities) have not been found. Therefore, the authors (Enomoto et al., 2017) investigated the difficulty of providing employment support to students with developmental disabilities in university career centers. Similarly, the authors made the free-expression answers the group by the similarity of the meaning, and generated the category. In addition, in this study, the authors analyzed the same free-expression answers. Next, the authors calculated the number of descriptions of each category and reported the categories with the most answers. As a result of this analysis, the generated categories are the following, and there were six of them. The authors named category I "the difficulty of urging the use of the career center." For example, category I was titled "when a student comes for consultation later than he or she should have and the support workers cannot provide early support." The authors also named category II "thc difficulty of a support worker's correspondence when using a career center." For example, category II included "When a student is unaware of a disability, it is difficult for a support worker to urge the student to accept support." The authors named category III "the difficulty of cooperating with a guardian." For example, category III included "Parents do not accept the fact that their children have disabilities, and they make such students hunt for jobs like healthy persons, and the students fail." The authors named category IV "the difficulty of cooperating with other sections in a university." For example, category IV included "Student information is not shared with the employment support section in its duty." The authors named category V "the difficulty of cooperation with the organs concerned outside a university." For example, category V included "After graduation, a student cannot take use procedure of a public external organization, and becomes unemployed." The authors named category VI "the difficulty of cooperating with a company." For example, category V included "Exploitation of the company which understands a disability and employs a student is difficult." It was <category II> that offered the most answers. Category II consisted of the following and it was three. The first was "The problem of a student's self-understanding." The second was "The problem which a student understands about work." The third was "Others: The problem of a capability side."

However, Enomoto et al. (2017) used qualitative analysis, which generates a category for free-expression answers. Thus, they had two types of problems in their research. The first problem was that it was hard to understand the concrete contents of the difficulty of providing support because the category generated had a high degree of abstraction. Therefore, the authors felt that it would be difficult to identify the key to providing support from the obtained result. The second problem was related to qualitative analysis: the reproducibility of formalities and the objectivity of the result were low when compared with quantitative analysis, but the method applied to the categories was qualitative analysis. Therefore, to clarify the difficulties in providing employment support for students with disabilities concretely and avoiding such difficulties in the future, it is necessary to conduct a more concrete and objective analysis.

As solution to the problems of qualitative analysis, text mining has attracted a great deal of attention as a method of analyzing free-expression answers in recent years. The reason is that text mining enables quantitative analysis, provided it can change the text in qualitative data into quantitative data. Thereby, it is believed that text mining enables analytic reproducibility and a high degree of objectivity in results. It further improves the reliability of research. However, the disadvantage of text mining is that it cannot capture unique information, which qualitative data can. With such uniqueness, it can be said to be a form of "narrative data-sidedness," although text mining contributes to increasing quantitative evidence in research, it also reduces qualitative evidence. However, in order to extract detailed information about employment support from free-expression answers, it is necessary to collateralize both quantitative evidence and qualitative evidence simultaneously.

While obtaining qualitative evidence from free-expression answers, in order to ensure objectivity, the authors advocated a new analysis method that combines text mining and tale analysis, as in Seino et al. (2016). For the purpose of this study, the authors have named this new analysis method "narrative analysis for integrative evidences." It is shown that this new analysis has an advantage over both quantitative analysis and qualitative analysis as it is a "mixed method" combining quantitative analysis and qualitative analysis. The reappearance of formalities was definitely enabled by quantitative analysis using text mining. Moreover, analysis of quantitative data raised the objectivity and reliability of the result. However, the contents of the free-expression answers were read in detail from the viewpoint of narratology by qualitative analysis using narrative analysis. Moreover, Seino et al. (2016) analyzed the employment of various disabled persons, including those with developmental disabilities, and suggested the possibility of using the new analysis method in research on employment support for persons with disabilities.

Accordingly, in this study, the authors analyzed afresh the free-expression answers that Enomoto et al. (2017) and others studied using qualitative analysis by employing the method that combines quantitative and qualitative analysis. Thereby, this study intends to acquire new information about employment support for students with developmental disabilities and clarify the effect of the new analysis method that Seino et al. (2016) advocated.

Furthermore, the "narrative generation system" is advocated as a comprehensive framework which organically unifies the whole "narrative phenomenon" from various sides (Ogata & Kanai, 2010). Furthermore, these researches apply the knowledge of other fields, such as pedagogy on developmental disability, personal support, text mining, and a narratology; psychology; engineering; and literature. Therefore, the authors believe that this research corresponds to "narrative generation system" theory research. Thus, it may be possible for suggestions regarding narrative generation to be produced as a secondary result of this research's process of analysis.

BACKGROUND

Definition of "Narrative"

There are a variety of definitions of term "narrative." The term "narrative" has a definition in the wider sense when used as a general term and another definition when used in the narrow sense of the term of "narratology." Narrative in the wider sense is understood as the "act of discussing and being discussed using language of the wide sense" (Yamada, 2007). On the other hand, narrative in the narrow sense refers to a reproduction of real or fictional events, and it is always accompanied by time restraints (Prince, 2003).

The free-expression answers treated by this research is told by language (Table 1). Therefore, it corresponds to the definition of a narrative in a broad sense. Moreover, some free-expression answers are accompanied by time chain. Therefore, a part corresponds also to the definition of a narrative in a narrow sense.

Table 1. Example of a question and free-expression answers

Question	When you offer support to a student with a developmental disability (or a student who is suspected of having such a disability), if it may be troubled, please let me know.
Answers	**Example 1:** A student has needs that he should understand the characteristic (it corresponds to a definition in wider sense).
	Example 2: A big difference appears from early time in employment volition by the domestic student who understood the obstacle and has corresponded, and the student who is not so (since it is accompanied by time chain, it corresponds also to a definition in narrow sense).

The Narrative Approach

Noguchi defined this narrative approach as "going closer to some reality with the clues in the forms of narratives" (Noguchi, 2005). The narrative approach focuses on the patient or client and emphasizes the integrity and individuality of the person. However, as a result of the case studies' one-sided interest in the narrative approach, there have been almost no statistical or experimental studies that have collected data (Noguchi, 2009).

Text Mining

Along with the development of text mining, natural language processing technology has been developed. From the mid-1990s, some researches, using text mining, have been conducted regarding feelings and evaluations of free descriptive sentences within the domain of natural language processing (Otsuka, Inui, & Okumura, 2007). The studies using free descriptive sentences within free-form answers can solve problems that are inherent in selective answers (Yasuda, 1970) because there is a re-experience-like possibility of consent (Mita, 1965). However, a problem of analyzing free descriptive sentences is that there is a lack of objectivity in the method of answering, which makes it difficult to analyze the data obtained (Arima & Tsuji, 1987; Tsuzuki, 1975). Additionally, the problem of the subjective interpretation of the results has been highlighted by Tsuzuki (1975).In response to these problems, text mining converts qualitative data into quantitative data, which are then classified automatically by a multivariate analysis. This is expected to solve the problems found in the earlier studies.

Literary Narratology and Psychological Narratology

Literary Narratology

The narrow sense of narratology is regarded as a literary theory. Narratology is the study of the nature, form, and function of narrative (Prince, 2003). According to narratology (Prince, 2003), the story concerns the content of the narrative while the discourse concerns the expressive side. Narratology employs both the analysis of story and that of discourse. Forster (1927) defined the components of narrative as "story" and "plot" (i.e., discourse). He observed, "Story talks about a case and an event according to progress of time," whereas the plot focuses on the causal relation of incidents and events. Propp (1968) described the fundamental components of any Russian folktale. In particular, he defined the narratological notions of "function" and characters' "roles." "Function" is a character's act defined from the viewpoint of its significance in the story. He described 31 types of "functions" that compose Russian folktales. Characters' "roles" are classified based on the range of performable "functions" by a character and, as a result, he described the following seven "roles:" Genette (1980) classified the narrative components into three: story, discourse, and narrating. In applied studies of narratology, some researchers analyze and generate stories based on the theories constructed by Propp and Genette. For example, Terada, Akimoto, Ono, and Ogata (2014) devised a conceptual dictionary that can provide the basic components of narrative; specifically, character, objects, and place.

Psychological Narratology

This study is considered a psychological narratology, used in the narrative approach. These theories are used to analyze the personal narratives and the social stories in the context of society and culture. Bruner (1986) classified forms of narrative into (1) "narrative mode," which includes the time-linking information about an event, and (2) "paradigmatic mode," which includes information about the necessary relations between multiple events as well as causal relations. Morgan (2000) views a story (corresponding to the narrative) as "an event connected on temporal axes in succession which becomes a plot (corresponding to the discourse)." Adam (1999) contended that narrative is composed of time, characters, predicates, and events that can change the predicates. There are some studies of narrative approaches to persons with disabilities. For example, there is research of the narrative approach to mental disorders (Buchanan- Barker & Barker, 2008).

Comparison of Two Narratologies

Literary narratology focuses on a literary narrative while a psychological story centers on social and personal stories. Both literary and psychological narratologies share some characteristics. For example, Bruner, and Morgan all reached the following consensus: narrative can be classified into two elements: (1) those lined up along the event in a time lapse (corresponding to the story) and (2) those lined up along the event in a causal relation (corresponding to the discourse). Also, an interest in the components of story is seen commonly in Propp (1968) and Adam (1999). The story consists of characters (including their roles and actions), functions, time, objects, places, predicates, and events that can affect the predicates. Additionally, Genette's (1980) classification of "voice" is divided into the time for narrating, a standard, and the persona of the narrator. Psychological narratology analyzes social and personal narratives, allowing the relationship between individuals, their culture, and society to be clarified.

The Significance and Originality of This Research

The significance of this research is that it focuses on the practice of providing employment support to students with developmental disabilities. From a practical perspective, this research describes the difficulty of providing employment support at the university level and shows that although it is important, there is little research on the subject. Therefore, the new key, which considers effective support, is acquired. As regards research, a more effective analysis method to analyze free-expression answers is shown. By conducting effective analysis on employment support, reproducibility and validity are high and individuality and concreteness may also be reflected. Thus, the new analysis method presented by the authors, which is a combination of text mining and story analysis, may unify evidence-based and narrative-based support for persons with disabilities In addition, the authors believe that the new analysis will result in application possibility for narrative generation and support.

EMPLOYMENT SUPPORT OF THE STUDENT WITH DEVELOPMENTAL DISABILITY

Purpose

With the above background in mind, this research conducted text analysis and analysis of the contents of a narrative (Story) on the free-expression answers supplied regarding difficulty in administering and providing employment support for students with developmental disabilities (unsure students were included). The primary purpose of this research is to obtain suggestions and business solutions to provide support for students with developmental disabilities. In addition, the secondary purpose is to obtain data on narrative generation through the process of this analysis.

The items examined to achieve these aims is as follows.

1. What elements in the free-expression answers are indicated regarding the subject of support?
2. What are the common features and differences in the results obtained between this research and the precedent research (Enomoto et al., 2017)?
3. What contributions can this research make regarding analysis of text mining and the contents of a narrative (Story), considering actual support and future research?
4. What can text mining and the contents of a narrative (Story) contribute to narrative generation and future research?

Methods

Survey

Self-conducted survey questionnaires were mailed to 751 career centers at four-year colleges all over the country, and they were returned by mail. Investigations were conducted between September and October 2014. The personnel of the career centers were asked to reply. Investigation consisted of multiple choice questions and a free-response question. For this research, the authors only analyzed the free responses. The contents of the question included whether the subject was "troubled by him when carrying out support towards working preparation to the student of developmental disability."

Narrative Analysis

Narrative analysis is the new analysis method that combines text mining and tale theory analysis and has been advocated by the authors.

Text Mining

Data analysis of free expression answers was conducted using KH Coder software (Ver.2. beta 32). The software was developed for an academic purpose and has the following functions necessary for text mining: the separation of words with a space; morphological analysis; dependency parsing; multivariate analysis, including correspondence and cluster analysis; document retrieval; and coating. The analysis consisted of extracting compound words, conducting morphological analysis, listing and searching extracted words, and conducting correspondence and cluster analysis. In particular, the KH Coder's Chasen function was employed in morphological analysis and "Term Extract" in KH Coder was used to extract compound words. Associated terms were coded. The unit of analysis was an individual respondent, and the same respondent using the same word multiple times was counted once.

Story Analysis

For this research, the authors performed text mining on the text data of the free-expression answers and analyzed the contents (Story) of the narrative based on the techniques of Seino, Haruna, and Ishizaki (2016). Seino et al. (2016) arranged the classification of the components of the Story of a narrative for the words used in the free-expression answers to reference elements, such as character types, predicates, places, and times.

Ethical Consideration

This research observed the research ethics indicated by the Japan Society of Vocational Rehabilitation.

Results

Reply Rate

Replies were obtained from 257 centers as a result of investigation (reply rate: 34.2%). Of these, 168 (65.4%) had supported students with developmental disabilities for less than two years. Moreover, 62 centers reported answers corresponding to the answer "This kind of support is troubling" (24.1% of the number of replies, 36.9% of the organizations which are experienced in support).

Analysis through Text Mining

Basic Data

In order to grasp the outline of the contents of the free-expression answers, the text data was analyzed using text mining. As a result of the morphological analysis after pretreatment, there were 1,193 difference words, from which a total of 475 words were extracted as candidates for analysis. The average of the number of times with which an extracted word appeared was 2.51 times, and standard deviation was 5.89.

Frequency of an Extracted Word

In order to clarify words commonly used by respondents, those that were used by five or more respondents were extracted (Figure 1). The number of extracted words was 31 as a result of analysis. Extracted words were not directly related to the contents of a question, and the extracted words included "guardian," "understanding," "cooperation," "time," "consciousness," etc. It is thought that these words have a high possibility of being connected with the concrete contents of a respondent's free-expression answers.

Figure 1. Word used by five or more persons (horizontal axis is number of respondents)

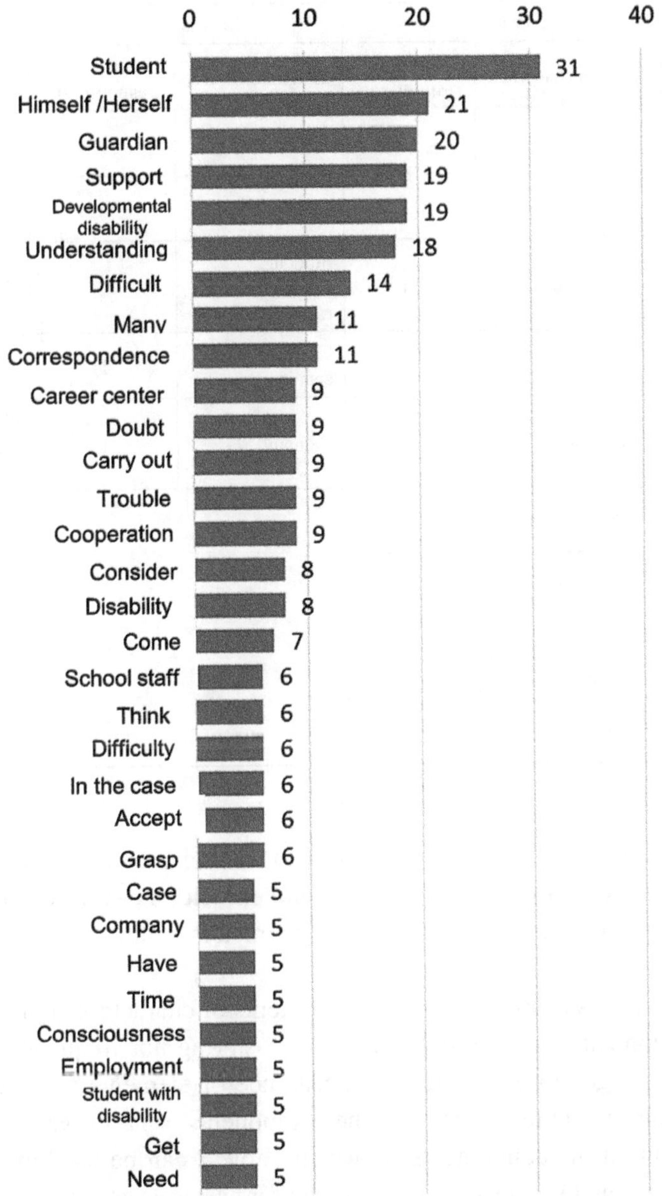

Analysis of the Contents of Narrative (Story)

Regarding the words used in the text data, the components of the Story were classified and arranged based on their context and the elements illustrating characters or acting as predicates, places, and times, using the analysis of Seino et al. (2016) as a reference, and the top ten words with many respective appearances are shown (Table 2). In addition, in order to clarify a meaning within a classification, re-extraction of the compound was performed. For example, six kinds of characters, including a student (for example, a student, the person himself/herself, and a disability studies student) with a developmental disability, a guardian and a school staff member, a company, an external organization, and a supporter

Table 2. Classification of words by component (top ten words)

Character		Predicate		Place		Time	
Extracted word	**Number of responders**	**Extracted word**	**Number of respondents**	**Extracted word**	**Number of respondents**	**Extracted word**	**Number of respondents**
Student	31	Support	19	Career center	9	Early Early time	3
Himself/ Herself	21	Understanding	18	In university	4	Future	2
Guardian	20	Correspondence	11	Student consultation room	2	Activity season	1
School staff	6	Carry out	9	Career support center	1	Time of consultation	1
Student with disability	5	Trouble	9	Campus	1	Nearness to graduation time	1
Company	5	Cooperation	9			After graduation	1
External organization	3	Consider	8				
Support staff	3	Come	7				
Specialist	2	Think	6				
Career counselor	1	Accept	6				

(such as a supporter, a specialist, and a career counselor) were extracted as a result of analysis. On the occasion that employment support was provided to a student with a developmental disability, the possibility that cooperation and the relationship of these characters would serve as an important element could be considered.

The result of story analysis showed the concrete contents of characters, a predicate, and a time and place. These concrete contents are acquired in neither clustering nor frequency analysis. In addition, concrete contents are arranged by frequency of appearance of elements. The components of a story (characters, predicate, place, and time) turn into the components of narrative generation. Accordingly, the concrete information on the components shown in Table 2 can be used as material for narrative generation. In addition, when it is considered as material for narrative generation of elements appearing with a higher frequency (as shown in Table 2), the narrative generated may serve as a story with a high possibility of becoming reality.

Hierarchical Cluster Analysis

In order to clarify the outline of an answer, hierarchical cluster analysis was conducted (Figure 2), where the minimum number of documents in which a word appears was set to two and the minimum number of appearances of a word was set to five. The distance between the words extracted set the distance between a Jaccard coefficient (Distance of Jaccard = 1-Jaccard coefficient) and a cluster using Ward's method, as in previous research. The distance between extraction words set up the distance between a Jaccard coefficient and a cluster by Ward's method like precedence research

Figure 2. Tree diagram of hierarchical cluster

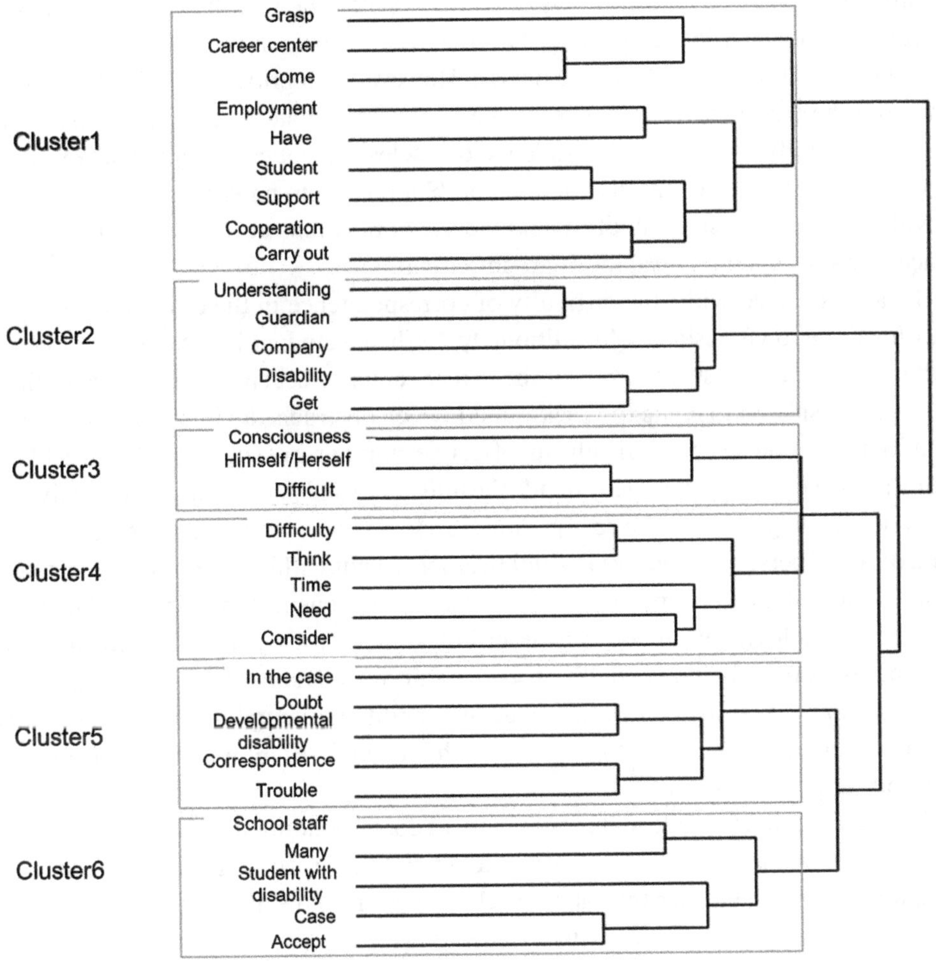

Each word was classified into six clusters as a result of analysis. Next, a document search was performed, and the meaning of the group of a cluster was interpreted by grasping the meaning of the context of the word contained and the meaning of the whole free-expression answer in which the word was contained. In addition, in order to improve the validity of the interpretation of a meaning, deliberations by two researchers were obtained regarding a disabled person's employment support. The words contained in clusters are shown in Figure 2.

As a result, cluster 1 was found to relate to the "subject's actual grasp of the supported student's obstacles." Specifically, answers included "It is difficult to grasp the actual condition of students prior to job-hunting activities," "It is difficult to grasp the condition of a student with disabilities who does not come to a career center, and support is difficult," "There are instances of individual support that are not tied to employment," and "The support itself cannot be carried out." On the other hand, "Cooperation with someone outside of the university or with a guardian is important" was also indicated in relation to support.

Next, cluster 2 was considered to relate to "the difficulty of obtaining information regarding a student's obstacles from a guardian or a company." Specifically, "When the guardian understands the student's obstacle, early support is possible and a record for the disabled person is created, allowing for employment to be secured that is appropriate for the person. However, in reality, it is difficult to obtain accurate information from the guardian" and "There are few companies that have a plan in place for students with disabilities that fully understand the students' obstacles. In that case, appropriate positions cannot be found." On the other hand, it was also noted that "Support from an early stage, employment that is consistent with a disabled person's abilities, and the use of positions at companies that understands the obstacles faced by students with disabilities are important."

Cluster 3 was associated with "the difficulty of correspondence in the case of a student who is not conscious of his or her own obstacles." Additionally, "When a student is not conscious of an obstacle, it is difficult to encourage the student to visit the career center or accept the existence of the obstacle."

Cluster 4 was considered to relate to "background which obstructs the implementation of a student's effective employment support." Specifically, for effective employment support to be possible, "Common understanding among persons concerned outside the university and persons within the university, as well as a mutual understanding between the person himself/herself and a guardian, are required"; "The use of a record for a disabled person is effective in finding employment within an appropriate framework"; and "It is necessary to advance an understanding of the obstacle to a business proprietor." On the other hand, the current state of employment support was described with the following: "Organization maintenance has not been performed in the university"; "It is difficult for a student with obstacles to be provided guidance in a group"; "It is difficult to tie a student's abilities to employment, if their condition has not been tracked from their time of entrance into a school"; and "Employment support should parallel mental care, and support takes time."

Cluster 5 was considered to relate to the "difficulty of corresponding with students with developmental disabilities." Specifically, the following were included: "Since few staff members possess technical knowledge, suitable correspondence that takes the characteristic of the obstacle into account is difficult"; "It is difficult to correspond adequately with a student who is in doubt of his or her developmental disabilities or tie him or her to external organizations"; and "Since the person himself/herself and his or her guardian do not understand an obstacle, support is difficult."

Cluster 6 was associated with the "difficulty of securing support obtained through collaboration with school staff or with a guardian's understanding." Specifically, "It is it is difficult for a school staff member who does not understand an obstacle to cooperate with a career center and provide support"; and "In cases where a guardian does not accept an obstacle, it is difficult to provide support that takes the obstacle into account" were noted.

DISCUSSION

Suggested Solution to the Issues Faced in the Provision of Employment Support for Students With Developmental Disabilities

From this research, the following six elements were identified as factors in employment support for students with developmental disabilities. These include "subject's actual grasp of the supported student's obstacles," "the difficulty of obtaining information regarding a student's obstacles from a guardian or a company," "the difficulty of correspondence in the case of a student who is not conscious of his or her own obstacles," "background which obstructs the implementation of a student's effective employment support," "difficulty of corresponding with students with developmental disabilities," and "difficulty of securing support obtained through collaboration with school staff or with a guardian's understanding."

Next, the common element was identified from the actual free-expression answers based on an element. The problems in common concrete support included the following: (1) Support staff cannot support students who do not come to a career center. (2) Neither students with disabilities nor their families have awareness or understanding of disability. (3) Neither school staff members nor companies have an understanding of disability. (4) Support takes time. (5) Support workers do not have expertise.

Based on this, the authors felt the need for the following efforts both inside and outside universities in the future: (1) early support and support that is provided for several hours, (2) disability acceptance and understanding among students with disabilities and their guardians, (3) maintenance of intramural support organizations, (4) mutual understanding with interested people from outside universities, (5) the university side and the mutual understanding of the person himself/herself and a guardian, (6) certification for persons with disabilities, and (7) promotion of understanding of disability by business proprietors.

Relationship With Precedent Research

The result of this research is compared with the result of Enomoto et al. (2017), who analyzed the same data through category generation. The contents of the six categories from which Enomoto et al. (2017) extracted the common features are the elements similarly extracted from the interpretation of the meaning of a cluster.

On the other hand, "cooperation within a university" and "cooperation with those outside the university" which were separated into different categories in the precedent research, were classified into the same cluster by this research. Moreover, in the precedent research, "support to which use of a center is urged" was used as a category name, and it does not represent a cluster with this research, having been positioned at a low rank. These items are considered because the viewpoints and rules of classification differ from each other due to the analysis method. Moreover, analysis of the contents of narrative (Story) in this research is conducted from a new viewpoint that is not included in the precedent research. Consequently, when considering support, new implications may be provided as a result of this research.

Suggestions for Support

First, since qualitative data is changed into quantitative data and text mining is used to support analysis, the methods applied in this study are more objective than the use of raw text data, potentially providing insight into representative factors. On the other hand, the subject's point of view is taken into consideration, and interpretation by an analyzer is necessary in order to grasp the relationship between the meanings of words and their contexts. However, analysis of the contents (Story) of a narrative through the arrangement of text data allows for a more structural analysis of free-expression answers. The perspective provided by this analysis may prove effective in future hypothesis formation. On the other hand, since the text data is generated by the subject, this analysis cannot be applied to an existing theory or component.

Suggestions for Narrative Generation

Analysis of text mining and the contents (Story) of a narrative can contribute to narrative generation in the following ways. If two or more text data exist, since existing text data can be broken down into fixed components of a Story, it will be possible to combine the existing elements in order to generate a new (or future) Story. Moreover, this story may function as a simulation, informing future support-related decisions. On the other hand, since the subject's perspective is limited (the component being analyzed) to the existing situation, in order to generate a new component in which a future situation is anticipated, technical knowledge related to the theme of the narrative and creative element development are required. In addition, this research analyzed the contents (Story) of a narrative and did not, therefore, take the narrative's expression (discourse) into account when classifying text data components of Story into a morpheme.

FUTURE RESEARCH DIRECTIONS

Based on the comprehensive framework of a narrative generation system, there is a possibility that "More detailed analysis of the text data of the described narrative," "Construction of a concept index through the use of actual data (such as that produced by this research)", "Computer simulation of narrative generation," and "Real-world application of these findings," etc., can be considered in cooperation with the researchers of other fields, such as literature and engineering. For example, the elements of the narrative investigated in this research can be disassembled and recombined in order to illuminate an underlying structure, which can assist with the generation of content specific to a student's particular situation. This Story is formed by the combination of the following elements: "Supporter (characters)," "At the time of support provided to a student (characters)," "In such a situation" (time and place)," "The levels of difficulty perceived (predicate)," "Such support was offered (predicate)," "The subject (characters) of one's other posts or an external organization," and "Results and subjects (predicate) perceived as a result of cooperation." If it becomes possible, the generated narrative could be considered for inclusion in a supporter's training materials as examples of support. One advantage of this method is that, since the actual example is not a complete narrative but a created one, the problem of personal information is conquerable. On the other hand, since the narrative's elements are extracted based on two or more actual occurrences, it is noted that realistic knowledge of a representative nature can be offered.

CONCLUSION

This research conducted quantitative analysis called "grasp of the quantitative index by text mining," using classification by cluster analysis of qualitative data extracted from free-expression answers. This was conducted as a complement to the qualitative analysis (Enomoto et al., 2017). Furthermore, a procedure that deepened the qualitative interpretation of the results was performed.

Although the subject was difficulty encountered in the provision of support for students with developmental disabilities, and the tangible elements of support administration were difficult to grasp in the precedent research (Enomoto et al., 2017), this research was able to use cluster analysis to extract concrete elements.

Moreover, although the dearth of statistical research on this subject using a narrative approach and survey data has been pointed out (Noguchi, 2009), proposals have been made regarding the analytical methods required for conquest of this subject. The authors believe that, in addition to the individuality and concreteness that are the advantages of qualitative data and qualitative analysis, the complex method proposed by this research can secure the objectivity that is an advantage of quantitative data and quantitative analysis. Thus, reliability can be obtained, offering significant implications. This research also contributes to suggestions for on-site practice by further adding qualitative narratology analysis to the complex method. There are limits to analytical abilities, for example, "The interpretation of a word or a text is influenced by an analyzer's knowledge and reading comprehension abilities" and "Since one free-expression answer is classified into two or more clusters, interpretation of the cluster's group is difficult." Moreover, the results obtained by this quantitative analysis of the contents of narrative (Story) do not provide sufficient examination of the subject, but the way in which a synthetic interpretation is performed is left as a subject of future study.

ACKNOWLEDGMENT

This work was supported by JSPS KAKENHI (Grant Numbers 15K13258 and 17K04253).

The data used in this study is data from the "survey about effective employment support for a college student with a developmental disability (or a student suspected of having a developmental disability)" which NPO Wing PRO (Kazuko Niibori, Chairman of the Board of Directors) conducted with the support of the Nippon Foundation. Thank you very much for the research partnership.

We would like to thank Editage (www.editage.jp) for English language editing.

REFERENCES

Adam, J. M. (1999). *Le récit*. Paris, France: Presses Universitaires de France.

Arima, M., & Tsuji, S. (1987). *Anketochosa no houhou* [Method of questionnaire survey]. Tokyo, Japan: Asakura Publishing.

Bruner, J. (1986). *Actual minds, possible worlds*. Cambridge, MA: Harvard University Press.

Enomoto, Y., Seino, K., & Nibori, K. (2017). The support situation to the student of the developmental disability in a career center Part3. In *Proceedings of Japan Academy for Comprehensive Rehabilitation 18th Conference*. Tokyo, Japan: Japan Academy for Comprehensive Rehabilitation.

Feldman, R., & Sanger, J. (2007). *The text mining handbook: Advanced approaches in analyzing unstructured data*. Cambridge, UK: Cambridge University Press.

Forster, E. M. (1927). *Aspects of the novel*. London, UK: Edward Arnold.

Genette, G. (1980). *Narrative discourse: An essay in method* (J. E. Lewin, Trans.). Ithaca, NY: Cornell University Press. (Original work published 1972)

Japan Student Services Organization. (2017). *Heisei 28 nendo syougai noaru gakusei no syugakusien nikansuru jittaichyosa* [A survey on study support for students with disabilities 2016]. Tokyo: Japan Student Services Organization.

Ministry of Education, Culture, Sports, Science, and Technology. (2017). Heisei 29 nendo gakkou ki-hon chyosa(sokuhochi) no kohyo nituite. Tokyo: Ministry of Education, Culture, Sports, Science and Technology.

Mita, M. (1965). *Gendainihon no seishinkouzou* [Mental structure of Japan]. Tokyo, Japan: Koubundo.

Morgan, A. (2000). *What is narrative therapy?* Adelaire, Australia: Dulwich Center Publication.

Noguchi, Y. (Ed.). (2005). Naratibu no rinshoshakaigaku [Clinical sociology of narrative]. Tokyo, Japan: Keiso shobo.

Noguchi, Y. (Ed.). (2009). Naratibu apurochi [Narrative approach]. Tokyo, Japan: Keiso shobo.

Ogata, T., & Kanai, A. (Eds.). (2010). *Monogatariron no jouhougaku josetsu: Monogatari seisei no shisou to gijutsu wo megutte* [An introduction to the informatics of narratology: About the thought and technologies of narrative generation]. Tokyo, Japan: Gakubunsha.

Otsuka, H., Inui, T., & Okumura, M. (2007). *Opinion mining engine*. Tokyo, Japan: Corona Publishing.

Prince, G. (2003). *A dictionary of narratology* (Revised edition). Lincoln, NE: University of Nebraska Press.

Propp, V. Y. (1968). *Morphology of the folktale* (L. Scott, Trans.). Austin, TX: University of Texas Press. (Original work published 1928)

Seino, K., Haruna, Y., & Ishizaki, S. (2016). Employment status and support needs of persons with disabilities in japan: An analysis of narrative using narratology and text mining on a national survey. In T. Ogata & T. Akimoto (Eds.), Computational and cognitive approaches to narratology (pp. 245-275). Hershey, PA: Information Science Reference (IGI Global).

Terada, T., Akimoto, T., Ono, J., & Ogata, T. (2014). A systematic description of proper noun concepts in the integrated narrative generation system. In *Proceedings of the Association for Natural Language 20th Conference* (pp. 217-220). Kyoto, Japan: The Association for Natural Language Processing.

Tsuzuki, A. (1975). Shitsumonshicyosa no igi [The significance of the questionnaire]. In M. Arima & E. Murakami (Eds.), *Shinrigakukenkyuhou 9* [Psychology Research Methods 9]. Tokyo, Japan: University of Tokyo Press.

Yamada, Y. (2007). *Shitsutekishinrigaku no houhou: Katari o kiku* [Method of qualitative psychology: Listening to narrative]. Tokyo, Japan: Shinyousha.

KEY TERMS AND DEFINITIONS

Employment: Being employed in public organizations, private firms, or administrative agencies with decent payment and contracts on either a full-time or part-time basis, or being self-employed, excluding welfare-based work or volunteer work with subminimum wages.

Employment for Persons With Disabilities: It refers to the employment of a person with a disability using the social system for persons with disabilities.

Employment Support: Support for employment preparation, job hunting, vocational life, etc.

Literary Narratology: The narrow sense of narratology is regarded as a literary theory.

Narrative Analysis: A classification and analysis modeled on a narratology.

Narrative in the Narrow Sense: A reproduction of a real or fictional event that is always accompanied by time restraints.

Narrative in the Wider Sense: The act of an individual narrating using his or her own language.

Psychological Narratology: These theories are used to analyze personal narratives and social stories in the context of society and culture.

Chapter 13
Practice and Modeling of Advertising Communication Strategy:
Sender-Driven and Receiver-Driven

Yoji Kawamura
Kindai University, Japan

ABSTRACT

Toward the building of a social/consumption simulation model, the objectives of this chapter are to understand in detail the practice of advertising communication through a framework aiming at quantification, to elucidate the goals and techniques of advertising communication, and to create a model for advertising communication strategies. First, the advertising communications goals, the advertising communications techniques, the motivations to become involved, and the consumer-generated contents are categorized. Next, the relationships between these categorized items are identified. Finally, the typical advertising communications strategies are identified and organized into three types models (two types of sender-driven strategies and one type of receiver-driven strategy). These models can be utilized to establish strategic rules for social simulations that include both senders and receivers of advertising.

INTRODUCTION

Changes in the Media Environment and the Use of Effectiveness Measures

As internet use has become more widespread, the flow of information through the use of consumer generated media (CGM) such as blogs and Twitter (Consumers to Corporations, Consumers to Consumers) has increased alongside the use of traditional mass media sources such as TV, newspapers, and leaflets (Corporations to Consumers). More and more energy is being put into attempts to utilize CGM in marketing strategies (Ikeo, 2003; Yamazaki, 2005; Ijichi, 2006; Ito, 2007) and a wide variety of "trial-and-error" style attempts are expected to continue in the foreseeable future. At the same time,

DOI: 10.4018/978-1-5225-4775-4.ch013

Copyright © 2018, IGI Global. Copying or distributing in print or electronic forms without written permission of IGI Global is prohibited.

the use of CGM has made it easier to collect information about consumers and has led to advances in the environment within which the effectiveness of communication is measured (Poynter, 2010; Sterne, 2011). In order for corporations to accurately plan and execute marketing strategies, it is necessary for them to utilize and integrate a variety of effectiveness measures that allow data collection using the CGM environment, and they must be able to quantitatively assess and analyze these attempts.

The Need for Social and Consumption Simulation Models That are Compatible with the CGM Environment

Increasingly active use of CGM communication has led to information cycling between corporations/society and consumers, as well as among consumers themselves, and has led to changes, such as increasing complexity in the structure of social and consumer communication. As a result, it is becoming increasingly difficult to predict and reproduce communication behaviors. In order to precisely assess, analyze, and predict the communication behaviors that are currently in circulation, it is necessary to carry out simulations based on some type of measurement model to anticipate consumer phenomena. Thus, it is necessary to create a common measurement model (hereafter referred to as the "social/consumption simulation model") that facilitates both the interpretation/analysis and the prediction of social and consumer phenomena. Social and consumer communication behavior in the CGM communication environment are undergoing dynamic changes that result from the content types produced by consumers and the timing of and related motivations for the release of these contents by consumers. When creating the social/consumption simulation model, it is necessary to model the information contents for the information cycles between corporations/society and consumers as well as among consumers themselves (corporate-generated contents, consumer-generated contents), the time coefficient (timing, frequency), and the driving forces (goals, methods, and strategies of communication as well as consumer-related factors).

Chapter Objective

Toward the building of a social/consumption simulation model, the objectives of this chapter are to understand in detail the practice of advertising communication through a framework aiming at quantification, to elucidate the goals and techniques of advertising communication, and to create a model for advertising communications strategies.

First is an explanation of the framework for the consumer behavior model, based on previous research, which will be used as the basis for this study. Next, the goals of advertising communication, types of media utilized, contents of the information that is being exchanged (corporation-generated contents, consumer-generated contents), and consumer-related motivational factors for advertising communication will be organized into a framework for this model based on advertising practices. The advertising communication techniques and related motivations as well as the consumer-generated contents will be categorized, and the relationships of consumer-generated contents and their related motivations with advertising communication techniques will be identified and described. Finally, there will be an attempt to summarize and create models for typical advertising communication strategies.

BACKGROUND

Previous Research on Consumer Behavior Models and Information Providers

The consumer behavior models known as the Awareness, Interest, Desire and Action (AIDA) model and the Attention, Interest, Demand, Memory, and Action (AIDMA) model were originated quite a long time ago (Strong, 1925). The Defining Advertising Goals for Measured Advertising Results (DAGMAR) approach to communication goals was originally proposed (Colley, 1961) based on the ideas contained in AIDA and AIDMA and currently remains in use as a measure of the effectiveness of advertising communication. Then, the Attention, Interest, Search, Action and Share (AISAS) model (Akiyama & Sugiyama, 2004; Morioka, Hasegawa, & Yamakawa, 2006), the Attention, Interest, Desire, Experience, Enthusiasm, and Share (AIDEES) model (Katahira, 2006), the Attention, Interest, Search, Trial, Action, and Repeat (AISTAR) model (Nomura Research Institute, 2007), the Spiral Model (Nishina, 2011), and other models that incorporated active consumer behaviors based on the expansion of the internet and the rise of CGM were proposed. However, the relationship between these conceptual models and a variety of effectiveness measures that allow data to be collected using the CGM environment has not been sufficiently examined.

The following groupings have been proposed as information providers that influence others: opinion leaders (Lazarsfeld, Berelson, & Gaudet, 1948), innovators (Rogers, 2003), market maven (Feick & Price, 1987), influencers (Eliashberg & Shugan, 1997), radical access members (RAM; Ikeda, 1997), active consumers (Hamaoka, 2002), leading consumers (Ikeda, 2008), and advanced consumers (Nishina, 2011), among others. Research that formulates (Bass, 1969; Kimura, 2008) the effect of these information providers and assesses and analyzes their effects (Ogawa, 2003; Yamamoto & Abe, 2007; Yamamoto & Katahira, 2008) has been conducted. Attempts at simulating the spread of information providers' word-of-mouth communication (customer reviews) have also been conducted (Hamaoka & Satomura, 2009; Ikeda, 2010; Yoshida, Ishii, & Arakaki, 2010). However, consumer models that utilize these simulations are simple and therefore do not sufficiently produce the desired results of the aforementioned consumer behavior model.

Previous Research in Marketing and Communications

There have been studies of corporate marketing and communications methods and practices that have summarized the strategies used in successful cases (Shimaguchi, Takeuchi, Katahira, & Ishii, 1998, 1999; Uotani, 2009) as well as those that have summarized marketing policy proposal manuals associated with successful cases (Wada, 1999; Bearingpoint, 2002; Sekizawa, Washida, & Bjorn, 2002; Tanaka & Ono, 2003). Currently, there are numerous such reference works. In general, they provide summaries of cases of specific corporations and products that succeeded and make marketing and communications strategy proposals based on those successful cases. However, the environment in which marketing and communications take place (media, needs, competition) is complex and changing at a bewildering pace. Thus, corporations and products that were presented just a few years ago as successful cases are often no longer popular after only a few years and, therefore no longer successful as they were unable to identify on an ad-hoc basis the factors that led to either the success or failure, and on what basis a corporation or product succeeded. They were unable to gain a structural understanding of marketing and communications. It is therefore impossible to launch a marketing or communications strategy based on past case studies. Rather, it is necessary to create a model with some sort of structure for both consumer and corporate communication methods (goals, techniques, strategies), understand the model for marketing and communications between corporations and consumers as a framework, and create an environment that allows careful analysis of why a communications method succeeded or failed, or if it succeeded, then what factors led to that success.

A Consumer Behavior Model and Analytical Framework That Can Be Used as a Basis for Research

Under these circumstances, a cyclical consumer behavior model known as iDEACCycle (Kawamura, 2013) was proposed as a basis for conducting predictions and simulations using a quantitative model. A variety of marketing and communications cases have been interpreted, assessed, and analyzed using this model, and an attempt has been made to categorize the cases (Kawamura, Kato, Tachibana, Okai, & Kinoshita, 2014). Here, the author analyzes attempts at promoting the marketing and communications information cycles between corporations and consumers.

The iDEACCycle considers the following three types of consumers (agents) and creates a model that identifies their characteristics using eight behavioral and psychological steps (Figure 1):

1. **Caster:** A person who has contact with a wide variety of media engages in purchasing and consumer activities based on deep information processing, and is, therefore, the source of ideas and information (that is, "casts out" ideas and information).
2. **Investigator:** A person who has contact with a wide variety of media and engages in purchasing and consumer activities based on deep information processing.
3. **Accepter:** A person who has passive contact with media, assimilates circumstances, and engages in purchasing and consumer activities.

Figure 1. Cyclical consumer behavior model iDEACCycle (Kawamura, 2013)

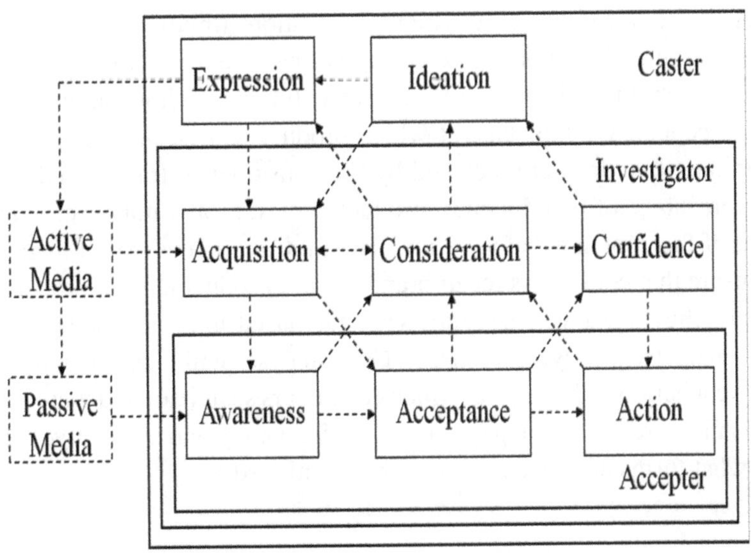

Here, the idea of "passive media" refers to media in which a consumer passively gains information without effort or cost. In contrast, "active media" refers to media in which the consumer makes some effort or bears some cost to actively obtain information.

The unique characteristic of this model is the fact that it is a model of the process that begins with a consumer receiving information stimuli (awareness, acquisition) from the media and then processing that information (acceptance, consideration, confidence), to the process of conceiving of an idea based on the processing of that information and then expressing (communicating) that information in the media. The cyclical consumer behavior model does not trace the ideas and behaviors of consumers in a linear fashion but rather provides a structure to the process by which their ideas and behaviors proceed in cyclical stages (in some cases, amplified or radiating). The model has the following characteristics, in contrast to previous consumer behavior models, as it:

- Allows one to gain a structural understanding of the process of communication that utilizes active media (homepages, CGM, participatory events, etc.) and facilitates the interpretation and analysis of the phenomena.
- Allows a more detailed understanding of the behavioral and psychological stages of consumers and allows a dynamic understanding of consumer behavior by creating a structural model of the relationships between the behavioral stages and media (passive, active) and the relationships between the behavioral and psychological stages.
- Creates a structural model of investigators (moderate involvement) and accepters (low involvement) based on the caster (high involvement) model.
- Allows the description, interpretation, and analysis of consumer behavior as a quantitative model through the use of a quantitative index and, at the same time, allows consumer behavior to be simulated through the use of the quantitative model as an agent.

The following provides the descriptions and the measurement indices for the eight behavioral and psychological stages. A framework for analyzing cases at each stage will also be presented.

1. **Awareness:** Awareness is the stage at which information stimuli from passive media reaches the consumer. It is measured based on the percentage of passive media the consumer receives and the frequency with which it is utilized. Case analyses will focus on how passive media are utilized.
2. **Acceptance:** Acceptance is the stage at which product names, product series names, company names, and product functions are received by the consumer in fragmented form. It is measured based on the percentage of brand names, product names, proper nouns, etc. that are recalled and the percentage of the contents that were understood. Case analyses will focus on what measures are taken to ensure that consumers recall brand names, product names, proper nouns, etc..
3. **Action:** Action is the stage at which products are purchased and consumed. It is measured based on product sales and the frequency of purchases. Case analyses will focus on purchasing performance.
4. **Acquisition:** Acquisition is the stage at which consumers search for and view information from active media. It is measured based on page views and frequency of use of active media. Case analyses will focus on what forms of active media are being utilized.

5. **Consideration:** Consideration is the stage at which consumers gain a good understanding of the functionality, effectiveness, cost-effectiveness, and suitability of products. It is measured based on the frequency that posted contents on customer review sites (keywords and associated terms that are related to product functions, effectiveness, cost-effectiveness, and suitability to consumers) appear. At this level, consumers consider the products more carefully than at Acceptance level, and therefore case analyses will focus on measures taken to ensure that consumers recall product functions, effectiveness, cost-effectiveness, and suitability to consumers.
6. **Confidence:** Confidence is that stage at which consumers make judgments regarding products and corporations based on Consideration and Acceptance. It is measured based on the rate of positive regard and the rate of purchase intent regarding a given corporation or product as well as the assessments of customer reviews (frequency with which keywords and associated terms related to product assessments appear). Case analyses will focus on measures taken to ensure consumer confidence using factors that create a favorable impression.
7. **Ideation:** Ideation is the stage at which consumers manifest ideas and awareness based Consideration and Confidence. It is measured based on the contents proposed on consumer-participation sites and planned events. Case analyses will focus on measures taken to ensure that consumers recall ideas and awareness of products and corporations.
8. **Expression:** Expression is the stage at which consumers post ideas and things they have recalled on active media. It is measured based on the frequency of posts and the frequency of participation on customer review sites and consumer-participatory sites. Case analyses will focus on how active media is utilized to post recalled ideas and awareness of products and corporations.

Consumer Behavior Model and Goals and Techniques of Communication

Corporations establish communication goals in accordance with the various consumer types, and they make use of a variety of communication techniques via media sites. For example, when focusing on Accepters (including both Investigators and Casters), communication techniques will add some type of "character" (an entertainer, etc.) to a product during a campaign for the purpose of promoting Awareness and Acceptance ("Awareness/Acceptance promotion") or will provide some type of special benefit (discounts, a giveaway present). When focusing on Investigators (including Casters), communication techniques such as product-related games are utilized for the purpose of promoting Investigator participation in order to promote Consideration, Confidence, and Acquisition of the product ("Relationship building"). When focusing on Casters, communication techniques such as providing information to consumers to gain their sympathy or recruiting consumers for product-related events are utilized for the purpose of promoting the Ideation of Casters in order to create Ideation and Expressions related to the product ("Ideation/Expression promotion").

In order to create a social/consumption simulation model, it is necessary to devise rules for the manipulation of variables (indices at each stage of the iDEACCycle) for the communication techniques that comprise the model.

In this chapter, an understanding of these communication techniques will be gained through the use of the iDEACCycle framework, and its structure will be analyzed.

Consumer Behavior Model and the Types of Information Handled

Nishina (2001) proposed an "integration model" as an advertisement effectiveness model and described the stages as follows: advertisement information processing->product/brand information processing and needs information processing->purchasing behavior information processing. When examining advertising communications, the information types handled include at least product/brand information and consumer needs information. When examining advertising communications that are designed to stimulate consumer attention and interest, the information handled also includes information related to fashions and events that sweep through society and information related to the daily lives of consumers.

In this chapter, the ways in which these various information types are utilized in advertising communications will be analyzed. The types that will be considered are information related to products and brands ("product-related information") and all types of information related to consumers (information related to fashions and events that sweep through society, information related to the daily lives of consumers, information related to consumers' needs: "consumer-related information"). The iDEACCycle mentioned above considers and analyzes product-related information and consumer-related information at each of the eight behavioral and psychological stages.

METHODS

Subjects

Hansoku Kaigi [Top Promotion] is a major monthly advertising communications journal in Japan.

In this chapter, the author analyzes the policies in 50 cases that were selected as the "Editors' best monthly promotions" in the journal (Sendenkaigi, 2011-2014).

Analytical Methods

First, the advertising communications goals, the advertising measures based on the iDEACCycle framework (use in the media and information contents of product-related information and consumer-related information at each of the iDEACCycle stages), and factors related to consumer participation in advertising communications will be identified in each of the cases based on the case descriptions (abstracts of contents, media, response etc.) of the editors' best monthly promotions report and additional surveys of the publicly available promotion-related sites. Identification and organization will be conducted through discussions by marketing communications researchers and promotion managers. Based on the results thus obtained, the advertising communications techniques, the motivations to become involved, and the consumer-generated contents will be categorized. Identification and categorization will be conducted through discussions by marketing communications researchers and promotion managers. Based on the results of the categorization, the relationships between advertising communications goals and advertising communications techniques and motivations to become involved, and the relationships between consumer-generated contents, the motivations to become involved, and advertising communications goals will be identified. Finally, based on the results thus obtained, the typical advertising communications strategies (patterns) will be identified and organized into a model.

RESULTS

Case Organization

The advertising communications measures in the 50 cases were identified based on the iDEACCycle framework. An example of the content types that were identified is shown in Table 1. This case takes up the example of the *Ore-tachi no yukikotan purojecuto* [Our yukikotan project] by Megmilk Snow Brand Co., Ltd. In this particular case, an advertisement communications policy that consisted of all the iDEACCycle stages in order to promote Ideation and Expression was utilized.

Categorization of Advertising Communications Techniques

Based on the results obtained, the author then categorized the advertising communications measures into advertising communications techniques. The main advertising communications techniques are listed below (1 to 4):

1. **Games:** Consumers' interest is aroused through the use of some type of game related to the product. In the cases examined, games that had to do with the product name, material, or characteristics were used. Interactive games in which consumers could enjoy themselves in the game "world" were

Table 1. An example of content types: Ore-tachi no yukikotan purojecuto by Megmilk Snow Brand Co., Ltd.

Goals of Advertising Communication	Ideation/Expression promotion	
Factors that Motivate Consumers to Contribute	Contest, Sharing	
Advertising Communication Measures Based on iDEACCycle Stages	Product-related Information	Consumer-related Information
Awareness (how passive media are utilized)	Journals, events, transport advertisement, product package.	Journals, events, transport advertisement, product package.
Acceptance (what measures are taken to ensure that consumers recall brand names, product names, proper nouns, etc.)	Brand name, product name.	Character public recruitment based on referendum.
Action (purchasing performance)	Sales of special product package and Christmas limited product package.	
Acquisition (what forms of active media are being utilized)	Web site.	Web site, Twitter.
Consideration (measures taken to ensure that consumers recall product functions, effectiveness, cost-effectiveness, and suitability to consumers)	Contents of product. History of product.	Contents of character. Event report.
Confidence (measures taken to ensure consumer confidence using factors that create a favorable impression)		Present of wallpaper and original theme song. Election by contest. Adoption of product character by contest.
Ideation (measures taken to ensure that consumers recall ideas and awareness of products and corporations)	Product character design.	
Expression (how active media is utilized to post recalled ideas and awareness of products and corporations)	Web site.	Web site.

used. By incorporating information about the product in the game, this technique creates "fans" who have a deeper awareness of the product. A relationship is created through Awareness, Acceptance, Acquisition, Consideration, Confidence, Ideation, and Expression of the consumer-related information (game-related information). This technique promotes Awareness, Acceptance, and Acquisition, which then leads to Consideration of and Confidence in the product-related information (Figure 2).

2. **Metonymy:** The use of some type of character (mainly entertainers) as part of advertising communications brings the corporation, product, and consumer into contact and creates a link to the characteristics of the character. In the cases examined, characters (in the broad sense, including singers, TV personalities, animated characters, games, sports figures, social involvement, etc.) are brought into contact with the product, corporation, and consumers. Consumers are brought into contact with characters that they are interested in, and then by linking information about the product to those characters, the technique creates "fans" who have a deep awareness of the product. The technique captures the attention of consumers through the use of the Awareness, Acceptance, Consideration of, and Confidence of consumer-related information (character-related information), promotes Awareness, Acceptance, Acquisition, and Consideration of product-related information, and this then leads to Confidence in the product-related information (Figure 2).
3. **Metaphor:** Alternate forms of communication of information (characters used as part of an advertising communications campaign, for example) can substitute for the characteristics of the corporation, product, or consumer. In the cases examined, sporting events were used to create an image for the product characteristics, and pieces of music or video were used to create an image for the product concept. This is similar to the technique of Metonymy mentioned in above, but the fact that information designed to promote the examination of product-related information is not presented, and the fact that alternatives to consumer-related information are used, are points that differ from Metonymy.
4. **Reticence, or Suspense:** Opportunities for the consumer to recall the product through contents or situations that provide advertising communications (in some cases, hiding some information or providing incomplete information) helps the consumer to expand on a "story" or "image." If the consumer's "story" is "consumption situation=>product acceptance=>consumption effect," then by omitting either "consumption situations," "product acceptance," or "consumption effect," the consumer can be made to fill in that part of the "story" (the consumer substitutes the missing section by creating his or her own story). By providing lifestyle-related information by sharing lifestyle information that the consumer is interested in, or preparing an experiential environment and then linking these to product information, the technique encourages consumers to post their feelings and ideas regarding consumption or the product. A relationship is created through the use of the Awareness, Acceptance, Acquisition, Consideration, and Expression of consumer-related information, which promotes the Awareness, Acceptance, Acquisition, and Consideration of product-related information, and this in turn leads to Confidence and Ideation of consumer-related information and Confidence, Ideation, and Expression of product-related information (Figure 2).

Although utilized only in a small number of cases, other techniques included "providing information" (providing information about the product directly), "invitations" (asking consumers to propose product functions), and "rewards" (giving consumers product-related presents). Because there was a tendency for these particular techniques to be utilized in the cases analyzed in this chapter, few of the simpler

Figure 2. Typical structures of main advertising communications techniques

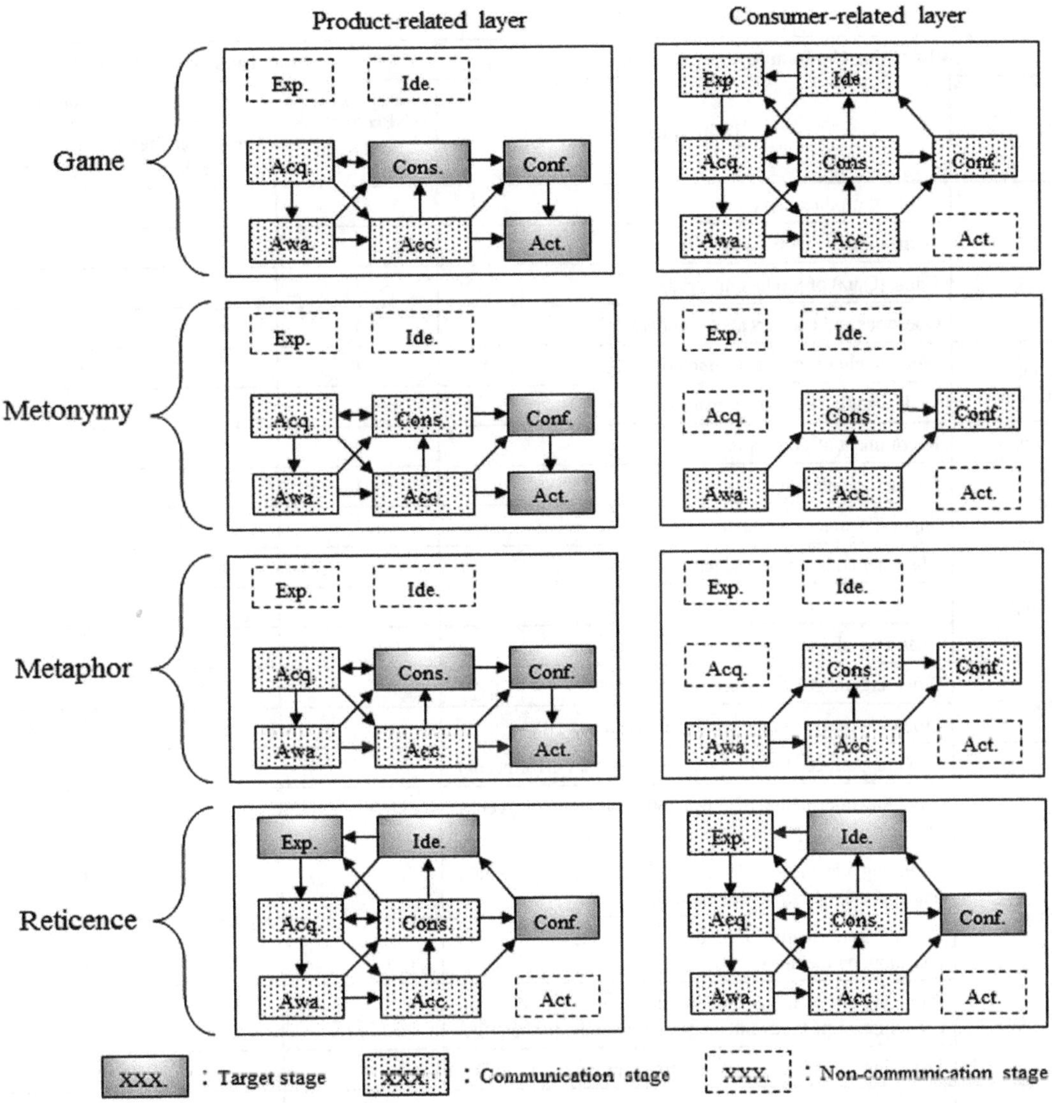

techniques were covered; however, the more complex techniques are generally the most commonly used. The relationships between advertising communications techniques and the main information contents handled are shown in Table 2. Of the 50 cases examined, 11 cases were product-related information and 39 were consumer-related information (18 cases of consumer lifestyle-related information and 21 cases of character-related information).

Categorization of Factors That Motivate Consumers to Contribute to Advertising Communications

Consumer motivations to become involved in advertising communications ("motivations to become involved") include a variety of factors. The following (1 to 5) are the results obtained by categorizing the motivations to become involved:

Table 2. The relationships between advertising communications techniques and the main information contents handled

Advertising Communications Techniques		Main Information Contents		
			Consumer-related	
Categories	Techniques	Product-related	Consumer lifestyle-related	Character-related
Game	Game of product name	3		
	Game of product characteristics	1		
	Game (Quiz) of product materials	1		
	Questions and answers about product	1		
Providing Information	Introduction of product characteristics	1		
	Understanding of product materials	1		
Invitations	Recruitment of product features	2		
Reward	Product gift planning	1		
	Support plan for consumers		1	
Metonymy	Character addition to products			14
	Character addition to company			1
	Character addition to consumers			3
Metaphor	Providing image of product concept			2
	Providing image of product characteristics			1
Reticence	Providing information of consumption situation (or needs)		1	
	Providing information of consumption situation (or scene) and product acceptance (or consumption method)		2	
	Providing information of consumption situation (or needs) and consumption effect (or benefit)		1	
	Providing information of product acceptance (or consumption method)		4	
	Providing information of product acceptance (or consumption method) and consumption effect (or benefit)		3	
	Providing information of consumption effect (or benefit)		6	
Total		11	18	21

1. **Reward:** Consumers are made to feel that they want to participate due to the promise of some reward (present, etc.).
2. **Gamification:** Consumers' interest and desire to participate is stimulated by some game-style element (game, contest, etc.).
3. **Collaboration:** Consumers are encouraged to make a commitment by raising their awareness through the creation of something (joint contents, commodification, etc.) in collaboration with the corporation.
4. **Sharing:** The existence of an environment in which corporations, consumers, and consumer groups, etc. can use the internet to share information makes consumers want to utilize that environment.

5. **Discovery:** Consumers obtain new information (experiences, ideas, counseling, etc.) from an information-sharing environment that serves as a base, and are, therefore, encouraged to enjoy making discoveries.

Categorization of Consumer-Generated Contents

The following (1 to 5) are the results of the categorization of consumer-generated contents based on contents identified as Ideations of advertising communications measures:

1. **Product evaluations:** Evaluations of products (ranking, etc.)
2. **Product functions:** Ideas, concepts, characters, etc. related to products
3. **Consumption situations:** Consumers' awareness of problems and scenes of their daily lives
4. **Consumption effects:** Feelings and opinions regarding the consumption of the product
5. **Other:** Contents related to society and daily life that are not closely related to the product

The Relationships Between Advertising Communications Goals and Techniques

The relationships between advertising communications goals and techniques are shown in Figure 3. There are 20 advertising campaigns with the main goal of Awareness/Acceptance promotion, with many of them (10 cases) using the technique of Metonymy, and 13 whose main goal was Relationship building, with many of them (five cases each) using the techniques of Games and Metonymy. There were also 17 cases whose main goal was Ideation/Expression promotion, with many of them (11 cases) using the technique of Reticence.

Figure 3. The relationships between advertising communications goals and techniques

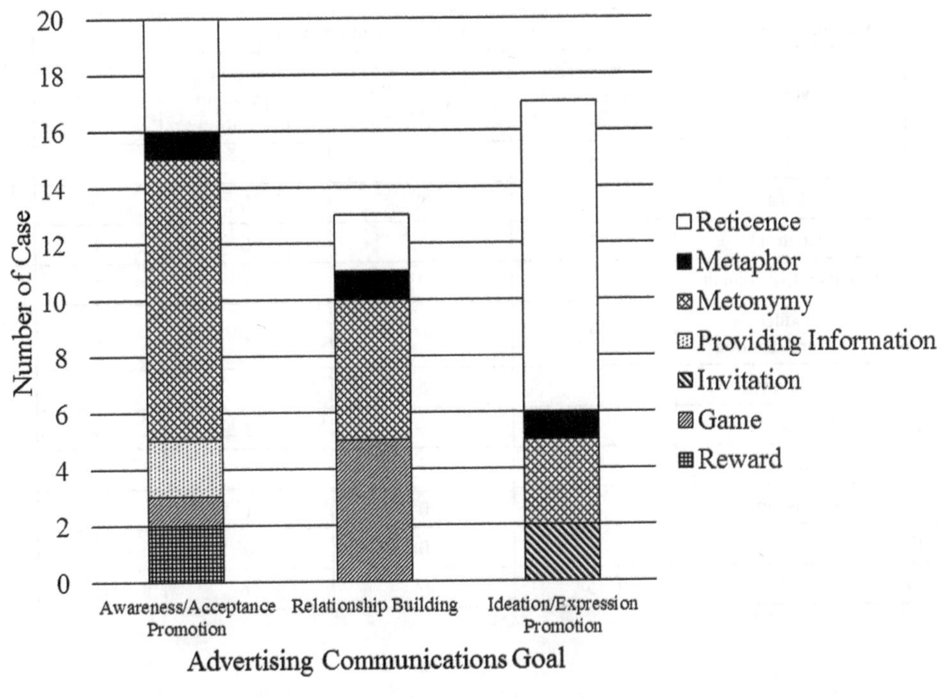

The Relationships Between Advertising Communications Goals and Motivations to Become Involved

The results of identifying and organizing the relationships between the factors related to motivations to become involved and advertising communications goals are shown in Table 3, and a graph showing the relationships between them is shown in Figure 4. Since even a single case may have multiple factors related to motivations to become involved, a total of 75 examples of factors were included.

Gamification accounted for a certain percentage of all advertising communications goals, as some time of game-style communication was conducted. However, although games themselves were utilized in a large number of cases (eight) in which the goal was Relationship building, contests were utilized in a large number of cases (six) in which the goal was Ideation/Expression promotion. When the goals were Relationship building and, particularly, Ideation/Expression promotion, and environments in which information could be shared were made available, consumers were encouraged to enjoy making discoveries using an environment in which information could be shared.

The Relationships Between Consumer-Generated Contents and Motivations to Become Involved/Advertising Communications Techniques

The relationships between consumer-generated contents and motivations to become involved/advertising communications techniques are shown in Table 4. A graph showing the relationships between consumer-generated contents and advertising communications techniques is shown in Figure 5.

Of the 50 cases examined, there were 27 that had consumer-generated contents. Of these, 11 included Gamification as the motivation to contribute and seven included Discovery as the motivation to contribute.

Table 3. The relationships between the factors related to motivations to become involved and advertising communications goals

Motivations to Become Involved		Advertising Communications Goals			Factors Total	Categories Total
Categories	**Factors**	**Awareness/ Acceptance Promotion**	**Relationship Building**	**Ideation/ Expression Promotion**		
Reward	Present	4	5	4	13	13
Gamification	Game	3	8	0	11	20
	Contest	1	2	6	9	
Collaboration	Collaborative content	1	2	1	4	5
	Product commercialization	0	0	1	1	
Sharing	Sharing information	1	6	15	22	22
Discovery	Experience	3	0	5	8	14
	Idea	1	1	3	5	
	Counseling	0	0	1	1	
Social contributions		1	0	0	1	1
Total		15	24	36	75	75

Figure 4. The relationships between advertising communications goals and the motivations to become involved

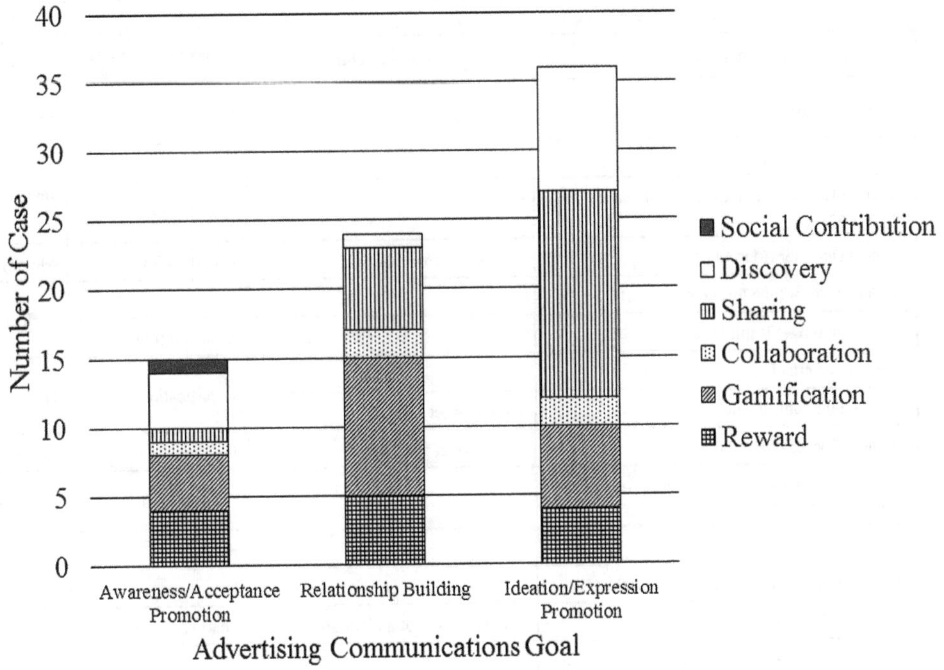

Figure 5. The relationships between consumer-generated contents and advertising communications techniques

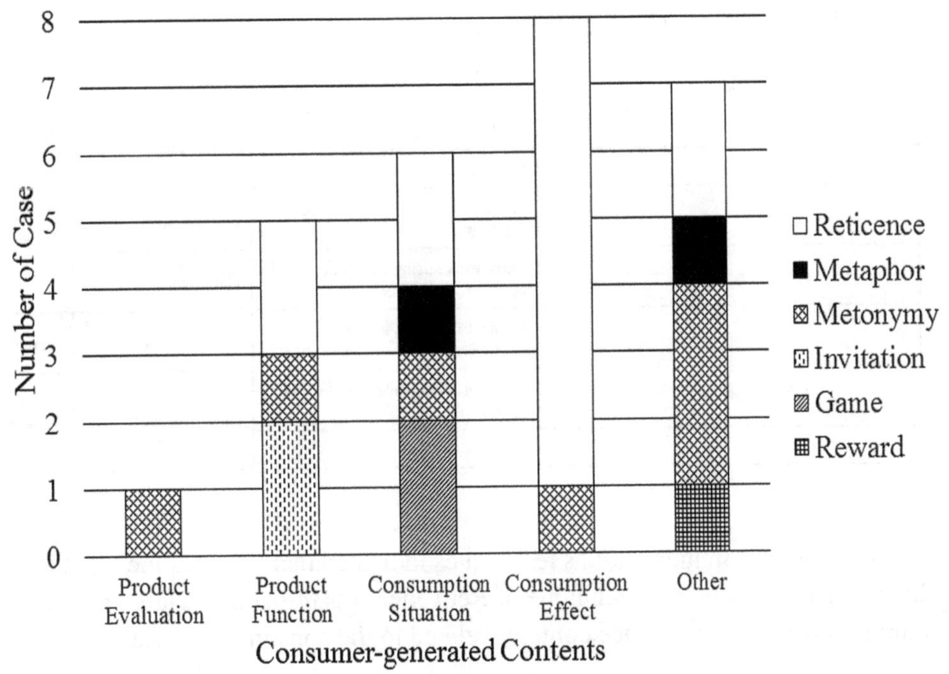

Table 4. The relationships between consumer-generated contents and motivations to become involved/ advertising communications techniques

Consumer-generated Contents			Motivations to Become Involved	Advertising Communications Techniques
Categories	**Product-related**	**Consumer-related**		
Product evaluations	Collaborate product ranking vote		Gamification	Metonymy
Product functions	Product/service (travel) planning		Reward	Invitation
	Service offer (idea to make cars and dealers interesting)		Gamification	
	Product character (Mascot design)	Character referendum	Gamification	Metonymy
	Product concept (one line composition)		Gamification	Reticence
	New menu (bowl) Inspiration		Collaboration	
Consump-tion situations	Tweet to the brand		Gamification	Game
	Tweet on the subject (life)	Funny Tweet		
	Product (Soccer shoes) Tweet	Tweet about high school soccer	Reward	Metonymy
	Consumption scene based on concept (words, pictures, animation)		Collaboration	Metaphor
	Consciousness about fragrance		Sharing	Reticence
	Product needs (Bedding suitable for me)		Discovery	
Consump-tion effects	Product (original curry) impression	An impression of an idol group etc.	Sharing	Metonymy
	How to drink merchandise (beverage) impression of recipe experience		Sharing	Reticence
	Item (beverage) opinion	Miss contest opinion exchange/ voting	Gamification	
	Consumption (yoghurt) impression	Ideas for continuing consumption	Discovery	
	New item (cleansing lotion) impression			
	New product (UV care) usage impression, image			
	Impression of using pillow experience			
	Impression of tenure experience			
Others		Challenge contents	Collaboration	Reward
		Graffiti on the coaster	Collaboration	Metonymy
		"Unreasonable event" planning for idols	Discovery	
		Entry works using assignment songs of "One Direction"	Gamification	
		Michael Jackson's image production, entry, video appearance	Gamification	Metaphor
		Shoot wrapping buses, post shoot photos	Gamification	Reticence
		Tweets about games		

Examination of advertising communications techniques indicated that 13 cases included Reticence and seven cases included Metonymy. The technique of Reticence was utilized in a large number of cases in order to encourage consumers to produce contents related to the consumption effect.

DISCUSSION

Based on the results of the above analyses, the author attempted to construct a model that included typical advertising communications strategies (patterns) for the three stages (low involvement, moderate involvement and high involvement) of consumers.

Strategies for Low-Involvement Consumers: Sender-Driven Strategy 1

Corporations utilize a sender-driven strategy for targeting consumers who have little involvement with products and advertising (mainly Accepters). Since the consumers are of the low-involvement type, they do not pay attention to information and advertisements associated with products and corporations. Therefore, attempts are made to promote their Awareness and Acceptance of products and corporations through the use of social contents that these consumers do pay attention to in order to involve them in the product and corporation. To achieve this, the following (1 and 2) are implemented:

1. **Advertising Communications Technique: Metonymy:** Advertising communication is used to link the product and corporate image and take advantage of characters (singers, TV personalities, cartoon characters, games, sports, social involvement, etc.) that the consumers pay attention to (see Figure 3, "metonymy" in "Awareness/Acceptance promotion").
2. **Motivation to Become Involved: Social Contents:** Consumers are provided with a reward of some kind once they achieve Awareness and Acceptance. However, since the main goal here is to create an opportunity for consumers to pay attention to the product and corporation, the reward need not be very substantial. Social contents that consumers pay attention to quickly and accurately are utilized and priority is placed on synergistically linking those contents to the characteristics of the product (see Table 2, "main information contents" in "metonymy").

Strategies for Moderate-Involvement Consumers: Sender-Driven Strategy 2

Corporations utilize a sender-driven strategy to target consumers with moderate involvement in products and advertisements (mainly Investigators). Since these consumers have a moderate level of involvement, they pay a certain amount of attention to information and advertisements associated with products and corporations. Therefore, by preparing environments in which corporations and consumers can share information about products that consumers pay attention to and by the consumer engaging in consumer-participatory communications using within this environment, relationships between the product, corporation, and consumers are created and strengthened. To achieve this, the following (1 and 2) are implemented:

1. **Advertising Communications Technique: Game and Metonymy:** First, an environment that allows the corporation and consumers to share information is prepared (see Figure 4, "sharing" in "Relationship building"). Next, using this environment as a type of advertising communication, games are provided for the purpose of deepening consumer understanding of the product and the corporation and to increase the amount of consumer goodwill toward the product and corporation

(see Figure 3, "game" in "Relationship building"). Characters (singers, TV personalities, cartoon characters, games, sports, social involvement, etc.), whose image matches that of the product and corporation that are utilized in the games, are then transferred to game-style consumer-participatory events (see Figure 3, "metonymy" in "Relationship building").

2. **Motivation to Become Involved: Gamification:** The consumer is rewarded once he or she engages in relationship building (participation in games, winning games, etc.) (see Table 3 and Figure 4, "reward" in "Relationship building"). However, priority is placed not on the reward itself, but rather on ensuring that the consumer enjoys the game that is implemented as a form of advertising communication (see Table 3 and Figure 4, "gamification" in "Relationship building"). To ensure that the consumer enjoys the game, it is necessary to create a game that the consumer will not become bored with. Thus, a variety of social contents are included in the game, and these contents encourage the consumer to consider the product and corporation more carefully and promote goodwill.

Strategies for High-Involvement Consumers: Receiver-Driven Strategy

Corporations utilize a receiver-driven strategy to target consumers with high involvement in products and advertising (Casters). Since the consumers have a high level of involvement, the strategy encourages consumers to become interested in and consider information and advertisements that are associated with the product and the corporation. There are also some cases in which consumers are requested to contribute something to a product or corporation they already have a significant intention of becoming involved with. Therefore, corporations prepare an environment in which the corporation and consumers can create information regarding products these consumers are already interested in. Then, by having consumers engage in consumer-participatory communications within this environment, corporations attempt to have consumers actively come up with opinions and ideas related to the product and the corporation and express those opinions and ideas. To achieve this, the following (1 and 2) are implemented:

1. **Advertising Communications Technique: Reticence:** First, an environment in which the corporation and consumers can share information is prepared (see Figure 4, "sharing" in "Ideation/Expression promotion"). Next, using this environment as a form of advertising communication, information related to the product, corporation, and consumers is provided and venues where consumers can have experiences are set up. However, not all of the information shared in this information-sharing environment is provided by the corporation (see Figure 3, "reticence" in "Ideation/Expression promotion"). By having consumers provide and supplement some of the contents, the corporation ensures that the information is jointly created and proliferated. Consumers can then utilize the information-sharing environment to provide each other with consumer-generated contents that can be quickly updated. This can then be utilized in consumer-participatory events whereby consumers provide stimulation to each other.
2. **Motivation to Become Involved: Gamification and Discovery:** Consumers are provided with some type of reward once they come up with ideas or express those ideas (by participating in and winning contests, etc.) (see Table 3 and Figure 4, "reward" in "Ideation/Expression promotion"). The reward must be appropriate to the amount of effort and time utilized by the consumer. Thus, it is not simply giving the consumer some type of present; rather, it is important to ensure that

the consumer-generated contents lead to the psychological reward of contributing to the corporation and consumer groups (see Table 3, "contest" in "Ideation/Expression promotion"). An information-creation environment is also prepared in which consumers provide each other with consumer-generated contents and provide each other with stimulation and discoveries (see Table 3 and Figure 4, "discovery" in "Ideation/Expression promotion").

SOLUTIONS AND RECOMMENDATIONS

In this chapter, the author confirmed advertising communications practices in detail using a framework designed to quantify the data in order to create a social/consumption simulation model. The author also elucidated the goals and techniques of advertising communications and created a model for advertising communications strategies.

As the iDEACCycle framework allows a more detailed understanding of the behavioral and psychological stages of consumers and allows a dynamic understanding of advertising communications between corporations and consumers, the author could identify the detail relationships (structures) between advertising communications goals and advertising communications techniques and motivations to become involved, and the relationships (structures) between consumer-generated contents, the motivations to become involved, and advertising communications goals. Based on the results thus obtained, the author could ide identify and organize the structural model of advertising communications strategies for the three stages (low involvement, moderate involvement and high involvement) of consumers.

FUTURE RESEARCH DIRECTIONS

As internet use becomes more widespread, environments that promote information sharing between corporations and consumers are becoming more common and, as a result, the number of corporations that utilize the receiver-driven strategy is increasing. Although the author described Reticence as the main technique used in the receiver-driven strategy, a variety of corporations are likely to utilize a trial-and-error process to identify what types of Reticence to use. If those attempts can be organized into a quantitative model for specific techniques, a more exact social/consumption simulation can be created.

CONCLUSION

In this chapter, the author created models for three types of advertising communications strategies (two types of sender-driven strategies and one type of receiver-driven strategy). These models can be utilized to establish strategic rules for social simulations that include both senders and receivers of advertising. Although the strategic rules have yet to be organized into a quantitative model, through attempts at quantifying them and through the combined use of these attempts and the iDEACCycle (a quantitative consumer behavior model), the author believes it will be possible in the future to implement social/consumption models that include both senders and receivers of advertising.

ACKNOWLEDGMENT

This work was supported by JSPS KAKENHI Grant Number 22500102. The analysis work was done based on the cooperation with Mr. Tachibana at Nissha Printing Communications, Inc.

REFERENCES

Akiyama, R., & Sugiyama, K. (2004). *Horisuthikku komyunikeishon* [Holistic Communication]. Tokyo, Japan: Sendenkaigi.

Bass, F. M. (1969). A new product growth for model consumer durables. *Management Science, 15*(5), 215–227. doi:10.1287/mnsc.15.5.215

Bearingpoint. (2002). *Kokyaku kando shugi: CRM kanzen tassei shinario* [Customer emotionalism: Achievement scenario for perfect CRM]. Tokyo, Japan: Diamond.

Colley, R. H. (1961). *Defining advertising goals for measured advertising results*. New York: Association of National Advertisers.

Eliashberg, J., & Shugan, S. (1997). Film critics: Influencers or predictors? *Journal of Marketing, 61*(2), 68–78. doi:10.2307/1251831

Feick, L. F., & Price, L. L. (1987). The market maven: A diffuser of marketplace information. *Journal of Marketing, 51*(1), 83–97. doi:10.2307/1251146

Hamaoka, Y. (2002). Akuthibu konshuma wo rikai suru [Understanding the active consumer]. *Hitotsubashi Business Review, 50*(3), 40–55.

Hamaoka, Y., & Satomura, T. (2009). *Shohishakan no sogo sayo nitsuiteno kiso kenkyu: kuchikomi e-kuchikomi wo chushin ni* [Basic research on the interaction between consumers: Focusing on word-of-mouth and e-word-of-mouth]. Tokyo, Japan: Keio University Press.

Ijichi, S. (2006). *CGM makethingu* [CGM marketing]. Tokyo, Japan: Asahi Communications.

Ikeda, K. (1997). *Nettowakingu komyunithi* [Networking community]. Tokyo, Japan: University of Tokyo Press.

Ikeda, K. (2008). Atarashii shohisha no shutsugen: Saiyosha kategori yoin no saikentou [The emergence of new consumers: Re-examination of the hiring category factor]. In Netto ga kaeru shohisha kodou: kuchikomi no eikyoryoku no jisshou bunseki [Consumer behavior that the internet changes: Empirical analysis on influence of word-of-mouth] (pp. 114-144). Tokyo, Japan: NTT Press.

Ikeda, K. (2010). *Kuchikomi to nettowahku no shakai shinri: Shohi to fukyu no sahbisu inobehshon kenkyu* [Social psychology of the word-of-mouth and network: Service innovation research on consumption and diffusion]. Tokyo, Japan: University of Tokyo Press.

Ikeo, K. (2003). *Netto komyunithi no mahkethingu senryaku* [Marketing Strategy of net community]. Tokyo, Japan: Yuhikaku.

Ito, F. (2007). *CGM: Shohisha hasshin medhia* [CGM: Consumer generated media]. Tokyo, Japan: Softbank Creative.

Katahira, H. (2006). Shohisha kodo moderu ha AIDMA kara AIDEES no jidai e [Consumer behavior model is changing from AIDMA to AIDEES]. *Nikkei BP LAP*, (18).

Kawamura, Y. (2013). Junkangata shohisha kodo moderu iDEACCycle no teian: Shohisha nikki chosa/intavu chosa wo motoni [A proposal of cyclical consumer behavior model iDEACCycle: Based on consumer dairy survey and interview survey]. *Japan Marketing Journal*, *33*(2), 95–109.

Kawamura, Y., Kato, T., Tachibana, K., Okai, G., & Kinoshita, S. (2014). Kokoku kyanpen no jirei ruikei no kokoromi: Junkangata shohisha kodo moderu iDEACCycle no kanten kara [An attempt of case categorization of advertising campaigns: From the view point of cyclical consumer behavior model iDEACCycle]. *Bulletin of Nikkei Advertising Research Institute*, (273), 10-16.

Kimura, H. (2008). Shohisha kobai purosesu wo donyu sita shinseihin fukyu moderu ni kansuru ichi kosatsu [A Study on new product diffusion model introduced the consumer purchasing process]. *Japan Marketing Journal*, *24*(3), 60–74.

Lazarsfeld, P. F., Berelson, B., & Gaudet, H. (1948). *The People's choice*. New York: Columbia University Press.

Morioka, S., Hasegawa, S., & Yamakawa, S. (2006). AISAS moderu ni miru kuchikomi no keisei katei ni okeru puranningu saho no teian [A proposal of planning manners on the formation process of word-of-mouth based on AISAS model]. *Japan Marketing Journal*, *26*(1), 29–39.

Nishina, S. (2001). *Kokoku koka ron: Joho shori paradaimu karano apurochi* [Advertisement effect theory: An approach from information processing paradigm]. Tokyo, Japan: Dentsu.

Nishina, S. (2011). Kokoku koka moderu no sogoka no kokoromi [An attempt of integration of advertisement effect model]. *Aoyama Journal of Business*, *46*(3), 111–124.

Nomura Research Institute. (2007). *Taishuka suru IT shohi* [IT consumption is popularizing]. Tokyo, Japan: Toyo Keizai Inc.

Ogawa, M., Sasaki, Y., Tsuda, H., Yoshimatsu, T., & Kokuryo, J. (2003). Damatte yondeiru hito tachi (ROM) no joho denpan kodo to sono kobai eno eikyo [Information propagation behaviors of silent readers (ROM) and its impact on purchasing]. *Japan Marketing Journal*, *22*(4), 39–51.

Poynter, R. (2010). *The handbook of online and social media research: Tools and techniques for market researchers*. New Jersey: John Wiley & Sons.

Rogers, E. M. (2003). *Diffusion of innovations* (5th ed.). New York: Free Press.

Sekizawa, H., Washida, Y., & Bjorn, M. (2002). *Shichueshon mahkethingu: Ketai jidai no shohi wo toraeru shin hasso* [Situation marketing: New idea to capture consumption in mobile age]. Tokyo, Japan: Kanki Press.

Sendenkaigi. (2011-2014). Henshubu ga eranda kongetsu no besuto puromoshon [Best promotion of this month selected by the editorial department]. In *Hansoku Kaigi* [Top Promotion] (pp. 153-200). Sendenkaigi.

Shimaguchi, M., Takeuchi, H., Katahira, H., & Ishii, J. (1998). *Mahkethingu kakushin no jidai 1: kokyaku sozo* [Age of marketing innovation 1: Customer creation]. Tokyo, Japan: Yuhikaku.

Shimaguchi, M., Takeuchi, H., Katahira, H., & Ishii, J. (1999). *Mahkethingu kakushin no jidai 4: burando kochiku* [Age of marketing innovation 4: Brand building]. Tokyo, Japan: Yuhikaku.

Sterne, J. (2011). *Social media metrics*. Wiley.

Strong, E. K. (1925). Theories of selling. *The Journal of Applied Psychology*, *9*(9), 75–86. doi:10.1037/h0070123

Tanaka, F., & Ono, A. (2003). *Raibu mahkethingu* [Live markething]. Tokyo, Japan: Toyo Keizai Inc.

Uotani, M. (2009). *Kokoro wo ugokasu mahkethingu: Coca-cola no burando kachi ha kousite tsukurareru* [Mind-moving marketing: Coca-Cola's brand value is thus created]. Tokyo, Japan: Diamond.

Wada, M. (1999). *Kankeisei mahkethingu to engeki shohi: Netsuretsu fan no sozo to iji no kozu* [Relationship marketing and theater consumption: Composition of enthusiastic fan creation and maintenance]. Tokyo, Japan: Diamond.

Yamamoto, A., & Abe, M. (2007). Sgohisha kan nettowahku wo riyou sita rekomendehshon ehjento [Recommendation agent using consumers network]. In Web mahkethingu no kagaku [Science of Web marketing] (pp. 165-191). Tokyo, Japan: Chikura Shobo.

Yamamoto, A., & Katahira, H. (2008). Infuruensa no hakken to kuchikomu no koka: AIDEES moderu no jissho bunseki [Discovery of influencers and effect of word-of-mouth: Empirical analysis of AIDEES model]. *Japan Marketing Journal*, *28*(1), 4–18.

Yamazaki, H. (2005). *Sosharu nettowahku mahkethingu* [Social network marketing]. Tokyo, Japan: Softbank Creative.

Yoshida, N., Ishii, A., & Arakaki, H. (2010). *Dai hitto no houteishiki: Sohsharu medhia no kuchikomi kouka wo suushikika suru* [Great hit equation: Mathematize the effects of social media's word-of-mouth]. Tokyo, Japan: *Discover*.

KEY TERMS AND DEFINITIONS

AIDA Model: A model of consumers' psychological/behavioral stages consisting of attention, interest, desire, action.

AIDEES Model: A model of consumers' psychological/behavioral stages consisting of attention, interest, desire, experience, enthusiasm, share.

AIDMA Model: A model of consumers' psychological/behavioral stages consisting of attention, interest, desire, memory, action.

AISAS Model: A model of consumers' psychological/behavioral stages consisting of attention, interest, search, action, share.

AISTAR Model: A model of consumers' psychological/behavioral stages consisting of attention, interest, search, trial, action, repeat.

DAGMAR Model: A model of consumers' psychological/behavioral stages consisting of unawareness, awareness, comprehension, conviction, action. DAGMAR is an acronym for defining adverting goals for measured advertising results.

High Involvement Consumers: A person who has contact with a wide variety of media engages in purchasing and consumer activities based on deep information processing and is, therefore, the source of ideas and information (that is, "casts out" ideas and information).

Low Involvement Consumers: A person who has passive contact with media, assimilates circumstances, and engages in purchasing and consumer activities.

Moderate Involvement Consumers: A person who has contact with a wide variety of media and engages in purchasing and consumer activities based on deep information processing.

Chapter 14
"The Dialogue Triangle" Effect and Structure for Prototyping on "Need–Solution Pairs":
The Development of the "Naruse Pedal," Which Prevents Mistakes When Stepping on a Vehicle Pedal

Akimitsu Hirota
Kindai University, Japan

ABSTRACT

Problem-solving behavior in a situation where the problem is not defined creates problems. However, concrete examples of the phenomenon are not shown. In order to capture this phenomenon, the authors investigated the process of pedal development for automobiles. The name of the pedal is called "Naruse pedal." Naruse pedal reduces accidents caused by mistakes in pressing foot on accelerator pedal and brake pedal. Naruse pedal has been reported by many media including the New York Times. The authors surveyed the development process of Naruse pedal. They show this development case and confirm the existence of simultaneity of needs and solution.

INTRODUCTION

In May 2016, an international long-jumping competition was held in Australia. Many of the athletes from the Olympic Games in Rio de Janeiro participated in this competition. One athlete, Markus Rehm, recorded a jump of 8 m 18 cm, which exceeded the distance required to participate in the Olympics (8 m 15 cm). This jump attracted significant attention because Rehm has a prosthetic right foot.

The sensation between a prosthetic foot and the ground can only be obtained from the area where the prosthetic foot is in contact with the person's leg. In order to compete equally with top athletes who do not have a physical disability, in addition to the actual physical training, it was necessary for Rehm to

DOI: 10.4018/978-1-5225-4775-4.ch014

Copyright © 2018, IGI Global. Copying or distributing in print or electronic forms without written permission of IGI Global is prohibited.

integrate his prosthetic foot as a part of his own body and to be able to use it freely. The right knee where the prosthetic foot is attached alters in shape slightly, depending on the temperature and the person's physical condition. Because the material used for the prosthetic foot is hard, pain may be produced in cases where the prosthetic foot does not fit perfectly to the knee as a result of slight changes in its shape. Naturally, for Rehm, this affects the outcome of a competition. It is essential to adjust the prosthetic foot in order for it to be integrated with the body even when there are temperature and physical changes. For these reasons, Rehm chose a career as a prosthetic orthotist. One reason for this decision is his ability to fully understand the feelings of other users of prostheses as he adjusts them. Additionally, because he himself is fitted with a prosthetic foot, he is able to quickly adjust it while relying on the senses he was born with and explore the relation between the prosthetic foot and his own movement.

In this study, the process of simultaneously discovering and resolving problems was confirmed through a case study of a user developing a product and using it himself. In addition, the role of prototyping in this process is considered.

BACKGROUND

Many of the previous studies on product innovation focused on problem-solving behavior (Clark & Fujimoto, 1991; Ogawa, 2000; Lester & Piore, 2004). One reason for focusing on problem solving is the assumption that the problem to be solved is defined. However, in recent years, it has been noted that product development is conducted in a situation in which the problems are not clarified, creating a condition in which problem discovery and solving take place simultaneously (Ishii, 1993, 2009, 2014; Lester & Piore, 2004; Von Hippel & Von Krogh, 2016). Moreover, the importance of solving problems of which customers are unaware (that is, the importance of discovering problems creatively) has also been pointed out (Ishii 2009, 2014; Lester & Piore, 2004; Takaoka & Kotler, 2016).

Incidentally, the existence of users called "lead users" who act in advance of future important markets and their contribution to market creation has been noted (Von Hippel, 1988, 2005; Ogawa, 2000, 2013). Lead users have the characteristics of discovering problems that manufacturers and other users were unaware of and realizing innovation by solving these problems (meeting these needs) themselves.

In this study, the occurrence of simultaneous problem discovery and solving in a case study of product development by a lead user is confirmed. Second, the requirements to realize the simultaneous creation of problem discovery and solving in a situation where the problem has not been defined are considered from the viewpoint of dialogue (Ishii, 1993, 2009; Lester & Piore, 2004).

MAIN FOCUS OF THE CHAPTER

"Naruse Pedal"

Present your perspective on the issues, controversies, problems, etc., as they relate to theme and arguments supporting your position. Compare and contrast with what has been, or is currently being done as it relates to the chapter's specific topic and the main theme of the book.

The Naruse Pedal is used to control both the acceleration and braking of a vehicle. It was developed by Mr. Masayuki Naruse (hereafter, Mr. Naruse), who is the representative director of Naruse Machinery

Co., Ltd. (Tamana City, Kumamoto Prefecture; hereafter Naruse Machinery). This pedal was developed for the purpose of reducing accidents caused by mistakenly stepping on a vehicle's accelerator or brake pedal, which has been a social issue in recent years. The trigger for its development was Mr. Naruse's own experience of losing control of his car around 1988. He mistakenly stepped on the accelerator pedal when he wanted to step on the brake pedal, and this experience of the vehicle moving differently to the way he intended left a deep impression on him. Fortunately, this incident did not result in an accident, but as a result of his experience of his car becoming out of control, as well as from the reports of accidents around that time that were caused by people mistakenly stepping on the wrong pedal, he started to develop a product, which he eventually commercialized after repeated trial and error. Since 1996, Naruse Machinery has sold these pedals and installed them for a fee in accordance with requests. As of November 2016, they had installed them in over 500 vehicles running on public roads in Japan.

A conventional vehicle has two pedals, an accelerator and a brake. The Naruse Pedal is also called "the one-pedal" because it integrates the accelerator and brake pedals into a single pedal. The Naruse Pedal consists of a "brake auxiliary pad" that is mounted on the existing brake pedal, an accelerator pedal that is integrated with the auxiliary pad, and an accelerator arm that is connected to the accelerator pedal via rollers. Only the accelerator pedal installed in commercially available vehicles is removed, and the Naruse Pedal is mounted on the brake pedal. A user drives with their right foot on the brake pedal. Because the driver steps on the pedal with their right foot only, the vehicle brakes even if they unconsciously step on the pedal. Therefore, it can reduce the phenomenon of the vehicle accelerating contrary to the intentions of the driver.[1] In addition, the Naruse Pedal's accelerator pedal is a slide-push type that is operated by pushing (sliding) it sideways to the right using the side of the right foot.

Figure 1. Naruse Pedal
Source: Naruse Machinery

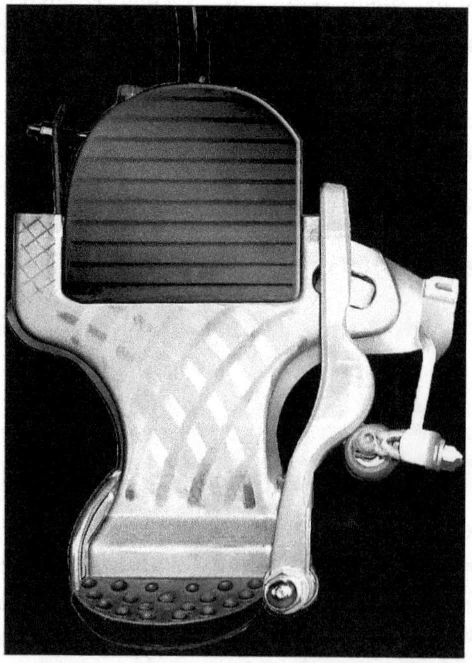

SURVEY METHOD

This paper is based on information obtained in interviews with Mr. Naruse, the developer of the Naruse Pedal, and other relevant parties who have had a relationship with the developer over many years and who fully understand the development of the Naruse Pedal. Information was also gathered from interviews with Mr. Naruse published in newspapers and magazines, and found on the Internet and television, as well as from patents filed by Mr. Naruse and others and from published patent publications.

The published information and interviews confirmed the characteristics of the Naruse Pedal and showed that its characteristic positions were selected based on a comparison with existing pedals.[2] The overwhelming majority of the published information was on the current Naruse Pedal (the third generation pedal). However, the first interview with Mr. Naruse confirmed the trigger for the development of the prototype and made it possible to ascertain the process that led to the specifications of the current pedal. After this, the characteristic positions of the Naruse Pedal were presented to Mr. Naruse, and the order of generation of these positions and the generation process were confirmed.

Mr. Naruse acquired the patent for the prototype that would become the current pedal in the United States in 1993, and then subsequently acquired it in Japan, Germany, the United Kingdom, France, and Italy in 1995. In Japan, he applied for and acquired 49 patents between 1999 and November 2016, including the model at the trial-and-error stage that led to the prototype of the current pedal. Based on the patent publications, 15 patents relating to pedals and 11 patents up to 2004 that became the current pedal specifications were selected as the subjects of the survey. After this, interviews were conducted with Mr. Matsunaga, along with a second interview with Mr. Naruse, and interviews with Mr. Arata and Mr. Ota. In addition, while linking the patent information, the A method of the KJ method was used to repeatedly enumerate and classify the keywords, link the classifications, and name the classifications.

DEVELOPMENT OF NARUSE PEDAL

Development in Situation in Which Problems Have Not Been Defined

Naruse Machinery, where Mr. Naruse is the representative director, is a company that develops and produces agricultural and fishery equipment, and it has a particularly large share of the laver-culture machinery market. From his previous work, Mr. Naruse had experience with the technologies used for metal machining and plant material processing. However, up to the development of the Naruse Pedal, he had no connection to the automotive industry (Nikkei Mechanical, September 2000). Therefore, Mr. Naruse had no knowledge of or experience with the design and development of automotive products or vehicles. However, because he had experience with the design and development of industrial machinery, he did possess knowledge about machinery design and development, metals processing, and materials, along with the experience and skills to actually create the prototype and product. In addition, because his company had these facilities, the environment was in place for him to quickly realize his idea as a prototype. The Naruse Pedal is a case study of user innovation. It was developed by Mr. Naruse as an individual for passenger cars using this sort of knowledge, experience, and environment.

Mr. Naruse provided the following description of the development of the Naruse Pedal, where the problems could not be found.

We could not find the problems. That was the feeling. We could not find the problems. To do this, we needed to find the problems. I think everything is like this. Once you find the problem, then you attempt to solve it in some way. When the problem is found, in some way or another, it (the solution) will come out. After proceeding to a certain extent, we could not find the problems. On evolving it to the third, fourth, and fifth iterations, the problems became visible to some extent, but in the case of evolving it 0–1 time, there were no problems, in that the problems were difficult to find. (Interview with Mr. Naruse.)

There are at least two types of development. In the first, the problems are clear (to a certain extent), and in the second, "the problems (issues) cannot be found," as in this case study. The Naruse Pedal can be said to be a case study in which the author can concretely confirm needs-solutions pairs,[3] in that the problem discovery and solving were conducted simultaneously in a situation in which the problems remained undiscovered, through repeated trial and error[4].

Actions and Product Redevelopment

Generally, when driving a vehicle, we perform the same stepping action with the same right foot when using both the accelerator pedal and the brake pedal. Therefore, in many cases, when the driver needs to use the brake pedal, it is necessary to move the right foot quickly and accurately from the accelerator pedal to the brake pedal. The Naruse Pedal has the following three characteristics. First, the brake pedal and accelerator pedal are operated using different actions. Second, the foot (generally, the right foot) that operates the brake pedal is in a fixed position when stopping and moving. Therefore, "the action of changing the pedal that is stepped on," which is one of the factors behind stepping on the wrong pedal, becomes unnecessary. Third, when stepping on the brake pedal, the drivers themselves and their actions are absolutely disconnected from the accelerator. In other words, a state is realized where the accelerator cannot be operated. These three characteristics of the Naruse Pedal create a state in which it is very difficult for the driver to think they are stepping on the brake but are actually accidentally stepping on the accelerator (Matsunaga, Hayashi, Sumida, Nishimura, & Koshi, 2011). In this way, the development of the Naruse Pedal considered the relationship between the pedal and the user and the actions needed to operate each of the pedals.

Creation of Operating Action From Fixing Position of Right Foot

In 1988, Mr. Naruse had the experience of stepping on the wrong pedal, but did not know what caused it.

First, he thought intuitively about whether it would be a good idea to prioritize the brake in the operating actions.[5] Therefore, he focused on fixing the position of the right foot, which operates both the brake and accelerator pedals, when driving. He conceived of a product that would create a state in which the right foot is always in a fixed position, making it easier to step on the brake pedal. This would make it possible to step on the brake without having to change the operating action during an emergency or when the driver panics. This would mean that even when acting unconsciously, the driver would step on the brake pedal and not cause the vehicle to accelerate or start moving by mistakenly stepping on the accelerator pedal.

In order to realize this state, Mr. Naruse processed metal and developed a device that held the heel. This device is attached to the floor of the driver's seat and when the heel of the right foot is set in it, the right

Table 1. Comparison of "Naruse Pedal" and existing pedals

	Pedal Type							
	"Naruse Pedal"				Existing Automatic Cars			
	Part of body performing operation action	Position of right foot when driving	Operation action	Part to be operated	Part of body performing operation action	Position of right foot when driving	Operation action	Part to be operated
Brake operation	Right foot (generally)	On the brake pedal, heel contact	Step on it	Brake pedal auxiliary pad (mounted on the existing brake pedal)	Right foot (generally)	-	Step on it	Brake pedal
Accelerator operation	Right foot (generally)	On the brake pedal, heel contact	Sideways push	Accelerator arm (connected to the existing throttle wire and throttle sensor)	Right foot (generally)	When driving:on the accelerator pedal when stopping:on the brake pedal	Step on it	Accelerator pedal

Source: prepared by the author

foot remains constantly on the brake pedal when driving. The accelerator is operated by a right turning action on the axis of the heel, and the accelerator pedal is operated with the toes or front part of the foot.

Problems Discovered Through "Trial Usage" Behavior

Mr. Naruse then actually installed the device that holds the heel into the vehicle and tested it. Certainly, as the right foot was always on the brake pedal, there was no change in action to step on the brake from the accelerator, and it was possible to quickly and correctly step on the brake pedal when it was necessary to do so. However, it was difficult to comfortably perform the accelerator operations, for which the frequency and time of operations are overwhelmingly larger than for the brake.[6]

At the same time, a problem with the brake pedal became clear. When driving, the right foot was always on the brake pedal. Therefore, with the prototype, it was necessary to maintain a state where the right foot "floated" on the brake pedal when driving. However, it was found to be generally difficult for drivers to continuously maintain this state when driving. Therefore, the problem occurred that the state became one of half braking when driving, and the brake light was constantly on.

Mr. Naruse explained the use of the prototype to clarify problems as follows.

(The fixed position of the heel) was centered on the brake. The foot is placed here and the heel is put on the brake's set line. We actually made it (the prototype) as we tried to do this. However, when you pushed it (the brake pedal) a little, naturally, we thought that fundamentally this would just be some sort of problem with (fixing) the heel when having to operate the pedal. (Interview with Mr. Naruse, words in parentheses added by the author)

By actually using the prototype, problem points that were not known when conceiving the idea and developing the prototype were clarified.

Operating Accelerator Through Sideways-Pushing (Sliding) Action

Mr. Naruse developed a prototype and then immediately used it for repeated trial-and-error in order to search for the position and shape of the pedal that would allow the driver to unconsciously operate the brake and only consciously operate the accelerator. The conclusion he finally reached was to have a sideways-pushing (sliding) action for the accelerator pedal.

As the sideways action (for the accelerator pedal) must be performed consciously, it (the use of the accelerator pedal) meant it would not be performed without the driver's conscious action to do so, compared to previously when it could be depressed unconsciously. In this way, the conclusion was that if you did not step on it (the existing accelerator pedal) previously, you also would not step on the (existing) accelerator. So we thought about it (to realize the sideways action). (Interview with Mr. Naruse, words in parentheses added by the author)

Therefore, he developed an accelerator arm that is operated with a sideways-pushing (sliding) action using the side of the right foot. A lead organ has a pedal called the "knee swell" that is operated by a sideways push of the knee to adjust the volume. Mr. Naruse got the idea for this solution from a childhood memory of watching an organ performance.

Solving Brake Pedal Problem and Discovering Additional Accelerator Pedal Problems

Because the position of the right foot is on the brake pedal, the problem became one of a state of half-braking, with the brake light constantly on, and it was necessary to solve this problem. As a solution, in 1998, he developed a brake pedal auxiliary pad that was divided into two parts in the middle part of the foot and moved based on the amount the brake was depressed. Stepping-on the brake auxiliary pad with the heel attached to the floor made possible an action of stepping on the same contact area for the sole of the foot and the pedal face, thereby making the stepping action smoother and solving the problem of half-braking and the brake light being constantly on.

A problem occurred with the accelerator bar prototype when Mr. Naruse mounted it in his own passenger car. The accelerator pedal is operated by the action of depressing it. It is possible to depress it with considerable force using the large muscles of the leg. The accelerator pedal in an existing passenger car is operated by the action of depressing it using the entire leg, with the hip joint as the fulcrum (patents publication, Japanese Unexamined Patent Publication 5-16692). Therefore, even women and the elderly are able to generate the necessary load to operate it. However, a sideways, sliding action with the foot made it hard to generate the same load, which made it difficult to operate the accelerator for long periods of time. To solve this problem, Mr. Naruse considered using powerful magnets to supplement the part of the necessary load that was lacking. Subsequently, up to 1999, he developed numerous and different prototypes, including some that incorporated a spring, in which the sideways push action changed the accelerator into a magnet. However, he was not able to reach the same level of operation as a conventional accelerator pedal.

Creation of Solution Information From Usage by Others

From around 1994, the pedal attracted attention because of its role in preventing accidents caused by stepping on the wrong pedal, and it was reported on by television and in newspapers and magazines. Inquiries and visits from engineers from automotive manufacturers also started to increase. These engineers visited Mr. Naruse and test drove a vehicle that was equipped with the Naruse Pedal. At that time, the operation of the accelerator arm using the right foot slide method had not yet reached a level of operation equivalent to that of a conventional pedal. In their conversations with Mr. Naruse after they had driven the car, the engineers remarked that the operations would be made easier by changing the rotating shaft (the fulcrum) of the accelerator bar from the top to the bottom.[7]

Based on the content of these conversations, Mr. Naruse produced an accelerator bar prototype. By placing the accelerator arm's rotating shaft at the bottom, he created a design in which it was integrated with the brake pedal auxiliary pad. Moreover, placing the rotating shaft at the bottom made possible a design in which the accelerator arm was separated into two parts, an upper part and a lower part. He called the upper part the arm, and the lower part the pedal, with the movement of the foot being transmitted via the roller. Further, by separating the accelerator arm into two parts, the outside parts of the accelerator pedal could be made with curved lines, with the roller moving along these curves. The way the curves were created made it possible to amplify and attenuate the amount of movement of the foot, and a large amount of movement could be transmitted to the accelerator bar with just a small movement of the foot. This made it possible to accelerate smoothly. Moreover, by separating it into two parts (the accelerator pedal and accelerator arm), the brake auxiliary pad and accelerator pedal could be integrated. Integrating the brake pedal and accelerator pedal created a structure in which the accelerator pedal and accelerator arm are connected via the roller. In this structure, when the brake pedal is depressed, the accelerator pedal and accelerator arm are separated, and the accelerator is shut off as a clutch mechanism ("accelerator cam clutch"), which results in increased safety.

CONSIDERATIONS

Third-Generation "Naruse Pedal"

As of 2017, the Naruse Pedal has reached its third generation. The first generation realized accelerator operations through the right-foot slide (sideways push) action. The second generation made the action of stepping on the brake pedal smoother and prevented the problem of the state of half-braking and the brake light being constantly on from the right foot being fixed on the brake pedal. The third generation integrated the brake pedal and accelerator pedal, made the slide action smoother, and shut off the accelerator pedal when the brake pedal was being operated.

Mr. Naruse's used a repeated trial-and-error method to answer questions about the actions taken by a driver (user) to operate the accelerator and brake and what kind of pedal specifications would realize these actions. He carried out the development with two constraints for this trial-and-error method. The first was the relations between the drivers (users) and the two pedals, along with the associated constraints on the required actions. The second was the constraint of the interface[8] with the accelerator and brake pedal of existing vehicles.

Problem Discovery and Simulating User Experiences

Product development is an activity used to solve the problems of customers (Clark & Fujimoto, 1991; Ogawa, 2000). This problem solving consists of four steps: awareness of the problem, generating choices, evaluation, and decision making (Clark & Fujimoto, 1991, Japanese translation, p. 47). Out of these, awareness of the problem entails being aware of customer needs and simulating future customer experiences (Clark & Fujimoto, 1991, Japanese translation, p. 44). However, when customer needs are unstable, uncertain, diverse, and ambiguous, it is not easy to clearly ascertain the potential future needs of customers and develop a product to meet these needs (Fujimoto, 2003, p. 122; Lester & Piore, 2004). Therefore, in a situation where it is difficult to be clearly aware of the needs, the ability to simulate customer experiences will affect a company's competitiveness (Clark & Fujimoto, 1991, Japanese translation, p. 46). However, it has been noted that in a situation that is highly opaque, there are times when the problem cannot be defined, and in such cases, there are limits to the problem-solving framework (Lester & Piore, 2004, p. 53).

Initial Stage of Development and Prototyping

Uncertainty is generally high in the initial stage of development. Therefore, there are situations in which even those responsible for the development cannot clearly define what is to be developed next. At this stage, for example, even if the developers carefully listen to customers' opinions, it will still be impossible to clearly define the project's goals (Lester & Piore, 2004). The developers go through a trial-and-error process to discover the development problems (Ishii, 1993; Lester & Piore, 2004). High-quality activities at this stage will increase the probability that the product will be a success (Song & Parry, 1996; Khurana & Rothenthal, 1998). Front loading is one method of problem solving (Thomke & Fujimoto, 2000), and it has been shown that rapid prototyping is one effective method of front loading (Thomke, 1998). Research in this field has produced many findings (Takeda, 2000; Gu & Fujimoto, 2000; Takeda, Nobeoka, & Aoshima, 2004). However, there has been insufficient research on ways to realize rapid prototyping at the initial stage of development.

Effects of Prototyping on Innovation

Dyer, Gregersen, and Christensen (2011) conducted a comparative study of approximately 500 innovators and approximately 5,000 management executives and clarified that there is one cognitive skill and four discovery abilities that are requirements to be an excellent innovator. The cognitive skill can be called associative thinking. The four discovery abilities are questioning ability, observational ability, networking ability, and experimental ability. Associative thinking is the ability to implement combinations of new pairings (Schumpeter, 1926). There are three experimental methods for experimental ability, which is one of the discovery abilities. The first is testing new experiences in a new environment. The second is breaking down the innovation into products, processes, and ideas, and the third is verifying the ideas through demonstration experiments and prototyping. Excellent innovators repeat and enlarge at least one of these three experimental methods (Dyer et al., 2011, Japanese translation, p. 155). Dyer et al. (2011) found that in order to obtain clues about the method that would produce success in the future, even when there is no way to succeed in the experiment (Dyer et al., 2011, Japanese translation, p. 170), in terms of the relationship between the experimental ability and the other discovery abilities, the amount of experimentation required to obtain new insights is practically inversely proportional to the amount of questions, observations, and networks that were asked, made, and created in advance, respectively (Dyer et al., 2011, Japanese translation, p. 168). In addition, experimental ability does not necessarily entail planning, and some things will be done by chance (Dyer et al., 2011, Japanese translation, p. 169). It has been noted that there are times when insights occur from the environment and constraints within which the experiment is conducted.

Need-Solution Pairs

Von Hippel and Von Krogh (2016) pointed out that in innovations, there are times when the needs and solutions are paired before the problem is defined. According to Von Hippel and Von Krogh (2016), as shown in Figure 2, the needs and solutions each have an area indicated in two dimensions (the X and Y axes), in which their respective so-called "landscapes"[9] of needs and solutions information[10] are distributed. Moreover, the heights of these areas are indicated by the Z axis.[11] Depending on the benefits from satisfying the height of the needs, the height of the solutions indicates the necessary cost. Problem solving is realized by "pairing" specific points in the two landscapes. Realizing pairing involves exploring the combinations of pairings, with the heights (Z axis) in each landscape as clues. The arrows in Figure 2 show the possible pairings found in the search.

Figure 2. Need-solution pairs
Source: prepared by the author based on Von Hippel and Von Krogh (2016)

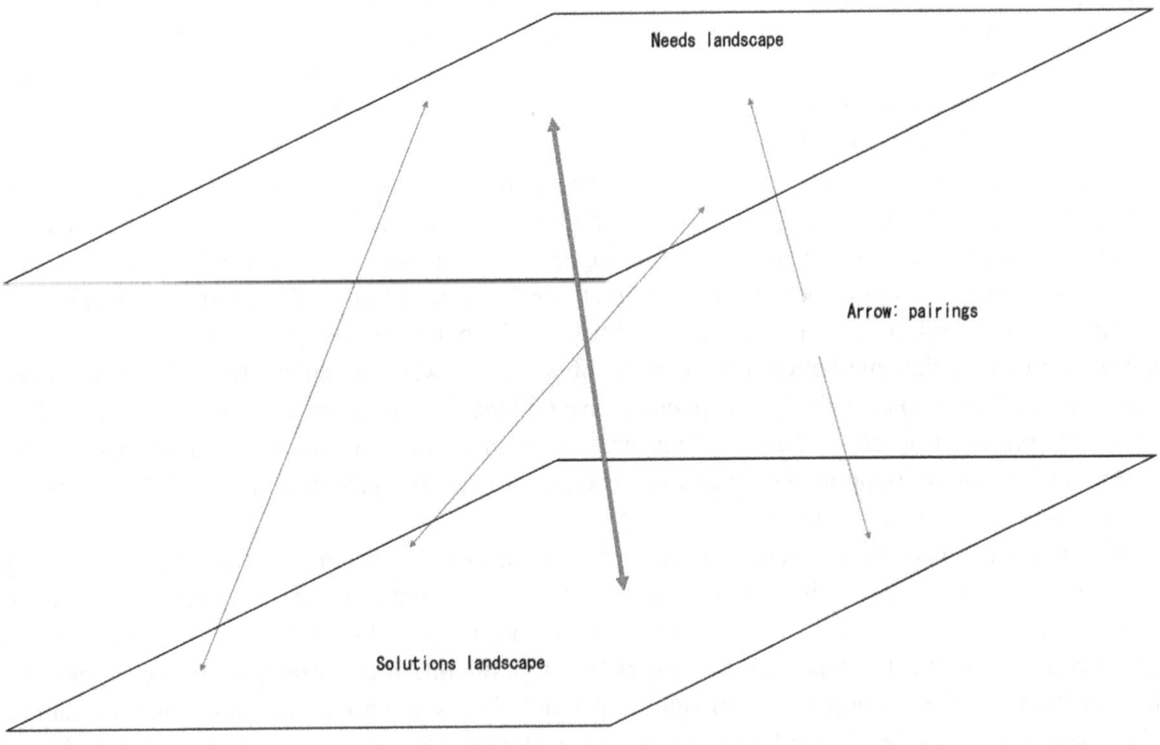

In the model of Von Hippel and Von Krogh (2016), need-solution pairs can be thought of as a model that is determined based on the state of the needs landscape (the solutions information distribution area) at a certain point in time.

Ishii (1993) also pointed out the same thing. He presented the viewpoint that the aspect where needs and solutions (seeds) connect is a protocol aspect where undefined and ambiguous needs and solutions are paired while mutually confirming each other. He considered this protocol aspect "not to be a one-way process of saying that the problem is raised and a solution sought, but a two-way process where the problem searches for the solution at the same time as the solution searches for the problem" (Ishii, 1993, p. 17). He also pointed out that these "are processes in which the menu of various solutions and the menu of various needs accidentally associate and crystalize" (Ishii, 1993, p. 18).

In their model, Von Hippel and Von Krogh (2016) noted the existence of problem solving in a state where the problem definition is ambiguous and showed the structure for mutual pairing using the landscape concept. However, they only explained the dynamism in the pairing (dynamic viewpoint) indicating the existence of the landscape Z axis in association with the pairing. They did not comment on this pairing process or the landscape transformation process.

Dialogue With Need-Solution Pairs

When developing a product that meets the needs that customers are not aware that they have, the developers are also in a state in which the problems to be solved have not been defined. Thus, at the initial stage of development, even if the developers listen carefully to the voices of their customers, because there is "radical uncertainty" in relation to the evaluation of the outcome, it is difficult to break down, classify, and clearly define the problems to be solved (Lester & Piore, 2004, 53–55). However, even in this sort of situation, developers must define the problems to be solved, and how problems are defined will have a major impact on the development's outcome (Lester & Piore, 2004, p. 55). In this sort of situation, the developers use a trial-and-error process to discover problems from the clues that are created in an unprincipled, accidental, and ad-hoc way (Ishii, 1993, p. 34; Lester & Piore, 2004, 56).

In this situation, the "dialogue" process is important to find the solutions while defining the problems (Ishii, 1993; Lester & Piore, 2004; Ishii, 2009). At first glance, the author might assume a dialogue to be between people. However, there is also "a dialogue between people (the plan) and resources" (Ishii, 1993, p. 165) and "a dialogue between people and things" as a result of people interacting deeply with the target (Ishii, 2009, p. 228). Ishii (1993) said that the dialogue between your own vision (the plan) and resources is a dialogue between the content of what you want to achieve (the plan) (needs and landscape) and the resources that you happen to have (at that time) in order to realize it (Ishii, 1993, p. 163) (solutions and landscape). Thus, the "resources combination is read and recombined" (Ishii, 1993, p. 165), and, while overlapping with the prior vision (plan) and compromising (Ishii, 1993, p. 165), a search is made for the realizable areas.

When the customers and developers are separate, the customers will express something in their daily behavior, and the developers will try to interpret this (Lester & Piore, 2004, p. 69). They express something through their words and deeds that connect to the needs created in their daily behavior, and this can be conveyed to the developers as the "others" through the interpreted dialogue. However, because they are "others," the developers' interpretation may not always be correct. As shown in the example of the development of the Naruse Pedal, the developers themselves interpret something obtained from their daily behavior as users, which is expressed through creation behavior, and We can visualize a development in which the dialogue taking place within a person and the dialogue between the separate customers and developers will be different in terms of speed and quality.

Two Behaviors in Trial and Error

Mr. Naruse developed the current version of the Naruse Pedal through repeated trial and error. One of the characteristics of this behavior is the act of immediately making a physical prototype based on an idea that a developer conceives of one day. This behavior is called "trial production." There was also the behavior of Mr. Naruse installing the prototype he produced in his own passenger car and actually using it. This behavior is called "trial usage." Both are trial-and-error behaviors. Trial production is a trial-and-error behavior of creating a prototype based on an idea and realizing it as a physical product (product realization[12]). Trial usage is the trial-and-error behavior of a user operating the product to be used in an everyday space while confirming the movements of the user's body. The information obtained through these two behaviors provides clues to the next prototype. The dialogue is realized through having a "specific target" and "daily behavior" (Lester & Piore, 2004, p. 69), and it can be considered that the specific target is the prototype (trial production) and the everyday behavior is the trial usage, in this case, of mounting the prototype on the vehicle.

"The Dialogue Triangle"

Mr. Naruse's dialogue was not limited to this because he repeated the trial production and trial usage while creating a picture in his mind about what sort of pedal action for the accelerator and brake would eliminate the problem of stepping on the wrong pedal. Moreover, from the information obtained from the trial production and trial usage, this picture in his mind of the pedal action was changed and re-created. In this way, it can be said that there is a dialogue between the actions that users want to be realized or the creation of experiences, and the behavior of the trial production and trial usage.

Upon confirming Mr. Naruse's development behavior from the viewpoint of this sort of dialogue, the author see that there were multiple dialogues. The first was the dialogue between the trial production and trial usage behaviors. The second was between the trial production and trial usage behaviors and the behavior to create the action that he wanted to realize. In this first dialogue, the question of how to reflect the respective behaviors was investigated through the dialogue. The second dialogue investigated the questions of what actions of users when operating the pedals will not cause them to "step on the wrong pedal," and at the same time, if such an action is realized, will it be possible to operate it easily compared to the operations of a conventional pedal. In this way, the simulation of "customer experiences in the future" (Clark & Fujimoto, 1991, Japanese translation, p. 46) was carried out through a dialogue between the trial production and trial usage. Clark and Fujimoto (1991) noted that when searching for the problem, it is necessary to create "customer experiences in the future." In this study, it was shown that the simulation is carried out through dialogue and that in some cases, this structure is realized through the dialogue between the trial production and trial usage.

In order to generate value in the narrow space between use and transmission (Ishii, 1993, p. 223), the realization of value is confirmed through the dialogue that leads to value creation and to raising the level of the value. In the Naruse Pedal case study, in the process of realizing innovation with new value, the following three behaviors were confirmed: ① a behavior to create user actions (experiences), ② "trial production" to create a physical prototype, and ③ "trial production" to realize actions (experiences).

Moreover, a mutual dialogue exists between these three behaviors. Here, this mutual dialogue is called "the dialogue triangle" (Figure 3). Mr. Naruse developed the Naruse Pedal as the user and innovator from a dialogue involving one person.

Landscape and "The Dialogue Triangle"

What kind of relationship is there between the landscapes of needs and solutions (Von Hippel & Von Krogh, 2016) and the dialogue triangle? The author shall continue the consideration while focusing on the two behaviors of trial production and trial usage.

The solutions landscape is vital for trial production. However, in a situation in which the problem is unknown, which information to select from within the solutions landscape is also unknown.[13] Therefore, clues can be obtained from the information created through the behavior of one's own trial usage and the

Figure 3. Dialogue triangle
Source: prepared by the author

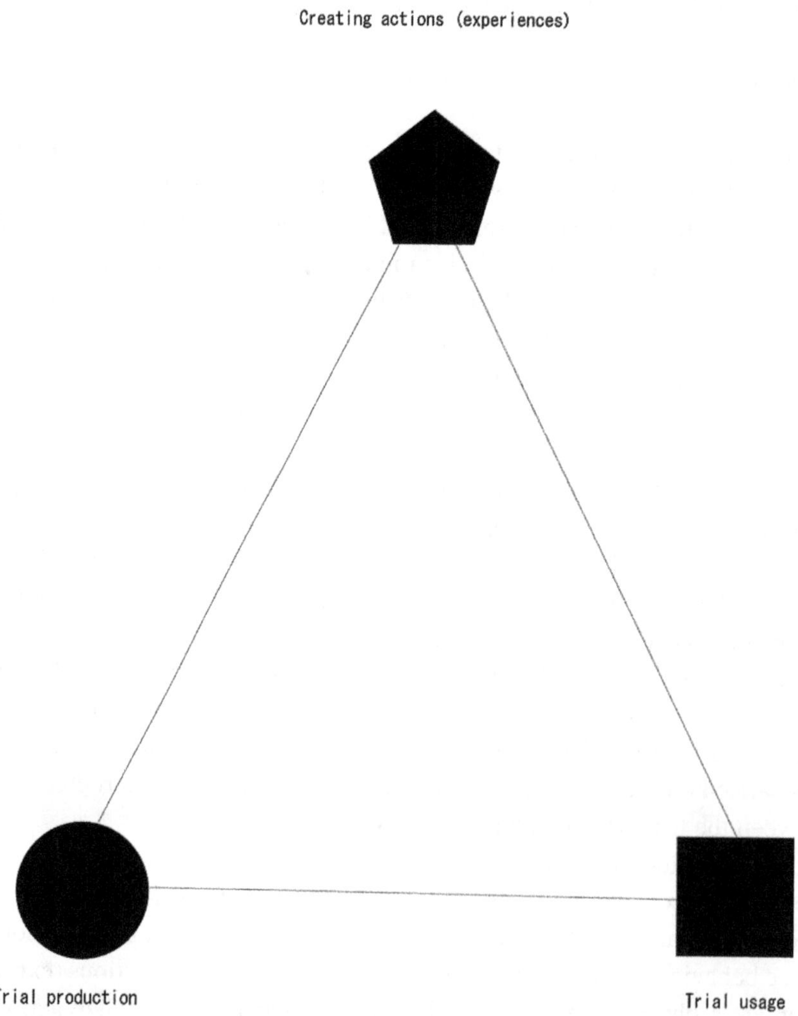

dialogue with the action to be realized, from searching the solutions landscape for related technologies and processing methods. At the same time, new information acquired through the trial production will accumulate in the solutions landscape.

In addition, the gap between the actions realized through using the prototype and the envisaged actions that accompany this, and the newly created actions, accumulate as needs in the needs landscape.

In other words, a two-way transfer of information is generated between the solutions landscape and the trial production behavior, and between the needs landscape and the trial usage behavior.

FUTURE RESEARCH DIRECTIONS

I discussed the role of prototypes in needs-solutions and pairs. Let's check about future research possibilities here.

Others with different similar experiences lead to landscape extension (mutual sharing) through shared experiences using the same prototype. In this case, the same prototype was a shared experience of using behavior in the same usage environment. This is considered to be an effect for promoting prototype innovation. This time the author confirmed the effect of different users using the same prototype. Besides that, there is a possibility that similar landscape expansion may occur in the sharing of actions that make the same prototype.

Figure 4. The dialogue triangle and landscapes
Source: prepared by the author based on Von Hippel and Von Krogh (2016)

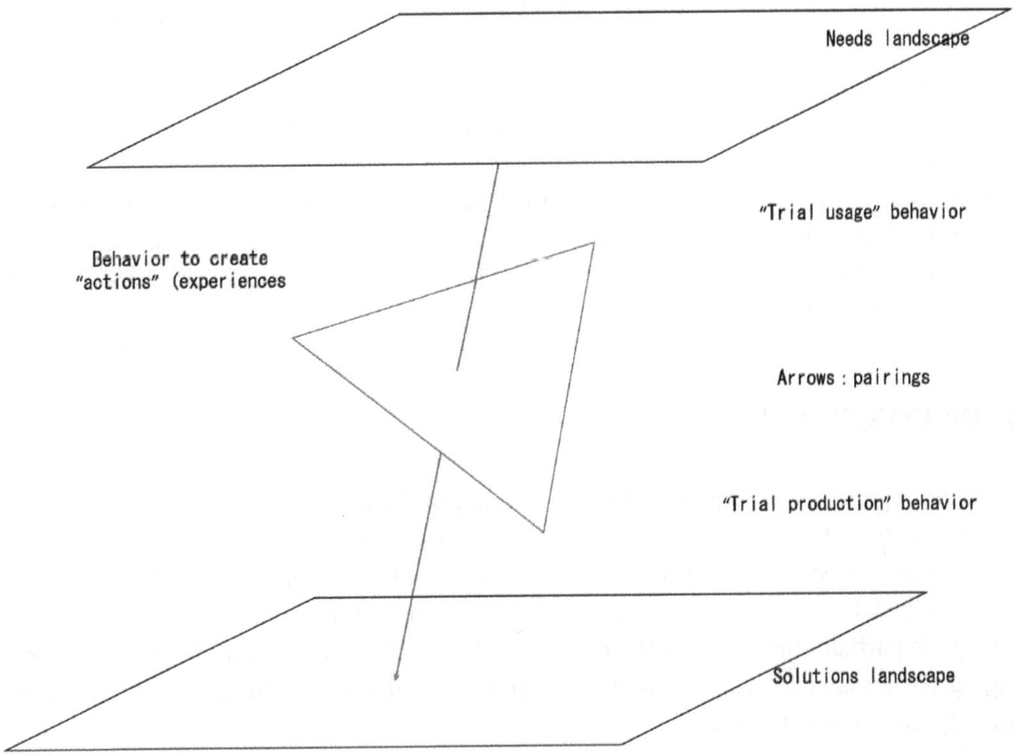

In addition, this result may lead to future studies on the effect of using prototype, association members of cooperative members and users / communities based on diverse knowledge and experience, related studies of subjects of dialogue to be shared and innovation.

CONCLUSION

The author have confirmed that there was a process involving simultaneous problem discovery and solving in the development of the Naruse Pedal, which was a situation where the problems were unclear. This situation was considered using the clues provided by the need-solution pairs (Von Hippel & Von Krogh, 2016) and dialogue framework (Ishii, 1993, 2009; Lester & Piore, 2004). Then, the behaviors of searching for combinations of the two landscapes, as indicated by Von Hippel and Von Krogh (2016), and the pairings were explained using the dialogue framework. In the process of realizing the innovation called the Naruse Pedal, the existence of dialogues with the prototypes as the medium was confirmed. Moreover, it was shown that there were three types of behaviors in the simultaneous problem discovery and solving processes, along with two dialogues toward pairing between the landscapes.

The three types of behaviors were the creation behavior, use behavior, and creation of actions (experiences).

The two dialogues were as follows. First, there was a mutual dialogue between the trial production and trial usage behaviors. Second, there was a dialogue between the trial production behavior, trial usage behavior, and the creation of actions (experiences).

The first and second dialogues took place in an integrated way and were called "the dialogue triangle" in this paper. It is possible that the dialogue triangle exists as the driving force behind the pairings in the need-solution pairs. Moreover, it was clarified that the prototype existed as the medium for this in the dialogues.

It is thought that in the future, these findings may lead to related studies on the effects of using prototypes, the organization of co-action members and user-community members based on diverse knowledge and experiences, and the targets of shared dialogue and innovation.

The process of dialogue is the process of narrative creation. It can be said that the process of narrative is leading to product design creation. The dialogue triangle is done to create a narrative that is called a user's experience. In the process of narrative, dialogue between "making" action and "using" action creates experience behavior.

ACKNOWLEDGMENT

I would like to express my gratitude for the cooperation in the interviews, provision of materials, and advice on this study that I received from Mr. Masayuki Naruse (Representative Director of Naruse Machinery), Mr. Katsuya Matsunaga (Emeritus Professor, Kyushu University), Mr. Akira Arata (Naruse Machinery one-pedal adviser), and Mr. Keitaro Ota (Ota Management Office).

This study is partially the result of the FY2016 KAKENHI (Grant-in-Aid for Scientific Research) (Challenging Exploratory Research) "Study on Prototyping and Value Creation in Design-driven Development" (grant no. 16K13392).

REFERENCES

Clark, K. B., & Fujimoto, T. (1991). *Product development performance.* Brighton, MA: Harvard Business School Press.

Dyer, J., Gregersen, H., & Christensen, C. M. (2011). *The innovator's DNA: mastering the five skills of disruptive innovators.* Brighton, MA: Harvard Business School Press.

Fujimoto, T. (2002). *Notes on the product-architecture concept, measurement, and strategy.* RIETI Discussion Paper Series 02-J-008, RIETI.

Fujimoto, T. (2003). *Capability development competition.* Tokyo: Chuokoron Shinsha Inc.

Goshi, K., & Katsuya, M. (2011). Safe driving education system by multimedia and network. *Proceedings of The 2011 International Workshop on Smart Info-Media System in Asia (SISA 2011).*

Hirota, A. (2010a). The framework for discovering "advanced similar fields" and the promotion of the "lead-user method"- innovation in Japanese competition-use swimwear products and utilizing the lead-user method. The Academic Association for Organization Science FY2010 Collection of Abstracts from the Research Presentations Conference. *Journal of the Academic Association for Organization Science,* 281-284.

Hirota, A. (2010b). The target of "similarity" in innovation and creating the "similarity" method – competition in the development of competition-use swimwear and the creation of innovation. *Quarterly Marketing Journal, 29*(4), 4–17.

Hirota, A. (2011). The framework for the discovery of "extreme users" and lead users. In *Japan Society of Marketing & Distribution FY2011 Collection of Papers Presented at the National Research Conference* (vol. 61, pp. 173-183). Kumamoto City, Japan: The Japan Society of Marketing and Distribution.

Hirota, A. (2013). Value-creation type innovation and customer-needs constraints – the management of dialogue when promoting value creation. In *Japan Society of Marketing & Distribution FY2013 Collection of Papers Presented at the National Research Conference* (vol. 63, pp. 47-57). Kusatsu, Japan: The Japan Society of Marketing and Distribution.

Hirota, A. (2016). The realization of prototypes in the product-design process – factors behind the realization of rapid prototyping. In *Japan Society of Marketing & Distribution FY2016 Collection of Papers Presented at the National Research Conference* (vol. 65, pp. 96-98). Chiba City, Japan: The Japan Society of Marketing and Distribution.

Hirota, A., Takemura, M., & Mizuno, M. (2014). User innovation and product standardization: Japanese experience. In *40th European International Business Conference.* Uppsala, Sweden: European International Business Academy.

Hirota, A., Takemura, M., & Mizuno, M. (2017). Design prototyping in the "fuzzy front end" of product development – rapid prototyping at the stage of high uncertainty. In *The ISPIM Innovation Forum 2017.* Toronto, Canada: ISPIM.

Hirota, A. (2017). The role of prototyping in creative moments (business insight). In *Japan Society of Marketing & Distribution FY2017 Collection of Papers Presented at the National Research Conference* (vol. 66, pp. 81-87). Kobe, Japan: The Japan Society of Marketing and Distribution.

Ogawa, S. (2000). *The logic of generating innovation*. Tokyo: Chikura Publishing.

Ishii, J. (2004). Marketing myths. Tokyo: Iwanami Shoten Inc. (originally published 1993)

Ishii, J. (2009). *Business insight – what is creation knowledge?* Tokyo: Iwanami Shoten Inc.

Ishii, J. (2010). The management of value created in the market. *Hitotsubashi Business Review*, *57*(4), 20–33.

Ishii, J. (2014). *The power to get close*. Tokyo: Sekigakusha Inc.

Lester, R. K., & Piore, M. (2004). *Innovation: the missing dimension*. Brighton, MA: Harvard Business School Press.

Matsunaga, K., & Yasuda, T. (1996). Experimental study of the new type of accelerator bar and brake pedal. In *The Japanese Association of Traffic Psychology 53rd Conference* (vol. 53, pp. 11-14). Tokyo: JATP.

Matsunaga, K., Hayashi, M., Sumida, Y., Nishimura, H., & Koshi, K. (2011). An experimental report to elucidate the mechanism for the occurrence of stepping-on the wrong pedal. In *Society of Automotive Engineers of Japan 2011 Spring Conference*. Tokyo: SAEJ.

Munakata, S. (2014). *Why is the use of the "brake that cannot be mistaken for an accelerator" not spreading?* Nikkei Business Online.

Ogawa, S. (2006). *The theory of competitive co-creation*. Tokyo: Hakuto-Shobo Publishing.

Ogawa, S. (2013). *User innovation*. Tokyo: Toyo Keizai Inc.

Sakurai, K. (2000, September). Save the reckless driving of the automatic car? New pedal. *Nikkei Mechanical,* 22-25.

Schumpeter, J. A. (1926). *The theory of economic development*. Cambridge, MA: Harvard University Press.

Takaoka, K., & Kotler, P. (2016). *Marketing Advice*. Tokyo: Chuko Laclef Shinsho.

Takeda, Y. (2000). *Product Realization Strategy*. Tokyo: Hakuto-Shobo Publishing.

Traffic and Safety Sciences FY2011 Research Project. (2012). *An analysis of the cause of errors when stepping-on the accelerator and brake and proposals for psychological and engineering countermeasures (II) report (2012)*. International Association of Traffic and Safety Sciences FY2011 Research Project (H2305)

Von Hippel, E. (1988). *The sources of innovation*. Oxford, UK: Oxford University Press.

Von Hippel, E. (1994). "Sticky information" and the locus of problem solving: Implications for Innovation. *Management Science*, *40*(4), 429–439. doi:10.1287/mnsc.40.4.429

Von Hippel, E., & Tyre, M. J. (1995). How learning by doing is done: Problem identification in novel process equipment. *Research Policy*, *24*(1), 1–12. doi:10.1016/0048-7333(93)00747-H

Von Hippel, E. (1998). Economics of product development by users: Impact of "sticky" local information. *Management Science*, *44*(5), 629–644. doi:10.1287/mnsc.44.5.629

Von Hippel, E. (2005). *Democratizing innovation*. Cambridge, MA: MIT Press.

Von Hippel, E., & Von Krogh, G. (2016). Crossroads—identifying viable "need-solution pairs"- problem solving without problem formulation. *Organization Science*, *27*(1), 207–221.

Yasuto, O., & Turner, P. M. (2013). Experimental study on preventing accidents caused by mistakenly stepping-on the accelerator pedal and brake pedal when driving a vehicle (2). In *Society of Automotive Engineers of Japan 2013 Spring Meeting*. Yokohama, Japan: SAEJ.

KEY TERMS AND DEFINITIONS

Dialogue: Interaction of the creation of projection and the representation. Other than the talks with a person and the person, the talks in a process making prototype, the talks in the process using the prototype, the talks with the experience that wants to come true exist.

Naruse-Pedal: This pedal was developed for the purpose of reducing accidents caused by mistakenly stepping on a vehicle's accelerator or brake pedal, which has been a social issue in recent years.

Pairing: A combination of a certain needs information that there is in a needs landscape and a certain solution information existing in a solution landscape.

Problem Finding: Discover a problem and solution in an action of the trial and error simultaneously.

Procedural Knowledge: Knowledge to come out of an experience through the practice.

Trial and Error: To investigate a combination of good combination through a trial by a combination of a certain needs information and a certain solution information.

ENDNOTES

1. Matsunaga et al. (1996) measured the effects from the Naruse Pedal in terms of shortening both the operating time (time to depress it) and stopping distance. In a comparison of measurements with the same seven subjects driving the same vehicle at the same speed (40 km/h), the operating time was reduced by an average of about 160 ms. The pedal was depressed in about one quarter of the time required for the existing pedal. In addition, the average braking distance was shortened for all of the subjects by approximately 1.6 m.
2. For example, when depressing the brake pedal, the accelerator arm from the sideways push (slide) action is separated from the accelerator pedal, which forcibly and mechanically withdraws the operations from the control of the driver.
3. Von Hippel and Von Krogh (2016).
4. Accidents caused by the driver stepping on the wrong pedal were confirmed as occurring in the 1980s when Mr. Naruse started to develop this pedal (Matsunaga et al., 2011). However, the reasons

for this were not clarified until the experiment of Matsunaga et al. (2011). Therefore, Mr. Naruse continued to develop this product without knowing the causes of this problem of stepping on the wrong pedal. The experiment of Matsunaga et al. (2011) explored and clarified the causes of the problem of stepping on the wrong pedal by setting experimental conditions that were close to real conditions. They concluded that it was highly likely that the cause involved the fact that the same right foot operated both the accelerator pedal and the brake pedal, and the action of stepping on the accelerator pedal, for which the frequency of a repeated fixed moment was overwhelmingly higher than that for the brake pedal, reached the level of a reflexive movement as a characteristic of the human movement system.

5 Interview with Mr. Naruse.

6 In general, the load required to depress the accelerator pedal of a domestically produced commercially available passenger car is about 1.5 kg (Interview with Mr. Naruse). Because this load assumes an action of pressing down using the large muscles of the entire leg, operating the pedal is not a problem even for women and the elderly. However, because the small muscles are used for the sideways push action, it was particularly difficult for women and the elderly to operate the pedal.

7 By setting the rotating shaft in the lower part, when the accelerator arm is operated, even with a small movement involving a sideways push of the right foot, the movement of the arm at the end of the upper part increases, which makes it easier to operate even when only applying a small force.

8 Removing the existing accelerator and brake pedals set in commercially available vehicles and attaching the Naruse Pedal requires constant linkages with the existing control systems and interfaces, which differ according to the individual vehicle types and manufacturers.

9 Landscape is a metaphor used to explain pairing. (Von Hippel & Von Krogh, 2016).

10 The information constituting the respective landscapes includes tacit elements (Von Hippel & Von Krogh, 2016).

11 The height is not shown in Figure 2.

12 Behavior to realize as a physical product the image a person has in their mind (Takeda, 2000, p. viii).

13 Cost can be considered to be the standard, but in the case of a cost standard, the problems are clarified only when the costs of the candidates for selection for the solution information can be compared.

Chapter 15
Collaboration for Supporting the Externalization of the Travel Narratives of the Elderly:
A Case Study

Nanae Shirozu
West Japan Marketing Communications Inc., Japan & Osaka University, Japan

Mitsunori Matsushita
Kansai University, Japan

ABSTRACT

The goal of this chapter is to explore a system to assist elderly travelers who are not familiar with computers in externalizing information about their travel experiences and in accumulating this information in the form of travel narratives. To accomplish this, the authors focused on dialogue about travel experiences and proposed a co-creation environment that supports interaction that elicits information about the travel experiences of the elderly. In this environment, an elderly person becomes a speaker, and a person close to the elderly person becomes a listener. Participatory observation and externalization interviews about travel experiences were conducted. In general, this study found that an elderly subject became more involved and responsive with more cohesive stories when paired with a listener equipped with relevant information. The design guidelines of the co-creation environment were formulated based on the findings.

INTRODUCTION

People have many different kinds of experiences in daily life. These experiences are often recorded as narratives by the individuals who experience them, often including information such as the details of an event that made an impression on the traveler and the thoughts they had as a result of the experience (Bolger, Davis, & Rafaeli, 2003). In the past, this content has been recorded and stored using analog media passed on from person to person in formats such as diaries and scrapbooks. This personal content

DOI: 10.4018/978-1-5225-4775-4.ch015

Copyright © 2018, IGI Global. Copying or distributing in print or electronic forms without written permission of IGI Global is prohibited.

has generally only been accessible to people who are familiar with the content's creator, such as family members and friends. For others who do not know the content's creator, access would be difficult or impossible.

This content, based on the creator's experiences, reflects the subjective point of view, or subjectivity, of the content creator. In this paper, subjectivity refers to the creator's personal thoughts, including the creator's knowledge or ideas. People's subjective experiences can be externalized as narratives, allowing others to know them. This can be valuable because experiences like war or disasters do not happen to everyone. Therefore, if a record of the experience is left for others, it becomes a social asset that can be used by future generations. Even if a record is personal, for example, a record describing the daily events of a person's unusual life, it will have value in that it describes part of the culture, customs, and life at that time.

The development of information and communication technologies (ICT) encourages the digitalization and deliberation of such narratives. Instances of ICT development include the expansion of the Internet and technologies' dissemination to individuals with high-performance computers, as well as the introduction and spread of small cameras and sensors. Social media is another example of the development of ICT; today, many people use social networking services such as Twitter and Facebook to share parts of their lives.

This improved ability for people to share their personal experiences increases the opportunity for people outside of a person's central social group, family, and friends to perceive the experiences of others and acquire useful information from those experiences. In addition, these newly shared pieces of information aid in maintaining relationships with friends and in meeting new acquaintances. In this way, ICT expands our means of communication.

Along with the expansion of ICT, however, the "digital divide," the gap between those who can access technology and those who cannot, has become a more and more serious problem (Friemel, 2016), particularly for elderly people. They tend to lack familiarity with communication via the Internet or with the operation of complicated information appliances. As a result, electronic records of the experiences of elderly people are difficult to accumulate. This means that, unlike information about the experiences of younger people, information about the experiences of elderly people cannot be shared and reused.

In recent years, several systems have been developed to help elderly people share their records electronically; however, despite the development of these systems, the problem still remains. One major reason for the persistence of this problem is that elderly people do not recognize the merit of using these systems. They often feel that these systems are not easy enough for them to use by themselves and that the time and cost required to learn to use them outweigh the value they provide. As a result, few systems penetrate their lives.

To change these circumstances, this paper will present design criteria to support the generation of content based on the experiences of elderly people. To begin, the authors will, under no circumstances, take the following approaches: (1) forcing users who are unfamiliar with information devices to use complex systems and (2) forcing users to use the systems alone. Instead of these approaches, this study employs an interaction model that takes the form of cooperative work. In this model, elderly people generate content while receiving assistance from others. The advantage of this interaction model is that the elderly subjects can concentrate on recalling and verbalizing their experiences. This assumes that the articulated experiences are recorded by people familiar with the subject (e.g., children, grandchildren, and caregivers), who, using the support system, serve as listeners and who turn the elderly person's narratives into content.

As an example of this, this chapter focuses on the "travel narrative," a story of a person's travel experience that is told to relay the experience to others after the storyteller has returned home. Travel narratives have always held great interest for people of all generations. This is a speaker's experience story based on what the traveler actually saw and heard, on location. This type of story draws the listener's interest. A travel narrative is also an opportunity to display objects acquired during travel, such as pictures of travel destinations and purchased souvenirs. This is a meaningful act from which the speaker draws pleasure and in which the speaker has the role of creating, articulating, and sharing experiences. However, listeners do not always have the same experiences as the speaker. The asymmetry of this experience may cause a one-way conversation dependent on the speaker's verbalizations. This implies that there is a possibility of a system hindering communication between speakers and listeners. The proposed interaction model assumes that a person close to the speaker will be the listener. In this model, the listener listens to frankly spoken stories of the elderly speaker's travel. The listener externalizes and records the spoken stories by linking them with information at sightseeing spots.

This chapter presents the following two points for developing a co-creation environment: (1) a method to support recalling and organizing an elderly person's experiences by facilitating communication using stories about travel and (2) a method for recording and making externalized experiences into content. First, the authors interviewed an elderly woman, subject A, about her travel experience. We confirmed an expected behavior, that she had prepared some materials (e.g., documents related to the sightseeing spot and photographs she took) as clues to help her tell the story of her travel. However, when the information she referred to was difficult to understand or not related to the travel topic, the conversation was interrupted. As a result, the speaker tended to talk unilaterally, without feedback from the interviewer. The documents and photographs she had were not sufficient to assist in organizing her travel experience into a cohesive narrative. As elderly people do not generally have all of the materials related to what they have experienced, and thus lose track of their narratives, it is difficult to organize cohesive travel narratives from their fragmented verbalizations.

To solve this problem, the authors created a prototype of a co-creation environment with the following functions. When the listener talks to the elderly person, the proposed system supports the dialogue by presenting information related to place the elderly person visited, triggered by the stories told by the speaker. By providing this information, the proposed system enhances speaker-listener communication and promotes the externalization of the elderly person's travel story. Through this system, the listener records the activities and memories of the elderly speaker in the form of an electronic map. The listener can then print this map on paper after finishing their conversation, and the elderly person can, through the printed map, look back on travel memories at any time, without using the system.

BACKGROUND

Travel serves as a form of entertainment for all generations. Greater numbers of people have the opportunity to casually visit famous sightseeing locations and historic sites more easily than before. Travelers' attributes are numerous, but in recent years, the number of elderly people engaged in leisure activities has actively increased. Elderly travelers tend to have more money to spend and time to travel compared to other generations. This paper focuses on these elderly travelers.

Information based on travel experiences can be utilized as content, not only by travelers keeping the information for memories, but also by externalizing it and recording it. For example, a travel note is content that explains the travel experience of a writer to a reader. When a traveler relays memories of traveling with others, presenting pictures taken during the trip serves as a topic of conversation. Travel content takes various forms, but this paper examines travel narratives. Travel narratives include facts such as good and bad things experienced by travelers.

In the field of nursing and social welfare, research on reminiscences and life reviews deal with the verbalization of past experiences by elderly people (Woods, Spector, Jones, Orrell & Davies, 2005).

Otake, for example, reports that it is useful for the elderly to recall memories by looking at old photographs and videos as a method to prevent dementia (Otake, Kato, Takagi, & Asama, 2009). Therefore, it is important to use this method to support the narrative articulation of elderly people's travel experiences. In the past, research on memory recall and communication support triggered by memories has been conducted (Balabanović, Chu, & Wolff, 2000). However, many elderly people have some problems that hinder communication, such as ambiguous memory and slow recollection, so communication between them and others may not be successful. If the listener can understand what the speaker wants to say and helps the speaker narrate his story, the problem of unsuccessful communication can be avoided. Unfortunately, there is often a general asymmetry of knowledge and experiences between the speaker and the listener, so the conversation becomes difficult to establish.

The purpose of this research is to help elderly people externalize information about travel experiences and to accumulate this information as the elderly persons' travel narratives. To accomplish this, this chapter focuses on dialogue about travel experiences and proposes a co-creation environment that supports interactions that elicit information about the experiences of the elderly. However, it is difficult for elderly people who are not familiar with computers to independently operate systems to record their own travel experience information. In this environment, elderly people concentrate speaking about their experiences, and the listeners (e.g., children, grandchildren, and caregivers) use the system to externalize and accumulate the travel experience information. This paper describes a co-creation environment designed to assist in recording experiences by repeating user observation through user-centered design.

EXTERNALIZATION OF TRAVEL EXPERIENCE INFORMATION

Baseline Interview

In order to investigate the characteristics of an elderly person's travel behavior during a trip and determine what records to create after the trip, a baseline interview was conducted with user/subject A, a woman in her 80s. The interview was held at her home on May 26, 2013. The listener/interviewer was a collaborator in this study, the interview subject's grandchild. The interview subject lives alone and does not have a computer or a smartphone. She travels with her friends and relatives once a year and photographs her trips with a disposable camera while traveling.

The method of questioning was a semi-structured interview, and the listener flexibly added questions according to the subject's answers. In the interview, the listener asked about the subject's preparation for travel, the means of gathering trip information, and the situation during the trip. The interview was recorded with a voice recorder after obtaining the subject's approval. Also, prior to the start of the interview, the subject was told the following: (1) "You can stop the interview at any time," (2) "You are not required to answer anything you do not want to answer," (3) "Your identity will be kept private," and (4) "You can use any tools and materials you need to answer."

As determined in the interview, the pleasure in traveling, for her, was to visit an environment away from home and to spend time talking and eating with family and friends. She rarely planned her trips herself, and the opportunity for travel and number of trips was influenced by her companions. Subject A was concerned that the number of available travel companions decreased year by year, as the travel participants were aging. She also expects that the frequency of travel will decrease as her physical condition may deteriorate, giving the pessimistic response, "I think I will not be able to go far in the future."

Immediately after the interview started, she gathered materials such as photographs taken at the destination and maps and guidebooks used during travel. While reading the prepared materials, she explained the events that occurred during the trip. When she had no materials related to the topic, she tried to remember events on-the-spot. Based on the results of this interview, it is suggested that materials related to traveling can be used to review the travel schedule and trigger conversation, and overall, they can be used as an impetus to externalize the travel experience.

Influence of Documents on Externalization

Based on the results of the baseline interview, the authors conducted a second interview with the hypothesis that it would be easier to review the travel experience with the subject while presenting materials related to the travel. The second interview was held subject A's home on June 17, 2013. As in the first interview, the listener was the subject's grandchild. In contrast with the first interview, she was asked to prepare travel-related materials in advance and to talk about one trip in detail. By observing the subject's behavior during the interview, the authors were able to examine the influence of the presentation of materials and information on the subject's externalization of the experience.

The subject began by stating that that the most impressive place on the recent trip was the coast of the Sea of Japan in Fukui Prefecture. When the listener inquired about the trip in detail, the subject relayed the memories of the trip while referring to the materials-in-hand that were related to the trip. However, when the materials were difficult to understand, or the title, date, and time written on the bag storing the photographs she took were ambiguous, it took her longer to speak. Also, the materials she had prepared were not necessarily related to the memories of the trip that she talked about, and sometimes there was no available information related to the topics of her trip. When there were no related materials, the listener searched the web for photos taken at the same location as the landscapes shown in the pictures the subject took, and then presented the photos on the display. However, the subject does not use a computer on a daily basis, so she misunderstood the image of the sightseeing location shown on the screen. Additionally, the subject did not give her full attention to the information retrieved by the listener, and since it took time for the listener to retrieve the information, the conversation was interrupted.

EFFECT OF THE PRESENTATION OF INFORMATION PROVIDED BY THE LISTENER

From the results of the two interviews, it was confirmed that presenting information related to travel is useful support for elderly subjects externalizing a travel experience. However, when information related to travel is limited, the dialogue between an elderly subject and the listener gets interrupted. In the case of the previous interview, the listener searched for the information on the web and presented it to the elderly subject, but communication was not smooth when the search result did not conform to the context of the topic or when searching took time. Therefore, in order to enable the listener to efficiently present relevant information, the information needed to be classified and structured in advance.

The authors observed the responses of elderly people to pre-classified and structured information by re-interviewing subject A on the same topic as before, this time using organized documents. The third interview was conducted on September 16, 2013 at the home of subject A. Prior to conducting the third interview, the authors gathered information on the coast of the Sea of Japan in Fukui prefecture, a topic discussed in the second interview. The sources of information were the official homepage about tourism in Fukui Prefecture, blog posts written by people visiting Fukui Prefecture, Wikipedia pages on Fukui prefecture, websites that present domestic event information, and guide maps on Fukui Prefecture.

This information was manually classified into seven types and structured as follows:

1. Useful information about destinations,
2. Tourist information near the destination,
3. Map information obtained from Google Maps API,
4. Store operating hours,
5. Weather during travel,
6. Specialties,
7. Annual events.

This interview also started after the subject had prepared materials, such as photographs and maps, that she related to the trip. The features observed in the interview are described below.

EFFECT OF STRUCTURED SUPPORT FOR REFLECTION

In the interview, interview subject A pointed to a picture taken of Mikata Goko, which is an area with five lakes, and talked about a visit there. At that time, the listener found and described the names and characteristics of each lake in Mikata Goko from the information classified in advance as "Useful information about destinations."

After hearing the explanation, the subject remembered having seen a sign with the name of the lake. In addition, while presenting a photograph, the subject talked about a memory of getting into a gondola lift to go to Itsuki-no-Sono, which is an area with a monument associated with famous Japanese singer Hiroshi Itsuki, on the summit around Mikata Goko. Therefore, the listener selected and presented the information categorized as "Tourist information near the destination" and relayed, "there is a large raccoon figure on the gondola lift's platform." The speaker said, "I saw a raccoon figurine; there was an incident in which my companion played with it, I could not recall (before) because there was no picture on hand."

Support Interpretation

In the picture taken by the subject, there was a landscape in front of the pond where a travel companion was swimming. Based on the pre-classified information, the listener told the subject that there was a pond where medaka were swimming and that there is a spot that tourists call "Vows Key" near the pond. She said, "I thought that I took a picture in front of a common pond, but I was aware that medaka were swimming in the pond." She also recalled wondering about a padlocked fence that was near the pond. From this result, it was observed that she reinterpreted travel experience information based on the information presented.

From the result of the third interview, when externalizing travel experience information, adaptively presenting relevant objective information makes it possible for the speaker's story to become concrete, and the speaker's memory was confirmed to have had a chance to connect. This is considered to conform to the encoding specificity principle (Tulving & Thomson, 1973).

In the third interview, the speaker was able to recall travel stories she did not talk about in the past two interviews. Even for listeners, it becomes easier to connect because the information is structured and becomes a topic in common with the speaker, rendering what tends to be a more interactive experience in communication.

DESIGN CRITERIA

Based on the knowledge gained from the interview, the authors have designed the following two functions for the system to support cooperative creation: (1) the function to present relevant information to promote the externalization of elderly people's travel experience, (2) the function for recording elderly people's externalized travel experience information.

The Function of Presenting Relevant Information

In the interview, when the elderly person talked about a travel experience, since the listener did not have the same experience, it was found that the information relayed by the elderly person and received by the listener was asymmetrical. Elderly people tend to speak subjectively and relay fragmentary travel experience information unilaterally.

The co-creation environment, at this point, presents objective information on the destination to the listener, so that the information the listener has and the elderly person relays coincide. A screenshot of the interface of the co-creation environment is shown in Figure 1. This interface is implemented with HTML and JavaScript, and it runs on a web browser.

In the interview, since the elderly subject could easily understand the travel experience information by pointing to the name of the location on the map, this study used Google Maps as a boundary object (Arias, Eden, Fischer, Gorman, & Scharff, 2000) for the basis of the co-creation environment. In order to display objective information on this map, the following additions were made: a tab for displaying sightseeing spots and traditional events, a function to record externalized travel experience information on a map, and a bar for displaying travel knowledge about tourist spots.

Objective information on travel destinations presented in the co-creation environment includes (1) sightseeing spots (e.g., Kehi Jingu, and Mikata Goko), (2) traditional events (e.g., festivals), (3) celebrities from the area (e.g., Ittosai Ito and Yasuo Kawasaki), (4) specialties (e.g., Echizen buckwheat and Echizen salt), and (5) useful information about destinations (e.g., Fukui Prefecture is ranked second in longevity nationwide).

In this research, Linked Data was adopted as a method for organizing and structuring information about destinations (Bizer, Heath, & Berners-Lee, 2009). An example of sightseeing information converted to Linked Data is shown in Figure 2. Figure 2 shows different means of transport to Mizushima and their costs, as information about Mizushima (the name of an uninhabited island) in Fukui prefecture, structured in RDF format. By expressing the information related to the trip in RDF form, it is connected to DBpedia (Bizer, Lehmann, et al., 2009), structured Wikipedia information converted into Linked Open Data, so more information can be obtained.

The following describes the functions of the co-creation environment.

- **Maps of sightseeing spots and traditional event information:**
  - When the co-creation environment is activated, information on sightseeing spots and traditional events is mapped with markers as shown in Figure 1-A. By clicking the marker on the map, you can view the detailed information. The detailed information displayed is (1) the name of a sightseeing spot and a traditional event, (2) a description, and (3) a picture of the place. Depending on the type of information, information on the time and location of the event is also displayed. When unnecessary information is presented on the map, the user can delete the marker by dragging and dropping the marker to the trash can icon on the lower left side of the screen. Also, taking into consideration the possibility that the topic changes to other surrounding areas during the conversation, a function that can change the display area is installed in the upper right corner of the screen (see Figure 1-B).
- **Useful information about destinations:**
  - Useful information about destinations flows in the bar at the top of the screen (see Figure 1-D). By reading the information, the user can obtain some information about the destination (e.g., local cuisine at the destination, traditional culture, etc.).

Figure 1. An overview of a co-creation environment

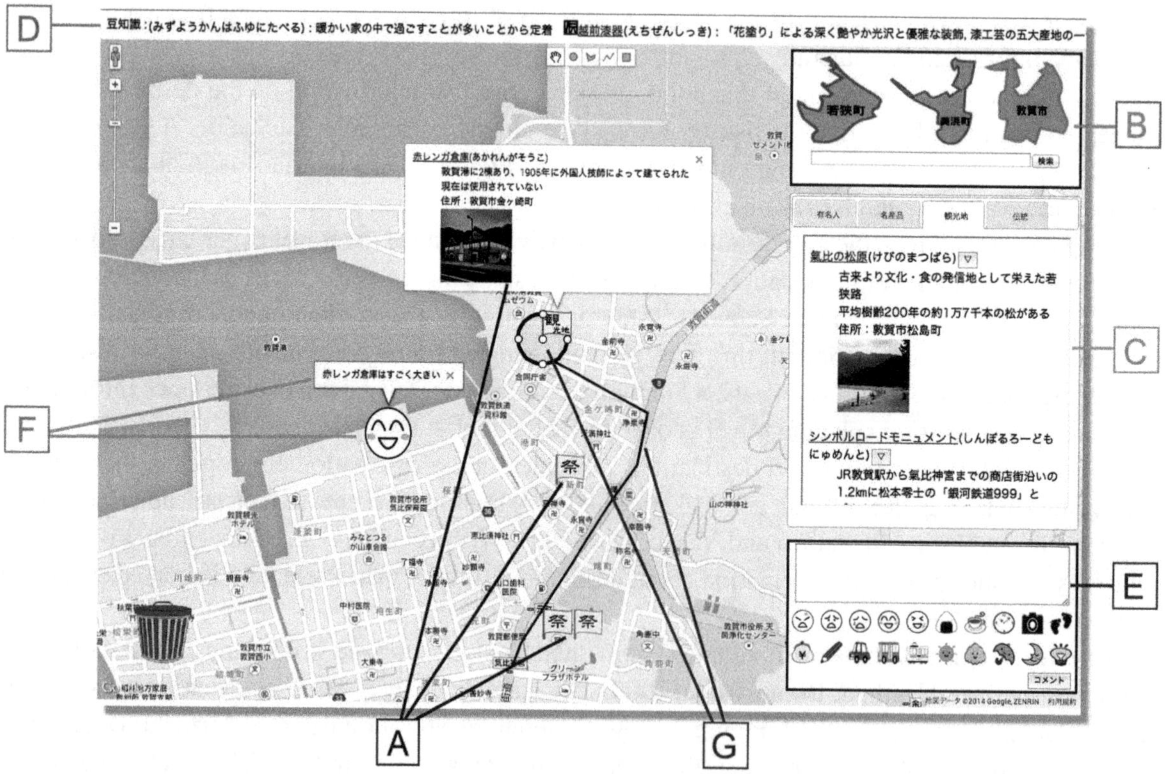

Figure 2. An example of structured information

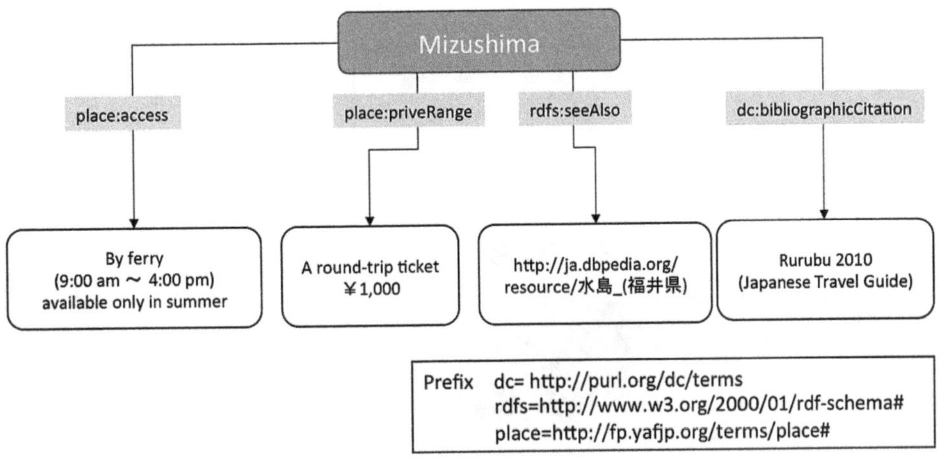

- **Tab for displaying information:**
    - In the tab placed on the right side of the co-creation environment (see Figure 1-C), the user can select four types of information: sightseeing spots, traditional events, celebrities from the area, and specialty items. By clicking on the heading of the information, the user can read detailed information (including explanations and images).

Recording Externalized Travel Experience Information

The co-creation environment has two ways to record externalized travel experience information on the map. The first is a function for recording travel experience information on a map as a comment with a stamp. Stamps are illustrations of 20 types of weather, transportation, and feelings.

When the listener inputs the travel experience information received from the elderly person in the comment field and selects and posts a stamp that matches the comment (see Figure 1-E), the stamp is placed on the map (see Figure 1-F). The user can freely move the stamp on the map by dragging, and if the stamp is clicked, the travel experience information recorded as a comment is displayed. The second is a function for drawing figures on the map. The user can draw four kinds of shapes: circles, straight lines, rectangles, and polygons. This function will be used when recording routes of movement or highlighting a specific area (see Figure 1 - G).

Output of the Recorded Travel Experience Information on Paper

The travel experience information from the elderly person that was recorded using the co-creation environment is then printed on paper (see Figure 3). As mentioned above, despite the widespread use of digital cameras and video cameras, elderly people, like the subject of the previous interview, use film cameras as a means of recording information about their experiences. Travel experience information can be associated with paper photographs taken by the elderly person by printing the recorded experience on paper. As a result, elderly people who are more familiar with analog information than digital are more often looking back on memories.

Figure 3. A printout of an elderly person's travel experience

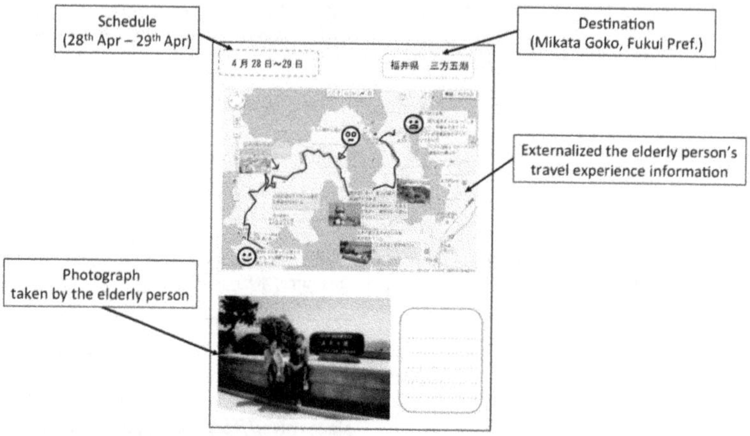

USER OBSERVATION USING THE CO-CREATION ENVIRONMENT

User observation was conducted using the interview subject as an experiment participant in order to investigate whether the listener and the elderly person could cooperate in order to accurately record the travel experiences of elderly people, using the co-creation environment. This user observation was conducted at the interview subject's home on January 5, 2014. As in the past interview, user observation involved travel in Fukui prefecture.

The listener mainly operated the co-creation environment, but in order to prepare an environment where the listener and the elderly person could see the screen together, a laptop PC for operation and a large display (Apple's Thunderbolt Display 27 inch) was prepared (see Figure 4). The cooperation creation environment was operated on the Web browser Firefox 26.0. The subject's behaviors were recorded using a video camera after obtaining the subject's agreement. In addition, the screen operated by the user was recorded using the screen recording function of QuickTime Player. The user observation ended in about one hour.

Figure 4. A snapshot of collaborative creation

Effect of Externalization of Travel Experience Information

In user observation, a total of 64 verbalizations from interview subject A were observed. The verbalizations were counted as a delimiter between cases where there was time before the next utterance and cases when the speaker changed. Of the 64 verbalizations, 43 contained travel experience information. The other 21 verbalizations were responses to questions from listeners and expressions of motivation for future travel. An example of the externalized travel experience information recorded by the co-creation environment is shown in Figure 5.

The information most referenced at the time of utterance was information about sightseeing spots presented in the co-creation environment (23 times) (see Table 1). This is presumably because the listener used information that was positively presented. However, the number of verbalizations about sightseeing locations exceeds the number of materials (7 times) that subject A possessed, so it can be seen that the information presented from the co-creation environment was useful to subject A. For example, she relayed information about an episode when she went to the top of the mountain around Mikata Goko and her companions got into the gondola lift; then, subject A took a cable car to the top of the mountain.

After listening to this topic, the listener offered information ("the riding capacity was 25 people") about the cable car, which was provided by the co-creation environment. As a result, subject A reported recalling that the inside of the car was wide. The listener asked subject A, "Did the gondola lift or cable car arrive at the top of the mountain first?" Subject A then relayed travel experience information: "The cable car arrived first; I waited for the companion who was delayed on the gondola lift at the top of the mountain."

Figure 5. An example of the externalized travel experience information recorded by the co-creation environment

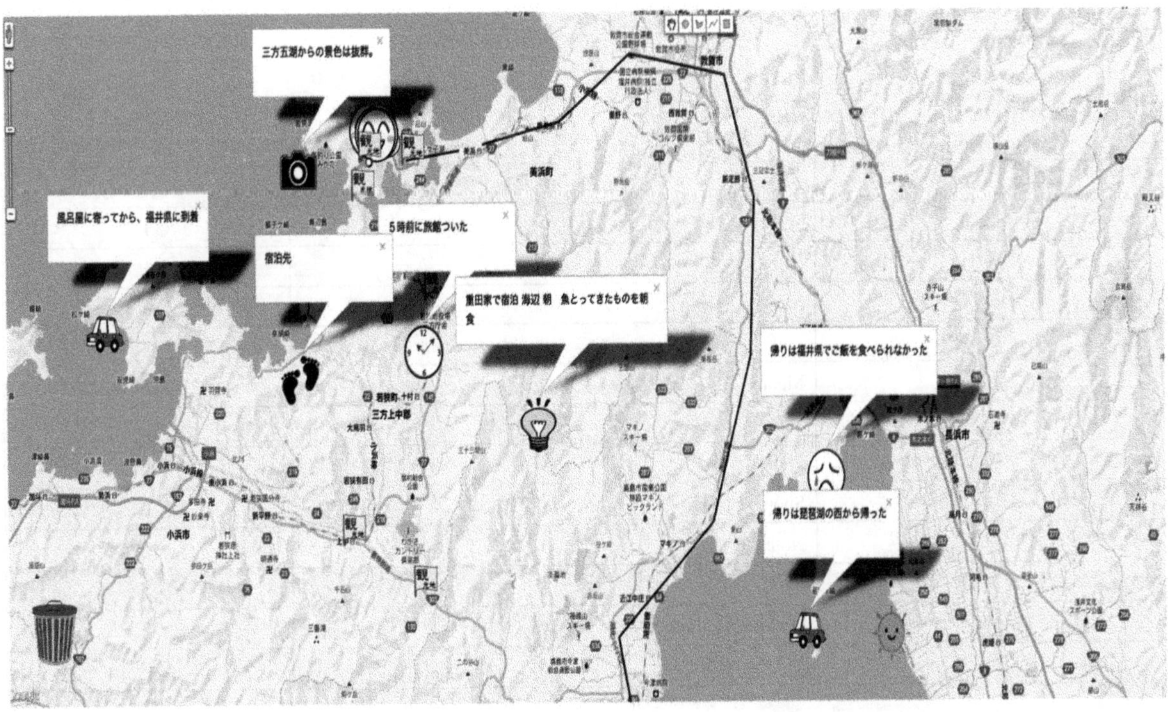

The information presented from the collaborative creative environment triggered a situation where the elderly subjects and listeners laughed with each other. By using the collaborative creative environment, it was possible to externalize the elderly subjects' travel experience information while promoting communication between the elderly people and the listeners.

As a result, subjects and listeners were able to recall or recognize new travel experience information that had not successfully become externalized with only photos and materials supplied by the elderly subjects. Examples include information about how a subject was traveling along the coast, that her planned destination for the future is near Fukui prefecture, and so on. This suggests that it is useful to share one map screen between the listener and the speaker. However, when listeners presented information that subject A did not experience, communication was stalled. For example, when listeners presented "People who live in Fukui Prefecture put Worcester sauce on Katsu-don (this is not a common way of eating in Japan)," subject A replied. "I don't know; is it delicious?"

Recording Externalized Travel Experience Information

Among 64 occurrences of vocalization by the elderly subject, listeners were able to record about 31.3% (20) vocal utterances using the co-creation environment. Listeners recorded utterances using the co-creation

Table 1. Types and frequencies of triggers that appeared in utterances

Types	Frequency
Co-creation environment (tourist information around the destination)	23
Materials owned by A	7
Co-creation environment (map)	6
Co-creation environment (search engine: Google)	2

Table 2. Frequencies of stamp usage

No.	Image of stamp	Frequency
②	Worry	1
③	Sadness	1
④	Joy	3
⑤	Fun	2
⑥	Meal	1
⑧	Time	1
⑨	Photo	1
⑪	Shopping	1
⑫	Notes	1
⑬	Car	3
⑯	Weather (sunny)	1
⑳	Discovery	1

environment while picking up the elderly subject's utterances, but often, the listener was confused as to which utterance to record. The stamps used when recording travel experience information on a map are shown in Figure 6, and the number of times the stamps were used is shown in Table 2. Of the 20 types of stamps (17 times in total), 12 were used. One problem with the stamping was that it was difficult for subject A to understand the meaning of the image on the stamp (for example, an illustration of a light bulb as an indication of discovery). In the future, it will be necessary to redesign the stamp considering the perceptions of the elderly. Since the co-creation environment is mainly used by listeners, listeners need to explain their reason to the elderly subject when moving the map. When moving the map, the listener had to tell the subject the name of the displayed place on the map and the features of the topography, but subject A also pointed to the map to request information, asking "Where is Tsuruga Bay?"

However, the listener was confused about which position on the map some experience information should be recorded at (e.g., experience information without location).

Response from Elderly Subjects to Printed Travel Experience Information

As mentioned above, it is assumed that elderly people store their information in the form of photographs. Thus, printing travel experience information externalized the memories recorded using the collaborative environment. After recording the travel experience information, the listener gave subject A a screenshot of the co-creation environment printed on paper. In response, subject A said, "I'm happy; I want to keep it as a document to remember the trip when I talk about it in the future."

The subject also said that it is easy to remember travel information when sharing information with other people through the printed travel experience information. In addition, she predicted that there would be more opportunities to take pictures on future trips for use in the co-creation environment. By storing photos taken by elderly subjects alongside travel experience information and information related to the sightseeing spot, it is expected that elderly subjects will be better able to recall events that occurred during travel (Tulving & Thomson, 1973).

USER OBSERVATION IN A CO-CREATION ENVIRONMENT

Section 5 explained the results of the externalization and the recording of travel experience information for subject A's travel in Fukui Prefecture, but it is not clear whether the same effect can be obtained when targeting other trips. In addition, this was the first time the listener and subject A collaborated, so some

Figure 6. A list of stamps

difference may be observed between the first user observation and the second user observation due to the user's improved understanding of the progress of co-creation.

Therefore, the second user observation was carried out with the following two purposes: (1) to confirm the reproducibility of cooperative creation based on a travel destination visited by subject A after the first user observation and (2) to determine how users who experienced cooperative creation behave in the second cooperative creation.

The second user observation was conducted at subject A's home on March 12, 2014. The topic was Amanohashidate in Miyazu City, Kyoto Prefecture, where the subject traveled in February of 2014, which was after the first user observation. The operating conditions of the co-creation environment were the same as those for the first user observation, and the listener asked subject A to prepare materials and photographs from the trip in advance. User behaviors under observation were visually recorded from the back using a video camera after obtaining agreement from subject A. In addition, the screen operated by the user was recorded using the screen recording function in QuickTime Player. User observation ended in about one hour. During user observation, a total of 67 vocal utterances from subject A were observed. Of the 67 vocalizations, 55 relayed travel experience information. The other 12 were answers (yes or no) to questions from the listener. Of the 67 utterances by the elderly subject, listeners were able to record about 19.4% (13 instances) of utterances using the co-creation environment. Stamps were used when recording travel experience information on a map and the number of times stamps were used is shown in Table 4. Of the 20 types of stamps, nine were used—13 times in total.

In the first observation, the information most referenced by subject A was information regarding sightseeing spots presented by the co-creation environment, but in the second user observation, the most commonly referenced information was the listener's utterance (23 times) (see Table 3). Unlike the first

Table 3. Types and frequencies of triggers that appeared in utterances in second observation

Types	Frequency
Co-creation environment (tourist information near the destination)	21
Materials owned by subject A	12
Co-creation environment (map)	2

Table 4. Frequencies of stamp usage in second observation

No.	Image of stamp	Frequency
②	Worry	1
③	Sadness	1
④	Joy	1
⑤	Fun	2
⑥	Meal	3
⑨	Photo	1
⑪	Shopping	1
⑬	Car	2
⑯	Weather (sunny)	1

user observation, subject A was not surprised when looking at the prepared information on the large display, and she remembered the progression of cooperative creation. Both the listener and A were at that point accustomed to using the co-creation environment, and their conversation was smooth.

When subject A traveled to Amanohashidate, this user observation was not scheduled. Nevertheless, the subject was taking action in preparation for the next cooperative creation while traveling (e.g., saving the receipt with the name of a shop she visited, shooting group photos, and taking notes on events at the travel destination).

In the first user observation, subject A's response was passive, but this time, she actively showed the listener the pictures she took and relayed the details of what happened during the trip. For example, when subject A described a place called Izushi, where she ate soba, the listener mispronounced the place's name. Then, subject A taught the correct pronunciation to the listener. This indicates that the listener, in a role focused on providing information, gained information from the travel experience of an elderly person. Based on the conversation, the listener received information from the co-creation environment that "the flavor of Izushi's buckwheat soba is rich with condiments." When the listener asked the subject whether there were condiments when she was eating soba, subject A showed a picture of a container of condiments. In this way, by collecting materials to facilitate recalling experiences while she was traveling, compared with the first user observation, the subject spoke actively and in a concrete manner.

FUTURE RESEARCH DIRECTIONS

Structuring Information

In user observation, some of the information presented by the co-creation environment contributed to the recall and externalization of travel experience information, but some information did not contribute. Particularly for traditional events and souvenirs, the degree of relevance was low depending on the season in which the speaker traveled. Therefore, it was necessary for the listener to understand the travel seasons by reading the explanation of the information presented by the co-creation environment. For example, even though subject A traveled in Fukui prefecture in spring, the listener asked if she ate Echizen crab, which is in season in the winter. Currently, information presented in the co-creation environment is categorized by region. In the future, the authors aim to present information more appropriately by applying constraints such as time and season.

In addition, when the user wants to know the details of presented information or to comprehensively search for related information, the current environment uses the method of clicking on the information headline and going to the Google search engine. However, in the baseline interview, it was confirmed that the display of the search result did not draw subject A's attention. In addition, taking time to locate information obstructs smooth communication. To solve this problem, using the Linked Data of information provides a solution (Bizer, Heath, et al., 2009).

The previous studies suggested that users can acquire information in a cross-sectoral manner using Linked Data, so that information can be presented according to changes in the topic of dialogue. For example, Shiramatsu et al. have structured background information on various problems in the community in a Linked Data model named SOCIA, which supports discussions related to community problems (Shiramatsu, Ozono, & Shintani, 2015). This application intends to deepen the understanding of the background knowledge of the agenda and encourage the formation of opinions by presenting relevant information stored in SOCIA to the participants in the discussion. The formed opinion is then structured and accumulated in SOCIA with the goal of being included as an element of further discussion. By structuring the information in this way, it is expected that more flexible and cross-sectional information access will be realized.

In the current prototype, information is created in advance by limiting the focus area, but in the future, it will be necessary to generate information automatically so that it can be applied to other areas as well. Also, by linking externalized travel experience information with location information alongside the provided information, the information can be utilized as reviews by users who are minorities on the web.

Although this chapter focused on talking about travel experiences, it is possible that the co-creation environment could also be used for different topics. For example, it may be able to support externalization of information known exclusively by the elderly, such as knowledge about previous wars, massive disasters, local history, and family history (Schwartz & Cook, 2002).

Promoting Behavior Change

In the baseline interview, the listener asked the user about the state of travel in general. The subject mentioned the possibility that the number of her trips will be reduced in the future because of possible non-availability of companions and about the likelihood that her health will deteriorate. However, when, through the co-creation environment, she learned about the famous products of the land she visited, she mused, “I would like to purchase those as a souvenir the next time I go” or “I will try to take more photos next time.” Remarks on her motivation to travel were obtained through those interactions. In fact, on the next trip, subject A took pictures of her travel group in front of the stores they visited, made memos recording events that occurred during the trip, and collected receipts and fliers from sightseeing spots.

This suggests the possibility that co-creation environments could promote the motivation to go on a journey and change a user’s behavior during the trip, in addition to aiding in the externalization of travel experiences and providing enhancements in communication. The co-creation environment could benefit from a list function that records what the user wants to do on the next trip, so the user can maintain the motivation generated by the co-creation environment in addition to gathering travel experience information.

Recording Travel Experiences

Travel experiences recorded through the observation of each user added up to about 20% to 30%. This result is not sufficient from the viewpoint of the efficiency of the externalization of travel experiences. The reason for this was (1) the listener concentrated on listening to the story too much, and (2) the listener took time to gather information. However, if the listener focuses on input work to improve the efficiency of recording, there is concern that the speaker might feel uncomfortable speaking with the listener and communication failure may recur. Therefore, it is necessary to determine an appropriate balance and clarify the improvements required in the system.

Travel experiences are more likely to be biased toward events that occurred during sightseeing or at accommodations than at events that occurred during travel. For example, suppose a listener attempts to record the events experienced by the speaker during her stay at a Japanese-style inn. In this case, the subject would have had various experiences at the same inn. When the listener places these multiple pieces of information at the same point on the map, a problem emerges regarding overlapping comments on the map. Therefore, in the future, the authors would like to conduct further study on the presentation of information in the co-creation environment.

CONCLUSION

The purpose of this research is to externalize information about travel experiences and accumulate the information as travel narratives from users who are not familiar with computers. To accomplish this, the paper focused on dialogue about travel experiences and proposed a co-creation environment that supports interaction that will elicit the experiences of elderly subjects. In this environment, an elderly person becomes a speaker, and a person close to the elderly person becomes a listener.

From the point of view of user-centered design focusing on elderly people, participatory observation of and interviews for the externalization of personal travel experiences were conducted. As a result, it was confirmed that externalization was facilitated by referring to items and pamphlets that were related to the subject's travel. Based on this finding, the design guideline functions of the co-creation environment are as follows: (1) a presentation function to visualize externalized travel experiences and (2) a record function for the externalized travel experiences.

This paper focused on the travel experience of a user A, a lead user, to verify the reproducibility of the developed environment in different trips made by user A. User observation was performed twice within the co-creation environment. In the first observation, it was verified that the co-creation environment successfully functioned. In the second observation, it was revealed that the subject was taking actions that were not seen in the previous observation, such as recording and collecting information and photography specifically intended to facilitate co-creation. This behavior can be regarded as behavior that was induced by her experiencing the first user observation. In addition, this study confirmed that in the second observation, the utterances of user A became positive and more concrete.

Among noted sequences in the observation, the listener utilized the information presented from the co-creation environment, and, as a result, mutual communication was achieved. This result suggests that the use of the proposed environment facilitated extracting information about travel experiences from elderly people and enabled recording and sharing the articulated experiences electronically. Although this chapter focused specifically on the elderly, future studies could experiment with different subjects and different areas to further investigate the usefulness of the co-creation environment.

REFERENCES

Arias, E., Eden, H., Fischer, G., Gorman, A., & Scharff, E. (2000). Transcending the individual human mind—creating shared understanding through collaborative design. *ACM Transactions on Computer-Human Interaction*, *7*(1), 84–113. doi:10.1145/344949.345015

Balabanović, M., Chu, L. L., & Wolff, G. J. (2000). Storytelling with digital photographs. In *Proceedings of the SIGCHI Conference on Human Factors in Computing Systems - CHI '00* (pp. 564–571). New York: ACM Press. doi:10.1145/332040.332505

Bizer, C., Heath, T., & Berners-Lee, T. (2009). Linked data - the story so far. *International Journal on Semantic Web and Information Systems*, *5*(3), 1–22. doi:10.4018/jswis.2009081901

Bizer, C., Lehmann, J., Kobilarov, G., Auer, S., Becker, C., Cyganiak, R., & Hellmann, S. (2009). DBpedia - A crystallization point for the Web of Data. *Journal of Web Semantics*, *7*(3), 154–165. doi:10.1016/j.websem.2009.07.002

Bolger, N., Davis, A., & Rafaeli, E. (2003). Diary methods: Capturing life as it is lived. *Annual Review of Psychology*, *54*(1), 579–616. doi:10.1146/annurev.psych.54.101601.145030 PMID:12499517

Friemel, T. N. (2016). The digital divide has grown old: Determinants of a digital divide among seniors. *New Media & Society*, *18*(2), 313–331. doi:10.1177/1461444814538648

Otake, M., Kato, M., Takagi, T., & Asama, H. (2009). Coimagination method: Communication support system with collected images and its evaluation via memory task. Lecture Notes in Computer Science, 5614, 403–411. doi: 10.1007/978-3-642-02707-9_46

Schwartz, J. M., & Cook, T. (2002). Archives, records, and power: The making of modern memory. *Archival Science*, *2*(1-2), 1–19. doi:10.1007/BF02435628

Shiramatsu, S., Ozono, T., & Shintani, T. (2015). SOCIA: Linked open data of context behind local concerns for supporting public participation. *International Journal of Advanced Computer Science and Applications*, *6*(2), 268–277. doi:10.14569/IJACSA.2015.060238

Tulving, E., & Thomson, D. M. (1973). Encoding specificity and retrieval processes in episodic memory. *Psychological Review*, *80*(5), 352–373. doi:10.1037/h0020071

Woods, B., Spector, A. E., Jones, C. A., Orrell, M., & Davies, S. P. (2005). Reminiscence therapy for dementia. *Cochrane Database of Systematic Reviews*, (2). doi:10.1002/14651858.CD001120.pub2 PMID:15846613

KEY TERMS AND DEFINITIONS

Behavior Change: A concept that refers to change in an automated behavior through the process of providing stimulus and making a person rethink, leading to the development of a new behavior.

Co-Creation Environment: A system that plays the role of complementing knowledge and skills to support cooperative work between two or more people.

Digital Divide: A social gap between those who can access information and communication technologies (ICT) and those who cannot.

Externalization: The process of expressing what a person has experienced in a form that others can recognize.

Personal Content: Content that reflects the subjectivity (e.g., thoughts, knowledge, or ideas) of the content creator, derived from the creator's personal experiences.

Structuring Information: A process for organizing and linking information related to a certain topic using a common format such as the resource description framework (RDF).

Travel Narrative: A story of a person's travel experience that is told to relay the experience to others after the storyteller has returned home.

Compilation of References

Abe, A. (1997). A criterion for hypotheses in abduction. In *Proc. of the 55th. Annual Conf. of IPSJ*, (*Vol. 2*, 6AH-4, pp. 573-574). Academic Press. (in Japanese)

Abe, A. (1998). Applications of abduction. In *Proc. of ECAI98 Workshop on Abduction and Induction in AI* (pp. 12-19). Academic Press.

Abe, A. (2002). User's interests change as chance discovery. In *Proc. of KES2002* (pp. 1291-1295). Academic Press.

Abe, A. (2015). The role of abduction in IMDJ. In *Proc. of IJCAI2015 International Workshop on Chance Discovery, Data Synthesis and Data Market* (pp. 59-64). Academic Press.

Abe, A. (2016). The possibility of the generation of literary works by computer. In T. Ogata & T. Akiomoto (Eds.), Computational and Cognitive Approaches to Narratology (pp. 75–89). Academic Press. doi:10.4018/978-1-5225-0432-0.ch002

Abe, A., & Hayashi, M. (2016a). On communication assistance via bots ---towards IMDJ. In *Proc. KES2016, Procedia Computer Science* (pp. 1657-1665). Academic Press. doi:10.1016/j.procs.2016.08.213

Abe, A., & Hayashi, M. (2016b). On communication via bots for the computational therapy. In *Proc. of Int'l Workshop on Language Sense on Computer in IJCAI2016* (pp. 61-66). Academic Press.

Abe, H., Ogata, T., & Hanada, K. (2008). Televi kōkoku no shot ni okeru brand dōnyū rhetoric no bunseki - Kōkoku no monogatari seisei system no ichi kikō no tameni [An analysis of brand introduction rhetoric in a shot in television commercial films: For a mechanism of an advertising narrative generation system]. In *Proceedings of the 16th Meeting of Literature, Cognition, and Computer Rereserch Group II in the Japanese Cognitive Science Society* (16G-05). Retrieved from http://www.ogata.soft.iwate-pu.ac.jp/LCC2_Web/LCC(II)Proceedings/Proceedings(16)/2008.11.15AbeOgataHanata.pdf

Abe, H., Ogata, T., & Hanada, K. (2008). Televi kōkoku no shot niokeru brand dōnyū rhteoric no bunseki - Kōkoku no monogatari seisei system no ichi kikō no tameni [An analysis of brand introduction rhetoric in a shot in television commercial films: For a mechanism of an advertising narrative generation system]. In *Proceedings of the 16th Meeting of Literature, Cognition, and Computer Rereserch Group II in Japanese Cognitive Science Society* (16G-05). Retrieved from http://www.ogata.soft.iwate-pu.ac.jp/LCC2_Web/LCC(II)Proceedings/Proceedings(16)/2008.11.15AbeOgataHanata.pdf

Abe, K. (1977). Mikkai. Tokyo: Shinchōsha.

Abe, A. (2000). Abductive analogical reasoning. *Systems and Computers in Japan, 31*(1), 11–19. doi:10.1002/(SICI)1520-684X(200001)31:1<11::AID-SCJ2>3.0.CO;2-E

Abe, K. (1973). *Hako-otoko* [The box man]. Tokyo: Shinchōsha.

Adam, J. M. (1999). *Le récit*. Paris, France: Presses Universitaires de France.

Akimoto, T. (2016). Exploratory approach to the computational modeling of narrative ability for artificial intelligence. *International Journal of Knowledge Engineering*, *2*(4), 170–176. doi:10.18178/ijke.2016.2.4.074

Akimoto, T. (2017). Computational modeling of narrative structure: A hierarchical graph model for multidimensional narrative structure. *International Journal of Computational Linguistics Research*, *8*(3), 92–108.

Akimoto, T., & Ogata, T. (2012). A narratological approach for narrative discourse: Implementation and evaluation of the system based on Genette and Jauss. In *Proceedings of the 34th Annual Conference of the Cognitive Science Society* (pp. 1272-1277). Tokyo: Japanese Cognitive Science Society.

Akimoto, T., & Ogata, T. (2013a). Discourse mechanism in narrative generation system: Proposal of a system introducing narrative discourse theory and reception theory. *Cognitive Studies*, *20*(4), 396–420.

Akimoto, T., & Ogata, T. (2013b). The expansion of paths in the mutual transformation mechanism of music and narrative. *International Journal of Cognitive Informatics and Natural Intelligence*, *7*(4), 44–63. doi:10.4018/ijcini.2013100103

Akimoto, T., & Ogata, T. (2014). Circulative narrative generation based on the mutual transformation between narrative conceptual structures and music in the integrated narrative generation system. *Journal of Robotics. Networking and Artificial Life*, *1*(3), 198–202. doi:10.2991/jrnal.2014.1.3.6

Akimoto, T., & Ogata, T. (2015). Experimental development of a focalization mechanism in an integrated narrative generation system. *Journal of Artificial Intelligence and Soft Computing Research*, *5*(3), 177–188. doi:10.1515/jaiscr-2015-0027

Akiyama, R., & Sugiyama, K. (2004). *Horisuthikku komyunikeishon* [Holistic Communication]. Tokyo, Japan: Sendenkaigi.

Akutagawa, R. (1922). Yabu no naka [In a grove]. *Shinchō*, 1.

Albert, R., Oltvai, Z. N., Barabasi, A. L., Jeong, H., & Tombor, B. (2000). The large-scale organization of metabolic networks. *Nature*, *407*(6804), 651–654. doi:10.1038/35036627 PMID:11034217

Alexander, C. (1966). A city is not a tree. *Design*, 46–55.

Allen, J. F. (1984). Towards a general theory of action and time. *Artificial Intelligence*, *23*(2), 123–154. doi:10.1016/0004-3702(84)90008-0

Amino, T., Kawamura, Y., & Ogata, T. (2002). Hierarchical generation of *geino*-idol stories: Toward *geino* information system and narrative marketing. In *Proceedings of* the *17th Congress of the International Association of Empirical Aesthetics* (pp. 549-552). Rome, Italy: University of Rome Tre.

Amino, T., Kawamura, Y., & Ogata, T. (2002a). Hierarchical generation of *geinō*-idol stories: Toward *geinō* information system and narrative marketing. In *Proceedings of 17th Congress of the International Association of Empirical Aesthetics* (pp. 549-552). Rome, Italy: University of Rome Tre.

Amino, T., Kawamura, Y., & Ogata, T. (2002b). Narrative generation of *geinō* characters and digital narrative marketing. In *Proceedings of the 16th Annual Conference of the Japanese Society for Artificial Intelligence* (3f2-10). Tokyo: Japanese Society for Artificial Intelligence.

Amino, T., & Ogata, T. (2000). *Geinōjin* no history bunseki to *geinōjin* simulation model [*Geinōjin* history analysis and a *geinōjin* simulation model]. In *Proceedings of the 7th Meeting of Literature, Cognition, and Computer Rereserch Group II in Japanese Cognitive Science Society*. Kofu, Japan: Yamanashi University.

Andersen, H. C. (2014). *The little mermaid: With original illustrations*. Hythlody Press. (Original work published 1837)

Anderson, T. S. (2015). From episodic memory to narrative in a cognitive architecture. In *Proceedings of 6th Workshop on Computational Models of Narrative* (pp. 2-11). Academic Press.

Aozorabunko. (2017). *Aozora bunko*. Retrieved October 5, 2017, from http://www.aozora.gr.jp/

Arias, E., Eden, H., Fischer, G., Gorman, A., & Scharff, E. (2000). Transcending the individual human mind—creating shared understanding through collaborative design. *ACM Transactions on Computer-Human Interaction*, *7*(1), 84–113. doi:10.1145/344949.345015

Arima, M., & Tsuji, S. (1987). *Anketochosa no houhou* [Method of questionnaire survey]. Tokyo, Japan: Asakura Publishing.

Aristotle, . (1997). *Poetics* (M. Heath, Trans.). London, UK: Penguin Classics.

Aruga, H., & Ogata, T. (1998). Structural analysis of tragic story and formalization of general rules. In *Proceedings of the 12th Annual Conference of the Japanese Society for Artificial Intelligence* (pp. 697-700). Tokyo: Japanese Society for Artificial Intelligence.

Asakawa, S. (2015). Neural network monogatari seisei moderu [A neural network narrative generation model]. In *Proceedings of 49th Special Interest Group on Language Sense Processing Engineering in Japanese Society for Artificial Intelligence* (pp. 15–21). Tokyo: Japanese Society for Artificial Intelligence.

Asakawa, S. (2015a). *Deep learning, big data, kikai gakushū mataha sono shinrigaku* [Deep learning, big data, machine learning or the psychology]. Tokyo: Shin'yōsha.

Asakawa, S. (2015b). Neural network monogatari seisei model [A neural network narrative generation model]. In *Proceedings of the 49th Special Interest Group on Language Sense Processing Engineering in Japaniese Society for Artificial Intelligence* (pp. 15-21). Tokyo: Japaniese Society for Artificial Intelligence.

Asakawa, S. (2016). *Python de taikensuru shinsō gakushū* [Deep learning to experience by Python]. Tokyo: Koronasha.

Asano, S. (2016). *Propp riron no kōsatsu - Nihon no irui-kon'intan no bunseki wo rei ni* [A consideration of Propp's theory: Based on examples of Japanese human-animal marriage stories] (Master dissertation). Yamagata University, Yamataga, Japan.

Avrahami, J., & Kareev, Y. (1994). The emergence of events. *Cognition*, *53*(3), 239–261. doi:10.1016/0010-0277(94)90050-7 PMID:7842635

Bae, B. C., Cheong, Y. G., & Young, M. R. (2011). Automated story generation with multiple internal focalization. In *Proceedings of the 2011 IEEE Conference on Computational Intelligence and Games* (pp. 211-218). Institute of Electrical and Electronics Engineers. doi:10.1109/CIG.2011.6032009

Bahdanau, D., Cho, K., & Bengio, Y. (2015). *Neural machine translation by jointly learning to align and translate*. Paper presented at The International Conference on Learning Representations (ICLR), San Diego, CA.

Bakhtin, M. (1984). *Problems of Dostoevsky's poetics* (C. Emerson, Trans.). University of Minnesota Press. (Original work published 1963)

Balabanović, M., Chu, L. L., & Wolff, G. J. (2000). Storytelling with digital photographs. In *Proceedings of the SIGCHI Conference on Human Factors in Computing Systems - CHI '00* (pp. 564–571). New York: ACM Press. doi:10.1145/332040.332505

Balzac, H. D. (2017). *Sarrasine* (C. Bell, Trans.). Projects Gutenberg. Retrieved October 15, 2017, 19:45, from http://onlinebooks.library.upenn.edu/webbin/gutbook/lookup?num=1826

Bando, T. (Director), & Ito, H. (Producer) (1995). *Tenshu monogatari* [Castle tower story] [Motion picture]. Japan: Shochiku.

Barabási, A. L., & Albert, R. (1999). Emergence of scaling in random networks. *Science*, *286*(5439), 509–512. doi:10.1126/science.286.5439.509 PMID:10521342

Barthes, R. (1975). *S/Z: An essay* (R. Miller, Trans.). Hill and Wang. (Original work published 1970)

Bass, F. M. (1969). A new product growth for model consumer durables. *Management Science*, *15*(5), 215–227. doi:10.1287/mnsc.15.5.215

Bateman, J., Henschel, R., & Rinaldi, F. (1995). *The generalized upper model 2.0*. Retrieved from http://www.darmstadt.gmd.de/publish/komet/gen-um/newUM.html

Bearingpoint. (2002). *Kokyaku kando shugi: CRM kanzen tassei shinario* [Customer emotionalism: Achievement scenario for perfect CRM]. Tokyo, Japan: Diamond.

Bentivogli, L., & Pianta, E. (2005). Exploiting parallel texts in the creation of multilingual semantically annotated resources: The MultiSemiCor Corpus. *Natural Language Engineering*, *11*(3), 247–261. doi:10.1017/S1351324905003839

Bergström, K. (2012). Creativity rules: How rules impact player creativity in three tabletop role-playing games. *International Journal of Role-Playing*, *3*, 4–17.

Birkhoff, G. (1967). *Lattice theory*. Providence, RI: Colloquium Publications, XXV, American Mathematical Society.

Bizer, C., Heath, T., & Berners-Lee, T. (2009). Linked data - the story so far. *International Journal on Semantic Web and Information Systems*, *5*(3), 1–22. doi:10.4018/jswis.2009081901

Bizer, C., Lehmann, J., Kobilarov, G., Auer, S., Becker, C., Cyganiak, R., & Hellmann, S. (2009). DBpedia - A crystallization point for the Web of Data. *Journal of Web Semantics*, *7*(3), 154–165. doi:10.1016/j.websem.2009.07.002

Bolger, N., Davis, A., & Rafaeli, E. (2003). Diary methods: Capturing life as it is lived. *Annual Review of Psychology*, *54*(1), 579–616. doi:10.1146/annurev.psych.54.101601.145030 PMID:12499517

Booth, W. C. (1983). *The rhetoric of fiction*. Chicago, IL: University of Chicago Press. doi:10.7208/chicago/9780226065595.001.0001

Bordwell, D. (1985). *Narration in the fiction film*. Madison, WI: University of Wisconsin Press.

Bordwell, D. (1988). *Ozu and the poetics of cinema*. London, UK: British Film Institute.

Bottou, L., & Bousquet, O. (2007). The tradeoffs of large scale learning. In Advances in Neural Information Processing Systems (vol. 20). Cambridge, MA: MIT Press.

Bowdle, B., & Gentner, D. (2005). The career of metaphor. *Psychological Review*, *112*(1), 193–216. doi:10.1037/0033-295X.112.1.193 PMID:15631593

Bowman, S. R., Vilnis, L., Vinyals, O., Dai, A. M., Jozefowicz, R., & Bengio, S. (2015). *Generating sentences from a continuous space*. arXiv, 1511.06349.

Boym, S. (2001). *The future of nostalgia*. New York, NY: Basic Books.

Brainerd, B., & Neufeldt, V. (1974). On Marcus' methods for the analysis of the strategy of a play. *Poetics*, *3*(2), 31–74. doi:10.1016/0304-422X(74)90013-8

Brecht, B. (1973). Engeki no tame no shō shikō genre [A principle for thinking theatre]. In Bertolt Brecht engeki ronshū I [Bertolt Brecht's drama theories collection I] (K. Senda, Trans.). Tokyo: Kawadeshobō-shinsha.

Brecht, B., & Willett, J. (1964). *Brecht on theatre: The development of an aesthetic*. New York, NY: Hill and Wang.

Bringsjord, S., & Ferrucci, D. A. (1999). *Artificial intelligence and literary creativity: Inside the mind of BRUTUS, a storytelling machine*. Lawrence Erlbaum.

Bringsjord, S., & Ferrucci, D. A. (2000). *Artificial intelligence and literary creativity*. Mahwah, NJ: Lawrence Erlbaum Associates, Inc. Publishers.

Broder, A., Kumar, R., Maghoul, F., Raghavan, P., Rajagopalan, S., Stata, R., & Wiener, J. et al. (2000). Graph structure in the web. *Computer Networks*, *33*(1), 309–320. doi:10.1016/S1389-1286(00)00083-9

Bruner, J. (1986). *Actual minds, possible worlds*. Cambridge, MA: Harvard University Press.

Bruner, J. (2003). *Making stories: Law, literature, life*. Cambridge, MA: Harvard University Press.

Caillois, R. (1958). *Les jeux et les hommes: Le masque et le vertige*. Paris: Gallimard.

Calvo, H., Daza-Arévalo, J. A., & Figueroa-Nazuno, J. (2016). Automatic story generation by learning from literary structures. Marietta, GA: Scholars' Press.

Camus, A. (1942). *L'Étranger*. Paris: Gallimard.

Camus, A. (1947). *La peste*. Paris: Gallimard.

Chambers, N., & Jurafsky, D. (2010). A database of narrative schemas. In *Proceedings of Seventh International Conference on Language Resources and Evaluation* (pp. 1614-1618). Academic Press.

Chatman, S. (1978). *Story and discourse: Narrative structure in fiction and film*. Ithaca, NY: Cornell University Press.

Chatman, S. (1990). *Coming to terms: The rhetoric of narrative in fiction and film*. Ithaca, NY: Cornell University Press.

Chiappe, D., & Chiappe, P. (2007). The role of working memory in metaphor production and comprehension. *Journal of Memory and Language*, *56*(2), 172–188. doi:10.1016/j.jml.2006.11.006

Christman, S. D., Sontam, V., & Jasper, J. D. (2009). Individual differences in ambiguous-figure perception: Degree of handedness and interhemispheric interaction. *Perception*, *38*(8), 1183–1198. doi:10.1068/p6131 PMID:19817151

Church, K., Dagan, I., Gale, W., Fung, P. N., Helfman, J., & Satish, B. (1993). Aligning parallel texts: Do methods developed for English-French generalize to Asian languages? In *Proceedings of the Pacific Asia Conference on Formal and Computational Linguistics* (pp.1-12). Taipei: Academica Sinica.

Clark, K. B., & Fujimoto, T. (1991). *Product development performance*. Brighton, MA: Harvard Business School Press.

Cohn, N. (2013). Visual narrative structure. *Cognitive Science*, *34*(3), 413–452. doi:10.1111/cogs.12016 PMID:23163777

Cohn, N. (2014). You're a good structure, Charlie Brown: The distribution of narrative categories in comic strips. *Cognitive Science*, *38*(7), 1317–1359. doi:10.1111/cogs.12116 PMID:24646175

Colley, R. H. (1961). *Defining advertising goals for measured advertising results*. New York: Association of National Advertisers.

Cooper, C. W., & Meyer, L. B. (1960). *The rhythmic structure of music*. Chicago, IL: Chicago UP.

Culpeper, J. (1996). Inferring character from texts: Attribution theory and foregrounding theory. *Poetics*, *23*(5), 335–361. doi:10.1016/0304-422X(95)00005-5

Cutting, J. E., Brunick, K. L., & Canden, A. (2012). Perceiving event dynamics and parsing Hollywood films. *Journal of Experimental Psychology*, *38*(6), 1476–1490. PMID:22449126

Cutting, J. E., & Iricinschi, C. (2014). Re-presentations of space in Hollywood movies: An event-indexing analysis. *Cognitive Science*, *35*, 1–23. PMID:25087776

Cutumisu, M. (2009). *Using behaviour patterns to generate scripts for computer role-playing games* (Doctoral dissertation). Department of Computing Science, University of Alberta, Edmonton, Canada.

Davey, B. A., & Priestley, H. A. (2002). *Introduction to Lattice and Order* (2nd ed.). Cambridge, UK: Cambridge University Press. doi:10.1017/CBO9780511809088

Davis, F. (1979). *Yearning for yesterday: A sociology of nostalgia*. New York: Free Press.

Deleuze, G. (1985). *L' Image-temps*. Paris, France: Les Editions de Minuit.

Deleuze, G. (1990). *Pourparlers*. Paris, France: Les Editions de Minuit.

Descartes, R. (1649). *Les passions de l'ame*. Paris: Henry Le Gras.

Dik, S. C. (1997). The theory of functional grammar (Vols. 1-2). Berlin: Mouton de Gruyter.

Dinu, M. (1968). Structures linguistiques probabilistes issues de l'étude du theatre [Probabilistic linguistic structures of theater studies]. *Cahiers de Linguistique Théorique et Appliquée*, *5*, 29–46.

Dinu, M. (1970). Contributions à l'étude mathématique du theatre [Contributions to the mathematical study of theatre]. *Revue Roumaine de Mathématiques Pures et Appliquées*, *15*, 521–543.

Dinu, M. (1977). How to estimate the weight of stage relations. *Poetics*, *6*(3-4), 209–227. doi:10.1016/0304-422X(77)90006-7

Dostoyevsky, F. (2008). *Demons* (R. A. Maguire, Trans.). London, UK: Penguin Books. (Original work published 1873)

Dostoyevsky, F. (2014). *Crime and punishment* (O. Ready, Trans.). London, UK: Penguin Books. (Original work published 1866)

Dubbelman, T. (2013). *Narratives of being there: Computer games, presence and fictional worlds* (Doctoral dissertation). Universiteit Utrecht, Utrecht, The Netherlands.

Dundes, A. (1965). *The structure of folklore*. Prentice Hall.

Dyer, J., Gregersen, H., & Christensen, C. M. (2011). *The innovator's DNA: mastering the five skills of disruptive innovators*. Brighton, MA: Harvard Business School Press.

DynaGloss. (2002). Retrieved May, 2002, from http://Seed.cs.colorado.edu/

Ebizō, I. (Jūichidaime). (n.d.). Retrieved from the Japanese Wikipedia: https://ja.wikipedia.org/wiki/%E5%B8%82%E5%B7%9D%E6%B5%B7%E8%80%81%E8%94%B5_(11%E4%BB%A3%E7%9B%AE)

Eisenstein, S. (Director) (1925). *Battleship Potemkin* [Motion picture]. Soviet Union.

Eisenstein, S. M. (1981). Montage [Montage]. In Eisenstein Zenshū Kankō Iinkai [Selected Writings of Eisenstein Publishing Committee], Tokyo: Kinema-Junpo. (Original works written 1936-1940)

Eisenstein, S. M. (1942). *The film sense* (J. Leyda, Trans.). New York, NY: Harcourt Brace.

Eisenstein, S. M. (1949). *Film form* (J. Leyda, Trans.). New York, NY: Harcourt Brace.

Eliashberg, J., & Shugan, S. (1997). Film critics: Influencers or predictors? *Journal of Marketing*, *61*(2), 68–78. doi:10.2307/1251831

Elman, J. L. (1990). Finding structure in time. *Cognitive Science, 14*(2), 179–211. doi:10.1207/s15516709cog1402_1

Endo, Y., & Ogata, T. (2004b). A rhetorical analysis of a Japanese comic for hyper-comic system. In *Proceedings of 18th Congress of the International Association of Empirical Aesthetics* (pp. 502-508). Rome, Italy: University of Rome Tre.

Endo, Y., & Ogata, T. (2003a). *Manga* no gensetsu gihō wo tōgōsuru wakugumi toshiteno hyper-comic [A hyper-comic as a framework for integrating the discource techniques of *manga*]. *Manga Studies, 4*, 113–132.

Endo, Y., & Ogata, T. (2003b). Narratology of *manga* and application to hyper-comic. In *Proceedings of the 29th Annual Conference of the Japanese Society for Artificial Intelligence* (2G2-03). Tokyo: Japanese Society for Artificial Intelligence.

Endo, Y., & Ogata, T. (2004a). Multilayered discourse in hyper-comic. In *Proceedings of the 9th International Symposium on Artificial Life and Robotics* (Vol. 1, pp. 49-52). Ōita, Japan: Oita University.

Enomoto, Y., Seino, K., & Nibori, K. (2017). The support situation to the student of the developmental disability in a career center Part3. In *Proceedings of Japan Academy for Comprehensive Rehabilitation 18th Conference*. Tokyo, Japan: Japan Academy for Comprehensive Rehabilitation.

Erdem, M. N. (2017). Narrative 3.0: Generating of user integrated narrative. In R. Yılmaz (Ed.), Narrative advertising models and conceptualization in the digital age (pp. 97-116). Hershey, PA: Information Science Reference (IGI Global).

Erdős, P., & Rényi, A. (1960). On the evolution of random graphs. *Publication of the Mathematical Institute of the Hungarian Academy of Sciences, 5*(1), 17–60.

Etō, J. (1970-1999). *Sōseki to sono jidai* [Sōseki and the age] (Vols. 1-5). Tokyo: Shinchōsha.

Etō, J. (1959). *Sakka ha kōdō suru* [Authors act]. Tokyo: Kōdansha.

Fainsilber, L., & Ortony, A. (1987). Metaphorical uses of language in the expression of emotions. *Metaphor and Symbolic Activity, 2*(4), 239–250. doi:10.1207/s15327868ms0204_2

Faloutsos, M., Faloutsos, P., & Faloutsos, C. (1999). On power-law relationships of the Internet topology. *Computer Communication Review, 29*(4), 251–262. doi:10.1145/316194.316229

Faulkner, W. (1929). *The sound and the fury*. London, UK: Jonathan Cape and Harrison Smith.

Faulkner, W. (1936). *Absalom, absalom!* Random House.

Feick, L. F., & Price, L. L. (1987). The market maven: A diffuser of marketplace information. *Journal of Marketing, 51*(1), 83–97. doi:10.2307/1251146

Feldman, R., & Sanger, J. (2007). *The text mining handbook: Advanced approaches in analyzing unstructured data*. Cambridge, UK: Cambridge University Press.

File:Rubin2.jpg. (2016, October 8). *Wikimedia Commons, the free media repository*. Retrieved September 29, 2017, from https://commons.wikimedia.org/w/index.php?title=File:Rubin2.jpg&oldid=209158772

Finlayson, M. A. (2012) *Learning narrative structure from annotated folktales* (Doctoral dissertation). Electrical Engineering and Computer Science, Massachusetts Institute of Technology, Cambridge, MA.

Fischer, G. (2000). Social creativity, symmetry of ignorance and meta-design. *International Journal Knowledge-Based Systems, 13*(7-8), 527-537.

Fischer, G. (2004). Social creativity: Turning barriers into opportunities for collaborative design. In *Proc. of the Participatory Design Conference (Pdc'04)* (pp. 152-161). Academic Press. doi:10.1145/1011870.1011889

Forster, E. M. (1956). *Aspects of the novel*. Boston, MA: Mariner Books. (Original work published 1927)

Forti, B. (2008). How could phenomenal consciousness be involved in mental function? *New Ideas in Psychology*, *27*(3), 312–325. doi:10.1016/j.newideapsych.2008.10.001

Freud, S. (1900). *Die traumdeutung*. Leipzig: Franz Deuticke.

Friemel, T. N. (2016). The digital divide has grown old: Determinants of a digital divide among seniors. *New Media & Society*, *18*(2), 313–331. doi:10.1177/1461444814538648

Fujii, S., Hasegawa, D., Nakano, T., & Hatori, T. (2011). Academic genealogies with respect to narrative in human and social sciences and their implication for public policies. *Journal of Japan Society of Civil Engineers*, *F5-67*(1), 32-45.

Fujii, S. (2016). *Nihon bungaku genryū-shi* [A history of origins in Japanese literature]. Tokyo: Seidosha.

Fujimoto, T. (2002). *Notes on the product-architecture concept, measurement, and strategy*. RIETI Discussion Paper Series 02-J-008, RIETI.

Fujimoto, T. (2003). *Capability development competition*. Tokyo: Chuokoron Shinsha Inc.

Fujiwara no Michitsuna no Haha. (1989). Kagerō nikki [Dragonfly diary]. In *Shin nihon koten bungaku taikei 24* [New Japanese classic literature collection 24]. Tokyo: Iwanamishoten. (Original work published around 975)

Fujiwara, A., & Ogata, T. (2014). Generalizing and expanding the Propp-based story content grammar using the structural analysis of folktales. In *Proceedings of the 13th Forum Information Technology* (Vol. 2, pp. 331-333). Tokyo: Information Processing Society of Japan.

Fukuda, I., Kurisawa, Y., & Ogata, T. (2013). Roles and the management mechanism of internal states of characters in a narrative generation system. In *Proceeding of the 27th Annual Conference of the Japanese Society for Artificial Intelligence* (2I4-2in). Tokyo: Japanese Society for Artificial Intelligence.

Fukuda, T. (1990). *Monogatari marketing* [Story marketing]. Tokyo: Takeuchishoten-shinsha.

Fukushima, H., Mutsumi, I., & Shigenori, T. (in press). The usage mechanism of Japanese ideophones in the description of taste: Morphological and co-occurrence analysis of the description words of wines and sakes. *International Journal of Computational Linguistics Research*.

Genette, G. (1972). *Discours du recit, essai de methode, Figures III*. Paris: Seuil.

Genette, G. (1972). *Discours du récit, Essai de méthode, Figures III*. Paris: Seuil.

Genette, G. (1972). Discourse du recit: Essai de method [Narrative discourse: An essay in method]. In *Figures III*. Paris: Seuil.

Genette, G. (1972). *Narrative discourse: An essay in method* (J. E. Lewin, Trans.). Cornell University Press. (Original work published 1972)

Genette, G. (1982). *Palimpsestes: La littérature au second degré*. Paris: Seuil.

Gentner, D. (1983). Structure mapping: A theoretical framework for analogy. *Cognitive Science*, *7*(2), 155–170. doi:10.1207/s15516709cog0702_3

Gerhard, N. (2010). *Algorithmic composition: Paradigms of automated music generation*. Berlin: Springer.

Gershoni, S., & Kobayashi, H. (2005). Symmetry and complementarity- a discussion and a qualitative demonstration with computer generated infinite patterns of natural scenes. In *Proceedings of The First International Workshop on Kansei* (vol. 68, pp. 89-90). The Society of Photographic Science and Technology of Japan.

Gervás, P., Lönneker-Rodman, B., Meister, J. C., & Peinado, F. (2006). Narrative models: narratology meets artificial intelligence. In *Proceedings of International Conference on Language Resources and Evaluation*, (pp. 44-51). Academic Press.

Gervás, P. (2009). Computational approaches to storytelling and creativity. *AI Magazine*, *30*(3), 49–62. doi:10.1609/aimag.v30i3.2250

Gervás, P. (2012). Story Generator Algorithms. In P. Hühn et al. (Eds.), *The living handbook of narratology*. Hamburg, Germany: Hamburg University Press.

Gervás, P. (2015). Computational drafting of plot structures for Russian folk tales. *Cognitive Computation*. doi:10.1007/s12559-015-9338-8 PMID:27642369

Glucksberg, S. (2001). *Understanding Figurative Language: From Metaphors to Idioms*. Oxford University Press. doi:10.1093/acprof:oso/9780195111095.001.0001

Glucksberg, S., & Haught, C. (2006a). Can Florida become *like* the next Florida? When metaphoric comparisons fail. *Psychological Science*, *17*(11), 935–938. doi:10.1111/j.1467-9280.2006.01807.x PMID:17176422

Glucksberg, S., & Haught, C. (2006b). On the relation between metaphor and simile: When comparison fails. *Mind & Language*, *21*(3), 360–378. doi:10.1111/j.1468-0017.2006.00282.x

Glucksberg, S., & Keysar, B. (1990). Understanding metaphorical comparisons: Beyond similarity. *Psychological Review*, *97*(1), 3–18. doi:10.1037/0033-295X.97.1.3

Glucksberg, S., McGlone, M., & Manfredi, D. (1997). Property attribution in metaphor comprehension. *Journal of Memory and Language*, *36*(1), 50–67. doi:10.1006/jmla.1996.2479

Godairiki koi no fujime. (1794). [Five great powers that secure love] [*Kabuki*]. Namiki Gohei I (Scenario). Kyōto, Japan: Nishi no Shibai (First performance).

Goertzel, B., & Pennachin, C. (Eds.). (2007). *Artificial General Intelligence. Cognitive Technologies*. Berlin: Springer. doi:10.1007/978-3-540-68677-4

Gomez-Gardenes, J., & Moreno, Y. (2004). Local versus global knowledge in the Barabási-Albert scale-free network model. *Physical Review. E*, *69*(3), 037103. doi:10.1103/PhysRevE.69.037103 PMID:15089443

Goshi, K., & Katsuya, M. (2011). Safe driving education system by multimedia and network. *Proceedings of The 2011 International Workshop on Smart Info-Media System in Asia (SISA 2011).*

Granek, E., & Ruttenberg, B. I. (2008). Changes in biotic and abiotic processes following mangrove clearing. *Estuarine, Coastal and Shelf Science*, *80*(4), 555–562. doi:10.1016/j.ecss.2008.09.012

Graves, A., Wayne, G., & Danihelka, I. (2014). *Neural Turing machines.* arXiv:1410.5401

Greimas, A. J. (1966). *Sémantique structurrale: Recherché de method.* Paris: Larousse.

Gruber, T. R. (1993). A translation approach to portable ontology specifications. *Knowledge Acquisition*, *5*(2), 199–220. doi:10.1006/knac.1993.1008

Guarino, N. (1998). Formal ontology and information systems. In N. Guarino (Ed.), *Formal Ontology in Information Systems. Proceedings of FOIS'98* (pp. 3-15). Amsterdam: IOS Press.

Gunji, M. (1963). *Kabuki no bigaku* [Aesthetics *of kabuki*]. Tokyo: Engeki-shuppansha.

Gunji, Y. P., & Haruna, T. (2010). A non-boolean lattice derived by double indiscernibility. *Lecture Notes in Computer Science*, *6190*, 211–225. doi:10.1007/978-3-642-14467-7_11

Gunji, Y. P., Niizato, T., Murakami, H., & Tani, I. (2010). Typ-Ken (an amalgam of type and token) drives Infosphere. *Knowledge, Technology & Policy*, *23*(1-2), 227–251. doi:10.1007/s12130-010-9107-7

Hamada, S. (2001). Four-layer structure of narratives. *Cognitive Studies: Bulletin of the Japanese Cognitive Science Society*, *8*, 319-326.

Hamaoka, Y. (2002). Akuthibu konshuma wo rikai suru [Understanding the active consumer]. *Hitotsubashi Business Review*, *50*(3), 40–55.

Hamaoka, Y., & Satomura, T. (2009). *Shohishakan no sogo sayo nitsuiteno kiso kenkyu: kuchikomi e-kuchikomi wo chushin ni* [Basic research on the interaction between consumers: Focusing on word-of-mouth and e-word-of-mouth]. Tokyo, Japan: Keio University Press.

Haniya, Y. (2003). Shirei [Death Spirits]. Tokyo: Kōdansha. (Original work published 1946-1995).

Hara, M. (2013). *Chikamatsu jōruri no sakugeki-hō* [The dramaturgy of Chikamatsu's jōruris]. Tokyo: Yagishoten.

Hasegawa, K. (2015). *Nihonshu techo* [Sake handbook]. Gakken Publishing.

Hashimoto, O. (2012). *Jōruri wo yomō* [Let's read jōruri]. Tokyo: Shinchōsha.

Hasumi, S. (1985). *Monogatari hihan josetsu* [An introduction to narrative criticism]. Tokyo: Chūōkōronsha.

Hasumi, S. (2014). *Bovary fujin ron* [A Theory of "Madam Bovary"]. Tokyo: Chikumashobō.

Heike Monogatari. (1991-1993). *Shin nihon koten bungaku taikei* (Vols. 44-45) [New Japanese classic literature collection (Vols. 44-45)]. Tokyo: Iwanamishoten.

Hemingway, E. M. (1929). *A farewell to arms*. Scribner.

Hemingway, E. M. (1940). *For whom the bell tolls*. Scribner.

Herrnstein-Smith, B. (1968). *Poetic closure*. Chicago, IL: Chicago UP.

Higson, A. (2014). Nostalgia is not what it used to be: Heritage films, nostalgia websites and contemporary consumers. *Consumption Markets & Culture*, *17*(2), 120–142. doi:10.1080/10253866.2013.776305

Higuchi, K. (2004). Quantitative analysis of textual data: Differentiaiton and coordination of two approches. *Sociological Theory and Methods*, *19*(1), 101–115.

Hinton, L., Nichols, J., & Ohala, J. J. (2006). *Sound symbolism*. Cambridge, UK: Cambridge University Press.

Hirota, A. (2010a). The framework for discovering "advanced similar fields" and the promotion of the "lead-user method"- innovation in Japanese competition-use swimwear products and utilizing the lead-user method. The Academic Association for Organization Science FY2010 Collection of Abstracts from the Research Presentations Conference. *Journal of the Academic Association for Organization Science,* 281-284.

Hirota, A. (2011). The framework for the discovery of "extreme users" and lead users. In *Japan Society of Marketing & Distribution FY2011 Collection of Papers Presented at the National Research Conference* (vol. 61, pp. 173-183). Kumamoto City, Japan: The Japan Society of Marketing and Distribution.

Hirota, A. (2013). Value-creation type innovation and customer-needs constraints – the management of dialogue when promoting value creation. In *Japan Society of Marketing & Distribution FY2013 Collection of Papers Presented at the National Research Conference* (vol. 63, pp. 47-57). Kusatsu, Japan: The Japan Society of Marketing and Distribution.

Hirota, A. (2016). The realization of prototypes in the product-design process – factors behind the realization of rapid prototyping. In *Japan Society of Marketing & Distribution FY2016 Collection of Papers Presented at the National Research Conference* (vol. 65, pp. 96-98). Chiba City, Japan: The Japan Society of Marketing and Distribution.

Hirota, A. (2017). The role of prototyping in creative moments (business insight). In *Japan Society of Marketing & Distribution FY2017 Collection of Papers Presented at the National Research Conference* (vol. 66, pp. 81-87). Kobe, Japan: The Japan Society of Marketing and Distribution.

Hirota, A., Takemura, M., & Mizuno, M. (2017). Design prototyping in the "fuzzy front end" of product development – rapid prototyping at the stage of high uncertainty. In *The ISPIM Innovation Forum 2017*. Toronto, Canada: ISPIM.

Hirota, A. (2010b). The target of "similarity" in innovation and creating the "similarity" method – competition in the development of competition-use swimwear and the creation of innovation. *Quarterly Marketing Journal*, *29*(4), 4–17.

Hirota, A., Takemura, M., & Mizuno, M. (2014). User innovation and product standardization: Japanese experience. In *40th European International Business Conference*. Uppsala, Sweden: European International Business Academy.

Hobbs, J. R., Stickel, M. E., Appelt, D. E., & Martin, P. (1993). Interpretation as abduction. *Artificial Intelligence*, *63*(1-2), 69–142. doi:10.1016/0004-3702(93)90015-4

Hoffman, D. D. (1983). The interpretation of visual illusions. *Scientific American*, *249*(6), 154–162. doi:10.1038/scientificamerican1283-154

Holbrook, M. B., & Schindler, R. M. (1991). Echoes of the dear departed past: Some work in progress on nostalgia. In R. H. Holman & M. R. Solomon (Eds.), *Advances in Consumer Research, 18* (pp. 330–333). Provo, UT: Association for Consumer Research.

Hollister, J. (2016). *A contextual approach to real time, interactive narrative generation* (Doctoral dissertation). University of Central Florida, Orlando, FL.

Honcho Nijushikō. (1766). [Japan's 24 paragons of filial piety] [*Ningyō jōruri*]. Ōsaka, Japan: Takemoto-za (First performance).

Hori, K. (2004). Do knowledge assets really exist in the world and can we access such knowledge?: Knowledge evolves through a cycle of knowledge liquidization and crystallization. LNAI, 3359, 1–13.

Hori, K. (1994). A system for aiding creative concept formation. *IEEE Transactions on Systems, Man, and Cybernetics*, *24*(6), 882–894. doi:10.1109/21.293507

Hori, K. (2007). *Sozo katsudo shien no riron to oyo* [Theories and applications of creativity support]. Tokyo: Ohmsha.

Hotta, T. (2013). The trick of information manipulation: surprise. *The Ryukoku Journal of Humanities and Sciences*, *34*(2), 193-204.

Hozumi, I. (1959). Naniwa miyage [Naniwa souvenir] (The first part). In Chikamatsu jōruri shū (vol. 2). Tokyo: Iwanamishoten. (Original work published 1738)

Huang, K. C. (2008). Effects of computer icons and figure/background area ratios and color combinations on visual search performance on an LCD monitor. *Displays*, *29*(3), 237–242. doi:10.1016/j.displa.2007.08.005

Huang, L., & Pashler, H. (2009). Reversing the attention effect in figure-ground perception. *Psychological Science*, *20*(10), 1199–1201. doi:10.1111/j.1467-9280.2009.02424.x PMID:19686294

Hubka, K. (1984). The dramatic syllables and hyper-syllables of Menander's 'Samia' and Plautus' 'Mercator'. *Poetics*, *13*(1-2), 83–100. doi:10.1016/0304-422X(84)90032-9

Hussey, K. A., & Katz, A. N. (2006). Metaphor production in online conversation: Gender and friendship status. *Discourse Processes*, *42*(1), 75–98. doi:10.1207/s15326950dp4201_3

Ichinotani Futaba Gunki. (1751). [Chronicle of the battle of Ichinotani] [*Ningyō jōruri*]. Ōsaka, Japan: Toyotake-za (First performance).

Ijichi, S. (2006). *CGM makethingu* [CGM marketing]. Tokyo, Japan: Asahi Communications.

Ikeda, K. (2008). Atarashii shohisha no shutsugen: Saiyosha kategori yoin no saikentou [The emergence of new consumers: Re-examination of the hiring category factor]. In Netto ga kaeru shohisha kodou: kuchikomi no eikyoryoku no jisshou bunseki [Consumer behavior that the internet changes: Empirical analysis on influence of word-of-mouth] (pp. 114-144). Tokyo, Japan: NTT Press.

Ikeda, K. (1997). *Nettowakingu komyunithi* [Networking community]. Tokyo, Japan: University of Tokyo Press.

Ikeda, K. (2010). *Kuchikomi to nettowahku no shakai shinri: Shohi to fukyu no sahbisu inobehshon kenkyu* [Social psychology of the word-of-mouth and network: Service innovation research on consumption and diffusion]. Tokyo, Japan: University of Tokyo Press.

Ikeo, K. (2003). *Netto komyunithi no mahkethingu senryaku* [Marketing Strategy of net community]. Tokyo, Japan: Yuhikaku.

Imabuchi, S., & Ogata, T. (2012). *A story generation system based on Propp theory: As a mechanism in an integrated narrative generation system. In Lecture Notes in Artificial Intelligence* (Vol. 7614, pp. 312–321). Berlin, Germany: Springer.

Imabuchi, S., & Ogata, T. (2012). A story generation system based on Propp theory: As a mechanism in an integrated narrative generation system. In *Lecture Notes in Artificial Intelligence* (Vol. 7614, pp. 312–321). Berlin: Springer. doi:10.1007/978-3-642-33983-7_31

Imabuchi, S., & Ogata, T. (2013). Methods for generalizing the Propp-based story generation mechanism. In Lecture Notes in Computer Science (Vol. 8210, pp. 333–344). Berlin: Springer. doi:10.1007/978-3-319-02750-0_36

Imabuchi, S., & Ogata, T. (2014a). Integrating the event generation mechanism in the Propp-based story generation mechanism into the integrated narrative generation system. *Journal of Robotics. Networking and Artificial Life*, *1*(2), 164–168. doi:10.2991/jrnal.2014.1.2.14

Imabuchi, S., & Ogata, T. (2014b). Propp ni motozuku story seisei system ni okeru tōjō-jinbutsu no kōsatsu [A consideration of characters in a Propp-based story generation system]. In *Proceedings of the 45th Special Interest Group on Language Sense Processing Engineering in Japanese Artificial Intelligence Society* (pp. 17-25). Tokyo: Japanese Artificial Intelligence Society.

Imao, T. (1970). *Henshin no shisō* [The theory of metamorphosis]. Tokyo: Hōsei University Press.

Inumaru, O. (2005). *Tempō jūichinen no chūshingura: Tsuruya Namboku kamikakete Sango taisetsu wo yomu* [Chushingura at Tempō 11: Reading Tsuruya Namboku's kamikakete Sango taisetsu]. Tokyo: Yūzankaku.

Iser, W. (1976). *Der akt des lesens.* Munchen, Germany: Wilhelm Fink Verlag.

Ishii, J. (2004). Marketing myths. Tokyo: Iwanami Shoten Inc. (originally published 1993)

Ishii, J. (2009). *Business insight – what is creation knowledge?* Tokyo: Iwanami Shoten Inc.

Ishii, J. (2010). The management of value created in the market. *Hitotsubashi Business Review, 57*(4), 20–33.

Ishii, J. (2014). *The power to get close.* Tokyo: Sekigakusha Inc.

Ishii, K., & Ogata, T. (1998). A study on the methodology of hypertext novels based on a prototyping. In *Proceedings of the 12th Annual Conference of the Japanese Society for Artificial Intelligence* (pp. 701-702). Tokyo: Japanese Society for Artificial Intelligence.

Ishii, R., & Ogata, T. (2006). Making of a narrative network from characters histories and making of tories by the tracing towards the general and automat processing of the hyper-comic system. In *Proceedings of the 20th Annual Conference of the Japanese Society for Artificial Intelligence* (2E3-3). Tokyo: Japanese Society for Artificial Intelligence.

Ito, F. (2007). *CGM: Shohisha hasshin medhia* [CGM: Consumer generated media]. Tokyo, Japan: Softbank Creative.

Izumi, K. (1917). *Tenshu monogatari* [Castle tower story]. Shinshōsetsu.

Izumu, K. (1919). *Yukari no onna* [A marginate woman]. Fujingahō.

Jakobson, R. (1960). Linguistics and poetics. In T. A. Sebeok (Ed.), *Style in language* (pp. 350–377). Cambridge, MA: MIT Press.

Japan Actors' Association, & the Organization for the Preservation of Kabuki. (2017). *Narukami - Kabuki enmoku an'nai* [Narukami: Kabuki play guide]. Retrieved October 20, 2017, from http://enmokudb.kabuki.ne.jp/repertoire/502

Japan Student Services Organization. (2017). *Heisei 28 nendo syougai noaru gakusei no syugakusien nikansuru jittaichyosa* [A survey on study support for students with disabilities 2016]. Tokyo: Japan Student Services Organization.

Jauss, H. R. (1970). Literaturgeschichte als provokation. Frankfurt am Main: Suhrkamp Verlag.

Jensen, R. (1999). *The dream society: How the coming shift from information to imagination will transform your business.* McGraw Hill.

Jhale, A., & Young, M. R. (2010). Cinematic visual discourse: Representation, generation, and evaluation. *IEEE Transactions on Computational Intelligence and AI in Games, 2*(2), 69–81. doi:10.1109/TCIAIG.2010.2046486

Jones, E. E., & Davis, K. E. (1965). From acts to dispositions; The attribution process in person perception. In L. Berkowitz (Ed.), Advances in experimental social psychology (Vol. 2, pp. 219–266). Academic Press. doi:10.1016/S0065-2601(08)60107-0

Jones, L., & Estes, Z. (2005). Metaphor comprehension as attributive categorization. *Journal of Memory and Language, 53*(1), 110–124. doi:10.1016/j.jml.2005.01.016

Jones, L., & Estes, Z. (2006). Roosters, robins, and alarm clocks: Aptness and conventionality in metaphor comprehension. *Journal of Memory and Language, 55*(1), 18–32. doi:10.1016/j.jml.2006.02.004

Joyce, J. (1922). *Ulysses.* Paris: Sylvia Beach.

Joyce, J. (1939). *Finnegans wake.* London: Faber and Faber.

Jurisica, I., Mylopoulos, J., & Yu, E. (1999). Using ontologies for knowledge management: An information systems perspective. In *Proceedings of Annual Conference of the American Society for Information Science* (pp. 380-401). Washington, DC: American Society for Information Science.

Kafka, F. (2009a). *The trial* (M. Michell, Trans.). Oxford, UK: Oxford University Press. (Original work published 1925)

Kafka, F. (2009b). *The castle* (A. Bell, Trans.). Oxford, UK: Oxford University Press. (Original work published 1926)

Kakas, A. C., Kowalski, R. A., & Toni, F. (1992). Abductive logic programming. *Journal of Logic and Computation*, *2*(6), 719–770. doi:10.1093/logcom/2.6.719

Kamada, M., & Ogata, T. (2013a). Analysis and imitation of the Japanese letter notation in narrative texts. In *Proceeding of the 27th Annual Conference of the Japanese Society for Artificial Intelligence* (2I4-5in). Tokyo: Japanese Society for Artificial Intelligence.

Kamada, M., & Ogata, T. (2013b). Monogatari seisei system ni okeru bun seisei kikō to moji hyōki kikō [The sentence generation and character representation mechanisms in a narrative generation system]. In *Proceedings of the 19th Annual Conference of the Association of Natural Language Processing* (pp. 698-701). Tokyo: Association of Natural Language Processing.

Kamikakete Sango taisetsu. (1825). [*Kabuki*]. Tsuruya Namboku IV (Scenario). Edo, Japan: Nakamura-za (First performance).

Kamozaki, M., Ohno, Y., & Thawonmas, R. (2008). Casting method considering emotions towards actions in a story generation system. *Journal of Digital Games Research*, *2*(1), 36–41.

Kanadehon chūshingura. (1748). [The treasury of loyal retainers] [*Ningyō jōruri*]. Namiki Sōsuke, Takeda Izumo II, Miyoshi Shōraku (Scenario). Ōsaka, Japan: Takemoto-za (First performance).

Kanai, A. (2001a). The story as a constraint on film. In *Proceedings of the Third International Conference on Cognitive Science* (pp. 503-506). Beijing, China: Academic Press.

Kanai, A. (2002). Film rhetoric and cognition. In *Proceedings of 17th Congress of the International Association of Empirical Aesthetics* (pp. 209-212). Takarazuka, Japan: Academic Press.

Kanai, A. (2003). Non-story type film rhetoric and cognitive effects. In *Proceedings of the Fourth International Conference on Cognitive Science* (pp. 259-264). Sydney, Australia: Academic Press.

Kanai, A. (2006). Reality of unfamiliar situations on moving image. In *Proceedings of 19th Congress of the International Association of Empirical Aesthetics* (pp. 800-803). Avignon, France: Academic Press.

Kanai, A. (2016). Non-story, nostalgia, and film cognition: Nostalgia-based narrative rhetoric composition. In T. Ogata & T. Akimoto (Eds.), Computational and cognitive approaches to narratology (pp. 385-399). Hershey, PA: Information Science Reference (IGI Global).

Kanai, A., & Ogata, T. (2004a). Aspect of non-story processing and film rhetoric composition in the narrative generation mechanism. In *Proceedings of The Ninth International Symposium on Artificial Life And Robotics (AROB 9th '04)* (pp.162-165). Beppu, Japan: Academic Press.

Kanai, A., & Ogata, T. (2004a). Aspect of non-story processing and film rhetoric composition in the narrative generation mechanism. In *Proceedings of The Ninth International Symposium on Artificial Life and Robotics* (*Vol. 1*, pp. 162–165). Academic Press.

Kanai, A., & Ogata, T. (2004b). Non-story processing on the film rhetoric composition system. In *Proceedings of 18th Congress of the International Association of Empirical Aesthetics* (pp. 433–436). Academic Press.

Kanai, A., & Ogata, T. (2004b). Non-story processing on the film rhetoric composition system. In *Proceedings of 18th Congress of the International Association of Empirical Aesthetics* (pp. 433-436). Lisbon, Portugal: Academic Press.

Kanai, A., Ogata, T., & Shinohara, K. (2002). Film rhetoric generation system for intensive cognitive effects. In *Proceedings of 2002 IEEE International Conference on Systems, Man and Cybernetics*. Hammamet, Tunisia: IEEE.

Kanai, A., Ogata, T., & Shinohara, K. (2002). Film rhetoric generation system for intensive cognitive system. In *Proceedings of IEEE International Conference on Systems, Man and Cybernetics (CD-ROM)*. The Institute of Electrical and Electronics Engineers.

Kanai, A. (2001b). Cognitive process model toward the rhetoric of the film. *Cognitive Studies*, *8*(2), 139–150.

Kanai, A. (2008). Eizo hensyu no ninchi kagaku [Cognitive science of film editing]. In A. Kanai & Y. Niwa (Eds.), *Eizo hensyu no riron to jissen* [Theory and practice of film editing] (pp. 13–38). Tokyo: Housei University Press.

Kanai, A. (2013). Eizō kankyō no monogatari to setsudan niyoru kihan riron: "Wakarinikusa" no ninchi wo megutte [Narratives of image environments and a critic theory by cutting: About the cognition of "incomprehensiveness"]. In *Media kankyō no monogatari to kōkyōken* [Narratives in media environments and public sphere] (pp. 193–229). Tokyo: Hōsei Daigaku Shuppankyoku.

Kanai, A. (2016). Non-story, nostalgia, and film cognition: Nostalgia-based narrative rhetoric composition. In T. Ogata & T. Akimoto (Eds.), *Computational and Cognitive Approaches to Narratology* (pp. 376–390). IGI Global. doi:10.4018/978-1-5225-0432-0.ch015

Kanai, A., & Kato, Y. (2001). Effect of advertising rhetoric on viewer's cognitive Process. *Journal of Advertising Science*, *42*, 87–100.

Kanai, A., & Kodama, K. (2010). Film Edit Design: Story and Irrational Cutting. *Cognitive Science*, *17*(3), 444–458.

Kanai, A., & Kodama, K. (2010). Film edit design: Story and irrational cutting. *Cognitive Studies*, *17*(3), 444–458.

Kanai, A., & Morohoshi, C. (2005). NS-narrative and film rhetoric composition system. In *Proceedings of Ninth International Conference on Information Visualisation* (pp.926-927). London: Academic Press. doi:10.1109/IV.2005.91

Kanai, A., & Niwa, Y. (2008). *Eizō henshū no riron to jissen* [Theories and practices of image editing]. Tokyo: Hōsei Daigaku Shuppankyoku.

Kanai, A., & Ogata, T. (2004). Aspect of non-story processing and film rhetoric composition in the narrative generation mechanism. In *Proceedings of the 9th International Symposium on Artificial Life and Robotics* (vol. 1, pp. 162-165). Oita: International Society of Artificial Life and Robotics.

Kanai, A., Ogata, T., & Shinohara, K. (2003). Identidal and different elements in film rhetoric generation. *Transactions of the Japanese Artificial Intelligence Soceity*, *18*(2G), 114–121. doi:10.1527/tjsai.18.114

Kanai, T., Takai, S., & Nakanisi, M. (2009). *Katari to katari no aida: Rashōmon teki genjitsu to ningen no responsibility (taiō, koō, sekinin)* [Between narration and deceiving: Rashomon-like reality and human responsibility (correnspondence, response, and responsibility)]. Kyōto, Japan: Nakanishiyashoten.

Kanjinchō. (1840). [The subscription list] [*Kabuki*]. Namiki Gohei III (Scenario). Edo, Japan: Kawarasaki-za (First performance).

Kanjinchō. (n.d.). Retrieved from the Japanese Wikipedia: https://ja.wikipedia.org/wiki/%E5%8B%A7%E9%80%B2%E5%B8%B3

Kan, S. (2010). *Rekishi no tetsugaku - Monogatari wo koete* [The philosophy of history: Beyond narratives]. Tokyo: Keisōshobō.

Karatani, K. (1993). *Origins of modern Japanese literature*. Durham, UK: Duke University Press. (Original work published 1980)

Katahira, H. (2006). Shohisha kodo moderu ha AIDMA kara AIDEES no jidai e [Consumer behavior model is changing from AIDMA to AIDEES]. *Nikkei BP LAP*, (18).

Kato, K., & Fujino, H. (2015). A narrative analysis of a university student from the table talk role-playing game circle: From the viewpoint of communication support. *Bulletin of Tokyo Gakugei University. Education in Science*, *66*(2), 333–339.

Katz, A. (1989). On choosing the vehicles of metaphors: Referential concreteness, semantic distances, and individual differences. *Journal of Memory and Language*, *28*(4), 486–499. doi:10.1016/0749-596X(89)90023-5

Kawabata, Y. (1948). Yukiguni. Tokyo: Sōgensha.

Kawabata, Y. (1955). Mizuumi. Tokyo: Shinchōsha.

Kawabata, Y. (1961). Nemureru bijo. Tokyo: Shinchōsha.

Kawamura, Y. (2016). An attempt of the commercial film production support system based on the image rhetoric of commercial film. In T. Ogata & T. Akimoto (Eds.), Computational and cognitive approaches to narratology (pp. 117-139). Hershey, PA: Information Science Reference (IGI Global). doi:10.4018/978-1-5225-0432-0.ch004

Kawamura, Y., & Ogata, T. (2000c). Kasō geinōjin character no jinsei [Lives of virtual characters]. In Y. kawaramu, S. Hamada & T. Ogata (Eds.). Literature and Cognition/Computer 6: Language and literature. Japanese Cognitive Science Society Technical Report (00-No. 32).

Kawamura, Y., & Ogata, T. (2002). A trial on narrative interpretation of *geinō* information system. In *Proceedings of IEEE, International Conference on Systems, Man and Cybernetics (CD-ROM)*. The Institute of Electrical and Electronics Engineers. doi:10.1109/ICSMC.2002.1175727

Kawamura, Y., Kato, T., Tachibana, K., Okai, G., & Kinoshita, S. (2014). Kokoku kyanpen no jirei ruikei no kokoromi: Junkangata shohisha kodo moderu iDEACCycle no kanten kara [An attempt of case categorization of advertising campaigns: From the view point of cyclical consumer behavior model iDEACCycle]. *Bulletin of Nikkei Advertising Research Institute*, (273), 10-16.

Kawamura, Y. (2013). Junkangata shohisha kodo moderu iDEACCycle no teian: Shohisha nikki chosa/ intavu chosa wo motoni [A proposal of cyclical consumer behavior model iDEACCycle: Based on consumer dairy survey and interview survey]. *Japan Marketing Journal*, *33*(2), 95–109.

Kawamura, Y., & Ogata, T. (2000a). *Geinō* soshiki model to image senryaku [A *geinō* organization model and the image strategies]. *Journal of Ōsaka University of Economics and Law*, *23*(2), 130–164.

Kawamura, Y., & Ogata, T. (2000a). *Geinōjin* image marketing system no tameno *geinōjin* homepage no bunseki [An analysis of *geinōjins*' homepages for a *geinōjin* image marketing system]. *Journal of Advertising Science*, *40*, 181–192.

Kawamura, Y., & Ogata, T. (2000b). A conceptual framework on *geinō* organization model for artificial *geinō* performers with lives. In *Proceedings of the 5th International Symposium on Artificial Life and Robotics* (pp. 793-796). Ōita, Japan: International Society of Artificial Life and Robotics.

Kawamura, Y., Ogata, T., & Kanai, A. (in press). Monogatari no wakugumi. [The framework of narrative] In T. Ogata, Y. Kawamura, & A. Kanai (Eds.), *Jōhō monogatariron - Jinkō chinō, ninchi, shakai katei to monogatari seisei* [Informational narratology: Artificial intelligence/cognition/social process and narrative generation]. Tokyo: Hakutōshobō.

Kawatake, T. (1992). *Kabuki: Its beauty and tradition* (C. Holmes, Trans.). Tokyo: Japan Arts Council.

Kawatake, T. (2003). *Kabuki: Baroque fusion of the arts*. Tokyo: The International House of Japan.

Kelley, H. H. (1967). Attribution theory in social psychology. In D. Levine (Ed.), Nebraska symposium on motivation (pp. 192-238). Lincoln, NE: University of Nebraska Press.

Kibakazari chūshingura. (1840). [Horse ornament Chūshingura] [*Kabuki*]. Namiki Gohei III (Ed.). Edo, Japan: Kawarasaki-za.

Kihara, Y. (2017). *Jikkensuru shousetsu tachi - Monogataru toha betssu no shikata de* [Experimental fiction: Otherwise than narrating]. Tokyo: Sairyūsha.

Kimishima, S. (2011). *Nihonshu kanzen guide* [Perfect sake guide]. Ikeda.

Kimura, H. (2008). Shohisha kobai purosesu wo donyu sita shinseihin fukyu moderu ni kansuru ichi kosatsu [A Study on new product diffusion model introduced the consumer purchasing process]. *Japan Marketing Journal*, *24*(3), 60–74.

Kingma, D. P., & Welling, M. (2014). *Auto-encoding variational Bayes*. arXiv:1312.6114

Kintsch, W. (2000). Metaphor comprehension: A computational theory. *Psychonomic Bulletin & Review*, *7*(2), 257–266. doi:10.3758/BF03212981 PMID:10909133

Kinyon, A. (2001). A language-independent shallow-parser compiler. In *Proceedings of the 39th ACL Annual Meeting (European Chapter)* (pp.322-329). Association for Computational Linguistics.

Kitamura, E. S. (2011). *Literature analysis with rough set derived lattice* (Unpublished doctoral dissertation). Kobe University, Kobe, Japan.

Kitamura, E. S., & Gunji, Y. P. (2010a). Evolving lattices for analyzing behavioral dynamics of characters in literary text. In *The 4th International Conference on the Foundations of Information Science*. tripleC-Cognition, Communication, Co-operation. Retrieved from http://triple-c.at/index.php/tripleC

Kitamura, E. S., & Gunji, Y. P. (2010b). Figure-ground analysis of characters in literary text. In *The 27th Annual Meeting of the Japanese Cognitive Science Society*. Nagoya, Japan: JCSS. Retrieved from http://www.jcss.gr.jp/meetings/jcss2010/proceedings.html

Kitamura, E. S., & Gunji, Y. P. (2012a). Figure-ground symmetry analysis of characters in literature. Symmetry: Culture and Science, 23(1), 67-96.

Kitamura, E. S. (2017). Time flow in character figure-ground relations in literary text--towards story generation. In *Proceedings of the Symposium on Reversible Time, Retardation and Anticipation in Quantum Physics, Biology and Cybernetics held as part of the 29th International Conference on System Research, Informatics & Cybernetics* (vol. 1, pp. 97-102). Tecumseh, Canada: The International Institute for Advanced Studies.

Kitamura, E. S., & Gunji, Y. P. (2011). Expressing implicit figure-ground character information from explicit literary text information. In *2011 IEEE/SICE International Symposium on System Integration (SII)* (pp. 946-950). Piscataway, NJ: IEEE Publication. doi:10.1109/SII.2011.6147576

Kitamura, E. S., & Gunji, Y. P. (2012b). Figure-ground characteristic of detective mystery The Murders in the Rue Morgue by Edgar Allan Poe. *International Journal of Advancements in Computing Technology*, *4*(22), 291–299. doi:10.4156/ijact.vol4.issue22.32

Kitamura, E. S., & Gunji, Y. P. (2014). Model of figure-ground cognition in literary text. *International Journal of Computing Anticipatory Systems*, *29*, 17–28.

Kobayashi, F., & Ogata, T. (2004). Narrative and music as variation: Transformation of musical structure based on narrative discourse theory. In *Proceedings of the 9th International Symposium on Artificial Life and Robotics* (Vol. 1, pp. 170-173). Ōita, Japan: International Society of Artificial Life and Robotics.

Koffka, K. (1935). *Principles of gestalt psychology*. London, UK: Routledge & Kegan Paul.

Kojiki. (1958). In *Nihon koten bungaku taikei 1* [Japanese classic literature collection 1]. Tokyo: Iwanamishoten.

Kristeva, J. (1980). *Desire in language: A semiotic approach to literature and art*. Columbia University Press. (Original work published 1969)

Kubo, M., & Abe, A. (2014). Critical points in conversations from the perspective of chance discovery. In *Proc. of KES2014* (pp. 969-978). Academic Press. doi:10.1016/j.procs.2014.08.178

Kudo, T. (2013). MeCab: Yet another part-of-speech and morphological analyzer (Version 0.996) [Software]. Available from http://taku910.github.io/mecab/

Kudo, A., Okada, T., & Chen, D. (2015). Writing style and revision of a novelist examined through real-time creative process data. *Cognitive Studies*, *22*(4), 573–590.

Kumagai, S., Funakoshi, S., Akimoto, T., & Ogata, T. (2012). Development of a language dictionary and a simple narrative sentence generation mechanism. In *Proceedings of the 26th Annual Conference of the Japanese Society for Artificial Intelligence* (1N1-OS-1a-3). Tokyo: Japanese Society for Artificial Intelligence.

Kumagai, T., Ogata, T., & Oikawa, H. (2010). The construction of a story based on characters' cognitions: The consideration of an aspect of narrative generation based on an analysis of novels. In *Proceedings of the 17th Annual Conference of the Japanese Society for Artificial Intelligence* (1I2-OS1b-4). Tokyo: Japanese Society for Artificial Intelligence.

Kurosawa, A. (Director), & Minoura, J. (Producer) (1950). *Rashōmon* [Motion picture]. Japan: Daiei.

Kybartas, B., & Bidarra, R. (2016). A survey on story generation techniques for authoring computational narratives. *IEEE Transactions on Computational Intelligence and AI in Games*, *9*(3), 39–253. doi:10.1109/TCIAIG.2016.2546063

Kyōganoko musume Dōjōji. (1753). [The dapple-patterned maiden at the Dōjōji temple] [*Kabuki* dance]. Fujimoto Tobun (Lyrics). Edo, Japan: Nakamura-za, (First performance).

Kyokutei Bakin. (2003-2004). *Nansō satomi hakkenden* [The eight dog chronicles] (Vols. 1-12). Tokyo: Shinchōsha. (Original work published 1814-1842)

Labov, W. (1972). *Language in the inner city: Studies in the Black English vernacular*. Philadelphia, PA: University of Pennsylvania Press.

Laird, J. E. (2012). *The Soar cognitive architecture*. Cambdidge, MA: The MIT Press.

Lakoff, G., & Johnson, M. (1980). *Metaphors We Live By*. The University of Chicago Press.

Lakoff, G., & Johnson, M. (1999). *Philosophy in the Flesh: The Embodied Mind and Its Challenge to Western Thought*. Basic Books.

Lakoff, G., & Núñez, R. (2000). *Where mathematics come from: How the embodied mind brings mathematics into being*. Basic Books.

Lang, R. R. (1999). A declarative model for simple narratives. In *Narrative Intelligence: Papers from the 1999 AAAI Fall Symposium* (Technical Report FS-99-01, pp. 134-141). North Falmouth, MA: AAAI.

Lang, R. R. (1999). A declarative model for simple narratives. In *Narrative intelligence: Papers from the 1999 AAAI fall symposium, Technical Report* (FS-99-01; pp. 134-141). Palo Alto, CA: Association for the Advancement of Artificial Intelligence.

Langxuan, Y. (2015). *The construction and evaluation of a design framework for narrative games for health* (Doctoral dissertation). Computer Science Program, Northeastern University, Boston, MA.

Lascarides, A., & Oberlander, J. (1992). Abducing temporal discourse. In *Proc. of 6th. Int'l Workshop on Natural Language Generation (LNAI-587)* (pp. 167-182). Academic Press.

Lazarsfeld, P. F., Berelson, B., & Gaudet, H. (1948). *The People's choice*. New York: Columbia University Press.

Lebowitz, M. (1985). Story-telling as planning and learning. *Poetics*, *14*(6), 483–502. doi:10.1016/0304-422X(85)90015-4

Lee, G. M. K. (2012). *Automated story-based commentary for sports* (Doctoral dissertation). Department of Computing Science, University of Alberta, Edmonton, Canada.

Leech, G. N. (1969). *A linguistic guide to English poetry*. London, UK: Longman.

Leiter, S. L. (2014). *Historical dictionary of Japanese traditional theatre (2nd ed.)*. Lanham, MD: Rowman & Littlefield.

Lem, S. (1984). *Imaginary Magnitude*. Orland, FL: Harcourt Brace Jevanovich. (Original work published 1973)

León, C. (2016). An architecture of narrative memory. *Biologically Inspired Cognitive Architectures*, *16*, 19–33. doi:10.1016/j.bica.2016.04.002

Lester, R. K., & Piore, M. (2004). *Innovation: the missing dimension*. Brighton, MA: Harvard Business School Press.

Lévi-Strauss, C. (1964). *Mythologiques 1: Le cru et le cuit*. Paris: PLON.

Li, B., & Riedl, M. O. (2015). Scheherazade: Crowd-powered interactive narrative generation. In *Proceedings of the 29th AAAI Conference on Artificial Intelligence* (pp. 4305-4306). Palo Alto, CA: Association for the Advancement of Artificial Intelligence.

Li, H., Zhu, K. Q., & Wang, H. (2013). Data-driven metaphor recognition and explanation. *Transactions of the Association for Computational Linguistics*, *1*, 379–390.

Loss, L., Bebis, G., Nicolescu, M., & Skurikhin, A. (2009). An iterative multi-scale tensor voting scheme for perceptual grouping of natural shapes in cluttered backgrounds. *Computer Vision and Image Understanding*, *113*(1), 126–149. doi:10.1016/j.cviu.2008.07.011

Lu, R., & Zhang, S. (2002). *Automatic generation of computer animation: Using AI for movie animation*. Berlin: Springer. doi:10.1007/3-540-45590-6

Lyotard, J-F. (1979). *La condition post moderne*. Paris: Les edition de Minuit.

Macklovitch, E., & Marie-Louise, H. (1996). Line 'em up: Advances in alignment technology and their impact on translation support tools. In *Proceedings of the 1996 AMTA* (pp. 145-156). The Association for Machine Translation in the Americas.

Mann, T. (1998). *Buddenbrooks* (H. T. L. Porter, Trans.). Vintage Books. (Original work published 1901)

Mann, T. (1999). *Doctor Faustus: The life of the German composer Adrian Leverkuhn as told by friend* (J. E. Woods, Trans.). Vintage Books. (Original work published 1947)

Marcus, S. (1970). *Poetica matematica* [Mathematical poetics, in Romanian]. Bucuresti, Romania: Editura Academiei R.S.R.

Martin, L. J., Ammanabrolu, P., Hancock, W., Singh, S., Harrison, B., & Riedl, M. O. (2017). Event representations for automated story generation with deep neural nets. In *Proceedings of KDD 2017 Workshop on Machine Learning for Creativity*. Retrieved from http://ml4creativity.mybluemix.net/papers/MartinEtAl-Event_Representations_for_Automated_Story-camera_ready.pdf

Matsunaga, K., & Yasuda, T. (1996). Experimental study of the new type of accelerator bar and brake pedal. In *The Japanese Association of Traffic Psychology 53rd Conference* (vol. 53, pp. 11-14). Tokyo: JATP.

Matsunaga, K., Hayashi, M., Sumida, Y., Nishimura, H., & Koshi, K. (2011). An experimental report to elucidate the mechanism for the occurrence of stepping-on the wrong pedal. In *Society of Automotive Engineers of Japan 2011 Spring Conference*. Tokyo: SAEJ.

Matsunaga, S. (2015). Narachibu wo bunkaisuru: Bideo gemu no naratoroji [Dissecting a narrative: A narratology for video games]. *Workshop of "Analytic Philosophy and Art", "Narrative of Game / Narrative of Music"*.

Matsuzaki, H. (2000). *Nihonshu guide book* [Sake guide book]. Shibata.

Mayama, S. (1982). *Genroku Chūshingura (1, 2)*. Tokyo: Iwanamishoten. (Original work published 1934-1941).

McCarthy, J., & Hayes, P. J. (1969). Some philosophical problems from the standpoint of artificial intelligence. In B. L. Webber & N. J. Nillson (Eds.), *Readings in artificial intelligence, 4* (pp. 431–450). Los Altos, CA: Morgan Kaufmann Publishers.

McIntyre, N., & Lapata, M. (2009). Learning to tell tales: A data-driven approach to story generation. In *Proceedings of Joint Conference of the 47th Annual Meeting of the Association for Computational Linguistics and the 4th International Joint Conference on Natural Language Processing of the Asian Federation of Natural Language Processing* (pp. 217-225). Suntec, Singapore: Academic Press. doi:10.3115/1687878.1687910

McRoy, S. W., & Hirst, G. (1993). Abductive explanation of dialogue misunderstandings. In *Proc. of EACL93* (pp. 277-286). Academic Press.

McRoy, S. W., & Hirst, G. (1995). The repair of speech act misunderstandings by abductive inference. *Computational Linguistics, 21*(4), 435–478.

Meehan, J. (1981). TAIL-SPIN. In R. Schank & K. Riesbeck (Eds.), *Inside computer understanding: Five programs plus miniatures* (pp. 197–226). Mahwah, NJ: Psychology Press.

Meehan, J. R. (1980). *The metanovel: Writing stories by computer*. Garland Publishing.

Meyerhold, V., Isahaya, Y., Iwate, T., & Ura, M. et al.. (2001). *Meyehold best selection* [Vsevolod Meyerhold Selected Writings]. Tokyo: Sakuhinsha.

Meyer, L. B. (1956). *Emotion and meaning in music*. Chicago, IL: Chicago UP.

Mihalcea, R., & Simard, M. (2005). Parallel texts. *Natural Language Engineering, 11*(3), 239–246. doi:10.1017/S1351324905003827

Mihnea, T. (1977). Combinatorics and dynamics of characters in drama. *Poetics*, *6*(3-4), 229–254. doi:10.1016/0304-422X(77)90007-9

Mikolov, T., & Yih, W., & Zweig, G. (2013). *Linguistic regularities in continuous space-word representations.* Paper presented at the 2013 Conference of the North American Chapter of the Association for Computational Linguistics: Human Language Technologies.

Mikolov, T., Sutskever, I., Chen, K., Corrado, G. S., & Dean, J. (2013). Distributed representations of words and phrases and their compositionality. In C. J. C. Burges, L. Bottou, M. Welling, Z. Ghahramani, & K. Weinberger (Eds.), Advances in neural information processing systems (Vol. 26, pp. 3111–3119). Curran Associates, Inc.

Ministry of Education, Culture, Sports, Science, and Technology. (2017). Heisei 29 nendo gakkou kihon chyosa(sokuhochi) no kohyo nituite. Tokyo: Ministry of Education, Culture, Sports, Science and Technology.

Mishima, Y. (1949). Kamen no kokuhaku. Tokyo: Kawadeshobō.

Mishima, Y. (1950). Ai no kawaki. Tokyo: Shinchōsha.

Mishima, Y. (1951, 1953). Kinjiki. Tokyo: Shinchōsha.

Mishima, Y. (1953). Manatsu no shi [Death in midsummer]. In Manatsu no shi [Death in midsummer]. Tokyo: Sōgensha.

Mishima, Y. (1954). Iwashiuri koi no hikiami [The sardine seller's net of love]. *Engekikai*, 11.

Mishima, Y. (1954). Shiosai. Tokyo: Shinchōsha.

Mishima, Y. (1956). Aoi no ue. In Kindai nōgaku shū. Tokyo: Shinchōsha.

Mishima, Y. (1956). Kindai nōgaku shū. Tokyo: Shinchōsha.

Mishima, Y. (1956). Kinkakuji. Tokyo: Shinchōsha.

Mishima, Y. (1956). Rokumeikan. Tokyo: Tokyo Sōgensha.

Mishima, Y. (1958). Hashi-zukushi. In Hashi-zukushi. Tokyo: Bungeishunjūsha.

Mishima, Y. (1960). Utage no ato. Tokyo: Shinchosha.

Mishima, Y. (1965). Mikumano mōde. In Mikumano mōde. Tokyo: Shinchōsha.

Mishima, Y. (1965). Sado kōshaku fujin. Tokyo: Kawadeshobō-shinsha.

Mishima, Y. (1968). Taiyō to tetsu. Tokyo: Kōdansha.

Mishima, Y. (1969). Haru no yuki. Tokyo: Shinchōsha.

Mishima, Y. (1969). Honba. Tokyo: Shinchōsha.

Mishima, Y. (1969-1971). *Hōjō no umi* [The sea of fertility]. Tokyo: Shinchōsha.

Mishima, Y. (1970). Akatsuki no tera. Tokyo: Shinchōsha.

Mishima, Y. (1970). Hatashi-eteinai yakusoku - Watasi no naka no 25 nen [A promise that has not played: 25 years in me]. *Sankei Shimbun* (Evening edition).

Mishima, Y. (1971). Tennin gosui. Tokyo: Shinchōsha.

Mishima, Y. (1991). Shibai nikki [Plays diary]. Tokyo: Chūōkōronsha. (Original work written 1942-1947)

Mishima, Y. (2000-2006). *Ketteiban Mishima Yukio Zenshū* [Complete Mishima Yukio Collection]. Tokyo: Shinchōsha.

Mishima, Y. (2003). Chikamatsu Hanji [On Chikamatsu Hanji]. In Mishima Yukio Zenshū 26 [Mishima Yukio Collection 26] (pp. 392-396). Tokyo: Shinchōsha. (Original work written 1943)

Mishima, Y. (1944). *Hanazakari no mori* [Forest in full bloom]. Tokyo: Shichijōshoten.

Mishima, Y. (1951). *Natsuko no bōken* [An adventure of Natsuko]. Tokyo: Asahi-Shimbunsha.

Mishima, Y. (1955). *Kōfukugō shuppan* [Kōfukugō sails]. Tokyo: Shinchōsha.

Mishima, Y. (1955). *Shizumeru taki* [A sinking waterfall]. Tokyo: Chūōkōronsha.

Mishima, Y. (1959). *Kyōko no ie* [Kyōko's house]. Tokyo: Shinchōsha.

Mishima, Y. (1962). *Utsukushii hoshi* [A beautiful star]. Tokyo: Shinchosha.

Mishima, Y. (1969). *Bunka bōei ron* [Discussion on the defence of culture]. Tokyo: Shinchōsha.

Mishima, Y. (1969). *Chinsetsu yumiharizuki* [A wonder tale: The moonbow]. Tokyo: Chūōkōronsha.

Mishima, Y. (1969). *Raiō no terrace* [The terrace of the leper king]. Tokyo: Chūōkōronsha.

Mishima, Y. (1969). *Tōron Mishima Yukio vs. Zenkyōtō - <Bi to Kyōdōtai to Tōdai Tōsō* [Discussions Mishima Yukio vs. Zenkyōtō: Beauty and community and Tokyo university dispute]. Tokyo: Shinchōsha.

Mishsima, Y. (1963). Gogo no eikō. Tokyo: Kōdansha.

Mita, M. (1965). *Gendainihon no seishinkouzou* [Mental structure of Japan]. Tokyo, Japan: Koubundo.

Miura, H. (2000). Naimaze [To blend]. In *Shinpan - Kabuki jiten* [New version: Encyclopedia of kabuki] (p. 310). Tokyo: Heibonsha.

Miyoshi, T. (1993). Mienai fukushū [Revenge invisible]. In *Mienai fukushū* [Revenge invisible]. Tokyo: Kōdansha.

Mizuhara, S. (Ed.). (2005). *Shinso-ban - Haiku sho saijiki* [Remodeled version: Handy glossary of seasonal words for haiku]. Tokyo, Japan: Ohizumi-shoten.

Mizutani, S. (1979a). Haiku-wo tsukuru keisanki [A computer program for generating haikus]. *Tokyo Joshi Daigaku Ronshu, 52,* 85-97. Retrieved from http://opac.library.twcu.ac.jp/opac/repository/1/4744/

Mizutani, S. (1979b). Futatabi haiku-wo tsukuru keisanki [One more a computer program for generating haikus]. *Tokyo Joshi Daigaku Ronshu, 63*, 106-103. Retrieved from http://opac.library.twcu.ac.jp/opac/repository/1/4833/

Montfort, N. (2007). *Generating narrative variation in interactive fiction* (Doctoral dissertation). Available from ProQuest. (AAI3271851)

Montfort, N. (2007). *Generating narrative variation in interactive fiction* (Doctoral dissertation). University of Pennsylvania, Philadelphia, PA.

Morgan, A. (2000). *What is narrative therapy?* Adelaire, Australia: Dulwich Center Publication.

Morioka, M. (2002). *Monogatari toshiteno mensetsu - Mimesis to jiko no hen'yō* [An interview as a narrative: Mimesis and self transformation]. Tokyo: Shin'yōsha.

Morioka, S., Hasegawa, S., & Yamakawa, S. (2006). AISAS moderu ni miru kuchikomi no keisei katei ni okeru puranningu saho no teian [A proposal of planning manners on the formation process of word-of-mouth based on AISAS model]. *Japan Marketing Journal*, *26*(1), 29–39.

Mori, Y., & Ogata, T. (2005). Hyper-comic no kōsō to hyper-link oyobi koma gōsei no jidōka [A plan of hyper-comic and the automatization of hyper-link and frame composition]. In *Proceedings of 19th Special Interest Group on Language Sense Processing Engineering in Japanese Society of Artificial Intelligence* (pp. 1–11). Tokyo: Japanese Society of Artificial Intelligence.

Mueller, E. T. (1990). *Daydreaming in humans and machines*. Ablex.

Mukařovský, J. (1970). Standard language and poetic language. In D. C. Freeman (Ed.), *Linguistics and literary style* (P. L. Garvin, Trans.; pp. 40–57). New York, NY: Holt, Rinehart and Winston.

Mukouyama, K., Shinohara, K., Kanai, A., & Ogata, T. (2002). Rhetorical analysis and automatic editing of the film. In *Proceedings of 17th Congress of the International Association of Empirical Aesthetics* (pp. 571-574). Academic Press.

Mukouyama, K., Shinohara, K., Kanai, A., & Ogata, T. (2002). Rhetorical analysis and automatic editing of the film. In *Proceedings of 17th Congress of the International Association of Empirical Aesthetics* (pp. 571-574). Rome, Italy: University of Rome Tre.

Mukouyama, K., Kanai, A., & Ogata, T. (2001). An analysis of the rhetoric of the film and an attempt to an editing system. In *Proceeding of the 15th Annual Conference of the Japanese Society for Artificial Intelligence* (1F1-11). Tokyo: Japanese Society of Artificial Intelligence.

Mukouyama, K., & Ogata, T. (1999). Transformation of time-order in narrative: A consideration based on movie films. In *Proceeding of the 13th Annual Conference of the Japanese Society for Artificial Intelligence* (pp. 492-493). Tokyo: Japanese Society of Artificial Intelligence.

Mukouyama, K., & Ogata, T. (2001). Monogatari eizō ni yoru ukete no ninchiteki kōka no bunseki [An analysis of cognitive effects of receivers using narrative moving image]. In *Proceedings of the 13th Annual Conference of the Japan Simulation & Gaming Association* (pp. 5-10). Tokyo: Japan Simulation & Gaming Association.

Munakata, S. (2014). *Why is the use of the "brake that cannot be mistaken for an accelerator" not spreading?* Nikkei Business Online.

Munday, J. (2009). *Introducing translation studies*. Abingdon, UK: Taylor & Francis Group.

Murai, H. (2014). Plot analysis for describing punch line functions in Shinichi Hoshi's microfiction. In *Proceedings of the 5th Workshop on Computational Models of Narrative (CMN'14)* (121-129). Dagstuhl, Germany: Schloss Dagstuhl--Leibniz-Zentrum fuer Informatik.

Murakami, H. (1985). Sekai no owari to hard boiled wonderland. Tokyo: Shinchōsha.

Murakami, H. (1994-1995). Nejimakidori chronicle. Tokyo: Shinchōsha.

Murakami, R. (1980). Coin locker babies. Tokyo: Kōdansha.

Murakami, R. (1997). In the miso soup. Tokyo: Yomiuri Shimbunsha.

Murakoshi, Y. (1998). Fukuzatsuka sareta nihongo no moji hyōki - Moji bunkaron [Complicated Japanese character representation: Study on the culture of characters]. *Atomi. English Studies*, *12*, 11–35.

Murasaki Shikibu (1993-1997). *Genji monogatari (1-5)*. Tokyo: Iwanamishoten.

Murasaki Shikibu. (1993-1997). Genji monogatari (1-5). Tokyo: Iwanamishoten.

Musil, R. (2017). *The man without qualities* (S. Wilkins, Trans.). Picador. (Original work publishued 1930, 1932)

Muto, T. (2016). Attitude of "surprise" in the Noh theory of Zeami. *International Cultural Studies, 22*, 59–72.

Nagaoka, C., & Ogata, T. (1999a). A method of computer game with NPCs that dynamically change. In *Proc. of the 13th Annual Conference of the Japan Society of Artificial Intelligence*, (pp. 165-166). Academic Press.

Nagaoka, C., & Ogata, T. (1999b). About a method of computer game based on autonomous NPC. In *Proc. of the 11th conference of Japan Association of Simulation & Gaming* (pp. 80-83). Academic Press.

Nakagami, K. (1977). Karekinada [The sea of withered trees]. Tokyo: Kawadeshobō-shinsha.

Nakagami, K. (1982). Sen'nen no yuraku [A thousand years of pleasure]. Tokyo: Kawadeshobō-shinsha.

Nakagawa, D. (2016). *Gendai game zenshi: Bunmei no yuugi shi kan kara* [Complete history of modern games: From a view of play history in a civilization]. Tokyo: Hayakawa Publishing.

Natsume, S. (1905-1907). Wagahai ha neko dearu. Tokyo: Ōkurashoten & Hattorishoten.

Natsume, S. (1908). Kōfu. Asahi-shimbun.

Natsume, S. (1908). Sanshirō. Asahi-shimbun.

Natsume, S. (1916). *Meian*. Asahi-shimbun.

Natsume, S. (1906). Kusamakura. *Shinshōsetsu*, 6.

Natsume, S. (1907). *Bungaku ron* [A theory of literature]. Tokyo: Ōkurashoten, Hattorishoten.

Natsume, S. (1907). *Gubijinsō* [Field poppy]. Asahi-shimbun.

Newell, A., & Simon, H. A. (1972). *Human problem solving*. Prentice Hall.

NHK Science & Technology Research Laboratories. (2017). *TVML - TV program making language: TVML toha nanika?* [What's TVML?]. Retrieved October 5, 2017, 11:00, from http://www.nhk.or.jp/strl/tvml/

Nishina, S. (2001). *Kokoku koka ron: Joho shori paradaimu karano apurochi* [Advertisement effect theory: An approach from information processing paradigm]. Tokyo, Japan: Dentsu.

Nishina, S. (2011). Kokoku koka moderu no sogoka no kokoromi [An attempt of integration of advertisement effect model]. *Aoyama Journal of Business*, *46*(3), 111–124.

Nitta, Y. (1986). Idiosyncratic gap: A tough problem to machine translation. In *Proceedings of the Computational Linguistics (COLING' 86)* (pp. 107-111). The Association for Computational Linguistics. doi:10.3115/991365.991394

Nitta, Y. (2012b). HAIKU no imi no keisiki teki kaishaku no kokoromi [An essay on a formal interpretation of HAIKU]. In *Proceedings of A-13-5 Thought and Language Session, IEICE Conference at Okayama University* (p. 215). Tokyo, Japan: The Institute of Electronics, Information and Communication Engineers.

Nitta, Y. (2012c). An approach to linguistic aesthetics by functional grammar. In *Proceedings of the 22nd Biennial Congress of the International Association of Empirical AESTHETICS (IAEA) 2012 Aug* (pp. 22-25). Rome, Italy: University of Rome Tre.

Nitta, Y. (2012d). Aesthetic sentence generation by functional grammar. *Economic Review of Nihon University, 82*(3), 9-17.

Nitta, Y. (2013). Silence of beautiful sentences - The mechanism of omission in HAIKU. In *Proceedings of the IEICE Conference on Study of Thought and Language. Meiji University., International General Research Laboratory* (*Vol. 114*, No. 442, pp. 73-78). Tokyo, Japan: The Institute of Electronics, Information and Communication Engineers.

Nitta, Y. (2015). On the formal generation of Haiku. In Technical Report of IEICE (2015-3) (Vol. 114, No. 465, pp. 23-26). Tokyo, Japan: The Institute of Electronics, Information and Communication Engineers.

Nitta, Y. (2001). The utility and problem of insufficient machine translation. *Economic Review of Nihon University*, *80*(4), 1–54.

Nitta, Y. (2002). Problems of machine translation: From a viewpoint of logical semantics. *Economic Review of Nihon University*, *72*(2), 23–42.

Nitta, Y. (2012a). *Kikai hon'yaku no Genri to Katsuyoho - Kotenteki kikai hon'yaku saihyoka no kokoromi* [Principle of machine translation and its practical usage: An attempt to reassess the value of classical transfer-based machine translation]. Tokyo, Japan: Akashi-shoten.

Nobuhara, Y. (Ed.), *Jikan, jiko, monogatari* [Time, self, and narrative]. Tokyo, Japan: Shunjusha.

Noe, K. (1996). *Monogatari no tetsugaku - Yanagita Kunio to rekishi no hakken* [The philosophy of narrative: Yanagita Kunio and the invention of a history]. Tokyo: Iwanamishoten.

Noguchi, Y. (Ed.). (2005). Naratibu no rinshoshakaigaku [Clinical sociology of narrative]. Tokyo, Japan: Keiso shobo.

Noguchi, Y. (Ed.). (2009). Naratibu apurochi [Narrative approach]. Tokyo, Japan: Keiso shobo.

Noma, H. (1952). *Shinkū chitai* [Zone of emptiness]. Tokyo: Kawadeshobō.

Nomura Research Institute. (2007). *Taishuka suru IT shohi* [IT consumption is popularizing]. Tokyo, Japan: Toyo Keizai Inc.

Nomura, K. (2014). *Stori sekai no tukurikata* [How to making a story world]. Tokyo: Shinkigensha.

Nonaka, R. (2015). *Bungaku no yōgo* [Terms of literature]. Tokyo: Shōhakusha.

Nuxoll, A. M., & Laird, J. E. (2004). A cognitive model of episodic memory integrated with a general cognitive architecture. In *Proceedings of International Conference on Cognitive Modeling* (pp. 220-225). Academic Press.

Nuxoll, A. M., & Laird, J. E. (2007). Extending cognitive architecture with episodic memory. In *Proceedings of the 22nd National Conference on Artificial Intelligence* (pp. 1560-1565). Academic Press.

Oda, J. (2007). Re-reinvestigation of Raimundus Lullus on creativity. In *Proceedings of the 26th Special Interest Group on Language Sense Engineering Research Group in Japanese Artificial Intelligence Society* (pp. 47-51). Tokyo: Japanese Artificial Intelligence Society.

Ōe, K. (2009). Suishi. Tokyo: Kōdansha.

Ōe, K. (1965). *Genshuku na tsunawatari* [Serious ropewalking]. Tokyo: Bungei-shunjū.

Ōe, K. (1973). *Kōzui ha waga tamashii ni oyobi* [The flood invades my spirit]. Tokyo: Shinchōsha.

Ōe, K. (1979). *Dōjidai game* [The game of contemporaneity]. Tokyo: Shinchōsha.

Ogata, T. (1995). *Monogatari seisei - Monogatari no tameno gihō to senryaku ni motozuku approach* [Narrative generation: An approach based on techniques and strategies for narrative] (Doctoral dissertation). The University of Tokyo, Tokyo, Japan.

Ogata, T. (1998). Proposal of computational narratology. *PSJ SIGNotes Computer and Humanities Abstract*, No.041 – 008. (in Japanese)

Ogata, T. (1999). Monogatari genre taikei no mōrateki kentō [A comprehensive consideration of a narrative genre system]. In N. Yoshimine, H. Akama, & A. Tokosumi (Eds.), Literature and Cognition/Computer 2: The Expansion of Literature. Japanese Cognitive Science Society Technical Report (00-No. 40).

Ogata, T. (1999a). Monogatari genre taikei no mōrateki kentō [A comprehensive consideration of a narrative genre system]. In N. Yoshimine, H. Akama & A. Tokosumi (Eds.), Literature and Cognition/Computer 2: The Expansion of Literature. Japanese Cognitive Science Society Technical Report (00-No. 40).

Ogata, T. (2002a). Expanded literary theory: Cognitive/computational expansion of literary theories and narratology. In *Proceedings of the 17th Congress of the International Association of Empirical Aesthetics* (pp. 163-166). Rome, Italy: University of Rome Tre.

Ogata, T. (2004b). Toward the consistent simulation of narrative discourse based on narratology. In *Proceedings of the Ninth International Symposium on Artificial Life and Robotics* (*Vol. 2*, pp. 579-584). Oita, Japan: Academic Press.

Ogata, T. (2008b). Ryūdō to kotei (2) [Fluidity and fixation (2)]. In *Proceedings of the 15th Meeting of Literature, Cognition, and Computer Rereserch Group II in the Japanese Cognitive Science Society* (15W-05). Retrieved from http://www.ogata.soft.iwate-pu.ac.jp/LCC2_Web/LCC(II)Proceedings/Proceedings(15)/15W-05Ogata.pdf

Ogata, T. (2014). Form and content in narrative generation: From the viewpoint of the implementation in an integrated narrative generation system. In Information Processing Society of Japan, Technical Reports, Natural Language Processing (2014-NL-217). Tokyo: Information Processing Society of Japan.

Ogata, T. (2015). Building conceptual dictionaries for an integrated narrative generation system. *Journal of Robotics, Networking and Artificial Life,* 270-284.

Ogata, T. (2016a). Computational and cognitive approaches to narratology from the perspective of narrative generation. In T. Ogata & T. Akimoto (Eds.), Computational and cognitive approaches to narratology (pp. 1-73). Hershey, PA: Information Science Reference (IGI Global). doi:10.4018/978-1-5225-0432-0.ch001

Ogata, T. (2016b). Kabuki as multiple narrative structures. In T. Ogata & T. Akimoto (Eds.), Computational and cognitive approaches to narratology (pp. 400-431). Hershey, PA: Information Science Reference (IGI Global).

Ogata, T. (n.d.a). Gaibu heno monogatari seisei mataha geinō jōhō system ni mukete [Narrative generation to outside or toward a geino information system]. In T. Ogata, Y. Kawamura & A. Kanai (Eds.), Jōhō monogatariron - Jinkō chinō, ninchi, shakai katei to monogatari seisei [Informational narratology: Artificial intelligence/cognition/social process and narrative generation]. Tokyo: Hakutōshobō. (in press)

Ogata, T. (n.d.a). Monogatari to ningen/shakai/kikai – Tajū monogatari kōzō kara ningen/kikai kyōsei-kei he [Narrative and human/society/machine: To human/machine co-existence system from multiple narrative structures]. In Jōhō monogatariron - Jinkō chinō, ninchi, shakai katei to monogatari seisei [Informational narratology: Artificial intelligence/cognition/social process and narrative generation]. Tokyo: Hakutōshobō. (in press)

Ogata, T. (n.d.b). Naibu heno monogatari seisei mataha watakushi monogatari ni mukete [Narrative generation to inside or toward "I" narratives]. In T. Ogata, Y. Kawamura, & A. Kanai (Eds.), Jōhō monogatariron - Jinkō chinō, ninchi, shakai katei to monogatari seisei [Informational narratology: Artificial intelligence/cognition/social process and narrative generation]. Tokyo: Hsakutōshobō.

Ogata, T. (n.d.b). Naibu heno monogatari seisei mataha watakushi monogatari ni mukete [Narrative generation to inside or toward I narratives]. In Jōhō monogatariron - Jinkō chinō, ninchi, shakai katei to monogatari seisei [Informational narratology: artificial intelligence/cognition/social process and narrative generation]. Tokyo: Hakutōshobō. (in press)

Ogata, T., & Akimoto, T. (Eds.). (2016). Computational and cognitive approaches to narratology. Hershey, PA: Information Science Reference (IGI Global). doi:10.4018/978-1-5225-0432-0

Ogata, T., & Kawamura, Y. (1997a). Historical process of contents creation and current strategy. In *Proceedings of the 7th International Forum on Tehcnology Management* (pp. 400-405). Kyōto, Japan: International Forum on Tehcnology Management.

Ogata, T., & Mori, Y. (2005). A systematic view of narrative discourse based on "hyper-comic" system with automatic generation mechanism. In *Proceedings of the 19th Annual Conference of the Japanese Society for Artificial Intelligence* (3D3-01). Tokyo: Japanese Society for Artificial Intelligence.

Ogata, T., & Ono, J. (2015). Language notation dictionaries and the use in an integrated narrative generation system. In IEICE Technical Report of Technical Committee on Natural Language Understanding and Models of Communication (Vol. 115, No. 69, pp. 25-30). Tokyo: Institute of Electronics, Information and Communication Engineers.

Ogata, T., & Terano, T. (1991). Explanation-based narrative generation using semiotic theory. In *Proceedings of Natural Language Processing Pacific Rim Symposium* (pp. 321-328). Tokyo: Special Interest Group of Natural Language Processing of Information Processing Society of Japan.

Ogata, T., & Terano, T. (1991). Explanation-based narrative generation using semiotic theory. In *Proceedings of Natural Language Processing Pacific Rim Symposium 1991* (pp. 321-328). Academic Press.

Ogata, T., Arai, T., & Ono, J. (2016). Using synthetically collected scripts for story generation. In *Proceedings of the 26th International Conference on Computational Linguistics: System Demonstrations* (pp. 253-257). Tokyo: The COLING 2016 Organizing Committee.

Ogata, T. (1997). *Geinō* character heno monogatarisei no fuyo - Joron-teki kōsatsu [Giving narrativity to *geinō* characters: An intoruductive consideration]. In *Proceedings of the 28th Annual Conference of the Japanese Academy of Advertising* (pp. 58-61). Tokyo: Japanese Academy of Advertising.

Ogata, T. (1997). Tajū monogatari kōzō no model [A model of multiple narrative structures]. In *Proceedings of the 9th Annual Conference of Japan Simulation & Gaming Association* (pp. 107-110). Tokyo: Japan Simulation & Gaming Association.

Ogata, T. (1999b). An attempt for systematization of narrative discourse theory from the viewpoint of narrative generation system. *Proceedings of IPSJ SIG Computers and the Humanities*, *99*(85), 31–38.

Ogata, T. (2000). Tajū monogatari kōzō no macro model - Simulation toshite no monogatari josetsu [The macro model of multiple narrative structures: an introduction to a narrative as a simulation]. *Simulation & Gaming*, *10*(1), 35–46.

Ogata, T. (2002b). The concept of system narratology: From the viewpoint of expanded literary theory. In *Proceedings of the 3rd International Workshop of Literature in Cognition and Computer in held in PRICAI2002* (W7-1, pp. 1-10). Tokyo: Japanese Society of Cognitive Studies.

Ogata, T. (2004): Toward the consistent simulation of narrative discourse based on narratology. In *Proceedings of the 9th International Symposium on Artificial Life and Robotics* (Vol. 2, pp. 579-584). Oita, Japan: International Society of Artificial Life and Robotics.

Ogata, T. (2007). To the rhetoric of story from Propp: Centering around the rhetoric of de-composition and re-composition. *Cognitive Studies*, *14*(4), 532–558.

Ogata, T. (2008). Monogatari seisei system ni okeru eizō kosei he mukete [Towards image editing in a narrative generation system]. In A. Kanai & Y. Niwa (Eds.), *Eizō henshū no riron to jissen* [Theories and practices of image editing] (pp. 165–235). Tokyo: Hōsei University Press.

Ogata, T. (2008a). Monogatari seisei systems ni okeru eizō kosei he mukete [Towards image editing in a narrative generation system]. In A. Kanai & Y. Niwa (Eds.), *Eizō henshu no riron to jissen* [Theories and practices of image editing] (pp. 165–235). Tokyo: Hōsei University Press.

Ogata, T. (2010). Shōsetsu - Ryūdō to kotei, sakuhin no hō he [Novels: Fluidity and fixation, towards a work]. In T. Ogata & A. Kanai (Eds.), *Monogatariron no jōhōgaku josetsu - Monogatari seisei no shisō to gijutsu wo megutte* [An introduction to informatics of narratology: Towards the thoughts and technologies of narrative generation] (pp. 130–169). Tokyo: Gakubunsha.

Ogata, T. (2011). Narrative generation system as the practice of "informatics of narratology.". *Journal of Japan Society for Fazzy Theory and Intelligent Informatics*, *23*(5), 14–24.

Ogata, T. (2014). Expanded literary theory for automatic narrative generation. In *Proceedings of Joint 7th International Conference on Soft Computing and Intelligent Systems and 15th International Symposium on Advanced Intelligent Systems* (pp. 1558-1563). Tokyo: Japan Society of Fuzzy Theory and Intelligent Informatics.

Ogata, T. (2015). Building conceptual dictionaries for an integrated narrative generation system. *Journal of Robotics. Networking and Artificial Life*, *1*(4), 270–284. doi:10.2991/jrnal.2015.1.4.6

Ogata, T. (2016c). Narrative generation of "zukushi": Towards its systematization through surveying *kabuki* and developing a proper noun conceptual dictionary in INGS. In *Proceedings of the 30th Annual Conference of the Japanese Society for Artificial Intelligence* (1K5-OS-06b-2). Tokyo: Japanese Society for Artificial Intelligence.

Ogata, T., & Akimoto, T. (2007). Towards the circular narrative generation based on the correspondences between language-based narrative and music: Systems development based on narrative rhetoric and fundamental considerations about the systems and the circular narrative generation. *Cognitive Studies*, *14*(3), 355–379.

Ogata, T., & Amino, T. (2002). Tajū monogatari kōzō to *geinō* character no monogatari seisei system [Multiple narrative structures and the narrative generation system of *geinō* characters] In *Proceedings of the 19th Annual Conference of the Japan Cognitive Science Society* (pp. 130-131). Aichi, Japan: Japan Cognitive Science Society.

Ogata, T., & Endo, Y. (2004). Narrative discourse theory and a hyper-comic system. In *Proceeding of the 18th Annual Conference of the Japanese Society for Artificial Intelligence* (2D2-01). Tokyo: Japanese Society for Artificial Intelligence.

Ogata, T., & Fujiwara, A. (2015). A generalization of the method of specifying each "function": For an expansion of the Propp-based story generation mechanism in an integrated narrative generation system. In *Proceeding of the 29th Annual Conference of the Japanese Society for Artificial Intelligence* (3G4-OS-05b-3). Tokyo: Japanese Society for Artificial Intelligence.

Ogata, T., Fujiwara, A., & Imabuchi, S. (2014). A way to relatively freely define the sequence of "functions" for a story: Generalizing a Propp-based Story Generation System. In *Proceedings of the 28th Annual Conference of the Japanese Society for Artificial Intelligence* (2F5-OS-01b-2in). Tokyo: Japanese Society for Artificial Intelligence.

Ogata, T., Hori, K., & Ohsuga, S. (1996). A basic framework for narrative conceptual structure generation based on narrative techniques and strategies. *Jinkō Chinō Gakkaishi*, *11*(1), 148–159.

Ogata, T., Hori, K., & Ohsuga, S. (1996). An analysis of narrative structure and generation process for narrative generation system. *Cognitive Studies, 3*(1), 72–109.

Ogata, T., & Hosaka, Y. (2004). Transformation of story in the story generation system based on narratology. In *Proceedings of the 9th International Symposium on Artificial Life and Robotics* (Vol.2, pp. 593-596). Oita, Japan: Oita University.

Ogata, T., & Kanai, A. (2010). *An introduction to informatics of narratology: Towards the thoughts and technologies of narrative generation.* Tokyo: Gakubunsha.

Ogata, T., & Kanai, A. (2010). *Monogatariron no jōhōgaku josetsu - Monogatari seisei no shisō to gijutsu wo megutte* [An introduction to informatics of narratology: Towards the thoughts and technologies of narrative generation]. Tokyo: Gakubunsha.

Ogata, T., & Kanai, A. (2010). *Monogatariron no jyohogaku jyosetsu: Monogatariseisei no shiso to gijyutsu wo megutte [An introduction to informatics of narratology: Towards the thoughts and technologies of narrative generation].* Tokyo, Japan: Gakubun-sha.

Ogata, T., & Kanai, A. (2010b). Story to shōhin = brand - Seisei ni muketa kōkoku no bunseki [Stories and products = brands: An analysis of advertisements towards narrative generation]. In T. Ogata & A. Kanai (Eds.), *Monogatariron no jōhōgaku josetsu - Monogatari seisei no shisō to gijutsu wo megutte* [An introduction to informatics of narratology: Towards the thoughts and technologies of narrative generation] (pp. 42–115). Tokyo: Gakubunsha.

Ogata, T., & Kanai, A. (Eds.). (2010). *Monogatariron no jouhougaku josetsu: Monogatari seisei no shisou to gijutsu wo megutte* [An introduction to the informatics of narratology: About the thought and technologies of narrative generation]. Tokyo, Japan: Gakubunsha.

Ogata, T., & Kawamura, Y. (1997b). Gendai minzoku kōgaku kōsō - Kenkyū keika to kongo no vision [A plan of contemporary folk engineering: The research process and future vision]. In *Proceedins of the 1997 Spring Conference of the Japanese Society of Management and Information* (pp. 161–164). Tokyo: Japanese Society of Management and Information.

Ogata, T., & Kawamura, Y. (1998). *Geinōjin* no monogatari simulation no kihon shisō [A basic theory of the narrative simulation of *geinōjins*]. *Bulletin of Nikkei Advertising Research Institute, 180*, 26–31.

Ogata, T., & Kawamura, Y. (1999). Monogatari sanshutsu soshikiron to *geinō* soshiki model [Narrative production organization and a geino organization model]. In *Proceedings of the 1999 Meeting of the Academic Association of Organizational Science* (pp. 219-222). Tokyo: Academic Association of Organizational Science.

Ogata, T., Kawamura, Y., & Kanai, A. (in press). *Jōhō monogatariron - Jinkō chinō, ninchi, shakai katei to monogatari seisei* [Informational narratology: Artificial intelligence/cognition/social process and narrative generation]. Tokyo: *Hakutōshobō.*

Ogata, T., & Morita, H. (2001). Story and discourse in narrative: From the viewpoint of narrative as simulation. *Simulation & Gaming, 11*(1), 40–49.

Ogata, T., & Mukouyama, K. (2001). The discourse analysis of movie film. In *Information Processing Society of Japan, Technical Reports Computers and the Humanities, CH-49*, 9–16.

Ogata, T., & Ono, J. (2016). A way for using the verb conceptual dictionary in an integrated narrative generation system: The use of co-occurrence information on verb concepts. *Journal of Robotics. Networking and Artificial Life, 3*(3), 209–212. doi:10.2991/jrnal.2016.3.3.15

Ogata, T., Tachibana, S., & Tomite, S. (2009). Monogatari gainen hyōgen kara no eizō no seisei to jidō camera work - "Tokyo monogatari" no bunseki to simulation [Image genertion from narrative conceptual representation and automatic camerawork: An analysis of "Tokyo story" and the simulation]. In *Proceedings of the 26th Annual Conference of the Japan Cognitive Science Society* (P2-32). Tokyo: Japan Cognitive Science Society.

Ogata, T., & Wanatabe, K. (1995). Jinkō chinō ni yoru kōkoku sakusei shien system no tame no monogatari-gata CF no kōzō bunseki to kōkoku no monogatari seisei katei no kentō [Structural analysis of narrative commercial films for advertising making support system by artificial intelligence and the consideration of the advertising narrative generation process]. *Journal of Advertising Science, 31*, 153–157.

Ogata, T., Wanatabe, K., Hori, K., & Ohsuga, S. (1993). Life style marketing heno monogatari seisei system no oyo [Application of a narrative generation system to life style marketing]. In *Proceedings of the Joint Conference of System Simposium and Intelligent System Simposium of the Society of Instrument and Control Engineers* (pp. 217-224). Tokyo: Society of Instrument and Control Engineers.

Ogata, T., Watanabe, K., Hori, K., & Ohsuga, S. (1995a). A basic framework of the application of narrative generation system for integrated support of marketing/advertisement. *Journal of the Japan Society for Management Information, 4*(1), 19–42.

Ogata, T., Watanabe, K., Hori, K., & Ohsuga, S. (1995b). Monogatari seisei system ni yoru kōkoku sōsaku shien wo mokuteki to shita televicomercial no kōzō bunseki [A structural of television commercial films for advertising creation support by a narrative generation system]. *Journal of Advertising Science, 30*, 1–22.

Ogawa, M., Sasaki, Y., Tsuda, H., Yoshimatsu, T., & Kokuryo, J. (2003). Damatte yondeiru hito tachi (ROM) no joho denpan kodo to sono kobai eno eikyo [Information propagation behaviors of silent readers (ROM) and its impact on purchasing]. *Japan Marketing Journal, 22*(4), 39–51.

Ogawa, S. (2000). *The logic of generating innovation.* Tokyo: Chikura Publishing.

Ogawa, S. (2006). *The theory of competitive co-creation.* Tokyo: Hakuto-Shobo Publishing.

Ogawa, S. (2013). *User innovation.* Tokyo: Toyo Keizai Inc.

Ohno, R. (Supervisory Editor) & Haiku-Bungakukan (Ed.). (1994). Handy-version introductory haiku saijiki. Tokyo: Kadokawa-shoten.

Ohsawa, Y., Benson, N. E., & Yachida, M. (1998). KeyGraph: Automatic indexing by co-occurrence graph based on building construction metaphor. In *Proc. Advanced Digital Library Conference (IEEE ADL'98)* (pp. 12-18). Academic Press. doi:10.1109/ADL.1998.670375

Ohsawa, Y., Kido, H., Hayashi, T., Liu, C., & Komoda, K. (2015). Innovation Marketplace on Data Jackets, for Valuating, Sharing, and Synthesizing Data, Knowledge-based Information. *Systems Practice, 30*, 83–97.

Ohsawa, Y., & Nishihara, Y. (Eds.). (2012). *Innovators' marketplace.* Springer Verlag. doi:10.1007/978-3-642-25480-2

Oikawa, H., & Ogata, T. (2010). Tōjō jinbutsu no ninchi jōhō wo motta monogari naiyō kikō jitsugen ni mukete - Shōsetsu no bunseki to system no teian [Towards the story generation mechanism with the cognitive information of characters: An analysis of a novel and the system proposition]. In *Proceedings of the 22th Meeting of Literature, Cognition, and Computer Rereserch Group II in Japan Cognitive Science Society* (22W-02). Retrieved from http://www.ogata.soft.iwate-pu.ac.jp/LCC2_Web/LCC(II)Proceedings/Proceedings(22)/22W-02Oikawa&Ogata.pdf

Oikawa, H., & Ogata, T. (2012). Tōjō jinbutsu no sōgo ninshiki kikō tosite no monogatari seisei no kōsatsu [A consideration of narrative generation as the mutual cognition mechanism of characters]. In *Proceedings of the 29th Annual Conference of the Japan Cognitive Science Society* (pp. 540-549). Nagoya, Japan: Japan Cognitive Science Society.

Okada, N., & Endo, T. (1992). Story generation based on dynamics of the mind. *Computational Intelligence*, *8*(1), 123–160. doi:10.1111/j.1467-8640.1992.tb00341.x

Omori, S. (1996). *Toki ha nagarezu* [Time does not flow]. Tokyo, Japan: Seidosha.

Ono, J., & Ogata, T. (2016b). A design plan of a game system including an automatic narrative generation mechanism: The entire structure and the world settings. In *Proceeding of the 2016 International Conference on Artificial Life and Robotics* (pp. 433-436). Academic Press. doi:10.2991/jrnal.2016.2.4.9

Ono, J., & Ogata, T. (2016c). Automatic generation mechanisms for games: For development of an automatic narrative generation game. In *Proc. of the 33rd Annual Meeting of the Japanese Cognitive Science Society* (pp. 175-180). Academic Press.

Ono, J., & Ogata, T. (2016d). Roles of non-player characters in an automatic narrative generation game using an integrated narrative generation system. In *Proc. of Forum on Information Technology 2016* (pp. 131-132). Academic Press.

Ono, J., & Ogata, T. (2016e). Generating stories by changing a world setting. In *Proc. of DiGRA Japan Annual Conference 2016* (pp. 63-66). Academic Press.

Ono, J., & Ogata, T. (2016f). A prototype system of a scene sequence expansion mechanism in an automatic narrative generation game based on TRPG method. In *Proc. of the 30th Annual Conference of the Japan Society of Artificial Intelligence* (1K4-OS-06a-6). Academic Press.

Ono, J., & Ogata, T. (2017a). Attribute information acquisition in a conceptual dictionary by using Wikipedia and the use in an automatic narrative generation game. In *Proc. of the 31th Annual Conference of the Japan Society of Artificial Intelligence*, (1D3-OS-29b-2in2). Academic Press.

Ono, J., & Ogata, T. (in press). Surprise-based narrative generation in an automatic narrative generation game. In T. Ogata & S. Asakawa. (Eds.), Content generation through narrative communication and simulation. Hershey, PA: Information Science Reference (IGI Global).

Ono, J., Tyo, I., & Ogata, T. (2012). Defamiliarization rhetoric and scenario generation for events using the constraints in conceptual system. In *Proc. of the 26th Annual Conference of the Japan Society of Artificial Intelligence*, (1N1-OS-1a-1). Academic Press.

Onodera, K., Kumagai, T., & Ogata, T. (2010). Monogatari naiyō no ichibu toshite no story sekai wo tsukuru system no shisaku to shōsetsu bunseki ni yoru sono kakuchō no kentō [A prototype system to create a story world as a part of a story and a consideration of its expansion by a novel analysis]. In *Proceedings of the 20th Meeting of Literature, Cognition, and Computer Rereserch Group II in Japan Cognitive Science Society* (20W-04). Retrieved from http://www.ogata.soft.iwate-pu.ac.jp/LCC2_Web/LCC(II)Proceedings/Proceedings(20)/20W-04onodera.pdf

Onodera, K., Akimoto, T., & Ogata, T. (2012). A state-event transformation mechanism for generating micro structures of story in an integrated narrative generation system. In *Proceedings of the 34th Annual Conference of the Cognitive Science Society* (pp. 2150-2155). Tokyo: Japanese Cognitive Science Society.

Ono, J., & Ogata, T. (2015). Selecting words and notation using literary data in the integrated narrative generation system. *Journal of Robotics. Networking and Artificial Life*, *2*(3), 194–199. doi:10.2991/jrnal.2015.2.3.13

Ono, J., & Ogata, T. (2016). A method of story generation for creating "surprise" using "gap techniques": An approach to an automatic narrative generation game based on table-talk role playing games. *Cognitive Studies.*, *24*(3), 410–434.

Ono, J., & Ogata, T. (2016a). Architecture of a narrative generation system based on a TRPG model: The use of an integrated narrative generation system for knowledge acquisition (Preliminary version). *Bulletin of Networking, Computing. Systems & Software*, *5*(1), 40–48.

Ono, J., & Ogata, T. (2016g). Implementation of a scene expansion mechanism using an event sequence: As a mechanism in an automatic narrative generation game. *International Journal of Knowledge Engineering.*, *2*(4), 165–169. doi:10.18178/ijke.2016.2.4.073

Ono, J., & Ogata, T. (2017). A method of story generation for creating "surprise" using "gap techniques": An approach to an automatic narrative generation game based on table-talk role playing games. *Cognitive Studies*, *24*(3), 410–434.

Ono, J., & Ogata, T. (2017b). Changing and transforming a story for a framework of an automatic narrative generation game. *Proc. of the 2017 international conference on artificial life and robotics.* doi:10.2991/jrnal.2017.4.1.16

Ōoka, S. (1952). Nobi. Tokyo: Sōgensha.

Ōoka, S. (1971). *Leyte senki* [A record of the battle of Leyte]. Tokyo: Chūōkōron-shinsha.

Ōoka, S. (1996). Akutagawa Ryūnosuke wo bengosuru - Jijitsu to shōsetsu no aida [Defending Akutagawa Ryunoske: Between a fact and a story]. In *Ōoka Shōhei Collection 14* (pp. 532–556). Tokyo: Iwanamishoten. (Original work published 1970)

Otake, M., Kato, M., Takagi, T., & Asama, H. (2009). Coimagination method: Communication support system with collected images and its evaluation via memory task. Lecture Notes in Computer Science, 5614, 403–411. doi: 10.1007/978-3-642-02707-9_46

Otsuka, H., Inui, T., & Okumura, M. (2007). *Opinion mining engine.* Tokyo, Japan: Corona Publishing.

Ozu, Y. (Director), & Yamamoto, T. (Producer) (1953). *Tokyo monogatari* [Tokyo story] [Motion picture]. Japan: Shōchiku.

Palmer, S., Davis, J., Nelson, R., & Rock, I. (2008). Figure-ground effects on shape memory for objects versus holes. *Perception*, *37*(10), 1569–1586. doi:10.1068/p5838 PMID:19065859

Parajanof, S. (Director) (1968). *The color of pomegranates* [Motion picture]. Soviet Union (Armenia).

Pawlak, Z. (1981). Information systems-theoretical foundations. *Information Systems*, *6*(3), 205–218. doi:10.1016/0306-4379(81)90023-5

Pawlak, Z. (1982). Rough sets. *International Journal of Computer and Information Science*, *11*(5), 341–356. doi:10.1007/BF01001956

Peinado, F., & Gervás, P. (2005). Creativity issues in plot generation. In *Workshop on Computational Creativity, Working Notes, 19th International Joint Conference on A.I.* (pp. 45-52). Academic Press.

Peirce, C. S. (1955). *Philosophical writings of Peirce.* Dover.

Peirce, C. S. (1974). *Collected papers of Charles Sanders Peirce.* Cambridge, MA: Harvard University Press.

Pemberton, L. (1989). A modular approach to story generation. In *Proceedings of the Fourth Conference on European Chapter of the Association for Computational Linguistics* (pp. 217-224). The Association for Computational Linguistics. doi:10.3115/976815.976845

Pérez y Pérez, R. (2014). The three layers evaluation model for computer-generated plots. In *Proceedings of the Fifth International Conference on Computational Creativity (ICCC 2014)* (220-229). Ljublijana, Slovenia: Jožef Stefan Institute.

Pérez y Pérez, R., & Sharples, M. (2001). MEXICA: A computer model of a cognitive account of creative writing. *Journal of Experimental & Theoretical Artificial Intelligence*, *13*(2), 119–139. doi:10.1080/09528130010029820

Pnueli, A. (1977). The temporal logic of programs. *Proceedings of the 18th IEEE Annual Symposium on Foundations of Computer Science*, (pp. 46-57). The Institute of Electrical and Electronics Engineers, Inc.

Poole, D., Goebel, R., & Aleliunas, R. (1987). Theorist: A logical reasoning system for defaults and diagnosis. In The Knowledge Frontier: Essays in the Representation of Knowledge (pp. 331-352). Springer-Verlag.

Porteous, J., Charles, F., & Cavazza, M. (2015). Using social relationships to control narrative generation. In *Proceedings of the 29th AAAI Conference on Artificial Intelligence (AAAI), Virtual Agents Demos*. Austin TX: AAAI.

Powers, R. (1995). *Galatea 2.2*. Harper Perennial.

Poynter, R. (2010). *The handbook of online and social media research: Tools and techniques for market researchers*. New Jersey: John Wiley & Sons.

Prince, G. (2003). *A dictionary of narratology* (Revised Ed.). Lincoln, NE: University of Nebraska Press.

Propp, V. (1968). *Morphology of the Folktale*. University of Texas Press.

Propp, V. Y. (1968). *Morphology of the folktale* (L. Scott, Trans.). Austin, TX: University of Texas Press. (Original work published 1928)

Proust, M. (2003). In search of lost time (T. Kilmartin, Trans.). Modern Library. (Original work published 1913-1927)

Rajaniemi, T. K., & Allison, V. J. (2009). Abiotic conditions and plant cover differentially affect microbial biomass and community composition on dune gradients. *Soil Biology & Biochemistry*, *41*(1), 102–109. doi:10.1016/j.soilbio.2008.10.001

Real Wine Guide. (2007–2009). *RWG* (vol. 19–26). Academic Press.

Reiter, R., & de Kleer, J. (1987). Foundation of assumption-based truth maintenance systems: Preliminary report. In *Proc. of AAAI87* (pp.183-188). AAAI.

Ricoeur, P. (1983–1985). *Temps et récit (Tome I–III)*. Paris, France: Seuil.

Riedl, M. O., & Young, R. M. (2010). Narrative planning: Balancing plot and character. *Journal of Artificial Intelligence Research*, *39*, 217–267.

Riesbeck, C. K., & Schank, R. C. (1989). *Inside case-based reasoning*. Mahwah, NJ: Lawrence Erlbaum.

Rogers, C. (1959). *Toward a theory of creativity, in creativity and its cultivation* (H. Anderson, Ed.). Harper & Row.

Rogers, E. M. (2003). *Diffusion of innovations* (5th ed.). New York: Free Press.

Roncero, C., & de Almeida, R. G. (2015). Semantic properties, aptness, familiarity, conventionality, and interpretive diversity scores for 84 metaphors and similes. *Behavior Research Methods*, *47*(3), 800–812. doi:10.3758/s13428-014-0502-y PMID:25007859

Rooney, R., Benson, C., & Hennessy, E. (2012). The apparent reality of movies and emotional arousal: A study using physiological and self-report measures. *Poetics*, *40*(5), 405–422. doi:10.1016/j.poetic.2012.07.004

Rubin, E. (1915). *Synsoplevede Figurer* [Visual Figures]. Retrieved July, 2010, from http://en.wikipedia.org/wiki/Rubin_vase

Rumelhart, D. E. (1975). Notes on a schema for stories. In D. G. Bobrow & A. Collins (Eds.), *Representation and understanding: Studies in cognitive science*. Academic Press. doi:10.1016/B978-0-12-108550-6.50013-6

Ryan, M.-L., & Thon, J.-N. (Eds.). (2014). *Storyworlds across media*. University of Nebraska Press.

Saito, Y., & Ogata, T. (1998). A consideration of a computational modeling of Freud's dream theory. In *Proceeding of the 12th Annual Conference of the Japanese Society for Artificial Intelligence* (pp. 703-706). Tokyo: Japanese Society for Artificial Intelligence.

Sakurai, K. (2000, September). Save the reckless driving of the automatic car? New pedal. *Nikkei Mechanical*, 22-25.

Sanmai no ofuda. (n.d.). Retrieved from the Japanese Wikipedia: https://ja.wikipedia.org/wiki/%E4%B8%89%E6%9E%9A%E3%81%AE%E3%81%8A%E6%9C%AD

Saraki, M. (Ed.). (2008). Seiki-Hyougen-to Text Mining [Regular expression and text mining]. Tokyo, Japan: Akashi-shoten.

Saraki, M., & Nitta, Y. (2005). The semantic classification of verb conjunction in the "Shite" Form. *Proceedings of Spring IECEI Conference* (A-13-3). Tokyo: The Institute of Electronics, Information and Communication Engineers.

Sarlej, M. (2014). *A lesson learned: Using emotions to generate stories with morals* (Doctoral dissertation). Computer Science and Engineering, University of New South Wales, Sydney, Australia.

Sato, K., Ochi, K., & Shimojima, Y. (2008). *Jidenteki kioku no shinrigaku* [Psychology of autobiographical memory]. Kyoto, Japan: Kitaohji shobo.

Sawa, K. (2015). *Logic as a complex network*. arXiv:1507.00840

Sawyer, S., & Tapia, A. (2005). The sociotechnical nature of mobile computing work: Evidence from a study of policing in the United States. *International Journal of Technology and Human Interaction*, *1*(3), 1–14. doi:10.4018/jthi.2005070101

Sayogoromo oshidori no tsurugiba. (1739). [*Ningyō jōruri*]. Namiki Sōsuke (Scenarios). Ōsaka, Japan: Toyotake-za (First performance).

Schank, R. C., & The Yale A.I. Project. (1975). *SAM: A story understander*. Research Report #43, Yale University, Department of Computer Science.

Schank, R. C. (1982). *Dynamic memory: A theory of reminding and learning in computers and people*. New York, NY: Cambridge University Press.

Schank, R. C., & Abelson, R. P. (1977). *Scripts, plans, goals, and understanding: An inquiry into human knowledge structures*. Lawrence Erlbaum.

Schank, R. C., & Riesbeck, C. K. (1981). *Inside computer understanding*. Lawrence Erlbaum.

Schumpeter, J. A. (1926). *The theory of economic development*. Cambridge, MA: Harvard University Press.

Schwartz, J. M., & Cook, T. (2002). Archives, records, and power: The making of modern memory. *Archival Science*, *2*(1-2), 1–19. doi:10.1007/BF02435628

Seino, K., Haruna, Y., & Ishizaki, S. (2016). Employment status and support needs of persons with disabilities in japan: An analysis of narrative using narratology and text mining on a national survey. In T. Ogata & T. Akimoto (Eds.), Computational and cognitive approaches to narratology (pp. 245-275). Hershey, PA: Information Science Reference (IGI Global).

Sekizawa, H., Washida, Y., & Bjorn, M. (2002). *Shichueshon mahkethingu: Ketai jidai no shohi wo toraeru shin hasso* [Situation marketing: New idea to capture consumption in mobile age]. Tokyo, Japan: Kanki Press.

Sekkyō. (1998). *Kojōruri sekkyō shū (Shin nihon koten bungaku taikei 90)* [A collection of old jōruris and sekkyōs (New Japanese classic literature collection 90)]. Tokyo: Iwanamishoten.

Sendenkaigi. (2011-2014). Henshubu ga eranda kongetsu no besuto puromoshon [Best promotion of this month selected by the editorial department]. In *Hansoku Kaigi* [Top Promotion] (pp. 153-200). Sendenkaigi.

Seto, K. (2003). *Kotoba wa aji wo koeru [Words excel the taste]*. Tokyo: Kaimeisha.

Sharples, M. (1996). An account of writing as creative design. In C. M. Levy & S. Ransdell (Eds.), *The science of writing: Theories, methods, individual difference and applications* (pp. 127–148). Lawrence Erlbaum.

Shigenori, T., & Masahiro, F. (1998). *Imizukeron> no tenkai [The evolution of the <sense-making theory>]*. Tokyo: Kinokuniya.

Shimaguchi, M., Takeuchi, H., Katahira, H., & Ishii, J. (1998). *Mahkethingu kakushin no jidai 1: kokyaku sozo* [Age of marketing innovation 1: Customer creation]. Tokyo, Japan: Yuhikaku.

Shimaguchi, M., Takeuchi, H., Katahira, H., & Ishii, J. (1999). *Mahkethingu kakushin no jidai 4: burando kochiku* [Age of marketing innovation 4: Brand building]. Tokyo, Japan: Yuhikaku.

Shin kokin waka shū. (1959). *Shin kokin waka shū* [The new collection of wakas, past and present]. Tokyo: Iwanamishoten. (Original work published the Kamakura era)

Shinohara, K., Yamauchi, N., Kawahara, S., & Tanaka, H. (2016). Takete and Maluma in action: A cross-modal relationship between gestures and sounds. *PLoS One*, *11*(9), e0163525. doi:10.1371/journal.pone.0163525 PMID:27682989

Shiramatsu, S., Ozono, T., & Shintani, T. (2015). SOCIA: Linked open data of context behind local concerns for supporting public participation. *International Journal of Advanced Computer Science and Applications*, *6*(2), 268–277. doi:10.14569/IJACSA.2015.060238

Shklovsky, V. (1965). Art as technique. In *Russian formalist criticism: Four essays* (L. T. Lemon & M. J. Reis, Trans. & Eds.). Lincoln, NE: University of Nebraska Press. (Original work published 1917)

Shklovsky, V. (1990). *Theory of prose* (B. Sher, Trans.). Dalkey Archive Press.

Shoenfield, J. R. (1967). *Mathematical logic* (Vol. 21). Reading, MA: Addison-Wesley.

Shutova, E. (2015). Design and evaluation of metaphor processing systems. *Computational Linguistics*, *41*(4), 579–623. doi:10.1162/COLI_a_00233

Si, M. (2010). *Thespian: A decision-theoretic framework for interactive narratives* (Doctoral dissertation). Faculty of the USC Graduate School, University of Southern California.

Siegenthaler, B. M., & Goldstein, J. (1967). Auditory and visual figure-background perception by adult aphasics. *Journal of Communication Disorders*, *1*(2), 152–158. doi:10.1016/0021-9924(67)90004-4

Singh, P., Barry, B., & Liu, H. (2004). Teaching machines about everyday life. *BT Technology Journal*, *22*(4), 227–240. doi:10.1023/B:BTTJ.0000047601.53388.74

Softbank. (n.d.). *Robot*. Retrieved from https://www.softbank.jp/en/robot/

Sophocles. (1994). Oedipus tyrannus. In *Ajax, Electra, Oedipus tyrannus* (H. Lloid-Jones, Trans.). Cambridge, MA: Harvard University Press. (Original work published around 429 BC)

Stam, R., Burgoyne, R., & Flitterman-Lewis, S. (1992). *New vocabularies in film semiotics: Structuralism, post-structuralism and beyond*. London: Routledge.

Steriadi-Bogdan, M. (1977). The evolution of the plot and problems of strategy in a detective play. *Poetics*, *6*(3-4), 375–382. doi:10.1016/0304-422X(77)90014-6

Stern, B. B. (1992). Historical and personal nostalgia in advertising text: The fin de siècle effect. *Journal of Advertising*, *21*(4), 11–22. doi:10.1080/00913367.1992.10673382

Sterne, J. (2011). *Social media metrics*. Wiley.

Stickel, M. E. (1988). A prolog-like system for computing minimum-cost abductive explanations in natural-language interpretation. In *Proc. of Int'l Computer Science Conf.* (pp. 343-350). Academic Press.

Stickel, M. E. (1989). Rationale and methods for abductive reasoning in natural language interpretation. In *Proc. of INt'l Scientific Symp. "Natural Language and Logic" (LNAI-459)* (pp. 233-252). Springer.

Strong, E. K. (1925). Theories of selling. *The Journal of Applied Psychology*, *9*(9), 75–86. doi:10.1037/h0070123

Sukeroku yukari no Edo-zakura. (1733). [Sukeroku: Flower of Edo] [*Kabuki*]. Edo, Japan: Ichimura-za (First performance).

Sukeroku. (n.d.). Retrieved from the Japanese Wikipedia: https://ja.wikipedia.org/wiki/%E5%8A%A9%E5%85%AD

Sutskever, I., Vinyals, O., & Le, Q. V. (2014). Sequence to sequence learning with neural networks. In Z. Ghahramani, M. Welling, C. Cortes, N. Lawrence, & K. Weinberger (Eds.), Advances in Neural Information Processing Systems (Vol. 27, 3104–3112). Montreal, Canada: Academic Press.

Swanson, R., & Gordon, A. S. (2012). Say Anything: Using textual case-based reasoning to enable open-domain interactive storytelling. *ACM Transactions on Interactive Intelligent Systems*, *2*(3), 16. doi:10.1145/2362394.2362398

Swartjes, I. (2010). *Whose story is it anyway? How improve informs agency and authorship of emergent narrative* (Doctoral dissertation). University of Twente, Enschede, The Netherlands.

Swartjes, I. M. T., Vromen, J., & Bloom, N. (2007). Narrative inspiration: using case based problem solving for emergent story generation. In A. Cardoso, & G. A. Wiggins (Eds.), *Proceedings of the Fourth International Joint Workshop on Computational Creativity* (pp. 21-28). London, UK: Goldsmiths, University of London.

Swift, J. (2005). *Gulliver's travels*. Oxford, UK: Oxford University Press. (Original work published 1726)

Szilas, N. (2015). Towards narrative-based knowledge representation in cognitive systems. In *Proceedings of 6th Workshop on Computational Models of Narrative* (pp. 133-141). Academic Press.

Tachibana, S., & Ogata, T. (2009). Extracting of rules for cameraworks in "Tokyo story" of Ozu. In *The 69th National Convention of Information Processing Society of Japan* (1ZD-1). Tokyo: Information Processing Society of Japan.

Taguchi, A. (2011). *Kabuki kara Edo wo yominaosu* [Reading again Edo from kabuki]. Tokyo: Yoshikawa-kobunkan.

Taiheiki. (1960-1962). *Nihon koten bungaku taikei 34-36* [Japanese classic literature collection 34-36]. Tokyo: Iwanamishoten. (Original work publishued the Muromachi era)

Takahashi, K. (1980). Nihon no akuryō [Demon of Japan]. Tokyo: Shinchōsha. (Original work published 1966-1968)

Takahashi, R. (1992-1993). *Mezon Ikkoku (1-10)* [Maison Ikkoku (1-10)]. Tokyo: Shōgakkan. (Original work published 1980-1987)

Takahashi, K. (1958). *Ri Shōin*. Tokyo: Iwanamishoten.

Takahashi, K. (1966). *Jashūmon* [Heretical faith]. Tokyo: Kawadeshobō-shinsha.

Takahashi, K. (1971). *Waga kaitai* [My dismantling]. Tokyo: Kawadeshobō-shinsha.

Takaoka, K., & Kotler, P. (2016). *Marketing Advice*. Tokyo: Chuko Laclef Shinsho.

Takeda, H. (2004). Upper Ontology. *Journal of Artificial Intelligence Japan, 19*(2), 172–186.

Takeda, Y. (2000). *Product Realization Strategy*. Tokyo: Hakuto-Shobo Publishing.

Tale of the Henike. (2012). (R. Tyler, Trans.). London: Penguin Books. (Original work published the Kamakura era)

Tanaka, F., & Ono, A. (2003). *Raibu mahkethingu* [Live markething]. Tokyo, Japan: Toyo Keizai Inc.

Taniguchi, T. (2010). *Komyunikeishon suru robotto wa tsukureruka* [Constructive Approach towards Symbol Emergence System]. Tokyo, Japan: NTT Publishing.

Tanizaki, J. (1925). Chijin no ai. Tokyo: Kaizōsha.

Tanizaki, J. (1931). Manji. Tokyo: Kaizōsha.

Tanizaki, J. (1946-1948). Sasameyuki. Tokyo: Chūōkōronsha.

Tanizaki, J. (1933). *Shunkinshō* [A portrait of shunkin]. Tokyo: Sōgensha.

Teodorescu-Brinzeu, P. (1984). The verbal zero-sign in theater. *Poetics, 13*(1-2), 47–56. doi:10.1016/0304-422X(84)90029-9

Terada, T., Akimoto, T., Ono, J., & Ogata, T. (2014). A systematic description of proper noun concepts in the integrated narrative generation system. In *Proceedings of the Association for Natural Language 20th Conference* (pp. 217-220). Kyoto, Japan: The Association for Natural Language Processing.

Thagard, P. (1989). Explanatory coherence. *Behavioral and Brain Sciences, 12*(03), 435–502. doi:10.1017/S0140525X00057046

Thorndyke, P. W. (1977). Cognitive structures in comprehension and memory of narrative discourse. *Cognitive Psychology, 9*(1), 77–110. doi:10.1016/0010-0285(77)90005-6

Tōkaido Yotsuya kaidan. (1825) [*The ghost stories at Yotsuya on the Tōkaido*] [*Kabuki*]. Tsuruya Namboku, et al. (Scenario). Edo, Japan: Nakamiura-za (First performance).

Tolstoy, L. (2010). War and peace (L. Maude, Trans.). Oxford, UK: Oxford University Press. (Original work published 1865-1869)

Tolstoy, L. (2009). *Ressurection* (A. Briggs, Trans.). London, UK: Penguin Books. (Original work published 1899)

Torreano, L., Cacciari, C., & Glucksberg, S. (2005). When dogs can fly: Level of abstraction as a cue to metaphorical use of verbs. *Metaphor and Symbol, 20*(4), 259–274. doi:10.1207/s15327868ms2004_2

Traffic and Safety Sciences FY2011 Research Project. (2012). *An analysis of the cause of errors when stepping-on the accelerator and brake and proposals for psychological and engineering countermeasures (II) report (2012).* International Association of Traffic and Safety Sciences FY2011 Research Project (H2305)

Troelstra, A. S., & Schwichtenberg, H. (2000). *Basic proof theory* (Vol. 43). Cambridge, UK: Cambridge University Press. doi:10.1017/CBO9781139168717

Truffaut, F. (1966). *Le cinema selon Alfred Hichicock*. Paris: Robert Laffont Editions.

Tsur, R. (2009). Metaphor and figure-ground relationship: comparisons from poetry, music, and the visual arts. In G. Brône & J. Vandaele (Eds.), *Cognitive Poetics: Goals, Gains and Gaps* (pp. 237–277). Berlin, Germany: Mouton de Gruyter.

Tsuru nyōbō. (2017). [Crane's return of a favor] (Y. Mori & M. Pertseva, Trans.). London, UK: YellowBirdProject.

Tsuzuki, A. (1975). Shitsumonshicyosa no igi [The significance of the questionnaire]. In M. Arima & E. Murakami (Eds.), *Shinrigakukenkyuhou 9* [Psychology Research Methods 9]. Tokyo, Japan: University of Tokyo Press.

Tulving, E. (1983). *Elements of episodic memory*. Oxford, UK: Oxford University Press.

Tulving, E., & Thomson, D. M. (1973). Encoding specificity and retrieval processes in episodic memory. *Psychological Review*, *80*(5), 352–373. doi:10.1037/h0020071

Turner, S. R. (1994). *The creative process: A computer model of storytelling and creativity*. Lawrence Erlbaum.

Ueda, K. (2006). *Hōdō-bangumi-fū scenario jidō seisei no kenkyū* [A study on automatic composition of news-story-like scenarios] (Master dissertation). Yamanashi University, Kofu, Japan.

Uotani, M. (2009). *Kokoro wo ugokasu mahkethingu: Coca-cola no burando kachi ha kousite tsukurareru* [Mind-moving marketing: Coca-Cola's brand value is thus created]. Tokyo, Japan: Diamond.

Utsumi, A. (2005). The role of feature emergence in metaphor appreciation. *Metaphor and Symbol*, *20*(3), 151–172. doi:10.1207/s15327868ms2003_1

Utsumi, A. (2007). Interpretive diversity explains metaphor-simile distinction. *Metaphor and Symbol*, *22*(4), 291–312. doi:10.1080/10926480701528071

Utsumi, A. (2011). Computational exploration of metaphor comprehension processes using a semantic space model. *Cognitive Science*, *35*(2), 251–296. doi:10.1111/j.1551-6709.2010.01144.x PMID:21429000

Utsumi, A., & Sakamoto, M. (2007a). Computational evidence for two-stage categorization as a process of adjective metaphor comprehension. *Proceedings of the Second European Cognitive Science Conference (EuroCogSci2007)*, 77–82.

Utsumi, A., & Sakamoto, M. (2007b). Predicative metaphors are understood as two-stage categorization: Computational evidence by latent semantic analysis. *Proceedings of the 29th Annual Meeting of the Cognitive Science Society (CogSci2007)*, 1587–1592.

Utsumi, A., & Sakamoto, M. (2010). Predicative metaphor comprehension as indirect categorization. *Proceedings of the 32nd Annual Meeting of the Cognitive Science Society (CogSci2010)*, 1034–1039.

Utsumi, A., & Sakamoto, M. (2011). Indirect categorization as a process of predicative metaphor comprehension. *Metaphor and Symbol*, *26*(4), 299–313. doi:10.1080/10926488.2011.609120

Utsumi, A., & Sakamoto, M. (2015). Discourse goals affect the process and product of nominal metaphor production. *Journal of Psycholinguistic Research*, *44*(5), 555–569. doi:10.1007/s10936-014-9305-7 PMID:24924472

Veale, T. (2009). Hiding in plain sight: figure-ground reversals in humour (commentary to Tsur). In G. Brône & J. Vandaele (Eds.), *Cognitive Poetics: Goals, Gains and Gaps* (pp. 279–288). Berlin, Germany: Mouton de Gruyter.

Veale, T., Shutova, E., & Beigman Klebanov, B. (2016). *Metaphor: A Computational Perspective*. Morgan & Claypool Publishers.

Vigliocco, G., & Vinson, D. P. (2007). Semantic representation. In M. G. Gaskell (Ed.), *The Oxford Handbook of Psycholinguistics* (pp. 217–234). Oxford University Press.

Visch, V. T., & Tan, E. S. (2009). Categorizing moving objects into film genres: The effect of animacy attribution, emotional response, and the deviation from non-fiction. *Cognition*, *110*(2), 265–272. doi:10.1016/j.cognition.2008.10.018 PMID:19118823

Von Hippel, E. (1988). *The sources of innovation.* Oxford, UK: Oxford University Press.

Von Hippel, E. (1994). "Sticky information" and the locus of problem solving: Implications for Innovation. *Management Science, 40*(4), 429–439. doi:10.1287/mnsc.40.4.429

Von Hippel, E. (1998). Economics of product development by users: Impact of "sticky" local information. *Management Science, 44*(5), 629–644. doi:10.1287/mnsc.44.5.629

Von Hippel, E. (2005). *Democratizing innovation.* Cambridge, MA: MIT Press.

Von Hippel, E., & Tyre, M. J. (1995). How learning by doing is done: Problem identification in novel process equipment. *Research Policy, 24*(1), 1–12. doi:10.1016/0048-7333(93)00747-H

Von Hippel, E., & Von Krogh, G. (2016). Crossroads—identifying viable "need-solution pairs"- problem solving without problem formulation. *Organization Science, 27*(1), 207–221.

Wada, M. (1999). *Kankeisei mahkethingu to engeki shohi: Netsuretsu fan no sozo to iji no kozu* [Relationship marketing and theater consumption: Composition of enthusiastic fan creation and maintenance]. Tokyo, Japan: Diamond.

Wang, L. N., Guo, J. L., Yang, H. X., & Zhou, T. (2009). Local preferential attachment model for hierarchical networks. *Physica A, 388*(8), 1713–1720. doi:10.1016/j.physa.2008.12.028

Wang, P. (2007). The Logic of Intelligence. In B. Goertzel & C. Pennachin (Eds.), *Artificial General Intelligence. Cognitive Technologies* (pp. 31–62). Berlin: Springer. doi:10.1007/978-3-540-68677-4_2

Watanabe, N. (2012). *Nihon shōsetsu gijutsushi* [A history of technologies of Japanese novels]. Tokyo: Shinchōsha.

Watanabe, T. (1989). *Kabuki - Kajō naru kigo no mori* [Kabuki: The forest of excessive signs]. Tokyo: Shin'yōsha.

Watanabe, T. (2013). *Kabuki - Kata no shinzui* [Kabuki: The essence of kata]. Tokyo: Kadokawa-gakugei-shuppan.

Watts, D. J., & Strogatz, S. H. (1998). Collective dynamics of'small-world'networks. *Nature, 393*(6684), 440–442. doi:10.1038/30918 PMID:9623998

Wayne, G., & Danihelka, I. (2014). *Neural turing machines.* arXiv:1410.5401

Werner, H., & Strauss, A. A. (1941). Pathology of figure-background relation in the child. *Journal of Abnormal and Social Psychology, 36*(2), 238–248. doi:10.1037/h0058060

White, H. (1980). The value of narrativity in the representation of reality. In W. J. T. Mitchell (Ed.), *On narrative.* Chicago, IL: The University of Chicago Press. doi:10.1086/448086

Williams-Whitney, D., Mio, J., & Whitney, P. (1992). Metaphor production in creative writing. *Journal of Psycholinguistic Research, 21*(6), 497–509.

Wilson, D. A., & Stevenson, R. J. (2006). *Learning to smell.* Baltimore, MD: Johns Hopkins UP.

Witwer, M. (2015). *Empire of imagination: Gary Gygax and the birth of Dungeons & Dragons.* London: Bloomsbury Publishing.

Woods, B., Spector, A. E., Jones, C. A., Orrell, M., & Davies, S. P. (2005). Reminiscence therapy for dementia. *Cochrane Database of Systematic Reviews,* (2). doi:10.1002/14651858.CD001120.pub2 PMID:15846613

Yamada, Y. (2007). *Shitsutekishinrigaku no houhou: Katari o kiku* [Method of qualitative psychology: Listening to narrative]. Tokyo, Japan: Shinyousha.

Yamaguchi, K., Nergui, M., & Otake, M. (2014). A robot presenting reproduced stories among older adults in group conversation. In H. J. Patthi Bin Hussain & Y. Zhu (Eds.), *Applied Mechanics and Materials* (Vol. 541–542, pp. 1120–1126). Murthy Rallapalli and Jamaluddin Mahmud. doi:10.4028/www.scientific.net/AMM.541-542.1120

Yamamoto, A., & Abe, M. (2007). Sgohisha kan nettowahku wo riyou sita rekomendehshon ehjento [Recommendation agent using consumers network]. In Web mahkethingu no kagaku [Science of Web marketing] (pp. 165-191). Tokyo, Japan: Chikura Shobo.

Yamamoto, Y. (2014). *Gensen nihonshu techo* [Selected sake handbook]. Sekai Bunka-sya.

Yamamoto, A., & Katahira, H. (2008). Infuruensa no hakken to kuchikomu no koka: AIDEES moderu no jissho bunseki [Discovery of influencers and effect of word-of-mouth: Empirical analysis of AIDEES model]. *Japan Marketing Journal*, *28*(1), 4–18.

Yamamura, M. (1988). Maiko satsujin jiken [A murder of an apprentice geisha]. In *Miyako odori satsujin jiken* [A murder of miyako dance] (pp. 7–53). Shinchōsha.

Yamane, T. (1996). *Chiyo-Jo's haiku seasons* (Y. Ishibashi & P. Donegan, Trans.). Matto City Publishing.

Yamane, I. (2005). Phenomenology of surprise. *Journal of Sugiyama Jogakuen University. Humanities*, *36*, 13–28.

Yamazaki, H. (2005). *Sosharu nettowahku mahkethingu* [Social network marketing]. Tokyo, Japan: Softbank Creative.

Yasuto, O., & Turner, P. M. (2013). Experimental study on preventing accidents caused by mistakenly stepping-on the accelerator pedal and brake pedal when driving a vehicle (2). In *Society of Automotive Engineers of Japan 2013 Spring Meeting*. Yokohama, Japan: SAEJ.

Yates-Glandorf, J. B. (Ed.). (1985). *Shakespeare's Romeo and Juliet. In the original and modern English. A parallel text edition*. Logan, IA: Perfection Learning Corporation.

Yılmaz, R. (Ed.). (2017). Narrative advertising models and conceptualization in the digital age. Hershey, PA: Business Science Reference (IGI-Global). doi:10.4018/978-1-5225-2373-4

Yokomitsu, R. (1931). Jikan [Time]. Chūōkōron, 4.

Yokomitsu, R. (1931). *Kikai* [Machine]. Tokyo: Hakusuisha.

Yokomitsu, R. (1932). *Shanghai*. Tokyo: Kaizōsha.

Yokomitsu, R. (1946). *Ryoshū* [Loneliness on a journey]. Tokyo: Kaizōsha.

Yoshida, N., Ishii, A., & Arakaki, H. (2010). *Dai hitto no houteishiki: Sohsharu medhia no kuchikomi kouka wo suushikika suru* [Great hit equation: Mathematize the effects of social media's word-of-mouth]. Tokyo, Japan: *Discover*.

Yoshikawa, K., & Miyoshi, T. (1952). *Shin-Toshi-sen* [Selected collection of new Tang-era Chinese poetries]. Tokyo, Japan: Iwanami-shoten.

Yoshimoto, T. (1965). *Gengo ni totte bi toha nanika* [What is beauty for language?]. Tokyo: Keisōshobo.

Yoshimoto, T. (1965). *Gengo nitotte bi toha nanika* [What is beauty for language?]. Tokyo: Keisōshobō.

Yoshimoto, T. (1966). *Jiritsu no shisō-teki kyoten* [An ideological base of self-reliance]. Tokyo: Tokumashoten.

Yoshimoto, T. (1968). *Kyōdō gensō ron* [Communal illusion]. Tokyo: Kawadeshobō-shinsha.

Yoshimoto, T. (1990). *Matthew-sho shiron, tenkōron* [Gospel of Matthew, political conversion]. Tokyo: Kōdansha.

Zhan, Y., Ono, J., & Ogata, T. (2012a). Single event and scenario generation based on movement and constraint in conceptual dictionary. In IEICE Technical Report of Technical Committee on Natural Language Understanding and Models of Communication, NLC2011-60 (Vol. 111, No. 427, pp. 65-70). Tokyo: Institute of Electronics, Information and Communication Engineers.

Zhang, Y., Ono, J., & Ogata, T. (2011). An advertising rhetorical mechanism for single event combined with conceptual dictionary in narrative generation system. In *Proceedings of 7th International Conference on Natural Language Processing and Knowledge Engineering* (pp. 340-343). The Institute of Electrical and Electronics Engineers. doi:10.1109/NLPKE.2011.6138221

Zhang, Y., Ono, J., & Ogata, T. (2012). Single event and scenario generation based on advertising rhetorical techniques using the conceptual dictionary in narrative generation system. In *Proceedings of the 4th IEEE International Conference on Digital Game and Intelligent Toy Enhanced Learning* (pp. 162-164). The Institute of Electrical and Electronics Engineers. doi:10.1109/DIGITEL.2012.46

Zhang, Y., Ono, J., & Ogata, T. (2011a). Defamiliarization rhetoric and scenario generation for events using the constraints in a conceptual system. In *Proceedings of the 26th Annual Conference of the Japanese Society for Artificial Intelligence* (1N1-OS-1a-1). Tokyo: Japanese Society for Artificial Intelligence.

About the Contributors

Takashi Ogata received his bachelor of social sciences in Waseda University in 1983. He received his M.S. in Tsukuba University in 1992 and his Ph.D. in the University of Tokyo in 1995. He has industrial experience since 1983 at software development companies. Having experienced Associate Professor of the Faculty of Engineering at Yamanashi University since 1997, he is Professor of the Faculty of Software and Information Science at Iwate Prefectural University since 2005. His major research interests include artificial intelligence, cognitive science, natural language processing, narratology and literary theories, an interdisciplinary approach to the development of narrative generation systems based on AI and narratology, and the application to narrative creation and business. He is a member of the Japanese Society for Artificial Intelligence, the Japanese Cognitive Science Society, and the Japanese Association for Natural Language Processing. He was also a main manager of Literature, Cognition and Computer research group at the JCSS. He received JSAI best paper award (1996), best paper award of Japan Academy of Advertising (1996), and other academic awards. He published academic books including "An Introduction to the Informatics of Narratology" (Ogata, T. & Kanai, A., 2010, Tokyo: Gakubunsha) and "Computational and Cognitive Approaches to Narratology" (Ogata, T. & Akimoto, T., 2016, IGI Global).

Shin Asakawa is an assistant professor in Tokyo Woman's Christian University. Main research topics are Neural networks modelings, Neuropsychology, Cognitive science, Cognitive psychology.

* * *

Akinori Abe received an M.E. and Doctor of Engineering (PhD) from the University of Tokyo in 1988 and 1991 respectively. His main research interests are abduction, analogical reasoning, data mining, Chance Discovery and language sense processing (rather emotional aspects of language processing). He worked in NTT Communication Science Laboratories from 1991 to 2000, NTT MSC (Malaysia) from 2000 to 2002, and ATR From 2002 to 2009. He also worked as an associate professor of IREIIMS, Tokyo Women's Medical Univ. and a visiting associate professor of Kobe Univ. Graduate School (Cooperation Course). In 2009 he returned to NTT Communication Science Laboratories. Then he moved to Faculty of Letters, Chiba University in April 2012. Since then he is a full professor of Chiba University.

Taisuke Akimoto is an assistant professor in the Graduate School of Computer Science and Systems Engineering, Kyushu Institute of Technology, Fukuoka, Japan. He received his Ph.D. from Iwate Prefectural University, Japan, in 2014. His research interests include artificial intelligence, informatics, and cognitive science. Especially, he interests a narrative-centered approach to artificial cultural intelligence. He is a member of the Japanese Society for Artificial Intelligence, Japanese Cognitive Science Society, and the Association for Natural Language Processing in Japan.

Yoko Enomoto received a Ph.D in Education from the University of Hiroshima, Japan. 2007-2010 Staff Research Investigator. Research Institute National Rehabilitation Center for Persons with Disabilities. 2014- Staff Research Investigator. NIVR.

Hiroki Fukushima is an Assistant Professor at Kyushu Women's University. He was the recipient of the JSAI Incentive Award 2013, and Good Design Award 2014 (in Japan).

Akimitsu Hirota (Ph.D, Kobe Univ.) is a Professor in Kindai University(Osaka Japan). Studied design thinking as a visiting professor at Stanford University Department of Mechanical Engineering (CDR:Center of Design Reserch) (2013-2014).Main research topic are Design-Thinking(Needs findings, Prototyping and Development for education program) and Co-creation(Find and specific for co-user(for example "Lead user", "Extreme User").

Akihito Kanai is a professor of media and communication studies at Hosei university. His current research interests include film cognition, film rhetoric, film narrative, and computational film composition.

Yoji Kawamura (M.B.A., Tsukuba University; B.S., Tokyo Institute of Technology) is professor of business administration at Kindai University. His majoring is modeling the various social (include business, advertising) phenomena based on the modeling of consumer and the system building for simulation. His published research has appeared in journals (in Japan) as Journal of Advertising Science, Japan Marketing Journal, Cognitive Studies, IPSJ Journal. He was received the 2005 Research Article Award given by Japan Academy of Advertising.

Eugene Kitamura obtained his Ph.D. in science from Earth and Planctary Science of Kobe University and his Ph.D. in Computer Science from the National Defense Academy of Japan. Trained in the school of thought of Internal Measurement, he offers an alternative approach to modeling natural phenomena in addition to the traditional external observer one.

Mitsunori Matsushita is currently a professor in the Faculty of Informatics, Kansai University. He received a B. E. degree in precision engineering in 1993 and a Master's degree and a Ph.D. in engineering science from Osaka University, Japan, in 1995 and 2003, respectively. From 1995 to 2008, he worked at the NTT Communication Science Laboratories, Nippon Telegraph, and Telephone Corporation. Since 2008, he has been working at Kansai University. His current interests include natural language understanding, information visualization, and interaction design. His primary awards are the IPSJ Best Paper Award (2003), the VRSJ Best Paper Award (2007), and the Laval Virtual Award (2013).

Shiho Miyazawa has Ph.D in Literature(Psychology) from the Waseda University, Japan. 2012-2013 Project Researcher. Tokyo Woman's Christian University 2013- Staff Research Investigator. NIVR.

Jumpei Ono received his B.S. and M.S. in Information Science from Iwate Prefectural University in 2010 and 2014. He is now pursuing his Ph.D. in the Iwate Prefectural University. His current research interest's narrative generation and games.

Koji Sawa obtained his Ph.D. in science from Earth and Planetary Science of Kobe University. Main research topics are Logic and Complex Networks.

Nanae Shirozu is currently a researcher at West Japan Marketing Communications Incorporation and is a Visiting Researcher at Osaka University. She received her M.S. and Ph.D. in Informatics from Kansai University in 2014 and 2017, respectively. Her research interests include human-computer interaction and behavioral change.

Akira Utsumi received Ph.D. from the University of Tokyo, Japan, in 1993. From 1993 to 2000, he was an assistant professor at Tokyo Institute of Technology. From 2000 to 2013, he was an associate professor at the University of Electro-Communications, and since 2013 he has been a professor. His current research interests include cognitive science of language, natural language processing, and pragmatics.

Index

S

T

V

W

Y

Purchase Print, E-Book, or Print + E-Book

IGI Global books can now be purchased from three unique pricing formats: Print Only, E-Book Only, or Print + E-Book. Shipping fees apply.

www.igi-global.com

Recommended Reference Books

ISBN: 978-1-4666-9728-7
© 2016; 344 pp.
List Price: $185

ISBN: 978-1-4666-9685-3
© 2016; 518 pp.
List Price: $235

ISBN: 978-1-4666-8751-6
© 2016; 2,308 pp.
List Price: $2,400

ISBN: 978-1-4666-8614-4
© 2016; 2,300 pp.
List Price: $2,415

ISBN: 978-1-4666-9970-0
© 2016; 733 pp.
List Price: $315

ISBN: 978-1-4666-9667-9
© 2016; 532 pp.
List Price: $295

Looking for free content, product updates, news, and special offers?
Join IGI Global's mailing list today and start enjoying exclusive perks sent only to IGI Global members.
Add your name to the list at **www.igi-global.com/newsletters.**

Publishing Information Science and Technology Research Since 1988

IGI Global
DISSEMINATOR OF KNOWLEDGE

www.igi-global.com | Sign up at www.igi-global.com/newsletters | facebook.com/igiglobal | twitter.com/igiglobal

Stay Current on the Latest Emerging Research Developments

Become an IGI Global Reviewer for Authored Book Projects

The overall success of an authored book project is dependent on quality and timely reviews.

In this competitive age of scholarly publishing, constructive and timely feedback significantly decreases the turnaround time of manuscripts from submission to acceptance, allowing the publication and discovery of progressive research at a much more expeditious rate. Several IGI Global authored book projects are currently seeking highly qualified experts in the field to fill vacancies on their respective editorial review boards:

Applications may be sent to:
development@igi-global.com

Applicants must have a doctorate (or an equivalent degree) as well as publishing and reviewing experience. Reviewers are asked to write reviews in a timely, collegial, and constructive manner. All reviewers will begin their role on an ad-hoc basis for a period of one year, and upon successful completion of this term can be considered for full editorial review board status, with the potential for a subsequent promotion to Associate Editor.

If you have a colleague that may be interested in this opportunity, we encourage you to share this information with them.

www.igi-global.com

InfoSci®-Books

A Database for Information Science and Technology Research

Maximize Your Library's Book Collection!

Invest in IGI Global's InfoSci®-Books database and gain access to hundreds of reference books at a fraction of their individual list price.

The InfoSci®-Books database offers unlimited simultaneous users the ability to precisely return search results through more than 80,000 full-text chapters from nearly 3,900 reference books in the following academic research areas:

Business & Management Information Science & Technology • Computer Science & Information Technology
Educational Science & Technology • Engineering Science & Technology • Environmental Science & Technology
Government Science & Technology • Library Information Science & Technology • Media & Communication Science & Technology
Medical, Healthcare & Life Science & Technology • Security & Forensic Science & Technology • Social Sciences & Online Behavior

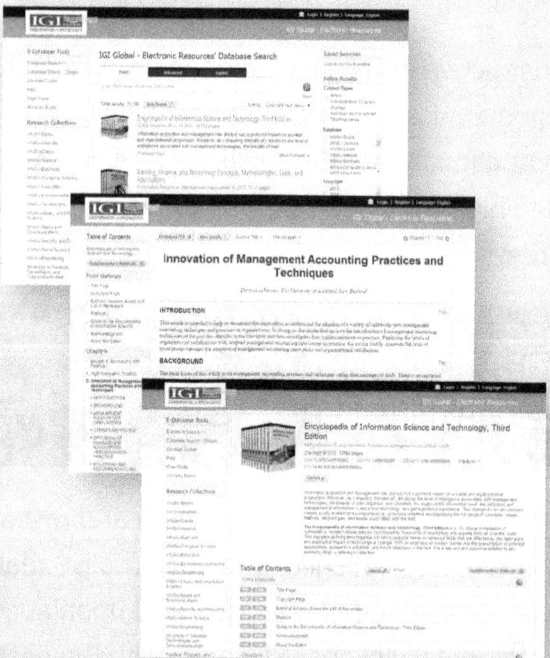

Peer-Reviewed Content:
- Cutting-edge research
- No embargoes
- Scholarly and professional
- Interdisciplinary

Award-Winning Platform:
- Unlimited simultaneous users
- Full-text in XML and PDF
- Advanced search engine
- No DRM

Librarian-Friendly:
- Free MARC records
- Discovery services
- COUNTER4/SUSHI compliant
- Training available

To find out more or request a free trial, visit: www.igi-global.com/eresources

IGI Global
DISSEMINATOR OF KNOWLEDGE
www.igi-global.com

IGI Global
DISSEMINATOR OF KNOWLEDGE
www.igi-global.com

IGI Global Proudly Partners with

eContent Pro International

Expert Copy Editing

eContent Pro International copy editors, with over 70 years of combined experience, will provide complete and comprehensive care for your document by resolving all issues with spelling, punctuation, grammar, terminology, jargon, semantics, syntax, consistency, flow, and more. In addition, they will format your document to the style you specify (APA, Chicago, etc.). All edits will be performed using Microsoft Word's Track Changes feature, which allows for fast and simple review and management of edits.

Additional Services

eContent Pro International also offers fast and affordable proofreading to enhance the readability of your document, professional translation in over 100 languages, and market localization services to help businesses and organizations localize their content and grow into new markets around the globe.

IGI Global Authors Save 25% on eContent Pro International's Services!

Scan the QR Code to Receive Your 25% Discount

The 25% discount is applied directly to your eContent Pro International shopping cart when placing an order through IGI Global's referral link. Use the QR code to access this referral link. eContent Pro International has the right to end or modify any promotion at any time.

Email: customerservice@econtentpro.com

econtentpro.com

Information Resources Management Association

Advancing the Concepts & Practices of Information Resources Management in Modern Organizations

Become an IRMA Member

Members of the **Information Resources Management Association (IRMA)** understand the importance of community within their field of study. The Information Resources Management Association is an ideal venue through which professionals, students, and academicians can convene and share the latest industry innovations and scholarly research that is changing the field of information science and technology. Become a member today and enjoy the benefits of membership as well as the opportunity to collaborate and network with fellow experts in the field.

IRMA Membership Benefits:

- **One FREE Journal Subscription**
- **30% Off Additional Journal Subscriptions**
- **20% Off Book Purchases**
- Updates on the latest events and research on Information Resources Management through the IRMA-L listserv.
- Updates on new open access and downloadable content added to Research IRM.
- A copy of the Information Technology Management Newsletter twice a year.
- A certificate of membership.

IRMA Membership $195

Scan code or visit **irma-international.org** and begin by selecting your free journal subscription.

Membership is good for one full year.

www.irma-international.org

IGI Global
DISSEMINATOR OF KNOWLEDGE
www.igi-global.com

Available to Order Now

Order through www.igi-global.com with **Free Standard Shipping**.

The Premier Reference for Information Science & Information Technology

100% Original Content

Contains 705 new, peer-reviewed articles with color figures covering over 80 categories in 11 subject areas

Diverse Contributions

More than 1,100 experts from 74 unique countries contributed their specialized knowledge

Easy Navigation

Includes two tables of content and a comprehensive index in each volume for the user's convenience

Highly-Cited

Embraces a complete list of references and additional reading sections to allow for further research

Included in: InfoSci®-Books

Encyclopedia of Information Science and Technology Fourth Edition

A Comprehensive 10-Volume Set

Mehdi Khosrow-Pour, D.B.A. (Information Resources Management Association, USA)

ISBN: 978-1-5225-2255-3; © 2018; Pg: 8,104; Release Date: July 2017

The **Encyclopedia of Information Science and Technology, Fourth Edition** is a 10-volume set which includes 705 original and previously unpublished research articles covering a full range of perspectives, applications, and techniques contributed by thousands of experts and researchers from around the globe. This authoritative encyclopedia is an all-encompassing, well-established reference source that is ideally designed to disseminate the most forward-thinking and diverse research findings. With critical perspectives on the impact of information science management and new technologies in modern settings, including but not limited to computer science, education, healthcare, government, engineering, business, and natural and physical sciences, it is a pivotal and relevant source of knowledge that will benefit every professional within the field of information science and technology and is an invaluable addition to every academic and corporate library.

Scan for Online Bookstore

Pricing Information

Hardcover: **$5,695** E-Book: **$5,695** Hardcover + E-Book: **$6,895**

Recommend this Title to Your Institution's Library: www.igi-global.com/books

www.ingramcontent.com/pod-product-compliance
Lightning Source LLC
LaVergne TN
LVHW062106300926
849161LV00010B/2387